PHILOSOPHY
OF THE
SOCIAL SCIENCES

Philosophy
of the
SOCIAL
SCIENCES

A Reader

EDITED BY

Maurice Natanson

UNIVERSITY OF CALIFORNIA AT SANTA CRUZ

RANDOM HOUSE · NEW YORK

FOURTH PRINTING

Library of Congress Catalog Card Number: 63-13982

MANUFACTURED IN THE UNITED STATES OF AMERICA BY
AMERICAN BOOK–STRATFORD PRESS, INC.

DESIGNED BY JEANETTE YOUNG

To

Alfred Schutz, 1899–1959

PHILOSOPHER AND SOCIAL SCIENTIST

FOREWORD

THE THEME of the essays which make up this book is the fundamental nature of the social world, and the approach to that theme is by way of the philosophy of the social sciences. Although specific methodological problems that arise in connection with the enterprise of social science are examined in various ways, the primary emphasis is on a broad philosophical viewing of the structure and texture of the world created by human beings, men aware of themselves as well as of each other. We may call the plenum of their meaningful action "Social Reality"; our concern here is with its rationale. Some indication of the scope and intent of the selections which follow as well as of the principles of organization that have led to their inclusion may help the reader to make an initial step toward understanding the editor's procedure.

Traditionally, anthologies of this sort (collections intended to be used as textbooks for college or university courses) are conceived as repositories for selected pages from the classics in the field. In belles-lettres the word "treasury" is a familiar if outmoded reminder of such pursuits. In these terms, one would expect a "reader" in the philosophy of the social sciences to be, for the most part, a gallery of famous names. The student is encouraged to read something by Comte, Marx, Durkheim, Pareto, etc. At the same time, he is warned that the fragments from these giants are no substitute for the real thing—the reading of their major works. Hopefully at least, such a reader will encourage the initiate to go on, to progress in his discipline. No doubt anthologies of this sort are helpful, but the present work cannot be included among their number. It is not a repository of bits of the classics; still less is it a gleaning from the full range of all major issues in the philosophy and methodology of the social sciences (unfortunately, there is no room to include a section on the sociology of knowledge or essays on the methodological problems of each of the social sciences). Instead, this volume is intended as a dialectical argument contrived to catch the student in its current and bear him along a course exciting enough to make him argue for himself. The pedagogic and moral implications of this procedure are developed in the Introduction. Here we shall enlarge on the procedure itself.

Two distinctively opposed philosophic attitudes are taken as polar positions underlying the social sciences: let us, for want of satisfying alternatives, call them "objective" and "subjective" *Weltanschauungen.* We are speaking, then, not of narrowly conceived ideas or systems of ideas that might be readily associated with the name of a particular thinker or school of thought, but rather of quite broad ways of seeing the social world, of fundamental conceptions of the social itself. But some further specifications can be made. Behaviorism, naturalism, empiricism, and positivism are least annoyed with an approach to the social sciences which strives for the location of "hard" data, which is concerned with exact measurement of social phenomena, which considers intersubjectively verifiable propositions as constituting the necessary core of any science, and which looks to social control as an ultimate, if distant, ideal of research in this domain. Finally, specific, limited, manageable methodological problems are generally seized upon by this camp as proper working material. Grand conceptual schemes, metaphysical systems, overarching patterns of social theory are willingly left to the "other side," those who are more nearly inclined to a "subjective" approach to social reality. In this group one might place thinkers who are not deeply offended or unduly upset by those who speak of "interpretive understanding" or *Verstehen*, or by those influenced by phenomenology and existentialism. The "subjective" emphasis is on trying to comprehend the way in which social life is lived by the actors on the social scene. The central, though by no means exclusive, emphasis is on the actor, not the observer. The attitudes, feelings, and conceptual awareness of the individual caught up in social reality and trying to come to terms with it involve, no doubt, much "soft" data. This is a challenge rather than something to regret for the "subjective" social scientist. These, then, are the antipodes of the universe of discourse explored by the writers included in this book. Assuming, as we do, that there *is* a universe of discourse shared, no matter how opposed some of the views may be, the central organizational problem is how best to bring the tension that underlies them to conceptual clarity. The answer which follows must be taken as one possible answer; there are others.

Just as the subject matter of the philosophy of the social sciences has been conceived here in terms of a fundamental argument, so the principle of selection governing the inclusion of essays has been formulated in dialectical terms. Wherever it has been possible and feasible, we have brought together essays, complete in themselves, which directly relate to each other. Thus, the ideal has been to include not bits but true units from writers who are aware of each other, who discuss each other's work, who examine each other's ideas in a controversial way. It has not been possible, for various reasons, to realize this ideal in all parts of the book. But we trust that in good measure the essays that follow do constitute a dialectic of a sort, an alive and at times kindly, at times belligerent, market place of ideas. It is hoped that the reader will find in both the explicit and the implicit alignments and antagonisms that comprise the discussion a sense of the mobile character of philosophical analysis. Certainly, he will discover soon enough that the dialectic between "objective" and "subjective" approaches to social reality is a gross oversimplification of the actual situation. No one will be surprised. There is no great battle in progress today in the social sciences between behaviorists and existentialists. Neither is there a struggle between positivists and phenomenologists. For the most part these labels are superficial and require much refinement before they can be utilized meaningfully. It is the thesis of this book, however, that they can be developed in a suggestive way without invoking the cliché of "straw men." For the pedagogic purposes of this book we prefer the overstatement of the case to what has been called "death by a thousand qualifications."

Adhering to a dialectical principle of selection and organization does not mean that what is decided upon is necessary or even, in every respect, superior to other possibilities. We can well conceive of a reader formed on similar lines which would make use of very different selections. It must be understood that sociology has been the social science we have leaned upon most; there is no reason why economics or anthropology could not have been given the same weight. Nor is it necessary to argue for the choice made. Here is one important, and we believe valid, way of creating an instrument that will encourage serious reflection on the philosophical problems of the social sciences. That there may be other ways of doing this is true and for our purposes irrelevant. Our case must rest with the book itself: the chapters which bear the argument, the Introduction which is addressed concretely to the student who may be trying to find his bearing in a new realm, the prefatory remarks which precede each Part and which are intended to serve as informal aids and suggestions (but not précis of the corresponding chapters or digestive tablets to be taken before reading), and the concluding Bibliography—which is decisively important if taken seriously.

But no book can be all things to all readers. Our guess is that what follows will strike a responsive chord in some and leave others quite untouched; this is preferable to a wide but tepid acceptance. Let us hope that if there are any who will be appalled by what they find here, they will be only men of extraordinary resentment. The word about them was given by Louis Armstrong: "There's some people, if they don't know, you can't tell them."

ACKNOWLEDGMENTS

ALTHOUGH A NUMBER of people have helped in a variety of ways in the preparation of this book, I have relied almost completely on my own judgment to make all major decisions. In the one or two cases where counter-suggestions were offered regarding the selections to be included, I decided to hold to my original choices. The blame, if not the credit, then, is mine alone. Nevertheless, others have helped materially, and I wish to acknowledge their advice and support. I thank Professor Charles H. Page for his sympathetic response to my proposal for this volume; Dr. Leon J. Goldstein and Professor Joseph A. Dowling for their critical suggestions; Professors Hans Jonas, George A. Lundberg, Fritz Machlup, Leo Strauss, Peter Winch, and Kurt H. Wolff for their informative aid; Mrs. Paul Henle for her kindness in making available and permitting me to quote from an unpublished paper by her late husband; Harvey and Marcelle Rabbin for their concern with the Merleau-Ponty translation and Professors Herbert Spiegelberg and Richard C. McCleary for their suggestions regarding that translation and Mr. B. Tolley who, through the persuasive offices of Professor A. L. Goodhart, helped with the translation of a legal term. The most perceptive aid has come from my wife, Lois

Natanson, whose response to what I've done has been warmly independent and richly sustaining. Random House has been consistently courteous to me, and I thank its College Department, in particular Mr. Charles D. Lieber, for his interest in this volume, and Mrs. Leonore C. Hauck for her patient, expert, and humane editorial guidance. My greatest and lasting indebtedness, however, is to the man to whose memory this book is dedicated.

M.N.

CONTENTS

PHILOSOPHY
OF THE
SOCIAL SCIENCES

INTRODUCTION

Human society is not merely a fact, or an event, in the external world to be studied by an observer like a natural phenomenon. Though it has externality as one of its important components, it is as a whole a little world, a cosmion, illuminated with meaning from within by the human beings who continuously create and bear it as the mode and condition of their self-realization.

—ERIC VOEGELIN

I

IT WAS Coleridge who said, "Every man is born an Aristotelian, or a Platonist."[1] We may take his remark as a theme relevant to the philosophy and methodology of the social sciences no less than to the history of ideas. For whether men view their social world as a vast architecture of concretely specifiable elements subject to gradual control or as a transcendent unity illuminated by the human spirit depends as much on their initial philosophic temperament as on their detailed arguments. There are styles of men no less than conceptual positions, and the student of social reality is faced, whether he recognizes it or not, with the generic

---

[1] From Samuel Taylor Coleridge's *Table Talk* in *Coleridge: Select Poetry and Prose*, p. 491.

problem of deciding what he shall take for granted in his intellectual career, what he shall set aside as "out of bounds" for his discipline, or what he shall let be done by that most famous of all colleagues—George. The choice at issue here is decisive for the kind of social science that will emerge during the next century; it is even more crucial for the life of the individual trying to find his own way in the labyrinth of the world. This Introduction takes as its point of departure the situation of the individual student—perhaps the present reader—concerned with understanding the relevance of philosophy for the social sciences and seeking, in this domain, the liberation of a set of questions.

II

The anatomy of the social world is familiar to its untutored beholder long before he undertakes sophisticated dissection. Each of us is part of a reality which has as one of its most subtle features the possibility that it may be placed in question, rendered an explicit object for investigation, description, or analysis. There is, then, a twofold aspect of every experience the individual has within the social order: something given, naively taken as part of the social world—for instance, the handshake that closes the business deal—may be treated as an example of a type or as an aspect of a type of structural relatedness that undergirds society. The dualism is overpowering: there is the event and the typification of the event, the social act and its conceptual articulation, human existence and its philosophic as well as sociological exploration. The student thinking about these matters is at once a concrete person at some determinate place in the world, in the midst of a situation, and a being whose human career is interrupted precisely at the moment when he catches himself *as* concrete, *as* situated, *as* involved in puzzling out these very issues. It is as if a double, your *Doppelgänger*, tapped you on the shoulder in the apparent spontaneity of a dance and asked you to observe yourself dancing while he took your partner. Analysis and immediacy fear each other's rights, and there is good reason to keep them separated. Unfortunately, this cannot be done by decree, nor is it clear that complete severance is even possible. Social events not only lend themselves to conceptualization; they are, to varying degrees, already typified when we locate them as objects for inspection. The problem, then, points to a special complexity: going one way we find the major questions of philosophic and sociological method; going the other way we are led to the central issues of what might be called an epistemology of the social world. We shall, in what follows, look in both directions.

If each moment of the social life of the concrete individual may, in principle, be taken by that person as problematic, as material for his own consideration, then there is indeed something paradoxical in speaking of the "concrete individual." And by the same logic, there is something strange about suggesting that "this Introduction takes as its point of departure the individual student." The person reading this page is as remote from the author as the author is from him. The notion of "concreteness" is suspicious at best; at worst, it sounds like a gimmick. Forcing the issue might lead to a discussion of certain aspects of existential philosophy, taken as an aesthetic bridge between an otherwise uncrossable gap. Our concern for the present, however, is not with Kierkegaard but with a methodological problem bearing its own style of paradox. To refer to the situation of the individual person is to do neither more nor less than enunciate the fact that the reader with suspicions distinguishes between himself and what others might wish to make of him, between his concreteness and its patronization. The weight of the issue rests on the methodological moment when the person realizes that he cannot formulate that distinction without self-embarrassment. Ordinarily, the distinction is first thrust upon him in some context of his education.

It is not uncommon for a beginner in the study of sociology to be shocked when he recognizes himself in the description given in a textbook account or one by his professor of, let us say, some aspect of middle-class American life. Until that time he may have been drowsing through the ritual of classroom attendance, peering busily at his neighbor's notes whenever he missed something said which everybody else appeared to be taking down, then lapsing back into that reverie made possible by a kind of auditory abulia, a distinctively collegiate disease often transmitted by lecturers. But at that moment, suddenly jolted into a wary wakefulness, he writhes as he hears tolled out in the presence of the total company those attributes that clearly point to him alone: it is he whose home life is being discussed; it is his family that subscribes to those magazines; *his* father is the one who twists the lion's tail each week; those are his friends, his relations, his opinions, his world. In short, he has been "found out"; but the incisive recognition here is self-recognition: for the first time he has secured a strangely new and vastly different vantage point, that of sociological description. The shock is devastating to some, of transitory significance to many. Those who are genuinely upset by their own social image are transposed into a new way of seeing; they achieve what Peter L. Berger has called "the precarious vision."[2] But the methodological implications of this transposition go deeper than the vocabulary of "upset" and "shock" might indicate. What is at issue ultimately is a philosophic upheaval, the self-discovery that makes philosophy possible.

Unlike its academic offspring, philosophy has a reflexive character. It cannot do away with the necessity of talking about itself, with the problems of what it means to undertake philosophical work. Although some of the results may prove unacceptable, philosophy is destined by the intrinsic nature of its own discipline to talk about itself: "meta-philosophical" talk is merely one dimension of talking philosophy at all, and it cannot be eliminated without eliminating the philosophical enterprise. It is this curious methodological involution which marks the reflexive character of philosophizing. In an analogous way, philosophy is committed to reflecting systematically on a variety of topics which appear "obvious" or "certain" to the nonphilosopher, and to raising questions about the meaning of such reflection. It is as if experience were interrogating itself through the agency of the philosopher's voice.

In the case of the social sciences the fundamental theme for methodological consideration is the existence of a social world, the primordial fact of there being social reality. Having that "datum" is in itself a step beyond (or beneath) the surprise of sociological vision. In the case of the student who suddenly sees himself as a typical member of a typical middle-class family the structure of his social world is grasped in its generality over and against the rest of that totality we call human experience. A distinct segment of

[2] See Peter L. Berger, *The Precarious Vision,* and compare p. 15 f.

the whole has been laid bare. In philosophy, on the other hand, the shock is qualitatively different. Not a part but the whole itself is in question, and the totality of human experience announces its sudden strangeness. Philosophical shock is the recognition that *what is* need not be at all, could be otherwise than it is, and that its being is, in the strictest sense of that word, remarkable.

It would be a mistake, however, to think that the difference between the sociological and philosophical angles of vision is a matter of how little or how much reality is placed in question. To repeat, the difference is qualitative. Sociological insight puts the social structure into relief, makes it viewable; philosophical reflection asks how it comes about that the individual's experience of social reality contains within it the possibility of asking philosophical questions regarding it. The sociology student, even in his newly won distress, takes it for granted that seeing himself "for the first time" is possible, unusual as the occurrence may be. The philosopher seizes the very familiarity of the everyday world and seeks its conceptual reconstruction. If nothing is taken for granted, then the philosopher himself is in question. True reflexivity is a different way of speaking of rigorous skepticism. The results may be shattering, for what lies at the focus of reflection is the dilemma we noted earlier: How is it possible for the concrete individual to grasp his uniqueness if the act of grasping is a generalized one? Or to put the matter differently: Is it not the case that being a philosopher engaged in asking fundamental questions about the nature of self and social reality is the fulfillment of one style of being? Genius alone may escape typification and transcend the dilemma; after all, there were two exceptions to Coleridge's dictum: Aristotle and Plato.

At this point we have glanced in the direction of philosophical and sociological method. It is time to look the other way toward the object of methodology, the social world known by the human beings who constitute it. The problems involved are those of the theory of knowledge, and they are met with at the juncture of science and epistemology. If there is such a "datum" as that of social reality (and even with quotation marks around it, the use of "datum" in this context is most peculiar) what manner of thing is it? *What* is it? Perhaps the story of the old lecturer is relevant here. He had been rereading the same set of notes to his classes for thirty-five years, and never had anything transpired in class which might interrupt the transferral of the material on his aged parchment to the fresh notebooks of his listeners. But in his last year of teaching something untoward did occur. He was in the middle of his thirty-sixth reading of the passage ". . . and so each year, that is to say, annually, over ninety million tons are deposited on the banks of the Mississippi . . ." when a student broke a generation of silence with the question, "Pardon me, Professor, but ninety million tons of *what?*" The old gentleman looked down toward the lectern, scrutinizing his notes, and finally looked up, replying, "It doesn't say."[3] It will be necessary to do a little better than our senior colleague, but delineating the "what" of the social is a perilous task.

For a modest beginning, we suggest that social reality is the sum of what can be meant by *our* world. We may point to a non-social object, a stone for example, but our pointing is part of the intersubjective world, the stone itself is not. The social, then, is grounded in the fact that men in their relatedness are capable of sharing the same object from different standpoints and perspectives. That you and I—that *we*—communicate with each other is less a curiosity of language than it is the presupposition of language, the condition for there being language at all. *What* is so shared is the meaning intended and grasped in the acts of communication. The handshake that consummates the business deal is in purely physical terms no more than an exercise in the mechanics of muscles, tendons, bone, cartilage, etc. From the standpoint of the social order, and the business world in particular, the handshake *is* a signification: it *means* that something has been agreed upon by the partners to the transaction, that the agreement has been concluded, fixed, or resolved in some form. Meaning in this sense refers to the object side of intention; it is what the intending points toward. Those acquainted with the procedures of the social world in its manifold levels act through the devices their neighbors understand, for the most part, in the same way. When cultural differences exist, *that* they exist is taken for granted, and techniques of translation from one social context to another are sought for and developed. Throughout our life with others in a

[3] I don't know where *he* heard it, but this one was told to me by Professor Burr Roney.

shared world the *what* of social reality is the meaning grasped by each of us of what is signified by external events. The distinctive feature of man's being in the social world is that he may and does reflect on his meaningful action, that he is able to treat meaning in a reflexive manner (the immanent beginning of philosophy) by understanding his own existence as life represented in the macrocosm of society.[4] Once again, the theme of individual and type is present. This time, however, it is transposed into a somewhat different form by our asking, What exactly is meant by an epistemology of the social world?

To raise an epistemological question is to inquire into the presuppositions for the experience of something. Following Kant, we might say that epistemology is concerned with determining the necessary conditions for the very possibility of experience. The emphasis, then, is upon experiencing, but it is clear that what is experienced is no less relevant to the discipline which calls itself the "theory of knowledge." An epistemology of the social world in these terms would have as its task the determination of those structural elements and forms of knowing which make the experience of the social order possible. Formidable as such an endeavor is, we have already located at least some of its main terms. To interpret meaning as the clue to the "what" of social reality is to suggest that meanings are socially shared precisely because intention goes beyond its material presentation. The vehicle or carrier of meaning is not the same as the meaning. What is signified by the handshake is the social event of agreement, and to the extent that the clasp of palms and fingers in the typical act we call "handshake" is a social act, the physical features of the event are irrelevant. In purely anatomical terms, the handshake of the business deal may be indistinguishable from that of the acknowledgment of an introduction, the ritual of receiving a diploma, or the rules of courtesy governing wrestlers about to meet in a ring. What is meant in each of these cases is quite different. To say that the handshake of the businessmen *is* the meaning is already to have interpreted the event as a social act. Each act, we may say, has a meaningful unity encased in or associated with a material embodiment. Once again, we are led back to the distinction between concreteness and generality. An epistemology of the social

[4] See Eric Voegelin, *The New Science of Politics.*

world is at the same time a study in the relationship between particulars and universals.

The problems, then, of philosophy and methodology of the social sciences and those of an epistemology of social reality are the inevitable terminals of one continuous line, and the student concerned with understanding himself and his world is confronted with a double challenge. The location of the particulars of experience involves the implicit possibility of their articulation in the context of a theoretical system. The methodological procedures necessary to the formulation of such a system are tied as much to the needs of theory as to the specific requirements of the material the theory is *about*. Again, there is a tension between the open possibilities of pure theory and its more nearly pedestrian responsibilities. Clarifying the nature of these responsibilities as well as possibilities means clarifying the nature of theory itself, and such an endeavor will lead ultimately to overarching questions about the maker of theories, the theorist in existential no less than methodological perspective.

III

It is almost the hallmark of discussions of the nature of theory that they begin with lamenting the confused state into which current usage has fallen. Such central terms as "method," "type," and "model" are held to be as greatly in need of standardization as is "theory" itself. A little later I will try to show that "standardization" in this domain is a most questionable notion and that the ideal of uniformity is based on philosophically problematic grounds. For the present, however, we might attend to a typical lament. "What is theory?" John Gillin asks as editor of a recent volume of essays by social scientists, "What useful purpose does it serve? What are the criteria of 'good' or useful theory? To some readers these questions may seem elementary or naive. Yet a perusal of the current theories in 'social science' will show that frequently little attention has been paid by their authors either to general canons of scientific theory or to the scientific requirements of theoretical formulations in their own fields."[5] And he

[5] John Gillin (ed.), *For a Science of Social Man*, p. 258.

goes on to suggest that theory and theorizing are far more wide-spread activities than the specialist or layman might realize:

> Every "normal" human being is, willy-nilly, a theorizer. This is merely to say that no normally intelligent member of the species Homo sapiens (with an I.Q. of, say, 90 or above) can look at anything without formulating a theory (or following some traditional formulation) about what he observes. To take a very trivial example, Joe Doakes hammers a nail into a board and the nail crumples. Doakes says to himself (if he has no audience), "That must be hard wood instead of soft wood." That statement of Doakes is a theoretical conclusion or theorem from certain implicit postulates. It is meant to explain the result he had from trying to drive the nail. Furthermore, it is a verifiable theorem. There are certain methods available to Doakes to determine whether or not the piece of wood involved is in fact northern oak or southern pine, or something else. Thus everyone theorizes."[6]

If professional social scientists are often remiss in making their theoretical assumptions explicit and well formed, it would appear to follow, on Gillin's premises, that the implicit theorizing done by ordinary men in daily life is even more in need of overt formulation and systematization—still another task for the social scientist. Burdened as he is, the scientist must take precautions in carrying his load. A rigorous concern with theory and methodology becomes a categorical imperative.

What, then, shall we understand by "theory" and "methodology"? Is every man a theorizer, as Gillin suggests? Or should the term be reserved for a more formal treatment of the problems of social science? A few traditional formulations of the meaning of theory, and methodology, may serve as a start toward a later reformulation. "A *theory*," N. S. Timasheff writes, "is a set of propositions complying, ideally, with the following conditions: one, the propositions must be couched in terms of exactly defined concepts; two, they must be consistent with one another; three, they must be such that from them the existing generalizations could be deductively derived; four, they must be fruitful—show the way to further observations and generalizations increasing the

[6] *Ibid.*

scope of knowledge."[7] And with regard to methodology Paul F. Lazarsfeld writes: "If coherence and precision are among the main objectives of the contemporary sociologist, then the very nature of his work involved decisions as to the direction of efforts, the selection of topics, the merit of procedures themselves. Sociologists are supposed to convert the vast and ever-shifting web of social relations into an understandable system of manageable knowledge. To discover and appraise the way in which this is being done is the object of methodological analysis. The sociologist studies man in society: the methodologist studies the sociologist at work."[8] Finally, with respect to the relationship between theory and methodology, Robert K. Merton distinguishes between "sociological theory, which has for its subject matter certain aspects and results of the interaction of men and is therefore substantive, and methodology, or the logic of scientific procedure."[9] The references to *sociological* theory and methodology should not, at this stage, present a serious obstacle to following the more general implications of theory and methodology as such for the comprehension of social reality. From these first formulations certain results are apparent:

1. Theory is held to be statable in the form of declarative sentences whose basic terms are capable of strict definition.

2. Systemic consistency is a necessary condition for an acceptable theory.

3. A pragmatic dimension informs the purpose of theory; an elegant theory may nevertheless be a barren one.

4. The logic of theory construction as well as the procedural problems of the activity of the social scientist are parts of the subject matter of methodology.

5. The form rather than the content of theory is of primary interest to the methodologist.

The utility of these distinctions is considerable. On their basis one may find a meaningful way of distinguishing between fact, the materials of observation, and the theoretical apparatus required to order and interpret those materials. In addition, the

---

[7] Nicholas S. Timasheff, *Sociological Theory*, pp. 9–10.

[8] Paul F. Lazarsfeld, "Problems in Methodology," in *Sociology Today*, pp. 39–40.

[9] Robert K. Merton, *Social Theory and Social Structure*, p. 86.

relationship between theory and methodology becomes manageable: the former is directed toward substantive issues, the latter toward procedural matters. Were all of this sufficient for the social scientist (and there are reasons to follow which suggest that it is not), it would still be insufficient for the student of social reality who has the focus of his attention on the question, What is the relevance of philosophy for both theory and methodology? A different way of posing this question is to ask what it is the philosopher does in these realms that is not done by the sociologist or economist or social psychologist who is primarily interested in theory or methodology. Rather than inquire whether the social scientist-theoretician doubles as a philosopher, we might do better to turn more directly to an alternative way of viewing the nature of theory and the province of methodology.

The reflexive character of philosophy mentioned earlier provides a clue to our present difficulties. The philosopher as theory builder must necessarily concern himself with the meaning and implications of his own activities. This is a distinctively systemic task, not a psychological obligation. Accordingly, it must be part of the function of a philosophy to ground its methodological operations. Modern philosophy from Descartes to Husserl is the clearest illustration of the recognition by philosophers that their own procedures are inescapably part of their proper worries, but this recognition is rooted in ancient philosophy as well. The dialogues of Plato are exercises in methodological self-examination. There is, then, a metatheoretical dimension to philosophy. Expressed simply, this means that a philosopher is obliged to take a sharp look at the ways in which his philosophy leads to specific results. The empiricist, rationalist, phenomenalist, and phenomenologist build theories which stand in a different relationship to their authors than do theories constructed by theoreticians in the various disciplines of the social sciences. The difference is important and must be made clear.

It is presumably the professional obligation of the empiricist philosopher to explain and defend the empiricist theory he constructs. But the sociologist who is empirically oriented is hardly expected to explain or defend the philosophical trappings of his theory. He may indicate his philosophical indebtedness or inclinations; he is not expected to pursue them with a passion. That, after all, is the philosopher's business. If some social scientists are philosophically sophisticated and do discuss philosophical problems, they are notable by their variance from the norm. The point at issue is not whether philosophers are more or less rigorous than social scientists; it is rather that philosophy is in its very nature different from social science. The difference in this instance is that a *philosophy* of the social sciences is beyond the province of the social sciences. This makes for distrust as much as for collaboration, and the rise of "interdisciplinary" research may, in part, be an implicit effort to overcome an initial unpleasantness.

There is no objection to characterizing theory in Timasheff's way, or methodology in the style of Lazarsfeld. It is what they do not tell us which is the point at issue. There is a philosophical level of theory and methodology which determines the orientation of these disciplines as they arise and develop in the social sciences. Undergirding sociological, economic, and other social science theory is the philosophic matrix which defines their basic nature. Since there is in the history of philosophy a vast array of different and competing systems and positions, it can hardly be said that the underlying matrix is uniform and without internal divergences. A different recommendation is in order. What characterizes the philosophic level of theory and methodology is the presence of a fundamental outlook, a synthesizing perspective. In short, I am suggesting that the philosophical dimension of social science theory is located in its *Weltanschauung*, its primordial way of looking at the world and trying to see it entire. But there is more involved in *Weltanschauung* than some sort of grand view of things. An appreciation of a fundamental viewing of social reality makes it clear that latent disagreements between theoreticians manifest themselves in terminological disorder. The reason that the vocabularies of social scientists cannot be cleaned up in some concerted operation and rendered uniform is that terminology is most often the reflection of an implicit *Weltanschauung*. Furthermore, the recalcitrance of many theoreticians and methodologists with regard to adopting a kind of theoretical Esperanto is rooted in the fact that among them there are serious philosophical differences.[10] Language can reflect underlying consensus; it

[10] See H. M. Kallen, "The Meanings of Unity Among the Sciences," in *Structure, Method, and Meaning.*

cannot create it. In this sense, appeals for theoreticians to clarify their arguments and make their presuppositions more explicit can be interpreted to mean that their *Weltanschauungen* must be understood for discussion to be productive. It cannot be assumed that philosophical hostilities will disappear if a call to clarification is sounded. Indeed, the sharpness of the differences fundamentally at issue puts in relief certain subordinate problems which those differences generate.

Of the many *Weltanschauungen* which underlie the history of ideas there are two styles of outlook which, as we have indicated in the Foreword, have been chosen for special consideration in the essays which follow in this book. Since they are implicitly or explicitly discussed throughout the book, we shall restrict ourselves here to some tangential remarks about them. The essential struggle between "objective" and "subjective" ways of seeing the world rests partly on the hopes one places in the development of science and the stress given to the unique possibilities of human consciousness. A naturalistic conception of consciousness places the individual within a world that promises to explain him in the course of its general business of explaining the natural order. A phenomenological view of social reality considers the intersubjective world as constituted in the activity of consciousness, with natural science being one aspect of the productivity of consciousness. The urge to build a science of man leads basically to a certain style of selection of problems, methods, and theories contrived to solve those problems. Thus, if the criterion of scientific achievement is the securing of empirically verifiable propositions incorporated in a theoretical instrument capable of adequate description and prediction, it will necessarily follow that what is to be admitted to begin with as a genuine problem must in principle meet the standards that will eventually be applied with respect to its solution. From the phenomenological perspective, there is a vast domain of pre- or proto-empirical experience which can be caught in the net of a philosophy which explores reality as immediately experienced by the individual. What is to count as "evidence" must meet the criterion of immediate presentation. Obviously, the "results" of these two outlooks are going to differ radically. The question posed by their disagreement is anterior to any possibility to choice of results. That question is: On what basis does one decide to assume one standpoint or the other, embrace one *Weltanschauung* or another? The issue reaches to a kind of philosophic bedrock, for one is asking whether in choosing between alternative systems of categories the basis for choice does not itself presuppose a *Weltanschauung*.[11] There are several ways in which this problem has been approached, depending on whether the discussion leads to the search for a "presuppositionless" philosophy or the rudiments of a sociology of knowledge. Neither of these possibilities can be explored here; instead we shall consider briefly a surface irruption produced by the wars of the *Weltanschauungen*.

It is clear that as a matter of fact the social scientist may come to philosophy because the concrete difficulties he faces in his day-to-day professional work lead him there. The theory of social roles, for example, may involve the most atheoretical mind in such issues as the nature of the self and the difference between aspects of the ego. In turn, these issues can hardly be examined rigorously without facing such disconcerting problems as the relevance of intersubjectivity and temporality for the genesis and development of the self. Before he knows what is happening, the social scientist who may abhor philosophical involvements finds himself in the midst of philosophical puzzles. And the student of social roles who may succeed, by bitter determination, in skirting the esoteric domain of the philosophers finds that in order to understand the literature in his special field he cannot ignore writers who, in turn, lean heavily upon the history of philosophy. Concretely: no student of social roles would think of remaining ignorant of the writings of George H. Mead. But if one turns to Mead (and goes beyond *Mind, Self and Society* to *The Philosophy of the Act* and the *Philosophy of the Present*), he finds that thinker caught up in the philosophies of Bergson and Whitehead. To understand social roles means to be forced to come to terms with philosophy. And since force is never a kindly guide, a certain resentment may remain.

Ideally, the social scientist who works in the field of theory should be a philosopher as well as, say, a sociologist or political scientist. Conversely, the philosopher of the social sciences should be, if perfection were to be realized, the master of the concrete

11 Compare Everett W. Hall, *Philosophical Systems*.

problems and materials as well as evolution of half a dozen assorted subjects ranging from anthropology to economics. In the history of the social sciences there have been notable examples of persons with encyclopedic range (Max Weber is the best known, perhaps) who never had to sacrifice depth for their remarkable coverage. Is it necessary to say that such instances are exceedingly rare and promise to be still rarer? What then is required of the social scientist concerned with philosophy and the philosopher interested seriously in the social sciences? The difficulty in giving straightforward answers at this point is indicative of a basic rift, the surface disturbance which points back to the conflict of *Weltanschauungen*. The social scientist may be irritated by the philosopher who is ignorant of the specific substantive problems the former faces but who loses no time in telling him "all about it."[12] The parallel complaint comes from the philosopher who hears the social scientist talk about "causation" in psychology, let us say, as though Hume and Kant had never lived. The exaggerated stereotypes on both sides tell us something about their more modified counterparts in reality: on the one hand, there is the Germanic philosopher who needs only to hear of a discipline in order to undertake a multivolumed treatise purporting to be a metaphysical prolegomenon to any future study of the subject; on the other hand, there is the kind of "behavioral scientist" who if asked whether he loved his mother, would reply that he couldn't answer until he had done a content analysis of their correspondence.

There are those who argue that better education is the way out of this impasse. That the sniping between philosophy and social science seems to be carried on, at times, by rather well-

[12] Ludwig von Mises writes that with regard to the general theory of human action "the errors of the philosophers are due to their complete ignorance of economics and very often to their shockingly insufficient knowledge of history. In the eyes of the philosopher the treatment of philosophical issues is a sublime and noble vocation which must not be put upon the low level of other gainful employments. The professor resents the fact that he derives an income from philosophizing; he is offended by the thought that he earns money like the artisan and the farm hand. Monetary matters are mean things, and the philosopher investigating the eminent problems of truth and absolute eternal values should not soil his mind by paying attention to them. No line of any contemporary philosopher discloses the least familiarity with even the most elementary problem of economics." (*Human Action*, pp. 32–33.)

educated individuals gives cause to hope that students may succeed where their professors have failed. Sociology, in particular, has been the target for much abuse, and there is no shortage of attack and counterattack between those (not always philosophers) who accuse sociology of being the mountain that labors to produce a mouse and their antagonists who charge the accusers with everything from illiteracy and incompetence to misguidedness and out-of-datedness.[13] The level of such haranguing is usually quite low, and, most often, the points really at issue are as obscure and antiquated as the disagreement itself. What is of significance is the underlying struggle; although the symptoms are often distant from the source they are no less indicative. Between those who speak of the "do-nothing methodologists . . . who sit around and philosophize when there is so much crucial work to be done"[14] and those who "sit around" there can be little meaningful discussion. We are forced back to a distinction between types of men. Without for a moment suggesting that the struggle is *between* Aristotelians and Platonists, at this point we may nevertheless extend Coleridge's metaphor. "I do not think it possible," he went on to say, "that any one born an Aristotelian can become a Platonist; and I am sure no born Platonist can ever change into an Aristotelian."[15]

We shall let Coleridge have the last word, but we need not give up the possibility of transposing the discussion to a new level. If there are radically different styles of theories and theorists, there is still the problem of whether the choice of style presupposes an existential commitment. To go back a step further, it should be realized that speaking of alternatives already implies decision among possibilities. Is there not at the base of all decisions a decision to decide? In the preceding discussion we have investigated facets of underlying theoretical alternatives: the relationship between concreteness and universality, the philosophical,

---

[13] See, for example, Russell Kirk, "Is Social Science Scientific?" *New York Times Magazine*, June 25, 1961; and Robert K. Merton, "Now the Case for Sociology," *Ibid.*, July 16, 1961. Also compare Edward Shils, "The Calling of Sociology," in *Theories of Society*, II, 1408–1409, and Charles H. Page, "Sociology as a Teaching Enterprise," in *Sociology Today*, pp. 581–585.

[14] Quoted in William Stephenson, *The Study of Behavior*, p. 1.

[15] *Op. cit.*

methodological and epistemological directions which a theory of social reality must trace out, the underlying tensions between opposing *Weltanschauungen* and the surface disturbances which reflect those tensions, and as a thematic motif, the Aristotelian and Platonist impasse. Antecedent to these alternatives, however, is the problem of the concrete individual's willingness, root determination to try to understand himself and his world. An openness and freedom toward knowledge are most often simply taken for granted in study and in reflection. They are grounded, nevertheless, in a primordial philosophic commitment of the most urgent sort, a commitment which marks the distance between reason and nihilism. The final turn of this discussion is toward the moral and pedagogic dimension of the philosophy of the social sciences.

IV

That the *particular*, the concrete event in experience, can become an object for inspection and so rendered universal has at least one fascinating yet alarming implication: the life of the individual, taken as a continuous fabric of particulars, may be viewed as a *universal* of sorts. In its typicality, the daily existence of a worker or a professional man or a civil servant has an emblematic dimension, for these concrete lives are nevertheless the expressions of possible styles of being. And there is an inescapable quality to the relationship between particular and universal. Implicitly or explicitly, unconsciously or self-consciously, the individual is a representamen of his type of life. In the case of the theorist as philosopher, the relationship is doubly strange, since, as we have suggested, an essential part of the philosopher's task is to scrutinize his own procedures and presuppositions. Leading the life of a theorist, then, becomes reflexively problematic for the very reason that theorizing must take into account the theorizer. The intimate connection between the two demands further analysis.

Observer and observed are ordinarily thought of as distinct entities. Even in the inquiries undertaken in the social sciences, there is the assumption that the scientist is methodologically divorced from the people and situations and relationships he studies.

Ideally, at least, this is what he strives for.[16] In the case of theoretical reflection, however, the problem of "objectivity" is not
at issue. Instead, we are confronted with a distinctively conceptual
and valuational phenomenon which cannot be thrust aside with
apologies about "psychological" idiosyncrasies. The philosopher-
theorist of social reality is himself part of the field he must
investigate; his own reality is a feature of social reality. This is
merely a further expression of the reflexive nature of all philosophical activity, but it does present a special difficulty for the
student who wishes to come to terms with his discipline by
finding some Archimedean point from which to operate. If the
theoretician is involved in some sort of reflexive regress, the
danger is that every conclusion is merely grist for a never-ending
further refinement in the philosophical mill. Such is not the case.
Given the radical reflection of the theorist who must face his
own activity, there emerges a cardinal theme for consideration
with regard to which both the scientist and the student must take
a stand. That theme is the nature of intellectual commitment, its
rationale and its existential implications.

The issue must be specified. In the natural sciences there is
a postulate of the uniformity of nature which is taken for granted
as the ground for all work. That physical reality lends itself to
scientific inquiry has been thoroughly demonstrated in the history
of science and provides more than a reasonable basis for assuming
that it will continue to do so in the future. But the assumption
remains an assumption. There can be no proof in any absolute
sense that the future will be like the past. For the purposes of
the enterprise of scientific work the postulation of uniformity
is sufficient. An analogous situation pertains in the sciences of
man. There, too, the assumption is that systematic analysis is
possible because social reality is, in principle, comprehensible.
Both assumptions, as well as the postulate that gives them methodological expression, rest upon a previous commitment that is
rarely stated and most often not even recognized. Before we are
interested in whether reality is knowable, we have already decided on whether knowing in itself is worthwhile. At the root of

16 Compare Edward A. Shils, "Social Inquiry and the Autonomy of
the Individual," in *The Human Meaning of the Social Sciences*.

all knowledge is a commitment in some form to its value. How one is to interpret that commitment is our present concern.

The paradox of the situation is apparent. If the conceptual apparatus of analysis and argumentation ordinarily used to support fundamental commitments itself rests upon the primordial *commitment to commitment*, it cannot be used, without circular reasoning, to validate the decision to know, to seek knowledge at all. It would seem that either we are confronted with an article of faith or that some order of pragmatic reasoning must be called into play. These possibilities must be considered. If basic commitment to knowledge rests upon an article of faith, then it has neither more nor less grounding than its contradictory, a refusal to seek to understand based on a fundamental lack of faith. If pragmatic considerations are going to be entertained as truly supporting arguments, then we are led to the plethora of human responses and motives, projections and satisfactions, which hardly yield any uniform results. Besides, to suggest that a commitment to knowledge is valid because it produces valid consequences presupposes that certain consequences will be recognized as valid and agreed upon as worth securing. Such recognition itself presupposes a value framework whose criteria must rest upon a fundamental commitment. It seems that either an extreme skepticism or a radical faith is the only consistent escape from these difficulties. Before accepting that conclusion another alternative must be considered.

Commitment to knowledge is at the heart of reason; the refusal of commitment is the essence of nihilism. Unless action in the social world be taken as a more or less conditioned and socio-psychologically motivated and sustained phenomenon, there is no completely persuasive argument, no *reason*, for the individual's continuing to bear the world he finds himself constantly within, perpetually straining to comprehend. But there is an order of decisive commitment at an existential level which may illuminate the meaning of both reason and nihilism as well as their dialectical interrelationship. By existential commitment we may understand an act in which the unique individual defines himself as a being who is the cause of order and purpose in the world. It is not an article of faith but the interior life of the person which is at issue in this order of commitment. The claim to the universal implications of such action rests upon the immediate experience of value and not a set of conceptual arguments. Instead of faith we have a structure of existence which is directly available to rational inspection.

Once again, the situation of the student of social reality might be taken as a base for clarifying these notions. The decision to do something meaningful in life rather than nothing at all can be examined apart from its manifold psychological and sociological background. The question at issue, then, is not, Why did an individual do something rather than nothing? but rather, In doing something or nothing what order of commitment is at the basis of decision? To speak of an existential commitment as grounding specific careers is merely to announce a descriptive possibility. The moral issue arises only when the individual is himself confronted in his actual existence with the reality of radical choice. Choosing a life which presupposes the validity of knowledge presents the person with the universal image hidden within his individual act: he has chosen to become that being who deems knowledge and reason intrinsically valuable. The relationship between particular and universal takes on a still more variegated significance. Furthermore, the very act of existential decision throws into relief the particularity of concrete existence, which otherwise remains taken for granted in the course of both daily life and much scientific investigation. The student who comes to see in the immediacy of commitment that his own life is a "concrete universal" (to borrow and adapt the language of Hegel) finds that the "decision to decide" is itself a moral act. Unhappily, such a realization carries with it some severe philosophical complications.

If the existential commitment to reason is possible, why not an equivalent commitment to unreason? Is it possible to have an existential nihilism? When asked for the purpose of his scholarly research, Weber answered: "I want to see how much I can stand."[17]

It is the affirming act which distinguishes the rationalist from the nihilist, not a disposition to optimism. More cautiously stated, nihilism can be defined as the refusal of existential commitment,

[17] See Reinhard Bendix, *Max Weber*, p. 9.

and the consistent nihilist can offer neither explanations for his choices nor reasons for his decisions. A rationale of nihilism at this fundamental level (and obviously we are not discussing political positions of the sort that have sometimes been called "nihilist") is a contradiction in terms. If one insists on speaking of a "commitment" to nihilism, it is an order of commitment which transcends explication as well as justification. It follows that the "decision to decide" is implicitly a celebration of the rationality of man and his determination to persist in trying to understand a reality that in itself offers little in the way of philosophical encouragement. At the same time, existential commitment illuminates the relationship between the concrete individual's life and the style of existence he has chosen. In the interplay between the concrete and the universal there arises a sense of social reality as the most matter of fact and yet the most remarkable of all things.

Despite our good intentions, the reader may have found the preceding discussion a bit grand for his tastes. What began as a statement of the province of the philosophy and methodology of the social sciences seems to have turned into a metaphysical arena for the encounter of existentialists and nihilists. It is as if one is invited to tea and finds himself suddenly ushered into a massive hall in which an ox is being roasted on a spit. Although I would insist that we have not gone as far from our starting point as it might seem, it might be judicious to turn to other matters, in particular to the complaints of the reader who might feel weary of the philosophical mazes of ultimate justification.

The student with little philosophical training or inclination who, nevertheless, has an open mind about what philosophy of the social sciences has to offer him also has a right to be heard. His interest, of course, is tied to the concrete problems he encounters in his study. What, then, has philosophy to say to him? Part of the answer to this question will be found after the reader has studied and discussed the essays which follow in this book, and after he has pursued and considered at least some of the works the titles of which appear in the Bibliography. Another part of the answer will emerge only with the passage of the time necessary to absorb basic philosophic challenges. This process cannot be ordered into a schedule. In the end, however, it may be that for some (and I hope they are few) very little will emerge from their flirtation with philosophy. One is tempted to speak of an academic Calvinism in this regard or to resound Coleridge's theme, but I prefer a different line, one which turns directly to the problems of the aphilosophical student of the social sciences as *he* experiences them.

A forthright listing of difficulties might help:

1. Is it really possible for a college senior majoring, let us say, in economics who has had but an introductory course in the field of philosophy to master the history of philosophy while he is studying the problems of philosophy and methodology of the social sciences in one semester or one year?

2. How can the reader grasp the problems of theory understood as *Weltanschauung* if he comes to that term without an appreciation of the history of ideas?

3. What difference does the relationship between particulars and universals make to the student of business administration who is simply trying to prepare for a job in management? And is it safe to tell a prospective employer in the course of an interview that you are concerned about nihilism?

4. Why isn't it more sensible to face methodological questions as they turn up in the course of actual study, in as reasonable a way as possible, instead of projecting vast conceptual schemes and employing the mysterious categories of philosophy?

5. What practical good results from the kind of study we are introducing here? Will it really make the student a better sociologist or historian or anthropologist?

6. Finally, assuming these questions are answered in a satisfactory way and the student is interested in making a start, where and how exactly shall he begin? Where is the door that leads into the fabulous mansion?

Before we comment on these genuine worries, it might be of some consolation to the worrier to learn that corresponding difficulties exist for the student of philosophy. How is he to come to terms with the overwhelming literature of the individual social sciences? Isn't he going to be accused of dilettantism despite his best efforts? And even if he gets into the literature of one social science, is it safe to assume that what he learns will carry over to the others? Once again, where does one really begin? If a convincing answer to all of these questions is unlikely, we may at least indicate a general direction the student might follow. First of all, it is hoped that this book of readings will serve as a guide to the individual seriously interested in a response to his difficulties. But as he might already suspect, philosophy is an unleasher of rude questions, not a guardian of salted truths. The reader who is looking for answers without being willing to suffer for his questions will find no solace in philosophy. On the other hand, the reader who is anxious to secure some theoretical foundation for his particular study of the social world will have the good fortune of making the acquaintance, in the pages of this book, of others who have shared his concern and who may understand his needs. There is, however, one type of reader who is unlikely to profit from what follows this Introduction. He is the fellow who, once having heard the word "methodology," is forever after blind to anything but what he conceives to be "methods" of doing things—the equivalent of the student in the natural sciences who understands by "methodology" reports on the latest techniques of setting up glassware in the chemistry laboratory. For this student it would be best if he got as far as reading these lines before writing his name in the book so that he could receive a full refund for it when he returns it to the store. This will not be his cup of tea.

For all students puzzled about just how to go about the study of theory and methodology I prescribe, in addition to steady doses of the chapters which follow, a reading of C. Wright Mills' essay "On Intellectual Craftsmanship."[18] It should provide a needed antidote to too much philosophizing, and if the reader finds contradictions between the advice given by Mills and the recommendations presented here, so much the better. But there should, at least, be one point of agreement. Neither theories nor methods, no matter how sophisticated their philosophical formulation, can be substitutes for intelligence and honesty. What is brilliant in the hands of a master sometimes becomes shoddy when taken over by a disciple. There is no alternative to

[18] This essay appears in C. Wright Mills, *The Sociological Imagination*, and is included in *Symposium on Sociological Theory*.

competence and responsibility within both science and philosophy. At the same time, competence and responsibility are not
enough.

It is unnecessary to dramatize the importance of philosophy
and its relevance for the social sciences. The student who remains fragmented in his disciplinary cell avoids the touch of
reality; the sense of security he gains is achieved at the expense
of his fundamental education. The moral and pedagogic dimension of the social sciences is illuminated by existential commitment. To the extent that the student struggles to grasp what it
means to be a being in the social world, the particular focus of
his work is broadened and deepened. Simultaneously *he* is broadened and deepened. If for no other reasons, philosophy serves a
heuristic function. But there are other reasons. To be concerned
with a segment of social reality is already to have some hint of
the nature of the whole. Although the social scientist as well as
the student may never be able to transcend the methodological
limits of his specialty, he can and ought to know that it is a
specialty within a wider range whose ultimate unity is social
reality itself, a metaphysical construction. Once again, the duality
of the concrete and the universal emerges. In the study of sociology or economics or political science it is ultimately the universal horizon of these fields which gives them a meaningful
placement in the hierarchy of all knowedge. The student who
fails to keep constantly before him the transcendent implications
of his concrete problems lacks a perspective vital to his life as
well as to his work. The ultimate reward of philosophy is to free
the philosopher from bondage to the fragmentation Nietzsche
warns against when he says: "*Ich habe meine Gründe vergessen*"
—I have forgotten why I ever began.[19]

[19] Quoted and translated in Karl Mannheim, *Ideology and Utopia*, p. 18.

PART I
Science
and
Society

··

Introduction to
PART I

THE OPPOSITION so obvious between the authors of the selections which follow immediately goes far beyond disagreements over matters of method or even, in one sense, theory. The radical cleavage between Lundberg and Simmel is a prime example of distinctively different *Weltanschauungen*, of qualitatively separate placements of the very meaning of science and the social. For Lundberg, scientific inquiry is restricted to phenomena which are subject to verification according to accepted canons of procedure. Thus, "All assertions about the *ultimate* 'reality,' 'nature,' 'essence,' or 'being' of 'things,' or 'objects' are therefore unverifiable hypotheses, and hence outside the sphere of science." Such notions as "mind," "feeling," and "motives" are meaningful for a scientific context only to the extent to which they are definable or translatable in operational terms. Some of the metaphysical language of antique science as well as some of the vocabulary of contemporary philosophical discourse can be salvaged by reducing them to units capable of controlled observation by competent witnesses. However, part of the vocabulary at issue is irreducible to a scientific denominator; it remains the "phlogiston" of the modern age. Finally, there is no line of demarcation in scientific methodology between the data of the natural and the social sciences. The social world, man included, of course, is an object for scientific investigation in essentially the same sense as any other aspect of reality. A science of the social is indeed possible, and the enterprise which seeks to establish it is already underway.

The world of Georg Simmel appears to be light-years away from that of Lundberg. The very title of his selection points to a primarily philosophical emphasis, for to ask, How is Society Possible? is, as Simmel indicates, to transpose Kant's question into social terms. Instead of the Newtonian framework that was the ground and the occasion for Kant's attempt to establish philosophy in strict form, Simmel's horizon is dominated by a concern for the manner in which sociation involves the concrete individual in the essential and invariant forms of social life. Those forms are the "apriorities" discussed in Simmel's essay. For the moment they may be understood, to use Kantian language, as the necessary conditions for the possibility of a certain range of experience. To call such essential forms "a priori" is only to emphasize their logical status, for such forms are prior to experience (in a logical rather than temporal sense) and their validity is independent of experience (without the suggestion that they are, like Plato's Ideas, reified in some metaphysical way). The search for the decisive universal grounds for the experience of social reality is, philosophically understood, an enterprise that is propaedeutic to social science.

At first glance, nothing would seem to have less in common than operationalism ("We say that anything is 'explained' or 'understood,' " Lundberg writes, "when we have reduced a situation to elements and correlations with which we are so familiar that we accept them as a matter of course so that our curiosity rests.") and Kantianism ("For Kant," writes Simmel, "nature is a particular way of cognizing, a picture growing through and in our cognitive categories."). Yet the historical motives underlying both have at least one line of convergence: Kant together with contemporary positivism was tremendously impressed with the achievements of mathematics and physics, and he tried to elucidate the epistemological source of their success. With that said, however, the great differences become manifest. Kant sought to illuminate the architecture of mind through a kind of inventory of forms and categories. One central result of this mode of philosophizing is that a philosophy of mind becomes a philosophy of consciousness, not a psychology of brain activity, but an exploration of the purely formative features of all perceptual activity. The methodological name for such investigation is transcendental philosophy, a style of analysis which is developed in nineteenth and twentieth century neo-Kantianism and phenomenology. Positivism, on the other hand, has little use for a priorism apart from its valid function in purely formal disciplines such as mathematics and logic. Its stress is rather on phenomena which are encountered in the course of behavior, phenomena already articulated in human experience, whose status and function in the social order become problematic to the social scientist. In these terms, a psychology of the mental would make more sense than a philosophy of consciousness. The former would be developed within the causal-genetic framework of natural science; the latter lends itself readily to the charge of being "metaphysical" in what is obviously a pejorative sense of that word.

If Lundberg and Simmel are that far apart, it might be asked what cause is served by bringing their writings together here. There are several answers possible. First, their writings are a testimony to the extreme dichotomy mentioned in the Foreword between "objective" and "subjective" approaches to social reality. In a way, the lack of dialogue between these thinkers is itself a communication to the reader. Second, the opposition set up in these first selections will reverberate throughout the volume, and a point made in the Introduction will find its embodiment: there are styles of thinkers as well as positions, and temperament is a philosophical theme. Third, these essays are broad enough in outlook to present the reader with some fundamental challenges regarding the nature of science and the reality which social scientists engage. What is the method of science? What are we to understand by the social? Despite their radical differences in approach, Lundberg and Simmel both raise these questions in interesting ways, whether directly or obliquely. Finally, both authors are involved in a study whose center is Man (or man). That Simmel would be happier with the capitalized form of the word and Lundberg more at ease with lower-case letters is a caution but not an absolute barrier to the posing of a large issue

which their work involves: the development of a philosophical
anthropology.

If it was Kant who posed the question of philosophical anthropology (What is Man?) in explicit terms, it is no less true
that this generative question has been resounded ever since his
time in increasingly sharper and yet more bewildering form. For
to ask the question (or to refrain from asking it) is to take a
stance with regard to the entire range of human experience. Man
is at issue; but also the concrete questioner is unsettled. In this
way we locate an aspect of the curious and powerful relationship
between universals and particulars which we spoke of in the Introduction. If Lundberg's conception of science and society
brackets the problem of the existential reality of the questioner
and would allow the meaningfulness of the question only in
empirically restricted terms, Simmel bases much of his sociology
upon the intrinsic fragmentation of the person. For him, Man is
a creature of partial possibilities and partial realizations: "All of
us are fragments, not only of general man, but also of ourselves."
It is this existential *aperçu* which marks the distance between the
"objective" and "subjective" approaches to social reality.

The Postulates of Science and Their Implications for Sociology[1]

GEORGE A. LUNDBERG

***

A. Science as a Technic of Adjustment

HUMAN SOCIOLOGY deals with the communicable adjustment technics which human groups have developed in their long struggle to come to terms with each other and with the rest of their environment. Science is, in the fields where it has been tried, the most conspicuously successful of these technics. As a human adjustment technic, science is primarily a *sociological* subject. Hence, if we start out with a brief consideration of this technic, we are not going outside our subject, but into a very vital aspect of it. Furthermore, since we wish to attempt to use this technic in the study of human group-behavior itself, it is not only permissible but necessary to consider first the implications of that approach.

All inquiry begins with an experienced tension or imbalance of some sort in the inquiring organism. "Tension" and "imbalance" are words used to describe the result of an imperfect adjustment. "Adjustment" is in turn a word used to describe the situation under which the activities of an organism come to rest

[1] Reprinted with the permission of the author, from his *Foundations of Sociology* (New York: The Macmillan Co., 1939, pp. 5–44).

NOTE: The Editor has made minor changes in the footnotes throughout the book in order to make them uniform.

or equilibrium.[2] The latter we define, as in physics, as the state of maximum probability in any organism or other system. We shall also refer to this state of maximum probability as the "normal" in any societal situation.

[2] It is still conventional in sociology to refer to adjustment in terms of an organism's "striving" or "need" for "certain ends." For many purposes this anthropomorphic terminology is useful. But for the sake of consistency with the terminology of other sciences, we propose to deal with the phenomena in question in a framework in which the terms "needs" and "ends" are unnecessary. It is possible to interpret the event of a stone rolling down a hill into a brook as a striving or a need of the stone for the brook, and in many other terms and frameworks of which ethnology furnishes various examples. But in the scientific frame of reference we have adopted and defined operationally such terms as "mass," "gravity," and "field of force," as more suitable for our purpose. That purpose in science is to explain as much as possible by as few terms or symbols as possible—the principle of parsimony. We adopt here the viewpoint of modern psychology that the behavior of nervous tissue and of organisms is explicable in the same basic terms as the behavior of other matter. In this orientation, "needs" become merely biophysical or biochemical imbalances in an organism or between it and its environment. Cf. J. Dewey, *Logic: The Theory of Inquiry*, p. 27: "The state of disturbed equilibration constitutes *need*." That organisms behave with reference to the anticipated results of the behavior is, of course, admitted, as is all other observed behavior. In our frame of reference such "ends" whenever they figure in a behavior situation exist in the form of symbols of some kind and organisms respond to these symbols just as they respond to other stimuli. These symbols and whatever they stand for are from our point of view merely part of the data of the situation, and have the same power of influencing conduct as any other phenomena that precipitate responses. The present treatment assumes an elementary knowledge of modern psychology and physiology.

The above position should dispel the curious notion that behavioristic or positivistic theory denies or ignores the problems of ends, values, etc., in behavior. For example R. K. Merton ("Durkheim's Division of Labor in Society," *American Journal of Sociology*, XL, 1934, 321) says: "For, if, as positivism would have us believe, logic and science can deal only with empirical facts, with sensa, then a science of social phenomena, on that score alone becomes impossible, since this attitude relegates to the limbo all ends [*sic*] i.e., subjective anticipations of *future* occurrences without a consideration of which human behavior becomes inexplicable." The symbols by and through which man anticipates the future or in terms of which he reacts to any "ends" are as tangible and objective phenomena as any other that precipitate behavior. If any positivist or behaviorist actually held such views as those attributed to them above, there would, of course, be ample ground for agitation on the part of the critics. But even J. B. Watson, whose more popular works are usually relied upon to furnish unguarded statements susceptible of such interpretation, was quite explicit and emphatic on the above point. "Let me make this fundamental point at once: that *saying* is doing—that is *behaving*. Speaking overtly or to ourselves (thinking) is just as objective a type of behavior as baseball." (*Behaviorism*, p. 6.)

When certain tensions are formulated verbally they tend to take the form of a question. The tentative, experimental answer to this question is called a hunch, a guess, a hypothesis, or a postulate. A tentative answer of this kind serves as a basis for the orderly assembling of data which will establish more firmly, modify, or refute the hypothesis. A hypothesis which is corroborated by repeated observations made by all qualified observers is thereupon called a principle or a law. Hunches, hypotheses, and guesses are produced, of course, by the responses of the organism to some situation, i.e., through data of experience, just as are the more adequately supported generalizations called principles or laws. "Hunches" differ from "principles" only in that the former rest upon more subjective (i.e., private, unverified), transitory, and quantitatively inadequate data. These characteristics frequently have misled men to believe that "hunches" are somehow generated spontaneously in the "mind"—a view which is here repudiated in favor of the position stated above.[3]

See also my paper "Is Sociology Too Scientific?" *Sociologus*, IX, 1933, 311–312. Also C. L. Hull, "Goal Attraction and Directing Ideas Conceived as Habit Phenomena," *Psychological Review*, XXXVIII, 505. Also note 20 below.

[3] It may be well to indicate briefly at this point my general position regarding the allegedly "mental" character of societal phenomena. For illustrative purposes I refer to some statements in the otherwise unobjectionable discussion by L. von Wiese and H. Becker, *Systematic Sociology*, ch. II, p. 33. E.g., "To be sure, our senses can perceive only *concrete objects*, in the form of discrete human bodies, and between them only the atmosphere, other organisms, and inorganic matter. *Plurality patterns themselves cannot be thus perceived* and can be made corporeally apparent only by symbols. Nevertheless, many of them are recognizable in our *internal world* of presentations, concepts and images. They live in the minds of tangible human beings, men, in the neuro-psychic patterns of human beings." [Italics mine.] (See also the section heading of the same page which reads: "Plurality patterns are not perceivable, but nevertheless are real." (!)) If we investigate wherein resides the "concreteness" of the "objects" which our senses perceive, we would probably be forced to agree with Bentley (*Behavior, Knowledge, Fact*, pp. 209–210), who in a brilliant chapter on "The Visibility of the Social," remarks: "Not that the words 'concrete' and 'abstract' have significance in modern scientific application; they are nebulous wraiths surviving from primitive man's attempts at description, serving today merely for the crudest contrasts and reports." When our senses perceive "concrete objects" we respond to behavior of some sort (i.e., light rays from an object strike the optic nerve). If this reaction ever becomes knowledge to us at all, i.e., if we symbolize it, we do so because the response (usually symbolized) fits into a system of past responses (also

In its maturest form the content of science consists of a body of verified propositions so related that under given rules (logic) the system is self-consistent and compatible with empirical observation. The more universally applicable these propositions are, i.e., the greater the variety of phenomena covered by the propo-

---

usually symbolized) as a frame of reference which gives the response meaning. If we say that certain social structures exist it is likewise because our senses react to some behavior. We symbolize this response into "presentations," "images," and "concepts." Then *these* (in common with our images of "concrete" objects) "live" in our "minds" and the minds of those to whom we may be able to communicate. In short, Wiese and Becker overlook in the above case the "concrete objects" (behavior) from which they derive their symbolic "image" of social structures, and in the other case overlook the *symbolic process* by which they derive the "images" of the "concrete objects"—in both cases because traditional philosophy and logic (symbolic systems) have thoroughly habituated us to (in fact require) such dichotomies between the "social" (human) and the "physical." The dichotomy is in the nature of a primary postulate taken over perhaps from theology. There is no support whatever for the postulate in modern science. Wiese and Becker come very near to my position later in the same section when they say: "Strictly speaking, a social structure never consists of human beings but of images, presentations and concepts which may be traced back to relationships. . . . *Relationship-structures exist only in and through human ideas.*" [Italics mine.] If they would say the same for *all* knowledge we would be agreed. I would say that our knowledge of "social" *and* "physical" structure-relationships consists of images, etc., which may be traced back to *that which* evoked them.

I am in full accord with the following estimate of Wiese's position by Bentley ("Sociology and Mathematics," *Sociological Review*, XXIII, 1931): "Turning to recent German sociology, the development of L. von Wiese is the one most fully in accord with what is here attempted. Taking his initiative from Simmel's presentation of forms of socialization as do all of the more important recent German sociologists, Wiese stresses as fundamental the immediate and direct observation of a realm of social fact. This is his 'sozial Optik' vital to his entire work. Differing from the present approach, however, he coordinates the social realm with the physical and psychical realms: accepting these latter as he finds them in their respective lines of scientific investigation: and demanding only for the social its full right to its own independent investigation, on a par with the others. In this social realm he finds possibilities of measuring and counting: and these are not mere borrowings from other sciences, but are peculiarly social techniques." (P. 160.) Because of this he asserts the existence of a peculiarly social space, "without, however, proceeding to a fully functional analysis of it in system with physical space presentations." The physical space therefore appears as an outlying or indirect "cause" of happenings in social space, and not as an intimately involved region of the full sociological investigation. (P. 161.)

Significant in this connection is Wiese's attempt to derive "sociologically

sitions, the more adequate is our knowledge of the field which they cover. Thus, nearly all empirically observed behavior of bodies from the point of view of their movement in space and time are "covered" by the general "principles" of physics. That is, events as "different" (from some points of view) as a man falling from a twentieth story window, a bullet fired into the air from a rifle, or drops of water in a rain storm, are all "explained" by the same basic principle.

No two cases of any of these events are ever identical in all respects nor are the natural conditions under which they occur ever the same. Yet by a process of ignoring all this variety and concentrating our attention on some single characteristic or aspect of the event (abstracting), we can make general statements that are equally true for all falling men, all rain drops, and all

---

usable materials through intensive analysis of words denoting relations, etc." He reports (Wiese-Becker, *Systematic Sociology*, p. 129) that a seminar at the University of Cologne devoted itself to lexicographic research over a period of years with the object of listing all words with "definite sociological meaning." "It soon became evident," he says, "that the plan covered too much territory, for in spite of relatively minute divisions of labor a full year was consumed in working through the letter A." While lists of such words may be of historical interest and while they may be suggestive of behavior phenomena to be looked for, the words thus found are unfortunately too frequently accorded quite other significance. It is assumed that since the word exists, it must have a counterpart in nature, and any system which leaves out the *word* is therefore defective. To include all words *as data* in sociology is obviously entirely different from including all the vague allusions of folklore-words in the vocabulary of scientific sociology. It is the latter tendency which is here under criticism.

In this connection I am also in agreement with the following criticism of a position which has been put forward by K. Lewin (*Principles of Topological Psychology*), and J. F. Brown (*Psychology and the Social Order*): "Although efforts have recently been made to distinguish two types of empirical statement, 'the language of data' and the 'language of constructs,' it appears evident to the psychologist that the dichotomy is artificial. A statement about a datum is a statement about a construct. The simple statement, 'I see red,' is a complex response conditional upon previous training and present circumstances of an organism and differs only in complexity from a statement such as, 'The oscillograph shows that the discharge takes place at a potential of 80 volts.' The notion of a language of Data is reminiscent of the concept of an absolute 'given' and since it can be shown that the immediately given experience is defined operationally as consisting of relatively elementary differential responses, we had best dispense with the distinction between data and constructs." (Pp. 99–100, S. S. Stevens, "Psychology: The Propaedeutic Science," *Philosophy of Science*, IV, 1936, 90–103.) See also note 7 below.

projectiles. This standardization of widely different events is achieved either through actual laboratory controls or through symbolic, usually statistical, devices. Thus are myriads of unique events of the most heterogeneous nature described, classified, summarized, and "explained" by showing that they are only special cases of a general rule or law already "understood" and in terms of which we have become accustomed to make adjustments to these events. We say that anything is "explained" or "understood" when we have reduced a situation to elements and correlations with which we are so familiar that we accept them as a matter of course so that our curiosity rests. By "element" we mean any component which we do not consider it necessary or possible further to analyze. Understanding a situation means, from the operational point of view, discovering familiar elements and correlations between them.[4]

As a result of his familiarity with the principles which govern (describe, explain) most of the events in the so-called "physical"[5] universe, man adjusts today to these events with relative

---

[4] Cf. P. W. Bridgman, *The Logic of Modern Physics*, p. 37. Failure to recognize this point has been the basis of much futile controversy such for example as the contention that statistics may *describe* but can never *explain* a situation. This position usually assumes that true "explanation" must always be in terms of lower levels, e.g., psychology in terms of physiology, physiology in terms of chemistry, etc. J. F. Brown (*op. cit.*), and K. Lewin (*A Dynamic Theory of Personality*), also seem to repudiate on other but equally fallacious grounds, the value of classification as a predictive device. If it has been established statistically that children lose their teeth at a certain age, then the classification of a child as of that age explains, in the sense defined above, the loss of his teeth and enables us to predict the event. Curiosity about the biological sequences leading up to that event is *also* desirable and the satisfaction of such curiosity (i.e., reducing the phenomenon to elements with which we are so familiar that we accept them as a matter of course) is a type of explanation on another level. Such explanation consists of classifying this particular phenomenon under some general and already established generalization of biology. That generalization is in the last analysis based on precisely the same kind of repeated observation as is the generalization that children of a certain age group lose their teeth. Such reduction is, of course, desirable in the pursuit of relatively comprehensive and unified knowledge and the suggestion by Brown and Lewin that we need *further* explanation of social phenomena in terms of the field structure within which they operate is quite true. It is an overstatement, however, to claim that classification is without explanatory or predictive value.

[5] I use the word "physical" in quotation marks in order to emphasize that I do not recognize this word as denoting, for scientific purposes, any unique character of the phenomena to which this word is usually used to

emotional equanimity. That is, his curiosity and other adjustments come to rest relatively easily and without the fears, doubts, angers, and magical practices which accompanied his adjustment to these events in prescientific times. The absence of reliable principles brings forth a vast amount of trial-and-error blundering and emotional squirmings in social adjustments as compared to our relatively systematic adjustments to the "physical" world. Scientific knowledge operates, therefore, as a sort of mental hygiene in the fields where it is applied. If the morning paper reports an earthquake, an eclipse, a storm, or a flood, these events are immediately referred to their proper place in the framework of science, in which their explanation, i.e., their relationship to other events, has already been worked out. Hence each new event of this character calls for very little, if any, "mental" or "emotional" strain upon the organism so far as our intellectual adjustment to it as an event is concerned.

Political and social upheavals, on the other hand, such as wars, revolutions, and crime are to most people a matter of shock and much personal recrimination and other emotionalism. Yet these societal events are "natural" in the same sense that "physical" events are "natural." "Natural" and "physical" are of course merely words by which we describe a relatively objective (corroborated) type of adjustment to the phenomena so designated. Unfortunately, it is at present very generally assumed that these terms represent not merely a type of adjustment technic on our part, but that such terms as "physical" and "natural" are inherent characterizations of *some* phenomena in the universe but not of others. The other type or types of data are variously and vaguely designated as "social," "cultural," "mental," and "spiritual." These terms, instead of being regarded as describing those situations to which we make at present a relatively subjective and emotional type of adjustment, are likewise *attributed to data as inherent characteristics*. The result of this semantic confusion has been a most mischievous separation of fields of knowledge into the

---

refer as contrasted with the phenomena designated "social," "cultural," etc. Since all phenomena are "physical" from my point of view, I retain the word only to designate a conventional distinction which must be defined, if at all, only in terms of the degree of universality and uniformity of responses of human beings to some phenomena as contrasted with others.

"natural" and "physical" on the one hand as against the "social" and "cultural" (mental, nonmaterial, spiritual) on the other. As a consequence, it has been assumed that the methods of studying the former field are not applicable to the latter. The generally admitted lag in the progress of the "social" as contrasted with the "physical" sciences has been a further result.

The history of science consists largely of the account of the gradual expansion of realms of the "natural" and the "physical" at the expense of the "mental" and the "spiritual." One by one "spiritual" phenomena have become "physical." This is not the place to review that history. It is readily available elsewhere and its implications for the point here under discussion are reasonably clear. The evolution of the concept of the "soul" is especially relevant, because its final stage of transition or translation by way of the "mind" into purely "physical" concepts is still under way. The resistance which this transition is encountering in some quarters is especially instructive because it illustrates the widespread linguistic confusion as to the nature of verbal symbols.

B. *The Postulates of Science*

To prevent constant digression and misunderstandings from arising, it is necessary in this connection to call attention explicitly to the postulates and their corollaries upon which this essay proceeds. This will seem to some to be a needless repetition and elaboration of the obvious. To others the postulates will seem unjustified. The implications of these assumptions will be set forth in this and subsequent chapters. Only as much of the reasoning will be given here as is necessary to make clear the assumptions themselves. The ultimate justification for the point of view adopted must wait upon the results it yields in clarifying thinking, in stimulating cumulatively productive research, and finally in providing that groundwork of knowledge on which alone effective practical adjustments can be made.

The basic postulates regarding the nature of "reality" and "knowledge" upon which all science proceeds may be briefly stated as follows:

1. All data or experience with which man can become concerned consist of *the responses of the organisms-in-environment*.

This includes the postulate of an external world and variations both in it and the responders to it.[6]

2. Symbols, usually verbal, are invented to represent these responses.

3. These symbols are the immediate data of all communicable knowledge and therefore of all science.

4. All propositions or postulates regarding the more ultimate "realities" must always consist of inference, generalizations, or abstractions from these symbols and the responses which they represent.

5. These extrapolations are in turn represented symbolically, and we respond to them as we respond to other phenomena which evoke behavior.

C. Corollaries and Implications for Sociology

Some of the corollaries and implications of these postulates, especially as they affect present methods in the social sciences, need to be emphasized and elaborated briefly.

1. THE INFERENTIAL NATURE OF KNOWLEDGE AND "REALITY"

In the first place according to these postulates, all statements about the nature of the universe or any part of it are necessarily a verbalization of somebody's responses to *that which* evoked these responses. The nature of that which evoked them must always be an inference from the immediate datum, namely, our symbolized sensory experience.[7] All assertions about the *ultimate*

---

[6] "Through the frosted windows of our senses we may say, if we please, that we receive impressions of what we call the 'external universe' or 'reality.' But it is not necessary to say anything so mystical—at least for the present. It is sufficient to recall that certain scientific philosophers are content to start from the sense impressions themselves as 'reality' without seeking for anything less familiar and more disputable. Einstein for one, in his paper of 1936, appears to be satisfied to identify reality provisionally with the sense impressions which others refer to a yet more recondite reality." (E. T. Bell, *The Handmaiden of the Sciences*, pp. 17, 18. See also note 14 below.)

[7] This statement should not be understood to mean that I consider sensory experience as an absolute datum or starting point in the sense that Hume and Hobbes (to mention no others before and since) seem to have held. I take rather the position of E. C. Singer (*Mind as Behavior*) which regards the immediate datum as an *ideal terminus* of abstraction. What we have to work with as immediate data are our *knowledge* of sensory experience, i.e., inferences (symbolic representations), from sensation. "The purely

"reality," "nature," "essence," or "being" of "things," or "objects" are therefore unverifiable hypotheses, and hence outside the sphere of science. Conversely, we assume that man and culture are definitely part of the cosmos. The *cosmos* is a word by which we designate the sum total of all the influences that precipitate responses in man. We assume further, that all phenomena of man and culture, in common with all nonhuman phenomena, are entirely contained within the cosmos and entirely dependent upon the energy transformations within that cosmos. We start with symbolized human responses as the immediate datum. As a metaphysical necessity we grant *that which* in the universe outside of the responding mechanism precipitates the response. After this is done, science is not concerned with the particular metaphysical hypotheses anyone may prefer to hold about the more ultimate nature of *that which* arouses responses.

2. WORDS AS OBJECTIVE PHENOMENA

It follows from the above that for scientific purposes all attempted distinctions, hypotheses, or assumptions regarding differences in the *ultimate* "nature" of so-called "physical" as contrasted with "social" data, between "material" and "immaterial," "mental," "spiritual," or "cultural" phenomena are ruled out. No relevant data (e.g., behavior designated by such words as "spiritual," etc.) are ruled out if they are manifest in human be-

---

objective world and the purely subjective datum of consciousness are two ideals toward which we can endlessly strive, modifying our notions of each as we change our understanding of the other. . . . It is only in this process of reconstruction that the concepts of 'consciousness' and 'object of consciousness' fall out—*they fall out together*, and together they grow apace. To follow the adventures of this pair is, I suspect, to be led deep into the heart of things." (P. 30.) For elaboration of the point see Singer, *op. cit.*, ch. 9 on "Sensation and the Datum of Science." See also W. James, *Principles of Psychology*, I, p. 508. See also John Dewey, *op. cit.*, p. 38: "In a proper conception of experience, inference, reasoning and conceptual structures are as experiential as is observation, and . . . the fixed separation between the former and the latter has no warrant beyond an episode in the history of culture." Also W. V. Metcalf, "The Reality of the Atom": "And just what is this fundamental philosophical distinction between 'percept' and 'concept'?—the 'percept' of the 'real' table and of the 'real' meteor, and the 'concept' of the atom? . . . Are they not both mental constructs of what we have come to believe exists in the external world? . . . The view that seems to me worth emphasizing is that *all* our beliefs in external reality are the result of inference from our subjective sense-data."

havior of *any observable kind*. At present we shall attempt to deal only with the more objective of these behaviors. But since objectivity is here regarded *not as a characteristic of things but as those ways of responding which can be corroborated by others*,[8] it follows that the framework of science affords place for all known or knowable data. Of course, the less developed our objectifying technics are for certain experiences (i.e., the "subjective" and "spiritual") the greater is the task of communicating them so that they can be verified (the test of objectivity). Indeed, this process of objectifying them may involve analysis, reclassification, and designation by new and strange symbols. Many terms at present employed probably will be abandoned entirely as devoid of content when the behavior phenomena to which they once referred has been more adequately described by other terms. As science has advanced, this has been true of all prescientific terms and categories. In this connection we encounter one of the chief obstacles to the translation of subjective experience into objective data, i.e., communicating the former and rendering them verifiable. Let us take only one illustration.

In the opinion of the best chemists as recently as 150 years ago, *phlogiston* was a necessary element in the explanation of combustion. The theory was that in all materials that burn there is present phlogiston, a substance without color, odor, taste, or weight. Even Priestley, to whom the discovery of oxygen is usually credited, continued to maintain during his lifetime the existence of phlogiston and the part it was supposed to play in combustion. By experiments involving much careful and accurate weighing, Lavoisier was able to demonstrate finally the unnecessary character of the hypothetical entity, phlogiston. Nevertheless, the older chemists of the day, thoroughly habituated to

8 Under this definition, objectivity is always a matter of degree and is always relative to the sensory equipment and general response capacities of responding organisms. The phenomena corroborated by everyone are thus considered the most objective. Corroboration by all or most "qualified observers" is frequently substituted for mere preponderance of general opinion in cases where the prestige of the "qualified" is such that we accept their responses as more valid than our own. This viewpoint is further elaborated later in this chapter. (See points 3 and 4). Cf. Aristotle: "Whatever appears true to everybody must be accepted as such; and he who denies the validity of universal opinion can hardly produce any more valid criterion of his own." (*Aristotle, from Natural Science, Psychology, and The Nicomachean Ethics*, trans. P. H. Wheelwright, p. 212.)

thinking about fire in terms of phlogiston continued to "feel"
that the new explanation "left something out." It did leave something out, namely, a *word* to which the chemists of the day had
become thoroughly habituated, and which was therefore as "real"
to them as the word "wood" or whatever other words are used
to symbolize the factors assumed to be present in a given fire.
However, we do not contend that by abandoning phlogiston,
modern chemists refuse to recognize a vital or relevant element
in the explanation of fire.

Today, however, a considerable number of students of
societal phenomena are still firmly convinced that the phenomena
with which they have to deal cannot be adequately described or
explained without, for example, a category called "mind," which
carries with it a whole vocabulary of subsidiary terms (thought,
experience, feeling, judgment, choice, will, value, emotion, etc.,
etc.). "We forget that these nouns are merely substitutes for
verbs and go hunting for the things denoted by the nouns; but
there are no such things; there are only the activities that we
started with."[9] By this oversight, also, we avoid the necessity of
defining operationally the behavior-units into which the phenomena of any field must be divided for scientific purposes. Any
attempt to deal in other words with the behavior which these
words are used to represent meets with the most determined resistance on the ground that "*something* has been left out." And
what has been left out? Why, "will," "feeling," "ends," "motives," "values," etc. These are the phlogiston of the social sciences. Argument or demonstration that the behavior represented
by these words is accorded full recognition within the present
framework of the "physical" sciences are to some apparently as
futile as were the arguments against phlogiston to Priestley. He
just knew that any system which left out the word phlogiston
was *ipso facto* fallacious. I have no doubt that a considerable part
of the present content of the social sciences will turn out to be
pure phlogiston. That fact will be discovered as soon as someone
attempts operational definitions of the vocabulary which at present confounds these sciences. Yet, it is on the basis of such words

[9] J. H. Robinson in *The Story of Human Error*, ed. J. Jastrow, p. 276.
The quotation is attributed to Professor Woodworth.

that we undertake to set up a separate universe[10] to which the methods of inquiry recognized in the other ("physical") universe is held not to apply. The Germans properly designate this former field as that of the "Geisteswissenschaften." The distinction between "science" and "social science" is, in fact, quite generally accepted as a matter of course. The present work continues, as a matter of necessity, to use the terminology here criticized because it is our purpose to communicate with the present generation. Also it is necessary to bring about the desired transition through the substitution of a new content for some of the old terms rather than abandoning them outright. Useless or undesirable words should be allowed to die as their content is taken over by new and more adequate terms. We contemplate a gradual transition to a dimensional and operational terminology.

The following illustration from contemporary sociological literature further illustrates the tendency to regard familiar words as essential components of situations: "There is an essential difference, from the standpoint of causation, between a paper flying before the wind and a man flying from a pursuing crowd. The paper knows no fear and the wind no hate, but without fear and hate the man would not fly nor the crowd pursue. If we try to reduce fear to its bodily concomitants we merely substitute the concomitants for the reality experienced as fear. *We denude the world of meanings for the sake of a theory itself a false meaning which deprives us of all of the rest.*"[11]

Note the essential nature of the words *hate* and *fear* in this analysis. Even their translation into terms of their behavior-referents is alleged to "denude the world of meanings." Now if anyone wishes to interpret the flying of a paper before the wind in terms of hate and fear, as has doubtless frequently been done in ages past, I know of no way of refuting the analysis for it is determined by the terms, the framework, and the meanings adopted. *These categories* are not given in the phenomenon. Neither are the categories I should use in scientific description so given. In fact, I have no objection to the words "fear" and "hate"

[10] E.g., M. Cohen's categorical statement "Psychic forces are not physical forces." *Reason and Nature*, p. 360.
[11] R. M. MacIver, *Society*, pp. 476–477. [Italics mine.]

if they are defined in terms of physico-chemical, biolinguistic, or sociological behavior subject to objective verification. I have no doubt, either, that descriptions in these terms would vary widely in different cases of flying objects. For this reason, I do not declare MacIver's analysis of the man and the crowd as *false*. I merely point out that possibly I could analyze the situation in a frame of reference not involving the words "fear" or "hate" but in operationally defined terms of such character that all qualified observers would independently make the same analysis and predict the behavior under the given circumstances. Such a demonstration would not, of course, constitute an adequate substitute explanation to some people any more than Lavoisier's interpretation of fire was satisfactory to Priestley. Indeed, that interpretation is still meaningless to those not familiar with the framework and terminology of chemistry and physics. On the other hand, the principle of parsimony requires that we seek to bring into the same framework the explanation of all flying objects. In an animistic culture the imputation of fear to all flying objects (under the above circumstances) fulfills this requirement. Gradually, however, this explanation was abandoned for all inorganic phenomena, and more recently for the lower animals. The fear-hate categories are not generally used in describing or "explaining" the approach of the amoeba to its food although even the amoeba approaches food that can move away in a different way than it approaches food which has no power of locomotion.

The idea that the same general laws may be applicable to both "physical" and societal behavior may seem fantastic and inconceivable to many people. It is literally inconceivable to those who do not possess the symbolic technology in terms of which alone it can be conceived. For this reason, it may be that the next great developments in the social sciences will come not from professed social scientists but from people trained in other fields. The contributions of men like Comte, Ward, and Pareto, all of them technically trained in other sciences and in mathematics, are significant in this connection. In present day psychology, likewise, the major contributions are being made by men trained in engineering, physiology, and other "physical" sciences. This does not mean the contribution of social scientists will be worthless. They have performed and will perform valuable services in pointing out data, problems, and difficulties in their field. With much data already available, scientists with more adequate technical equipment will probably make the most important contributions to systematic sociology for some time to come. In the meantime, the general scientific and technical equipment of social scientists is, of course, rapidly improving.

The doctrine that man is the one unique object in the universe whose behavior cannot be explained within the framework found adequate for all others is, of course, a very ancient and respectable one. We merely make the contrary assumption in this work. From the latter point of view a paper flying before the wind is interpreted as the behavior of an object of *specified characteristics* reacting to a stimulus of *specified characteristics* within a specified field of force. Within this framework we describe the man and the crowd, the paper and the wind. The characteristics of these elements (and they may be specified to any degree desired) would never be the same in any two cases of wind and paper or of men and crowds. But it is the faith of science that sufficiently general principles can be found to cover all these situations, and that through these principles reliable predictions can be made of the probability of specific events.

3. THE RELATIVITY OF "EXISTENCE" AND "REALITY"

It will be observed that the above position regards "existence" and "reality" as always relative to some responding organism and that these words designate nothing absolute or final of the type usually implied by such words as "truth" and "fact." The only metaphysical position necessary and compatible with science is a postulate conceding the existence of *whatever* precipitates our responses, but making no further statements whatever about the absolute nature, characteristics, or temporal-spatial qualities of these postulated entities. Phenomena exist for those organisms which respond to the stimuli in question but do not exist for organisms which do not so respond. If "wall" is defined as that which obstructs the movement of a person toward a given place, the existence of the wall is predicated upon that observed behavior of the person. To a micro-organism whose movement is in no way hindered by that which obstructs the person, the wall does not exist under the definition we have adopted. "Existence," "reality," the verb "is" as a mystical general designation, and a large number of similar words, and rules of logic constructed from them, are merely words designating behavior and behavior relationships. Apart from this behavior, the words are without content for science.

The deepseated nature of these language habits and the rules of logic couched in these terms cause many people to feel that the bottom drops out of all "sensible" discourse unless *certain* things (as contrasted with the mere postulate of *something*) can be declared to *exist* quite irrespective of anybody's responses to them. If this position is assumed, it follows that *someone must declare what things do so exist*. In spite of the mischief and obscurantism which has resulted from this position throughout history, contemporary scientists, and especially social scientists, are still inclined to cling to some "eternal verities" specified or implicitly taken for granted by themselves. They still undertake to discard new theories precisely on the same ground as did certain contemporaries of Galileo, namely, the conflict of these theories with "ultimate realities."[12] The latter are assumed to be given in nature and self-evident to all decent and competent persons. We are usually so thoroughly habituated to the "ultimate realities" as to be unaware of the origin of these word-habits and impatient of any inquiry into that subject. The most vigorous critics of *past* obscurantists are likely to be also the most passionate defenders of the current faith. Did not their present beliefs triumph over "Falsehood," "Error," "Superstition," etc. and does not this sufficiently establish the former as "Truth" now finally "discovered"? Because of their mistaken notion that these words are absolute *entities* of some sort instead of an organism's designation of certain types of responses entirely relative to itself, they follow precisely in the footsteps of the popes and the priests for whom they profess such contempt.

Scientists had better confine themselves to a modest postulate of "*x*" which precipitates our responses and the nature of which we tentatively infer from these responses. The justification of even the postulate of the "*x*" had better be its demonstrable efficiency in helping us comprehend our world rather than in vociferous declarations about its "existence" and its "truth." Then

---

[12] See A. Einstein and L. Infeld, *The Evolution of Physics*, p. 33.

if, for example, the time ever comes when the data of experience are more adequately comprehended by the assumption of a round rather than an elliptical orbit of the earth or any other modification in even the most widely accepted viewpoints, we can with full freedom and consistency adopt such a view.

Informed scientists in other fields have, of course, accepted this view of even their most stable formulations. Einstein and Infeld have expressed the viewpoint with admirable clarity in the following passage:

> In our endeavor to understand reality we are somewhat like a man trying to understand the mechanism of a closed watch. He sees the face and the moving hands, even hears its ticking, but he has no way of opening the case. If he is ingenious he may form some picture of a mechanism which could be responsible for all the things he observes, but he may never be quite sure his picture is the only one which could explain his observations. *He will never be able to compare his picture with the real mechanism and he cannot even imagine the possibility or the meaning of such a comparison.* But he certainly believes that, as his knowledge increases, his picture of reality will become simpler and simpler and will explain a wider and wider range of his sensuous impressions. He may also believe in the existence of the ideal limit of knowledge and that it is approached by the human mind. He may call this ideal limit the objective truth.[13] [Italics mine.]

The same authors have also recognized a point too frequently overlooked by those who believe that past theories were merely a morass of error serving no purpose but to obscure the truth now so happily finally attained. Say Einstein and Infeld: "The new theory shows the merits as well as the limitations of the old theory and allows us to regain our old concepts from a higher level. This is true not only for the theories of electric fluids and

---

[13] *Ibid.* It is interesting to note that this, on the whole, excellent statement runs afoul of itself on account of the speech habits which even these authors are unable to avoid when they attempt popular exposition. Note the contradiction in the sentence in italics in the text. My criticism in the text is directed at precisely this linguistic habit of talking about *"real* mechanisms" of which we "cannot *even imagine* the possibility or meaning" as compared to our conception of them!

field, but for all changes in physical theories, however revolutionary they may seem. . . . To use a comparison, we could say that creating a new theory is not like destroying an old barn and erecting a skyscraper in its place. It is rather like climbing a mountain, gaining new and wider views, discovering unexpected connections between our starting point and its rich environment. But the point from which we started out still exists and can be seen, although it appears smaller and forms a tiny part of our broad view gained by the mastery of the obstacles on our adventurous way up."[14]

[14] *Ibid.*, pp. 158, 159. Cf. also the following passages from these authors:

"The [electromagnetic] field *did not exist* for the physicist of the early years of the nineteenth century." (p. 157.)

"There would be no place in our new physics, for both field and matter, *field being the only reality*," . . . But we have not yet succeeded in formulating a pure field physics. For the present we must still assume the existence of both: field and matter." (pp. 258, 260.) [Italics mine.]

"The reality created by modern physics is, indeed, far removed from the reality of the early days. But the aim of every physical theory still remains the same. . . . Quantum physics formulates laws governing crowds and not individuals. Not properties but probabilities are described, not laws disclosing the future of systems are formulated, but laws governing the changes in time of the probabilities and relating to great congregations of individuals." (pp. 312–313.)

"But what I am trying to do is to push the analysis so far back that we are asking ourselves what it means to say that a world really 'exists' independently of ourselves and our sensations. I am trying to point out that any meaning I find in making such a statement is found in things *which I do* and experience, of which I am aware." (P. W. Bridgman, *The Intelligent Individual and Society*, pp. 152–153.) [Italics mine.]

The following statement by A. P. Weiss has, I think, never been improved upon:

"Metaphysics, for the behaviorist, is merely a name for special types of linguistic habits that have been acquired by reading other books on metaphysics, rhetoric, grammar, etc. A metaphysical analysis is essentially an analysis of a verbal statement of some sort into other verbal statements that are historically related. . . . One of the problems of science is that of determining the antecedent conditions which precede the appearance of some experimental or technical result. Next the antecedents of the antecedents are isolated, and so the investigations are continued backward until a stage is reached beyond which experimental analysis or observation has not gone. The usefulness of any guess as to the nature of unobserved antecedents depends upon how well the guess is verified when the experimental technique will have been refined to the point at which a testing of the validity of the guess or prediction is possible. Thus, until recently by following this method, the chemist regarded the atom, of which he postulated about ninety different kinds, as the ultimate unit or element in the structure of matter. As experimentation became more refined, the guess of ninety different kinds

The above reasoning applies with equal validity to our most firmly established orientations and to our more transient theories. It is not likely that we shall have to revise our notion of the earth's shape. But it is highly likely that we shall have to abandon or thoroughly revise some of our most profoundly held notions

---

of elements was not verified. A new guess was proposed by the physicists, —the electron-proton hypothesis, in which the number of units was reduced to two. For the physicist, then, the electron-proton hypothesis is a guess as to what would be observed visually with a microscope of sufficient magnifying power. On the whole it is to be expected that the physicist who *uses* the microscope, *performs* the laboratory analysis and then *reports* the results, should be better qualified to guess the nature of the antecedents of what he observes than the professional metaphysician who has available only the verbal report of the physicist.

"The metaphysical problem as it presents itself for analysis, can only be a study of the biosocial antecedents of the language responses (metaphysical discussions) recorded in the literature as the verbo-motor responses of individuals who, for the time being, are classified as metaphysicians. The *scientific* solution is thus narrowed down to an investigation of the metaphysician's heredity and training. All metaphysical discussions, no matter how profound and involved they may be, are in the *last* analysis nothing but language responses and linguistic habits derived from other language responses. In science, observation and the analysis of experiential conditions play a much larger part. When the metaphysical problem is stated in the form of the question, What are the essentials of reality? the term *reality* for the behaviorist is merely a word stimulus which individuals of a given social status use to designate the fact that the responses occurring at any one moment might be more complex and varied than they actually are if the bodily response mechanism were more complex than it really is.

"Thus I may affirm that the clock in my room has an existence or reality aside from my reactions to it because of the following behavior conditions. Suppose one of my responses is that of counting the ticks. The number of ticks that can be counted seems to be unlimited, but the manner of counting may be continuous or intermittent. The alternative responses of counting or not counting are not determined by the nature of the clock. That is, if I had installed an automatic counter for the ticks, the visual readings of this counter would be correlative with *continuous* auditory counting, but not with *intermittent* auditory counting. In terms of behavior this only means that some responses (oral counting) and other responses (visual counting) are sometimes correlated, sometimes not, and that the cause of this correlation is some condition (clock) that is independent of my own body.

"Reality is merely the term that designates this type of relationship between responses. It is the basis of the fiction of an external world of stimuli. This particular fiction, as a form of behavior, has persisted. Another fiction, characterized as solipsism, has never been generally adopted. According to this fiction my own responses are the only responses that ever occur. Certainly I have never found myself doing anything else. When I am not reacting (as in dreamless sleep) there is only oblivion. For the behaviorist,

about man and human society. The resistance which behaviorism encountered some years ago in psychology and sociology even in some scientific circles suggests that science had better make no absolute and final declarations about "existence," "reality," and "truth," in any field. Sociology especially had better keep clear of such declarations. It is quite common for researchers in sociology to be told that however rigorous has been their devotion to all the requirements of scientific method, their results unfortunately do not square with "the very nature of the thing" studied; its "true or real content" has been missed, and so forth.[15] The mere objectivity of findings in the sense of corroboration by other workers is not enough from the point of view I am attacking. The findings must also, and primarily, square with some "objective reality" (*represented only by certain words*) which is declared to "exist" independently of anybody's observations or corroboration.

Fortunately, scientists are likely to go about their business without too much attention to these strictures. They record their observations, analyze and synthesize them according to rules that experience has shown yield a certain kind of result. If, when they are through, it seems more sensible to say the earth is round rather than flat, they say so, suffer persecutions, but go on their way. They have done it in the past, and will doubtless do it in the future, even when it does to "the very nature" of man and society what Darwinism did. I have taken here an epistemological position compatible with such developments.

4. THE VISIBILITY AND OBJECTIVITY OF SOCIETAL PHENOMENA

Within our universe of discourse, then, all data are known to us only through human responses and we infer both the existence and the characteristics of any phenomena from these responses. A taboo, a custom, an "idea," or a belief is, therefore, as a datum, as "tangible," "real," observable, measurable, and otherwise sus-

---

then, the problem of the nature of reality is a biosocial problem of tracing out the type of behavior which corresponds to the assumption that there is an external reality of which man is only a part and that this assumption has survived longer (produced better co-operation between individuals) than any other." (A. P. Weiss, *A Theoretical Basis of Human Behavior*, pp. 44–47.)

[15] See, for example, ch. II, note 41, *Foundations of Society*.

ceptible of scientific study as is a stone, a table, or a horse. The contrary assumption flows from the fact that the responses aroused through certain senses, notably of touch and sight, being responses for which the most highly developed objective symbols have been invented, are therefore assumed to possess a "tangibility" which events that have not yet been thus symbolized do not have. Now the words "tangibility," "reality," etc., may be used profitably to describe a degree of objectification of our responses to some data while such terms as "intangible," "spiritual," "nonmaterial," describe a lesser degree of objectivity of responses. But these terms cannot be used to indicate intrinsic characteristics of data in the present frame of reference. The alleged greater "tangibility" of certain "physical" events resides not in the events, but in our more highly objectified methods of responding to them. *That response* which we call custom, affection, pain, anger, the welfare of our grandchildren, the Future Life, or what not, consists of reactions of sense receptors to stimuli from outside or inside the organism as truly as our experience of a stone or a tree.

This point is fundamental and must be taken quite literally if we really contemplate bringing societal phenomena within the framework of natural science. We must be able to show that symbols such as honor, duty, loyalty, etc., and the behavior which they represent are as observable and objective data as are baseball, the seasonal flight of birds, or the jump of an electric spark. "Baseball," "flight," and "spark" are words by which one person communicates to another certain of his responses to whatever phenomena precipitate these responses. Honor, duty, and loyalty are another group of such words designating people's responses to other phenomena. The capacity of a word or any other stimulus to evoke a given response depends upon our conditioning, at some time in our existence as an organism, to respond in a given way in a given stimulus-response situation. All of these words stand for behavior of some sort. To the extent that numbers of individuals use the same word to designate similar behavior phenomena (i.e., to the extent that numbers of individuals behave in a given way in a given situation) it is conventional to designate the phenomena to which they respond as objective. Phenomena are objective in science to the extent that this criterion of agreement, corroboration, or verifiability is satisfied.

Failure to grasp this relativistic meaning of objectivity is perhaps the basic reason for fundamental misunderstandings in the social sciences. The common objection to the position advanced in this book, usually designated as behavioristic or positivistic, is that it cannot, it is said, take account of what men feel or think.[16] In elaboration of this statement Cooley's "bold statement that the solid facts of social life are the facts of the imagination" is quoted.[17] "My friend is best defined," it is said, "as what I imagine he will do and say to me on occasion"—a surprisingly behavioristic statement. The point is further illustrated by the statement that "when John and Tom meet there are six persons present. There is John's real self (known only to his Maker) [*sic*], John's idea of himself, and John's idea of Tom, and, of course, three corresponding Toms. Cooley goes on to say that there are really twelve or more, including John's idea of Tom's idea of John's idea of Tom. In these 'echoes of echoes of echoes' of personality we have an *a fortiori* consideration of the importance of *the subjective aspect of conduct*."[18] [Italics mine.]

If it is assumed that any social scientist, behaviorist or other, proposes to ignore any or all of the above data, it is not surprising that the thought has caused considerable agitation. No supporter of such a view is ever cited by the critics, and I have never in the course of a considerable survey of the literature encountered an exponent of the position. The better known authorities, including the most extreme behaviorists, have specifically disavowed any such view.[19] Not only have the behaviorists apparently failed to communicate what their position is, but they have succeeded in arousing in their critics nightmares of vast proportions. The obvious fact is that communication has broken down on this subject. Whether the fault lies at the sending or the receiving end is not immediately relevant. The important thing is to clarify the position if possible, since the possibility of objective study of phe-

---

[16] E. Faris, "The Primary Group: Essence and Accident," *American Journal of Sociology*, XXXVIII, 1932, 44.
[17] *Ibid.*, p. 45.
[18] *Ibid.*
[19] See J. B. Watson, *op. cit.* (See note 2 above.)

nomena of the kind illustrated above is obviously basic to a science of sociology.

I hold that "echoes" and "shadows" are just as truly physical phenomena subject to objective scientific study as are the phenomena which shadows and echoes reflect. The charge that we propose to ignore the phenomena of "imagination," "thought," or "consciousness" is as unwarranted as would be a similar charge that physicists deny the phenomena of shadows and echoes. The physicist demands verifiable sensory evidence of echoes and shadows exactly as he does of original noises that echo or of objects that cast shadows. The sociologist must similarly demand sensory evidences of the imaginings, thoughts, and other phenomena of "consciousness." When he has such evidences he is as much interested in the phenomena of what men think and feel as in any other data. Imaginings, thoughts, and feelings manifest themselves if at all through symbolic or other neuro-muscular behavior. As such they are as proper subject for scientific study as are all other phenomena. This holds for all so-called introspective phenomena as well as for phenomena assumed to originate outside of the observer. (Actually, of course, all *responses* are "subjective" or "introspective" in the sense that the response occurs before it is communicated.)

The assumed inaccessibility of the data of consciousness to objective study arises from the undeveloped state of the technic for such study.[20] No behaviorist questions the scientific validity

[20] The relatively undeveloped state of the methods of study of symbolic behavior has, of course, given rise to the usual conclusion that these phenomena are, as T. Parsons has said, "outside the range of scientific observation and analysis." (*The Structure of Social Action*, p. 421.) In this work, the author says: "It will be maintained and the attempt made in considerable detail to prove that *in this sense* [as a general framework for understanding human behavior] *all of the versions of positivistic social thought constitute untenable positions*, for both empirical and methodological reasons." [P. 125. Italics in the original.] In so far as a single statement may be selected as illustrative of the type of consideration which the author has in mind, the following is suggestive with respect to the matter here under discussion: "If a stone is at the same time a religious symbol, there is a double symbolic reference when the word 'stone,' or a particular of that class, is spoken or thought: first, a reference of the word to the object; second, that of the object, in turn, to that which it symbolizes. In the case of an imaginary entity, the situation is *in essentials* the same, except that the immediate reference of the original linguistic symbol is not mediated through sense data *in the same way*. Zeus is not experienced *in the same*

of a physician taking his own temperature, pulse count, or recording by any method subject to verification, his observation of the behavior of any part of his organism in relation to stimuli of whatever kind, societal or "physical." It is a problem of developing an objective terminology and instruments with which to observe and describe experience which is now very inadequately communicable or subject to verification. "The possibility of one man's observing another's mental processes, like the possibility of observing another's digestion becomes a question of developing laboratory technique."[21] This technic need not contemplate substituting our experience for his directly. Like all other knowledge it is usually inferred from objective signs. In short, it is only a matter of what degree of objectivity we shall require before we can use them as a basis for scientific generalizations. Of course, we are using and should continue in the meantime to use these data for all they are worth in their present form.

The same reasoning holds for the common assumption that a strictly behavioristic description of societal behavior denies "the relevance of anticipated social ends as a partial determinant of social action."[22] Anticipated ends, in the sense of "conscious" prevision, whenever they become stimuli to action, exist as words or other symbols to which the organism responds as it does to other stimuli. The same is true of memories, "values," "meanings," "ideals," "ideas," and all the rest of the phenomena which are alleged to be unapproachable by the accepted methods of science. Again, the error lies in assuming that the telic character or purposiveness which we like to attribute to societal behavior is an intrinsic character of the behavior rather than our way of de-

---

sense as a stone." [P. 423. Italics mine.] I assume that the author means by imaginary entities precisely the type of "imaginings" and "echoes" I have discussed in the main text and, if so, that discussion also applies to this illustration. To me, the significant admission is that the imaginary situation is *"in essentials* the same," for I consider the essential similarity in this context to be the observability and the possibility of objectively designating the phenomenon. If so, it is, as I have noted in the main text, entirely unnecessary that there should be any other "sameness" in the situations. In short, echoes and shadows may be "mediated" in a vast variety of ways, but we do not therefore contend that they are not experienced "in the same sense."

[21] M. A. Copeland, "Desire, Choice and Purpose from a Natural-Evolutionary Viewpoint," *Psychological Review*, XXXIII, 1926, 145.

[22] See R. K. Merton, *op. cit.*, p. 321. See note 2 above.

scribing it. All phenomena *may* be described in teleological, theological, or magical terms. We have merely abandoned the practice of ascribing "malice" to the tree which falls "in order to" block our path, or of attributing "planning" to the amoeba in approaching its food.

Physicists have likewise lost interest in the question of whether an echo or a shadow is "objective," "real," or "exists." The investigation and description of an "echo of an echo of an echo" proceeds according to the same principles as the investigation and description of any other noise. When we adopt this attitude toward the "intangibles" which so bedevil and frustrate contemporary sociological theory, we shall presently find that certain metaphysical questions of "existence," "reality," "subjectivity," and "tangibility" can take their place with the question of how many angels can stand on the point of a needle and other profound issues that agitated learned men of other ages.

Full inquiry into the conditions affecting the observed behavior is required in any case. If it is desired to designate a certain type of conditions common among human beings by the term "malice," there is no objection to doing so. It is the use of the word as a substitute for the investigation of the conditions that is here under criticism. As convenient classifications of types of data there is, likewise, no objection to designating some as "physical" and "material" and others as "cultural," "social," or even "spiritual," provided we do not make assumptions that these classifications affect the method by which we know the phenomena in question, i.e., through sensory responses of some kind. It is true that both an iron fence and a taboo will keep men from touching an object or going to a certain place. It is also true that the taboo will have this effect only upon the behavior of men conditioned to a certain culture, while the fence may have the same effect on all men. Therefore, by men in general, greater objectivity is ascribed properly to the fence. But *to the men conditioned by the given culture*, the taboo has the same degree of objectivity, the test of objectivity in either case being the observed behavior of the men. From this behavior of the men, the existence, meaning, objectivity, and other characteristics of both fence and taboo is inferred. Obviously, the fact that we ascribe equal degrees of objectivity to two things for given groups of men does not mean that we claim they are the "same," "alike," or "similar" in any or all *other* respects. The fact to keep in mind is that all existence, data, reality, or being is relative to some observer and, of course, to his frame of reference. Obviously, to some of the lower animals with different sensory apparatus and background of experiences, many data sensed by all men do not exist and *vice versa*. Likewise, different men sense different things. Things which all or nearly all men respond to in very much the same way, i.e., an iron fence, we call relatively objective, physical, material, tangible, etc. Things to which only relatively few, or only one, respond in the same way without special cultural conditioning are termed subjective, intangible, spiritual, etc. We are not contending that the data called intangible and spiritual today may not be properly so described. We merely point out wherein their intangibility resides, so that, if we develop response technics which permit the checking and corroboration of the responses to things today called intangible, they would then be tangible. Whether this can ever be done to some "subjective" data remains to be seen. In any case we are more likely to make progress in this quest if we assume as a working hypothesis that it can be done. We have no choice but to proceed on that hypothesis if we wish to bring these data within the domain of science.

5. MEANING AS A TYPE OF CLASSIFICATION

Much of the difficulty which the above position seems to involve is the result of a failure to recognize that within the framework here advanced, words themselves, spoken or written, are just as truly entities to which we respond as all other objects are. Under other orientations, words are frequently unique and mysterious, not to say magical, entities, because it is alleged, we respond to their *meanings* rather than to the words as objects or as "physical" stimuli. This is a confusion flowing from the assumptions dealt with under our first postulate. Our response to a stone is also to its meaning to us, i.e., the conditioning we have undergone to the word "stone." Prior to such conditioning it has no "meaning" to us (in the sense of knowledge) and calls for no response as a symbol. All words (stone as well as taboo) are symbolic designations of some behavior phenomenon to which we respond. It is our response which gives it "meaning."[23] The meaning of anything we respond to at all is implicit in the response and part of it. We do not respond symbolically to that which has *no* meaning to us. Meaningless things, words, or symbols are a contradiction in terms; the very fact that we call them meaningless proves that they have *that* meaning, i.e., we so classify them. We use the expression to designate, of course, phenomena that do not fit in consistently with the frame of reference in which we try to place them. A "nonsense" syllable, for example, has meaning *as such*. What we mean when we call it meaningless is that it does not have *a certain kind* of meaning that other syllables in a given language have.

To say that a statement is meaningless is obviously as meaningful a statement as any other. Only *words* or *statements* (symbols) about the world (not objects *per se* which are only inferences from responses) can have meaning. We encounter here, the old question as to whether we can "think" without symbols. This question can be resolved only by an arbitrary definition of "thinking." Since all responses that have any scientific import involve symbolic systems, we take the generally accepted view that all thinking involves symbols and that only when symbolized do "objects" or behavior have meaning.

6. CATEGORIES AS GENERALIZED HABITS

What has been said above about words in general also applies to categories and classifications of phenomena. The limitations of man's sense organs permit him to respond only to certain aspects of the whole universe (i.e., everything that might be responded to) at any one time. We mean by an "aspect," "segment," "field," or "part," any situation to which our neural organization allows us to respond as a unit while responding in a secondary way to the relation of this situation to a larger situation in which the former is considered as encompassed. The problems that confront us at a given time define and evoke selective responses. We designate them as parts or wholes according to their individual

23 See J. F. Markey, *The Symbolic Process and Its Integration in Children*, pp. 141, 142, 146, 147. Also J. Dewey, *Experience and Nature*, p. 322 and G. H. Mead, "The Genesis of Self and Social Control," *International Journal of Ethics*, XXXV, 1924–1925, 251–277.

sufficiency for the adjustment-needs of the occasion. On this basis, we designate some situations as "wholes" and others as "parts." It follows, of course, that what is regarded as a "whole" with reference to one situation may be regarded as a "part" with reference to another, and *vice versa*. Thus a cell may be a whole and the solar system a part, according to the frame of reference adopted. The words are therefore merely designations of types of response, not intrinsic qualities or characteristics of objects or situations as is implied by some writers on "Gestalt" psychology.[24] In other words, all aspects, segments, parts, or other categories or classifications, including the classification of the sciences, are defined by whatever behavior the organism finds relevant to its adjustment needs (including the intellectual needs of a given organism at a given time) to restore that balance the disturbance of which we postulate as the occasion for any or all behavior. The lines of

[24] See W. Köhler, *Gestalt Psychology*. Also K. Kaffka, *Principles of Gestalt Psychology*.

I am unable to see that there is anything in the approach of these and other authors of the so-called "Gestalt school" which justifies its designation as a unique "school." Their experimental work is frequently excellent, but I find no difficulty in interpreting their findings in the behavioristic terms of A. P. Weiss or other competent behavioristic writers. Much of the "Gestalt" attack seems to me to be directed at a bogey usually called the "atomistic-mechanistic" approach, the alleged sponsors of which are usually not cited, and I have been unable to find anyone who supports the position referred to. In so far as the Gestalt position can be identified with the field theory as advanced by J. F. Brown (*Psychology and the Social Order*), I find myself largely in agreement with it. But the whole-part relationship to which Gestalt psychology is supposed to have made special contributions does not seem to me to have been at all clarified by the turgid treatment of Gestalt writers. Fine literary phrases such as "the whole is more than the sum of its parts," derive their impressiveness chiefly from their obscurity. The problem when objectively examined is quite simple. Consider the much quoted illustration of hydrogen and oxygen considered separately and in the compound H_2O. Is the latter "more than the sum of" the former? The question has no sensible operational meaning. All that needs to be pointed out is that hydrogen and oxygen act upon *different sense organs* (or act differently upon the same sense organs) when combined into H_2O than when uncombined. That they should give us a *different* sensation in combination than in separation is, therefore, no mystery requiring weird philosophical conjuring about the whole-part relationship. One is neither more nor less than the other. They produce different sensations, each of which is equally "real," "whole," and otherwise a legitimate phenomenon for study. This is perhaps generally recognized with respect to such phenomena as are used in the above illustration. But when the same problem rises as between "man" and "society" it sometimes gives rise to protracted futile discussion.

classification which we impose upon phenomena "are not walls of separation, but more like the parallels and meridians of the globe, which in no way mar its continuity but make our sphere intelligible and comprehensible from our various points of view."[25]

The number of different aspects of the universe to which it is possible for the human organism to respond probably are practically unlimited. The permutations and combinations possible among such a multiplicity of factors as those to which the human senses are sensitive, as well as the constantly appearing new aspects resulting from the phenomena of evolution or change in man himself, his technology, and his environment make the social universe alone a field within which an almost unlimited number of classifications of phenomena (selective responses) are possible.

The broadest and most general classification of aspects of the universe which any species will make consists of those aspects which involve the adjustment needs of all or nearly all individuals. The broad divisions of the universe introduced by some of the ancients such as earth, air, fire, water; man, as distinct from other animals; distinctions between body, soul, and mind, etc., represent designations of aspects of the universe calling for special types of responses to which practically all people were called upon to make common-sense adjustments of certain fairly uniform kinds. For example, it is found that changing one's position from point to point by walking is under given conditions always possible on land but not on water. Air, likewise, is an aspect of the universe to which all are compelled to make specific responses different from those adapted to locomotion on land and water. The constant verification of these responses by everyone, permits universal assent to the imputation of certain characteristics to each of these aspects of man's environment. This is how *all* phenomena come to have attributed to them their generally recognized characteristics. That is, we assign to *that which* arouses *certain responses, words designating the qualities or characteristics which differentiate these responses from other responses.* Earth is that which supports us when we walk, water is that which does not support us if we try to walk on it but which is definable in terms of our *other* responses to it, etc., etc.

[25] J. A. Thomson and P. Geddes, *Life: Outlines of General Biology,* II, p. 1413.

We delimit the total universe, therefore, into aspects, categories, and classifications on the basis of the differential responses with which we are compelled to adjust. These adjustments consist, of course, of observably different behaviors. In the human species, these different behaviors are represented by different words. To these aspects of the universe to which nearly all men respond in nearly the same way we attribute high objectivity, "reality," "existence," "being," etc. This is the basis of "common sense," the experiential precursor of science. There are other aspects with reference to which the uniformity of response is not so easily observable or verifiable and for which the descriptive symbols are not as yet so easily checkable against the behavior for which they are alleged to stand. To these aspects we therefore attribute lesser objectivity, lesser "reality," etc. The point to be observed is that the *divisions, categories, classifications,* and *groupings* of the phenomena of the universe are *words representing* differential *responses of man.* The objectivity of any aspect of the universe (situation) as contrasted with another, therefore, depends upon its capacity to evoke uniform responses from large numbers of people.[26] Since the overwhelming majority of these responses in the human species become known to others only through verbal behavior, the objectivity of phenomena depend largely upon the possibility of communicating accurately the meaning of words so as to insure that a given person uses a given word to represent the same kind of experience that other people use the word to represent. This we achieve chiefly through specifying in terms already highly objectified, and ultimately in overt behavior of some sort, such as pointing to an object, or going through the *operations* which we use the new term to designate.

It is quite essential to remember this basic nature of all categories in order to avoid becoming involved in insoluble metaphysical questions of ultimate reality, as we have pointed out above, and in order not to create the impression that the various classifications of human groupings to be reviewed in the later chapters represent anything more ultimate than ways of responding to aspects of the universe to which adjustment of some sort is

[26] See L. L. Bernard, "The Evolution of Social Consciousness and of the Social Sciences," *Psychological Review,* 1932, 147–164, for a discussion of the reasons for the earlier development of some sciences.

made. On the scientific level that adjustment consists chiefly of the need of scientists to relieve the intellectual tension which comes of inability to fit certain phenomena into a coherent framework so that their curiosity can come to rest.

The postulates, axioms, and assumptions, and the corollaries we draw from them, constitute a symbolic frame of reference or universe of discourse, the origin and properties of which will be further discussed elsewhere. No orderly discussion is possible without such a framework for it is only by reference to some such framework that individual statements about phenomena have meaning. Since the elementary rules of grammar of any language constitute the most general of such frameworks, we usually take the reference for granted and do not state postulates explicitly. As a result we assume too lightly that the knowledge regarding which we have developed familiar verifying technics has an inherency in the universe, instead of being only a more uniform way of responding. In short, frames of reference and universes of discourse are themselves merely comprehensive ways of responding to large configurations of data. ". . . Both mathematics and scientific theories," says Bell, "are nothing more immortal than convenient man-made maps for the correlation of human experiences."[27] We here make the same statement about any and all theories and generalizations whatsoever. Their "truth" or validity will rest on the same practical test upon which we estimate the adequacy of any other response, namely, whether it achieves the adjustment sought.

7. THE UTILITARIAN TEST OF ALL THOUGHT-SYSTEMS

The above orientation calls for no theoretical argument, therefore, as to the "truth" of our system as against theological and philosophical terms and postulates *within their own system*. Many theologies are quite as logical, comprehensive, and self-sufficient theoretical systems as is science. Thus the postulate of an omnipresent, omniscient, and just God, or of a devil directing the affairs of the universe provides a frame into which events may be fitted according to certain general rules of logic, i.e., of verbal syntax. The postulate of the earth as a flat body around which the sun and the other planets move is another frame of reference

[27] E. T. Bell, *op. cit.*, pp. 104, 105.

into which common-sense observations may be fitted logically. The postulate of a round earth moving around the sun is an alternative frame of reference. The only legitimate criterion for judging frames of reference, as such, is the degree to which they are consistent with themselves. From the standpoint of the use of a given frame as a chart or compass for practical adjustments, the criterion becomes, of course, its practical adequacy, i.e., its usefulness in securing the desired adjustment. By the first criterion several widely disparate systems may be equally defensible. By the second criterion, one system will, under given circumstances, tend to be superior (on the ground noted) to others. These two criteria must not be confused. Under the first criterion the postulates of the present work should be judged by their self-consistency, the possibility of logically deducing from them theorems capable of empirical verification, and their compatibility with the general framework of science. Under the second criterion they must be judged by their simplicity, their generality, and by their capacity to provide a basis for practical adjustments.

The futile scholastic discussion of many subjects especially affecting man and the social order owe their futility to the failure to designate explicitly the frame of reference, the postulates, and the rules upon which the discussion proceeds. This failure is in turn due to the common assumption that frames of reference are in some way inherent in the universe instead of being pure constructions for our convenience—"ways of looking at things."

The conditions under which men live, including their cultural heritage determines, of course, in a broad way what frames of reference will be invented at any given time. The point of view here presented, for example, is the result of the tension which comes of trying to live in an intellectual world which is half scientific and half something else. Although the thought pattern of science is bearing down on us from every side, we nevertheless try to avoid its full implications in the sociological realm on the ground that the latter involve "mental" or "spiritual" factors. Out of these factors it is attempted to erect a separate order of being or of knowledge called "Geisteswissenschaft." In the meantime, the incompatibility of the assumptions behind such a view in the light of increasing psychological knowledge about the nature of the "mental" categories, is destroying the basis for the distinction.

Since failure to recognize the essential nature of propositions, postulates, and frames of reference as discussed above results in the most widespread and fundamental misunderstandings and futile arguments, these essential points cannot be too strongly emphasized. It must be admitted too that scientists as well as their opponents frequently overlook these considerations. The tirades against religion, theology, and other systems of thought by erstwhile adherents to these faiths who have recently discovered "science" are often evidence of a mistaken notion regarding the nature of both science and the faiths of the fathers. *All* of these systems are merely adjustment technics which have been found more or less satisfactory to their adherents *under given conditions* at different times. As times and conditions change, all of these frames of reference, including present science, may be expected to prove inadequate, and be abandoned for radically different postulates, and may proceed perhaps, according to different technics and systems of logic.

The tests of the adequacy ("truth") of any system at any given time will in any event be determined by certain empirical tests, notably whether the system affords a rationale of the adjustments that have to be made and whether it aids in planning those adjustments. The vogue of "physical" science today springs from just such demonstrable relevance in an industrial, mechanical age in which adjustments to remote environments have become necessary through highly developed means of communication. The same conditions have, of course, forced the "social" sciences in the same direction and will ultimately, I think, compel them to align themselves completely with the "physical." But it is impossible to show that the orientations of science have any greater (or as great) relevance to the practical adjustments of life in a convent or a monastery (and some of the present academic counterparts of these societies) than theology. Different ways of life demand different ways of thought. In abandoning here a traditional distinction between the "physical" and the "social," "mental," and "spiritual" we are not doing so under the delusion of having "discovered" "new," "absolute" truth. Neither do we deny, ignore, or abolish any phenomena whatsoever. Philosophies may themselves be considered sociologically as systems of verbal behavior, but their declared objectives and objects (entities allegedly represented by the words employed) need not be considered in a scientific framework unless the phenomena designated by the words used can be verified. We aim merely to discuss from a certain explicit point of view the *same* behavior phenomena with which all other sociological systems (including all the theologies and social philosophies) deal, and to organize them as far as possible according to the general pattern of science. The "truth," the merits, or the advantages of this point of view will have to be determined by the same practical usefulness which has given modern science in other fields its prestige and its following as against the thoughtways it has supplanted.

8. THE NONETHICAL NATURE OF SCIENCE[28]

It should be clear from the above that it is the primary function of all science to formulate the sequences that are observable in *any* phenomena in order to be able to predict their recurrence. I shall specify in a later chapter what I consider to be the particular field of sociology. In the meantime, it is desirable to point out, as another corollary of the position stated above, that questions of ethics or of what "ought to be" must not in science be confused with what observations indicate. Nor must sociological problems be confused with "social" problems in the sense of adjustments deemed desirable by anyone in any time, place, or circumstance. The prevention of crime is a social problem. The relationship between criminality and population density or any other social condition is a sociological problem. Sociological and all other scientific questions have to do with the formulation of verifiable relationships. Social questions have to do with other and more general readjustments of social conditions with reference to any goals toward which man may aspire.

The fact that there is a relationship between these fields is no reason for confusing them. It is entirely permissible for society to maintain educational institutions and courses to transmit to the

[28] I have dealt elsewhere in some detail with this subject. See especially, "Science, Scientists, and Values," *Social Forces*, XXX, 1932, 373–379. Also see *Can Science Save Us?*, 2d ed., pp. 30–41.

young a knowledge of past and current social events from the viewpoint of the dominant ethical and social system that prevails or which is idealized at any given time. Orientation courses, courses in reform, ethics, idealism, religion, current events, and social work are doubtless a useful and necessary part of the educational program of contemporary society. If it is found administratively convenient or otherwise advisable to give this instruction in departments of sociology and by "sociologists" that is again a practical question of educational administration. To confuse such subject matter with scientific problems, however, is mere confusion and cannot lead to the solution of scientific problems. If we give little attention to traditional "social" problems in the present work it is not because we are not personally interested in these problems as all members of human society are likely to be, but because we do not wish to confuse them with certain *other* problems with which we wish to concern ourselves.

As we shall see in later chapters, the approach to societal phenomena here proposed provides a place for all societal data whatsoever including those conventionally designated as ethical, idealistic, spiritual, or esthetic. It does not follow that we must adopt the conventional categories in terms of which these phenomena are treated in other systems. Only *the behavior designated by these conventional categories* is entitled to recognition. Much confusion results from overlooking the fact that no theory legitimately can be required to adopt the *categories* of another theory. Take, for example, the constant demand upon thoroughgoing social scientists as to how they propose within their frame of reference to deal with "spiritual" data—what about "values," "ideals," "ethics," the good, the true, and the beautiful? Frightened by the prestige of the source from which these inquiries frequently come, the sociologist, himself often a bit worried over his own heterodoxy, makes ludicrous attempts to provide within a scientific framework place for *categories* which have no place in that framework any more than scientific categories have a place in a theological framework. It is not necessary for a priest to give an account of the cellular structure of the Holy Ghost. The only answer which a scientist needs to give to the question as to how "spiritual" data are to be handled within the scientific framework is to point out that all the *observable behavior* covered by this category is readily and fully provided for in the scientific framework. The *category itself* clearly does not have to be, and should not be, incorporated, any more than the categories of science can or need be incorporated into theology.

The root of this difficulty lies, of course, in the naive conceit of man which induces him to believe that any word which he may invent inevitably has a necessary counterpart in nature or in supernatural regions. A slight sophistication in the nature and functions of language would render obsolete the major controversies of the day in sociological theory, as hundreds of similar time-honored discussions of other philosophical subjects have been rendered obsolete by the advancement of science.

D. Conclusion

We have enumerated above the major postulates of science and their corollaries which have special significance for sociology. Many of these points will be further elaborated in the next two chapters of *Foundations of Sociology*.

Our principal concern in the present chapter has been to emphasize that the apparent difference between the data of the "physical" and the social sciences springs chiefly from a failure to recognize that the immediate data of *all* sciences are human responses to whatever arouses those responses. Much of scientific development depends, as we shall see, upon the type of symbols we develop to represent the phenomena to which we respond. We need only suggest in this connection what would be the state of any of our sciences if arabic numerals, the zero, and the calculus had never been invented. With these symbols and the rules governing their use, any fourth-grade child can solve problems—relevant, important problems—which staggered the most brilliant intellect of ancient Greece. Clearly it makes a difference with what symbolic equipment we approach our scientific tasks. It would be strange indeed if this lesson from the other sciences should be entirely inapplicable to the study of sociological problems.

This point has been emphasized not so much to minimize the uniqueness and intricacy of societal phenomena as to suggest the type of approach to which these difficulties are most likely to yield. It is not necessary to argue that societal and "physical" data are the "same," or "similar." No phenomena in the universe are identical, and to admit that societal phenomena are "different" from "physical" is a highly irrelevant concession in the present context unless we further specify *in what respect* we allege they are different. *All* phenomena are different in some respects. *All* of them are similar in one highly vital respect, namely, in that they are all known, if at all, through sense experience conceptualized and organized into the patterns determined by the nature of the human organism as conditioned by all its environments. This is the only similarity relevant to the present discussion because we are concerned at present only with the means by which valid knowledge of *any* phenomena is achieved. Are the means by which we know societal phenomena fundamentally different from the means by which we know physical phenomena? If they are not, then it is as irrelevant for our present purpose to enumerate "differences" between "physical" and societal phenomena as it would be to claim that the differences between ants, spiders, and grasshoppers preclude a science of biology. Indeed, all discussion of similarities and differences of phenomena without specifying explicitly or through the context with respect to what aspect of the phenomena we are concerned may be said to be quite meaningless. Such discussion is not uncommon in sociological treatises on differences between societal and "physical" phenomena.

Much has been said in this connection about the ability of "physical" scientists to bring their "subject-matters" (i.e., the referents of their symbolized responses) into the laboratory and otherwise manipulate them. This possibility varies considerably with different sciences. The solar system has never been brought into any laboratory. Astronomical laboratories do contain very ingenious symbolic and mechanical representations of the astronomical aspects of that system and remarkable instruments for observing it. These every science must unquestionably develop. Beyond this, the question of laboratory conditions becomes one of convenience and technical and mechanical ingenuity. Already it is possible to observe illuminating sociological situations in the laboratory through sound and motion pictures not to mention the extensive sociological experiments involving laboratory observations of children and college students.

In short, most of us have been brought up in a world in

which we are taught that the physical sciences deal with metals, fluids, gases, and such "matter" which we like to describe with such reassuring sounds as "tangible," "visible," "actual," "real." The phenomena of the social sciences, on the other hand, we have been taught to consider "intangible," and "invisible" entities described by words like customs, mores, competition, sovereignty, justice, etc., etc. Yet these words if they mean anything at all, certainly refer to *behavior—events* impinging on our senses. The aspects of the universe with which chemists and physicists deal, and which folk-language designates by such broad categories as metals, fluids, and gases refer just as certainly to *other* behavior events. Yet such is the tendency for us to project upon nature the structure of our language that we develop a superstitious reverence for the categories which, as we shall see in the next chapter, are merely constructs which man somewhere, sometime, found a convenient framework within which to assort his experiences.[29]

[29] It is unfortunately not possible here to give an adequate account of the full extent to which linguistic and semantic difficulties at present handicap the social sciences. The reader is urged to supplement the present chapter by readings from the following sources. The first two sources are popular and elementary treatises. S. Chase, *The Tyranny of Words*. T. W. Arnold, *The Folklore of Capitalism*. P. W. Bridgman, *The Logic of Modern Physics*. C. K. Ogden and I. A. Richards, *The Meaning of Meaning*. A. Korzybski, *Science and Sanity*. J. F. Markey, *The Symbolic Process and Its Integration in Children*. By far the best brief source is C. W. Morris, "Foundations of the Theory of Signs," in *International Encyclopedia of Unified Science*, I, Univ. of Chicago Press, 1938. Consider, for example, the following extracts:

"No contradiction arises in saying that every sign has a designatum but not every sign refers to an actual existent. Where what is referred to actually exists as referred to, the object of reference is a *denotatum*. It thus becomes clear that, while every sign has a designatum, not every sign has a denotatum. A designatum is not a thing, but a kind of object or class of objects—and a class may have many members, or one member, or no members. The denotata are the members of the class. This distinction makes explicable the fact that one may reach in the icebox for an apple that is not there and make preparations for living on an island that may never have existed or has long since disappeared beneath the sea." (P. 5.)

By "actual existent" Morris here apparently means those stimuli-phenomena which evoke universal or at least very general confirmatory responses in all or large numbers of men. The explanation of the behavior of reaching for the apple which "is there" and the apple which "is not there" lies in the description of the sequence or combination of events leading up to the reaching. This set of events will be different in the two cases, but subject to description within the same framework. Morris continues:

To those who still find that these traditional frameworks serve their purposes, the present essay has nothing to offer. There are doubtless also those who still find the pre-Copernican astronomy, pre-Newtonian physics, and pre-Darwinian biology quite adequate to their needs. But they will perhaps find themselves increasingly disturbed by the intrusions and by-products of the scientific quest as represented by our technological age. Frequently the findings of that quest will, as Veblen said, "go beyond the breaking-point of their jungle-fed spiritual sensibilities." At such times they will "furtively or by an overt breach of consistency . . . seek comfort in marvelous articles of savage-born lore."[30] Take, for example, the following honest confession of a distinguished president of Columbia University in 1873. President Barnard had himself specialized in the natural sciences, served as president of the American Association for the Advancement of Science, and was noted for his liberal views. With reference to the doctrine of evolution he said:

"The interpreter of a sign is an organism; the interpretant is the habit of the organism to respond, because of the sign vehicle, to absent objects which are relevant to a present problematic situation as if they were present. In virtue of semiosis an organism takes account of relevant properties of absent objects, or unobserved properties of objects which are present, and in this lies the general instrumental significance of ideas. Given the sign vehicle as an object of response, the organism expects a situation of such and such a kind and, on the basis of this expectation, can partially prepare itself in advance for what may develop. The response to things through the intermediacy of signs is thus biologically a continuation of the same process in which the distance senses have taken precedence over the contact senses in the control of conduct in higher animal forms; such animals through sight, hearing, and smell are already responding to distant parts of the environment through certain properties of objects functioning as signs of other properties. This process of taking account of a constantly more remote environment is simply continued in the complex processes of semiosis made possible by language, the object taken account of no longer needing to be perceptually present. (Pp. 31–32.)

. . . "If, following the lead of the pragmatist, mental phenomena be equated with sign responses, consciousness with reference by signs, and rational (or "free") behavior with the control of conduct in terms of foreseen consequences made available by signs, then psychology and the social sciences may recognize what is distinctive in their tasks and at the same time see their place within a unified science. Indeed, it does not seem fantastic to believe that the concept of sign may prove as fundamental to the sciences of man as the concept of cell for the biological sciences." (p. 42).

30 T. Veblen, *The Place of Science in Modern Civilization*, pp. 26, 27.

Much as I love truth in the abstract I love my sense of immortality still more; and if the final outcome of all the boasted discoveries of modern science is to disclose to men that they are more evanescent than the shadow of the swallow's wing upon the lake . . . if this, after all is the best that science can give me, give me then, I pray, no more science. I will live on in my simple ignorance, as my fathers did before me; and when I shall at length be sent to my final repose, let me . . . lie down to pleasant, even though they may be deceitful dreams.[31]

To those who find themselves in this unhappy predicament I can only say with Bentley:

I can deeply sympathize with anyone who objects to being tossed into such a floating cosmology. Much as I have stressed its substantiality, I can hardly expect everyone to feel it. The firm land of "matter" or even of "sense" or "self" is pleasanter, if only it stands firm. To anyone whose tasks can be performed on such ground, I have not the slightest thought of bringing disturbance. But for many of us tasks are pressing, in the course of which our firmest spots of conventional departure themselves dissolve in function. When they have so dissolved, and when we are so involved, there is no hope of finding refuge in some chance island of "fact" which may appear. The continents go, and the islands. The pang may be like that felt by a confirmed landsman at his first venture on the ocean, but the ocean in time becomes familiar and secure. Or, if I may change the figure, the fledgling will vastly prefer his firm nest to falling with untried wings. But the parent sciences are pushing; the nest, even, is disintegrating; and there is air for flight, even though it is not so vividly felt and seen as the sticks and straws of the nest.[32]

[31] Quoted by S. Ratner, "Evolution and the Rise of the Scientific Spirit in America," *Philosophy of Science*, III, 1936, 115. For a good summary of the present scientific status of "materialism" see W. Seifriz, "A Materialistic Interpretation of Life," *Philosophy of Science*, VI, 1939, 266–284.
[32] A. F. Bentley, *Behavior, Knowledge, Fact*, p. 183.

How Is Society Possible?[1]

GEORG SIMMEL

KANT ASKED and answered the fundamental question of his philosophy, "How is nature possible?" He could do so only because nature for him was nothing but the representation of nature. It was so not merely in the sense that "the world is my representation" and that we can therefore speak of nature too as only a content of consciousness, but also in the sense that what we call nature is the special way in which the mind assembles, orders, and shapes sense perceptions. These given perceptions of color, taste, tone, temperature, resistance, and smell pass through our consciousness in the accidental sequence of our subjective experience. In themselves, they are not yet nature. They rather become nature, and they do so through the activity of the mind which combines them into objects and series of objects, into substances and attributes, and into causal connections. In their immediate givenness, Kant held, the elements of the world do not have the

---

[1] Translated by Kurt H. Wolff, in *Georg Simmel, 1858–1918: A Collection of Essays, with Translations and a Bibliography*, ed. Kurt H. Wolff (Columbus, Ohio: Ohio State University Press, 1959), pp. 337–356. Used by permission of the publisher. Originally: "Exkurs über das Problem: Wie ist Gesellschaft möglich?" *Soziologie. Untersuchungen über die Formen der Vergesellschaftung* ([1908] 3d ed.; Munich and Leipzig: Duncker und Humblot, 1923), pp. 21–31.

interdependence which alone makes them intelligible as the unity of nature's laws. It is this interdependence which transforms the world fragments—in themselves incoherent and unstructured—into nature.

The Kantian image of the world grows from a most peculiar play of contrasts. On the one hand, sense impressions are purely subjective: they depend upon a physicopsychical organization (which may differ from individual to individual) and upon the contingency of their provocations. They become objects as they are absorbed by the forms of our intellects and are transformed thereby into fixed regularities and into a consistent picture of "nature." On the other hand, these perceptions are what is really "given," the content of the world which we must simply accept, and the guarantee of an existence that is independent of us. Thus it is precisely the fact that our intellect forms perceptions into objects, systems, and uniformities which strikes us as subjective, that is, as something which *we* add to the given, as intellectual functions which, though unchangeable themselves, would have constructed a nature with a different content had they had different sense materials to work upon. For Kant, nature is a particular way of cognizing, a picture growing through and in our cognitive categories. Therefore, the question, "How is nature possible?"—that is, "What conditions are necessary for nature to be?"—is resolved by means of an inquiry into the forms which constitute the essence of our intellect. It is they which call forth nature itself.

It is very suggestive to treat as an analogous matter the question of the aprioristic conditions under which society is possible. Here, also, we find individual elements. In a certain sense, they too, like sense perceptions, stay forever isolated from one another. They, likewise, are synthesized into the unity of society only by means of a conscious process which correlates the individual existence of the single element with that of the other, and which does so in certain forms and according to certain rules. However, there is a decisive difference between the unity of a society and the unity of nature. It is this: In the Kantian view (which we follow here), the unity of nature emerges in the observing subject exclusively; it is produced exclusively by him in the sense materials, and on the basis of sense materials, which are in themselves heterogeneous. By contrast, the unity of society needs no observer. It is directly realized by its own elements because these elements are themselves conscious and synthesizing units. Kant's axiom that connection, since it is the exclusive product of the subject, cannot inhere in things themselves, does not apply here. For societal connection immediately occurs in the "things," that is, the individuals. As a synthesis, it too, of course, remains purely psychological. It has no parallels with spatial things and their interaction. Societal unification needs no factors outside its own component elements, the individuals. Each of them exercises the function which the psychic energy of the observer exercises in regard to external nature: the consciousness of constituting with the others a unity is actually all there is to this unity. This does not mean, of course, that each member of a society is conscious of such an abstract notion of unity. It means that he is absorbed in innumerable, specific relations and in the feeling and the knowledge of determining others and of being determined by them. On the other hand, it should be noted that it is quite possible for an observing outsider to perform an additional synthesis of the persons making up the society. This synthesis would proceed as if these persons were spatial elements, but it is based only upon the observer himself. The determination of which aspect of the *externally* observable is to be comprehended as a unity depends not only on the immediate and strictly objective content of the observable but also upon the categories and the cognitive requirements of the subjective psyche. Again, however, society, by contrast, is the objective unit which needs no outside observer.

Things in nature are further apart than individuals are. In the spatial world, each element occupies a place it cannot share with any other. Here, there is nothing analogous to human unity, which is grounded in understanding, love, or common work. On the other hand, spatial elements fuse in the observer's consciousness into a unity that is not attained by the assemblage of individuals. For here, the objects of the synthesis are independent beings, psychic centers, personal units. They therefore resist the absolute fusion (in an observer's mind) to which, by contrast, the "self-lessness" of inanimate things must yield. Thus, a number of people is a unit to a much greater extent, really, but to a much lesser extent, ideally, than are the units "décor," which is formed by table, chairs, couch, carpet, and mirror, or "landscape" (or its "picture" in a painting), which is made up of river, meadow, trees, and house.

Society is "my representation"—something dependent upon the activity of consciousness—in quite a different sense from that in which the external world is. For the other individual has for me the same reality which I have myself, and this reality is very different from that of a material thing. Kant insists that I am precisely as certain of the existence of spatial objects as I am of my own existence. But by "my own existence" he can understand only the particular contents of my subjective life. For its basis, the very basis of representation, the feeling of the existing ego, is unconditional and unshakable to a degree not attained by any representation of a material object. This very certainty, however, whether we can account for it or not, also extends to the *you*. And as the cause or as the effect of this certainty, we feel the *you* as something independent of our representation of it, as something that exists with exactly the same autonomy as does our own existence. And yet, this selfness of the other does not preclude his being made our representation. In other words, something which can by no means be resolved into our representation, nevertheless becomes its content, and thus its product.

This phenomenon is the fundamental psychologico-epistemological paradigm and problem of sociation. Within our own consciousness we very clearly distinguish between two things. One is the basic character of the ego, the precondition of all representing, which does not have the problematic nature of its contents, a nature which can never be completely eliminated; and the other is these contents themselves. In their coming and going, in their doubtfulness and corrigibility, all of these contents always present themselves as the mere products of the former, products of that absolute and ultimate force and existence which is our psychic being. And although we also *think* the other *mind*, we must nevertheless ascribe to it the very conditions, or rather freedom from conditions, of our own ego. We think that the other mind has the same maximum degree of reality, as distinguished from its mere contents, which our own self possesses, as distinguished from its contents.

Owing to these circumstances, the question of how society is possible implies a methodology which is wholly different from that for the question of how nature is possible. The latter question is answered by the forms of cognition, through which the subject synthesizes the given elements into nature. By contrast, the former is answered by the conditions which reside a priori in the elements themselves, through which they combine, in reality, into the synthesis, society. In a certain sense, the entire content of this book [*Soziologie*], as it is developed on the basis of the principle enunciated, is the beginning of the answer to this question. For it inquires into the processes—those which, ultimately, take place in the individuals themselves—that condition the existence of the individuals as society. It investigates these processes, not as antecedent causes of this result, but as part of the synthesis to which we give the inclusive name of "society."

But the question of how society is possible must be understood in a still more fundamental sense. I said that, in the case of nature, the achieving of the synthetic unity is a function of the observing mind, whereas, in the case of society, that function is an aspect of society itself. To be sure, consciousness of the abstract principle that he is forming society is not present in the individual. Nevertheless, every individual knows that the other is tied to him—however much this knowledge of the other as fellow sociate, this grasp of the whole complex as society, is usually realized only on the basis of particular, concrete contents. Perhaps, however, this is not different from the "unity of cognition." As far as our conscious processes are concerned, we proceed by arranging one concrete content alongside another, and we are distinctly conscious of the unity itself only in rare and later abstractions. The questions, then, are these: What, quite generally and a priori, is the basis or presupposition which lies behind the fact that particular, concrete processes in the individual consciousness are actually processes of sociation? Which elements in them account for the fact that (to put it abstractly) their achievement is the production of a societal unit out of individuals?

The sociological apriorities envisaged are likely to have the same twofold significance as those which make nature possible. On the one hand, they more or less completely determine the actual processes of sociation as functions or energies of psychological processes. On the other hand, they are the ideational, logical presuppositions for the perfect society (which is perhaps never realized in this perfection, however). We find a parallel in the law of causation. On the one hand, it inheres and is effective in the actual processes of cognition. On the other hand, it constitutes truth as the ideal system of perfect cognition. And it does so irrespective of whether or not this truth obtains in the temporal and relatively accidental psychological dynamics in which causation actually operates—irrespective, that is, of the greater or lesser degree to which the actual, consciously held truth approximates the ideally valid truth.

To ask whether such an inquiry into the conditions of the process of sociation should or should not be called an epistemological inquiry is merely a question of terminology. The phenomenon which arises from these conditions and which receives its norms from their forms does not consist of cognitions but of concrete processes and actual situations. Nevertheless, what I have in mind here and what (as the general idea of sociation) must be examined in regard to its conditions *is* something cognitive, namely, the consciousness of sociating or of being sociated. This consciousness is perhaps better called a "knowing" than a "cognizing." For here, the subject is not confronting an object of which he will gradually gain a theoretical picture. The consciousness of sociation is, rather, the immediate agent, the inner significance, of sociation itself. It is the processes of interaction which signify the fact of being sociated to the individual—not the abstract fact, to be sure, but a fact capable of abstract expression. What forms must be at the basis of this fact? What specific categories are there that man must bring along, so to speak, so that this consciousness may arise? And what, therefore, are the forms which come to the fore in the consciousness once this consciousness has arisen (namely, society as a fact of knowledge)? The discussion of these questions may well be called the epistemology of society. In what follows, I shall try to give an example of such epistemological studies by sketching some of these a priori effective conditions or forms of sociation (which cannot, however, in contrast to the Kantian categories, be designated by a single word).

(1) The picture of another man that a man gains through

personal contact with him is based on certain distortions. These are not simple mistakes resulting from incomplete experience, defective vision, or sympathetic or antipathetic prejudices. They are fundamental changes in the quality of the actual object perceived, and they are of two types. We see the other person generalized, in some measure. This is so, perhaps, because we cannot fully represent to ourselves an individuality which deviates from our own. Any re-creation of a person is determined by one's similarity to him. To be sure, similarity is by no means the only condition of psychological insight, for dissimilarity, too, seems required in order to gain distance and objectivity. In addition, aside from the question of similarity or dissimilarity, an intellectual capacity is needed. Nevertheless, *perfect* cognition presupposes perfect identity. It seems, however, that every individual has in himself a core of individuality which cannot be re-created by anybody else whose core differs qualitatively from his own. And the challenge to re-create is logically incompatible with psychological distance and objective judgment which are also bases for representing another. We cannot know completely the individuality of another.

All relations among men are determined by the varying degrees of this incompleteness. Whatever the cause of this incompleteness, its consequence is a generalization of the psychological picture that we have of another, a generalization that results in a blurring of contours which adds a relation to other pictures to the uniqueness of this one. We conceive of each man —and this is a fact which has a specific effect upon our practical behavior toward him—as being the human type which is suggested by his individuality. We think of him in terms not only of his singularity but also in terms of a general category. This category, of course, does not fully cover him, nor does he fully cover it. It is this peculiarly incomplete coincidence which distinguishes the relation between a human category and a human singularity from the relation which usually exists between a general concept and the particular instance it covers. In order to know a man, we see him not in terms of his pure individuality, but carried, lifted up or lowered, by the general type under which we classify him. Even when this transformation from the singular to the typical is so imperceptible that we cannot recognize it immediately; even when all the ordinary characterological concepts such as "moral" or "immoral," "free" or "unfree," "lordly" or "slavish," and so on, clearly appear inadequate, we privately persist in labeling a man according to an unverbalized type, a type which does not coincide with his pure, individual being.

This leads to a further step. It is precisely because of the utter uniqueness of any given personality that we form a picture which is not identical with its reality but which at the same time does not coincide with a general type. The picture we form is the one the personality would show if the individual were truly himself, so to speak, if he realized, toward a good or toward a bad side, for better or worse, his ideal possibility, the possibility which lies in every individual. All of us are fragments, not only of general man, but also of ourselves. We are outlines not only of the types "man," "good," "bad," and the like but also of the individuality and uniqueness of ourselves. Although this individuality cannot, on principle, be identified by any name, it surrounds our perceptible reality as if traced in ideal lines. It is supplemented by the other's view of us, which results in something that we never are purely and wholly. It is impossible for this view to see anything but juxtaposed fragments, which nevertheless are all that really exist. However, just as we compensate for a blind spot in our field of vision so that we are no longer aware of it, so a fragmentary structure is transformed by another's view into the completeness of an individuality. The practice of life urges us to make the picture of a man only from the real pieces that we empirically know of him, but it is precisely the practice of life which is based on those modifications and supplementations, on the transformation of the given fragments into the generality of a type and into the completeness of the ideal personality.

In practice, this fundamental process is only rarely carried to completion. Nevertheless, within an existing society it operates as the a priori condition of additional interactions that arise among individuals. Every member of a group which is held together by some common occupation or interest sees every other member not just empirically, but on the basis of an aprioric principle which the group imposes on every one of its participants. Among officers, church members, employees, scholars, or members of a family, every member regards the other with the unquestioned assumption that he is a member of "my group." Such assumptions arise from some common basis of life. By virtue of it, people look at one another as if through a veil. This veil does not simply hide the peculiarity of the person; it gives it a new form. Its purely individual, real nature and its group nature fuse into a new, autonomous phenomenon. We see the other not simply as an individual but as a colleague or comrade or fellow party member —in short, as a cohabitant of the same specific world. And this inevitable, quite automatic assumption is one of the means by which one's personality and reality assume, in the imagination of another, the quality and form required by sociability.

Evidently, this is true also of the relations of members who belong to different groups. The civilian who meets an officer cannot free himself from his knowledge of the fact that this individual is an officer. And although his officership may be a part of this particular individuality, it is certainly not so stereotypical as the civilian's prejudicial image would have it. And the same goes for the Protestant in regard to the Catholic, the businessman in regard to the bureaucrat, the layman in regard to the priest, and so on. In all these cases, reality is veiled by social generalization, which, in a highly differentiated society, makes discovering it altogether impossible. Man distorts the picture of another. He both detracts and supplements, since generalization is always both less and more than individuality is. The distortions derive from all these a priori, operative categories: from the individual's type as man, from the idea of his perfection, and from the general society to which he belongs. Beyond all of these, there is, as a heuristic principle of knowledge, the idea of his real, unconditionally individual nature. It seems as if only the apprehension of this nature could furnish the basis for an entirely correct relation to him. But the very alterations and new formations which preclude this ideal knowledge of him are, actually, the conditions which make possible the sort of relations we call social. The phenomenon recalls Kant's conception of the categories: they form immediate data into new objects, but they alone make the given world into a knowable world.

(2) There is another category under which the individual views himself and others and which transforms all of them into

empirical society. This category may be suggested by the proposition that every element of a group is not only a societal part but, in addition, something else. However trivial it may seem, this fact nevertheless operates as a social a priori. For that part of the individual which is, as it were, not turned toward society and is not absorbed by it, does not simply lie beside its socially relevant part without having a relation to it. It is not simply something outside society to which society, willingly or unwillingly, submits. Rather, the fact that in certain respects the individual is not an element of society constitutes the positive condition for the possibility that in other respects he is: the way in which he is sociated is determined or codetermined by the way in which he is not. The chapters of this book discuss, among other things, several types whose essential sociological significance lies in the very fact that in some fashion or other they are excluded from society (for which their existence, nevertheless, is important). Such types are the stranger, the enemy, the criminal, even the pauper. But this peculiar relationship to society not only holds for such generalized types as these but, albeit with innumerable modifications, for any individual whatever. The proposition is not invalidated by the fact that at every moment we are confronted, as it were, by relations which directly or indirectly determine the content of every moment: for the social environment does not surround all of the individual. We know of the bureaucrat that he is not only a bureaucrat, of the businessman that he is not only a businessman, of the officer that he is not only an officer. This extrasocial nature—a man's temperament, fate, interests, worth as a personality—gives a certain nuance to the picture formed by all who meet him. It intermixes his social picture with non-social imponderables—however little they may change his dominant activities as a bureaucrat or businessman or officer.

Man's interactions would be quite different if he appeared to others only as what he is in his relevant societal category, as the mere exponent of a social role momentarily ascribed to him. Actually, individuals, as well as occupations and social situations, are differentiated according to how much of the non-social element they possess or allow along with their social content. On this basis, they may be arranged in a continuum. One pole of the continuum is represented by an individual in love or friendship.

What this individual preserves for himself after all the developments and activities devoted to the friend or beloved are taken
care of is almost nothing. In his case, there is only a single life that
can be viewed or lived from two sides, as it were: from the inside, from the *terminus a quo* of the subject and in the direction
of the beloved, and from the *terminus ad quem*, by which, too,
this life is covered without residue. A very different tendency is
illustrated by the formally identical phenomenon of the Catholic
priest, where the clerical function entirely supersedes and absorbs
his individual existence. In the first of these two extreme sub-
types, the non-social element, which exists in addition to the
social, disappears, because its content has completely vanished in
the individual's turning toward another person. In the second
case, it disappears because the corresponding type of content itself has completely disappeared.

The opposite pole of the continuum is found in certain phenomena characteristic of modern culture with its money economy.
Here the individual, inasmuch as he produces, buys, sells, and in
general performs anything, approaches the ideal of absolute objectivity. Except in the highest leading positions, the individual
life and the tone of the total personality is removed from the
social action. Individuals are merely engaged in an exchange of
performance and counter-performance that takes place according
to objective norms—and everything that does not belong to this
pure objectivity has actually disappeared from it. The personality
itself, with its specific coloration, irrationality, and inner life, has
completely absorbed the non-social element and, in a neat separation, has left to the social activities only those energies which are
specifically appropriate for them.

Actually, social individuals move between these two extremes.
They do so in such a way that the energies and characteristics
which are directed back toward the individual have significance
at the same time for the actions and attitudes which are directed
toward another. There is an extreme case, namely, the notion that
this social activity or mood is something separate from the rest
of the personality, that the personality's non-social existence and
significance do not enter into social relations. Clearly, even this
notion, however, has its effect upon the attitude which the subject
holding it adopts toward others and upon the attitude which

others adopt toward him. The a priori of empirical social life consists of the fact that life is not entirely social. The reservation of a part of our personalities so as to prevent this part from entering into interaction has an effect upon our interactions which is twofold. In the first place, through general psychological processes it has its effect upon the social structure of the individual. In the second place, the formal fact itself, the part that exists outside the individual, affects this structure.

A society is, therefore, a structure which consists of beings who stand inside and outside of it at the same time. This fact forms the basis for one of the most important sociological phenomena, namely, that between a society and its component individuals a relation may exist as if between two parties. In fact, to the degree that it is more open or more latent, this relation, perhaps, always does exist. Society shows possibly the most conscious, certainly the most general, elaboration of a fundamental form of general life. This is that the individual can never stay within a unit which he does not at the same time stay outside of, that he is not incorporated into any order without also confronting it. This form is revealed in the most transcendent and general as well as in the most singular and accidental contexts. The religious man feels himself fully seized by the divine, as if he were merely a pulse-beat of its life. His own substance is given over unreservedly, if not in a mystical, undifferentiated fusion, to that of the absolute. But in spite of this, in order to give this fusion any significance whatever, he must preserve some sort of self-existence, some sort of personal counter, a differentiated ego, for whom the absorption in this divine all-being is a never ending task. It is a process that neither would be possible metaphysically, nor could be felt religiously, if it did not start from the existence of the individual: to be one with God is conditioned in its very significance by being other than God.

We do not have to adduce this experience of the transcendental. The same form of life is expressed in the idea that man's relation to nature is as a part of the totality of nature, an idea which the human mind has vindicated throughout its history. We view ourselves as incorporated into nature, as one of its products, as an equal of all other natural products, as a point which the stuffs and forces of nature reach and leave just as they circulate through flowing water and a blossoming plant. Yet we have the feeling of being independent and separate from all these entanglements and relationships, a feeling that is designated by the logically uncertain concept "freedom." We have a feeling that we represent a counter and contrast to this process, whose elements we nevertheless are. The most radical formulation of this feeling is found in the proposition that nature is merely a human imagination. In this formulation, nature, with all its undeniable autonomy and hard reality is made part of the individual self, although this self, with all its freedom and separate existence and contrast to "mere" nature, is nevertheless a link in it. In its most general form, the very essence of the relation between nature and man is that man comprises nature in spite of the fact that it is independent and very often hostile; that which is, according to man's innermost life-feeling, outside of him, must necessarily be his medium and element.

This formula is no less valid in regard to the relation between individuals and the groups to which they are socially tied or, if these groups are subsumed under the over-all concept or feeling of sociation, in regard to the relation among individuals in general. On the one hand, we see ourselves as products of society. The physiological succession of our ancestors, their adaptations and peculiarities, the traditions of their work and knowledge and belief—the whole spirit of the past as it is crystallized in objective forms determines the pattern and content of our lives. The question has even been raised as to whether the individual is anything more than a vessel in which elements existing before him are mixed in varying measures. For even if these elements ultimately are produced by the individual himself, his contribution is only minimal; only as individuals converge in species and society do the factors arise whose synthesis results in any discernible degree of individuality. On the other hand, we see ourselves as members of society. In this capacity we depend on it. By our life and its meaning and purpose, we are as inextricably woven into society, as a synchronic, coexisting phenomenon, as we are, as products, into diachronic, successive society.

In our capacity as natural objects we have no self-existence. The circulation of natural forces passes through us as through completely self-less structures, and our equality before the laws of nature resolves our existence without residue into a mere example of the necessity of these laws. Analogously, as social beings we do not live around any autonomous core. Rather, at any given moment, we consist of interactions with others. We are thus comparable to a physical body which consists merely of the sum of numerous sense impressions and does not have its own existence. Yet we feel that this social diffusion does not entirely dissolve our personalities. We feel this, not only because of the reservations already mentioned, that is, because of particular contents whose significance and development inhere exclusively in the individual and find no room whatever in the social sphere; nor only because the unifying center, the individual phenomenon, in the formation of social contents is not itself social (just as the artistic form, though composed of color spots on canvas, cannot be derived from the chemical nature of the colors); but also because, although it may be possible to explain the whole content of life completely in terms of social antecedents and interactions, this content must also be considered under the category of the individual life, as the individual's experience, as something exclusively oriented toward the individual. The two—social and individual—are only two different categories under which the same content is subsumed, just as the same plant may be considered from the standpoint of its biological development or its practical uses or its aesthetic significance. In the same way, the standpoint from which the life of the individual is conceived and structured may be taken from within as well as from without the individual. With all its socially derivable contents, a total life may be interpreted as the centripetally directed fate of its bearer as legitimately as—with all the elements that are reserved for the individual—it may be conceived of as the product and component of social life.

We thus see how the fact of sociation puts the individual into the dual position which I discussed in the beginning: The individual is contained in sociation and, at the same time, finds himself confronted by it. He is both a link in the organism of sociation and an autonomous organic whole; he exists both for society and for himself. The essence and deepest significance of the specific sociological a priori which is founded on this phenomenon is this: The "within" and the "without" between individual and society are not two unrelated definitions but define together the fully homogeneous position of man as a social animal. His existence, if we analyze its contents, is not only partly social and partly individual, but also belongs to the fundamental, decisive, and irreducible category of a unity which we cannot designate other than as the synthesis or simultaneity of two logically contradictory characterizations of man—the characterization which is based on his function as a member, as a product and content of society; and the opposing characterization which is based on his functions as an autonomous being, and which views his life from its own center and for its own sake.[2] Society consists not only of beings that are partially non-sociated, as we saw earlier, but also of beings which, on the one hand, feel themselves to be complete social entities, and, on the other hand—and without thereby changing their content at all—complete personal entities. And we do not deal here with two unrelated, alternative standpoints such as we adopt, for instance, when we look at an object in regard to either its weight or its color; for we are dealing with two elements that together form the unit we call the social being, that is, with a synthetic category. The phenomenon parallels the concept of causation. It, too, is an a priori unit, in spite of the fact that it covers two elements which are heterogeneous in content, cause and effect. We do perform the synthesis "social being." We are capable of constructing the notion of society from the very idea of beings, each of whom may feel himself as the *terminus a quo* and the *terminus ad quem* of his developments and destinies and qualities. And we do construct this concept of society, which is built up from that of the potentially autonomous individual, as the *terminus a quo* and the *terminus ad quem* of the individual's very life and fate. This capacity constitutes an a priori of empirical society. It makes possible the form of society as we know it.

(3) Society is a structure composed of unequal elements. The "equality" toward which democratic or socialistic efforts are directed—and which they partly attain—is actually an equivalence of people, functions, or positions. Equality in people is impossible because of their different natures, life contents, and destinies. On

---

[2] It is true, of course, that in given cases these may actually develop as two unrelated characteristics and that they may even be in mutual conflict.

the other hand, the equality of everybody with everybody else in an enslaved mass, such as we find in the great oriental despotisms, applies only to certain specific aspects of existence—political or economic aspects, for example—never to the total personality. For innate qualities, personal relations, and decisive experiences inevitably make for some sort of uniqueness and irreplaceability in both the individual's self-evaluation and his interactions with others.

Society may be conceived as a purely objective system of contents and actions connected by space, time, concepts, and values. In such a scheme, personality, the articulation of the ego (in which, nevertheless, the dynamics of society is located) may be ignored. However, the elements of this system are heterogeneous. Every action and quality within it is individual and is irrevocably located in its specific place. Society appears as a cosmos whose complex nature and direction are unlimited, but in which every single point can be fixed and can develop only in a particular way because otherwise the structure of the whole would change. What has been said of the structure of the world in general—that not a single grain of sand could have a shape different from what it has or be in a position different from its actual position without first conditioning the alteration by a change of the whole and without entailing such a change in the whole—is true of the structure of society, of society considered as a web of qualitatively differentiated phenomena.

This image of general society finds a small-scale analogy (infinitely simplified and stylized) in bureaucracy. A bureaucracy consists of a certain order of positions, of a predetermined system of functions. It exists as an ideal structure, irrespective of the particular occupants of these positions. Every new entrant finds within it a clearly defined place which has waited for him, so to speak, and to which his individual talents must be suited. In society at large, what here is a conscious, systematic determination of functions is a deeply entangled play and counterplay of them. Positions within society are not planned by a constructive will but can be grasped only through an analysis of the creativity and experience of the component individuals. Empirical, historical society is therefore vastly different from a bureaucracy because of its irrational and imperfect elements. From certain value standpoints, some of these elements must be condemned. Nevertheless, the phenomenological structure of society is the sum of the objective existences and actions of its elements and the interrelations among these existences and actions. It is a system of elements each of which occupies an individual place, a co-ordination of functions and function-centers which have objective and social significance, although they are not always valuable. Purely personal and creative aspects of the ego, its impulses and reflexes, have no place in this system. To put it otherwise: The life of society (considered not psychologically but phenomenologically, that is, exclusively in regard to its social contents) takes its course as if each of its elements were predestined for its particular place in it. In spite of all discrepancies between it and ideal standards, social life exists as if all of its elements found themselves interrelated with one another in such a manner that each of them, because of its very individuality, depends on all others and all others depend on it.

We are thus in a position to see the a priori which we must now discuss. This a priori provides the individual with the basis for, and offers the "possibility" of, his being a member of a society. An individual is directed toward a certain place within his social milieu by his very quality. This place which ideally belongs to him actually exists. Here we have the precondition of the individual's social life. It may be called the general value of individuality. It is independent both of its development into a clear, consciously formed conception and of its realization in the empirical life-process. In the same way, the apriority of causality as a determining precondition of cognition depends neither on its conscious formulation in specific concepts nor on the behavior of reality, as we grasp it psychologically, in accord or discord with it. For our cognition is based on the premise of a pre-established harmony that exists between our psychological energies, however individualized they may be, and external, objective existence. This existence always remains immediate, no matter how many attempts there have been to show, metaphysically or psychologically, that it is the intellect's own product. In a similar fashion, social life presupposes an unquestionable harmony between the individual and society as a whole. This harmony, of course, does not preclude violent ethical and eudaemonistic dissonances. If social reality were determined by this presupposition of harmony alone, without the interference of other factors, it would result in the perfect society. It would be perfect, however, not in the sense of ethical or eudaemonistic perfection, but of conceptual perfection; it would be not the *perfect* society but the perfect *society*. The a priori of the individual's social existence is the fundamental correlation between his life and the society that surrounds him, the integrative function and necessity of his specific character, as it is determined by his personal life, to the life of the whole. In so far as he does not realize this a priori or does not find it realized in society, the individual is not sociated and society is not the perfect system of interactions called for by its definition.

This situation is shown with particular sharpness in the phenomenon of vocation. Antiquity, to be sure, did not know this concept in its connotation of personal differentiation in a society articulated by a division of labor. But even antiquity knew its root, the idea that socially effective action is the unified expression of the inner qualification of the individual, the idea that by functioning in society the wholeness and permanence of subjectivity becomes practically objective. Yet in antiquity this relationship was exemplified by contents that were much less heterogeneous than they are today. Its principle is expressed in the Aristotelian axiom that some individuals are by nature destined to slavery; others, to domination. The more highly developed concept of vocation refers to a peculiar phenomenon: On the one hand, society within itself produces and offers to the individual a place which—however different in content and delimitation it may be from other places—can be filled by many individuals, and which is, for this reason, something anonymous, as it were. On the other hand, this place, in spite of its general character, is nevertheless taken by the individual on the basis of an inner calling, a qualification felt to be intimately personal. For such a thing as vocation to be possible, there must exist that harmony, whatever its origin, between the structure and development of society, and individual qualities and impulses. It is this general premise that constitutes the ultimate basis of the idea that for every personality there exist a position and a function in society to which he is called and which he must seek and find.

Empirical society becomes possible because of the a priori that finds its most obvious expression in the concept of vocation. Nevertheless, like the other a prioris thus far discussed, it cannot be designated by a simple slogan like those which it is possible to use for the Kantian categories. The processes of consciousness which formulate sociation—notions such as the unity of the many, the reciprocal determination of the individuals, the significance of the individual for the totality of the others and vice versa—presuppose something fundamental which finds expression in practice although we are not aware of it in its abstractness. The presupposition is that individuality finds its place in the structure of generality, and, furthermore, that in spite of the unpredictable character of individuality, this structure is laid out, as it were, for individuality and its functions. The nexus by which each social element (each individual) is interwoven with the life and activities of every other, and by which the external framework of society is produced, is a causal nexus. But it is transformed into a teleological nexus as soon as it is considered from the perspective of the elements that carry and produce it—individuals. For they feel themselves to be egos whose behavior grows out of autonomous, self-determined personalities. The objective totality yields to the individuals that confront it from without, as it were; it offers a place to their subjectively determined life-processes, which thereby, in their very individuality, become necessary links in the life of the whole. It is this dual nexus which supplies the individual consciousness with a fundamental category and thus transforms it into a social element.

It is a rather irrelevant question to ask whether the epistemological analyses of society exemplified in these sketches belong to social philosophy or to sociology proper. Perhaps they are tangential to both. At any rate, the nature of the sociological problem, as outlined earlier, and its delimitation from philosophical problems do not suffer from this question. They no more suffer from it than do the notions of day and night from the phenomenon of dawn, or the concepts of man and animal from the possibility that one day perhaps we may find intermediate stages in which the characteristics of both are fused in a way that we can no longer separate them conceptually. The sociological inquiry is directed toward abstracting from the complex phenomenon called social life that which is purely society, that is, sociation. It eliminates from the purity of this concept everything which does not constitute society as a unique and autonomous form of existence, although it can be realized only historically in society. It thus has its clearly defined problem area, whose center does not shift its position, although its periphery may, at present or forever, touch on other areas so that it becomes blurred.[3]

[3] A brief concluding paragraph is omitted.—Ed.

For
FURTHER READING

The whole of Lundberg's *Foundations of Sociology* gives a full statement of his position. He has also written *Social Research* and *Can Science Save Us?* Lundberg considers Stuart C. Dodd's *Dimensions of Society* to be an elaboration of the methodological implications of *Foundations of Sociology*. See Paul H. Furfey, *The Scope and Method of Sociology*, ch. 2, for further literature by and about Lundberg.

Several volumes of translations into English from the writings of Simmel have recently appeared: *The Sociology of Georg Simmel* and *Conflict* and *The Web of Group-Affiliations*. Some essays by and about Simmel appear in *Georg Simmel 1858–1918* (a good bibliography is included). These volumes are either edited or translated by Kurt H. Wolff. There is a book on *The Social Theory of Georg Simmel* by Nicholas J. Spykman. For a shorter introduction see Rudolf Heberle, "The Sociology of Georg Simmel," in *An Introduction to the History of Sociology* (ed. Harry Elmer Barnes).

For a general survey of the range of social science see Kaspar D. Naegele, "Some Observations on the Scope of Sociological Analysis," in *Theories of Society* (ed. Parsons, Shils, Naegele, and Pitts), Vol. I, and compare Edward Shils, "The Calling of Sociology," in Vol. II of the same work. On the controversy over the methodological status of social science see F. A. Hayek, *The Counter-Revolution of Science* and compare its critical discussion by May Brodbeck, "On the Philosophy of Social Sciences," *Philosophy of Science*, Vol. XXI, 1954 (this discussion is continued in the same issue by Alan Gewirth, "Subjectivism and Objectivism in the Social Sciences," and Richard S. Rudner, "Philosophy and Social Science"). Compare Barbara Wootton, *Testament for Social Science*, ch. 2; Felix Kaufmann, *Methodology of the Social Sciences*, chs. 1, 3, 4, 10, 11, 12, 14; Ludwig von Mises, *Human Action*, pp. 1–91; and Ernest Nagel, *The Structure of Science*, chs. 13, 14. Two articles by Maurice Mandelbaum are also recommended: "Societal Facts," *British Journal of Sociology*, Vol. VI, 1955 (reprinted in *The Structure of Scientific Thought*, ed. Edward H. Madden); and "Societal Laws," *British Journal for the Philosohy of Science*, Vol. VIII, 1957.

NOTE: Full bibliographical citations are given at the end of the volume for all titles that are mentioned elsewhere in the book.

PART II
Theory
and
Practice

Introduction to
PART II

━━

THE RELATIONSHIP between theory and practice has been viewed in a number of ways: some regard the liaison as highly improper, some predict divorce proceedings, others speak of a marriage of convenience, and a few remain under the impression that the principals are consummate lovers. In different guises, the essays which follow are reflections on this notorious affair. The terminals of the discussion are the opening sentence of the piece by Winch and Machlup's title, for those, reported by the former, who would speak of the social sciences as being in their infancy make an assumption which is given a close analytic examination by the latter. To this extent (and a fuller reading of both authors would lead us to add a qualifying "and to this extent only"), Winch and Machlup are in agreement about the inadvisability of regarding social science as a presently inferior version of natural scientific achievement. Before one can ask, How can the social sciences perfect themselves? it is necessary to know whether "imperfect" is a reliable term of discourse in this context. Hence Machlup's prior question, Are the Social Sciences Really Inferior? Winch, on the other hand, turns his attention to the nexus between "social studies, philosophy and the natural sciences." The clue to their relationship is the initial placement one makes of the nature of philosophical inquiry.

The fear that theory may overpower practice is, in a way, another version of the concern to keep science free of philosophical tampering. The concern on the part of those who distrust intellection that goes on in plush furniture is that purely conceptual analysis may distort practical problems and tend to deflect their solution. A deeper source of anxiety is the uncertain status of knowledge itself—whether its ultimate validation lies in its utility or in its intrinsic nature. Jonas's paper cuts across or cuts under the dualism of theory and use. His "thesis is that to modern theory in general, practical use is no accident but is integral to it, or that 'science' is technological by its nature." This claim rests upon an understanding of the nature of action, which has as a cardinal dimension knowledge itself. Instead of action being subordinated to the category of external force and movement, the latter become modalities of the former. But one consequence of Jonas's thesis is that the term "theory" requires more refined specification. A distinction is made between knowledge concerned with the desirability of ends and knowledge which deals with the means to those ends. In turn, knowledge of means is of two types: science and applied science. If a theory of science and applied science is possible with respect to action, a theory of the concrete exercise of judgment is held to be impossible: "Thus there is theory and use of theory, but no theory of the use of theory." Whether the reader is persuaded by Jonas's argument will depend in part on whether he accepts this claim.

Theory and use, then, far from being uneasy partners may instead be understood as intimates. But the critics of theory are far from agreement as to its proper interpretation. Here, once again, is the quarrel between social "scientists" and social "humanists" to which Lowe refers and which Asch and Hula are concerned with in their comments. But in mentioning the "uneasy compromise between these extremes" sought for by those who view both alternatives, radically taken, with some alarm, Lowe points to an order of "instrumentalism" (which the reader should not confuse with its pragmatic form) designed to make the compromise more than an eclectic apology. Such instrumentalism sets aside the problem of the prediction of social phenomena as they are found in a given situation in favor of a restricted model of a system (the discussion, of course, is restricted to economics, though the implications are wider) in which postulated goals are delineated together with the means seen as formally compatible with achieving these goals. Whether such a delimitation of the social field is enough to mediate between "scientists" and "humanists" is an open question, but it offers a vantage point from which the reader may consider Machlup's remarks on the "Predictability of Future Events." If the economist is, in the course of his professional activity, called upon to make predictions of at least the general shape of future events, he may have as another but quite related methodological province that of "instrumental" analysis. It might be suggested that if instrumentalism capitalizes on the hypothetical form of assertion, it may qualify, in Jonas's terms, as applied science. If this is so, the status of the execution of the theory of such science might lead to further thoughts about "theory of the use of theory."

How one goes about theorizing and practicing in social science depends, then, on some rather fundamental commitments to philosophically charged categories. Whether such commitment is sophisticated and highly self-conscious or totally naive does not alter the matter; if anything it complicates it. At least one great function of philosophy (even if it is considered to be merely a heuristic one) is to elucidate the assumptions of those who are proud and those who are simple. In the course of such elucidation it seldom fails that marginal doubts and deeply rooted suspicions are forced to account for themselves. Philosophy thrives on embarrassment. At the same time, it is usually the case that elucidated assumptions sort out types of thinkers and styles of thought. Winch's discussion of the "underlabourer" conception of philosophy may be taken as an extension of the problem of *Weltanschauung* explored in the Introduction and exemplified in the abortive dialogue between Lundberg and Simmel. This theme will be resounded in other parts of this book, and its climax will be reached in the concluding Part, "Philosophical Perspectives." There the reader will find "A. J. Ayer's distinction between the 'pontiffs' and the 'journeymen' of philosophy" that is referred to by Winch. Readers are welcome to play the game of dual classifications that so many thinkers have enjoyed. First, however, they might consider William James's characterization of "The Tender-Minded and the Tough-Minded" (in his *Pragmatism*) and Isaiah Berlin's beauty, *The Hedgehog and the Fox*. Nowadays any voyager in these waters eventually makes a call at the port of C. P. Snow's *The Two Cultures and the Scientific Revolution*. From there he goes on for himself.

The opposed *Weltanschauungen* that are evident throughout this section are partly positions analytically presented in the essays and partly representations of the philosophical orientations of the authors themselves. In some instances it would be difficult as well as unfair to label the writers, but there are intimations of a rather wide range of influences evident here. Some of these sources turn out to be unexpected alliances, as in the case of Winch's Wittgensteinian defense of an approach to the social sciences that is closest, in many respects, to that of Max Weber. The coming together of such diverse motives suggests that "scientists" and "humanists" may have their arguments taken out of their hands by those who are prepared to carry them forward in newly enlivened terms. A transvaluation of entrenched positions may give rise to a reappraisal of theory and practice. Philosophy remains the only ground on which to judge whether a breakthrough is not merely another name for a regrouping of traditional forces.

Philosophical Bearings[1]

PETER WINCH

::

1. Aims and Strategy

THAT the social sciences are in their infancy has come to be a
platitude amongst writers of textbooks on the subject. They will
argue that this is because the social sciences have been slow to
emulate the natural sciences and emancipate themselves from the
dead hand of philosophy; that there was a time when there was
no clear distinction between philosophy and natural science; but
that owing to the transformation of this state of affairs round
about the seventeenth century natural science has made great
bounds ever since. But, we are told, this revolution has not yet
taken place in the social sciences, or at least it is only now in
process of taking place. Perhaps social science has not yet found
its Newton but the conditions are being created in which such a
genius could arise. But above all, it is urged, we must follow the
methods of natural science rather than those of philosophy if we
are to make any significant progress.

I propose, in this monograph, to attack such a conception of
the relation between the social studies, philosophy and the natu-

[1] Reprinted from Peter Winch, *The Idea of a Social Science: and Its
Relation to Philosophy* (London: Routledge & Kegan Paul, 1958, pp. 1–24),
with the permission of the publisher and the approval of the author.

ral sciences. But it should not be assumed on that account that what I have to say must be ranked with those reactionary antiscientific movements, aiming to put the clock back, which have appeared and flourished in certain quarters since science began. My only aim is to make sure that the clock is telling the right time, whatever it may prove to be. Philosophy, for reasons which may be made more apparent subsequently, has no business to be anti-scientific: if it tries to be so it will succeed only in making itself look ridiculous. Such attacks are as distasteful and undignified as they are useless and unphilosophical. But equally, and for the same reasons, philosophy must be on its guard against the extra-scientific *pretensions* of science. Since science is one of the chief shibboleths of the present age this is bound to make the philosopher unpopular; he is likely to meet a similar reaction to that met by someone who criticizes the monarchy. But the day when philosophy becomes a popular subject is the day for the philosopher to consider where he took the wrong turning.

I said that my aim was to attack a current conception of the relations between philosophy and the social studies. Since that conception involves two terms, what may appear to some a disproportionately large portion of this book must be devoted to discussing matters whose bearing on the nature of the social studies is not immediately evident. The view I wish to commend presupposes a certain conception of philosophy, a conception which many will think as heretical as my conception of social science itself. So, however irrelevant it may at first appear, a discussion of the nature of philosophy is an *essential* part of the argument of this book. This opening chapter, then, cannot safely be skipped as a tiresome and time-wasting preliminary.

This may be more convincing if I briefly outline the general strategy of the book. It will consist of a war on two fronts: first, a criticism of some prevalent contemporary ideas about the nature of philosophy; second, a criticism of some prevalent contemporary ideas about the nature of the social studies. The main tactics will be a pincer movement: the same point will be reached by arguing from opposite directions. To complete the military analogy before it gets out of hand, my main war aim will be to demonstrate that the two apparently diverse fronts on which the war is being waged are not in reality diverse at all; that to be clear about the nature of philosophy and to be clear about the nature of the social studies amount to the same thing. For any worthwhile study of society must be philosophical in character and any worthwhile philosophy must be concerned with the nature of human society.

2. *The Underlabourer Conception of Philosophy*

I will call the conception of philosophy which I want to criticize the "underlabourer conception," in honour of one of its presiding geniuses, John Locke. The following passage from the Epistle to the Reader which prefaces Locke's *Essay Concerning Human Understanding*, is often quoted with approval by supporters of the underlabourer conception.

> The commonwealth of learning is not at this time without master-builders, whose mighty designs, in advancing the sciences, will leave lasting monuments to the admiration of posterity: but everyone must not hope to be a Boyle or a Sydenham; and in an age that produces such masters as the great Huygenius and the incomparable Mr. Newton, with some others of that strain, it is ambition enough to be employed as an under-labourer in clearing the ground a little, and removing some of the rubbish that lies in the way to knowledge.

Locke's view is echoed in A. J. Ayer's distinction between the "pontiffs" and the "journeymen" of philosophy; it is translated into the idiom of much modern philosophical discussion by A. G. N. Flew, in his introduction to *Logic and Language* (First Series); and it has many points of contact with Gilbert Ryle's conception of philosophy as "informal logic."[2]

I will try to isolate some of the outstanding features of this view which are most relevant for my present purpose. First, there is the idea that "it is by its methods rather than its subject-matter that philosophy is to be distinguished from other arts or sciences." That obviously follows from the underlabourer conception; for according to it philosophy cannot contribute any positive understanding of the world on its own account: it has the purely

[2] Cf. G. Ryle, *Dilemmas.*

negative role of removing impediments to the advance of our understanding. The motive force for that advance must be sought in methods quite different from anything to be found in philosophy; it must be found, that is, in science. On this view philosophy is parasitic on other disciplines; it has no problems of its own but is a technique for solving problems thrown up in the course of non-philosophical investigations.

The modern conception of what constitutes the "rubbish that lies in the way to knowledge" is very similar to Locke's own: philosophy is concerned with eliminating linguistic confusions. So the picture we are presented with is something like this. Genuine new knowledge is acquired by scientists by experimental and observational methods. Language is a tool which is indispensable to this process; like any other tool language can develop defects, and those which are peculiar to it are logical contradictions, often conceived on the analogy of mechanical faults in material tools. Just as other sorts of tool need a specialist mechanic to maintain them in good order, so with language. Whereas a garage mechanic is concerned with removing such things as blockages in carburetors, a philosopher removes contradictions from realms of discourse.

I turn now to a further, connected, implication of the under-labourer conception. If the problems of philosophy come to it from without, it becomes necessary to give some special account of the role of metaphysics and epistemology within philosophy. For though it may be plausible to say that the problems of the philosophy of science, the philosophy of religion, the philosophy of art, and so on, are set *for* philosophy by science, religion, art, etc., it is not at all obvious what sets the problems for metaphysics and epistemology. If we say that these disciplines are autonomous with regard to their problems, then of course the underlabourer conception collapses as an exhaustive account of the nature of philosophy. Some writers have suggested that metaphysics and epistemology are just the philosophies of science and of psychology respectively in disguise, but I have never seen this view defended in any detail and it is certainly not *prima facie* plausible to anyone who is at all familiar with the history of these subjects. Others again have said that metaphysical and epistemological discussions are an entirely spurious form of activity and do not belong to any respectable discipline at all. But they treat of questions which have a habit of recurring and such a cavalier attitude soon begins to ring somewhat hollow. It is in fact a good deal less popular than once it was.

Another widely held view is that championed, for instance, by Peter Laslett in his editorial introduction to *Philosophy, Politics and Society*. According to this view, the preoccupation with epistemological questions, which has for some time characterized philosophical discussion in Great Britain, is to be construed as a temporary phase, as a period of examining and improving the *tools* of philosophy, rather than as the very stuff of philosophy itself. The idea is that, when this work of re-tooling has been done, it is the duty of the philosopher to return to his more important task—that of clarifying the concepts which belong to other, non-philosophical disciplines.

In the first place this interpretation is unhistorical, since epistemological questions have always been central to serious philosophical work, and it is difficult to see how this could be otherwise. More importantly, Laslett's view involves a reversal of the true order of priority within philosophy: epistemological discussion is represented as important only in so far as it serves a further end, namely to advance the treatment of questions in the philosophies of science, art, politics, etc. I want to argue, on the contrary, that the philosophies of science, art, politics, etc.— subjects which I will call the "peripheral" philosophical disciplines —are important only in relation to epistemology and metaphysics. But before I can show this in detail, I must first attempt to examine the philosophical foundations of the underlabourer conception of philosophy.

3. Philosophy and Science

That conception is in large part a reaction against the "master-scientist" view of the philosopher, according to which philosophy is in direct competition with science and aims at constructing or refuting scientific theories by purely *a priori* reasoning. This is an idea which is justly ridiculed; the absurdities to which it may lead are amply illustrated in Hegel's amateur pseudo-scientific speculations. Its philosophical refutation was provided by Hume:

If we would satisfy ourselves . . . concerning the nature of
that evidence, which assures us of matters of fact, we must
enquire how we arrive at the knowledge of cause and effect.
I shall venture to affirm, as a general proposition, which admits of no exception, that the knowledge of this relation is
not, in any instance, attained by reasonings *a priori;* but arises
entirely from experience, when we find that any particular
objects are constantly conjoined with each other. Let an
object be presented to a man of ever so strong natural reason
and abilities; if that object be entirely new to him, he will
not be able, by the most accurate examination of its sensible
qualities, to discover any of its causes or effects.[3]

Now this is admirable as a critique of *a priori* pseudo-science. But
the argument has also frequently been misapplied in order to
attack *a priori* philosophizing of a sort which is quite legitimate.
The argument runs as follows: new discoveries about real matters
of fact can only be established by experimental methods: no
purely *a priori* process of thinking is sufficient for this. But since
it is science which uses experimental methods, while philosophy is
purely *a priori*, it follows that the investigation of reality must
be left to science. On the other hand, philosophy has traditionally
claimed, at least in large part, to consist in the investigation of the
nature of reality; either, therefore, traditional philosophy was attempting to do something which its methods of investigation
could never possibly achieve, and must be abandoned; or else it
was mistaken about its own nature, and the purport of its investigations must be drastically reinterpreted.

Now the argument on which this dilemma is based is fallacious: it contains an undistributed middle term. The phrase "the
investigation of the nature of reality" is ambiguous, and whereas
Hume's argument applies perfectly well to what that phrase con-
veys when applied to *scientific* investigation, it is a mere *ignoratio
elenchi* as applied to *philosophy*. The difference between the respective aims of the scientist and the philosopher might be expressed as follows. Whereas the scientist investigates the nature,
causes and effects of *particular* real things and processes, the
philosopher is concerned with the nature of reality as such and

[3] D. Hume, *Enquiry into Human Understanding*, Section IV, Part I.

in general. Burnet puts the point very well in his book on *Greek Philosophy* when he points out (on pages 11 and 12) that the sense in which the philosopher asks, "What is real?" involves the problem of man's relation to reality, which takes us beyond pure science. "We have to ask whether the mind of man can have any contact with reality at all, and, if it can, what difference this will make to his life." Now to think that this question of Burnet's could be settled by experimental methods involves just as serious a mistake as to think that philosophy, with its *a priori* methods of reasoning, could possibly compete with experimental science on its own ground. For it is not an empirical question at all, but a *conceptual* one. It has to do with the *force of the concept* of reality. An appeal to the results of an experiment would necessarily involve begging the question, since the philosopher would be bound to ask by what token those results themselves are accepted as "reality." Of course, this simply exasperates the experimental scientist—rightly so, from the point of view of his own aims and interests. But the force of the philosophical question cannot be grasped in terms of the preconceptions of experimental science. It cannot be answered by generalizing from particular instances since a particular answer to the philosophical question is already implied in the acceptance of those instances as "real."

The whole issue was symbolically dramatized on a celebrated occasion in 1939 when Professor G. E. Moore gave a lecture to the British Academy entitled "Proof of an External World." Moore's "proof" ran roughly as follows. He held up each of his hands in succession, saying "Here is one hand and here is another; therefore at least two external objects exist; therefore an external world exists." In arguing thus Moore seemed to be treating the question "Does an external world exist?" as similar in form to the question "Do animals with a single horn growing out of their snout exist?" This of course would be conclusively settled by the production of two rhinoceri. But the bearing of Moore's argument on the philosophical question of the existence of an external world is not as simple as the bearing of the production of two rhinoceri on the other question. For, of course, philosophical doubt about the existence of an external world covers the two hands which Moore produced in the same way as it covers everything else. The whole question is: Do objects like Moore's two hands qualify as inhabitants of an external world? This is not to say that Moore's argument is completely beside the point; what is wrong is to regard it as an experimental "proof," for it is not like anything one finds in an experimental discipline. Moore was not making an experiment; he was *reminding* his audience of something, reminding them of the way in which the expression "external object" is in fact used. And his reminder indicated that the issue in philosophy is not to prove or disprove the existence of a world of external objects but rather to *elucidate the concept* of externality. That there is a connection between this issue and the central philosophical problem about the general nature of reality is, I think, obvious.

4. The Philosopher's Concern with Language

So much, at present, for the relation between philosophy and science. But I have yet to show why the rejection of the master-scientist conception of the philosopher need not, and should not, lead to the underlabourer conception. I have spoken of Moore reminding us how certain expressions are in fact used; and I have emphasized how important in philosophy is the notion of elucidating a concept. These are ways of speaking which *prima facie* fit the underlabourer conception very well. And in fact what is wrong with that conception in general is to be looked for not so much in any downright false doctrine as in a systematically mistaken emphasis.

   Philosophical issues do, to a large extent, turn on the correct use of certain linguistic expressions; the elucidation of a concept is, to a large extent, the clearing up of linguistic confusions. Nevertheless, the philosopher's concern is not with correct usage as such and not all linguistic confusions are equally relevant to philosophy. They are relevant only in so far as the discussion of them is designed to throw light on the question how far reality is intelligible[4] and what difference would the fact that he could have a grasp of reality make to the life of man. So we have to

   [4] I am aware that this is a somewhat old-fashioned sounding way to talk. I do so in order to mark the difference between the philosopher's concern with reality and that of, e.g., the scientist. I take this opportunity of saying that I owe the statement of the philosopher's kind of interest in language, in the next paragraph, to an unpublished talk by Mr. Rush Rhees on "Philosophy and Art."

ask how questions of language, and what kinds of question about language, are likely to bear upon these issues.

To ask whether reality is intelligible is to ask about the relation between thought and reality. In considering the nature of thought one is led also to consider the nature of language. Inseparably bound up with the question whether reality is intelligible, therefore, is the question of how language is connected with reality, of what it is to *say* something. In fact the philosopher's interest in language lies not so much in the solution of particular linguistic confusions for their own sakes, as in the solution of confusions about the nature of language in general.

I will elaborate this point polemically, referring to T. D. Weldon's *Vocabulary of Politics*. I choose this book because in it Weldon uses his interpretation of the concern which philosophy has with language to support a conception of the relations between philosophy and the study of society, which is fundamentally at variance with the conception to be commended in this monograph. Weldon's view is based on an interpretation of recent developments in philosophy in this country. What has occurred, he says, is that "philosophers have become extremely self-conscious about language. They have come to realise that many of the problems which their predecessors have found insuperable arose not from anything mysterious or inexplicable in the world but from the eccentricities of the language in which we try to describe the world."[5] The problems of social and political philosophy, therefore, arise from the eccentricities of the language in which we try to describe social and political institutions, rather than from anything mysterious in those institutions themselves. In accordance with the underlabourer conception of philosophy, which Weldon is here faithfully following, he regards philosophy as having a purely negative role to play in advancing our understanding of social life. Any positive advances in this understanding must be contributed by the methods of empirical science rather than by those of philosophy. There is no hint that discussion of the central questions of metaphysics and epistemology themselves may (as I shall later argue) have light to throw on the nature of human societies.

In fact those questions are cavalierly brushed aside in the very

[5] T. D. Weldon, *Vocabulary of Politics*, ch. 1.

statement of Weldon's position. To assume at the outset that one can make a sharp distinction between "the world" and "the language in which we try to describe the world," to the extent of saying that the problems of philosophy do not arise at all out of the former but only out of the latter, is to beg the whole question of philosophy.

Weldon would no doubt reply that this question has already been settled in a sense favourable to his position by those philosophers who contributed to the developments of which he is speaking. But even if we overlook the important fact that philosophical issues can never be settled in that way, that the results of other men's philosophizing cannot be assumed in one's own philosophical work as can scientific theories established by other men—even, I say, if we overlook this, the work of Wittgenstein, the most outstanding contributor to the philosophical development in question, is just misinterpreted if it is taken to support Weldon's way of speaking. This is obvious enough in relation to Wittgenstein's *Tractatus Logico-Philosophicus*, as can be seen from two representative quotations. "To give the essence of proposition means to give the essence of all description, therefore the essence of the world."[6] "That the world is *my* world shows itself in the fact that the limits of my language (of the only language I can understand) mean the limits of *my* world."[7]

It is true that these ideas in the *Tractatus* are connected with a theory of language which Wittgenstein afterwards rejected and which Weldon would also reject. But Wittgenstein's methods of argument in the later *Philosophical Investigations* are equally incompatible with any easy distinction between the world and language. This comes out clearly in his treatment of the concept of seeing an object *as* something: for example, seeing the picture of an arrow as in flight. The following passage is characteristic of Wittgenstein's whole approach:

> In the triangle I can see now *this* as apex, *that* as base—now *this* as apex, *that* as base.—Clearly the words 'Now I am seeing this as the apex' cannot so far mean anything to a learner who has only just met the concepts of apex, base, and so on.—

[6] L. Wittgenstein, *Tractus Logico-Philosophicus*, 5.4711.
[7] *Ibid.*, 5.62.

But I do not mean this as an empirical proposition.

'Now he's seeing it like *this*', 'now like *that*' would only be said of someone *capable* of making certain applications of the figure quite freely.

The substratum of this experience is the mastery of a technique.

But how queer for this to be the logical condition of someone's having such and such an *experience!* After all, you don't say that one only 'has toothache' if one is capable of doing such-and-such.—From this it follows that we cannot be dealing with the same concept of experience here. It is a different though related concept.

It is only if someone *can do*, has learnt, is master of, such-and-such, that it makes sense to say he has had *this* experience.

And if this sounds crazy, you need to reflect that the *concept* of seeing is modified here. (A similar consideration is often necessary to get rid of a feeling of dizziness in mathematics.)

We talk, we utter words, and only *later* get a picture of their life.[8]

We cannot say then, with Weldon, that the problems of philosophy arise out of language *rather than* out of the world, because in discussing language philosophically we are in fact discussing *what counts as belonging to the world*. Our idea of what belongs to the realm of reality is given for us in the language that we use. The concepts we have settle for us the form of the experience we have of the world. (It may be worth reminding ourselves of the truism that when we speak of the world we are speaking of what we in fact mean by the expression "the world": there is no way of getting outside the concepts in terms of which we think of the world, which is what Weldon is trying to do in his statements about the nature of philosophical problems. The world *is* for us what is presented through those concepts. That is not to say that our concepts may not change; but when they do, that means that our concept of the world has changed too.)

[8] L. Wittgenstein, *Philosophical Investigations*, II, xi.

5. *Conceptual and Empirical Enquiries*

This misunderstanding of the way in which philosophical treat-
ments of linguistic confusions are also elucidations of the nature
of reality leads to inadequacies in the actual methods used for
treating such questions. Empiricists like Weldon systematically
underemphasize the extent of what may be said *a priori:* for them
all statements about reality must be empirical or they are un-
founded, and *a priori* statements are "about linguistic usage" as
opposed to being "about reality." But if the integrity of science is
endangered by the *over*-estimation of the *a priori*, against which
Hume legitimately fought, it is no less true that philosophy is
crippled by its *under*-estimation: by mistaking conceptual enquiries into what it makes sense to say for empirical enquiries
which must wait upon experience for their solution.

The misunderstanding is well illustrated in the following passage from Hume himself. He is discussing the extent and nature
of our knowledge of what will happen in the future and arguing
that nothing in the future can be logically guaranteed for us by
our knowledge of what has been observed to happen in the past.

> In vain do you pretend to have learned the nature of
> bodies from past experience. Their secret nature, and con-
> sequently all their effects and influence may change, without
> any change in their sensible qualities. This happens some-
> times, and with regard to some objects: Why may it not
> happen always and with regard to all objects? What logic,
> what process of argument secures you against this supposi-
> tion?[9]

Hume assumes here that since a statement about the uniform behaviour of *some* objects is a straightforward empirical matter
which may at any time be upset by future experience, the same
must be true of a statement about the uniform behaviour of all
objects. This assumption is very compelling. Its compellingness
derives from a healthy unwillingness to admit that anyone can
legislate *a priori* concerning the course of future experience on
the basis of purely logical considerations. And of course we cannot
thus legislate against a breakdown in the regular order of nature,

[9] D. Hume, *op. cit.*, Section IV, Part II.

such as would make scientific work impossible and destroy speech, thought, and even life. But we can and must legislate *a priori* against the possibility of *describing* such a situation in the terms which Hume attempts to use: in terms, that is, of the properties of objects, their causes and effects. For were the order of nature to break down in that way these terms would be no longer applicable. Because there may be minor, or even major, variations *within* such an order without our whole conceptual apparatus being upset, it does not follow that we can use our existing apparatus (and what other are we to use?) to describe a breakdown in the order of nature as a whole.

This is not merely verbal quibbling. For the whole philosophical purport of enquiries like Hume's is to clarify those concepts which are fundamental to our conception of reality, like *object, property of an object, cause and effect.* To point out that the use of such notions necessarily presupposes the continuing truth of *most* of our generalizations about the behaviour of the world we live in is of central importance to such an undertaking.

The importance of this issue for the philosophy of the social sciences will become more apparent later on. I shall argue, for instance, that many of the more important theoretical issues which have been raised in those studies belong to philosophy rather than to science and are, therefore, to be settled by *a priori* conceptual analysis rather than by empirical research. For example, the question of what constitutes social behaviour is a demand for an elucidation of the *concept* of social behaviour. In dealing with questions of this sort there should be no question of "waiting to see" what empirical research will show us; it is a matter of tracing the implications of the concepts we use.

6. The Pivotal Role of Epistemology Within Philosophy

I can now offer an alternative view of the way in which the problems of epistemology and metaphysics are related to those in what I have called the peripheral philosophical disciplines. Everything I have so far said has been based on the assumption that what is really fundamental to philosophy is the question regarding the nature and intelligibility of reality. It is easy to see that this question must lead on to a consideration of what we mean by "intelligibility" in the first place. What is it to understand something, to grasp the sense of something? Now if we look at the contexts in which the notions of understanding, of making something intelligible, are used we find that these differ widely amongst themselves. Moreover, if those contexts are examined and compared, it soon becomes apparent that the notion of intelligibility is systematically ambiguous (in Professor Ryle's phrase) in its use in those contexts: that is, its sense varies systematically according to the particular context in which it is being used.

The scientist, for instance, tries to make the world more intelligible; but so do the historian, the religious prophet and the artist; so does the philosopher. And although we may describe the activities of all these kinds of thinker in terms of the concepts of understanding and intelligibility, it is clear that in very many important ways, the objectives of each of them differ from the objectives of any of the others. For instance, I have already tried, in Section 3, to give some account of the differences between the kinds of "understanding of reality" sought by the philosopher and the scientist respectively.

It does not follow from this that we are just punning when we speak of the activities of all these enquirers in terms of the notion of making things intelligible. That no more follows than does a similar conclusion with regard to the word "game" when Wittgenstein shows us that there is no set of properties common and peculiar to all the activities correctly so called.[10] There is just as much point in saying that science, art, religion and philosophy are all concerned with making things intelligible as there is in saying that football, chess, patience and skipping are all games. But just as it would be foolish to say that all these activities are part of one supergame, if only we were clever enough to learn how to play it, so is it foolish to suppose that the results of all those other activities should all add up to one grand theory of reality (as some philosophers have imagined: with the corollary that it was their job to discover it).

On my view then, the philosophy of science will be concerned with the kind of understanding sought and conveyed by the scientist; the philosophy of religion will be concerned with the way in which religion attempts to present an intelligible pic-

[10] Cf. *Philosophical Investigations*, I, pp. 66–71.

ture of the world; and so on. And of course these activities and
their aims will be mutually compared and contrasted. The purpose of such philosophical enquiries will be to contribute to our
understanding of what is involved in the concept of intelligibility,
so that we may better understand what it means to call reality
intelligible. It is important for my purposes to note how different
is this from the underlabourer conception. In particular, the philosophy of science (or of whatever enquiry may be in question)
is presented here as autonomous, and not parasitic on science itself, as far as the provenance of its problems is concerned. The
motive force for the philosophy of science comes from within
philosophy rather than from within science. And its aim is not
merely the negative one of removing obstacles from the path of
the acquisition of further scientific knowledge, but the positive
one of an increased philosophical understanding of what is involved in the concept of intelligibility. The difference between
these conceptions is more than a verbal one.

It might appear at first sight as if no room had been left for
metaphysics and epistemology. For if the concept of intelligibility
(and, I should add, the concept of reality equally) are systematically ambiguous as between different intellectual disciplines, does
not the philosophical task of giving an account of those notions
disintegrate into the philosophies of the various disciplines in
question? Does not the idea of a *special* study of epistemology rest
on the false idea that all varieties of the notion of intelligibility
can be reduced to a single set of criteria?

That is a false conclusion to draw, though it does provide a
salutary warning against expecting from epistemology the formulation of a set of *criteria* of intelligibility. Its task will rather be
to describe the conditions which must be satisfied if there are to
be any criteria of understanding at all.

7. Epistemology and the Understanding of Society

I should like here to give a preliminary indication of how this
epistemological undertaking may be expected to bear upon our
understanding of social life. Let us consider again Burnet's formulation of the main question of philosophy. He asks what difference
it will make to the life of man if his mind can have contact with

reality. Let us first interpret this question in the most superficially obvious way: it is clear that men do decide how they shall behave on the basis of their view of what is the case in the world around them. For instance, a man who has to catch an early morning train will set his alarm clock in accordance with his belief about the time at which the train is due to leave. (If anyone is inclined to object to this example on the grounds of its triviality, let him reflect on the difference that is made to human life by the fact that there are such things as alarm clocks and trains running to schedule, and methods of determining the truth of statements about the times of trains, and so on.) The concern of philosophy here is with the question: What is involved in "having knowledge" of facts like these, and what is the general nature of behaviour which is decided on in accordance with such knowledge?

The nature of this question will perhaps be clearer if it is compared with another question concerning the importance in human life of knowing the world as it really is. I am thinking of the moral question which so exercised Ibsen in such plays as *The Wild Duck* and *Ghosts:* How far is it important to a man's life that he should live it in clear awareness of the facts of his situation and of his relations to those around him? In *Ghosts* this question is presented by considering a man whose life is being ruined by his ignorance of the truth about his heredity. *The Wild Duck* starts from the opposite direction: here is a man who is living a perfectly contented life which is, however, based on a complete misunderstanding of the attitude to him of those he knows; should he be disillusioned and have his happiness disrupted in the interests of truth? It is necessary to notice that our understanding of both these issues depends on our recognition of the *prima facie* importance of understanding the situation in which one lives one's life. The question in *The Wild Duck* is not whether that is important, but whether or not it is *more* important than being happy.

Now the interest of the epistemologist in such situations will be to throw light on *why* such an understanding should have this importance in a man's life by showing what is involved in having it. To use a Kantian phrase, his interest will be in the question: How is such an understanding (or indeed any understanding) possible? To answer this question it is necessary to show the central role which the concept of understanding plays in the activities which are characteristic of human societies. In this way the discussion of what an understanding of reality consists in merges into the discussion of the difference the possession of such an understanding may be expected to make to the life of man; and this again involves a consideration of the general nature of a human society, an analysis, that is, of the concept of a human society.

A man's social relations with his fellows are permeated with his ideas about reality. Indeed, "permeated" is hardly a strong enough word: social relations are expressions of ideas about reality. In the Ibsen situations which I just referred to, for example, it would be impossible to delineate the character's attitudes to the people surrounding him except in terms of his ideas about what they think of him, what they have done in the past, what they are likely to do in the future, and so on; and, in *Ghosts*, his ideas about how he is biologically related to them. Again, a monk has certain characteristic social relations with his fellow monks and with people outside the monastery; but it would be impossible to give more than a superficial account of those relations without taking into account the religious ideas around which the monk's life revolves.

At this point it becomes clearer how the line of approach which I am commending conflicts with widely held conceptions of sociology and of the social studies generally. It conflicts, for instance, with the view of Emile Durkheim:

> I consider extremely fruitful this idea that social life should be explained, not by the notions of those who participate in it, but by more profound causes which are unperceived by consciousness, and I think also that these causes are to be sought mainly in the manner according to which the associated individuals are grouped. Only in this way, it seems, can history become a science, and sociology itself exist.[11]

It conflicts too with von Wiese's conception of the task of sociology as being to give an account of social life "disregarding the cultural aims of individuals in society in order to study the in-

---

[11] See Durkheim's review of A. Labriola, *Essais sur la conception matérialiste de l'histoire, Revue Philosophique*, XLIV, 1897, 645–651.

fluences which they exert on each other as a result of community life."[12]

The crucial question here, of course, is how far any sense can be given to Durkheim's idea of "the manner according to which associated individuals are grouped" *apart* from the "notions" of such individuals; or how far it makes sense to speak of individuals exerting influence on each other (in von Wiese's conception) in abstraction from such individuals' "cultural aims." I shall try to deal explicitly with these central questions at a later stage in the argument. At present I simply wish to point out that positions like these do in fact come into conflict with philosophy, conceived as an enquiry into the nature of man's knowledge of reality and into the difference which the possibility of such knowledge makes to human life.

[12] See R. Aron, *German Sociology*, p. 8.

The Practical Uses of Theory[1]

HANS JONAS

I

IN HIS COMMENTARY to Aristotle's "On the Soul," Thomas Aquinas
wrote as follows:

> All knowledge is obviously good because the good of any
> thing is that which belongs to the fulness of being which all
> things seek after and desire; and man as man reaches fulness
> of being through knowledge. Now of good things some are
> just valuable, namely, those which are useful in view of some
> end—as we value a good horse because it runs well; whilst
> other good things are also honourable: namely, those that
> exist for their own sake, for we give honour to ends, not
> to means. Of the sciences some are practical, others specula-
> tive; the difference being that the former are for the sake of
> some work to be done, while the latter are for their own sake.

[1] This essay, together with the comments which follow by Solomon E.
Asch, Erich Hula, and Adolph Lowe, appeared in *Social Research* (Vol.
XXVI, No. 2, Summer 1959, pp. 127–166), and are reprinted by permission
of that journal and with the approval of the authors. Professor Jonas has
made minor corrections in his paper.

The speculative sciences are therefore honourable as well as good, but the practical are only valuable.[2]

About three and a half centuries later, Francis Bacon wrote in *The Great Instauration* as follows:

> I would address one general admonition to all: that they consider what are the true ends of knowledge, and that they seek it not either for pleasure of the mind, or for contention, or for superiority to others . . . but for the benefit and use of life, and that they perfect and govern it in charity. . . . [From the marriage of the Mind and the Universe] there may spring helps to man, and a line and race of inventions that may in some degree subdue and overcome the necessities and miseries of humanity . . . For the matter in hand is no mere felicity of speculation, but the real business and fortunes of the human race, and all power of operation . . . And so those twin objects, *human knowledge* and *human power*, do really meet in one.[3]

Here are two opposing statements of the aim and very meaning of knowledge and, consequently, of its relation to possible use, or to "works." On this old theme the present discourse attempts to offer some comments unavailable to the original contestants but available to us in the light of the new "necessities and miseries of humanity," which are besetting us, so it seems, precisely as a concomitant of that use of knowledge which Bacon envisaged as the remedy for humanity's old necessities and miseries.

Aquinas and Bacon obviously speak of two different things. In assigning different ends to knowledge, they speak in fact of different kinds of knowledge, having also different kinds of things

---

[2] A. M. Pirotta, ed., *Sancti Thomae Aquinatis in Aristotelis Librum de 'Anima Commentarium*, Lectio 1, § 3. The above quotation is from the translation by K. Foster and S. Humphries, *Aristotle's De Anima in the Version of William of Moerbeke and the Commentary of St. Thomas Aquinas*, p. 45.

[3] From the Prooemium of Francis Bacon, *The Great Instauration*. The four sentences of the quotation occur in the text in that order, but widely scattered. An additional quotation from the Prooemium may instance Bacon's direct criticism of classical theory: "And for its value and utility it must be plainly avowed that that wisdom which we have derived principally from the Greeks is but the boyhood of knowledge, and has the characteristic property of boys: it can talk, but it cannot generate; for it is fruitful of controversies but barren of works."

for their subject. Taking Aquinas first, who of course speaks for Aristotle, the "speculative" (that is, theoretical) sciences of his statement are about things unchangeable and eternal—the first causes and intelligible forms of Being—which, being unchangeable, *can* be contemplated only, not involved in action: theirs is *theoria* in the strict Aristotelian sense. The "practical sciences," on the other hand, are "arts," not "theory"—a knowledge concerning the planned changing of the changeable. Such knowledge springs from experience, not from theory or speculative reason. The guidance that theory *can* provide with regard to the arts consists not in promoting their invention and informing their procedures, but in informing their user (if he partakes in the theoretical life) with the wisdom to use those arts, like all things, wisely, that is, in proper measure and for proper ends. This may be called a practical benefit of theory through the enlightening effect which it has on the whole person of its votaries beyond its immediate actuality. But this benefit is not in the nature of a "use" made of theory as a means, and is anyway a second best in response to the necessities of man: the best is the sustained activity of pure thought itself, where man is most free.

So far Aristotle and Aquinas. It is the "necessities of humanity" which assume first place in Bacon's scheme: and since art is man's way of meeting and conquering necessity, but has not hitherto enjoyed the benefit of speculative reason (mainly by the latter's fault), Bacon urges that the two be brought into a new relationship in which their former separation is overcome. This involves a revision of both, but first, in causal order, of speculative science, which has so long been "barren of works." Theory must be so revised that it yields "designations and directions for works," even has "the invention of arts" for its very end, and thus becomes itself an art of invention. Theory it is nonetheless, as it is discovery and rational account of first causes and universal laws (forms). It thus agrees with classical theory in that it has the nature of things and the totality of nature for its object; but it is such a science of causes and laws, or a science of such causes and laws, as then makes it possible "to command nature in action." It makes this possible because from the outset it looks at nature *qua* acting, and achieves knowledge of nature's laws of action by itself engaging nature in action—that is, in experiment, and therefore on terms set by man himself. It yields directions for works because it first catches nature "at work."

A science of "nature at work" is a mechanics, or dynamics, of nature. For such a science Galileo and Descartes provided the speculative premises and the method of analysis and synthesis. Giving birth to a theory with inherently technological potential, they set on its actual course that fusion of theory and practice which Bacon was dreaming of. Before I say something more of that kind of theory which lends itself to technical application, and indeed has intrinsic reference to this kind of use, I must say something about use as such.

II

What is use for? The ultimate end of all use is the same as the end of all activity, and this is twofold: preservation of life, and betterment of life, that is, promotion of the good life. Put negatively, as suggested by Bacon's pair "necessities and miseries," the twofold end is to ward off extinction and to overcome misery. We note the emergency aspect that Bacon gives to human endeavor, and thus to knowledge as part of that endeavor. He speaks of lifting or lessening an adverse and pressing condition, whereas Thomas, with Aristotle, speaks positively of attaining "fulness of being," or perfection. Bacon's negative emphasis invests the task of knowledge with a kind of physical and moral urgency altogether strange and novel in the history of theory, but increasingly familiar since his time.

The difference in emphasis admits, however, of common ground: assuming mere preservation (which takes precedence in both cases) to be assured in its basic conditions, misery means denial of a good life; its removal then means betterment, and therefore by both accounts, that of Aristotle and that of Bacon, the ultimate aim of all doing beyond that minimum necessary for survival is the good life or human happiness. Leaving the term "happiness" in all the ambiguity it must have until we determine what happiness may consist in, we may thus state as the ground common to Bacon and Aristotle that the "what for" of all use, including that of knowledge, is happiness.

Whose happiness? If, as Bacon holds, knowledge is to do

away with the miseries of mankind, it is the happiness of mankind which the pursuit of knowledge has for its aim. If, as Aristotle holds, man as man reaches fulness of being through, or rather in, knowledge, it is the happiness of the knower which the pursuit of pure knowledge achieves. In both cases there is, then, a supreme "use" to theoretical knowledge. To Aristotle it consists in the good that knowledge works in the soul of the knower, that is, in the condition of knowing itself as the perfection of the knower's being.

Now, to claim this ennobling effect for knowledge makes sense only when theory is knowledge of the noblest, that is, most perfect, objects. There being such objects is indeed the condition of there being "theory" in the classical sense of the word; and conversely, failing such objects the contemplative ideal of classical philosophy becomes pointless. Assuming the condition as given, then theory, as intellectual communion with those objects—and through such communion modifying the subject's own condition—does not merely promote but in its actuality constitutes happiness: a happiness termed "divine," and therefore but briefly obtainable in the lives of mortals. Hence in this case possession and use of theory are the same. If there is a further "use" of it beyond its own activity—and therefore a contribution to happiness of a more "human" (as distinct from "divine") kind—it consists, as we have seen, in the wisdom it confers on the person for the conduct of his life in general, and in the comprehension which, from the summit of speculation, transfuses his understanding of all things, including common things. But although theory through wisdom may deliver its possessor from the spell of common things, and thereby increase his moral freedom from their necessity, it does not increase his physical control over and use of them (rather tends to limit the latter), and leaves the realm of necessity itself unaffected.

Since Bacon's time it has been the other alternative that matters. To him and those after him, the use of knowledge consists in the "fruits" it bears in our dealing with the common things. To bear that fruit the knowledge itself must be one of common things—not derivatively so, as was classical theory, but primarily and even before becoming practical. This is indeed the case: the theory that is thus to be fruitful is knowledge of a universe which, in the absence of a hierarchy of being, consists of common things entirely. Since freedom can then no longer be located in a cognitive relation to the "noblest objects," knowledge must deliver man from the yoke of necessity by meeting necessity on its own ground, and achieves freedom for him by delivering the things into his power. A new vision of nature, not only of knowledge, is implied in Bacon's insistence that "the mind may exercise over the nature of things the authority which properly belongs to it." The nature of things is left with no dignity of its own.[4] All dignity belongs to man: what commands no reverence can be commanded, and all things are for use. To be the master of nature is the right of man as the sole possessor of mind, and knowledge, by fitting him to exercise this right, will at last bring man into his own. His own is "the kingdom of man," and it consists in his sovereign use of things. Sovereign use means more use—not merely potential but actual and, strange to say, even necessary use. Control, by making ever more things available for more kinds of uses, enmeshes the user's life in ever more dependencies on external objects. There is no other way of exercising the power than by making oneself available to the use of the things as they become available. Where use is forgone the power must lapse, but there is no limit to the extension of either. And so one master is exchanged for another.

Even the laying hold of power in the first place is not quite so free as the appeal to man's legitimate authority suggests. For not only is man's relation to nature one of power, but nature herself is conceived in terms of power. Thus it is a question of either ruling or being ruled; and to be ruled by a nature not noble or kindred or wise means slavery and hence misery. The exercise of

---

[4] "The works of God . . . show the omnipotency and wisdom of the Maker, but not his image: and therefore therein the heathen opinion differeth from the sacred truth; for they supposed the world to be the image of God, and man to be an exact or compendious image of the world, but the Scriptures never vouchsafe to attribute to the world that honour, as to be the image of God, but only the work of His hands; neither do they speak of any other image of God, but man" (Bacon, *Works*, ed. J. Spedding and R. L. Ellis, III, p. 349 f.). Leo Strauss adduces this passage in support of the statement: "The division of philosophy into natural and human philosophy is based on the systematic distinction between man and world, which Bacon makes in express controversy against ancient philosophy" (*The Political Philosophy of Hobbes*, p. 91, n. 1).

man's inherent right is therefore also the response to a basic and continuous emergency: the emergency of a contest decreed by man's condition. The attack of knowledge, being a defense against necessity, is itself a function of necessity, and retains this aspect throughout its career, which is a continuous response to the new necessities created by its very progress.

III

For knowledge to be beneficial to man's estate it must be "perfected and governed in charity." This is to say that whoever administers the course and the use of theory must take the necessities and miseries of humanity to heart. The blessings of knowledge are not in the first place for the knower but for his not-knowing fellowmen—and for himself only in so far as he is one of them. Unlike the magician, the scientist does not acquire in his own person the power that springs from his art. He hardly even acquires, and certainly does not own, the knowledge itself in his own person: since this knowledge is a collective enterprise, his fractional contribution goes into the common stock, of which the scientific community is the depository and society as a whole should be the beneficiary. Among the benefits that knowledge grants through power over things is relief from toil: leisure then, but not the scientist's own, is here a fruit of knowledge. The classical pattern was the opposite: leisure was a condition of theory, antecedently assured to make theory possible, not something to be achieved by its exertions. Modern theoretical activity, far from being use of leisure, is itself a toil and part of the common toil of humanity, however gratifying to the toiler. This alone shows that modern theory does not, in human terms, take the place of classical theory.

Furthermore, the need for charity or benevolence in the use of theory stems from the fact that power can be for evil as well as for good. Now charity is not itself among the fruits of theory in the modern sense. As a qualifying condition of its use—which use theory itself does not specify, let alone determine—it must spring from a source transcendent to the knowledge that the theory supplies.

Here a comparison with the classical case is instructive.

Though Plato does not call it by that name, the responsibility that compels the philosopher to return to the "cave" and help his fellowmen imprisoned there is an analogue to Bacon's charity or pity. But also how different! In the first place, since of theory in the Platonic sense the activity as well as the object is noble, it will itself be the source of benevolence in its adepts for whatever part they may take in the active life. Non-benevolent action would be inconsistent with the light they partake of through the highest knowledge. No such contradiction obtains between the insights of science and their potential non-benevolent use. Secondly, though in Plato's scheme the "descent" into the active life is not by inclination but by duty, and this duty is proximately enforced by the state, its ultimate sanction emanates from the object of contemplation itself, namely "the good," which is not envious and impels its own communication; thus no additional and heterogenic principle is required to provide the ground of responsibility. Finally, the returning philosopher's action in the cave is concerned not with the managing of things, but with the ordering of lives; in other words, it is not technical but political, informed by the vision of order in the intelligible world. Thus it is an "application" that derives its motive, its model, and its standard of what is beneficial from the one and self-sufficient theory. Such "application" can be exercised only in person by the authentic adepts of theory; it cannot be delegated, as can and must be the application of the "know-how" of technical science.

By contrast, modern theory is not self-sufficiently the source of the human quality that makes it beneficial. That its results are detachable from it and handed over for use to those who had no part in the theoretical process is only one aspect of the matter. The scientist himself is by his science no more qualified than others to discern, nor even is he more disposed to care for, the good of mankind. Benevolence must be called in from the outside to supplement the knowledge acquired through theory: it does not flow from theory itself.

Why is this so? One answer is commonly expressed in the statement that science is "value-free" (*wertfrei*), with the corollary that values are not objects of knowledge, or at any rate of scientific knowledge. But why is science divorced from value, and value considered non-rational? Can it be because the validation of value requires a transcendence whence to derive it? Relation to an objective transcendence lies today outside theory by its rules of evidence, whereas formerly it was the very life of theory.

"Transcendence" (whatever else the term comprises) implies objects higher than man, and about such was classical theory. Modern theory is about objects lower than man: even stars, being common things, are lower than man. No guidance as to ends can be derived from them. The phrase "lower than man," implying a valuation, seems to contradict the asserted "value-freedom" of science. But this value-freedom means a neutrality as much of the objects as of the science: of the objects, their neutrality toward whatever value may be "given" them. And that which lacks intrinsic value of its own is lower than that by reference to which alone it may receive value, namely, man and human life, the only remaining source and referent of value.

What then about the sciences of man, like psychology or sociology? Surely it cannot be said of them that the objects of science are lower than man? Their object is man. Is it not true that with them value re-enters the universe of science? And cannot spring from them, as dealing with source and reference of all value, a valid theory of value? But here we have to distinguish: Valuation as a fact of human behavior indeed becomes known in the human sciences—but not value itself. And facetious as it may sound: in so far as they are *sciences* their object too is "lower than man." How so? For a scientific theory of him to be possible, man, including his habits of valuation, has to be taken as determined by causal laws, as an instance and part of nature. The scientist does take him so—but not himself while he assumes and exercises his freedom of inquiry and his openness to reason, evidence, and truth. Thus man-the-knower apprehends man-qua-lower-than-himself and in doing so achieves knowledge of man-qua-lower-than-man, since all scientific theory is of things lower than man the knower. It is on that condition that they can be subjected to "theory," hence to control, hence to use. Then man-lower-than-man explained by the human sciences—man reified—can by the instructions of these sciences be controlled (even "engineered") and thus used.

Charity then, or even love (as love of mankind rather than

person), in trying to make such use a charitable or beneficent one, does not correct but rather confirms the lower status. And as the use of what is lower-than-man can only be for what is lower and not for what is higher in the user himself, the knower and user becomes in such use, if made all-inclusive, himself lower than man. And all-inclusive it becomes when it extends over the being of one's fellowmen and swallows up the island-kingdom of the person. Inevitably the manipulator comes to see himself in the same light as those his theory has made manipulable; and in the self-inclusive solidarity with the general human lowliness amidst the splendor of human power his charity is but self-compassion and that tolerance which springs from self-contempt: we are all poor puppets and cannot help being what we are. Benevolence then degenerates to condoning and conniving.

Even when of a purer and less ambiguous kind, benevolence alone is insufficient to insure beneficial use of science. As a disposition to refrain from harming, it is of course as indispensable in this context as it is in the fellowship of men in general. But in its positive aspect good will is *for* the good and must therefore be informed by a conception of what is the good. Whence such a conception can derive and whether it can be raised to the rank of "knowledge" must here be left undecided. If there is a knowledge of it, not science can supply it. Mere benevolence cannot replace it—nor even love, if love without reverence; and whence can reverence come except from a knowledge of what is to be revered? But even if a guiding knowledge of the good, that is, true philosophy were available, it might well find its counsel to be of no avail against the self-generated dynamics of science in use. To this theme I shall return at the end. Now I must say something more about the specifically modern practice-theory relation itself and the ways it works, rather than what it works for.

IV

We speak of *using* when we apply something as a means toward an end. As the end is distinct from the means, so normally is the means distinct from its application. That is to say, the means has a prior existence of its own and would continue to be what it is even if never so applied at all. Whether this holds fully for theory too, or for every theory, we have reason to doubt. But in speaking of uses of theory that much is conceded that theory, however used, is also something by itself.

Being something by itself is not necessarily to be neutral to possible use. Use may be essential, or it may be accidental, to that which can serve as a means. Some things, though having a substantive being of their own once they exist, do so *as* means from the outset. A tool, for example, owes its very being to the purpose beyond itself for which it was designed. If not put to such service it misses its raison d'être. To other things use comes as it were as an afterthought on the part of a user: for them, being used is accidental, extraneous to the being they have in their own independent right. In the first category are mainly man-made things, like hammers or chairs, in the second mainly natural ones, like horses or rivers. Theory is certainly man-made, and it has uses; but whether use is essential or accidental to it may well depend on the kind of theory one considers, as also on the kind of use. Mathematics, for example, differs in this respect from physics. My thesis is that to modern theory in general, practical use is no accident but is integral to it, or that "science" is technological by its nature.

Practical is a use which involves external action, resulting in a change in the environment (or preventing a change). External action requires the use of external, physical means, and moreover some degree of information, which is an internal, non-physical thing. But all action which is not strictly routine, and not purely intuitive, requires more than that, namely deliberation, and this can be as to ends and as to means: as to ends—for example, whether desirable, and whether generally possible; as to means—for example, which as such suitable, and which here and now available. In all these respects, *knowledge* (if not necessarily theory) enters into the conditions and conduct of action and is made use of.

Obviously it is a different kind of knowledge which has to do with the desirability of ends, and a different kind that has to do with feasibility, means, and execution. Again, within the latter kind, the knowledge which pronounces on possibility in principle is different from the one which maps, still in the abstract, possible

ways of realization, and this from the discernment of the course
of action most practicable in the given circumstances. We have
here a scale descending from the general to the particular, from
the simple to the complex, and at the same time from theory to
practice, which is complexity itself. The knowledge of possibility
rests on the universal principles of the field, its constitutive laws
(the terminal points of what Galileo called the "resolutive
method"); that of typical ways of coming-to-be on more complex and more specific causal patterns, embodying the first principles and providing models for rules of action ("compositive
method"); the knowledge, finally, of what to do now is entirely
particular, placing the task within the context of the whole, concrete situation. The first two steps are both within theory, or
rather, they each *can* have their developed theory. The theory in
the first case we may call science proper, such as theoretical
physics; the theory in the second case, derivative from it in logic,
if not always in fact, we may call technological or applied science—which, it must be remembered, is still "theory" in respect
to action itself, as it offers the specific rules of action as parts of a
reasoned whole and without making a decision. The particular
execution itself has no theory of its own and can have none.
Though applying the theory, it is not simply derivative of it but
involves decision based on *judgment;* and there is no science of
judgment (as little as there is one of decision)—that is, judgment
cannot be replaced by or transformed into science, much as it can
avail itself of the findings and even of the intellectual discipline of
science and is itself a kind of knowledge, a cognitive faculty.
Judgment, says Kant, is the faculty of subsuming the particular
under the universal; and since reason is the faculty of the universal, and science the operation of that faculty, judgment as concerned with particulars is necessarily outside science and strictly
the bridge between the abstractions of the understanding and the
concreteness of life.

In the first stage, that of pure science, the form of propositions is categorical: A is P, B is P, . . . In the applied stage, the
form is hypothetical: if P is to be, then either A or B . . . must
be provided. In the deliberations of practical judgment, the propositional form is problematical: particulars f, g, . . . available in
the situation, do perhaps (not, partially) fit the demands of uni-

versal A, or B, . . . ; may therefore be (not, more, less) suitable for bringing about P. Invention is typically such a combination of concrete judgment with abstract science.

It is in this realm of concrete judgment and choice that the practical use of theory comes about. Whence it follows that the use of theory does not itself permit of a theory: if it is enlightened use, it receives its light from deliberation, which may or may not enjoy the benefits of good sense. But this knowledge of use is different not only from the knowledge of the theory used in the case but from that of any theory whatsoever, and it is acquired or learned in ways different from those of theory. This is the reason why Aristotle denied there being a science of politics and practical ethics; the where, when, to whom . . . cannot be reduced to general principles. Thus there is theory and use of theory, but no theory of the use of theory.

At the opposite end of the scale is the knowledge concerning ends repeatedly alluded to—of which today we do not know whether it admits of theory, as once it was held eminently to do. This knowledge alone would permit the valid discrimination of worthy and unworthy, desirable and undesirable uses of science, whereas science itself only permits discrimination of its correct or incorrect, adequate or inadequate, effectual or ineffectual use. But it is with this very science which is not in doubt that we must now concern ourselves, asking what features intrinsically fit this type of theory for use in the world of things.

V

Of theory formation one of its nineteenth-century masters, Heinrich Hertz, had this to say: "We form images or symbols of the external objects; the manner in which we form them is such that the *logically* necessary consequences of the images are invariably the images of the *materially* necessary consequences of the corresponding objects."[5]

This is an elliptic statement. For the "images or symbols" formed and used are not of the immediate external objects such as

[5] H. Hertz, *Prinzipien der Mechanik*, p. 1, taken from H. Weyl, *Philosophy of Mathematics and Natural Science*, p. 162.

rocks and trees, or even of whole classes or general types of such, but symbols for the residual products of a speculative analysis of the given objects and their states and relations—residues which admit of none but symbolic representation, yet by hypothesis are presumed to underlie the objects and are thus treated as "external objects" themselves in substitution for the original objects.

The key term here is "analysis." Analysis has been the distinctive feature of physical inquiry since the seventeenth century: analysis of *working* nature into its simplest dynamic factors. These factors are framed in such identical quantitative terms as can be entered, combined, and transformed in equations. The analytical method thus implies a primary *ontological reduction* of nature, and this precedes mathematics or other symbolism in its application to nature. Once left to deal with the residual products of this reduction, or rather, with their measured values, mathematics proceeds to reconstruct from them the complexity of phenomena in a way which can lead beyond the data of the initial experience to facts unobserved, or still to come, or to be brought about. That nature lends itself to this kind of reduction was the fundamental discovery, actually the fundamental anticipation, at the outset of mechanical physics.

With this reduction, "substantial forms," that is, wholeness as an autonomous cause with respect to its component parts, and therefore the ground of its own becoming, shared the fate of final causes. In Newtonian physics the integral wholeness of form, on which classical and mediaeval ontology was based, is broken up into elementary factors for which the parallelogram of forces is a fitting graphic symbol. The presence of the future, formerly conceived as potentiality of becoming, consists now in the calculability of the operation of the forces discernible in a given configuration. No longer something original in its own right, form is the current compromise among the basic actions of aggregate matter. The falling apple is not so much elevated to the rank of cosmic motion as the latter is brought down to the level of the falling apple. This establishes a new unity of the universe, but of a different complexion from the Greek one: the aristocracy of form is replaced by the democracy of matter.

If, according to this "democracy," wholes are mere sums, then their seemingly genuine qualities are due to the quantitatively more or less involved combination of some simple substrata and their dynamics. Generally complexity and degrees of complexity supplant all other ontological distinctions. Thus for purposes of explanation the parts are called upon to account for the whole, and that means that the primitive has to account for the more articulated, or, in older parlance, *the lower for the higher*.

With no hierarchy of being but only distributions of a uniform substratum, all explanation has to start from the bottom and in fact never leaves it. The higher is the lower in disguise, where the disguise is provided by complexity: with the latter's analysis, the disguise dissolves, and the appearance of the higher is reduced to the reality of the elemental. From physics this schema of explanation has penetrated all provinces of knowledge, and it is now as much at home in psychology and sociology as in the natural sciences where it originated. No longer is the realm of passion characterized by the absence of reason, but reason is characterized as a disguise and servant of passion. The transcendental philosophy of a society is but the ideological superstructure to (and thus a disguise of) its vital interests, which reflect organic needs, which depend on physical constitution. The rat in the maze tells us what we are. Always the lower explains the higher and in the course of analysis emerges as its truth.

Now this ontological analysis has *per se* technological implication prior to any application in fact. The latter is possible only because of the manipulative aspect inherent in the theoretic constitution of modern science as such. If it is shown how things are made up of their elements, it is also shown, on principle, how they can be made up out of such elements. Making, as distinct from generating, is essentially putting together pre-existing materials or rearranging pre-existing parts. Similarly, scientific cognition is essentially analysis of distribution, that is, of the conditions in which elements are interrelated, and is not burdened with the task of comprehending the essence of those elements themselves. Not what they are but how they function under such specified conditions, that is, in such combinatorial relations, is the theme that science can and does pursue. This restriction is basic to the modern conception of knowledge; for, unlike substantial natures, distributions of conditions can be reconstructed, even freely constructed, in mental models and so allow of understanding. Again, unlike "natures," they may be actually repeated or modified in human imitation of nature, that is in technique, and so allow of manipulation. Both understanding and making are here concerned with relations and not with essences. In fact, understanding of this sort is itself a kind of imaginary making or re-making of its objects, and this is the deepest cause for the technological applicability of modern science.

Early in the eighteenth century, Vico enunciated the principle that man can understand only what he has made himself. From this he reasoned that not nature, which as made by God stands over against man, but history, which is of man's own making, can be understood by man. Only a *factum*—what has been made—can be a *verum*. But in opposing this principle to Cartesian natural science, Vico overlooked the fact that, if only "has been made" is widened to "can be made," the principle applies to nature even better than to history (where in fact its validity is doubtful). For according to the mechanistic scheme the knowledge of a natural event deals, as we have seen, not with the God-created part of the situation—the intrinsic nature of the substances involved—but with the variable conditions which, given those substances, determine the event. By reenacting those conditions, in thought or in actual manipulation, one can reproduce the event without producing the substratum. To understand the substratum itself is as much beyond man's powers as to produce it. But the latter is beyond the powers even of nature, which, once created in its substantial entities, goes on "creating" only by manipulating them, that is, by the shift of relations. Conditions and relations are the vehicle for created nature's noncreative productions, just as they are the vehicle for created man's cognition of nature and also for his technical imitation of nature's ways of production. This was the meaning of Bacon's famous maxim that nature can be commanded only by being obeyed. Nature's quasi-technical modes of making—or nature as its own artificer and artifact—is the at once knowable and imitable aspect of it, whereas essences in themselves are unknowable because unmakable. The metaphor of "nature's workshop," into which science is to pry in order to learn her procedures, popularly expresses the point that the distinction between natural and artificial, so basic to classical philosophy, has lost its meaning. "I do not," wrote Descartes, "recognize any difference between the machines made by craftsmen and the diverse bodies put together by nature alone . . . all the rules of mechanics belong to physics, so that all things which are artificial are thereby natural" (*Principles* IV, art. 203).[6] In the same vein, Descartes could say "Give me matter and motion, and I shall make the world once more"—a saying impossible in the mouth of a pre-modern thinker. To know a thing means to know how it is or can be made and therefore means being able to repeat or vary or anticipate the process of making. It does not matter whether man can always actually, with the forces at his command, provide the factors making up the required conditions and, therefore, himself produce their result. Man cannot reproduce a cosmic nebula, but assuming he knows how it is produced in nature, he would on principle be able to produce one too if he were sufficiently large, powerful, and so on, and this is what to know a nebula means. To put it in the form of a slogan, the modern knowledge of nature, very unlike the classical one, is a "know-how" and not a "know-what," and on this basis it makes good Bacon's contention that knowledge is power.

This, however, is not the whole story of the technological aspect inherent in scientific theory. Theory is an internal fact and internal action. But its relation to external action may be not only that of means to end by way of application, but also the reverse: that is, action may be employed in the service of theory as theory may be employed in the service of action. Some com-

---

[6] But do "all the rules of mechanics" equal "*all* the rules of physics"? The readily conceded truth that the former "belong to" physics may serve to cover the very different subreption that they exhaust the book of rules of physics (i.e., of nature). —The complete passage in the *Principles*, from which the above quotation is taken, is of capital importance as the enunciation of a really new principle, which has since dominated natural science and natural philosophy. Its technological implications are obvious. The new doctrine of a uniform nature, here emerging from the ruins of the mediaeval edifice, naively assumes an identity of macro- and micro-modes of operation, which more recent physics has found wanting. But even apart from any later discoveries, one could have objected at the outset on logical grounds that from the fact of machines working by natural principles entirely it does not follow that they work by the entire natural principles, or, that nature has no other modes of operation than those which man can utilize in his constructions. But this very view of nature (not the innocent one of human mechanics) was Descartes' true conviction: its spirit alone, going far beyond a mere experiment with Occam's razor, accounts for the supreme confidence of the next statement quoted in the text.

plementarity of these two aspects suggests itself from the outset: it may be that only that theory which has grown out of active experience can be turned to the active changing of experience; or only that theory can become a means to practice which has practice among its own means. That this is the case becomes obvious when we consider the role of experiment in the scientific process.

The alliance contemplated by Bacon between knowing and changing the world is indeed much more intimate than the mere delegation of theoretical results to practical use, that is, the *post factum* application of science, would make it. The procedure of science itself, if it is to yield practically relevant results, has to be practical, namely, experimental. We must "close with nature" and do something to it in order to make it yield its secrets through the response we have elicited, "seeing," as Bacon says, "that the nature of things betrays itself more readily under the vexations of art than in its natural freedom." Thus in two different respects modern science is engaged in the active changing of things: on the small scale of the experiment it effects change as a necessary means of knowing nature, that is, it employs practice for the sake of theory; the kind of theory gained in this way lends itself to, and thus invites, the large-scale changes of its technical application. The latter, in turn, becomes a source of theoretical insights not to be gained on the laboratory scale—in addition to furnishing the tools for more effective laboratory work itself, which again in turn yields new increments of knowledge, and so on in a continuous cycle. In this way the fusion of theory and practice becomes inseparable in a way which the mere terms "pure" and "applied" science fail to convey. Effecting changes in nature as a means and as a result of knowing it are inextricably interlocked, and once this combination is at work it no longer matters whether the pragmatic destination of theory is expressly accepted (for example by the "pure" scientist himself) or not. The very process of attaining knowledge leads through manipulation of the things to be known, and this origin fits of itself the theoretical results for an application whose possibility is irresistible—even to the theoretical interest, let alone the practical, whether or not it was contemplated in the first place.

VI

At the same time the question as to what is the true human end, truth or use, is entirely left open by the fact of the union as such and is in essence not affected by the conspicuous preponderance of the practical element. The answer is determined by the image of man, of which we are uncertain. Certain it is from what we have learned that if "truth" be the end it cannot be the truth of pure contemplation. The modern discovery that knowing nature requires coming to grips with nature—a discovery bearing beyond the field of natural science—has permanently corrected Aristotle's "contemplative" view of theory. More, of course, was involved in the ideal of the contemplative life than a conception merely of theoretical method: more than the latter's correction must also be involved in a legitimate farewell to the ideal—a farewell the more bidden with a heavy heart the more understood in its necessity.

It was Aristotle's contention that we act in order to intuit and not intuit in order to act—on which the favorite modern comment is that it reflects nothing but the attitude of a leisure class in a slave society. Rarely in our pragmatic climate is the trouble taken to ask whether Aristotle, socially biased or not, might not be right. He was, after all, not deaf to the demands of "reality." That the necessities of life have to be taken care of first he explicitly states, this being the task allotted to civilization; only he considered this task to be finite, not infinite, or interminable, as it is likely to appear to modern thought on the basis of different attitudes and experiences. Even with these it is well to consider the Greek reasoning in the matter, so as to put the contemporary dynamism of the active life in its proper perspective. Some simple considerations will still be found pertinent. Thus Aristotle's reasoning that we make war in order to have peace is unanswerable, and the generalization that we toil in order to find rest is at least eminently reasonable.[7] Clearly, then, the rest to be found must not consist in suspension of activity, but must itself be a kind of life, that is, have its content in an activity of its own—which to Aristotle was "thought." Now, when full due is given to the sanity

[7] *Nicomachean Ethics*, X, 7, 1177b 4 f.

and appeal of this classical stance, it must be said that it implies views both of civilization and of thought which, rational as they are, have in the light of modern experience become questionable concerning civilization, and untenable concerning thought.

As to civilization, Aristotle takes for granted that once it has reached a working equilibrium between legitimate wants and means for their satisfaction it can devote its surplus to making possible the philosophical life, the life of thought, the true goal of man. Today we have good reason for disbelief in the very attainment of such an equilibrium. We therefore see no better use (in fact, no choice) for the "surplus" than to be fed back into the active process for that adjustment of its constantly generated disequilibrium which results in progress—a self-feeding automatism in which even theory is of necessity involved as factor and function at once, and to which we cannot see (let alone set) a limit. But, if infinite, then the process of civilization calls for the constant care of the best minds—that is: for their constant employment in the "cave."

And as for "thought" itself, the modern adventure of knowledge has corrected the Greek view of it in yet another respect than that of its possible detachment from practice, and for all we know as definitively. To the Greeks, be it Plato or Aristotle, the number of the truly knowable things is finite, and the apprehension of first principles, whenever obtained, is definitive—subject to intermittent renewal but not to obsolescence through new discovery and better approximation. To the modern experience of knowledge it is inconceivable that any state of theory, including the conceptual system of first principles governing it, should be more than a temporary construct to be superseded by the next vista to which it opens itself the way when all its implications are matched against all the facts. In other words, the *hypothetical* character of modern science *ipso facto* qualifies each of its explanatory and integrating attainments as setting a new problem rather than granting the object for ultimate beholding.

At the root of this difference is, of course, the difference between modern nominalism, with its understanding of the tentative nature of symbolism, as against classical realism. To the latter, concepts reflect and match the self-existing forms of being, and these do not change; to the former, they are products of the human mind, the endeavor of a temporal entity and therefore subject to change. The element of infinity in Greek *theoria* concerned the potential infinity of satisfaction in beholding the eternal, that which never changes; the element of infinity in modern theory concerns the interminableness of the process by which its tentative hypotheses are revised and absorbed into higher symbolical integrations. Thus the idea of potentially infinite progress permeates the modern ideal of knowledge with the same necessity as it does the modern ideal of technical civilization;[8] and so, even apart from the mutual involvement of the two, the contemplative ideal has become invalid, nay, illogical, through the sheer lack of those presumed ultimates, the abiding "noblest objects," in whose apprehension knowledge would come to rest and turn from search into contemplation.

VII

It seems then that practice and theory conspire to commit us to unceasing dynamism, and with no abiding present our life is ever into the future. What Nietzsche has called "sovereign becoming" is upon us, and theory, far from having where to stand beyond it, is chained to its chariot, in harness before it or dragged in its tracks—which, it is hard to tell in the dust of the race, and sure is only that not theory is the charioteer.

There are those who cheer the surge that sweeps them along and disdain to question "whither?"; who hail change for its own sake, the endless forward thrust of life into the ever new, unknown, the dynamism as such. Yet, surely, for change to be valuable it is relevant *what* entity changes (if not toward what), and this underlying whatness must in some way be definable as that nature of "man as man" which qualifies the endless consummation of its possibilities in change as a worthwhile enterprise. Some image then is implied in the affirmation of change itself. But, if an image, then a norm, and if a norm, then also the freedom of negation, not only the surrender of affirmation; and this freedom itself transcends the flux and points to another sort of theory.

---

[8] And as it permeates the modern idea of nature or reality itself: the very doctrine of being, not merely that of knowledge and of man, has become engulfed in the symbolism of process and change.

That theory would have to take up the question of ends which the radical vagueness of the term "happiness" leaves open and on which science, committed to provide the means for happiness, cannot pronounce. The injunction to use it in the interest of man, and to the best of his interest, remains empty as long as it is not known what the best interest of man is.

Faced with the threat of catastrophe we may feel excused from inquiring into ends, since averting catastrophe is a non-debatable first end, suspending all discussion of ultimate ends. Perhaps we are destined to live for long with such pressing emergencies of our own making that what we can do is shoring-up and short-term remedy, not planning for the good life. The former surely needs no philosophy; to meet the recurrent emergency that kind of knowledge would seem competent which has helped to create it—technological science, for it did help create it in each instance by successfully meeting its predecessor.

But if ever we entrust or resign ourselves wholly to the self-corrective mechanics of the interplay of science and technology, we shall have lost the battle for man. For science, with its application governed solely by its own logic, does not really leave the meaning of happiness open: it has prejudged the issue, in spite of its own value-freedom. The automatism of its use—in so far as this use carries beyond the recurrent meeting of the recurrent emergency created by itself—has set the goal of happiness in principle: indulgence in the use of things. Between the two poles of emergency and indulgence, of resourcefulness and hedonism, set up by the ever expanding power over things, the direction of all effort and thereby the issue of the good tends to be predecided. But we must not let that issue be decided by default.

Thus even with the pressure of emergencies upon us we need a view beyond them to meet them on more than their own terms. Their very diagnosis (wherever it is not a case of extremity) implies at least an idea of what would not be an emergency, as that of sickness implies the idea of health; and the anticipation of success inherent in all struggle against danger, misery, and injustice must face the question of what life befits man when the emergency virtues of courage, charity, and justice have done their work.

VIII

Whatever the insights of that "other" theory called philosophy, and whatever its counsels, there is no stopping the use of scientific theory which propels us into the flux, for stopping its use means stopping theory itself; and the course of knowledge must not be stopped—if not for its gains, then in spite of its costs.

Nor is a return to the classical position open to honesty and logic. Theory itself has become a process, and one, as we have seen, which continuously involves its own use; and it cannot be "possessed" otherwise. Science is, therefore, theory and art at once. But whereas in other arts having the skill and using it are different, so that its possessor is free to use it or not, and to decide when, the skill of science as a collective property begets its use by its own momentum, and so the hiatus between two stages, where judgment, wisdom, freedom can have their play, is here dangerously shrinking: the skill possesses its possessor.

Theory itself has become a function of use as much as use a function of theory. Tasks for theory are set by the practical results of its preceding use, their solutions to be turned again to use, and so on. Thus theory is thoroughly immersed in practice.

With this mutual feedback mechanism theory has set up a new realm of necessity, or what may be called a second nature in place of the first nature from whose necessity theory was to liberate man. To this second nature, no less determinative for being artificial, man is as subject as he was to original nature, and theory itself is under it while constantly engaged in its further making.

If we equate the realm of necessity with Plato's "cave," then scientific theory leads not out of the cave; nor is its practical application a return to the cave: it never left it in the first place. It is entirely of the cave and therefore not "theory" at all in the Platonic sense.

Yet its very possibility implies, and its actuality testifies to, a "transcendence" in man himself as the condition for it. A freedom beyond the necessities of the cave is manifest in the relation to truth, without which science could not be. This relation—a capacity, a commitment, a quest, in short, that which makes science humanly possible—is itself an extra-scientific fact. As much, therefore, as science is of the cave by its objects and its uses, by its originating cause "in the soul" it is not. There is still "pure theory" as dedication to the discovery of truth and as devotion to Being, the content of truth: of that dedication science is the modern form.

To philosophy as trans-scientific theory the human fact of science can provide a clue to a theory of man, so that we may know again about the essence of man—and through it, perhaps, even something of the essence of Being. Whenever such knowledge will again be with us, it can provide a basis for the supremely useful and much needed knowledge of ends. Pending that event, unforeseeable today as to when and if, we have to live with our poverty—comforted perhaps by the recollection that once before the "I know that I know not" has proved a beginning of philosophy.

SOLOMON E. ASCH

Comment[9]

Although our age is dominated by the fact of science, its relation to the ends of human life is not sufficiently an object of critical examination. Science has altered in the most decisive ways not only our conceptions but our everyday experience of nature; it has transformed our material environment, and brought us face to face with new problems. Despite these profound changes, and those still to come, there is not enough reflection on the relation of science to other concerns. Most people know of science mainly

[9] See note 1 on p. 119.

by its practical achievements, and only dimly apprehend its spirit; they think of it largely as an instrument to the production of goods. Scientists too are often oblivious of the wider significance of what they are doing. Specialization has proceeded so far that one can do not only competent but distinguished work without reflecting on the nature of science. Yet there is a need for a continuous appraisal of its intellectual and moral consequences. The paper of Dr. Jonas is a welcome contribution to this discussion.

So much has science become part of our existence that it is hard to recapture the sense of distrust it has aroused in thoughtful persons. Yet the effort may be enlightening. Let us therefore consider the "case" against science.

Science tells us much about the machinery of the world, but not about its worth. Science is mute about all questions of worth, including the worth of science itself. Those who engage in science are like skilled workers who know how to construct the most exquisite musical instrument, but are deaf to the sounds it utters. Science is essentially a worldly activity that does not satisfy our yearning for answers about the highest good; it has little if anything to say about beauty or justice. Indeed, it stifles the sense of urgency about these vital concerns. By riveting us to the control and manipulation of things, it commits us to a perpetual seeking after goals that turn out to be only means to other goals that are equally transient.

Even the knowledge that science gives us, although highly effective, eliminates much of the world that is familiar and that matters most to us. The procedures of science uncompromisingly exclude the form, structure, and significance of events as they are given to us naively, replacing them with a more abstract and strange order. It constantly strives to refer unique and qualitatively diverse events to a few uniform underlying relations. The consequence is a great simplification that amounts to impoverishment, if our naive experience is taken as the standard. The claim follows that the procedures of science, which make it necessary to comprehend the complex in terms of the simple, turn into a systematic reduction of the articulate to the primitive, in general of the higher to terms of the lower. The *what* of things—their individual, intimate character—eludes us in direct proportion to our successes. Thus the human mind, which creates the concepts of science, is driven by some inexorable necessity to the construction of a world that is increasingly alien to it.

By a final irony, the science of man, far from redressing the balance, itself appears under the necessity of reading man out of its picture. Thoughts, joys, and sorrows become equally transformed as soon as we turn them into objects of study; the sense and pathos of these phenomena elude scientific investigation. What can neural discharges and glandular secretions tell us about sympathy and suffering? Indeed, a future science of man looms as a threat of a new kind. By treating man as an object, we may learn to manipulate and control him too, without troubling to consider the significance of what we are doing.

The conclusions drawn from these appraisals of the limitations of science are well known. One takes the form of asserting that the methods of science are not relevant to decisions concerning ends. A more particular inference, in agreement with the former, states that the data of science can be usefully employed, but only in the choice of means. These statements deserve to be taken seriously. But the preceding remarks have, somewhat deliberately, overstated the "case" against science. They slight some essential points; to ignore these is to distort the human relevance of science.

No discussion of science is adequate that fails to note the extraordinary change of temper it has ushered in. Philosophy and religion aim at comprehensive answers to the questions of our origin and destiny. Science breathes another spirit. Its first requirement is certainty. It turns first to observation, and is content to postpone, indefinitely if necessary, other questions of great moment. It prefers the minutest truth to the most alluring exaggeration. This priority can appear misplaced. Science does not take the most direct path to a universal philosophy, and may therefore be charged with not putting first things first. But this temper of science needs to be better understood by its critics; it is the kind of limitation that is a source of strength.

Science does replace the familiar character of events with a more abstract order. But there is at least one region, that of psychology, where scientific understanding requires that we take directly into account the actual content, structure, and significance of experience. This is, I believe, the case for many questions of human thinking and feeling, of aesthetic and ethical sensitivity. It is most doubtful that we can have a psychology of persons and of relations between persons on any other basis. Nor is it likely that the data of experience are needed only as a scaffolding, to be discarded as our knowledge advances. Investigation in human psychology often requires us to start with the naively given form and structure of events. These dictate the kind of analysis that is fruitful. It is not too much to say that complex psychological events can be studied without submitting them first to the kind of analysis that loses sight of their most striking properties. This indeed has been a central thought of gestalt theory, the further consequences of which still remain to be explored.

It is not accurate enough to say that science is silent about ends, that it is an indifferent instrument. This is to overlook the fact that science gives expression to ends that are deeply rooted in the nature of man. It is a unique example of man's search for truth. In this respect it is a worthy discipline for the human intellect. It is also a humane corrective to arrogance of mind; it teaches us to put up with uncertainty and ignorance, and the necessity under which we are revising our ideas to fit the nature of things. The investigator always faces phenomena of unsuspected subtlety, which must extort an admission of fallibility; at the same time the spirit of inquiry is incompatible with terror or abject surrender. The enterprise of science reveals our limitations while it fosters our independence.

Those who first built the foundations of science were driven by a thirst for understanding and a delight in the patterns of nature. It is easy to lose sight of this fact today when, for the first time, we have a technology of science, one that is affecting also its practitioners. With specialization, modern investigators may be increasingly lacking in philosophical outlook, and even lose a sense of the coherence of the scientific enterprise. But it is questionable whether profound changes in understanding can, even in the future, come in the absence of the spirit that guided the early steps.

One can agree with the critics of science that it does not teach principles of justice or supplant the search for beauty. Science is only one human activity, and it is to be judged by what it does rather than by what should in the first place not be expected of it. One can go further and say that science is to be ultimately judged by the contribution it makes to the ideal side of our life. Some of the necessary evidence for this appraisal is at hand; is it too much to expect that science will not remain altogether silent about the nature and destiny of mankind?

ERICH HULA

Comment [10]

Dr. Jonas has given us a breathtaking philosophical account of the relentless onward march of modern science and technology. What has been the effect of its sweep upon theory and practice in politics?

The new necessities and miseries to which, as Dr. Jonas has rightly pointed out, the modern pursuit of knowledge has given rise are most notorious in the realm of politics. The magnitude and complexity of the political problems that statesmanship is expected to solve are today, and will be in the future, infinitely greater than they ever were prior to the scientific age. The prospect is the more frightening because the political ordering of human affairs was never a simple matter. Unrest and change have throughout history sapped the foundations of political societies and institutions almost as soon as they were established. How much stronger are the dynamic forces pressing on political life in all parts of the world now that mankind seems to be definitely committed to "the endless thrust into the ever-new and unknown"! How much more difficult is the governance of modern mass society, which the unceasing series of technical inventions and economic changes has brought into being, than was the gov-

[10] See note 1 on p. 119.

ernance of the smaller communities of the past! How much more complex is the problem of international peace when its dimensions are global, as they are today, than it was when nature, not yet conquered by man, assured the coexistence of at least those whom its barriers kept physically apart from one another! Finally, how much less terrifying was the specter of war then than it is at present! By delivering things into man's power, by achieving his mastery over nature, science—whatever it has accomplished for the betterment of life—has brought the self-extinction of the human race within the reach of the possible. Indeed, politics today means dealing with emergencies, one following the other ever more rapidly.

The greater magnitude and complexity of the practical problems to be solved is not the only effect that the pursuit of science in modern times has had on politics. Its influence on the theory of politics and on conceptions of its practical uses has been no less profound. In fact, time and again it has been asserted that while the progress of the physical sciences may have aggravated the practical problems of politics, the progress of social and political science, if only it follows the path of the former, will eventually provide mankind with the technical tools for coping with those problems successfully.

Only lately, however, practically only in our own time, has this vision of a political science patterned on the model of the physical sciences led to massive and concrete attempts to transform the vision into reality. For a long time the influence on political science of the procedures used in modern natural science was negative rather than positive. Thus the insistence on applying to the study of political phenomena requirements and methods similar to those to which the natural scientists have subjected themselves set in motion the lengthy process that resulted in the separation from one another of political philosophy, political theory, and political science. In his new work, just published, Arnold Brecht has given us a masterful account of that momentous process.[11] Moreover, the increasing prestige of the physical sciences could not fail to effect a depreciation of political philosophy and theory in so far as their objects and procedures place

[11] A. Brecht, *Political Theory.*

them outside of what came to be considered political science proper.

Attempts actually to realize the vision of a political science based on the rigorous application of the principles of the physical sciences have taken shape somewhat slowly. The most radical manifestation and the very culmination of this development are the current efforts of an increasing number of political scientists, mostly American, to engage in strictly empirical investigation of all facts bearing on human behavior in politics. Their ultimate and most ambitious objective is to build a scientific system or general theory of human political behavior, and to make scientific the conduct of politics, international and domestic. While originally one could speak only of a common "research orientation" as the uniting bond of these scholars,[12] they have rapidly grown into a school, setting itself apart from political scientists working along more traditional lines of research.

Needless to say, empirical research holds a rightful place and is likely to play an increasingly important role in political science. Its recent concentration on human political processes rather than on the machinery of government has helped us to realize the limits set to the effectiveness of political and legal institutions, once greatly overrated by political scientists. The study of human behavior in politics is not only a worthwhile pursuit of theoretical knowledge; it can also be useful from a practical point of view. Nor is there any reason to object to its employment of quantitative methods, or to deny the significance and the validity of its results. Doubts begin to arise, however, when the moral realm of man, a free agent, is equated to the realm of physical things, and when the absolutist claim is made that the quantitative approach to the questions of politics is the only scientific and promising one.

How little such a claim is justified is borne out by the narrow sphere in which the quantitative approach has so far proved fruitful. It is indeed no accident that the search for uniformities of political behavior has been directed chiefly to the investigation and analysis of electoral behavior. Only mass behavior offers a

[12] See H. S. Kariel, "Political Science in the United States: Reflections on One of Its Trends," *Political Studies*, IV, 1956, 113; also D. E. Butler, *The Study of Political Behaviour*.

sufficiently large number of comparable instances on which relevant generalizations and predictions can be based. But even in this limited field, quantitative measurement is a problematic and insufficient means for piercing through the political realities, and is bound to remain so, all possible and likely future technical improvements of the methods of measurement notwithstanding. In the first place, the selection of the factors to which the voting behavior is correlated is determined by conclusions founded on preconceived, not necessarily valid ideas on what motivates political attitudes, as is clearly suggested by the overemphasis in voting studies on the economic motive. Moreover, the actual reason why a person votes one way or another is ultimately inscrutable. Unlike the physical scientist, with his canons of experimental testing, the social scientist is hardly ever able to identify all variable factors in the situation he is exploring, or to repeat his experiment under the same conditions.

More recently the study of political processes and political behavior has been extended to decision-making on the governmental level, in relation to both domestic and foreign policy matters. The empirical investigation of decision-making "as an action process," "analyzed in terms of a generalized conceptual scheme," is expected finally to yield the components of a general behavioral theory. Again it is undoubtedly a worthwhile undertaking to find out how legislative, executive, and judicial bodies actually arrive at their decisions. Moreover, theory can undoubtedly contribute to the rationality of decision-making, in so far as it can help to clarify the choices open to the decision-maker. But it is an entirely different matter to assume, as the behaviorists do, that refinements of the methods applied in individual case studies and refinements of the theoretical formulations will sooner or later enable us "to predict, within limits, policy outcomes from a knowledge of processes."[13]

The basic fallacy of this expectation is that it underrates the degree to which decisions are bound to remain based on contingent factors, varying in varying combinations from one case to the other. For this very reason Edmund Burke not only denied

[13] R. C. Snyder and G. D. Paige, "The United States Decision to Resist Aggression in Korea: The Application of an Analytical Scheme," *Administrative Science Quarterly*, III, 1958, 343.

that theory can provide the light needed by practice but also insisted that history, from which he thought "much political wisdom may be learned," is valuable for the statesman only "as habit, not as precept."[14] Indeed, though one can very well visualize that the future statesman will be surrounded by brilliant experts in decision-making, one wonders whether he will therefore be any the less a lonely man, acting and having to act on hunches and in compliance with the commands of his conscience. Discretion is an ineradicable element of decision-making, and the limits set to reducing it are narrow.

There is a strange irony about the efforts of the behavioral school. Their advocacy of a strictly empirical theory and science has been largely prompted by a desire to narrow, if not to close, the gap between political theory and practice. Admittedly, some behavioral investigations have actually added to our knowledge of political realities and enriched the knowledge of usable political techniques as well. But one wonders how many more have yielded only irrelevant results, or merely confirmed what we have already known through the application of less rigorous methods. In fact, the most ambitious and ingenious adepts of the school have become bogged down in purely methodological exercises, or, as one critic has put it, in a methodology of methodology.[15] They are paying the price for disregarding Aristotle's warning that "it is the mark of an educated mind to expect that amount of exactness in each kind which the nature of the particular subject admits." The remoteness from practical life, characteristic of these methodological inquisitions, is strikingly illustrated by the esoteric jargon in which they are presented. One need not be Molière's M. Jourdain not to recognize it as prose.

In spite of the increasing distance that actually separates this type of empirical theory from the practical concerns of politics, the fact remains that its proponents envisage and advocate a blending of political science and practice, similar to the merging of physical science and practice that Dr. Jonas has described to us. The political ordering of human affairs is looked upon as a task of

---

[14] See L. Strauss, *Natural Right and History*, p. 294 f.

[15] A. A. Rogow, "Comment on Smith and Apter: or, Whatever Happened to the Great Issues?" *American Political Science Review*, LI, 1957, 765.

social-political technology or engineering, applying the behavioral laws of politics.

One is entitled to wonder how an allegedly purely descriptive theory of political behavior, which purposely dispenses with moral speculation, could be able to fulfill the normative function of setting the goals of political society. The answer to this puzzling question must be sought in an entirely unscientific assumption—"unscientific" from the point of view of the scientists themselves. The ends, according to this assumption, are somehow or other given. Moreover, they happily coincide with the ends of democratic society. Thus, like the technician, the political scientist has to concern himself only with the means for attaining preestablished ends.[16] This assumption, or belief rather, reveals more clearly than anything else the utopian streak in behavioral science. "Never forget," Erasmus wrote in the sixteenth century, "that 'dominion,' 'imperial authority,' 'kingdom,' 'majesty,' 'power' are all pagan terms, not Christian. The ruling power of a Christian state consists only of administration, kindness, and protection."[17] In the nineteenth century utopian and scientific socialists were foreseeing and foretelling the advent of the day when the government of men over men would be replaced by the administration of things. In our own time computing machines are added to the technique of manipulating reified man.

The persistence of the political realities suggested by the "pagan terms" is what limits the theoretical value and the practical usefulness of a political science that cannot possibly enlighten us on those central political concepts, or on the political problems they signify.[18] At the same time, the persistence of the perennial great issues of politics justifies, nay makes imperative, our perseverance in the traditional approaches to the study of the vital and pressing political problems. True, political scientists who follow the traditional lines of deductive theorizing and descriptive approach cannot claim, and do not even attempt, to prove by exact scientific procedures the validity of their conclusions and observations. But their contributions to the knowl-

[16] See Kariel, *op. cit.*, p. 120 f.
[17] Quoted by F. Caspari, "Erasmus on the Social Functions of Christian Humanism," *Journal of the History of Ideas*, VIII, 1947, 95, n. 38.
[18] See H. J. Morgenthau, *Dilemma of Politics*, p. 29 f.

edge and practice of politics need not therefore be any less substantial and relevant, as the record of the illustrious political writers of the past convincingly proves. If political scientists today want to live up to the standards set by those writers, they must, in particular, shirk as little as their predecessors did the discussion of the great moral issues of the political world in which they live. They must not even shirk the greatest of those issues, raised anew by the destructive potentialities of modern science and technology. Dr. Jonas has suggested that the course of knowledge must not be stopped. Surely, such an unqualified dictum, if it is meant to be unqualified, is open to challenge, and deserves probing. The question of the substantive criteria to be applied in controlling the pursuit of knowledge is no doubt as formidable and difficult to answer as is the question of the authority that ought to exercise such control. But it can no longer be shirked.

ADOLPH LOWE

Comment[19]

I

I should like first of all to associate myself with Professor Jonas' spirited defense of the "truth value" of theory and its philosophical implications. His point is well taken at a time when even educated public opinion has come to judge the value of theory mainly by its usefulness as a technical tool. In the restrained language of the philosopher, Professor Jonas has voiced the anguish of some of our greatest natural scientists who, in pondering the practical use made of their findings, almost wish they had discovered less.

As a social scientist I can only envy them their worries. In

[19] See note 1 on p. 119.

our fields we certainly do not suffer as yet from a superabundance of theoretical findings that would lend themselves to practical application. The call to philosophical self-examination may be a challenge to the physical scientists, who for the last three hundred years have sworn by the Baconian creed—but with us the Baconian revolution has only just started. Moreover, such a revolution means with us a break with a tradition of more than two thousand years, a break that is by no means generally welcomed. True, there is an extreme group whose members demand, in the name of the unity of science, that we fully commit ourselves to the methods that have proved so successful in physics and chemistry. But these social "scientists" are confronted by social "humanists," who refuse to submit man and society to the technique of pointer readings, rather hankering after the days when speculative wisdom held the place now occupied by "research." And the rest of us seek some uneasy compromise between these extremes.

Of course, we all agree that social studies must refer to *some* reality, and that, in this sense, our theories must be applicable. But opinions divide when we ask how our theories are to be formed, and to what sort of reality they are to apply.

The answer of the "scientists" is unambiguous. For them the only subject of study is everyday experience—not that mysterious substratum of such experience which ancient and mediaeval philosophers proclaimed as "true" or "essential" reality. And for the scientists there is only one method appropriate to the study of man, as to that of nature: detached observation, in order that the "facts" can speak for themselves—and all the more clearly the better the observer succeeds in cutting himself loose from the observed object.

To this the "humanists" reply that everyday social reality is subject to the flux of history, amenable at best to description but not to theory, that is, to meaningful generalization. To arrive at such generalizations we must ascend from the kaleidoscope of experience to the realm of norms. It is with the "good society" that social theory is concerned. Hence it must not sever its ties with that domain where criteria are established, namely philosophy. And since the student, in studying society, studies the likes of himself, it is through his participation rather than his aloofness that laws of the social process are discovered.

It is my conviction that total victory for either of these positions would spell defeat for the social sciences. Only if a region of inquiry can be opened up in which both the scientific and the humanist approach play their characteristic roles may we ever hope to gain knowledge of man—knowledge rather than figment, and of man rather than of social atoms. To indicate the direction in which such a reconciliation might be achieved, let me now say a word about my specialty, economics.

II

Economics offers an instructive example for the problem at issue because, among all the social sciences, it has far the most ambitious pretensions. We economists have by now adopted all the trimmings of the "exact" sciences, including the progressive mathematization of our models. Like them we claim the power to predict from alleged empirical laws. Of course, when it comes to practical performance we resemble fumbling meteorologists rather than precise astronomers. This, I fear, is the impression we created last year when we tried to forecast the course of the recent recession, and to prescribe remedies for its cure. And, what is rather baffling, on such occasions our most sophisticated econometrics does hardly better than certain old-fashioned rules of thumb. Thus it would be rather difficult to prove that the practical usefulness of our theories has increased in proportion with the refinement of method.

This apparent paradox disappears when we look beneath the surface. All the scientific innovations of recent economics have left untouched one fundamental assumption that was introduced more than two hundred years ago. It concerns the incentive that is supposed to motivate buyers as well as sellers, namely the desire to minimize expenditure and to maximize receipts. As is well known, this heroic simplification has been challenged again and again by psychologists, sociologists, and historians. But in the present context I would rather insist that a strong case can be made for the realism of this assumption in the era of nineteenth-century capitalism. Then, under the pressure of mass poverty, unbridled competition, and a Puritan value system, maximizing behavior was indeed a condition for survival; the limits for deci-sion-making were narrow indeed. Hence a model that was origi-nally abstracted from non-human mechanical phenomena—phe-nomena "lower" than man—could for a time serve as a fair image, and even as a basis for prediction, of economic processes.

Unfortunately this model can no longer cope with the com-plexities of the modern economy. The consummation of the in-dustrial revolution is radically altering the social environment of the market, at least in the democratic West. It has liberated the broad masses from the bondage of extreme scarcity; self-organi-zation of producers and the interventions of the welfare state have mitigated the fierceness of competition; and the inherited system of values is giving way to capriciousness, typical of an "affluent society." A wide spectrum of incentives and expectations is supplanting the earlier single-mindedness of buyers and sellers, and it cannot surprise us that predictions based on the traditional model should miss the target by an increasing margin—a di-vergence that is highlighted by the very precision of mathematical techniques.

Now this is an argument against the dominant constructs in economic theory, but not against theorizing as such: perhaps we can devise more complex models that will take account of the rising tolerance of the system for unorthodox behavior. But this would hardly improve the prospects for prediction. Once we take the transitory nature of our social "constants" seriously, we may have to be satisfied with short-term inferences from current ob-servations—accepting the status of social meteorologists. At any rate, unless Madison Avenue and Pennsylvania Avenue combine with the "organization men" in imposing a new conformity on market behavior, the economics of the later twentieth century is likely to be less an exact science than was the economics of the early nineteenth century.

III

This, at least, is the conclusion so long as we impose on economic theory the task of discovering empirical laws, universal or statistical, to describe and predict the actual course of events. But is there an alternative task?

Suppose that, rather than studying the causes of today's state of affairs and predicting therefrom the state of tomorrow, we were to postulate a *goal* for the economic system to attain, and then to investigate the requirements for the realization of that goal. More specifically, instead of pronouncing on the likely effects of a wage rise or a technical change, we can ask: given the goal of full employment free from inflationary pressures, or the goal of a five percent annual rate of growth, or of the conversion of output to stated defense needs—which changes in income, consumption, investment, and the physical order of production must occur in order that the goal can be reached either at maximum speed or with minimum input of resources, or in accordance with some other criterion of optimization? Once the required adjustment path has thus been determined, we can further ask: what behavior on the part of buyers and sellers in the markets of commodities and services is best suited to set the system on the required path and to keep it there? And finally: what incentives and expectations must prevail for the required behavior pattern to materialize?

Because this procedure studies the means appropriate to postulated ends, I call it "instrumental." Such instrumental analysis treats as unknowns what in predictive analysis is treated as a known, namely behavior and motivations. Instrumentalism can do so because it is not concerned with all the possible behavior patterns and motivations that the real world exhibits. It focuses in each case on only those patterns that are compatible with the attainment of the goal. This analytical task can be solved with deductive strictness provided we define with sufficient precision the initial state of the system, the goal itself, and the criteria for optimization. Now it is the business of empirical research to describe the initial position. But who answers for the choice of the goal and of the criteria of optimization, criteria that decide on the propriety of the means?

Modern welfare economics has taught us that such goals and criteria cannot be deduced within the framework of economics proper. Yet it by no means follows that they need be chosen arbitrarily. Here the basic unity of the science of man and society becomes methodologically fruitful. If it is true that, within economics, certain adjustment processes and behavior patterns can be derived as means from the postulated goal of, say, full employment, this goal of full employment itself can be derived, in political science, by the same procedure from the more comprehensive goal of, say, political stability. There comes into the open a hierarchy and an interplay of relations wherein the ends of one branch of the social sciences are established as means in another.

Of course, all these partial goals and criteria must be vindicated by some ultimate goal and criterion. At this point instrumentalism is driven beyond itself toward that philosophical decision that is Professor Jonas' basic concern. It is the decision on what is the "good life." Though fraught with grave risks and ambiguities, such decisions are put to us all the time, and also the skeptic must take them, even if unawares more often than not. Full awareness of these implications warns the "humanists" among us not fully to surrender to the world of facts. But the "scientists" among us must insist that this step beyond the facts be taken only once, at the very beginning, when ultimate criteria are explicitly postulated. From then on fact-finding and analysis alone must rule our work.

Much more than is possible on this occasion should be said in order to interpret instrumentalism as an alternative approach to social study. But it should be clear that the manner in which instrumentalism tries to fuse pure and applied theory differs fundamentally from the method employed in the natural sciences. There we search for regularities in events the surface of which we cannot penetrate. Here, by relating individual actions and motivations to collective goals, we not only participate in what we observe but bear a more than scientific responsibility for our results. In this way instrumentalism tries to reconcile the Baconian turn with the one immutable law in the kingdom of man: that its design is never fully "given," but is always set for us as a task —*nicht "gegeben" sondern "aufgegeben."*

Are the Social Sciences
Really Inferior?[1]

FRITZ MACHLUP

IF WE ASK whether the "social sciences" are "really inferior," let us first make sure that we understand each part of the question.

"*Inferior*" to what? Of course to the natural sciences. "Inferior" in what respect? It will be our main task to examine all the "respects," all the scores on which such inferiority has been alleged. I shall enumerate them presently.

The adverb "*really*" which qualifies the adjective "inferior" refers to allegations made by some scientists, scholars, and laymen. But it refers also to the "inferiority complex" which I have noted among many social scientists. A few years ago I wrote an essay entitled "The Inferiority Complex of the Social Sciences."[2] In that essay I said that "an inferiority complex may or may not be justified by some 'objective' standards," and I went on to discuss the consequences which "the *feeling* of inferiority"—conscious or subconscious—has for the behavior of the social scientists who are suffering from it. I did not then discuss whether the complex has

[1] Reprinted from *The Southern Economic Journal* (Vol. XXVII, No. 3, January 1961, pp. 173–184), with the permission of that journal and the approval of the author.

[2] Published in *On Freedom and Free Enterprise: Essays in Honor of Ludwig von Mises*, ed. Mary Sennholz, pp. 161–172.

an objective basis, that is, whether the social sciences are "really" inferior. This is our question to-day.

The subject noun would call for a long disquisition. What is meant by *"social sciences,"* what is included, what is not included? Are they the same as what others have referred to as the "moral sciences," the "Geisteswissenschaften," the "cultural sciences," the "behavioral sciences"? Is Geography, or the part of it that is called "Human Geography," a social science? Is History a social science —or perhaps even *the* social science *par excellence,* as some philosophers have contended? We shall not spend time on this business of defining and classifying. A few remarks may later be necessary in connection with some points of methodology, but by and large we shall not bother here with a definition of "social sciences" and with drawing boundary lines around them.

The Grounds of Comparison

The social sciences and the natural sciences are compared and contrasted on many scores, and the discussions are often quite unsystematic. If we try to review them systematically, we shall encounter a good deal of overlap and unavoidable duplication. None the less, it will help if we enumerate in advance some of the grounds of comparison most often mentioned, grounds on which the social sciences are judged to come out "second best":

1. Invariability of observations
2. Objectivity of observations and explanations
3. Verifiability of hypotheses
4. Exactness of findings
5. Measurability of phenomena
6. Constancy of numerical relationships
7. Predictability of future events
8. Distance from every-day experience
9. Standards of admission and requirements

We shall examine all these comparisons.

Invariability of Observations

The idea is that you cannot have much of a science unless things recur, unless phenomena repeat themselves. In nature we find many factors and conditions "invariant." Do we in society? Are not conditions in society changing all the time, and so fast that most events are unique, each quite different from anything that has happened before? Or can one rely on the saying that "history repeats itself" with sufficient invariance to permit generalizations about social events?

There is a great deal of truth, and important truth, in this comparison. Some philosophers were so impressed with the invariance of nature and the variability of social phenomena that they used this difference as the criterion in the definitions of natural and cultural sciences. Following Windelband's distinction between generalizing ("nomothetic") and individualizing ("ideographic") propositions, the German philosopher Heinrich Rickert distinguished between the generalizing sciences of nature and the individualizing sciences of cultural phenomena; and by individualizing sciences he meant historical sciences.[3] In order to be right, he redefined both "nature" and "history" by stating that reality is "nature" if we deal with it in terms of the *general* but becomes "history" if we deal with it in terms of the *unique*. To him, geology was largely history, and economics, most similar to physics, was a natural science. This implies a rejection of the contention that all fields which are normally called social sciences suffer from a lack of invariance; indeed, economics is here considered so much a matter of immutable laws of nature that it is handed over to the natural sciences.

This is not satisfactory, nor does it dispose of the main issue that natural phenomena provide *more* invariance than social phenomena. The main difference lies probably in the number of factors that must be taken into account in explanations and predictions of natural and social events. Only a small number of reproducible facts will normally be involved in a physical explanation or prediction. A much larger number of facts, some of them probably unique historical events, will be found relevant in an explanation or prediction of economic or other social events. This is true, and methodological devices will not do away with the difference. But it is, of course, only a difference in degree.

The physicist Robert Oppenheimer once raised the question whether, if the universe is a *unique* phenomenon, we may assume

[3] H. Rickert, *Die Grenzen der naturwissenschaftlichen Begriffsbildung*.

that *universal* or *general* propositions can be formulated about it. Economists of the Historical School insisted on treating each "stage" or phase of economic society as a completely unique one, not permitting the formulation of universal propositions. Yet, in the physical world, phenomena are not quite so homogeneous as many have liked to think; and in the social world, phenomena are not quite so heterogeneous as many have been afraid they are. (If they were, we could not even have generalized concepts of social events and words naming them.) In any case, where reality seems to show a bewildering number of variations, we construct an ideal world of abstract models in which we create enough homogeneity to permit us to apply reason and deduce the implied consequences of assumed constellations. This artificial homogenization of types of phenomena is carried out in natural and social sciences alike.

There is thus no difference in invariance in the sequences of events in nature and in society as long as we theorize about them —because in the abstract models homogeneity is assumed. There is only a difference of degree in the variability of phenomena of nature and society if we talk about the real world—as long as heterogeneity is not reduced by means of deliberate "controls." There is a third world, between the abstract world of theory and the real unmanipulated world, namely, the artificial world of the experimental laboratory. In this world there is less variability than in the real world and more than in the model world. But this third world does not exist in most of the social sciences (nor in all natural sciences). We shall see later that the mistake is often made of comparing the artificial laboratory world of manipulated nature with the real world of unmanipulated society.

We conclude on this point of comparative invariance, that there is indeed a difference between natural and social sciences, and that the difference—apart from the possibility of laboratory experiments—lies chiefly in the number of relevant factors, and hence of possible combinations, to be taken into account for explaining or predicting events occurring in the real world.

Objectivity of Observations and Explanations

The idea behind a comparison between the "objectivity" of observations and explorations in the natural and social sciences may be conveyed by an imaginary quotation: "Science must be objective and not affected by value judgments; but the social sciences are inherently concerned with values and, hence, they lack the disinterested objectivity of science." True? Frightfully muddled. The trouble is that the problem of "subjective value," which is at the very root of the social sciences, is quite delicate and has in fact confused many, including some fine scholars.

To remove confusion one must separate the different meanings of "value" and the different ways in which they relate to the social sciences, particularly economics. I have distinguished eleven different kinds of value-reference in economics, but have enough sense to spare you this exhibition of my pedagogic dissecting zeal. But we cannot dispense entirely with the problem and overlook the danger of confusion. Thus, I offer you a bargain and shall reduce my distinctions from eleven to four. I am asking you to keep apart the following four meanings in which value judgment may come into our present discussion: (a) The analyst's judgment may be biased for one reason or another, perhaps because his views of the social "Good" or his personal pecuniary interests in the practical use of his findings interfere with the proper scientific detachment. (b) Some normative issues may be connected with the problem under investigation, perhaps ethical judgments which may color some of the investigator's incidental pronouncements—obiter dicta—without however causing a bias in his reported findings of his research. (c) The interest in solving the problems under investigation is surely affected by values since, after all, the investigator selects his problems because he believes that their solution would be of value. (d) The investigator in the social sciences has to explain his observations as results of human actions which can be interpreted only with reference to motives and purposes of the actors, that is, to values entertained by them.

With regard to the first of these possibilities, some authorities have held that the social sciences may more easily succumb to temptation and may show obvious biases. The philosopher Morris Cohen, for example, spoke of "the subjective difficulty of maintaining scientific detachment in the study of human affairs. Few human beings can calmly and with equal fairness consider both sides of a question such as socialism, free love, or birth-control."[4]

[4] M. Cohen, *Reason and Nature*, p. 348.

This is quite true, but one should not forget similar difficulties in the natural sciences. Remember the difficulties which, in defer-ence to religious values, biologists had in discussions of evolution and, going further back, the troubles of astronomers in discussions of the heliocentric theory and of geologists in discussions of the age of the earth. Let us also recall that only 25 years ago, German mathematicians and physicists rejected "Jewish" theorems and theories, including physical relativity, under the pressure of na-tionalistic values, and only ten years ago Russian biologists stuck to a mutation theory which was evidently affected by political values. I do not know whether one cannot detect in our own period here in the United States an association between political views and scientific answers to the question of the genetic dangers from fallout and from other nuclear testing.

Apart from political bias, there have been cases of real cheat-ing in science. Think of physical anthropology and its faked Pilt-down Man. That the possibility of deception is not entirely beyond the pale of experimental scientists can be gathered from a splendid piece of fiction, a recent novel, *The Affair*, by C. P. Snow, the well-known Cambridge don.

Having said all this about the possibility of bias existing in the presentation of evidence and findings in the natural sciences, we should hasten to admit that not a few economists, especially when concerned with current problems and the interpretation of recent history, are given to "lying with statistics." It is hardly a coincidence if labor economists choose one base year and business economists choose another base year when they compare wage increases and price increases; or if for their computations of growth rates expert witnesses for different political parties choose different statistical series and different base years. This does not indicate that the social sciences are in this respect "superior" or "inferior" to the natural sciences. Think of physicists, chemists, medical scientists, psychiatrists, etc., appearing as expert witnesses in court litigation to testify in support of their clients' cases. In these instances the scientists are in the role of analyzing concrete individual events, of interpreting recent history. If there is a difference at all between the natural and social sciences in this respect, it may be that economists these days have more oppor-tunities to present biased findings than their colleagues in the physical sciences. But even this may not be so. I may underestimate the opportunities of scientists and engineers to submit expert testimonies with paid-for bias.

The second way in which value judgments may affect the investigator does not involve any bias in his findings or his reports on his findings. But ethical judgments may be so closely connected with his problems that he may feel impelled to make evaluative pronouncements on the normative issues in question. For example, scientists may have strong views about vivisection, sterilization, abortion, hydrogen bombs, biological warfare, etc., and may express these views in connection with their scientific work. Likewise, social scientists may have strong views about the right to privacy, free enterprise, free markets, equality of income, old-age pensions, socialized medicine, segregation, education, etc., and they may express these views in connection with the results of their research. Let us repeat that this need not imply that their findings are biased. There is no difference on this score between the natural and the social sciences. The research and its results may be closely connected with values of all sorts, and value judgments may be expressed, and yet the objectivity of the research and of the reports on the findings need not be impaired.

The third way value judgments affect research is in the selection of the project, in the choice of the subject for investigation. This is unavoidable and the only question is what kinds of value and whose values are paramount. If research is financed by foundations or by the government, the values may be those which the chief investigator believes are held by the agencies or committees that pass on the allocation of funds. If the research is not aided by outside funds, the project may be chosen on the basis of what the investigator believes to be "social values," that is, he chooses a project that may yield solutions to problems supposed to be important for society. Society wants to know how to cure cancer, how to prevent hay fever, how to eliminate mosquitoes, how to get rid of crab grass and weeds, how to restrain juvenile delinquency, how to reduce illegitimacy and other accidents, how to increase employment, to raise real wages, to aid farmers, to avoid price inflation, and so on, and so forth. These examples suggest that the value component in the project selection is the same in the natural and in the social sciences. There are instances, thank God, in which the investigator selects his project out of sheer intellectual curiosity and does not give "two hoots" about the social importance of his findings. Still, to satisfy curiosity is a value too, and indeed a very potent one. We must not fail to mention the case of the graduate student who lacks imagination as well as intellectual curiosity and undertakes a project just because it is the only one he can think of, though neither he nor anybody else finds it interesting, let alone important. We may accept this case as the exception to the rule. Such exceptions probably are equally rare in the natural and the social sciences.

4 – Now we come to the one real difference, the fourth of our value-references. Social phenomena are defined as results of human action, and all human action is defined as motivated action. Hence, social phenomena are explained only if they are attributed to definite types of action which are "understood" in terms of the values motivating those who decide and act. This concern with values—not values which the investigator entertains but values he understands to be effective in guiding the actions which bring about the events he studies—is the crucial difference between the social sciences and the natural sciences. To explain the motion of molecules, the fusion or fission of atoms, the paths of celestial bodies, the growth or mutation of organic matter, etc., the scientist will not ask why the molecules want to move about, why atoms decide to merge or to split, why Venus has chosen her particular orbit, why certain cells are anxious to divide. The social scientist, however, is not doing his job unless he explains changes in the circulation of money by going back to the decisions of the spenders and hoarders, explains company mergers by the goals that may have persuaded managements and boards of corporate bodies to take such actions, explains the location of industries by calculations of such things as transportation costs and wage differentials, and economic growth by propensities to save, to invest, to innovate, to procreate or prevent procreation, and so on. My social-science examples were all from economics, but I might just as well have taken examples from sociology, cultural anthropology, political science, etc., to show that explanation in the social sciences regularly requires the interpretation of

phenomena in terms of idealized motivations of the idealized persons whose idealized actions bring forth the phenomena under investigation.

An example may further elucidate the difference between the explanatory principles in non-human nature and human society. A rock does not say to us: "I am a beast,"[5] nor does it say: "I came here because I did not like it up there near the glaciers, where I used to live; here I like it fine, especially this nice view of the valley." We do not inquire into value judgments of rocks. But we must not fail to take account of valuations of humans; social phenomena must be explained as the results of motivated human actions.

The greatest authorities on the methodology of the social sciences have referred to this fundamental postulate as the requirement of "subjective interpretation," and all such interpretation of "subjective meanings" implies references to values motivating actions. This has of course nothing to do with value judgments impairing the "scientific objectivity" of the investigators or affecting them in any way that would make their findings suspect. Whether the postulate of subjective interpretation which *differentiates* the social sciences from the natural sciences should be held to make them either "inferior" or "superior" is a matter of taste.

Verifiability of Hypotheses

It is said that verification is not easy to come by in the social sciences, while it is the chief business of the investigator in the natural sciences. This is true, though many do not fully understand what is involved and, consequently, are apt to exaggerate the difference.

One should distinguish between what a British philosopher has recently called "high-level hypotheses" and "low-level generalizations."[6] The former are postulated and can never be *directly* verified; a single high-level hypothesis cannot even be *indirectly*

---

[5] H. Kelsen, *Allgemeine Staatslehre*, p. 129. Quoted with illuminating comments in A. Schutz, *Der sinnhafte Aufbau der sozialen Welt.*

[6] R. B. Braithwaite, *Scientific Explanation: A Study of the Function of Theory, Probability and Law in Science.*

verified, because from one hypothesis standing alone nothing follows. Only a *whole system* of hypotheses can be tested by deducing from some set of general postulates and some set of specific assumptions the logical consequences, and comparing these with records of observations regarded as the approximate empirical counterparts of the specific assumptions and specific consequences.[7] This holds for both the natural and the social sciences. (There is no need for *direct* tests of the fundamental postulates in physics—such as the laws of conservation of energy, of angular momentum, of motion—or of the fundamental postulates in economics—such as the laws of maximizing utility and profits.)

While entire theoretical systems and the low-level generalizations derived from them are tested in the natural sciences, there exist at any one time many unverified hypotheses. This holds especially with regard to theories of creation and evolution in such fields as biology, geology, and cosmogony; for example (if my reading is correct), of the theory of the expanding universe, the dust-cloud hypothesis of the formation of stars and planets, of the low-temperature or high-temperature theories of the formation of the earth, of the various (conflicting) theories of granitization, etc. In other words, where the natural sciences deal with non-reproducible occurrences and with sequences for which controlled experiments cannot be devised, they have to work with hypotheses which remain untested for a long time, perhaps forever.

In the social sciences, low-level generalizations about recurring events are being tested all the time. Unfortunately, often several conflicting hypotheses are consistent with the observed facts and there are no crucial experiments to eliminate some of the hypotheses. But every one of us could name dozens of propositions that have been disconfirmed, and this means that the verification process has done what it is supposed to do. The impossibility of controlled experiments and the relatively large number of relevant variables are the chief obstacles to more efficient verification in the social sciences. This is not an inefficiency on the part of our investigators, but it lies in the nature of things.

[7] F. Machlup, "The Problem of Verification in Economics," *Southern Economic Journal*, XXII, 1955, 1–21.

Exactness of Findings

Those who claim that the social sciences are "less exact" than the natural sciences often have a very incomplete knowledge of either of them, and a rather hazy idea of the meaning of "exactness." Some mean by exactness measurability. This we shall discuss under a separate heading. Others mean accuracy and success in predicting future events, which is something different. Others mean reducibility to mathematical language. The meaning of exactness best founded in intellectual history is the possibility of constructing a theoretical system of idealized models containing abstract constructs of variables and of relations between variables, from which most or all propositions concerning particular connections can be deduced. Such systems do not exist in several of the natural sciences—for example, in several areas of biology—while they do exist in at least one of the social sciences: economics.

We cannot foretell the development of any discipline. We cannot say now whether there will soon or ever be a "unified theory" of political science, or whether the piecemeal generalizations which sociology has yielded thus far can be integrated into one comprehensive theoretical system. In any case, the quality of "exactness," if this is what is meant by it, cannot be attributed to all the natural sciences nor denied to all the social sciences.

Measurability of Phenomena

If the availability of numerical data were in and of itself an advantage in scientific investigation, economics would be on the top of all sciences. Economics is the only field in which the raw data of experience are already in numerical form. In other fields the analyst must first quantify and measure before he can obtain data in numerical form. The physicist must weigh and count and must invent and build instruments from which numbers can be read, numbers standing for certain relations pertaining to essentially non-numerical observations. Information which first appears only in some such form as "relatively" large, heavy, hot, fast, is later transformed into numerical data by means of measuring devices such as rods, scales, thermometers, speedometers. The economist can begin with numbers. What he observes are prices and sums of moneys. He can start out with numerical data given to him without the use of measuring devices.

The compilation of masses of data calls for resources which only large organizations, frequently only the government, can muster. This, in my opinion, is unfortunate because it implies that the availability of numerical data is associated with the extent of government intervention in economic affairs, and there is therefore an inverse relation between economic information and individual freedom.

Numbers, moreover, are not all that is needed. To be useful, the numbers must fit the concepts used in theoretical propositions or in comprehensive theoretical systems. This is rarely the case with regard to the raw data of economics, and thus the economic analyst still has the problem of obtaining comparable figures by transforming his raw data into adjusted and corrected ones, acceptable as the operational counterparts of the abstract constructs in his theoretical models. His success in this respect has been commendable, but very far short of what is needed; it cannot compare with the success of the physicist in developing measurement techniques yielding numerical data that can serve as operational counterparts of constructs in the models of theoretical physics.

Physics, however, does not stand for all natural sciences, nor economics for all social sciences. There are several fields, in both natural and social sciences, where quantification of relevant factors has not been achieved and may never be achieved. If Lord Kelvin's phrase, "Science is Measurement," were taken seriously, science might miss some of the most important problems. There is no way of judging whether nonquantifiable factors are more prevalent in nature or in society. The common reference to the "hard" facts of nature and the "soft" facts with which the student of society has to deal seems to imply a judgment about measurability. "Hard" things can be firmly gripped and measured, "soft" things cannot. There may be something to this. The facts of nature are perceived with our "senses," the facts of society are interpreted in terms of the "sense" they make in a motivational analysis. However, this contrast is not quite to the point, because the "sensory" experience of the natural scientist refers to the *data*, while the "sense" interpretation by the social scientist of the ideal-typical inner experience of the members of society refers to basic *postulates* and intervening variables.

The conclusion, that we cannot be sure about the prevalence of non-quantifiable factors in natural and social sciences, still holds.

Constancy of Numerical Relationships

On this score there can be no doubt that some of the natural sciences have got something which none of the social sciences has got: "constants," unchanging numbers expressing unchanging relationships between measurable quantities.

The discipline with the largest number of constants is, of course, physics. Examples are the velocity of light ($c = 2.99776 \times 10^{10}$ cm/sec), Planck's constant for the smallest increment of spin or angular momentum ($h = 6.624 \times 10^{-27}$ erg sec), the gravitation constant ($G = 6.6 \times 10^{-8}$ dyne cm^2 gram^{-2}), the Coulomb constant ($e = 4.8025 \times 10^{-10}$ units), proton mass ($M = 1.672 \times 10^{-24}$ gram), the ratio of proton mass to electron mass ($M/m = 1836.13$), the fine-structure constant ($\alpha^{-1} = 137.0371$). Some of these constants are postulated (conventional), others (the last two) are empirical, but this makes no difference for our purposes. Max Planck contended, the postulated "universal constants" were not just "invented for reasons of practical convenience, but have forced themselves upon us irresistibly because of the agreement between the results of all relevant measurements."[8]

I know of no numerical constant in any of the social sciences. In economics we have been computing certain ratios which, however, are found to vary relatively widely with time and place. The annual income-velocity of circulation of money, the marginal propensities to consume, to save, to import, the elasticities of demand for various goods, the savings ratios, capital-output ratios, growth rates—none of these has remained constant over time or is the same for different countries. They all have varied, some by several hundred per cent of the lowest value. Of course, one has found "limits" of these variations, but what does this mean in comparison with the virtually immutable physical constants? When it was noticed that the ratio between labor income and na-

---

[8] M. Planck, *Scientific Autobiography and Other Papers*, p. 173.

tional income in some countries has varied by "only" ten per cent over some twenty years, some economists were so perplexed that they spoke of the "constancy" of the relative shares. (They hardly realized that the 10 per cent variation in that ratio was the same as about a 25 per cent variation in the ratio between labor income and non-labor income.) That the income velocity of circulation of money has rarely risen above 3 or fallen below 1 is surely interesting, but this is anything but a "constant." That the marginal propensity to consume cannot in the long run be above 1 is rather obvious, but in the short run it may vary between .7 and 1.2 or even more. That saving ratios (to national income) have never been above 15 per cent in any country regardless of the economic system (communistic or capitalistic, regulated or essentially free) is a very important fact; but saving ratios have been known to be next to zero, or even negative, and the variations from time to time and country to country are very large indeed.

Sociologists and actuaries have reported some "relatively stable" ratios—accident rates, birth rates, crime rates, etc.—but the "stability" is only relative to the extreme variability of other numerical ratios. Indeed, most of these ratios are subject to "human engineering," to governmental policies designed to change them, and hence they are not even thought of as constants.

The verdict is confirmed: while there are important numerical constants in the natural sciences, there are none in the social sciences.

Predictability of Future Events

Before we try to compare the success which natural and social sciences have had in correctly predicting future events, a few important distinctions should be made. We must distinguish hypothetical or conditional predictions from unconditional predictions or forecasts. And among the former we must distinguish those where all the stated conditions can be controlled, those where all the stated conditions can be either controlled or unambiguously ascertained before the event, and finally those where some of the stated conditions can neither be controlled nor ascertained early enough (if at all). A conditional prediction of the third kind is such an "iffy" statement that it may be of no use unless one can know with confidence that it would be highly improbable for these problematic conditions (uncontrollable and not ascertainable before the event) to interfere with the prediction. A different kind of distinction concerns the numerical definiteness of the prediction: one may predict that a certain magnitude (a) will change, (b) will increase, (c) will increase by at least so-and-so much, (d) will increase within definite limits, or (e) will increase by a definite amount. Similarly, the prediction may be more or less definite with respect to the time within which it is supposed to come true. A prediction without any time specification is worthless.

Some people are inclined to believe that the natural sciences can beat the social sciences on any count, in unconditional predictions as well as in conditional predictions fully specified as to definite conditions, exact degree and time of fulfilment. But what they have in mind are the laboratory experiments of the natural sciences, in which predictions have proved so eminently successful; and then they look at the poor record social scientists have had in predicting future events in the social world which they observe but cannot control. This comparison is unfair and unreasonable. The artificial laboratory world in which the experimenter tries to control all conditions as best as he can is different from the real world of nature. If a comparison is made, it must be between predictions of events in the real natural world and in the real social world.

Even for the real world, we should distinguish between predictions of events which we try to bring about by design and predictions of events in which we have no part at all. The teams of physicists and engineers who have been designing and developing machines and apparatuses are not very successful in predicting their performance when the design is still new. The record of predictions of the paths of moon shots and space missiles has been rather spotty. The so-called "bugs" that have to be worked out in any new contraption are nothing but predictions gone wrong. After a while predictions become more reliable. The same is true, however, with predictions concerning the performance of organized social institutions. For example, if I take an envelope, put a certain address on it and a certain postage stamp, and deposit it in a certain box on the street, I can predict that after three or four days it will be delivered at a certain house thousands of miles away. This prediction and any number of similar predictions will prove correct with a remarkably high frequency. And you don't have to be a social scientist to make such successful predictions about an organized social machinery, just as you don't have to be a natural scientist to predict the result of your pushing the electric-light switch or of similar manipulations of a well-tried mechanical or electrical apparatus.

There are more misses and fewer hits with regard to predictions of completely unmanipulated and unorganized reality. Meteorologists have a hard time forecasting the weather for the next 24 hours or two or three days. There are too many variables involved and it is too difficult to obtain complete information about some of them. Economists are only slightly better in forecasting employment and income, exports and tax revenues for the next six months or for a year or two. Economists, moreover, have better excuses for their failures because of unpredictable "interferences" by governmental agencies or power groups which may even be influenced by the forecasts of the economists and may operate to defeat their predictions. On the other hand, some of the predictions may be self-fulfilling in that people, learning of the predictions, act in ways which bring about the predicted events. One might say that economists ought to be able to include the "psychological" effects of their communications among the variables of their models and take full account of these influences. There are, however, too many variables, personal and political, involved to make it possible to allow for all effects which anticipations, and anticipations of anticipations, may have upon the end results. To give an example of a simple self-defeating prediction from another social science: traffic experts regularly forecast the number of automobile accidents and fatalities that are going to occur over holiday weekends, and at the same time they hope that their forecasts will influence drivers to be more careful and thus to turn the forecasts into exaggerated fears.

We must not be too sanguine about the success of social scientists in making either unconditional forecasts or conditional predictions. Let us admit that we are not good in the business of prophecy and let us be modest in our claims about our ability to predict. After all, it is not our stupidity which hampers us, but chiefly our lack of information, and when one has to make do with bad guesses in lieu of information the success cannot be great. But there is a significant difference between the natural sciences and the social sciences in this respect: Experts in the natural sciences usually do not try to do what they know they cannot do; and nobody expects them to do it. They would never undertake to predict the number of fatalities in a train wreck that might happen under certain conditions during the next year. They do not even predict next year's explosions and epidemics, floods and mountain slides, earthquakes and water pollution. Social scientists, for some strange reason, are expected to foretell the future and they feel badly if they fail.

Distance from Every-day Experience

Science is, almost by definition, what the layman cannot understand. Science is knowledge accessible only to superior minds with great effort. What everybody can know cannot be science.

A layman could not undertake to read and grasp a professional article in physics or chemistry or biophysics. He would hardly be able to pronounce many of the words and he might not have the faintest idea of what the article was all about. Needless to say, it would be out of the question for a layman to pose as an expert in a natural science. On the other hand, a layman might read articles in descriptive economics, sociology, anthropology, social psychology. Although in all these fields technical jargon is used which he could not really understand, he might *think* that he knows the sense of the words and grasps the meanings of the sentences; he might even be inclined to poke fun at some of the stuff. He believes he is—from his own experience and from his reading of newspapers and popular magazines—familiar with the subject matter of the social sciences. In consequence, he has little respect for the analyses which the social scientists present.

The fact that social scientists use less Latin and Greek words and less mathematics than their colleagues in the natural science departments and, instead, use everyday words in special, and often quite technical, meanings may have something to do with the attitude of the layman. The sentences of the sociologist, for example, make little sense if the borrowed words are understood in their non-technical, every-day meaning. But if the layman is told of the special meanings that have been bestowed upon his words, he gets angry or condescendingly amused.

But we must not exaggerate this business of language and professional jargon because the problem really lies deeper. The natural sciences talk about nuclei, isotopes, galaxies, benzoids, drosophilas, chromosomes, dodecahedrons, Pleistocene fossils, and the layman marvels that anyone really cares. The social sciences, however,—and the layman usually finds this out—talk about— him. While he never identifies himself with a positron, a pneumococcus, a coenzyme, or a digital computer, he does identify himself with many of the ideal types presented by the social scientist, and he finds that the likeness is poor and the analysis "consequently" wrong.

The fact that the social sciences deal with man in his relations with fellow man brings them so close to man's own everyday experience that he cannot see the analysis of this experience as something above and beyond him. Hence he is suspicious of the analysts and disappointed in what he supposes to be a portrait of him.

Standards of Admission and Requirements

High-school physics is taken chiefly by the students with the highest I.Q.'s. At college the students majoring in physics, and again at graduate school the students of physics, are reported to have on the average higher I.Q.'s than those in other fields. This gives physics and physicists a special prestige in schools and universities, and this prestige carries over to all natural sciences and puts them somehow above the social sciences. This is rather odd, since the average quality of students in different departments depends chiefly on departmental policies, which may vary from institution to institution. The preeminence of physics is rather general because of the requirement of calculus. In those universities in which the economics department requires calculus, the students of economics rank as high as the students of physics in intelligence, achievement, and prestige.

The lumping of all natural sciences for comparisons of student quality and admission standards is particularly unreasonable in view of the fact that at many colleges some of the natural science departments, such as biology and geology, attract a rather poor average quality of student. (This is not so in biology at universities with many applicants for a pre-medical curriculum.) The lumping of all social sciences in this respect is equally wrong, since the differences in admission standards and graduation requirements among departments, say between economics, history, and sociology, may be very great. Many sociology departments have been notorious for their role as refuge for mentally underprivileged undergraduates. Given the propensity to overgeneralize, it is no wonder then that the social sciences are being regarded as the poor relations of the natural sciences and as disciplines for which students who cannot qualify for *the* sciences are still good enough.

Since I am addressing economists, and since economics departments, at least at some of the better colleges and universities, are maintaining standards as high as physics and mathematics departments, it would be unfair to level exhortations at my present audience. But perhaps we should try to convince our colleagues in all social science departments of the disservice they are doing to their fields and to the social sciences at large by admitting and keeping inferior students as majors. Even if some of us think that one can study social sciences without knowing higher mathematics, we should insist on making calculus and mathematical statistics absolute requirements—as a device for keeping away the weakest students.

Despite my protest against improper generalizations, I must admit that averages may be indicative of something or other, and that the average I.Q. of the students in the natural science departments is higher than that of the students in the social science department.[9] No field can be better than the men who work in it. On this score, therefore, the natural sciences would be superior to the social sciences.

The Score Card

We may now summarize the tallies on the nine scores.

1. With respect to the invariability or recurrence of obser-

[9] The average I.Q. of students receiving bachelor's degrees was, according to a 1954 study, 121 in the biological sciences, and 122 in economics, 127 in the physical sciences, and 119 in business. See D. Wolfe, *America's Resources of Specialized Talent: The Report of the Commission on Human Resources and Advanced Training*, pp. 319–322.

vations, we found that the greater number of variables—of relevant factors—in the social sciences makes for more variation, for less recurrence of exactly the same sequences of events.

2. With respect to the objectivity of observations and explanations, we distinguished several ways in which references to values and value judgments enter scientific activity. Whereas the social sciences have a requirement of "subjective interpretation of value-motivated actions" which does not exist in the natural sciences, this does not affect the proper "scientific objectivity" of the social scientist.

3. With respect to the verifiability of hypotheses, we found that the impossibility of controlled experiments combined with the larger number of relevant variables does make verification in the social sciences more difficult than in most of the natural sciences.

4. With respect to the exactness of the findings, we decided to mean by it the existence of a theoretical system from which most propositions concerning particular connections can be deduced. Exactness in this sense exists in physics and in economics, but much less so in other natural and other social sciences.

5. With respect to the measurability of phenomena, we saw an important difference between the availability of an ample supply of numerical data and the availability of such numerical data as can be used as good counterparts of the constructs in theoretical models. On this score, physics is clearly ahead of all other disciplines. It is doubtful that this can be said about the natural sciences in general relative to the social sciences in general.

6. With respect to the constancy of numerical relationships, we entertained no doubt concerning the existence of constants, postulated or empirical, in physics and in other natural sciences, whereas no numerical constants can be found in the study of society.

7. With respect to the predictability of future events, we ruled out comparisons between the laboratory world of some of the natural sciences and the unmanipulated real world studied by the social sciences. Comparing only the comparable, the real worlds—and excepting the special case of astronomy—we found no essential differences in the predictability of natural and social phenomena.

8. With respect to the distance of scientific from every-day

experience, we saw that in linguistic expression as well as in their main concerns the social sciences are so much closer to pre-scientific language and thought that they do not command the respect that is accorded to the natural sciences.

9. With respect to the standards of admission and requirements, we found that they are on the average lower in the social than in the natural sciences.

The last of these scores relates to the current practice of colleges and universities, not to the character of the disciplines. The point before the last, though connected with the character of the social sciences, relates only to the popular appreciation of these disciplines; it does not aid in answering the question whether the social sciences are "really" inferior. Thus the last two scores will not be considered relevant to our question. This leaves seven scores to consider. On four of the seven no real differences could be established. But on the other three scores, on "Invariance," "Verifiability," and "Numerical Constants," we found the social sciences to be inferior to the natural sciences.

The Implications of Inferiority

What does it mean if one thing is called "inferior" to another with regard to a particular "quality"? If this "quality" is something that is highly valued in any object, and if the absence of this "quality" is seriously missed regardless of other qualities present, then, but only then, does the noted "inferiority" have any evaluative implications. In order to show that "inferiority" sometimes means very little, I shall present here several statements about differences in particular qualities.

> "Champagne is inferior to rubbing alcohol in alcoholic content."
> "Beef steak is inferior to strawberry jello in sweetness."
> "A violin is inferior to a violoncello in physical weight."
> "Chamber music is inferior to band music in loudness."
> "Hamlet is inferior to Joe Palooka in appeal to children."
> "Sandpaper is inferior to velvet in smoothness."
> "Psychiatry is inferior to surgery in ability to effect quick cures."
> "Biology is inferior to physics in internal consistency."

It all depends on what you want. Each member in a pair of things is inferior to the other in some respect. In some instances it may be precisely this inferiority that makes the thing desirable. (Sandpaper is wanted *because* of its inferior smoothness.) In other instances the inferiority in a particular respect may be a matter of indifference. (The violin's inferiority in physical weight neither adds nor detracts from its relative value.) Again in other instances the particular inferiority may be regrettable, but nothing can be done about it and the thing in question may be wanted none the less. (We need psychiatry, however much we regret that in general it cannot effect quick cures; and we need biology, no matter how little internal consistency has been attained in its theoretical systems.)

We have stated that the social sciences are inferior to the natural sciences in some respects, for example, in verifiability. This is regrettable. If propositions cannot be readily tested, this calls for more judgment, more patience, more ingenuity. But does it mean much else?

The Crucial Question: "So What?"

What is the pragmatic meaning of the statement in question? If I learn, for example, that drug E is inferior to drug P as a cure for hay fever, this means that, if I want such a cure, I shall not buy drug E. If I am told Mr. A is inferior to Mr. B as an automobile mechanic, I shall avoid using Mr. A when my car needs repair. If I find textbook K inferior to textbook S in accuracy, organization, as well as exposition, I shall not adopt textbook K. In every one of these examples, the statement that one thing is inferior to another makes pragmatic sense. The point is that all these pairs are *alternatives* between which a choice is to be made.

Are the natural sciences and the social sciences alternatives between which we have to choose? If they were, a claim that the social sciences are "inferior" could have the following meanings:

1. We should not study the social sciences.

2. We should not spend money on teaching and research in the social sciences.

3. We should not permit gifted persons to study social sciences and should steer them toward superior pursuits.

4. We should not respect scholars who so imprudently chose to be social scientists.

If one realizes that none of these things could possibly be meant, that every one of these meanings would be preposterous, and that the social sciences and the natural sciences can by no means be regarded as alternatives but, instead, that both are needed and neither can be dispensed with, he can give the inferiority statement perhaps one other meaning:

5. We should do something to improve the social sciences and remedy their defects.

This last interpretation would make sense if the differences which are presented as grounds for the supposed inferiority were "defects" that can be remedied. But they are not. That there are more variety and change in social phenomena; that, because of the large number of relevant variables and the impossibility of controlled experiments, hypotheses in the social sciences cannot be easily verified; and that no numerical constants can be detected in the social world—these are not defects to be remedied but fundamental properties to be grasped, accepted, and taken into account. Because of these properties research and analysis in the social sciences hold greater complexities and difficulties. If you wish, you may take this to be a greater challenge, rather than a deterrent. To be sure, difficulty and complexity alone are not sufficient reasons for studying certain problems. But the problems presented by the social world are certainly not unimportant. If they are also difficult to tackle, they ought to attract ample resources and the best minds. Today they are getting neither. The social sciences are "really inferior" regarding the place they are accorded by society and the priorities with which financial and human resources are allocated. This inferiority is curable.

For

FURTHER READING

For discussions of theory in social science see: Talcott Parsons, *The Structure of Social Action*, ch. 1, his "The Present Position and Prospects of Systematic Theory in Sociology," in *Twentieth Century Sociology* (ed. Gurvitch and Moore), and his "General Theory in Sociology," in *Sociology Today* (ed. Merton, Broom, and Cottrell); also, Robert K. Merton, "The Bearing of Sociological Theory on Empirical Research" and "The Bearing of Empirical Research on Sociological Theory," in his *Social Theory and Social Structure* (revised ed.). The theories of Parsons, Merton, and others are examined in *Modern Social Theories* (ed. Loomis and Loomis). Also see *The Social Theories of Talcott Parsons* (ed. Max Black). Relevant articles will be found in *Modern Sociological Theory* (ed. Becker and Boskoff) and *Symposium on Sociological Theory* (ed. Llewellyn Gross).

The following titles have a more specific focus in one or more of the social sciences: James G. Miller, "Toward a General Theory for the Behavioral Sciences," in *The State of the Social Sciences* (ed. Leonard D. White); *Handbook of Social*

Psychology (ed. Gardner Lindzey), Vol. I; Benjamin B. Wolman, *Contemporary Theories and Systems in Psychology; The Human Meaning of the Social Sciences* (ed. Daniel Lerner); T. W. Hutchison, *The Significance and Basic Postulates of Economic Theory;* Lionel Robbins, *An Essay on the Nature and Significance of Economic Science;* Fritz Machlup, "Why Bother with Methodology?" *Economica* (New Series), Vol. III, 1936; *Theory and Practice in Historical Study* (Social Science Research Council, 1946); Lewis W. Beck, "The 'Natural Science Ideal' in the Social Sciences," *Scientific Monthly*, Vol. LXVIII, 1949; Symposium on "Causality in the Social Sciences" by Lewis S. Feuer and Ethel M. Albert, *Journal of Philosophy*, Vol. LI, 1954. For historical surveys see Nicholas S. Timasheff, *Sociological Theory*, and Don Martindale, *The Nature and Types of Sociological Theory*. For other titles relevant to anthropology, political science, etc., consult *A Reader's Guide to the Social Sciences* (ed. Bert F. Hoselitz).

PART III
Concepts, Constructs, and Theory Formation

....

PART III

Introduction to
PART III

■■

THE CENTRAL DIALECTIC of this volume is contained in the following Part, for here it has been possible not only to pose some
major questions of philosophy of the social sciences but also
to include interrelated selections whose authors comprise a
contemporary forum of methodological discussion. The range of
issues presented and explored is great, and we must restrict ourselves here to outlining only a few of the problems involved.
Underlying the discussion of functionalism, naturalism, behaviorism, phenomenology, etc., is the following cluster of generic
themes about which the authors move more or less explicitly:
(1) the natural versus the social sciences; (2) the nature of interpretive understanding (*Verstehen*); (3) the typifications of social
science; (4) the exploration of the "life-world" (*Lebenswelt*) of
social reality. The horizon of each theme leads outward through
a maze of related problems, but a preliminary statement of what
is involved in each case may provide a point of departure for appreciating the dialectic as a whole.

    1. *The natural versus the social sciences.* The contributors
to this Part may be grouped into three divisions: those who represent an essentially naturalistic, empiricistic or positivistic position

(Nagel and Hempel), those who are phenomenologists (Schutz and Natanson), and those whose orientation is toward an "enlightened" naturalism which tries to mediate between the first two camps (Lavine and Goldstein). It should not be necessary to add that these labels are rough and can serve only to confuse matters unless the reader remembers that they are working approximations which refer primarily to the following essays and not, necessarily, to the entire range of each author's productivity. The basis for the division is the difference in philosophic stance with respect to the interpretation of the relationship between the natural and the social sciences. Simply stated, Nagel and Hempel hold that the problems of the social world are not in principle qualitatively different, to the inquiring scientist, from those of the natural sciences and that, therefore, essentially the same methodological procedures can be and ought to be employed in both domains. For Schutz and Natanson, social reality is made up of the meanings which actors on the social scene give to their actions and to their situations. The consciousness or subjectivity of the actor is the axis of social action, and the cardinal problem of the philosophy of the social sciences is the illumination and reconstruction of the essential features of subjectivity as it founds and structures a social world. The mediating positions of Lavine and Goldstein are directed toward two goals: the former claiming that naturalism has failed to account for the philosophic status of its own method (while holding that such failure can be overcome in essentially naturalistic terms) and the latter arguing that naturalism and phenomenology are more nearly complementary disciplines interested in different levels of description and analysis than they are conflicting theories of the same reality. All of these distinctions and claims are carried further in related themes.

2. *The nature of interpretive understanding* (Verstehen). Here again the split between naturalists and phenomenologists is decisive with a mediating influence present. In this instance the conflict is over the methodological status and utility of a fundamental feature of Max Weber's position (though the method of *Verstehen* has other sources as well—Wilhelm Dilthey, for example), the claim that social action must be understood as grounded in the meanings intended by actors, that we understand social action by grasping the meaning which an act has for

the actor who performs it, that the procedure involved in such understanding turns upon the conceptual clarification of the motives and goals that shape the world of a fellow man as *he* interprets and articulates its meaning. The debate over Weber's notion of *Verstehen* can be summarized by Nagel's stress on the claim that "the method of *Verstehen* does not, by itself, supply any *criteria* for the validity of conjectures and hypotheses concerning the springs of human action" and Schutz's insistence on treating Weber's postulate of subjective interpretation as being primarily (though not exclusively) a structural feature of common-sense life rather than of social scientific inquiry. At this level *Verstehen* is understood "as the way in which common-sense thinking finds its bearings within the social world and comes to terms with it."

3. *The typifications of social science.* As Hempel points out, the notion of "type" has been used by social scientists in a number of different senses. He distinguishes between "classificatory types" in which types are understood as classes, "extreme types" which operate on a principle of comparison, and "ideal types" which are constructions "invoked as a specific device for the explanation of social and historical phenomena." Schutz, on the other hand, stresses a radical distinction between the types (and the whole logic of typification) which he finds embedded in the matrix of daily life and common-sense thinking and those formally constructed by the social scientist for concrete purposes of inquiry. The former may become the objects investigated by the latter, but this is not to say that their formal character (their essential structure) is synonymous with the scientist's mode of procedure. Rather, for Schutz, the overpowering methodological problem which the philosopher of the social sciences faces is how he can succeed in formulating a theory which both confronts the phenomena of social life with all its embedded types and formulates its descriptions, analyses, and results in terms of a theory which derives its strength from the typifications of the social scientist. Is it possible to be true to both life and science?

4. *The exploration of the "life-world"* (Lebenswelt) *of social reality.* The term *Lebenswelt* was used by the founder of the phenomenological movement, Edmund Husserl, to refer to the immediately experienced world each of us lives in, un-

mediated by the sophistications of science, and which each of us interprets for himself. The importance of this "life-world" is not its status as knowledge but its focus as the meaningful ground of human action. The phenomenologist's concern with the *Lebenswelt* as a theme for social science is twofold: To begin with, the typifications of the social world are aspects of the life-world in so far as the individual caught up in daily life utilizes them naively with no realization that daily life itself presupposes such philosophical problems as that of intersubjectivity and of there *being* a social world. Apart from this, however, the *Lebenswelt* is seen as a *constituted* structure, that is, a vast network of meaningful relationships which have a developmental history in the activity of consciousness as much as they do in historical genesis. The miracle of daily life is that the experience it implies is in fact realized by the persons who comprise it. The phenomenologist, then, is interested in both a descriptive account of the structure of the life-world and a constitutive examination of its coming into being. Whether philosophical naturalism offers a complement to any aspect of this style of thought depends upon appreciating the underlying *Weltanschauungen* as much as upon the delineation of levels of analysis. If "subjectivists" and "objectivists" can be encouraged to speak the same language, it is still uncertain whether they have anything to say to each other.

NOTE: Since much of the discussion in the selections which follow in this Part presupposes some knowledge of the position of Max Weber, the reader should turn to Weber's *The Theory of Social and Economic Organization*, especially pp. 87–123.

Problems of Concept and
Theory Formation
in the Social Sciences[1]

ERNEST NAGEL

I

THE STUDY of human institutions and human behavior in institutional settings has been under cultivation for at least as long as has inquiry into physical and biological phenomena. But few will question the assertion that in no area of social study have a body of knowledge and systems of explanatory theory been achieved, which compare in scope, precision, and reliability with what the natural sciences have to offer. To be sure, systems of "social physics" have been proposed in the past as adequate for all human cultures and for all periods of history. Most of these explanatory systems are so-called "single-factor" theories. They identify some one "factor"—such as geography, race, economic structure, to mention but a few—as the "basic determinant" in terms of which the organization and development of societies are to be understood. However, none of these ambitious hypotheses has been able to survive critical scrutiny; and even in restricted domains of social study, such as economics, the empirical worth

[1] Reprinted from *Science, Language, and Human Rights* (American Philosophical Association, Eastern Division, Philadelphia: University of Pennsylvania Press, 1952, Vol. I, pp. 43–64), with the permission of the publisher and the approval of the author.

of the theories currently in development is still a seriously debated matter.

In consequence, the right of any existing department of social study to the title of a "genuine science" has been repeatedly challenged. It is idle to debate an issue so stated, for it is little more than a dispute over the use of an honorific label. In any case, it is preposterous to deny that social scientists have produced valuable descriptive studies of many social phenomena, that they have thrown much light on the interdependence of a variety of social processes, or that they have devised techniques of measurement and empirical analysis possessing varying degrees of actual and potential usefulness. On the other hand, many professional students of human affairs believe it is premature to attempt comprehensive theories for their subject matters; and most of them are indeed occupied with less ambitious though doubtless also less impressive tasks. Moreover, there is an influential group of thinkers who claim it is a fundamental error to measure the achievements of the social sciences by standards borrowed from the natural sciences; and they maintain that the construction of "abstract" theories which require to be warranted by objective evidence, like the theories of physics, is not the appropriate goal of social inquiry. The social sciences thus present a scene not only of widely diverse undertakings, but also of acute methodological controversy between different schools of inquiry.

Anyone who proposes to discuss the social sciences, with the intent of comparing their theoretical structures and their logical methods with those of the natural sciences, is thus in a quandary. There is little general agreement as to what social theory ought to be, and as to what social theory ought to accomplish; and in any case, whatever sense is attached to the word "theory," there is no theoretical treatise in these disciplines comparable in scope and authority with those current in physics, chemistry, or biology. Whatever material is selected for analysis is likely to be judged by many students as unrepresentative, and the analysis itself as irrelevant to the central problems of social inquiry. But this risk is unavoidable. In this paper I wish to examine some issues that seem to me perennial in the social sciences, and to discuss them in the context of an approach in them that is extensively exploited at present. Many outstanding investigators of human affairs believe that the best hope for their disciplines lies in the systematic cultivation of "functional" analyses of social processes and institutions; and some of them even proclaim functionalism to be a full-fledged "theory" of social phenomena. It is to a few broad problems raised by functionalism that the following somewhat desultory comments are addressed.

II

Since functional analysis in the social sciences is often a self-conscious attempt to adopt a type of explanation common in biology, and especially physiology, let me begin with a brief consideration of functional explanations in biological science. In biology, a functional account is an analysis of the structure and operations of various parts of an organism (or a system that includes living bodies) with the objective of exhibiting the manner in which certain characteristic activities or features of the organism (or system) are maintained, despite variations in its external and internal environment.

Now it is demonstrable that functional analyses in biology do not differ in kind or method from the so-called "causal" explanations in the physical sciences with which they are often contrasted. For in the first place, a functional account in biology traces the objective effects which follow from the operation of various components of an organic system upon that system as a whole or upon some of its other parts. In consequence, the formulations of the relations of dependence that are thus discovered do not differ in content from formulations which simply specify the conditions (whether necessary or sufficient) under which events of a specified type occur. In fact, statements in biology that have a teleological form are translatable without loss of meaning into statements of a nonteleological kind. To say, for example, that the function of the human kidney is to maintain a certain chemical balance in the blood is to assert nothing different from saying that in the absence of kidneys in the normal human body the chemical composition of the blood does not remain approximately constant. In the second place, though physiologists conduct their experiments upon individual organic systems, their conclusions are intended to be valid not only for the particular systems actually investigated, but for all systems of a stated type. In short, physiological analyses terminate in general statements or laws. Moreover, in the process of ascertaining the functions of various parts of an organic system, explicit use is made of generalized knowledge obtained in prior inquiries, and frequently of theories established by the physical sciences. In the third place, though the systems studied in biology are "self-maintaining" or "goal-directed," while the systems explored by the physical sciences are usually not of this nature, biologists no longer find it necessary to postulate purposes or special vital agents to account for the self-regulative character of the systems they investigate. Indeed, as the current literature on servo-mechanisms makes evident, it is now possible to define what distinguishes self-maintaining systems from those which are not, in terms that are neutral to the distinction between the living and the nonliving. In any event, biologists have succeeded in a number of cases in explaining the self-maintenance of organisms entirely in terms of the organization of their parts, and of compensatory physiochemical changes in those parts. On the other hand, a critical biology recognizes that a teleological analysis is always relative to a specified system and a designated set of structures and activities. For the operation of a given organ will in general have a variety of consequences, so that to ask for *the* function of an organ is to ask for the consequences of its operation for *one among several* systems of which it may be a component. But this relativity of functional explanations does not make them illegitimate, and does not preclude the possibility of there being objective warrant for them. And finally, successful functional analysis in biology is not contingent upon the prior acceptance of any particular theory of organic processes. In particular, it does not rest upon the far-going assumption that the continued existence and operation of every part is indispensable to the organism, or that the actual behavior of each distinguishable component of an organic system is dependent on the character and mode of behavior of every other component. If by "theory" one understands an explicit formulation of determinate relations between a set of variables, in terms of which a fairly extensive class of empirically ascertainable regularities (or laws) can be explained (always provided that suitable boundary conditions for the application of the theory are supplied), and if the pursuit of functional analyses in biology is called "functionalism," then functionalism is not a biological theory. It is at best but a precept for orienting inquiry to the study of conditions and mechanisms of self-maintenance.

III

These brief reminders of the character of teleological analyses in biology will prove to be pertinent to the examination of functionalism in the social sciences, to which I now turn. However, despite their conviction of its great promise, proponents of functionalism in the social sciences are not in general formal agreement as to its content. I shall nevertheless take for my point of departure a statement of it which is by now classic, even though it is not fully representative of current functionalists' views and even if not all professed functionalists subscribe to it in its entirety. In an account of functionalism in anthropology, Malinowski explained that a functionalist analysis of culture

aims at the explanation of anthropological facts at all levels of development by their function, by the part which they play within the integral system of culture, by the manner in which they are related to each other within the system, and by the manner in which this system is related to the physical surroundings. . . . The functional view of culture insists therefore upon the principle that in every type of civilization, every custom, material object, idea and belief fulfills some vital function, has some task to accomplish, represents an indispensable part within a working whole.[2]

But what is functionalism on this statement? Is it a hypothesis concerning the interrelations of social phenomena, is it simply a program for inquiry, is it both? The explicit insistence that every item discoverable in a culture is indispensable to it as a "working whole," inclines one to believe that it falls under the first alternative; but the remainder of the statement suggests that it is to be subsumed under the second. However, if func-

[2] B. Malinowski, "Anthropology," *The Encyclopaedia Britannica,* Supplementary I, 132–133.

tionalism is a "theory" about civilizations, it must agree with available empirical evidence; and there is ample evidence to show that societies are not in general the tightly knit "organic" systems which this theory proclaims them to be, so that functionalism in this version must be judged as false. On the other hand, if functionalism is construed as a methodological precept, then the above statement appears to be fully conveyed by the imperative: "There are relations of dependence between cultural objects, and between cultural objects and their physical environment. Look for them!" But if this translation is not a complete caricature, it is difficult to understand why functionalism should be so widely hailed as a fresh and promising approach to the study of social phenomena. In point of fact, the content of functionalism (whether it is construed to be a theory or a program) is meager to the vanishing point, unless formulations of it such as the above are supplemented by a variety of material assumptions about the organization and the operation of societies. At the same time, the ambiguity just noted pervades not only the writings of Malinowski, but also the literature of functionalism in other areas of social study.

IV

But I hasten to more substantial issues. Although it is usually quite clear in biology what are the activities of an organic system which must be maintained if the system is to endure, the corresponding question in the social sciences does not in general admit of a ready answer. For in biology there are certain familiar and generally acknowledged inclusive functions, such as respiration or reproduction, without whose continued maintenance the organism or the species will perish. In the social sciences, on the other hand, there is much less explicit agreement as to what are the indispensable activities and structures of social systems—except when specifically biological needs of human beings are in question. The problem obviously involves complicated matters of empirical fact and analysis, though it is often settled by a tacit use of moral principles. For example, though Hayek's recent polemics against deliberate social planning employ the arguments of an implicit functionalism, his arguments have force only if one accepts the moral assumptions underlying them.[3] In the absence of explicit agreement on what are the "essential" requirements of society, the functionalist's injunction to study the manner in which "the integral system of culture" is maintained, is frequently a concealed endorsement of some particular social ideal. But in any event, the characterization of a process or set of conditions as "functional" or "dysfunctional," according as it contributes to or detracts from the "integration and effectiveness" of a social system, is empirically empty unless there is an antecedent specification of what is to be integrated and for what a process is effective. For every occurrence is functional for some things and at the same time dysfunctional for others, as indeed a critical biology makes plain.

Some recent functionalists, if I understand them, seek to outflank these difficulties by frankly recognizing the relativity of teleological analyses of social systems. They propose systematically articulated "structural" categories allegedly so general as to comprehend all types of institutions. (For example, one proposal distinguishes between configurations of institutions according as they stress norms of conduct binding upon all members of a society indiscriminately, or norms which involve reference to special relations between individuals; and the proposal further distinguishes between configurations according as they promote social stratification on the basis of individual achievement, or on the basis of possession of special attributes. At least four types of social structure are thus recognized.) A functional analysis will therefore show just what, and in what manner, various social processes contribute to the maintenance of designated structural features of a social system. If I am correct in my reading of this version of functionalism, it makes central the possibility of alternate patterns of social organization. It thereby not only makes explicit the relativity of functional analyses, but also keeps distinct questions of actual fact from questions of social policy. The present and eventual worth of the categorical schemas thus far proposed is by no means clear, and is certainly disputable. But it is safe to say that without some such "structural" categories functionalism cannot intelligibly maintain this distinction, and cannot consistently escape basic confusion.

[3] F. A. Hayek, *The Counter-Revolution of Science*, pp. 90–92.

V

It is therefore a mistaken claim which asserts that functional analyses (or for that matter any responsible inquiry into human affairs) are necessarily committed to some pattern of cultural values, and which concludes that "objectivity" in any relevant sense of this difficult word is impossible in the social sciences. I will begin with a quotation from Max Weber, whose views on this issue continue to exercise enormous influence. Weber maintained that it is the distinctive task of the social sciences to analyze phenomena in terms of their "cultural significance," and in this respect he was a functionalist despite his vigorous dissent from certain functionalist tendencies. But he also declared that

> The *significance* of a configuration of cultural phenomena and the basis of this significance cannot . . . be derived and rendered intelligible by a system of analytical laws, however perfect it may be, since the significance of cultural events presupposes a *value-orientation* toward these events. The concept of culture is a *value-concept*. Empirical reality becomes "culture" to us because and insofar as we relate it to value ideas. It includes those segments and only those segments of reality which have become significant to us because of this value-relevance. Only a small portion of existing concrete reality is colored by our value-conditioned interest and it alone is significant to us. It is significant because it reveals relationships which are important to us due to their connection with our values. . . . The focus of attention on reality under the guidance of values which lend it significance and the selection and ordering of the phenomena which are thus affected in the light of their cultural significance is entirely different from the analysis of reality in terms of laws and general concepts.

Weber finally concluded that

> an "objective" analysis of cultural events, which proceeds according to the thesis that the ideal of science is the reduction of empirical reality to "laws" is meaningless. . . . The transcendental presupposition of every *cultural science* lies

not in our finding a certain culture or any "culture" in general to be *valuable* but rather in the fact that we are *cultural beings*, endowed with the capacity and the will to take a deliberate attitude towards the world and to lend it *significance*.[4]

It would take more pages than are at my disposal to unravel the ambiguities in these pronouncements, or to separate what seems to me sound in them from what is false. I must limit myself to but one point. Why is the fact that an inquirer selects his material for study in the light of the problems that interest him, of greater moment for the logic of social inquiry than it is for the logic of natural science? If a social scientist discovers that the outcome—and in this sense the "significance"—of certain forms of individual activity is the perpetuation of a free economic market, in what way is his concentration upon processes that maintain this particular institution rather than something else, of greater relevance in evaluating the adequacy of his explanation than is, for the corresponding question, the concern of the physiologist with processes that maintain a relatively constant internal temperature of the human body? Were we not human beings, but were nevertheless capable of engaging in inquiry, we might perhaps show no interest either in the conditions that maintain a free market or in the conditions that make possible the homeostasis of human temperature. But there is no ascertainable difference on this score between the natural and the social sciences. The traits selected for study, with a view to discovering their conditions and consequences, may indeed be dependent on the fact that the investigator is a "cultural being"; but there is no reason whatever for believing that the validity of his conclusions is dependent on that fact in the same way.

It may be said, however, that some point of view is required in selecting materials in the conduct of social inquiry, that the "point of view determines what is important and what is unimportant in the confusing maze of human events," and that since questions of importance involve problems of valuation, it is impossible to eliminate bias from the study of human affairs.[5] But

[4] M. Weber, " 'Objectivity' in Social Science and Social Policy," in this book, pp. 382–383, 386–387.

[5] M. R. Cohen, *The Meaning of Human History*, p. 80.

this argument is a *non-sequitur*, and gains its apparent plausibility from confounding several senses in which valuations may enter into inquiry. It should be noted in the first place that if the argument is sound, it applies equally to inquiries in both the natural and social sciences. In the second place, it is undoubtedly correct that the scientist brings certain "values" to his investigations, and imposes certain demands upon the course of his inquiry. But the only values which are relevant in this connection are the values and standards implicit in the enterprise of obtaining warranted knowledge. Doubtless such standards change with the development of science, and doubtless also these changes are frequently associated with other cultural variations. But evidence is completely lacking to support the currently fashionable belief that even when the specific problem initiating an inquiry is carefully formulated and understood, individuals may be so disparate in their "cultural values" as to preclude in principle the possibility of agreement between them concerning the *validity* of a proposed solution for it. And in the third place, though judgments of importance are unavoidable in all inquiries, in the natural as well as the social sciences, such judgments are not necessarily "subjective" in any pejorative sense. In particular, they need not be made in terms of some "private" set of values, since standards of relative importance can be explicitly formulated, and the question whether these standards are satisfied in a given case can be settled, at least in principle and when sufficient evidence is available, by customary methods of empirical investigation. To be sure, men's interests may be discordant, and the standards accepted by some in ascribing degrees of relative importance may be different from the standards accepted by others. It does not follow, however, that two apparently contradictory judgments of relative importance are necessarily incompatible; for the appearance of contradiction may merely indicate the use of different criteria by which the *meaning* of "relative importance" is tacitly specified. Interests may clash, they may not be arbitrable by rational methods, and they may eventuate in the adoption of alternate principles for selecting and organizing empirical material. But once the meanings of terms have been decided upon and a principle of selection adopted, the clash of interests plays no *logical* role in establishing the cognitive worth of a proposed explanation of social phenomena.

It is also frequently argued, to quote one fairly typical statement of the point, that a social scientist

> cannot wholly detach the unifying social structure that, as a scientist's theory, guides his detailed investigations of human behavior, from the unifying structure which, as a citizen's ideal, he thinks ought to prevail in human affairs and hopes may sometime be more fully realized. His social theory is thus essentially a program of action along two lines which are kept in some measure of harmony with each other by that theory—action in assimilating social facts for purposes of systematic understanding, and action aiming at progressively molding the social pattern, so far as he can influence it, into what he thinks it ought to be.[6]

Now it is undoubtedly difficult in many inquiries to prevent our hopes and wishes from coloring the conclusions we draw; and it has taken centuries of devoted effort even in the natural sciences to develop habits and techniques of investigation which safeguard the course of inquiry against the intrusion of irrelevant personal factors. But to say this is to assume the possibility of distinguishing between fact and hope, for otherwise the statement becomes unintelligible. Even if it is invariably the case, as the above quotation maintains, that social scientists pursue a double line of activity, the claim that they do so makes clear sense only if it is possible to adjudicate between, on the one hand, contributions to theoretical understanding whose validity does not depend on allegiance to any social ideal, and on the other hand contributions toward the realization or perpetuation of some such ideal. Accordingly, the difficulty noted is a remediable practical difficulty. It can be overcome, as is often recognized, not by futile resolutions to remain unbiased, but through the self-correcting processes of science as a social enterprise. For the tradition of modern science encourages the free exchange and criticism of ideas; and it permits and welcomes competition in the quest for knowledge on the part of independent investi-

[6] E. A. Burtt, *Right Thinking*, p. 522.

gators, whatever may be their prior doctrinal commitments. It would be ignorance to claim that these self-corrective processes have operated or are likely to operate in social inquiry as readily as they have in the natural sciences. But it would be a confusion in analysis to conclude that therefore there is a basic difference in the character of warranted knowledge in these two areas of inquiry.

VI

I must now turn to issues of a different order. In the study of biological functions the imputation of motives, attitudes, and purposes to organic systems or their parts is strictly irrelevant. In the study of social phenomena such imputation is highly pertinent. What is the significance of this fact for the objectives and the methods of the social sciences?

According to an influential school of functionalists, all socially significant human behavior is an expression of motivated psychic states, so that the "dynamism" of social processes is identified with the "value-oriented" behavior of human individuals. An inquiry that is properly a *social* study has been therefore said to begin only with the question: "What motives determine and lead the individual members and participants in [a given] community to behave in such a way that the community comes into being in the first place and that it continues to exist?"[7] In consequence, the social scientist cannot be satisfied with viewing social processes simply as the sequential concatenations of "externally related" events; and the establishment of correlations, or even of universal relations of concomitance, cannot be his ultimate goal. For he must not ignore the fact that every social change involves the assessment and readjustment of human activities relating means to ends (or "values"). On the contrary, he must construct "ideal types" or "models of motivation," in terms of which he seeks to "understand" overt social behavior by imputing springs of action to the actors involved in it. But these springs of action are not accessible to sensory observation; and the social scientist who wishes to understand social phenomena must imaginatively identify himself with its participants, and

[7] M. Weber, *The Theory of Social and Economic Organization*, p. 107.

view the situation which they face as the actors themselves view it. Social phenomena are indeed not generally the *intended* resultants of individual actions; nevertheless the central task of social science is the explanation of phenomena as the unintended outcome of springs of action—of psychic states which are familiar to us solely from our own "subjective" experiences as volitional agents.

In consequence, there is said to be a radical difference between explanations in the social and in the natural sciences. In the latter we allegedly understand the "causal nexus" of events only in an external manner; in the former we can grasp the peculiar unity of social processes, since these involve a dynamic synthesis of subjective urges, values, and goals, on the one hand, and the external environment on the other. A purely "objective" or "behavioristic" social science is thus declared to be a vain hope. For in the words of one recent writer, proponents of behaviorism in social science

> fail to perceive the essential difference from the standpoint of causation, between a paper flying before the wind and a man flying from a pursuing crowd. The paper knows no fear and the wind no hate, but without fear and hate the man would not fly nor the crowd pursue. If we try to reduce it to its bodily concomitants we merely substitute the concomitants for the reality expressed as fear. We denude the world of meanings for the sake of a theory, itself a false meaning which deprives us of all the rest. We can interpret experience only on the level of experience.[8]

In short, since social science seeks to establish "meaningful" connections and not merely relations of concomitance, its goal and method are fundamentally different from those of natural science.

I will not take time to comment here at length on the psychological preconceptions underlying this rejection of behaviorism, nor on the adequacy with which behaviorism is portrayed. Only one point requires brief mention in this connection. It is surely not the case that we must ourselves undergo (whether actually or in imagination) other men's psychic experiences in order to know that they have them, or in order to predict their

[8] R. M. MacIver, *Society*, p. 530.

overt behaviors. But if this is so, the alleged "privacy" or "sub-jectivity" of mental states has no bearing on the acquisition of knowledge concerning the character, the determinants, and the consequences of other men's dispositions and actions. A historian does not have to be Hitler or even be capable of reënacting in imagination Hitler's frenzied hatreds, to write competently of Hitler's career and historical significance. For knowledge is not a matter of having images, whether faint or vivid; it is not a reduplication of, or a substitute for, what is claimed to be known. Knowledge involves the discovery through processes of con-trolled inference that something is a sign of something else; it is statable in propositional form; and it is capable of being verified through sensory observation by anyone who is prepared to make the effort to do so. It is therefore just as possible to know that a man is in a state of fear or that a crowd is animated by hatred, without recreating in imagination such fears and hatreds, as it is to know that a man is running away or that a crowd is pursuing him without an imaginary exercise of one's legs. It is possible to discover and know these things on the evidence supplied by the overt behaviors of men and crowds, just as it is possible to dis-cover and know the atomic constitution of water on the evidence supplied by the physical and chemical behavior of that substance.

But I must consider at greater length the claim that since the social sciences seek to "understand" social phenomena in terms of "meaningful" categories of human experience, the "causal-func-tional" approach of the natural sciences is not applicable in social inquiry. The abstract pattern of such "meaningful" explanations appears to be as follows. Let A be some complex set of conditions (e.g., membership in certain religious groups) under which a phenomenon B occurs (e.g., the development of modern forms of capitalistic enterprise). The social agents involved in A and B are then assumed to possess certain feelings, beliefs, etc.: A^1 (e.g., belief in the sacredness of a worldly calling) and B^1 (e.g., prizing of honesty, orderliness, and abstemious labor), respectively. Here A^1 and B^1 are supposedly "meaningfully" related, because of our familiarity with motivational patterns in our own experience; and the relations between A and A^1, as well as between B and B^1, are are also of the same alleged kind. Accordingly, the "external" connection between A and B is "meaningfully" explained, when each is "interpreted" as an expression of certain "motivational" states A^1 and B^1 respectively, where the connection between the latter is "understood" in a peculiarly intimate way.

But do such explanations require a special kind of logic, distinctive of the social sciences? At the risk of belaboring the obvious, I must state the grounds for maintaining that the answer is negative. The imputation of emotions, attitudes, and purposes as an explanation of overt behavior is a twofold hypothesis; it is not a self-certifying one, and evidence for it must be supplied in accordance with customary canons of empirical inquiry. The hypothesis is twofold: for on the one hand, it assumes that the agents participating in some social phenomenon are in certain psychological states; and on the other hand, it also assumes definite relations of concomitance between such states, and between such states and certain overt behaviors. But as the more responsible exponents of "meaningful" explanations themselves emphasize, it is in general not easy to obtain competent evidence for either assumption. We may identify ourselves in imagination with a trader in grain, and conjecture what course of action we would take were we confronted with the problems of a fluctuating market. But conjecture is not fact, however necessary conjecture may be as part of the process of discovering what is fact. None of the psychological states which we imagine the subjects of our study to possess may in reality be theirs; and even if our imputations should be correct, none of the overt actions which allegedly issue from those states may appear to us as "understandable" or "reasonable" in the light of our own experiences. If the history of anthropological research proves anything, it surely testifies to the errors students commit when they interpret the actions of men in unfamiliar cultures in terms of categories drawn uncritically from their limited personal lives.

Moreover, do we "understand" the nature and operation of human motives and their issuance in overt behavior more adequately and with greater certitude, than we do the occurrences studied in the natural sciences? Do we understand more clearly and know with greater certainty why an insult tends to produce anger, than why a rainbow is produced when the sun's rays strike raindrops at a certain angle? The question is rhetorical, for the obvious answer is "no." We may feel assured that if an illiterate and impoverished people revolts against its masters, it does so not because of adherence to some political doctrine but because of economic ills. But this assurance may only be the product of familiarity and a limited imagination; and the sense of penetrating comprehension that we may associate with the assertion, instead of guaranteeing its universal truth, may be only a sign of our provincialism. The contrast that is drawn between "understanding" in terms of "meaningful" categories and the merely "external" knowledge of causal relations which the natural sciences are alleged to provide is indeed far from clear. When we "meaningfully" explain the flight of a man from an angry crowd by imputing to him a fear of physical violence, we surely do not postulate in him a special agency called "fear" which impels him to run; nor do we intend by such an imputation that a certain immediate quality of the man's experience is the determinant of his action. What I think we are asserting is that his action is an instance of a *pattern of behavior* which human beings exhibit under a variety of circumstances, and that since some of the relevant circumstances are realized in the given situation the person can be expected to manifest a certain particular form of that pattern. But if something like this is the content of explanations in terms of "meaningful" categories, there is no sharp gulf separating them from explanations that involve merely "external" knowledge of causal connections.

One final comment in this connection. While the "dynamism" of social processes is in general identified by many functionalists with the "motivational" character of human action, some of them have maintained that all social change must be understood in terms of those particular variations in motivation that are called "values." Thus, it has been argued that if we wish to ascertain why there has been a pronounced increase in the divorce rate in the U.S. during the past fifty years, a satisfactory explanation must be of the type which stipulates

> a change in valuation affecting the status of the family. The general indication is that divorce is more prevalent in those areas where the continuity of the family through several generations has less significance in the schema of cultural values than formerly or elsewhere.

More generally, the claim has been made that "In so far as we are able to discover the changes of the evaluative schema of social groups we can attain, and thus only, a unified explanation of social change."[9]

It is not my concern to take sides in an issue of material fact, and in any case I am not qualified to do so in this particular one. But it is relevant to ask how an assumed alteration in a schema of cultural values can be established. The obvious procedure would be to take as evidence for such a change the explicit statements of the persons involved, whether these statements take the form of personal confessions, public speeches, or the like. However, explicit statements of the kind required are not generally available; and even when they are, they cannot always be taken at their face value. For there is often a great disparity between what men verbally profess and what they actually practice, and individuals may continue their verbal allegiance to a set of ideals even though their mode of living has been radically transformed. Students of human affairs are thus compelled to base their conclusions as to what are the operative evaluative schemas in a given society on evidence that is largely drawn from the overt behavior of men—from their conduct of business affairs, their mode of recreation, their domestic arrangements, and so on.

There is in fact a risk that explanations of social change in terms of alterations in value-schemas collapse into tautologies, which simply restate in different language what is presumably explained. For example, if a change in the divorce rate is the sole evidence for the assumption that there has been a shift in the value associated with the continuity of the family, a proposed explanation of the former change by the latter is a spurious one. It does not follow that all explanations in terms of variations in evaluative schemas are necessarily sterile. It does follow, however, that if such sterility is to be avoided, the concept of a value-schema must be construed as a highly compact formulation of various regularities (most of which are perhaps never explicitly codified, or codified only in vague terms) between types of human behavior.

The point I wish to make is that in imputing a certain schema of values to a community, one is imputing to its mem-

9 R. M. MacIver, *Social Causation*, pp. 338, 374.

bers certain attitudes. But an attitude is not something that can be established by introspection, whether in the case of our own persons or of others. An attitude is a dispositional or latent trait; and it is comparable in its *theoretical* status with viscosity or electrical resistance in physics, even if, unlike the latter, it can be usefully defined for sociopsychological purposes only in statistical terms. In any event, the concept is cognitively valuable only in so far as it effects a systematic organization of manifest data obtained from overt human responses to a variety of conditions, and only in so far as it makes possible the formulation of regularities in such responses. Whether, in point of fact, explanations of social changes in terms of variations in attitudes have a greater systematizing and predictive power than explanations employing different substantive concepts, is not the point at issue, and it cannot be settled by dogmatic *a priori* claims. But if these comments are well taken, there is nothing in such explanations which differentiates them in principle from explanations in the natural sciences, or which requires for their validation a distinctive logic of inquiry.

VII

I will conclude, as I have begun, with some general reflections on the social sciences. Many commentators in recent as well as in earlier years have been in despair over the state of these disciplines, and have doubted the possibility of developing comprehensive and reliable theories of social processes. One reason, though by no means the only one, commonly advanced for this scepticism is the "historical" character of social phenomena—that is, the variation of modes and conditions of social processes with different societies and periods. It is therefore frequently asserted that unlike a law in the natural sciences, an assumed regularity in social matters is at best valid only within a specified institutional setting and only for a limited duration. Snell's law is presumably true for the refraction of light throughout the universe; but the variation of fertility rate with social status which obtains in one community at one time is generally different from what is found in the same or a different community at another time.

It would be futile to dismiss such scepticism as without

foundation, or to deny that human actions are modified by their cultural environment which itself is in constant change. It must be admitted, at least as a possibility, that all social "laws" may have only a narrowly restricted universality. Nevertheless, the scepticism when it is wholesale often has its source in two misconceptions upon which I wish to comment briefly. One of them is the tacit assumption that celestial mechanics is the paradigm of any science worthy of the name; the other is the failure to distinguish between instability or variability in the specific materials and organization of systems, and an abstract uniformity which may nevertheless be pervasive in all the systems.

It has been maintained, for example, that if a science of society

> were a true science, like that of astronomy, it would enable us to predict the essential movements of human affairs for the immediate and the indefinite future, to give pictures of society in the year 2000 or the year 2500 just as astronomers can map the appearance of the heavens at fixed points of time in the future. Such a social science would tell us exactly what is going to happen in the years to come and we should be powerless to change it by an effort of will.[10]

But since "owing to the development of human experience, men . . . are always growing and changing," so that "closed schemes cannot be made out of the data of the social sciences," it is concluded that there cannot be a "social science in any valid sense of the term as employed in real science."[11]

It needs little argument to show that the circumstances which permit long-range predictions in astronomy do not prevail in other branches of natural sciences, and that in this respect celestial mechanics is not a typical physical science. Such predictions are possible because for all practical purposes the solar system is an isolated sytem which will remain isolated, so there is reason to believe, during an indefinitely long future. In most other domains of physical inquiry, however, this condition is not in general satisfied. Moreover, in many cases we are ignorant of the appropriate initial and boundary conditions, and cannot

[10] C. A. Beard, *The Nature of the Social Sciences*, p. 29.
[11] *Ibid.*, pp. 26, 33, 37.

make precise forecasts even though available theory is adequate for that purpose. We can predict with reasonable accuracy the motion of a pendulum, because both the theory and the specific factual data for the system are known; but because we have no reason to assume that the system will continue to be immune indefinitely from external perturbations, the predictions can be made safely only for a limited period. On the other hand, we cannot predict with great accuracy where a fallen leaf will be carried by the wind in ten minutes, because though physical theory is in principle capable of resolving the problem, we do not have the requisite knowledge of the relevant initial conditions. It is clear, therefore, that inability to forecast the indefinite future is not unique to the study of human affairs.

It is, moreover, an obvious error to believe that theoretical knowledge is possible only in those domains in which effective human control is lacking. Crude ores can be transformed into refined products not because no theory for such changes is available, but in large measure just because there is. And conversely, a domain does not cease to be a field for theoretical knowledge if, when suitable techniques have been developed, changes in that domain for which hitherto there has been no control become controllable. Will the principles of meteorology stop being valid, should we discover some day how to manufacture the weather? Men are able to alter various aspects of their social organizations; but this does not establish the impossibility of a "real" science of human affairs.

The fact that social processes vary with their institutional settings, and that the specific uniformities found to hold in one culture are not pervasive in all societies, does not therefore preclude the possibility that these specific uniformities are specializations of relational structures invariant for all cultures. For the admitted differences between the ways in which different societies are organized may be the consequences simply of differences in the specific elements which enter into an invariant pattern of relations. Consider the following purely physical phenomena: a lightning storm, the behavior of a mariner's compass, and the formation of an optical image on the ground glass of a camera. These are quite heterogeneous occurrences, and there is no antecedent reason for suspecting that they illustrate a common set of principles. But as is well known, they can all be understood in terms of modern electromagnetic theory; and though different special laws hold for them, the theory can explain them all when suitable initial and boundary conditions are supplied for each instance.

Despite the variability and instability of social phenomena, they may nevertheless be subsumable under a common theory in an analogous way—though whether this is more than a fancy is at present any man's guess. But some things are fairly clear. If a comprehensive social theory is ever achieved, it will not be a theory of historical development, according to which societies and institutions succeed one another in a series of inevitable changes. Those who are seeking a comprehensive social theory by charting the rise and decline of civilizations, are looking for it in the wrong place. The theory will undoubtedly have to be highly abstract, if it is to cut across the actual cultural differences in human behavior. Its concepts will have to be apparently remote from the familiar and obvious traits found in any one society; its articulation will involve the use of novel algorithmic techniques; and its application to concrete materials will require special training of high order. But above all, it will have to be a theory for which a method of evaluating evidence must be available which does not depend on the vagaries of special insights and private intuitions. It will have to be a theory which, in its method of articulating its concepts and evaluating its evidence, will be continuous with the theories of the natural sciences.

Typological Methods in the Social Sciences[1]

CARL G. HEMPEL

1. Introduction

THE CONCEPT of type has played a significant role in various phases of the development of empirical science. Many of its uses are by now of historical interest only; but some branches of research, especially psychology and the social sciences, have continued up to the present to employ typological concepts for descriptive and for theoretical purposes. In particular, various typologies of character and physique have been propounded as providing fruitful approaches to the study of personality; the investigation of "extreme" or "pure" types of physical and mental constitution has been advocated as a source of insight into the functioning of "normal" individuals; and as for social science, the use of ideal types has been declared one of the methodological characteristics which distinguish it essentially from natural science.

Considering these recent uses of typological concepts and

[1] Reprinted from *Science, Language, and Human Rights* (American Philosophical Association, Eastern Division, Philadelphia: University of Pennsylvania Press, 1952, Vol. I, pp. 65–86), with the permission of the publisher and the approval of the author. The present title is used at Professor Hempel's request. The article was originally entitled "Symposium: Problems of Concept and Theory Formation in the Social Sciences."

the various claims concerning their peculiar significance, it appears to be a matter of some interest and importance to have a reasonably clear understanding of their logical status and their methodological function. Now, there exists a voluminous literature on the subject, but a large part of it suffers from a definite inadequacy of the logical apparatus used for the analysis of the issues at hand. In particular, many of the studies devoted to the logic of typological concepts use only the concepts and principles of classical logic, which is essentially a logic of properties or classes, and thus is incapable of dealing adequately with relations and with quantitative concepts. In a manner illustrative of this situation, Max Weber, who so impressively champions the method of ideal types in the social sciences, makes a clear negative statement about their logical status: they cannot be defined by *genus proximum* and *differentia specifica*, and concrete cases cannot be subsumed under them as instances[2]—i.e., they are not simply class, or property, concepts; but when it comes to a positive characterization, he resorts to much less precise, and often metaphorical, language. An ideal type, according to Weber, is a mental construct formed by the synthesis of many diffuse, more or less present and occasionally absent, concrete individual phenomena, which are arranged, according to certain one-sidedly accentuated points of view, into a unified analytical construct, which in its conceptual purity cannot be found in reality; it is a utopia, a limiting concept, with which concrete phenomena can only be compared for the purpose of explicating some of their significant components.[3] This characterization, and many similar accounts which Weber and others have given of the nature of ideal types, are certainly suggestive, but they lack clarity and rigor and thus call for further logical analysis.

In addition to the logical status of typological concepts, some of the methodological claims which have been made for them appear to me to warrant reëxamination.

The present paper, then, is an attempt to explicate in outline the logical and methodological character of typological concepts, and to appraise their potential significance for the purposes they

---

[2] M. Weber, "'Objectivity' in Social Science and Social Policy," in this book, p. 399.

[3] *Ibid.*, pp. 396–399.

are intended to serve. The proposed investigation will naturally have to use some of the concepts and principles of contemporary logic; but it will not employ any symbolic devices. Our explicatory efforts will repeatedly invite comparative glances at concept formation in the natural sciences. By thus undertaking a comparative examination of certain aspects of the methodology of natural and social science, I hope this study will justify its inclusion in the present symposium on the concept of theory in the social and the physical sciences.

It is a familiar fact that the term "type" has been used in several quite different senses. I propose to distinguish here three main kinds of type concepts, which for brief reference, and pending further clarification, will be called classificatory, extreme, and ideal types. These will now be considered in turn.

2. Classificatory Types

The classificatory use of type concepts is illustrated by Ernst Kretschmer's rather influential typological theory of character and physique,[4] in which types are construed as classes. In this case, the logic of typological procedure is the familiar logic of classification, which requires no discussion here. Methodologically, classificatory type formation, like any other kind of classification in empirical science, is subject to the requirement of systematic fruitfulness: The characteristics which serve to define the different types should not merely provide neat pigeonholes to accommodate all the individual cases in the domain of inquiry, but should lend themselves to sound generalization and thus offer a basis for prediction. Thus, e.g., constitutional typologies often aim at defining their types by reference to certain physical properties which are empirically associated with a variety of psychological traits, so that every type represents a cluster of concomitant characteristics. This objective is the methodological kernel of the search for "natural" as distinguished from "artificial" classes or types.

---

[4] E. Kretschmer, *Physique and Character*. On the theory and technique of classificatory type formation in contemporary social research, see P. F. Lazarsfeld and A. H. Barton, "Qualitative Measurement in the Social Sciences: Classification, Typologies, and Indices," in *The Policy Sciences*, ed. D. Lerner and H. D. Lasswell.

In connection with classificatory types, brief reference should be made to the use of the term "typical" in the sense of "average," for that usage evidently presupposes a classification. Thus, the statement that the typical American college undergraduate is, say, 18.9 years old, purports to state the average value of a certain magnitude for a specified class. But since there are different kinds of average, and since none of these provides much information without an added measure of dispersion, it is clear that for any serious scientific purpose this use of the term "typical" has to be supplanted by a more precise formulation in statistical terms.

3. *Extreme Types*

Attempts at typological classification in empirical science are often frustrated, however, by the realization that those characteristics of the subject matter which are to provide the defining basis of the classification cannot fruitfully be construed as simple property concepts determining, as their extensions, classes with neatly demarcated boundaries. Thus, e.g., if we try to formulate explicit and precise criteria for the distinction of extravert and introvert personalities it soon becomes clear that the adoption of classificatory criteria drawing a precise boundary line between the two categories would prove an "artificial," theoretically sterile procedure: it appears much more natural, much more promising systematically, to construe the two concepts as capable of gradations, so that a given individual will not be qualified either as extravert or as introvert, but as exhibiting each of the two traits to a certain extent. The purely extravert and the purely introvert personalities thus come to be conceived as "extreme" or "pure" types, of which concrete instances are rarely if ever found, but which may serve as conceptual points of reference or "poles," between which all actual occurrences can be ordered in a serial array. This general conception underlies several of the recent and contemporary systems of psychological and physical types, such as, e.g., Sheldon's theory of physique and temperament.[5]

What is the logical form of these "extreme" or "pure" type

[5] W. H. Sheldon, *The Varieties of Human Physique;* and W. H. Sheldon, *The Varieties of Temperament.*

concepts? Clearly, they cannot be construed as class concepts: individual cases cannot be subsumed under them as instances, but can only be characterized as to the extent to which they approximate them. In other words, if the term "*T*" represents an extreme type, an individual *a* cannot be said either to be *T* or to be non-*T;* rather, *a* may be, so to speak, "more or less *T*." But exactly how is this "more or less" to be objectively defined? A description, however vivid, of an extreme type with which concrete cases are to be compared does not by itself provide standards for such comparison; at best, it may suggest a program of research, focusing attention upon certain empirical phenomena and regularities and stimulating efforts toward the development of a precise conceptual apparatus suited for their description and theoretical interpretation. But if an extreme type is to function as a legitimate scientific concept in scientific statements with clear objective meaning, then explicit criteria for the "more or less" of comparison must be provided. These criteria may take a nonnumerical, "purely comparative" form, or they may be based on quantitative devices such as rating scales or measurement.

The formally simplest, purely comparative form of an extreme-type concept *T* can be specified by laying down criteria which determine, for any two individual cases *a*, *b* in the domain under investigation, whether (i) *a* is more *T* than *b*, or (ii) *b* is more *T* than *a*, or (iii) *a* is just as much *T* as is *b*. For the concept of pure introversion as an extreme type, for example, this would require objective criteria determining, for any two individuals *a*, *b* whether they are equally introverted and, if not, which of them is the more introverted. Thus, an extreme type *T* of the purely comparative or ordering kind is defined, not by *genus* and *differentia* in the manner of a class concept, but by specifying two dyadic relations, "more *T* than" and "as much *T* as." Now, if the criteria defining those relations are to yield an ordering of all particular cases in a linear array reflecting increasing *T*-ness, then they must meet certain formal requirements: "more *T* than" must be an asymmetrical and transitive relation, "as much *T* as" must be symmetrical and transitive, and the two together must satisfy a trichotomy law to the effect that any two particular cases *a*, *b* meet the defining conditions for exactly one of the three alternatives (i), (ii), (iii) mentioned above.[6]

The kind of ordering concept here characterized is well illustrated by the definition, in mineralogy, of a purely comparative concept of hardness by reference to the scratch test: A mineral *a* is said to be harder than another, *b*, if a sharp point of a sample of *a* will scratch the surface of a sample of *b*, but not conversely. If neither of the materials is harder than the other, they are said to be of the same hardness. The two relations thus defined might be said to determine a purely comparative extreme type of hardness; but this terminology would tend to obscure rather than clarify the logic of the procedure, and it is not actually used.

In psychology and the social sciences, it is difficult, to say the least, to find fruitful objective criteria, analogous to those based on the scratch test, which will determine a purely comparative typological order. We find therefore that proponents of extreme-type concepts, insofar as they provide precise criteria and not merely suggestive programmatic characterizations, either end by construing their types as classes after all or else specify their typological orders by reference to rating scales or measuring procedures, which define a numerical "degree of T-ness," as it were. The first course is illustrated by Kretschmer's typology of physique and character: it uses the parlance of pure types for an intuitive characterization of the material to be investigated, while for exact formulations, it construes each of the main types as a class and accommodates the intermediate cases in some additional classes, designated as "mixed types." The second course is exemplified by Sheldon's typology of physique, which assigns to each individual a specific position on each of three seven-point scales representing the basic type traits of the theory: endomorphy, mesomorphy, and ectomorphy.

But once suitable "operational" criteria of a strictly comparative or of a quantitative kind have been specified, the pure types lose their special importance: they simply represent extreme places in the ranges defined by the given criteria, and from a systematic point of view, the typological terminology is no more significant than it would be to say that the specific electric

[6] For details, see: C. G. Hempel and P. Oppenheim, *Der Typusbegriff im Lichte der neuen Logik*, ch. 3.

conductivity of a given material indicated how close it came to the extreme, or pure, type of a perfect conductor.

The use of extreme-type concepts of the kind here considered reflects an attempt to proceed from the classificatory, qualitative level of concept formation to the quantitative one; ordering concepts of the purely comparative kind representing an intermediate stage. As long as explicit criteria for their use are lacking, they have, as we noted, essentially a programmatic but no systematic status; and once suitable criteria have been specified, the parlance of extreme types becomes unnecessary, for there are no logical peculiarities which differentiate extreme-type concepts from the other comparative and quantitative concepts of empirical science; their logic is the logic of ordering relations and of measurement; henceforth, we will therefore refer to them also as ordering types.

Methodologically, ordering as well as classificatory typologies belong, as a rule, to an early stage in the growth of a scientific discipline, a stage which is concerned with the development of a largely "empirical" concept system and with its use for description and for low-grade generalization. Systematic fruitfulness, which is an essential requirement for all stages of concept formation, here consists, in the simplest case, in a high correlation between the criteria which "operationally define" a typological order (such as certain anthropometric indices, say) and a variety of other graded traits (such as further anatomical and physiological indices or psychological characteristics). For quantitative scales, such correlations may assume, in favorable cases, the form of a proportionality of several variables (analogous to the proportionality, at constant temperature, of the specific electric and thermic conductivities of metals), or they may consist in other invariant relationships expressible in terms of mathematical functions.[7]

[7] A fuller discussion of the logic and methodology of ordering and quantitative procedures may be found in C. G. Hempel, *Fundamentals of Concept Formation in Empirical Science*, especially Section 11.

On the use of such procedures in typological studies, cf. Lazarsfeld and Barton, *op. cit.*, Hempel and Oppenheim, *op. cit.*, and R. F. Winch, "Heuristic and Empirical Typologies: A Job for Factor Analysis," *American Sociological Review*, XII, 1947, 68–75.

4. Ideal Types and Explanation in the Social Sciences

As was mentioned in the first section, ideal types, too, are usually presented as the results of isolating and exaggerating certain aspects of concrete empirical phenomena, as limiting concepts which are not fully exemplified but at best approximated in reality.[8] Despite the suggestion conveyed by this description, I think that an adequate logical reconstruction has to assign to ideal types a status different from that of the extreme or pure types discussed above. For ideal types—or, as Howard Becker aptly calls them, constructed types—are usually introduced without even an attempt at specifying appropriate criteria of order, and they are not used for the kind of generalization characteristic of ordering types; rather, they are invoked as a specific device for the explanation of social and historical phenomena. I shall try to argue now that this conception reflects an attempt to advance concept formation in sociology from the stage of description and "empirical generalization," which is exemplified by most classificatory and ordering types, to the construction of theoretical systems or models. In order to amplify and substantiate this view, it will be necessary to examine more closely the character and function of ideal types as conceived by its proponents.

According to Max Weber and some writers holding similar views, the use of ideal types makes it possible to explain concrete social or historical phenomena, such as the caste system in India or the development of modern capitalism, in their individuality and uniqueness. Such understanding is held to consist in grasping the particular causal relationships which interconnect the relevant elements of the total occurrence under examination. If such re-

---

[8] For detailed exposition and critical discussion of the concept of ideal type as used in social science, see especially the following works, which have served as guides in the present attempt at analysis and reconstruction: M. Weber, *On the Methodology of the Social Sciences.* M. Weber, *The Theory of Social and Economic Organization.* A. von Schelting, *Max Weber's Wissenschaftslehre.* T. Parsons, *The Structure of Social Action,* ch. 16. H. Becker, *Through Values to Social Interpretation.*

Further stimulating critical discussions of the concept of ideal type may be found in: F. Kaufmann, *Methodenlehre der Sozialwissenschaften,* especially Section 6 of the second part. J. W. N. Watkins, "Ideal Types and Historical Explanation," *The British Journal for the Philosophy of Science,* III, 1952, 22–43.

lationships are to afford a sociologically significant explanation they must be, according to this view, not only "causally adequate" but also meaningful, i.e., they must refer to aspects of human behavior which are intelligibly actuated by valuation or other motivating factors. Weber characterizes the principles expressing those connections as "general empirical rules" concerning the ways in which human beings are prone to react in given situations; the "nomological knowledge" conveyed by them is said to be derived from our own experience and from our knowledge of the conduct of others. Weber mentions Gresham's law as a generalization of this kind: it is empirically well substantiated by the pertinent information available, and it is "a rationally clear interpretation of human action under certain conditions and under the assumption that it will follow a purely rational course."[9]

As for specific ways of discovering meaningful explanatory principles, Weber mentions the method of empathic understanding but adds the reminder that it is neither universally applicable nor always dependable. And indeed, as is made clear by the fuller argument presented in Professor Nagel's paper, the subjective experience of empathic identification with a historical figure, and of an immediate—almost self-evidently certain—insight into his motivations, constitutes no knowledge, no scientific understanding at all, though it may be a guide in the search for explicit general hypotheses of the kind required for a systematic explanation. In fact, the occurrence of an empathic state in the interpreter is neither a necessary nor a sufficient condition of sound interpretation or understanding in the scientific sense: not necessary, for, as Professor Nagel's illustration shows, an appropriate theory of psychopathic behavior may provide the historian with an explanation of some phases of Hitler's actions even in the absence of empathic identification; not sufficient, for the motivational hypotheses suggested by the empathic experience may be factually unsound.

Weber himself stresses that verification of subjective interpretation is always indispensable; he adds that in the absence of adequate experimental or observational data, "there is available

[9] *The Theory of Social and Economic Organization*, p. 98; cf. also pp. 107–109.

only the dangerous and uncertain procedure of the 'imaginary experiment' which consists in thinking away certain elements of a chain of motivation and working out the course of action which would then probably ensue, thus arriving at a causal judgment."[10] By thus establishing what *would* have happened *if* certain specified constituents of the situation had been different, this method yields "judgments of objective possibility," which form the basis of causal imputation in the social sciences. Those judgments evidently have the form of contrary-to-fact conditionals, and students of the currently much discussed logic of counterfactuals might be interested in Weber's fascinating illustration of the proposed method by reference to interpretive problems of historiography, among them the question of the significance of the Persian Wars for the development of Western culture;[11] Weber's discussion of these topics shows how well he was aware of the close connection between contrary-to-fact conditionals and general laws.

An ideal type, then, is meant to serve as an interpretive or explanatory schema embodying a set of "general empirical rules" which establish "subjectively meaningful" connections between different aspects of some kind of phenomenon, such as purely rational economic behavior, a capitalistic society, a handicraft economy, a religious sect, or the like. But then, in intent at least, ideal types represent not concepts properly speaking, but rather theories; and the idea naturally suggests itself that if those theories are to serve their purpose, they must have a character quite similar to that of the theory of ideal gases, say.[12] To elaborate and substantiate this conception, I will first try to show that the alleged differences between the explanatory use of ideal types and the method of explanation in natural science are spurious; then (in section 5) I will attempt a brief compara-

---

[10] *Ibid.*, p. 97.

[11] *The Methodology of the Social Sciences*, pp. 164–188. An illuminating amplification and examination of Weber's analysis may be found in von Schelting, *op. cit.*, pp. 269–281.

[12] Parallels between ideal types and certain idealizations in physics have often been drawn, of course (cf., e.g., Weber, *The Theory of Social and Economic Organization*, p. 110; Becker, *op. cit.*, p. 125). It seems important, however, to make explicit the similarities involved and to show that they do not accord with the claim of a status *sui generis* for ideal-type concepts in the social sciences.

tive analysis of the status of "idealized" concepts, and the corresponding theories, in natural and social science.

In natural science, to explain a concrete event means to explain the occurrence of some repeatable characteristic (a rise in temperature, the presence of corrosion, a drop in blood pressure, etc.) in a particular, i.e., at a specified place or in a specified object at a given moment or during a certain period of time (the air in New Haven during the morning hours of September 5, 1952, the hull of a specified ship, patient John Doe at a given time). Explanation of a concrete event does not and cannot reasonably mean an account of *all* the repeatable characteristics of a given particular, say b. For the latter include the fact that in such and such directions and at such and such spatiotemporal distances from b, there are particulars having such and such repeatable properties; as a consequence, to explain *all* the repeatable aspects of b is tantamount to explaining every concrete fact in the universe—past, present, and future. Evidently this kind of explaining a concrete occurrence "in its uniqueness" is no more accessible to sociology than it is to physics; in fact, even its precise *meaning* is quite problematic. Thus, all that can be significantly sought is the explanation of the occurrence of some repeatable characteristic U (which may be quite complex, of course) in a given particular b. The task of explaining Western capitalism in its uniqueness, for example, has to be construed in this fashion if it is to be at all significant; and it is then strictly analogous to the problem of explaining the solar eclipse of March 18, 1950. In either case, there are certain characteristics—their combination is referred to as U above—for whose occurrence an explanation is sought (in the case of the eclipse, e.g., those characteristics might include the fact that the eclipse was annular, not visible in the United States, of a duration of 4 hours and 42 minutes, etc.), but there are innumerable other characteristics for which no account is intended (such as, say, the number of newspapers in which the event was described). It is worth noting here that the event thus to be explained, $U(b)$ for short, is still unique because the particular b is unrepeatable.

In natural science, to explain a unique concrete event, say $U(b)$, amounts to showing that it had to be expected in view of certain other concrete events which are prior to or contemporaneous with it, and by virtue of specifiable general laws or theories. Formally, such explanation consists in the deduction of "$U(b)$" from those general principles and from the "boundary conditions" describing the antecedent and contemporaneous concrete occurrences.

As Max Weber's writings clearly show, an adequate explanation of a concrete event in sociology or historiography has to be of essentially the same character. Reliance on empathic insight and subjective "understanding" provides no warrant of objective validity, no basis for the systematic prediction or postdiction of specific phenomena; the latter procedures have to be based on general empirical rules, on nomological knowledge. Weber's limitation of the explanatory principles of sociology to "meaningful" rules of intelligible behavior, on the other hand, is untenable: many, if not all, occurrences of interest to the social scientist require, for their explanation, reference to factors which are "devoid of subjective meaning," and accordingly also to "non-understandable uniformities," to use Weber's terminology. Weber acknowledges that the sociologist must accept such facts as causally significant data, but he insists that this does "not in the least alter the specific task of sociological analysis . . ., which is the interpretation of action in terms of its subjective meaning."[13] But this conception bars from the field of sociology any theory of behavior which foregoes the use of "subjectively meaningful" motivational concepts. This either means a capricious limitation of the concept of sociology—which, as a result, might eventually become inapplicable to any phase of scientific research—or else it amounts to an *a priori* judgment on the character of any set of concepts which can possibly yield explanatory sociological theories. Clearly, such an *a priori* verdict is indefensible, and indeed, the more recent development of psychological and social theory shows that it is possible to formulate explanatory principles for purposive action in purely behavioristic, nonintrospective terms.

In discussing, next, the role of experiments-in-imagination, which are, of course, well known also in the natural sciences, it will be useful to distinguish *two kinds of imaginary experiment: the intuitive and the theoretical.* An intuitive experiment-in-

[13] *The Theory of Social and Economic Organization*, p. 94.

imagination is aimed at anticipating the outcome of an experimental procedure which is just imagined, but which may well be capable of being actually performed. Prediction is guided here by past experience concerning particular phenomena and their regularities, and occasionally by belief in certain general principles which are accepted as if they were *a priori* truths; thus, e.g., in "explaining" the equidistribution of results obtained in rolling a regular die, or in anticipating similar results for a game with a regular homogeneous dodecahedron, certain rules of symmetry, such as the principle of insufficient reason, are often invoked; and similar principles are sometimes adduced in imaginary experiments involving levers and other physical systems with certain symmetry features. Imaginary experiments of this kind are intuitive in the sense that the assumptions and data underlying the prediction are not made explicit and indeed may not even enter into the conscious process of anticipation at all: past experience and the—possibly unconscious—belief in certain general principles function here as suggestive guides for imaginative anticipation rather than as a theoretical basis for systematic prediction.

The theoretical kind of imaginary experiment, on the other hand, presupposes a set of explicitly stated general principles—such as laws of nature—and it anticipates the outcome of the experiment by strict deduction from those principles in combination with suitable boundary conditions representing the relevant aspects of the experimental situation. Sometimes, the latter is not actually realizable, as when the laws for an ideal mathematical pendulum or for perfectly elastic impact are deduced from more general principles of theoretical mechanics. The question what *would* happen *if*, say, the thread of a pendulum were infinitely thin and perfectly rigid and if the mass of the pendulum were concentrated in the free end point of the thread is answered here, not by "thinking away" those aspects of a physical pendulum that are at variance with this assumption and then trying to envisage the outcome, but by rigorous deduction from available theoretical principles. Imagination does not enter here; the experiment is imaginary only in the sense that the situation it refers to is not actually realized and may indeed be technically incapable of realization.

The two types of experiment-in-imagination here distinguished constitute extreme types, as it were, which are rarely realized in their pure form: in many cases, the empirical assumptions and the reasoning underlying an imaginary experiment are made highly, but not fully, explicit. Galileo's dialogues contain excellent examples of this procedure, which show how fruitful the method can be in suggesting general theoretical insights. But, of course, intuitive experiments-in-imagination are no substitute for the collection of empirical data by actual experimental or observational procedures. This is well illustrated by the numerous, intuitively quite plausible, imaginary experiments which have been adduced in an effort to refute the special theory of relativity; and as for imaginary experimentation in the social sciences, its customary reliance on empathy underscores its fallibility. Professor Nagel's example of an attempt to anticipate the behavior of a trader in grain provides a good illustration of this kind of mental experimentation. Thus, the results of intuitive experiments-in-imagination cannot strictly constitute evidence pertinent to the test of sociological hypotheses; rather, the method has an essentially heuristic function: it serves to *suggest* hypotheses, which must then be subjected, however, to appropriate objective testing procedures.

The imaginary experiments mentioned by such writers as Max Weber and Howard Becker as a method of sociological inquiry are obviously of the intuitive variety; their heuristic function is to aid in the discovery of regular connections between various constituents of some social structure or process. These connections can then be incorporated into an ideal type and thus provide the basis for the explanatory use of the latter.

5. Ideal Types and Theoretical Models

We have argued that since ideal types are intended to provide explanation, they must be construed as theoretical systems embodying testable general hypotheses. To what extent is this conception reconcilable with the frequent insistence, on the part of proponents of the method, that ideal types are not meant to be hypotheses to be verified by empirical evidence, that deviation from concrete fact is of their very essence? As a point of departure in dealing with this question, let us consider more closely

how those who hold such views conceive of the application of
ideal-type concepts to concrete phenomena. There are few precise statements on this subject; perhaps the most explicit formulation has been given by Howard Becker, in an effort to develop
what he terms "a logical formula for typology." Becker suggests
that ideal, or constructed, types function in hypotheses of the
form "If P then Q," where P is the type invoked, and Q is
some more or less complex characteristic.[14] Concerning the application of such hypotheses to empirical data, Becker says: "In the
very nature of type construction, however, the consequent seldom if ever follows empirically, and the antecedent is then empirically 'false.' If Q' then P'."[15] By this deviation from empirical
fact, by the occurrence of Q' rather than Q, a constructed type
acquires what Becker calls "negative utility": it initiates a search
for factors other than those embodied in P to account for the
discrepancy.[16] In this manner, according to Becker, "constructive
typology makes *planned* use of the proviso 'All other conditions
being equal or irrelevant' for the purpose of determining the
'inequality' or 'relevance' of the 'other conditions.' "[17]

This view calls for closer analysis, for it suggests—perhaps
unintentionally—the use of the *ceteris paribus* clause for a con-
ventionalistic defense of typological hypotheses against any
conceivable disconfirming evidence.[18] To illustrate this point, let
us imagine, by way of analogy, a physicist propounding the
hypothesis that under ideal conditions, namely in a vacuum near
the surface of the Earth, a body falling freely for t seconds will

[14] *Op. cit.*, pp. 259–264. Becker describes the connection between P and
Q as one of "objective probability." But since he uses the expression "If P
then Q" in an inference of the *modus tollens* form, which does not hold for
probabilistic implication—i.e., for statements of the form, "If P then probably Q"—it seems more adequate to construe Becker's remark as meaning
that "If P then Q" is a typological hypothesis expressing an empirical generalization in Weber's sense. Such a generalization, like any other empirical
hypothesis, can of course be only probable, and never certain, relatively
to any body of pertinent factual evidence.
[15] *Op. cit.*, p. 262.
[16] M. Weber has similarly pointed to the heuristic utility of ideal types;
cf. e.g., " 'Objectivity' in Social Science and Social Policy," in this book,
pp. 396, 407–409; *The Theory of Social and Economic Organization*, p. 111.
[17] H. Becker, *op. cit.*, p. 264.
[18] On the use of the *ceteris paribus* clause, see also the excellent discussion in F. Kaufmann, *Methodology of the Social Sciences*, pp. 84 f, 213 f.

cover a distance of exactly $16t^2$ feet. Suppose now that a careful experiment yields results differing from those required by the hypothesis. Then clearly the physicist cannot be content simply to infer that the requisite ideal conditions were not realized: in addition to this possibility, he has to allow for the alternative that the hypothesis under test is not correct. To state the point now in terms of Becker's general schema: we could infer that P is not realized only if, in addition to the observational finding Q', we could take the truth of the hypothesis "If P then Q" for granted; but for this assumption, we surely have no warrant; in fact, it would make the entire test pointless. Thus, from the occurrence of Q', we can infer only that either P was not realized or the hypothesis, "If P then Q," is false.

Now, it might seem that we may with assurance assert our typological hypothesis if only we qualify it by an appropriate *ceteris paribus* clause and thus give it the form: "All other factors being equal or irrelevant, Q will be realized whenever P is realized." Evidently, no empirical evidence can ever disconfirm a hypothesis of this form since an apparently unfavorable finding can always be attributed to a violation of the *ceteris paribus* clause by the interference of factors other than those specifically included in P. In other words, the qualified hypothesis can be made unexceptionable by the convention to plead violation of the *ceteris paribus* clause whenever an occurrence of P is not accompanied by an occurrence of Q. But the very convention that renders the hypothesis irrefutable also drains it of all empirical content and thus of explanatory power: since the protective clause does not specify *what* factors other than P have to be equal (i.e., constant) or irrelevant if the prediction of Q is to be warranted, the hypothesis is not capable of predictive application to concrete phenomena. Similarly, the idea of testing the given hypothesis becomes pointless. It is significant to note here by contrast that in the formulation of physical hypotheses, the *ceteris paribus* clause is never used: all the factors considered relevant are explicitly stated (as in Newton's law of gravitation or in Maxwell's laws) or are clearly understood (as in the familiar formulation of Galileo's law, which is understood to refer to free fall in a vacuum near the surface of the Earth); all other factors are asserted, by implication, to be irrelevant. Empirical test is therefore significant, and the discovery of discordant evidence requires appropriate revisions either by modifying the presumed functional connections between the variables singled out as relevant, or by explicitly introducing new relevant variables. Ideal-type hypotheses will have to follow the same pattern if they are to afford a theoretical explanation of concrete historical and social phenomena rather than an empirically vacuous conceptual schematism.

But is it not true, after all, that in physics as well, there are theories, such as those of ideal gases, of perfectly elastic impact, of the mathematical pendulum, of the statistical aspects of a game played with perfect dice, etc., which are not held to be invalidated by the fact that they possess no precise exemplification in the empirical world? And could not ideal types claim the same status as the central concepts of those "idealized" theories? Those concepts refer to physical systems satisfying certain extreme conditions which cannot be fully, but only approximately, met by concrete empirical phenomena. Their scientific significance lies, I think, in the following points: (a) The laws governing the behavior of the ideal physical systems are deducible from more comprehensive theoretical principles, which are well confirmed by empirical evidence; the deduction usually takes the form of assigning certain extreme values to some of the parameters of the comprehensive theory. Thus, e.g., the laws for an ideal gas are obtainable from more inclusive principles of the kinetic theory of gases by "assuming" that the volumes of the gas molecules vanish and that there are no forces of attraction among the molecules—i.e., by setting the appropriate parameters equal to zero. (b) The extreme conditions characterizing the "ideal" case can at least be approximated empirically, and whenever this is the case in a concrete instance, the ideal laws in question are empirically confirmed. Thus, e.g., the Boyle-Charles law for ideal gases is rather closely satisfied by a large variety of gases within wide, specifiable ranges of pressure and temperature (for a fixed mass of gas), and it is for this reason that the law can be significantly invoked for explanatory purposes.

The preceding analysis suggests the following observations on the "ideal" and the empirical aspects of ideal-type concepts in the social sciences:

(i) "Ideal" constructs have the character not of concepts in the narrower sense, but of theoretical systems. The introduction of such a construct into a theoretical context requires, therefore, not definition by *genus* and *differentia*, but the specification of a set of characteristics (such as pressure, temperature, and volume in the case of an ideal gas) *and* of a set of general hypotheses connecting those characteristics.

(ii) An idealized concept *P* does *not*, therefore, function in hypotheses of the simple form "If *P* then *Q*." Thus, e.g., the hypothesis "If a substance is an ideal gas then it satisfies Boyle's law," which is of that form, is an analytic statement entailed by the definition of an ideal gas; it cannot serve explanatory purposes. Rather, the hypotheses characterizing the concept of ideal gas connect certain quantitative characteristics of a gas, and when they are applied to concrete physical systems, they make specific empirical predictions. Thus, to put the point in a somewhat oversimplified form, what enters into physical theory is not the concept of ideal gas at all, but rather the concepts representing the various characteristics dealt with in the theory of ideal gases; only they are mentioned in the principles of thermodynamics.

(iii) In the natural sciences at least, a set of hypotheses is considered as characterizing an ideal system only if they represent what might be called *theoretical*, rather than *intuitive*, idealizations; i.e., if they are obtainable, within the framework of a given theory, as special cases of more inclusive principles. Thus, e.g., the formula for the mathematical pendulum as empirically discovered by Galileo did not constitute a theoretical idealization until after the establishment of more comprehensive hypotheses which (a) have independent empirical confirmation, (b) entail the pendulum formula as a special case, (c) enable us to judge the degree of idealization involved in the latter by giving an account of additional factors which are relevant for the motion of a physical pendulum, but whose influence is fairly small in the case of those physical systems to which the formula is customarily applied.

No theory, of course, however inclusive, can claim to give a completely accurate account of any class of empirical phenomena; it is always possible that even a very comprehensive and well-confirmed theory may be improved in the future by the inclusion of further parameters and appropriate laws: the most comprehensive theory of today may be but a systematic idealization within the broader theoretical framework of tomorrow.

Among the ideal-type concepts of social theory, those used in analytical economics approximate most closely the status of idealizations in natural science: the concepts of perfectly free competition, of monopoly, of economically rational behavior on the part of an individual or a firm, etc., all represent schemata for the interpretation of certain aspects of human behavior and involve the idealizing assumption that noneconomic factors of the sort that do in fact influence human actions may be neglected for the purposes at hand. In the context of rigorous theory construction, those ideal constructs are given a precise meaning in the form of hypotheses which "postulate" specified mathematical connections between certain economic variables; frequently, such postulates characterize the ideal type of behavior as maximizing a given function of those variables (say, profit).

In two important respects, however, idealizations in economics seem to me to differ from those of the natural sciences: first of all, they are intuitive rather than theoretical idealizations in the sense that the corresponding "postulates" are not deduced, as special cases, from a broader theory which covers also the nonrational and noneconomic factors affecting human conduct. No suitable more general theory is available at present, and thus there is no theoretical basis for an appraisal of the idealization involved in applying the economic constructs to concrete situations. This takes us to the second point of difference: the class of concrete behavioral phenomena for which the "idealized" principles of economic theory are meant to constitute at least approximately correct generalizations is not always clearly specified. This of course hampers the significant explanatory use of those principles: an ideal theoretical system, as indeed any theoretical system at all, can assume the status of an explanatory and predictive apparatus only if its area of application has been specified; in other words, if its constituent concepts have been given an empirical interpretation which, directly or at least mediately, links them to observable phenomena. Thus, e.g., the area of application for the theory of ideal gases might be indicated, roughly speaking, by interpreting the theoretical parameters "P," "V," "T" in terms of the "operationally defined" magnitudes of pressure, volume, and temperature of gases at moderate or low pressures and at moderate or high temperatures. Similarly, the empirical applicability of the principles of an ideal economic system requires an interpretation in empirical terms which does not render those principles analytic; hence the interpretation must not amount to the statement that the propositions of the theory hold in all cases of economically rational behavior—that would be simply a tautology; rather, it has to characterize, by criteria logically independent of the theory, those kinds of individual or group behavior to which the theory is claimed to be applicable. In reference to these, it has then to attach a reasonably definite "operational meaning" to the theoretical parameters, such as "money," "price," "cost," "profit," "utility," etc. In this fashion, the propositions of the theory acquire empirical import: they become capable of test and thus susceptible to disconfirmation—and this is an essential characteristic of all potential explanatory systems.

The results of the preceding comparison between the ideal constructs of economics with those of physics should not be considered, however, as indicating an essential methodological difference between the two fields. For in regard to the first of our two points of comparison, it need only be remembered that much effort in sociological theorizing at present is directed toward the development of a comprehensive theory of social action, relatively to which the ideal constructs of economics, in so far as they permit of empirical application, might then have the status of theoretical rather than intuitive idealizations. And quite apart from the attainability of that ambitious goal, it is clear that an interpretation is required for any theoretical system which is to have empirical import—in the social no less than in the natural sciences.

The ideal types invoked in other fields of social science lack the clarity and precision of the constructions used in theoretical economics. The behavioral regularities which are meant to define a given ideal type are usually stated only in more or less intuitive terms, and the parameters they are meant to connect are not explicitly specified; finally, there is no clear indication of the area of empirical applicability and consequent testability claimed for the typological system. In fact, the demand for such testability is often rejected in a sweeping manner which, I think, the preceding discussion has shown to be inconsistent with the claim that ideal types provide an understanding of certain empirical phenomena.

If the analysis here outlined is essentially sound, then surely ideal types can serve their purpose only if they are introduced as interpreted theoretical systems, i.e., by (a) specifying a list of characteristics with which the theory is to deal, (b) formulating a set of hypotheses in terms of those characteristics, (c) giving those characteristics an empirical interpretation, which assigns to the theory a specific domain of application, and (d), as a long-range objective, incorporating the theoretical system, as a "special case," into a more comprehensive theory. To what extent these objectives can be attained cannot be decided by logical analysis; but it would be self-deception to believe that any conceptual procedure essentially lacking in the first three respects can give theoretical understanding in any field of scientific inquiry. And to the extent that the program here outlined can actually be carried through, the use of "ideal types" is at best an unimportant terminological aspect, rather than a distinctive methodological characteristic, of the social sciences: the method of ideal types becomes indistinguishable from the methods used by other scientific disciplines in the formation and application of explanatory concepts and theories.

6. Conclusion

In sum, then, the various uses of type concepts in psychology and the social sciences, when freed from certain misleading connotations, prove to be of exactly the same character as the methods of classification, ordering, measurement, empirical correlation, and finally theory formation used in the natural sciences. In leading to this result, the analysis of typological procedures exhibits, in a characteristic example, the methodological unity of empirical science.

Concept and Theory Formation
in the Social Sciences[1]

ALFRED SCHUTZ

THE TITLE of my paper refers intentionally to that of a Symposium held in December, 1952, at the annual meeting of the American Philosophical Association.[2] Ernest Nagel and Carl G. Hempel contributed highly stimulating comments on the problem involved, formulated in the careful and lucid way so characteristic of these scholars. Their topic is a controversy which for more than half a century has split not only logicians and methodologists but also social scientists into two schools of thought. One of these holds that the methods of the natural sciences which have brought about such magnificent results are the only scientific ones and that they alone, therefore, have to be applied in their entirety to the study of human affairs. Failure to do so, it has been maintained, prevented the social sciences from developing systems of explanatory theory comparable in precision to those offered by the natural sciences and makes

---

[1] This article appeared originally in *The Journal of Philosophy* (Vol. LI, No. 9, April 29, 1954, pp. 257–273) and is reprinted with corrections in Alfred Schutz, *Collected Papers I: The Problem of Social Reality*, ed. and intro., by Maurice Natanson with a preface by H. L. Van Breda, The Hague: Martinus Nijhoff, 1962, pp. 48–66. It is reprinted here with the permission of *The Journal of Philosophy* and Martinus Nijhoff. The 1962 text has been used.

[2] Included in this book, pp. 189–230.

debatable the empirical work of theories developed in restricted domains such as economics.

The other school of thought feels that there is a basic difference in the structure of the social world and the world of nature. This feeling led to the other extreme, namely the conclusion that the methods of the social sciences are *toto coelo* different from those of the natural sciences. In order to support this position a variety of arguments was proffered. It has been maintained that the social sciences are idiographic, characterized by individualizing conceptualization and seeking singular assertory propositions, whereas the natural sciences are nomothetic, characterized by generalizing conceptualization and seeking general apodictic propositions. The latter have to deal with constant relations of magnitude which can be measured and can perform experiments, whereas neither measurement nor experiment is practicable in the social sciences. In general, it is held that the natural sciences have to deal with material objects and processes, the social sciences, however, with psychological and intellectual ones and that, therefore, the method of the former consists in explaining, that of the latter in understanding.

Admittedly, most of these highly generalized statements are untenable under closer examination, and this for several reasons. Some proponents of the characterized arguments had a rather erroneous concept of the methods of the natural sciences. Others were inclined to identify the methodological situation in one particular social science with the method of the social sciences in general. Because history has to deal with unique and non-recurrent events, it was contended that all social sciences are restricted to singular assertory propositions. Because experiments are hardly possible in cultural anthropology, the fact was ignored that social psychologists can successfully use laboratory experiments at least to a certain extent. Finally, and this is the most important point, these arguments disregard the fact that a set of rules for scientific procedure is equally valid for all empirical sciences whether they deal with objects of nature or with human affairs. Here and there, the principles of controlled inference and verification by fellow scientists and the theoretical ideals of unity, simplicity, universality, and precision prevail.

This unsatisfactory state of affairs results chiefly from the fact that the development of the modern social sciences occurred during a period in which the science of logic was mostly concerned with the logic of the natural sciences. In a kind of monopolistic imperialism the methods of the latter were frequently declared to be the only scientific ones and the particular problems which social scientists encountered in their work were disregarded. Left without help and guidance in their revolt against this dogmatism, the students of human affairs had to develop their own conceptions of what they believed to be the methodology of the social sciences. They did it without sufficient philosophical knowledge and stopped their effort when they reached a level of generalization which seemed to justify their deeply felt conviction that the goal of their inquiry could not be reached by adopting the methods of the natural sciences without modification or implementation. No wonder that their arguments are frequently ill-founded, their formulations insufficient, and that many misunderstandings obfuscate the controversy. Not what social scientists *said* but what they *meant* is therefore our main concern in the following.

The writings of the late Felix Kaufmann[3] and the more recent contributions by Nagel[4] and Hempel[5] have criticized many fallacies in the arguments proposed by social scientists and prepared the ground for another approach to the problem. I shall here concentrate on Professor Nagel's criticism of the claim made by Max Weber and his school that the social sciences seek to "understand" social phenomena in terms of "meaningful" categories of human experience and that, therefore, the "causal functional" approach of the natural sciences is not applicable in social inquiry. This school, as Dr. Nagel sees it, maintains that all socially significant human behavior is an expression of motivated psychic states, that in consequence the social scientist cannot be satisfied with viewing social processes simply as concatenations of "externally related" events, and that the establishment of correlations or even of universal relations of concomitance cannot be his ultimate goal. On the contrary, he must construct "ideal types" or "models of motivations" in terms

[3] Especially his *Methodology of the Social Sciences*.
[4] In this book, pp. 189–209.
[5] *Ibid.*, pp. 210–230.

of which he seeks to "understand" overt social behavior by imputing springs of action to the actors involved in it. If I understand Professor Nagel's criticism correctly, he maintains:

1) That these springs of action are not accessible to sensory observation. It follows and has frequently been stated that the social scientist must imaginatively identify himself with the participants and view the situation which they face as the actors themselves view it. Surely, however, we need not undergo other men's psychic experiences in order to know that they have them or in order to predict their overt behavior.

2) That the imputation of emotions, attitudes, and purposes as an explanation of overt behavior is a twofold hypothesis: it assumes that the agents participating in some social phenomenon are in certain psychological states; and it assumes also definite relations of concomitance between such states, and between such states and overt behavior. Yet none of the psychological states which we imagine the subjects of our study to possess may in reality be theirs, and even if our imputations should be correct none of the overt actions which allegedly issue from those states may appear to us understandable or reasonable.

3) That we do not "understand" the nature and operations of human motives and their issuance in overt behavior more adequately than the "external" causal relations. If by meaningful explanation we assert merely that a particular action is an instance of a pattern of behavior which human beings exhibit under a variety of circumstances and that, since some of the relevant circumstances are realized in the given situation, a person can be expected to manifest a certain form of that pattern, then there is no sharp gulf separating such explanations from those involving merely "external" knowledge of causal connections. It is possible to gain knowledge of the actions of men on the evidence supplied by their overt behavior just as it is possible to discover and know the atomic constitution of water on the evidence supplied by the physical and chemical behavior of that substance. Hence the rejection of a purely "objective" or "behavioristic" social science by the proponents of "meaningful connections" as the goal of social sciences is unwarranted.

Since I shall have to disagree with Nagel's and Hempel's findings on several questions of a fundamental nature, I might be permitted to start with a brief summary of the no less important points on which I find myself happily in full agreement with them. I agree with Professor Nagel that all empirical knowledge involves discovery through processes of controlled inference, and that it must be statable in propositional form and capable of being verified by anyone who is prepared to make the effort to do so through observation[6]—although I do not believe, as Professor Nagel does, that this observation has to be sensory in the precise meaning of this term. Moreover, I agree with him that "theory" means in all empirical sciences the explicit formulation of determinate relations between a set of variables in terms of which a fairly extensive class of empirically ascertainable regularities can be explained.[7] Furthermore, I agree wholeheartedly with his statement that neither the fact that these regularities have in the social sciences a rather narrowly restricted universality, nor the fact that they permit prediction only to a rather limited extent, constitutes a basic difference between the social and the natural sciences, since many branches of the latter show the same features.[8] As I shall try to show later on, it seems to me that Professor Nagel misunderstands Max Weber's postulate of subjective interpretation. Nevertheless, he is right in stating that a method which would require that the individual scientific observer identify himself with the social agent observed in order to understand the motives of the latter, or a method which would refer the selection of the facts observed and their interpretation to the private value system of the particular observer, would merely lead to an uncontrollable private and subjective image in the mind of this particular student of human affairs, but never to a scientific theory.[9] But I do not know of any social scientist of stature who ever advocated such a concept of subjectivity as that criticized by Professor Nagel. Most certainly this was not the position of Max Weber.

I also think that our authors are prevented from grasping the point of vital concern to social scientists by their basic philosophy of sensationalistic empiricism or logical positivism, which identifies experience with sensory observation and which assumes that the only alternative to controllable and, therefore,

---

[6] *Ibid.*, p. 202.
[7] *Ibid.*, p. 192.
[8] *Ibid.*, p. 206 f.
[9] *Ibid.*, pp. 201–203.

objective sensory observation is that of subjective and, therefore, uncontrollable and unverifiable introspection. This is certainly not the place to renew the age old controversy relating to the hidden presuppositions and implied metaphysical assumptions of this basic philosophy. On the other hand, in order to account for my own position, I should have to treat at length certain principles of phenomenology. Instead of doing so, I propose to defend a few rather simple propositions:

1) The primary goal of the social sciences is to obtain organized knowledge of social reality. By the term "social reality" I wish to be understood the sum total of objects and occurrences within the social cultural world as experienced by the common-sense thinking of men living their daily lives among their fellow-men, connected with them in manifold relations of interaction. It is the world of cultural objects and social institutions into which we all are born, within which we have to find our bearings, and with which we have to come to terms. From the outset, we, the actors on the social scene, experience the world we live in as a world both of nature and of culture, not as a private but as an intersubjective one, that is, as a world common to all of us, either actually given or potentially accessible to everyone; and this involves intercommunication and language.

2) All forms of naturalism and logical empiricism simply take for granted this social reality, which is the proper object of the social sciences. Intersubjectivity, interaction, intercommunication, and language are simply presupposed as the unclarified foundation of these theories. They assume, as it were, that the social scientist has already solved his fundamental problem, before scientific inquiry starts. To be sure, Dewey emphasized, with a clarity worthy of this eminent philosopher, that all inquiry starts and ends within the social cultural matrix; to be sure, Professor Nagel is fully aware of the fact that science and its self-correcting process is a social enterprise.[10] But the postulate of describing and explaining human behavior in terms of controllable sensory observation stops short before the description and explanation of the process by which scientist B controls and verifies the observational findings of scientist A and the conclusions drawn by him. In order to do so, B has to know what

10 *Ibid.*, p. 199.

A has observed, what the goal of his inquiry is, why he thought the observed fact worthy of being observed, *i.e.*, relevant to the scientific problem at hand, etc. This knowledge is commonly called understanding. The explanation of how such a mutual understanding of human beings might occur is apparently left to the social scientist. But whatever his explanation might be, one thing is sure, namely, that such an intersubjective understanding between scientist B and scientist A occurs neither by scientist B's observations of scientist A's overt behavior, nor by introspection performed by B, nor by identification of B with A. To translate this argument into the language dear to logical positivism, this means, as Felix Kaufmann[11] has shown, that so-called protocol propositions about the physical world are of an entirely different kind than protocol propositions about the psycho-physical world.

3) The identification of experience with sensory observation in general and of the experience of overt action in particular (and that is what Nagel proposes) excludes several dimensions of social reality from all possible inquiry.

a) Even an ideally refined behaviorism can, as has been pointed out for instance by George H. Mead,[12] merely explain the behavior of the observed, not of the observing behaviorist.

b) The same overt behavior (say a tribal pageant as it can be captured by the movie camera) may have an entirely different meaning to the performers. What interests the social scientist is merely whether it is a war dance, a barter trade, the reception of a friendly ambassador, or something else of this sort.

c) Moreover, the concept of human action in terms of common-sense thinking and of the social sciences includes what may be called "negative actions," *i.e.*, intentional refraining from acting,[13] which, of course, escapes sensory observation. Not to sell certain merchandise at a given price is doubtless as economic an action as to sell it.

d) Furthermore, as W. I. Thomas has shown,[14] social reality contains elements of beliefs and convictions which are real

[11] *Op. cit.*, p. 126.

[12] *Mind, Self and Society.*

[13] See M. Weber, *The Theory of Social and Economic Organization*, p. 88.

[14] See W. I. Thomas, *Social Behavior and Personality*, ed. E. H. Volkart, p. 81.

because they are so defined by the participants and which escape sensory observation. To the inhabitants of Salem in the seventeenth century, witchcraft was not a delusion but an element of their social reality and is as such open to investigation by the social scientist.

e) Finally, and this is the most important point, the postulate of sensory observation of overt human behavior takes as a model a particular and relatively small sector of the social world, namely, situations in which the acting individual is given to the observer in what is commonly called a face-to-face relationship. But there are many other dimensions of the social world in which situations of this kind do not prevail. If we put a letter in the mailbox we assume that anonymous fellow-men, called postmen, will perform a series of manipulations, unknown and unobservable to us, with the effect that the addressee, possibly also unknown to us, will receive the message and react in a way which also escapes our sensory observation; and the result of all this is that we receive the book we have ordered. Or if I read an editorial stating that France fears the re-armament of Germany, I know perfectly well what this statement means without knowing the editorialist and even without knowing a Frenchman or a German, let alone without observing their overt behavior.

In terms of common-sense thinking in everyday life men have knowledge of these various dimensions of the social world in which they live. To be sure, this knowledge is not only fragmentary since it is restricted principally to certain sectors of this world, it is also frequently inconsistent in itself and shows all degrees of clarity and distinctness from full insight or "knowledge-about," as James[15] called it, through "knowledge of acquaintance" or mere familiarity, to blind belief in things just taken for granted. In this respect there are considerable differences from individual to individual and from social group to social group. Yet, in spite of all these inadequacies, common-sense knowledge of everyday life is sufficient for coming to terms with fellow-men, cultural objects, social institutions—in brief, with social reality. This is so, because the world (the natural and the social one) is from the outset an intersubjective world and because, as shall be pointed out later on, our knowledge of it is in

15 *Principles of Psychology*, I, p. 221 f.

various ways socialized. Moreover, the social world is experienced from the outset as a meaningful one. The Other's body is not experienced as an organism but as a fellow-man, its overt behavior not as an occurrence in the space-time of the outer world, but as our fellow-man's action. We normally "know" what the Other does, for what reason he does it, why he does it at this particular time and in these particular circumstances. That means that we experience our fellow-man's action in terms of his motives and goals. And in the same way, we experience cultural objects in terms of the human action of which they are the result. A tool, for example, is not experienced as a thing in the outer world (which of course it is also) but in terms of the purpose for which it was designed by more or less anonymous fellow-men and its possible use by others.

The fact that in common-sense thinking we take for granted our actual or potential knowledge of the meaning of human actions and their products, is, I suggest, precisely what social scientists want to express if they speak of understanding or *Verstehen* as a technique of dealing with human affairs. *Verstehen* is, thus, primarily not a method used by the social scientist, but the particular experiential form in which common-sense thinking takes cognizance of the social cultural world. It has nothing to do with introspection; it is a result of processes of learning or acculturation in the same way as the common-sense experience of the so-called natural world. *Verstehen* is, moreover, by no means a private affair of the observer which cannot be controlled by the experiences of other observers. It is controllable at least to the same extent to which the private sensory perceptions of an individual are controllable by any other individual under certain conditions. You have just to think of the discussion by a trial jury of whether the defendant has shown "pre-meditated malice" or "intent" in killing a person, whether he was capable of knowing the consequences of his deed, etc. Here we even have certain "rules of procedure" furnished by the "rules of evidence" in the juridical sense and a kind of verification of the findings resulting from processes of *Verstehen* by the Appellate Court, etc. Moreover, predictions based on *Verstehen* are continuously made in common-sense thinking with high success. There is more than a fair chance that a duly stamped and addressed letter put in a New York mailbox will reach the addressee in Chicago.

Nevertheless, both defenders and critics of the process of *Verstehen* maintain, and with good reason, that *Verstehen* is "subjective." Unfortunately, however, this term is used by each party in a different sense. The critics of understanding call it subjective, because they hold that understanding the motives of another man's action depends upon the private, uncontrollable, and unverifiable intuition of the observer or refers to his private value system. The social scientists, such as Max Weber, however, call *Verstehen* subjective because its goal is to find out what the actor "means" in his action, in contrast to the meaning which this action has for the actor's partner or a neutral observer. This is the origin of Max Weber's famous postulate of subjective interpretation, of which more will have to be said in what follows. The whole discussion suffers from the failure to distinguish clearly between *Verstehen* 1) as the experiential form of common-sense knowledge of human affairs, 2) as an epistemological problem, and 3) as a method peculiar to the social sciences.

So far we have concentrated on *Verstehen* as the way in which common-sense thinking finds its bearing within the social world and comes to terms with it. As to the epistemological question: "How is such understanding or *Verstehen* possible?" Alluding to a statement Kant made in another context, I suggest that it is a "scandal of philosophy" that so far a satisfactory solution to the problem of our knowledge of other minds and, in connection therewith, of the intersubjectivity of our experience of the natural as well as the socio-cultural world has not been found and that, until rather recent times, this problem has even escaped the attention of philosophers. But the solution of this most difficult problem of philosophical interpretation is one of the first things taken for granted in our common-sense thinking and practically solved without any difficulty in each of our everyday actions. And since human beings are born of mothers and not concocted in retorts, the experience of the existence of other human beings and of the meaning of their actions is certainly the first and most original empirical observation man makes.

On the other hand, philosophers as different as James, Bergson, Dewey, Husserl, and Whitehead agree that the common-sense knowledge of everyday life is the unquestioned but always questionable background within which inquiry starts and within which alone it can be carried out. It is this *Lebenswelt*, as Husserl calls it, within which, according to him, all scientific and even logical concepts originate; it is the social matrix within which, according to Dewey, unclarified situations emerge, which have to be transformed by the process of inquiry into warranted assertibility; and Whitehead has pointed out that it is the aim of science to produce a theory which agrees with experience by explaining the thought-objects constructed by common sense through the mental constructs or thought objects of science.[16] For all these thinkers agree that any knowledge of the world, in common-sense thinking as well as in science, involves mental constructs, syntheses, generalizations, formalizations, idealizations specific to the respective level of thought organization. The concept of Nature, for instance, with which the natural sciences have to deal is, as Husserl has shown, an idealizing abstraction from the *Lebenswelt*, an abstraction which, on principle and of course legitimately, excludes persons with their personal life and all objects of culture which originate as such in practical human activity. Exactly this layer of the *Lebenswelt*, however, from which the natural sciences have to abstract, is the social reality which the social sciences have to investigate.

This insight sheds a light on certain methodological problems peculiar to the social sciences. To begin with, it appears that the assumption that the strict adoption of the principles of concept and theory formation prevailing in the natural sciences will lead to reliable knowledge of social reality is inconsistent in itself. If a theory can be developed on such principles, say in the form of an ideally refined behaviorism—and it is certainly possible to imagine this—then it will not tell us anything about social reality as experienced by men in everyday life. As Professor Nagel himself admits,[17] it will be highly abstract, and its concepts will apparently be remote from the obvious and familiar traits found in any society. On the other hand, a theory which aims at

[16] See this book, p. 302 f.—Ed.
[17] *Ibid.*, p. 209.

explaining social reality has to develop particular devices foreign to the natural sciences in order to agree with the common-sense experience of the social world. This is indeed what all theoretical sciences of human affairs—economics, sociology, the sciences of law, linguistics, cultural anthropology, etc.—have done.

This state of affairs is founded on the fact that there is an essential difference in the structure of the thought objects or mental constructs formed by the social sciences and those formed by the natural sciences.[18] It is up to the natural scientist and to him alone to define, in accordance with the procedural rules of his science, his observational field, and to determine the facts, data, and events within it which are relevant for his problem or scientific purpose at hand. Neither are those facts and events pre-selected, nor is the observational field pre-interpreted. The world of nature, as explored by the natural scientist, does not "mean" anything to molecules, atoms, and electrons. But the observational field of the social scientist—social reality—has a specific meaning and relevance structure for the human beings living, acting, and thinking within it. By a series of common-sense constructs they have pre-selected and pre-interpreted this world which they experience as the reality of their daily lives. It is these thought objects of theirs which determine their behavior by motivating it. The thought objects constructed by the social scientist, in order to grasp this social reality, have to be founded upon the thought objects constructed by the common-sense thinking of men, living their daily life within their social world. Thus, the constructs of the social sciences are, so to speak, constructs of the second degree, that is, constructs of the constructs made by the actors on the social scene, whose behavior the social scientist has to observe and to explain in accordance with the procedural rules of his science.

Thus, the exploration of the general principles according to which man in daily life organizes his experiences, and especially those of the social world, is the first task of the methodology of the social sciences. This is not the place to outline the procedures of a phenomenological analysis of the so-called natural attitude

[18] Some of the points dealt with in the following are presented more elaborately in "Common-Sense and Scientific Interpretation of Human Action," in this book, pp. 302–346.

by which this can be done. We shall briefly mention only a few problems involved.

The world, as has been shown by Husserl, is from the outset experienced in the pre-scientific thinking of everyday life in the mode of typicality. The unique objects and events given to us in a unique aspect are unique within a horizon of typical familiarity and pre-acquaintanceship. There are mountains, trees, animals, dogs—in particular Irish setters and among them my Irish setter, Rover. Now I may look at Rover either as this unique individual, my irreplaceable friend and comrade, or just as a typical example of "Irish setter," "dog," "mammal," "animal," "organism," or "object of the outer world." Starting from here, it can be shown that whether I do one or the other, and also which traits or qualities of a given object or event I consider as individually unique and which as typical, depends upon my actual interest and the system of relevances involved—briefly, upon my practical or theoretical "problem at hand." This "problem at hand," in turn, originates in the circumstances within which I find myself at any moment of my daily life and which I propose to call my biographically determined situation. Thus, typification depends upon my problem at hand for the definition and solution of which the type has been formed. It can be further shown that at least one aspect of the biographically and situationally determined systems of interests and relevances is subjectively experienced in the thinking of everyday life as systems of motives for action, of choices to be made, of projects to be carried out, of goals to be reached. It is this insight of the actor into the dependencies of the motives and goals of his actions upon his biographically determined situation which social scientists have in view when speaking of the subjective meaning which the actor "bestows upon" or "connects with" his action. This implies that, strictly speaking, the actor and he alone knows what he does, why he does it, and when and where his action starts and ends.

But the world of everyday life is from the outset also a social cultural world in which I am interrelated in manifold ways of interaction with fellow-men known to me in varying degrees of intimacy and anonymity. To a certain extent, sufficient for many practical purposes, I understand their behavior, if I understand their motives, goals, choices, and plans originating in *their* biographically determined circumstances. Yet only in particular situations, and then only fragmentarily, can I experience the Others' motives, goals, etc.—briefly, the subjective meanings they bestow upon their actions, in their uniqueness. I can, however, experience them in their typicality. In order to do so I construct typical patterns of the actors' motives and ends, even of their attitudes and personalities, of which their actual conduct is just an instance or example. These typified patterns of the Others' behavior become in turn motives of my own actions, and this leads to the phenomenon of self-typification well known to social scientists under various names.

Here, I submit, in the common-sense thinking of everyday life, is the origin of the so-called constructive or ideal types, a concept which as a tool of the social sciences has been analyzed by Professor Hempel in such a lucid way. But at least at the common-sense level the formation of these types involves neither intuition nor a theory, if we understand these terms in the sense of Hempel's statements.[19] As we shall see, there are also other kinds of ideal or constructive types, those formed by the social scientist, which are of a quite different structure and indeed involve theory. But Hempel has not distinguished between the two.

Next we have to consider that the common-sense knowledge of everyday life is from the outset socialized in many respects.

It is, first, structurally socialized, since it is based on the fundamental idealization that if I were to change places with my fellow-man I would experience the same sector of the world in substantially the same perspectives as he does, our particular biographical circumstances becoming for all practical purposes at hand irrelevant. I propose to call this idealization that of the reciprocity of perspectives.[20]

It is, second, genetically socialized, because the greater part of our knowledge, as to its content and the particular forms of typification under which it is organized, is socially derived, and this in socially approved terms.

It is, third, socialized in the sense of social distribution of

[19] *Ibid.*, pp. 221 f., 227.
[20] See "Common-Sense and Scientific Interpretation of Human Action," in this book, pp. 310–312.—Ed.

knowledge, each individual knowing merely a sector of the world and common knowledge of the same sector varying individually as to its degree of distinctness, clarity, acquaintanceship, or mere belief.

These principles of socialization of common-sense knowledge, and especially that of the social distribution of knowledge, explain at least partially what the social scientist has in mind in speaking of the functional structural approach to studies of human affairs. The concept of functionalism—at least in the modern social sciences—is not derived from the biological concept of the functioning of an organism, as Nagel holds. It refers to the socially distributed constructs of patterns of typical motives, goals, attitudes, personalities, which are supposed to be invariant and are then interpreted as the function or structure of the social system itself. The more these interlocked behavior patterns are standardized and institutionalized, that is, the more their typicality is socially approved by laws, folkways, mores, and habits, the greater is their usefulness in common-sense and scientific thinking as a scheme of interpretation of human behavior.

These are, very roughly, the outlines of a few major features of the constructs involved in common-sense experience of the intersubjective world in daily life, which is called *Verstehen*. As explained before, they are the first level constructs upon which the second level constructs of the social sciences have to be erected. But here a major problem emerges. On the one hand, it has been shown that the constructs on the first level, the common-sense constructs, refer to subjective elements, namely the *Verstehen* of the actor's action from his, the actor's, point of view. Consequently, if the social sciences aim indeed at explaining social reality, then the scientific constructs on the second level, too, must include a reference to the subjective meaning an action has for the actor. This is, I think, what Max Weber understood by his famous postulate of subjective interpretation, which has, indeed, been observed so far in the theory formation of all social sciences. The postulate of subjective interpretation has to be understood in the sense that all scientific explanations of the social world *can*, and for certain purposes *must*, refer to the subjective meaning of the actions of human beings from which social reality originates.

On the other hand, I agreed with Professor Nagel's statement that the social sciences, like all empirical sciences, have to
be objective in the sense that their propositions are subjected to
controlled verification and must not refer to private uncontrollable experience.

How is it possible to reconcile these seemingly contradictory
principles? Indeed, the most serious question which the methodology of the social sciences has to answer is: How is it possible to
form objective concepts and an objectively verifiable theory of
subjective meaning-structures? The basic insight that the concepts formed by the social scientist are constructs of the constructs formed in common-sense thinking by the actors on the
social scene offers an answer. The scientific constructs formed on
the second level, in accordance with the procedural rules valid
for all empirical sciences, are objective ideal typical constructs
and, as such, of a different kind from those developed on the first
level of common-sense thinking which they have to supersede.
They are theoretical systems embodying testable general hypotheses in the sense of Professor Hempel's definition.[21] This device
has been used by social scientists concerned with theory long
before this concept was formulated by Max Weber and developed by his school.

Before describing a few features of these scientific constructs, let us briefly consider the particular attitude of the theoretical social scientist to the social world, in contradistinction to
that of the actor on the social scene. The theoretical scientist—
qua scientist, not qua human being (which he is, too)—is not
involved in the observed situation, which is to him not of practical but merely of cognitive interest. The system or relevances
governing common-sense interpretation in daily life originates in
the biographical situation of the observer. By making up his
mind to become a scientist, the social scientist has replaced his
personal biographical situation by what I shall call, following
Felix Kaufmann,[22] a scientific situation. The problems with
which he has to deal might be quite unproblematic for the human
being within the world and vice versa. Any scientific problem is

[21] This book, p. 223 f.
[22] *Op. cit.,* pp. 52, 251.

determined by the actual state of the respective science, and its solution has to be achieved in accordance with the procedural rules governing this science, which among other things warrant the control and verification of the solution offered. The scientific problem, once established, alone determines what is relevant for the scientist as well as the conceptual frame of reference to be used by him. This and nothing else, it seems to me, is what Max Weber means when he postulates the objectivity of the social sciences, their detachment from value patterns which govern or might govern the behavior of the actors on the social scene.

How does the social scientist proceed? He observes certain facts and events within social reality which refer to human action and he constructs typical behavior or course-of-action patterns from what he has observed. Thereupon he co-ordinates to these typical course-of-action patterns models of an ideal actor or actors, whom he imagines as being gifted with consciousness. Yet it is a consciousness restricted so as to contain nothing but the elements relevant to the performing of the course-of-action patterns observed. He thus ascribes to this fictitious consciousness a set of typical notions, purposes, goals, which are assumed to be invariant in the specious consciousness of the imaginary actor-model. This homunculus or puppet is supposed to be interrelated in interaction patterns to other homunculi or puppets constructed in a similar way. Among these homunculi with which the social scientist populates his model of the social world of everyday life, sets of motives, goals, roles—in general, systems of relevances—are distributed in such a way as the scientific problems under scrutiny require. Yet—and this is the main point— these constructs are by no means arbitrary. They are subject to the postulate of logical consistency and to the postulate of adequacy. The latter means that each term in such a scientific model of human action must be constructed in such a way that a human act performed within the real world by an individual actor as indicated by the typical construct would be understandable to the actor himself as well as to his fellow-men in terms of common-sense interpretation of everyday life. Compliance with the postulate of logical consistency warrants the objective validity of the thought objects constructed by the social scientist; compliance with the postulate of adequacy warrants their compatibility with the constructs of everyday life.[23]

As the next step, the circumstances within which such a model operates may be varied, that is, the situation which the homunculi have to meet may be imagined as changed, but not the set of motives and relevances assumed to be the sole content of their consciousness. I may, for example, construct a model of a producer acting under conditions of unregulated competition, and another of a producer acting under cartel restrictions, and then compare the output of the same commodity of the same firm in the two models.[24] In this way, it is possible to predict how such a puppet or system of puppets might behave under certain conditions and to discover certain "determinate relations between a set of variables, in terms of which . . . empirically ascertainable regularities . . . can be explained." This, however, is Professor Nagel's definition of a theory.[25] It can easily be seen that each step involved in the construction and use of the scientific model can be verified by empirical observation, provided that we do not restrict this term to sensory perceptions of objects and events in the outer world but include the experiential form, by which common-sense thinking in everyday life understands human actions and their outcome in terms of their underlying motives and goals.

Two brief concluding remarks may be permitted. First, a key concept of the basic philosophic position of naturalism is the so-called principle of continuity, although it is under discussion whether this principle means continuity of existence, or of analysis, or of an intellectual criterion of pertinent checks upon the methods employed.[26] It seems to me that this principle of continuity in each of these various interpretations is fulfilled by the characterized device of the social sciences, which even establishes continuity between the practice of everyday life and the conceptualization of the social sciences.

Second, a word on the problem of the methodological unity of the empirical sciences. It seems to me that the social scientist

[23] See this book, p. 342 f.–Ed.
[24] See F. Machlup, *The Economics of Seller's Competition*, p. 9 f.
[25] This book, p. 192; see also pp. 234–235 above.
[26] *Ibid.*, pp. 250–261, 262–265.

can agree with the statement that the principal differences between the social and the natural sciences do not have to be looked for in a different logic governing each branch of knowledge. But this does not involve the admission that the social sciences have to abandon the particular devices they use for exploring social reality for the sake of an ideal unity of methods which is founded on the entirely unwarranted assumption that only methods used by the natural sciences, and especially by physics, are scientific ones. So far as I know, no serious attempt has ever been made by the proponents of the "unity of science" movement to answer or even to ask the question whether the methodological problem of the natural sciences in their present state is not merely a special case of the more general, still unexplored, problem how scientific knowledge is possible at all and what its logical and methodological presuppositions are. It is my personal conviction that phenomenological philosophy has prepared the ground for such an investigation. Its outcome might quite possibly show that the particular methodological devices developed by the social sciences in order to grasp social reality are better suited than those of the natural sciences to lead to the discovery of the general principles which govern all human knowledge.

Note to Naturalists on the Human Spirit[1]

THELMA Z. LAVINE

The idealists may have lacked scientific knowledge and techniques. But it is often hard not to feel that they have possessed most of the human wisdom. . . . The idealists appear to have the edge on insights, on the discrimination of values, on the appreciation of the richness and variety of the factors demanding organization. . . . Naturalistic philosophizing must become as rich as the idealistic philosophies by incorporating the facts and experiences they emphasized within its own more adequate framework. . . .

> —J. H. RANDALL, JR., *Naturalism and the Human Spirit*, ed. Y. H. Krikorian, pp. 375–376.

SEVEN YEARS after the appearance of this passage does it not occasionally still seem to the reflective naturalist that the idealists have the edge on insights, that they possess most of the human wisdom? Yet the various essays in Mr. Krikorian's volume have laid bare the misunderstandings and untruths in the centuries-old, frequently stereotyped criticisms of naturalism, especially as applied to the present-day position. The characteristic, recurrent

[1] Reprinted from *The Journal of Philosophy* (Vol. L, No. 5, February 26, 1953, pp. 145–154), by permission of that journal and with the approval of the author.

charges against naturalism (such as materialism, physicalism, reductionism, uncritical experimentalism, naive scientism, naive empiricism, naive realism, inability to cope with human or cultural phenomena) seem for the most part to have been adequately refuted. Why, then, need a naturalist experience the anxiety of occasional doubt? How does it happen that Mr. Randall's boldly un-naturalistic terms, "wisdom," "insights," "appreciation," are so well suited to articulate this doubt?

Perhaps some light may be thrown upon these questions by examining the formulation of what some of the contributors to this symposium offered as the central tenet of the naturalistic position.

There is for naturalism no knowledge except that of the type ordinarily called scientific. But such knowledge can not be said to be restricted by its method to any limited field of subject matter—to the exclusion, let us say, of the processes called history and the fine arts. For . . . there is no serious way to approach controlled hypotheses as to what the answers should be except by inspection of the relevant evidence and by inductive inference from it.[2]

For naturalism as a philosophy the universal applicability of the experimental method is a basic belief. . . . The naturalist as experimentalist . . . must proceed with the belief that mental phenomena, like all other phenomena, can be understood by means of the experimental method.[3]

If naturalism is to be interpreted in terms of a principle or postulate of continuity, the postulate does not concern a continuity of existence, such as Professor Dewey suggests, but of analysis. To postulate the continuity of analysis is to demand, if one is a naturalist, that the investigation into all problems in all subject matters employ the methods of the special sciences or methods which may be incorporated by the special sciences. The naturalistic principle may be stated as the resolution to pursue inquiry into any set of phenomena by means of methods which administer the checks of

2 W. R. Dennes, "The Categories of Naturalism," *op. cit.*, p. 289.
3 Y. H. Krikorian, "A Naturalistic View of Mind," *op. cit.*, p. 242.

intelligent experiential verification in accordance with the contemporary criteria of objectivity.[4]

Positively, naturalism can be defined as the continuity of analysis—as the application of what all the contributors call "scientific methods" to the critical interpretation and analysis of every field.[5]

Even apart from their contexts,[6] these strikingly similar statements of basic principle may serve to reveal certain difficulties in the current naturalistic position as being sufficiently pervasive to warrant serious attention.

(1) The dominating concern with the unrestricted applicability of scientific method tends unfortunately to reduce naturalism itself to a mere uncompromising testimonial to the universal adequacy of that method. Naturalism is left with only a negative function: watchdog of scientific method, sniffing out interloping methods. A naturalism that is content to be defined by a principle of continuity of analysis conceived of in terms of experiment and empirical verifiability must also be agreeable to forfeiting its status as a positive,[7] i.e., constructive philosophy.[8]

(2) A related difficulty stems from the failure to distinguish at all times between the method stipulated by naturalism for inquiry into all types of subject matter and the method of naturalism itself. If naturalism views "itself," however, as nothing but a methodological principle, it is easy to see why more care was not devoted to distinguishing itself from the scientific method it recommends. Naturalism as mere "controlling methodological

---

[4] T. Z. Lavine, "Naturalism and the Sociological Analysis of Knowledge," *op. cit.*, pp. 184–185. A portion of this passage was quoted by Mr. Virgil Hinshaw, "Levels of Analysis," *Philosophy and Phenomenological Research*, XI, 1950, 213–220. Mr. Hinshaw criticizes both naturalism and logical positivism for failing to perceive that "science and philosophy are radically different pursuits." The present article is in a sense a rejoinder, and will contend that there is a method common to philosophy and to the large non-experimental areas of all the special sciences; moreover, that this method is utilized by empirical areas within the social sciences.

[5] J. H. Randall, Jr., "Epilogue: The Nature of Naturalism," *op. cit.*, p. 385.

[6] And omitting, for lack of space, the many other versions of this tenet which appear throughout the volume, as well as in naturalistic writing elsewhere.

[7] As opposed to negative.

[8] Some of the contributors to this symposium are explicitly agreeable to this forfeiture. Cf., e.g., W. R. Dennes, *op. cit.*, pp. 271, 288–289.

principle" or as "criticism" is in the limbo of methodology, concerning which methodological questions are rarely raised. The failure to raise clearly the question: *"What is the method of naturalism?"* even more than the failure to provide a clear answer, has two unhappy results. It has, firstly, suggested to some[9] that the method of naturalism is the method of the sciences. Yet who should know better than a naturalist that only science uses scientific method? Secondly, an even less desirable result of not inquiring into the method of naturalism is that naturalists have thereby cut themselves off from that insight into their own philosophy which can lead them out of the *cul-de-sac* of a position which is nothing but a methodological principle.

(3) It is difficult to escape the impression of an exaggerated experimentalism in the conception of scientific method in the quotations above,[10] as well as exaggeration in the roles given to causal, conditional, functional, and genetic operations within scientific method. Although Mr. Randall commends Mr. Nagel for not going along with "the way in which most of the other authors rather cavalierly identify 'scientific method' with experimentation,"[11] nevertheless Mr. Randall himself does go along, at least to the extent of speaking of a "single intellectual method" affirmed by naturalism, which "reformulates that method in experimental terms."[12] For his part, Mr. Nagel, as author of the essay on logic, understandably sees fit to point out that ". . . a naturalistic philosophy must be consistent with its own assumptions. . . . If it aims to give a coherent and adequate account of the various principles employed in acquiring scientific knowledge, it can not maintain that all of them are empirical generalizations when some are not subject to experimental refutation."[13] Mr. Nagel is concerned with such non-experimental components of scientific inquiry as symbolic systems, symbolic operations,

[9] Sometimes naturalists write as if their philosophic position were open sesame to performance in all the sciences.
[10] Also elsewhere in current naturalistic literature.
[11] *Op. cit.,* p. 380.
[12] *Op. cit.,* p. 373. Cf. also, e.g., Mr. Dennes, *op. cit.,* p. 289.
[13] "Logic without Ontology," *op. cit.,* p. 211. Cf. also, in Mr. Nagel's essay, p. 223: "Nowhere is the systematic undervaluation of the constructive function of thought in inquiry more glaring than in the widespread neglect of the role played by symbolic manipulations in scientific procedure. The more comprehensive and integrated a theoretical system is, the more obvious does the need for such manipulations appear." *Et seq.*

norms for theory construction and for the direction of inquiry. However, in the essay "The Categories of Naturalism," the staunchness of Mr. Dennes's naturalistic position seems to compel him to insist that "analysis of categories and methods used in explanation is an activity not totally different from the scientific. . . . And all questions about the superior convenience of one set of definitions (whether of categories or of any other terms) over others are questions that can be settled only on the basis of many scientifically determined probabilities."[14] Not only here but over and over again in contemporary naturalistic writing on scientific inquiry recurs the conception of a "single intellectual method" (viz., experimentation). What varies is the degree of attention and skill devoted to sweeping the non-experimental under the rug.

(4) Such an unremitting experimentalism would seem to corroborate the frequent charge that naturalism is still materialistic and still taking "science" to mean the physical sciences.[15] Sensitivity to the problems of the social sciences, it might be thought, would surely have modified the rigorousness with which the "single intellectual method" is defended. On the contrary, nothing is affirmed more often or more clearly in these essays than the "universal and unrestricted" applicability of scientific method and the inadequacy of attempting to reduce the "richness and variety of . . . human experience" to anything else; the very title of the book is emblematic of these commitments on the part of contemporary naturalism. How does it happen, then, that nowhere in this volume is there any discussion, e.g., of the crucial problem of scientific method for the social sciences? It appears that naturalism has thus far been able to satisfy its new-found concern with the human spirit by recommending the method of experimentation to the social sciences. But behaviorism, making the same recommendation long ago, at least attempted to justify it.

The present short paper will attempt no more than to make *one tentative suggestion* pertinent to the four points of criticism

---

[14] *Op. cit.*, pp. 293–294. It will be argued below that "scientific probabilities" may indeed constitute empirical checks upon "definitions." However, the *determination of definitions* proceeds by a method which is not that of scientific experimentation, and this distinction of method, it will be urged, cannot be glossed over.

[15] Cf., e.g., Mr. Sheldon's review of the symposium on naturalism, "Critique of Naturalism," *Journal of Philosophy*, XLII, 1945, 253–270.

just listed. These four points: naturalism's surrendering of the status of constructive philosophy for that of methodological principle, the failure to raise the question of its own method as distinguished from that of science, the neglect of elements other than the experimental in scientific method, the omission of the problems of social science method—these points may, for present purposes, be summed up as the incapacity to recognize and to cope with the variety of non-experimental elements in scientific and in philosophic inquiry.

The non-experimental in inquiry may, from the point of view of traditionally experimentalistic naturalistic theory, be called, following Mr. Parsons, a residual element, i.e., one of those elements "defined theoretically by their failure to fit into the positively defined categories of the system."[16] As is frequently the case with entities negatively identified, the non-experimental is markedly heterogeneous. Some of the more conspicuous types of the non-experimental element in the special sciences and in the traditional divisions of philosophy are: (1) reflective and critical analysis of fundamental categories and of crucial concepts, principles, and criteria in philosophy and in the sciences;[17] (2) the syn-

[16] Cf. T. Parsons, *The Structure of Social Action*, pp. 17–18: "Every system, including both its theoretical propositions and its main relevant empirical insights, may be visualized as an illuminated spot enveloped by darkness. The logical name for the darkness is, in general, 'residual categories.' . . . If, as is almost always the case, not all the actually observable facts of the field, or those which have been observed, fit into the sharply, positively defined categories, they tend to be given one or more blanket names which refer to categories negatively defined, that is, of facts known to exist, which are even more or less adequately described, but are defined theoretically by their failure to fit into the positively defined categories of the system. The only theoretically significant statements that can be made about these facts are negative statements—they are *not* so and so. . . . *The surest symptom of impending change in a theoretical system is increasingly general interest in such residual categories.* [Italics the present writer's.] Indeed, one kind of progress of theoretical work consists precisely in the carving out from residual categories of definite positively defined concepts and their verification in empirical investigation."

[17] Cf. Mr. C. I. Lewis, *Mind and the World Order*, p. 236: "Probably these modes of thought embodied in logic and in the forms of language are more fundamental than others. And very likely what we recognize as explicit categories are always superficial as compared with more deep-lying forms which only the persistent and imaginative student can catch, in some vague and fleeting insight. . . ." Once again, cf. Mr. Dennes, *op. cit.*, p. 293, on "analysis of categories": "The determination of what people mean by the terms they use is a matter of scientific inference as much as is the determination of the probability of any opinion expressed in those terms."

thesizing of scientific materials into general theory; (3) the use of symbolic systems in the construction of scientific theories; (4) the critical study of methodological problems such as that of the validity requirements for different types of subject matter; (5) critical interpretation of dominant culture-categories and attitudes; (6) analysis of the relations between cognitive and other values and the creative synthesis of these values into "a wisdom which would influence the conduct of life";[18] (7) critical examination of the norms of systematization, classification, regulation of research, concept construction in the sciences.

All of these varied inquiries are, it will be observed, commonly held to be "philosophical." Nor has the method common to these inquiries lacked for a name: among others, the method of reflection; intellectual intuition; criticism; dialectic; the philosophical method; and most recently, the phenomenological method. Like most of these, the term "method of understanding" (*Verstehen*) smacks of the idealistic tradition. It is here suggested, nevertheless, because it has the merit of designating the above non-experimental elements in scientific and in philosophic theory, while lacking the compounded vagueness of "dialectic" and the taint of privacy that attaches to "intellectual intuition." Moreover, unlike "method of reflection" and "criticism," *Verstehen* may serve to denote synthetic as well as merely analytic operations. Finally, in sociology, where it originates,[19] *Verstehen* signifies primarily the understanding of concrete motivation, and thus offers promise, at least, of throwing across a bridge from the non-experimental to a subject matter (motivation) which may be rendered susceptible of experimental check.

The present writing will confine itself to pointing out that the method of understanding may be said to have the function of *interpreting meaning* (*Sinndeutung*) and appears to be directed

---

Cf. footnote 14. While there is nothing "unscientific" about "vague and fleeting insight" into "deep-lying forms," the method by which such insight is gained is not "inference" in the sense in which Mr. Dennes uses that term.

[18] J. Dewey, *Democracy and Education*, p. 378.

[19] And is called, following M. Weber, *verstehende Soziologie*, usually translated as "interpretive" or "interpretative" sociology. Cf. especially the writing of Mr. H. Becker.

upon three major types of objects:[20] (1) the interpretation of the various theoretical elements in scientific and philosophic inquiry which are the objects of the seven characteristically non-experimental inquiries just discussed, and which have provoked this "note to naturalists"; (2) the interpretation of motivation in concrete human action, e.g., the motivation, rational or irrational, underlying the failure of a considerable percentage of the eligible U.S. population to go to the polls, even in national elections; (3) the interpretation of symbolic action, i.e., action which can be given significance only in terms of a system of symbolic meanings, as, for example,[21] the anthropologist interprets ritualistic behavior or the psychoanalyst interprets neurotic behavior. But methodological analysis of the characteristics of *Verstehen* common to these three types of objects, as well as of the *verstehende* operations relevant specifically to each type of object, present problems which lie far beyond the province of this brief paper.[22] For the social scientific problems of motivation and symbolism, to which the method of understanding is crucial, are manifold and largely unexplored, while the third object of *Verstehen*, the non-experimental factors in inquiry, has been the perennial cross of naturalistic theory.

The naturalist who views with alarm any entanglement with such "idealistic" matters as these should perhaps be reminded that what is being urged upon him is not philosophic conversion, but only recognition of the potential utility to the naturalistic position of much that is entailed in the method of *Verstehen*. Surely, in the first place, the attempt to link philosophy with some of the special sciences is in accord with naturalistic tradition; and specifically, the use of social scientific materials gives promise of a

[20] Cf. T. Parsons, *op. cit.*, pp. 635–637 *et passim*.

[21] Perhaps in no other areas of inquiry is there greater dependence upon the *verstehende* method than in cultural anthropology and in psychoanalysis, nor a greater need for critical analysis of it.

[22] The writings of W. Dilthey, H. Rickert, and M. Weber remain the most adequate literature concerning *Verstehen*; and along with these A. von Schelting, *Max Weber's Wissenschaftslehre*. In English, cf., in addition to T. Parsons, *op. cit.*, M. Weber, *The Theory of Social and Economic Organization*, pp. 87–112; H. A. Hodges, *Wilhelm Dilthey*; T. F. Abel, *Systematic Sociology in Germany*; H. Becker, *Through Values to Social Interpretation*; F. Znaniecki, *Social Actions*; also articles by A. Salomon, A. Schutz, and P. Sorokin.

naturalistic reconstruction of the problems of philosophy as fruitful as the great historical naturalistic reconstructions in terms of
physics, physiology, and biology.[23]

Secondly, what is here being suggested is that those present
difficulties of naturalism stemming from its incapacity to admit
and to treat effectively the various types of non-experimental elements in inquiry may be resolved by a naturalistically reconstructed method of *Verstehen*. In this reconstruction the most
important single task is working out a set of controls for the
verstehendes element in philosophic and scientific theory which
will serve, as do the controls in experimentation, as empirical
checks.[24] Nor is the task one which naturalism has never previously undertaken: Professor Dewey has often labored at formulating the nature and significance of the "empirical method in
philosophizing."[25] Unfortunately, his and most other attempts to
specify controls for *Verstehen* have usually culminated in metaphor rather than in applicable checks:[26] for example, in proposals
that theoretical elements should meet such tests as making the
relevant empirical materials more "coherent," or constitute a
"path" or "road" "leading back" to the empirical, or that they
render experience or bodies of data "more significant," or that
they be "fruitful" in production of research. Supplanting these
metaphorical tests with applicable empirical criteria is perhaps
the most pressing need of contemporary naturalism.

A naturalistically reconstructed method of *Verstehen* would
make possible the revising of the naturalistic methodological principle to incorporate *Verstehen* and would thus make this principle
a more accurate statement of naturalistic aims. For naturalists do
not so much seek to deny the fact of the various non-experimen-

---

[23] Another way of stating the relation of the method of *Verstehen* to
naturalistic tradition is that a naturalistic treatment of the method of understanding would constitute the naturalizing of the traditional idealistic view
(beginning with Kant) of mind as active, and imposing meaning or interpretation upon the given. Cf. the writer's "Knowledge as Interpretation: An
Historical Survey," *Philosophy and Phenomenological Research*, X, 1950,
526–540; XI, 1950, 88–103.

[24] Various schema for empirical checks and for experiment-equivalents
have already made their appearance in *verstehende* sociology. Cf., e.g.,
M. Weber, *op. cit.*, pp. 96–98; T. Parsons, *op. cit.*, pp. 610–614, 724–743.

[25] His own unabating creativity made this type of problem unavoidable.

[26] Cf., e.g., *Experience and Nature*, 2d ed., ch. 1.

tal elements in inquiry as they fear the uncontrolled philosophic vagaries which are apt to result from acknowledging them.[27] Once naturalistic safeguards were provided for *Verstehen*, this new content might modify the form of the principle of continuity of analysis as follows: *The naturalistic principle is the resolution that inquiry into any area be subject to the single intellectual criterion of pertinent empirical checks upon the methods employed.* This is to say that *the nerve of the naturalistic position is not insistence upon a "single intellectual method" but upon a single intellectual criterion for whatever method may be feasible.* What is crucial, of course, is the concept of the pertinence of empirical checks to given methods. Programmatically, this means, as indicated above, that naturalists be willing to recognize the non-experimental element in inquiry and to investigate ways in which this element may be harnessed to empirical tests. Too rigid an acceptance of experimental controls as a model would be neither pertinent nor workable.

The four points in criticism of present-day naturalism raised earlier in this discussion may now be briefly re-appraised in the light of the suggestion of the method of controlled *Verstehen* for naturalistic consideration. These points were: (1) naturalism's surrendering of the status of constructive philosophy for that of methodological principle; (2) its failure to raise the question of its own method as distinguished from that of science; (3) its neglect of elements other than the experimental in scientific method; (4) its omission of the problems of social science method.

(1) If continuity of analysis is conceived of in terms of controlled *Verstehen* as well as controlled experimentation, the naturalist can continue to promote the potent corrective force of experiential verification without accepting this negative function as exhaustive of his present-day intellectual contribution.[28] An

[27] E.g., in his own essay, "A Naturalistic View of Mind" (*op. cit.*), Mr. Krikorian does not hesitate to concede that consciousness *does* exist and to move on toward the important problem of how to make responsible statements about it.

[28] Cf. J. Dewey, *Philosophy and Civilization*, p. 10: "In the historic role of philosophy, the scientific factor, the element of correctness, of verifiable applicability, has a place, but it is a negative one. . . . This fact confers upon scientific knowledge an incalculably important office in philosophy. But . . . the exclusion of the inconsistent is far from being identical with a positive test which demands that only what has been scientifically

empirically controlled *Verstehen* would permit the naturalist to resume with impunity his traditional cultural role—interpreter of experience by means of reflective analysis upon scientific method and its findings.

(2) *Verstehen* is the sole method of philosophy. Alternative philosophies cannot differ in the method they employ, but only in the types of terms they select as the objects of reflection. What distinguishes naturalism from other philosophies and at the same time is the basis of the intimacy of its relationship to science is the fact that naturalism limits the terms to be reflected upon to those which, whether experimental or *verstehende* in derivation, may be incorporated by scientific method and its findings. This limitation, in turn, makes empirical controls for naturalistic *Verstehen* possible.

(3) A naturalism that apprehends the function of *Verstehen* in both science and philosophy must reject the "single intellectual method" interpretation of scientific inquiry. In accordance with the revised naturalistic principle, continuity of analysis can not be established by the single intellectual method of experimentation, but only by the single intellectual criterion of applying empirical checks to the methods analytically distinguishable within scientific inquiry.

(4) The startling inarticulateness on the part of naturalism with regard to the social sciences may be ascribed to the experimentally-minded naturalist's avoidance of a troubled area in which the crucial problems involve *Verstehen* of concrete motivation as well as of a-temporal theoretical meaning.[29] Investigation into the possibility of devising empirical controls for the variety of *verstehende* elements in the social sciences holds out the promise, in these days of failure of nerve, that naturalism may yet "supply

---

verifiable supply the entire content of philosophy. It is the difference between imagination that acknowledges responsibility to logical compatibility with demands of ascertained facts, and a complete abdication of all imagination in behalf of a prosy literalism."

[29] Cf. T. Parsons, *op. cit.*, p. 636. It is important in social science to distinguish "a-temporal meaning" in the sense of theoretical elements in inquiry from the same term when used to signify conceptual systems (e.g., Calvinism) as held subjectively by individuals.

an intellectual polity,"[30] "a wisdom which would influence the conduct of life."[31]

Naturalism released from these self-imposed restrictions could indeed be described in Mr. Randall's *verstehende* words, "as the concern to treat the total subject-matter of idealistic metaphysics, with all its sensitivity to the complex range of human culture . . ."[32] in terms of methods which are relevant as well as reliable.

[30] J. Dewey, *Philosophy and Civilization*, p. 12.
[31] J. Dewey, *Democracy and Education*, p. 378.
[32] J. H. Randall, Jr., *op. cit.*, p. 374. Unfortunately, Mr. Randall continues: ". . . in terms of a scientific and experimental method"!

On the Method of *Verstehen* as the Sole Method of Philosophy[1]

ERNEST NAGEL

MISS LAVINE's *Note* is a puzzling one, and for two reasons. The "difficulties" she claims to find in current naturalism are only doubtfully genuine; and the specific recommendation she offers to naturalists for overcoming those difficulties is of questionable worth. The following comments are brief expansions of these dicta.

(1) Miss Lavine does not explain what she understands by "a positive, i.e., constructive philosophy," and I am far from certain that I have grasped her meaning. But in any event, I have not succeeded in seeing why a philosophy that is content to be defined by "a principle of continuity of analysis" must therefore be content to forfeit its status as a positive philosophy. The adoption of that definitional principle is no obvious bar to the acceptance of whatever conclusions may be reached through the use of an intellectual method which requires experiment and empirical verifiability as warrants for knowledge of matters of fact. And indeed, even if everything written by naturalists except what is contained in the *Naturalism* volume is ignored, many of the essays in that volume amply show that naturalists do subscribe to quite a variety

[1] Reprinted from *The Journal of Philosophy* (Vol. L, No. 5, February 26, 1953, pp. 154–157), by permission of that journal and with the approval of the author.

of fairly general conclusions which can count as components in a constructive philosophy.

If judgment is based on an adequate sampling of naturalist publications, and not simply on the essays in the *Naturalism* volume, none of the other "difficulties" listed by Miss Lavine appears to be actual. Few if any contemporary naturalists identify scientific method with overt experimental activity, or fail to recognize (and in varying degrees to analyze) the function in scientific inquiry of such so-called "non-experimental" factors as the interpretation of data in terms of theoretical conceptions, the construction of symbolic systems, or the derivation of consequences from postulated premises. In point of fact, this much is clear from the *Naturalism* volume itself, and Miss Lavine's quotations from it do not establish a contrary claim. Moreover, it is not evident on what ground naturalists can be justly charged with neglect of the intellectual methods of the social sciences, or with failure to analyze the nature of philosophic method—even though no essay in the *Naturalism* volume is devoted to either theme. The fairly extensive writings of Cohen and Dewey, to mention but two names, on methodological issues in history, economics, jurisprudence, political and social theory, as well as in philosophy proper, contain obvious disproofs of those accusations.

(2) Accordingly, since I have not experienced the "difficulties" in current naturalism which Miss Lavine has discovered, I am prevented from recognizing the cogency of her recommendation as to how those alleged difficulties may be circumvented. But however this may be, I find little merit in her proposed "intellectual method of *Verstehen*" for achieving a "positive" naturalistic philosophy.

As Miss Lavine's *Note* makes clear, the "method of *Verstehen*" has been prominent in the methodological writings of one school of sociologists during the past half century. According to the proponents of that method it is distinctive of and unique to the social sciences; and it consists in supplying interpretations and explanations of social action by imputing to social agents "subjective states of mind," "motivational attitudes," and "intended meanings." Two questions thus arise: Is this method, as Miss Lavine contends, "the sole method of philosophy," is it exclusively pertinent to the actual content of philosophical inquiry? Does the method hold any special promise for philosophical analysis in those contexts in which the method is relevantly employable, and does it supply adequate canons for responsible knowledge?

(a) Current naturalism, like most other standpoints in the philosophical enterprise, is concerned with issues in moral and social theory. But it is also concerned with much else—for example, with questions bearing on the foundations of logic, mathematics, and the natural sciences, and with problems provoked by the structures of physical and organic processes. Now does Miss Lavine seriously propose the method of *Verstehen*, as formulated by its proponents in the social sciences, as relevant to all these matters? Or is she using the phrase "the method of *Verstehen*" in some unusual and unexplained sense, perhaps simply as a blanket term for whatever intellectual method or methods philosophers actually employ in their analyses? Or is she prepared to exclude from philosophy, in order to obtain for the method of *Verstehen* the status of being the sole philosophic method, the consideration of everything that does not pertain to human behavior? Since these alternatives seem to me preposterous, I do not believe that Miss Lavine can be recommending any of them. But I am also at a loss to say just what she is proposing.

(b) In discussing the adequacy of the method of *Verstehen* it is essential to distinguish between that method conceived as a way of *generating* suggestive hypotheses for explaining social action, and that method conceived as a way of *validating* proposed explanations. Now there is respectable evidence to show that the method understood in the first sense frequently functions usefully in certain areas of inquiry, for many distinguished social scientists have proclaimed it to be a source of fertile ideas. It is nevertheless worth noting that equally distinguished students of human affairs have not found in that method a fruitful heuristic technique; and it is still a matter of warm debate among sociologists whether explanations of social behavior in terms of "subjective states of mind" are adequate to the goals of social inquiry.

On the other hand, it is generally recognized that the method of *Verstehen* does not, by itself, supply any *criteria* for the validity of conjectures and hypotheses concerning the springs of human action. There is at least little current disagreement over the point that an imaginative recreation of motives and intended meanings, imputed to others to account for their behavior, requires to be supplemented by independent "objective" evidence, if the proposed explanation of behavior is to count as a warranted one. Miss Lavine seems to be fully aware of all this, for she advocates a naturalistic "reconstruction" of the method of *Verstehen* so that it would provide "a set of controls" for the "non-experimental" elements in philosophic and scientific theory.

But why then should naturalists adopt the method of *Verstehen* as their method of philosophizing? If, as Miss Lavine suggests, the nerve of naturalism is the insistence "upon a single intellectual criterion for whatever method may be feasible," there is no reason for their committing themselves to that method, for the method admittedly does not supply such a criterion. Nor is there any reason for assuming that even if that method were reconstructed in accordance with her specifications, it would provide intellectual criteria comparable in scope, precision, and reliability to those already in use or in process of being forced (as in modern theories of statistical inference), for evaluating the worth of evidence or the adequacy of theoretical constructions.

In common with other naturalists, Miss Lavine is actuated by the aim of fertilizing naturalistic philosophy through the establishment of intimate relations between philosophic inquiry and other areas of study. However, if the above comments are well-taken, her proposal as to how this end is to be achieved would not enrich naturalism, but merely ally it with a program of analysis possessing an unusually limited scope.

What Is the Method of Naturalism?[1]

THELMA Z. LAVINE

IT IS REGRETTABLE that the force of Mr. Nagel's acumen should have been expended upon (a) a somewhat orthodox denial of the weaknesses I tried to show in naturalism and upon (b) a repudiation of the method of *Verstehen* in a sense quite distinct from the one I used. I shall take up the two main points of his criticism.

(1) Mr. Nagel claims that he has not "experienced" the weaknesses in naturalism which I have tried to point out. This is undoubtedly true, since his remarks on this score furnish an unintended instance of some of those very weaknesses. In response to my statement that a naturalism that is content to be defined by a principle of continuity of analysis conceived of in terms of experiment and empirical verifiability "must be agreeable to forfeiting its status as a positive (as opposed to negative), i.e., constructive philosophy," Mr. Nagel holds that the principle is "no obvious bar to the acceptance of whatever conclusions may be reached through the use of an intellectual method which requires experiment and empirical verifiability as warrants for knowledge of matters of fact."

[1] Reprinted from *The Journal of Philosophy* (Vol. L, No. 5, February 26, 1953, pp. 157–161), by permission of that journal and with the approval of the author.

Now the conclusions which are reached by the method of experiment and empirical verification are commonly termed scientific conclusions. Undeniably, the principle of continuity of analysis does not bar the "acceptance" of scientific conclusions. But the point which I am making lies precisely here: What is entailed in the concept of "acceptance of scientific conclusions"? Further, what is the relationship between acceptance of scientific conclusions and the philosophy of naturalism? Does Mr. Nagel maintain that the acceptance of scientific conclusions constitutes philosophy, and specifically, the philosophy of naturalism? Surely in the most common usage of the term "acceptance," acceptance of scientific conclusions does not by itself entail any philosophical operations whatsoever and is unworthy of being designated as naturalistic.

It may be, however, that Mr. Nagel holds to another meaning of "acceptance," for he adds that "naturalists do subscribe to quite a variety of *fairly general conclusions* which can count as *components* in a constructive philosophy." (Italics mine.) Here it appears that Mr. Nagel is discussing a second order of conclusions, not those *of* the method of experiment and empirical verification but "fairly general conclusions" which are presumably derived in some way *from* the conclusions of scientific method. Moreover, these "fairly general conclusions," once arrived at, become in turn, according to Mr. Nagel, the "components" in a philosophy which, having been constructed, may be called naturalism. It appears, then, that many diverse operations must be performed upon the conclusions of the method of experiment and empirical verification in the construction of a naturalistic philosophy. The question, therefore, finally emerges: What is the nature of these operations? What method does the naturalist bring to bear upon the conclusions of science?

Whatever be their nature, these and no other types of operation constitute the functions of the naturalist. Whether in ethics or logic or metaphysics or epistemology or aesthetics or methodology, the operations performed by the naturalist are not the experimental and verificatory operations of the scientist, moving toward further scientific conclusions. The largely unexamined area upon which attention must be focused is this: the operations which the naturalist performs and the method he may be said to be employing when he moves from the conclusions of science to the conclusions of the naturalistic philosophy.

To assert, as does Mr. Nagel, that the naturalist accepts the conclusions reached through "the method requiring experiment and empirical verifiability as warrants for knowledge of matters of fact," or that naturalists "subscribe to quite a variety of fairly general conclusions" drawn from such warranted knowledge, is to obliterate the distinction between the experimental and (empirically) verificatory method of science and the method of naturalism. And insofar as naturalism views itself as methodologically grounded in continuity of analysis with the special sciences, conceived of in terms of experiment and empirical verifiability, it is cut off from recognition of its own philosophic operations and method, while at the same time being unable to pursue the type of method which it advocates. As a result, naturalistic treatment of the non-experimental element in method, scientific and philosophic, is less than adequate; and naturalistic excursions into other areas frequently consist merely in negative criticism of philosophic writings which have not availed themselves of the relevant scientific findings, coupled with the recommendation that the given problems be handed over to the special sciences. Thus naturalism endangers its status as a constructive philosophy, i.e., as a philosophy which provides interpretation of the phenomena it proposes to discuss. A philosophy which gives explicit theoretical sanction to no method but that of experiment and empirical verification has but a dim philosophic future.

As to the character of the method of naturalism, I have hazarded the view that insofar as the naturalist is engaged in anything more than pointing toward the propositions of science, his method is the perennial one of reflection, analytic and critical, and of intellectual intuition, synthetic and imaginative. The philosophic method is carried out by various types of intellectual operations, which these remarks can not undertake to examine. This method is what, among other things, teachers of philosophy may be presumed to teach, and its exercise is perhaps most clearly visible among graduate students at every stage of quest and commitment.

Accordingly, there is no distinction between the naturalist and the proponents of other philosophies in respect to method, but only in respect to their selection of terms for treatment by the philosophic method. As has been stated above, the terms selected by the naturalist for philosophic treatment are exclusively those which can be incorporated within scientific method and its conclusions. The characterization of naturalism as "acceptance" of scientific conclusions may thus be seen to be a misguided attempt to express the fact of this exclusive selectivity.

Mr. Nagel denies that "contemporary naturalists identify scientific method with overt experimental activity, or fail to recognize (and in varying degrees to analyze) the function in scientific inquiry of . . . so-called 'non-experimental' factors." I agree that there is ample acknowledgment on the part of naturalists of elements other than the experimental in scientific method (and in philosophy). But the point that I have tried to make is that this acknowledgment, which is, of course, inevitable, has not received theoretical status. Insofar as elements other than the experimental have entered into naturalistic formulations, these elements have tended to remain residual, i.e., to be regarded as *non*-experimental, and so to be unexplored. I have been attempting to examine the theoretical significance of the non-experimental in science and philosophy.

Finally, Mr. Nagel disclaims any neglect of the social sciences on the part of naturalism and cites the writings of Cohen and Dewey as "obvious disproofs" of such neglect. I do not wish to analyze or evaluate here the contributions to the social sciences which Cohen and Dewey may have made, but surely it is worthy of comment that these writers, both of them by now remote from present theoretical problems in the social sciences, should be offered as evidence of contemporary concern with these matters.

(2) It would be fruitless to discuss here the adequacy of *Verstehen* as the method of philosophy and of the non-experimental element in science, since Mr. Nagel treats *Verstehen* as being directed toward only one of the three types of objects which I outlined above, and is thus engaged in rejecting a conception which I have not proposed. Mr. Nagel's limitation of *Verstehen* to the understanding of subjective states of mind is an unduly narrow one, as some social scientists have seen, for sciences which have the responsibility of treating a-temporal systems of rational meanings and non-rational symbolic systems in relation to concrete motivation.

Moreover, in my suggestion of *Verstehen* as the philosophic method, I do not view philosophy as merely borrowing from the social sciences. The concept of *Verstehen* is of comparatively recent philosophic origin. It attempts to analyze interpretive activity insofar as its objects are meanings. A naturalistic study of the logic of this type of interpretive activity would enlighten not only philosophy but a number of the social sciences. Such a study would, of course, avail itself of whatever explorations of the dimensions of the problem may have been made by such interested sciences as cultural anthropology, Gestalt psychology, sociology, and psychoanalysis.

Finally, I am not suggesting that, despite its difficulties, "naturalists adopt the method of *Verstehen* as their method of philosophizing" but rather that they recognize that *Verstehen* in the form of reflective and intuitive interpretation of theoretical meaning is the sole method which they can and *in fact do* employ; and that this method does not preclude empirical controls. And is not an explicit commitment to the traditional philosophic role of reflective interpretation in part, at least, the clue to the idealists' "edge on insights"?

A Study in Philosophy and the Social Sciences[1]

MAURICE NATANSON

MY INTENTION in this essay is not to survey either the historical or the structural relationships between philosophy and the social sciences, but rather to focus on a basic systematic problem in methodology: the philosophical character and implications of the methods of social-scientific inquiry. By "methodology" I understand the underlying conceptual framework in terms of which concrete studies in history, sociology, economics, and the like are carried out, and in terms of which they receive a general rationale. Therefore I am not concerned here with the nature of specific techniques that social scientists utilize, or with their evaluation. Instead, I am interested in what I take to be a distinctly philosophical task, the analysis of the underlying presuppositions of the conceptual systems employed by social scientists in virtue of which their scientific enterprise is carried out. Methodology in the sense in which I am using it thus implies a certain order of philosophical commitment.

[1] This article appeared originally in *Social Research* (Vol. XXV, No. 2, Summer 1958, pp. 158–172), and is reprinted in Maurice Natanson, *Literature, Philosophy, and the Social Sciences: Essays in Existentialism and Phenomenology,* The Hague: Martinus Nijhoff, 1962, pp. 155–166. It is reprinted with the permission of *Social Research* and Martinus Nijhoff and with the approval of the author.

The framework for my remarks is historically oriented, however, since I wish to begin with two major methodological approaches to the task of social-scientific inquiry. The approaches in question will provide us with a point of departure for a discussion of social-scientific methodology, its relationships with natural-scientific inquiry, and its general philosophical implications. Such a discussion looks toward the concrete problem of this paper, which is an analytic, critical comparison of naturalistic and phenomenological approaches to the methodology of the social sciences. It shall be my purpose to point out certain crucial inadequacies in the naturalistic interpretation of social science—inadequacies that can be overcome, it seems to me, by a phenomenological approach.

II

Let me begin, then, with a statement of two positions. I use the designation "naturalism" in this context to refer to that approach to social science which holds that the methods of the natural sciences, scientific method generally, are not only adequate for the understanding of social phenomena but indeed constitute the paradigm for all inquiry in this field. A conjoint thesis of naturalism is that of the qualitative continuum between problems of the natural and of the social sciences. William R. Dennes expresses this point quite clearly: "There is for naturalism no knowledge except that of the type ordinarily called 'scientific.' But such knowledge cannot be said to be restricted by its method to any limited field of subject matter—to the exclusion, let us say, of the processes called 'history' and the 'fine arts.' "[2]

Thelma Z. Lavine presents the thesis of naturalism in this way: "The naturalistic principle may be stated as the resolution to pursue inquiry into any set of phenomena by means of methods which administer checks of intelligent experiential verification in accordance with the contemporary criteria of objectivity. The significance of this principle does not lie in the advocacy of empirical method, but in the conception of the regions where that method is to be employed. That scientific

[2] W. R. Dennes, "The Categories of Naturalism," in *Naturalism and the Human Spirit*, ed. H. Krikorian, p. 289.

analysis must not be restricted in any quarter, that its extension to any field, to any special set of phenomena, must not be curtailed—this is the nerve of the naturalistic principle. 'Continuity' of analysis can thus mean only that all analysis must be scientific analysis."[3]

It follows clearly that naturalistic methodology is held to be applicable to the problems of the social sciences—in fact, that a proper theory of the social sciences would have to be founded in these terms. In the words of Ernest Nagel, it would have to be a theory that, "in its method of articulating its concepts and evaluating its evidence," would be "continuous with the theories of the natural sciences."[4]

The second approach is radically different. It directly argues that the phenomena of the social sciences are not qualitatively continuous with those of the natural sciences, and that very different methods must be employed to study social reality. Here it is maintained that what is needed above all is a way of looking at social phenomena which takes into primary account the intentional structure of human consciousness, and which accordingly places major emphasis on the meaning social acts have for the actors who perform them and who live in a reality built out of their subjective interpretation.

Obviously the label "phenomenological" is less than satisfactory for this total approach, since it neither derives directly from the philosophy of Edmund Husserl nor is always philosophically compatible with principles of Husserlian phenomenology. Nevertheless, I prefer the term "phenomenological" to the possible alternative "subjective," for although the former may be misunderstood, the latter is necessarily misinterpreted in the context of its present meaning if it is equated, as unfortunately it generally is, with personal or private or merely introspective, intuitive attitudes. I shall therefore use "phenomenological" as a generic term to include all positions that stress the primacy of consciousness and subjective meaning in the interpretation of social action.

The clearest expression of this standpoint is offered by Max

[3] T. Z. Lavine, "Naturalism and the Sociological Analysis of Knowledge," *ibid.*, pp. 184–185.
[4] E. Nagel, in this book, p. 209.

Weber: "Sociology . . . is a science which attempts the interpretive understanding of social action in order thereby to arrive
at a causal explanation of its course and effects. In 'action' is
included all human behaviour when and in so far as the acting individual attaches a subjective meaning to it. Action in this sense
may be either overt or purely inward or subjective; it may consist of positive intervention in a situation, or of deliberately
refraining from such intervention or passively acquiescing in
the situation. Action is social in so far as, by virtue of the subjective meaning attached to it by the acting individual (or individuals), it takes account of the behaviour of others and is
thereby oriented in its course."[5]

Contemporary discussion of the problems of the social sciences has been dominated by the dialogue between representatives of the two camps. Most of the characteristic problems of
social-scientific methodology have been at issue: criteria of
verification, the status of so-called introspective reports, the use
of models in explanation, the applicability of mathematical or
formalistic modes of description to social phenomena. But underlying all of these topics there is what I consider to be the root issue for the entire range of problems involved: the question of
the nature and status of knowledge as such in science as such. At
the basis of all methodological analysis there lies an essentially
epistemological problem, that of the critique of knowledge. It is
this problem I am interested in exploring at present. To carry out
such an exploration requires that we turn to the epistemological
grounding of the naturalistic and phenomenological approaches.

As we have seen, it is the central contention of the naturalistic school that the methods of natural science constitute the
proper means for inquiring into social phenomena. Now if we
distinguish between methods in the sense of concrete techniques
and methods in the philosophical sense of conceptual instruments,
it is clear that the naturalist's thesis is directed to a level concerned with the kind of knowledge involved in social science.
In other words, the naturalist is suggesting that the concepts of
the social sciences, as well as the theoretical matrix for those concepts, are identical or ought to be made identical with those of
the natural sciences.

[5] M. Weber, *The Theory of Social and Economic Organization*, p. 88.

But at what level is this suggestion offered? Is the suggestion itself a proper part of scientific discourse? Is the analysis of the conceptual structure of a system within the province of science? Is the working out of a system of scientific explanation to take place within the framework of natural science? Are philosophical questions about natural science to be treated as problems within the methodology of natural science? All of these questions lead back to a foundational one: is an epistemological analysis of the kind of knowledge involved in natural-scientific discourse to be taken at the same level with natural-scientific problems, and therefore to be answered in terms of the criteria of explanation provided by natural science? The immediate question is then whether natural science can talk about itself philosophically in natural-scientific terms. But before turning to the paradox I think is involved here, let us glance at the epistemological problem relevant to the phenomenological approach.

To decide that the problems of the social sciences are first of all phenomenological means that social action is understood as founded on the intentional experience of the actors on the social scene. The kind of theoretical framework erected in accordance with this insight is distinctively philosophical, that is, questions about the nature and status of intentional experience may themselves be raised and resolved within the same framework. A phenomenological approach has then this unique characteristic: questions about its own methods and procedures are part of its structural content. Since a phenomenological system is not bound to criteria taken over from a non-philosophical or a supra-philosophical domain, it may consider immanent problems. For the same reason a philosophical system may, indeed must, consider its own procedures and articulation as part of its field for inquiry. The point is that a phenomenological approach lends itself completely to philosophical self-scrutiny.

At the conceptual level, then, the method of natural science and the method of social science are radically different; the former is rooted in a theoretical system that may never take itself as the object of its inquiry without transcending its own categories; the latter, in its phenomenological character, necessarily becomes self-inspecting yet remains within the conceptual system involved, that of philosophical analysis. Furthermore, whereas a phenomenological approach begins by raising the question of its own philosophical status, the naturalistic standpoint cancels out the possibility of self-inspection by its own claim that natural science provides the essential method for stating and evaluating philosophical claims.

It might appear that this analysis of naturalism does not do justice to its precisely philosophical character, that it fails to acknowledge the status of naturalism as a philosophy that reflects on nature and experience. Rather than replying to this caution directly, I prefer to consider it first in the context of a fairly recent statement by a philosopher in the naturalist tradition who approaches this criticism of naturalism in an especially forceful manner.

III

In a 1953 article Thelma Z. Lavine, herself a contributor to the earlier volume entitled *Naturalism and the Human Spirit*, reflects on certain problems raised in that volume concerning philosophical naturalism, and addresses herself to a criticism of the fundamental method of naturalistic inquiry.[6] Although her purpose is a reconstruction of naturalism in the light of her criticisms, rather than an abandonment of the position, her critical remarks are directly relevant to the present discussion.

Miss Lavine presents four basic charges that she thinks naturalism must face: "(1) naturalism's surrendering of the status of constructive philosophy for that of methodological principle; (2) its failure to raise the question of its own method as distinguished from that of science; (3) its neglect of elements other than the experimental in scientific method; (4) its omission of the problems of social science method."[7] Her statement of the first two charges will suffice for an account of her general argument:

> The dominating concern with the unrestricted applicability of scientific method tends unfortunately to reduce naturalism itself to a mere uncompromising testimonial to the universal adequacy of that method. Naturalism is left with only

[6] T. Z. Lavine, in this book, pp. 250–261.
[7] *Ibid.*, p. 259.

a negative function: watchdog of scientific method, sniffing out interloping methods. A naturalism that is content to be defined by a principle of continuity of analysis conceived in terms of experiment and empirical verifiability must also be agreeable to forfeiting its status as a positive, i.e., constructive philosophy . . . A related difficulty stems from the failure to distinguish at all times between the method stipulated by naturalism for inquiry into all types of subject matter and the method of naturalism itself. If naturalism views "itself," however, as nothing but a methodological principle, it is easy to see why more care was not devoted to distinguishing itself from the scientific method it recommends. Naturalism as mere "controlling methodological principle" or as "criticism" is in the limbo of methodology, concerning which methodological questions are rarely raised. The failure to raise clearly the question: *"What is the method of naturalism?"* even more than the failure to provide a clear answer, has two unhappy results. It has, firstly, suggested to some that the method of naturalism is the method of the sciences. Yet who should know better than a naturalist that only science uses scientific method? Secondly, an even less desirable result of not inquiring into the method of naturalism is that naturalists have thereby cut themselves off from that insight into their own philosophy which can lead them out of the *cul-de-sac* of a position which is nothing but a methodological principle.[8]

I have quoted here at length because I believe that this statement on its own account deserves more serious attention than it was given in Ernest Nagel's reply to it,[9] and because, coming from a naturalist, it is doubly interesting.

For Miss Lavine the way out of this naturalistic impasse is provided by a reconstructed "method of understanding" or *Verstehen*, which has, among other things, the "merit of designating the . . . non-experimental elements in scientific and in philosophic theory."[10] "What is here being suggested," she writes, "is that those present difficulties of naturalism stemming

---

[8] *Ibid.*, pp. 252–253.
[9] This book, pp. 262–265.
[10] *Ibid.*, p. 256.

from its incapacity to admit and to treat effectively the various non-experimental elements in inquiry may be resolved by a naturalistically reconstructed method of *Verstehen*. In this reconstruction the most important single task is working out a set of controls for the *verstehendes* element in philosophic and scientific theory which will serve, as do the controls in experimentation, as empirical checks."[11] Of course, it is Miss Lavine's view that such a reconstruction *is* possible within the naturalistic framework. I would like to challenge this contention.

First, it is necessary to be clear about the meaning of *Verstehen*. The translation "understanding" is not a happy one, because *Verstehen* signifies a certain kind of understanding relevant primarily to human behavior. *Verstehen* is interpretive understanding. If we go back to Max Weber's conception of the subjective interpretation of meaning in social action, we will have a clearer notion of what is at issue here. Weber maintains that the primary task of the sociologist is to understand the meaning an act has for the actor himself, not for the observer. The kind of understanding involved is precisely that of *Verstehen*.

What is sought in such explanatory understanding is the total character of the intentional framework of the actor, which alone provides the key to the meaning of a specific act he performs. A particular act is referred back interpretively to the intentional matrix that is the ground of its meaning. "Thus," Weber writes, "for a science which is concerned with the subjective meaning of action, explanation requires a grasp of the complex of meaning in which an actual course of understandable action thus interpreted belongs. In all such cases, even where the processes are largely affectual, the subjective meaning of the action, including that also of the relevant meaning complexes, will be called the 'intended' meaning. This involves a departure from ordinary usage, which speaks of intention in this sense only in the case of rationally purposive action."[12] *Verstehen*, then, for Weber, is the operation concerned with explicating the structure of subjective interpretation of meaning. But this is not all that *Verstehen* signifies.

Alfred Schutz has pointed out that *Verstehen* has at least

11 *Ibid.*, p. 258.
12 *Op. cit.*, pp. 95–96.

three different levels of application. It may be understood "as the experiential form of common-sense knowledge of human affairs . . . as an epistemological problem, and . . . as a method peculiar to the social sciences."[13] It is the failure to distinguish these different levels which explains, in part, much of the confusion involved in the criticisms directed against Weber's postulate of the subjective interpretation of meaning. These criticisms are usually generated by the following assumptions: first, that Weber is saying that a different kind of knowledge is involved in understanding social phenomena from that involved in understanding natural phenomena; second, that the method of *Verstehen* consists in an empathic response to or imaginative reconstruction of another person's motivation in social action; third, that Weber's postulate of subjective interpretation involves a "subjectivism" that renders the method of *Verstehen* not only unscientific but even anti-scientific; and fourth, that the method of *Verstehen* offers no criteria for scientific explanation. As Ernest Nagel puts it, "the method of *Verstehen* does not, by itself, supply any *criteria* for the validity of conjectures and hypotheses concerning the springs of human action."[14]

All of these assumptions are false and completely misleading. A review of the three levels of *Verstehen* presented by Schutz will enable us to see what Weber *is* advocating. To say, in line with the first of those levels, that *Verstehen* is "the experiential form of common-sense knowledge of human affairs" means that as a matter of fact men in daily life do interpret one another's actions by seeking to grasp the meaning intended by fellow men. Consider some of the language involved at this level. "What did he really mean by that?" "Why don't you say what you mean?" "Who does he think he's fooling?" If overt statements and actions were always taken at face value, taken as true indicators of the speaker's opinions and attitudes, sincerity would be a meaningless term, politics would be without a subject matter, and history would be the chronicle of human vegetation. Common-sense interpretation turns out to be a highly complicated instrument. Motive, attitude, intent, and purpose are the primary structures looked to as the *real* basis for understanding overt be-

[13] This book, p. 240.
[14] *Ibid.*, p. 264.

havior. *Verstehen* at the level of common sense is the actual mode of understanding utilized by actors in daily life to interpret one another's actions.

"As a method peculiar to the social sciences," another level of application formulated by Schutz, *Verstehen* is concerned with the typifications of interpretation found in common-sense life, and endeavors to provide a theoretical system suitable for their clarification. This theoretical system has as its guiding principle the subjective interpretation of meaning, but how this principle is utilized depends on the particular way in which the theoretical system is understood. There are two aspects to the system. First, it is the theoretical foundation for a method of interpreting social phenomena, that is, it provides the general concepts in terms of which the method of *Verstehen* is comprehensible. But second, it is a philosophical foundation for comprehending the intentional structure of social action.

For this reason it makes good sense to say, with Schutz, that *Verstehen* may be understood in a third application "as an epistemological problem." Here there are again two aspects to be grasped. *Verstehen* is concerned epistemologically with the cardinal philosophical problem of the social sciences, that of intersubjectivity; at this point it endeavors to pose the problem rather than to resolve it. But a second meaning of *Verstehen* involved here is that of philosophical method itself; in this sense it is synonymous with what might be termed metaphilosophical inquiry, that is, a necessarily *a priori*, dialectical, categorial analysis of philosophical procedures. Since philosophy is necessarily reflexive in character, since a philosopher must necessarily concern himself with the critique of his own enterprise (in its systematic rather than psychological context), it follows that metaphilosophy is an indispensable part of philosophical analysis. *Verstehen* is as essential to philosophical life as it is to common-sense life.

The misunderstandings involved in the criticisms of Weber presented before are now manifest. It is not that a different *kind* of knowledge is involved in the social sciences as compared with the natural sciences, but that the object of knowledge is different. The social sciences are concerned with the intentional dimension of social reality. Again, the "method" of *Verstehen* is not that of empathic or imaginative response, but rather a conceptual clarification of the interpretive understanding descriptively involved in the affairs of common-sense men in daily life. Furthermore, the "subjectivism" of Weber's postulate of interpretation does not mean that private, intuitive, unverifiable elements are involved in the understanding of social action, but that the very structure of social action is built out of the intentional character of human life.[15] Finally, to argue, as Nagel does, that "the method of *Verstehen* does not, by itself, supply any *criteria* for the validity of conjectures and hypotheses concerning the springs of human action"[16] is to confound several senses of "method" and to ignore what is distinctive about Weber's leading principle. *Verstehen* is not concerned at any level with providing empirical criteria for determining the validity of hypotheses; as a philosophically directed method it is concerned rather with the conceptual framework within which social reality may be comprehended.

Interestingly enough, this interpretation of the method of *Verstehen* as metaphilosophically oriented is in complete agreement with Miss Lavine's presentation of *Verstehen* as "designating the . . . non-experimental elements in scientific and in philosophic theory."[17] Indeed, it is her claim that "*Verstehen* is the sole method of philosophy. Alternative philosophies cannot differ in the method they employ, but only in the types of terms they select as the objects of reflection."[18] But now it is Miss Lavine's contention that *Verstehen*, understood in this sense, may be appropriated by a reconstructed naturalism and thus provide what amounts to a philosophical grounding for the naturalistic position. I am in complete agreement with Miss Lavine's criticisms of naturalism, and with her conclusion that the method of *Verstehen* is needed to correct the central inadequacies she has indicated. I do not agree, however, that a reconstruction of *Verstehen* is possible in naturalistic terms. My reasons follow.

It seems to me, first of all, that Miss Lavine, having distinguished between methods of science and philosophical analysis, between "the method stipulated by naturalism for inquiry into all

[15] *Ibid.*, pp. 245–246.
[16] *Ibid.*, p. 264.
[17] *Ibid.*, p. 256.
[18] *Ibid.*, p. 260.

types of subject matter and the method of naturalism itself,"[19] lapses into the very evil she is attacking when she recommends a *Verstehen* reconstructed in such a way that empirical controls are built into it. It may be well, however, to quote her own conception of what such an empirically controlled *Verstehen* would involve:

A naturalistically reconstructed method of *Verstehen* would make possible the revising of the naturalistic methodological principle to incorporate *Verstehen* and would thus make this principle a more accurate statement of naturalistic aims. For naturalists do not so much seek to deny the fact of the various non-experimental elements in inquiry as they fear the uncontrolled philosophic vagaries which are apt to result from acknowledging them. Once naturalistic safeguards were provided for *Verstehen*, this new content might modify the form of the principle of continuity of analysis as follows: *The naturalistic principle is the resolution that inquiry into any area be subject to the single intellectual criterion of pertinent empirical checks upon the methods employed.* This is to say that *the nerve of the naturalistic position is not insistence upon a "single intellectual method" but upon a single intellectual criterion for whatever method may be feasible.* What is crucial, of course, is the concept of the pertinence of empirical checks to given methods.[20]

If *Verstehen* is offered by Miss Lavine as "the sole method of philosophy," which is then to be the method of naturalism, I do not see how it can be consistently suggested that "naturalistic safeguards" can be "provided for *Verstehen*." It was the philosophical status of naturalistic safeguards which was placed in question by Miss Lavine in her criticisms of naturalism. To reinvoke naturalistic criteria as correctives for a reconstructed naturalistic method is to take a step forward and follow with a step back. Moreover, Miss Lavine sacrifices the central point of her argument when, after making it clear that *Verstehen* is the essence of philosophical method, she reverts to a notion of

[19] *Ibid.*, p. 252.
[20] *Ibid.*, pp. 258–259.

Verstehen in the narrow sense of method as a conceptual device. *Verstehen* in the broad sense cannot be "incorporated" into naturalistic methodology, because it is itself foundational; the meaning of methodological incorporation is part of the subject matter of *Verstehen*. What Miss Lavine wishes to do is quite clear. She wants to found naturalism philosophically without departing from naturalistic method. But her own placement of naturalism "in the limbo of methodology" should have warned her away from such an undertaking, and her insight into the character of *Verstehen* as the fundamental method of philosophical inquiry might have suggested a way out: the transcension of naturalism in favor of a phenomenological standpoint.

IV

Thus far I have used the term "phenomenological" to designate a general style of social science which takes human consciousness and its intended meanings as the proper locus for the understanding of social action. In this sense such American social scientists as W. I. Thomas, Cooley, and G. H. Mead, in addition to the European school influenced directly by Max Weber, are all representatives of the phenomenological standpoint. Now, however, I wish to narrow my usage of the term to the technical meaning in contemporary philosophy given to it by Edmund Husserl, and suggest that Husserlian phenomenology not only is capable of providing a philosophical grounding for the social sciences but is distinctively suited to the philosophical task of *Verstehen*. Husserl's doctrine of the intentionality of consciousness provides an immediate entrance into the questions at issue. √

All perceptual acts, in the broad Cartesian sense, have a directional character, an active movement that intends some object. Unlike the naive, real object of common sense or natural science, the intentional object is merely the correlate of the act of intending. The intentional object, or noema in Husserl's language, is the object as *meant*, as *intended* in the acts of thinking, remembering, willing, imagining, and the like. Phenomenology is a discipline concerned with the description of the phenomenon in so far as it is given to consciousness by way of the acts of intentionality. Since the entire range of intentional activity is taken as the subject matter for phenomenological investigation, the intentional life of actors in social reality is clearly included in the phenomenological domain. And here philosophical and sociological concerns merge into a single concordant venture: the attempt to comprehend social action in terms of the intentional meanings consciousness ascribes to its objects. Phenomenology is precisely, therefore, philosophical *Verstehen.*

In addition to its methodological rapport with the structure of social life, phenomenology is also a philosophy that claims to be self-founding. Determining whether it is truly a presuppositionless philosophy depends first on understanding in what sense that phrase is used by Husserl, a problem outside the province of this paper. But it is proper to suggest here that by a self-founding philosophy Husserl meant a position that attempts an absolute scrutiny of its own concepts, postulates, principles, and general procedures, by referring them back in each case to their experiential roots in the intentional life of consciousness. Therefore what distinguishes Husserlian phenomenology from all other positions is its insistence on a method that is reflexive, that places in radical question its own enterprise, and that seeks to found its results on a transcendental ground rendered apodictic by the instrument of phenomenological reduction. In contradistinction to naturalism, then, phenomenology not only is able to ground its own method but is defined by its insistence on doing so. Phenomenological philosophy is phenomenologically derived and phenomenologically realized.

Finally, the phenomenological approach to social reality fulfills the method of *Verstehen* since it offers a *philosophy* of the social world, rather than techniques or devices in the narrower methodological sense. And the social world at issue for the phenomenologist is the original, forceful, meaning-laden reality in which we exist. It is this world, the world of the natural attitude, which requires the interpretive understanding of *Verstehen.* When the naturalist approches social reality in terms of the methods of natural science, he forfeits his philosophical concern with a crucial dimension of reality and indeed reduces himself to limbo. Phenomenology claims to reconstruct social action by providing a fundamental clarification of its intentional structure within the framework of a comprehensive philosophy. It claims to return us to the social world in its full richness and urgent complexity. These are its claims. The demonstration of what is claimed involves another story, one much more difficult to tell.

The Phenomenological and Naturalistic Approaches to the Social[1]

LEON J. GOLDSTEIN

I

IN AN INTERESTING ESSAY not long ago, Maurice Natanson contrasted two approaches to the study of sociocultural phenomena and concluded that one of them, the naturalistic, is entirely wanting and not adequate to dealing with such phenomena, and that the other, the phenomenological, is, on the contrary, entirely suited to the task.[2] It seems to me, however, that he has said too much, and in the course of what follows I want to show that far from opposing one another, these two approaches are complementary and both of them necessary if we are to have a full account of the phenomena in question. Each does a different job, and there is no reason why we cannot have both.

The terms "phenomenological" and "naturalistic" suggest schools or procedures within philosophy, and I think it best if I make some preliminary remarks as to how I intend the distinction between them in this paper. It is not my intention when speaking of the phenomenological approach to speak of the ap-

[1] This article appeared in *Methodos* (Vol. XIII, No. 51–52, 1961, pp. 225–238), and is reprinted with the permission of that journal and the approval of the author.
[2] Maurice Natanson, "A Study in Philosophy and the Social Sciences," in this book, pp. 271–285.

plication to the social of the methods of Edmund Husserl and his followers. I do not know whether the approach I mean to deal with is or is not phenomenological in that sense, but for what it is worth the reader may be informed that Alfred Schutz seems to think that it is,[3] Hans Neisser that it is not,[4] and Natanson himself takes both views,[5] depending on whether he intends phenomenology in a broad or a narrow sense. For the purpose of the distinction that I want to make, "the phenomenological approach" will mean one that is primarily oriented toward description, not theory formation, and in which the vantage point of subjectivity, in a way to be made clear, is of first importance.

By the naturalistic approach I shall mean any concern with the social not from the standpoint of subjectivity. Naturalistic social science seeks to explain how sociocultural phenomena come to be as they are, how they develop and change. For reasons which have been sufficiently discussed by well-known methodologists[6] and will simply be assumed here, such explanation presupposes reference to general laws. But I do not think that one can say that it is the utilization of general propositions that distinguishes the naturalistic from the phenomenological approach, for a descriptive or phenomenological account of the social world can always be formulated so as to contain general propositions. Our account might say that things are such in our social world that if anyone having specificable social characteristics were to find himself in a given situation he would act in a determinate way. Most anyone in the given society may be expected to *understand* the action, thus the element of subjectivity is seen to be entirely compatible with generality. (This is not to say that people ordinarily bother to set out the common characteristics of their social life in the form of general propostions, and it is not unreasonable to think that many, even most, people of a given community could not do so if asked. Nevertheless,

[3] A. Schutz, "Concept and Theory Formation in the Social Sciences," in this book, pp. 231–249.

[4] H. P. Neisser, "The Phenomenological Approach in Social Science," *Philosophy and Phenomenological Research*, XX, 1959, 209 f.

[5] M. Natanson, in this book, pp. 273 and 283 f.

[6] E.g., C. G. Hempel and P. Oppenheim, "Studies in the Logic of Explanation," *Philosophy of Science*, XV, 1948, 135–175; and C. G. Hempel, "The Function of General Laws in History," *Journal of Philosophy*, XXXIX, 1942, 35–48.

people generally know what to expect of their fellow participants in the social and cultural life of their community; they seem to "know" implicitly what the ethnographer or sociologist sets forth explicitly).

I have still to make clear, even in a preliminary sort of way, what I mean by the naturalistic approach to the social. In a paper written some twenty years ago but only recently discovered and posthumously published, Schutz opposes to the subjectivism of his favored phenomenological approach what he calls objectivism.[7] "Objectivism" does not refer to just one specific alternative to phenomenology in social science, but seems to be used as a general name for all social research which does not take as its task the attempt to understand some social world from the standpoints of those who live in that world. At the extreme position of the objectivist spectrum, Schutz finds behaviorism, but, unlike the view he seems to hold in his later paper to which reference has been made,[8] he recognizes that there are alternative objectivist possibilities. "There is rather a basic attitude conceivable— and, in fact, several of the most successful social scientists have adopted it—which accepts naively the social world with all the alter egos and institutions in it as a meaningful universe, *meaningful namely for the observer* whose only scientific task consists in describing and explaining his and his co-observers' experiences of it."[9] Whether or not it is fair to speak here of naive acceptance, I do agree with Schutz that we can, and do, have social science the purpose of which is to make intelligible to the observer the social phenomena he elects to study. This is a social science which takes as its point of departure not the living experiences of the members of a society, but, rather, the questions that the investigator thinks are worth answering.[10] It is this kind

[7] A. Schutz, "The Social World and the Theory of Social Action," *Social Research*, XXVII, 1960, 203 f.

[8] A. Schutz, "Concept and Theory Formation in the Social Sciences," where on p. 237 of this book and elsewhere it is clear that he takes the alternative to his views to be some form of behaviorism.

[9] A. Schutz, "The Social World and the Theory of Social Action," 205 f.; my italics.

[10] For an instance of complete refusal to see any point of view other than that of the participants in the social world being studied as worthy of consideration, see G. Dalton, "A Note of Clarification on Economic Surplus," *American Anthropologist*, 1960, LXII, 483–90. Dalton considers that

of social science that I intend by the term "naturalistic social science," and I think that it is this kind of social science that Natanson finds wanting.

It seems, then, that naturalistic social science is one kind of nonsubjective social science subsumed by Schutz under the rubric "objective." We have seen that in addition to this he recognizes and rejects an approach he calls "behavioristic." I must confess that I am not able to make any sense of the idea that there can be such a thing as behavioristic social science, though I can appreciate the polemical value it may have for a subjectivist who wishes to make his opponents seem to be defending an impossible position. Behaviorism, if it can be carried off at all, seems to be an orientation in the study of individual behavior or psychology and purports to describe such behavior using only terms which refer to overt or public movements and the like. Since meanings of some sort and in some sense are necessary—as we shall see in the sequel—for human action to be understood as social, there cannot possibly be a behavioristic approach to the study of sociocultural phenomena.

Perhaps advocates of the view that only the phenomenological approach is ultimately tenable think behaviorism is the extreme alternative to their position because it is obviously the extreme alternative to views they hold in psychology. There, too, subjectivists have inclined to think that *the* purpose of psychological investigation is to present an account of the mental life from the standpoint of the subject himself. One need not, of course, deny that this is a possible subject for study, but I do think it a mistake to conclude therefrom that no other approach in psychology is possible. I should imagine that if those who follow behavioristic procedures emerge with conclusions which do not violate the accepted canons of scientific procedure, if, that is, their results are confirmable by others and their predictions realized, anyone would admit that their discipline is a scientific one. What I am saying is rather like Rollo May's suggestion that what both Kierkegaard and Freud have to say about anxiety is

a question raised from any other standpoint is an imposition of the "values" of the investigator upon the people being studied (p. 487), and reserves the honorific adjective "empirical" solely for the standpoint of the subjects (p. 489).

useful and admissible even though they seem to be pursuing different lines of investigation. "What powerfully struck me then was that Kierkegaard was writing about *exactly what my fellow patients and I were going through*. Freud was not; he was writing on a different level, giving formulations of the psychic mechanisms by which anxiety came about."[11] Kierkegaard's approach was to offer a subjectively oriented account of anxiety, and the acceptability of his work depends upon the extent to which it results in descriptions of anxiety that actually accord with the experience of those who experience it. That Freud's results do not accord with such experiences does not invalidate them, for they are judged by different criteria entirely, namely those of scientific method. In just this way we may distinguish between those criteria with reference to which we are to judge the work of behaviorism and those relevant to assessing psychological descriptions from the standpoint of subjectivity. For those who prefer only the latter to rule out the possibility of the former on the ground that psychology *must* characterize the mental life as it is experienced is simply dogmatism. It seems, however, that this view of psychology came to be accepted by behaviorists, who then proceeded to deny that there was a subjective standpoint at all. And this is clearly incredible. One may suggest that the source of both dogmatism and incredibility is the treatment, by denizens of both camps, of the methodological prescriptions of their respective procedures as if they were more fundamentally metaphysical, and on that basis proscribing entirely what failed to be in accord with them.

To return to our present purpose, I think it is not difficult to see that the same sort of distinction I have been making for psychology can be made for social science. And so we may come to recognize that far from confronting each other as incompatible ways of studying the same phenomena of experience, the phenomenological and the naturalistic approaches to the social are simply different undertakings for the purpose of acquiring different kinds of knowledge. I do not wish to suggest that they are so disparate that there is no point of contact between them; rather, on the contrary, I hope that one of the conclusions

[11] R. May, "Kierkegaard and Freud," *The New School Bulletin*, XVII, February 15th, 1960; May's italics.

which will emerge from the discussion to follow is that the two approaches are complementary and, in fact, mutually require one another.

Schutz himself may be pointing in the direction of our distinction when he says the following: "The fathers of behaviorism had no other purpose than that of describing and explaining real human acts within a real human world. But the fallacy of this theory consists in the substitution of a fictional world for social reality by promulgating methodological principles as appropriate for the social sciences which, though proved true in other fields, prove a failure in the realm of intersubjectivity."[12] Implicit in this statement is recognition of the fact that the behaviorists could do whatever job behaviorism is capable of doing within that area of investigation suited to their methods, but that it was a mistake to extend them beyond their proper limits. The notion that they substituted "a fictional world for social reality," is just Schutz's way of saying that they treated their methodological principles as metaphysical ones, thus imposing unwarranted restrictions upon the possibility of theoretical developments.

Schutz then goes on to recognize that it is possible to do useful social scientific work which does not treat the social world from the standpoint of subjectivity. In his own words: "Doubtless *on a certain level* real scientific work may be performed and has been performed without entering into the problems of subjectivity. We can go far ahead in the study of social phenomena, like social institutions of all kinds, social relations, and even social groups, without leaving the basic frame of reference, which can be formulated as follows: What does all this mean for us, the scientific observer?" But this, he adds, "does not alter the fact that this type of social science does not deal directly and immediately with the social life-world, common to us all, but with skilfully and expediently chosen idealizations and formulizations of the social world which are not repugnant to its facts."[13] Schutz's view is that no matter how well it does its work, naturalistic social science is defective and inferior precisely because it fails to deal directly with the common social world as it pre-

[12] A. Schutz, "The Social World and the Theory of Social Action," 205.

[13] *Ibid.*, p. 207; my italics.

sents itself to those who experience it. He also holds that it is always possible to go back to the subjective standpoint and that we must go back to it if our interest is at all in the social. He holds that even naturalistic social science rests upon the phenomenological standpoint. I think that in what follows it will emerge that there is a sense in which this is justified. Yet I think, too, that there are problems confronting social science which can only be resolved along naturalistic lines. Our problem, then, is not to arrange the approaches to the study of sociocultural phenomena in an hierarchical order and so conclude that the phenomenological approach is or is not higher than the naturalistic, but, rather, to sketch the purposes and domains of each and to pay some attention to their possible points of contact.

II

Professor de Laguna is entirely correct in her claim that what the phenomenologists call the *"Lebenswelt,"* the social world the description of which Schutz and Natanson both take to be preeminently the task of social science, and what anthropologists describe as the cultural world are, in the end, two ways of referring to the same data of experience.[14] The main point of those who defend the phenomenological standpoint is that human action is informed by meanings, and that it is purposive in a way that only meaningful behavior can be. This means that to observe an action as if it were simply a physical event in a physically causal nexus would not enable the observer to apprehend the action as social, as something which cannot be reduced to the non-social. As long as we confine our attention to investigations of the social world which the investigator shares with the people he studies, it is easy to take the meanings which are involved for granted,[15] and by concentrating attention upon the behavior of individuals to ignore the fact that we have to do with more than individual behavior in a behavioristic sense.

If I prick my finger, or cut it or bruise it, I am very likely to

[14] G. A. de Laguna, "The *Lebenswelt* and the Cultural World," *Journal of Philosophy*, LVII, 1960, 777–791.

[15] The behavior is taken to be natural and its meaningful-conventional character overlooked.

put it into my mouth. My companions may express concern, but they certainly find nothing odd in my response to the accident, as they might, say, if a man of my age were to be seen sucking his thumb. Likely, they think that putting the hurt finger in my mouth has some beneficial effect, and likely, too, they would expect that most sensible people share their belief. Of course, the subject never comes up for discussion and these beliefs are rarely explicitly elicited, yet I suppose that most readers will agree that what I have just said obtains for most of the people they know. But once an anthropologist was riding somewhere in the western part of the United States in the company of an American Indian, and, catching his finger in some appurtenance of his saddle, he hurriedly put the finger into his mouth only to find himself an object of amusement to his companion.[16] To the Indian, the sudden act of the anthropologist was odd, even silly, and apparently made no sense as a sequel to the accident. Presumably for him, the "theory" which underlay the anthropologist's action had no standing at all: it was not an element of his own culture and he simply never heard of it. Instances of this kind can be multiplied indefinitely, and we shall be satisfied simply to add a few words of Raymond Firth, who observes that "if the anthropologist is travelling in the Plateau of Northern Nigeria . . . he may meet men from the Bi Rom and other pagan tribes living there. They will probably shake their clenched fists in the air as he approaches. According to his fears or his politics, he may interpret this as a symbol of anger or of solidarity among fellow-workers. In time, he will find it is merely the normal greeting."[17] Firth calls this "contextualization," and means that in time the anthropologist comes to understand the sense of the behavior as he comes to appreciate its context.

The experiences of anthropologists when they first try to get their bearings in a new community entirely different from their own amply evidence the fact that the behavior of people when observed but not understood within the context of the way of life it exemplifies is entirely unintelligible. I do not say that this

---

[16] I believe I heard this story from Professor George P. Murdock, in an anthropology seminar at the Yale Graduate School. It was intended to illustrate the notion of "covert culture."

[17] R. Firth, *Elements of Social Organization*, p. 23.

understanding is of the motives of the particular agent whose behavior is observed, though, of course, there are times when these motives are quite central to any effort to make sense of his behavior. These are times when he, behaving as the rational agent he sometimes is, does what he does in order to effect some end in view, and unless we are cognizant of the end we are neither able to make sense of what he does nor to assess the adequacy of his action. But much of human action is not purposive in this way yet, nevertheless, cannot be made intelligible without the kind of understanding that is simply not to be had if one limits one's apprehension of it to accord with the prescriptions of behaviorism. What must be understood to make sense of such action is the mode of social existence which makes this sort of behavior the thing to expect or the thing to do. To think that the kind of understanding called for is of "subjective states of mind"[18] is simply to miss the point, for it seems to suggest that its advocates treat all social action as if it were the purposive behavior of rational agents. And this is surely not the case.

My last remarks may seem to have a peculiar effect upon our notion of social inquiry from the standpoint of subjectivity for they seem to suggest that such inquiry is not concerned with the idiosyncratic standpoint of the individual, though this is the only standpoint which is actually that of a subject. It may well be that those—or many of those—who have defended some version of the phenomenological standpoint in social science would find any attempt to limit the centrality of the idiosyncratic standpoint unacceptable. We have seen, for example, that Schutz objects to those who would place emphasis upon the standpoint of the observer rather than that of the participant in social action, and since the participant is always a particular individual one might think that this requires that only the discovery of the individual's particular purpose in doing what he does will suffice to make it intelligible. The difficulty with such a view, however, is that there is no reason for thinking that every—perhaps even most—human action is done with an end in view, and this would seem to result in that much such action could not be made intelligible as social-meaningful rather than biological-behavioral.

[18] E. Nagel, "On the Method of *Verstehen* as the Sole Method of Philosophy," in this book, p. 264.

Actually, we do not have to impose such a narrow interpretation upon Schutz, for it seems clear enough that writers such as he and Natanson take the regularities of social life to be part of the *Lebenswelt* that phenomenological social science is called upon to describe, and these are not subjective in the idiosyncratic sense. The standpoint, then, that this approach is supposed to make explicit is that which the actor may be thought to acquire in the course of his enculturation and which comes to inform his life and actions, even though he need not be explicitly aware of it as one standpoint among others. The behavior of the subject becomes intelligible to the observer when the observer has come to understand the presuppositions of social action in the subject's community. If the observer is an enculturated member of the same community and not a scientific observer then the understanding is un-selfconscious and not explicit. If he is not, then his understanding is likely the outcome of the kind of painstaking effort we have come to expect from ethnographers. For the first, the activity in question makes sense and is natural. For the second, it is intelligible in light of what he has come to know about the culture of the actor.

In sum, the purpose of the phenomenological approach to the study of social behavior is to make explicit what is implicit in the social action of the members of a given community. In a sense, Schutz is right in seeing this as the exploration of the social from the standpoint of the subject or the actor in that the whole point of the investigation is to reveal just what precisely it is that makes the actor's action intelligible. Yet the ordinary—naive—actor acts in ways he takes to be "natural" and not the consequence of adherence to a standpoint. That it is the consequence of such adherence is precisely the point of view of the observer. In view of the way that writers like Schutz make so much of their claim that the standpoint of the subject is the only *real* standpoint for the study of social phenomena, this may seem somewhat paradoxical.

III

I think that from what we have already said, it is possible to argue that between the phenomenological and the naturalistic conception of the social there is really no fundamental difference.

Such an argument would be based upon the facts that the phenomenological social scientist does not concern himself with the merely idiosyncratic and the naturalistic social scientist does not adopt the standpoint of behavioristic psychology. For both of them social inquiry has to do with socially meaningful action, action the entire point of which depends upon the presence of shared meanings or values.

But even if the idea of the social implicit in the work of both phenomenological and naturalistic social science is identical, it is still the case that some social research is not phenomenological. Not all social inquiry is directed toward determining the character of the system of shared meanings in terms of which the action of the members of a given society is seen to make sense. In seeking such intelligibility one assumes that some system of ideas or what have you exists and that one must only discover what it is in order to discover the standpoint of the acting subject.[19] To think that this approach exhausts the possibilities of work in the social sciences, however, is simply to think that we cannot ask of any such system of ideas—or any system of institutional arrangements which are reflected in the system of ideas— how it came to be as it is. But here we find ourselves trying *to account for the development* of a particular social world, and this is not the same as trying to constitute that social world in order to understand the activities of those whose world it is. Only the latter is pointed at the recovering of the standpoint of subjectivity as this is intended by Schutz and Natanson. The kind of inquiry I am now concerned about, however, is, to speak metaphorically, outside of the given standpoint and seeks to account for it. Consequently, it is clearly not social science of the sort that the phenomenological philosophers insist is the only proper way to achieve the most desirable kind of social knowledge.

Any historical account which is not an attempt to reconstitute a social world which once was but is no more, but is, rather, an attempt to trace the development of institutions, must, per-

---

[19] A Wittgensteinian version of the phenomenological approach may be found in P. Winch, *The Idea of a Social Science: and Its Relation to Philosophy*, in this book pp. 101-118. For a criticism of it in the spirit of the present section of the paper, see my review in *The Philosophical Review*, LXVIII, 1960, 411-14.

force, fail to satisfy the requirement of the phenomenological approach. While at each stage in the development recounted one may hope to reconstruct the standpoint which renders intelligible the actions of the men and women whose standpoint it is, it is clear enough that the sweep of the development as presented cannot possibly be from the subjective standpoint of any of the actors in question but must be entirely from that of the observer or historian. The development as reconstructed is introduced for the purpose of making sense of what the observer finds before him, namely, the sundry documents, artifacts and such like which constitute his historical evidence.[20] Presumably, the historian purports to be characterizing the standpoint of the people and leading actors with whom he is concerned, but that in no way alters our point that his characterization is made from the standpoint of himself confronting the evidence which lies before him. Given the nature of historical research, this is the only standpoint which is possible to him. (It may be noted, by the way, that one may always take ethnography, presumably the model of phenomenological social science, as being entirely like history in the respect just noted. Instead of dealing with documents and artifacts, the ethnographer is faced with the task of making intelligible his observations or his field notes. We have tended to think of the ethnographer as *reconstructing* the subjective standpoint of the people whose actions he observes, but we can just as easily think of him as *postulating* that standpoint in order to explain what he observes. This latter way of putting the matter would be part of an attempt to characterize the standpoint of the ethnographer himself, part of a methodological account of ethnography.)[21]

Just as historians may be interested in the development of events, institutions, and the like in the course of time, so too sociologists and anthropologists. It will serve no purpose of this paper to deal in any detail with the kind of investigation that such scholars call "diachronic," and it will suffice to call passing attention to the fact that the development characterized cannot possibly be in accord with the subjective standpoint of given actors. It may be agreed that each stage of the development is a

[20] Cf. L. J. Goldstein, "Evidence and Events in History," *Philosophy of Science*, XXIX, 1962, 174–182.
[21] *Ibid.*, p. 183.

reconstruction of a subjective standpoint, but what is done in such investigations is not to confront subjects engaged in action in order to discover the standpoint which renders their action intelligible—something which can only be done at the very most with contemporary actors who must always be at the end of the sequence of development—but rather to assume or postulate past stages or standpoints in order to render present practice or presently existing evidence intelligible.

In addition to such investigations, there is also the interest of at least some social scientists in the formulation of general laws, and it is easily seen that such formulation can hardly be the reconstruction of a subjective standpoint. It was noted above that the phenomenological approach to the social involves the discovery of the expected regularities characteristic of the social world being reconstructed. It might be thought that the formulation of these regularities represents a contribution to theoretical social science—hence that such theory is phenomenological—but this would be mistaken. Though from the standpoint of the acting individual we have to do with a recurrent phenomenon, from the standpoint of describing a given social world we have to do with a single fact: this is a social world in which when such-and-such is the case then some determinate sequel may be anticipated. But there are other social worlds in which it is not the case, and so our formulation is not a general or theoretical statement about social worlds. This recurrence may be said to form part of the constant background for the action of those who participate in the given social world, but the discovery of its presence there is hardly a theoretical matter. On the contrary, it is the task of theory, together with history, to explain how the given feature of the social world has come to be as it is. Our explanation refers to antecedent conditions, i.e., must make use of history, but in order to render intelligible or to justify the claim that the present feature emerged out of the antecedent condition one must have recourse to some system of theoretical social science.[22] Whatever one wants to say about such laws, they surely cannot be reconstructed subjective standpoints, since their purpose here is to help us understand the transition from one such standpoint to another. And, indeed, even if we were not explicitly aware of

[22] Cf. C. G. Hempel, *op. cit.*

their purpose here, enough is known about the logic of scientific theory and the general character of scientific propositions to see that it simply would make nonsense to think of theoretical social science as being the reconstruction of a subjective standpoint. Such propositions are intended to state that the elements of systems characterized in determinate ways bear certain specified or specifiable relationships to one another. To rule these out of social science on the ground that they do not conform to the ideal of a phenomenological social science would be most arbitrary indeed. I find it difficult to believe that writers such as Schutz and Natanson actually intend that this be done.

IV

We have seen that there are at least two kinds of approach to the study of the social and that to suggest that only the so-called phenomenological approach is true to the reality of its subject-matter is somewhat arbitrary. Indeed, if one were required to choose between the two approaches, we shall see that it is the phenomenological approach which would have to be rejected in favor of the naturalistic. But there is really no reason for not adopting a position of methodological tolerance and keeping what may be derived from both of these procedures.

If one agrees with the phenomenologist that inquiry must proceed from the standpoint of the subject, I do not see how one may gainsay the fact that the ultimate subject of any investigation is the investigator himself. No account of what the investigator does, or, more generally, no attempt to characterize the methodology of the sort of investigation it is, can fail to conclude that what is produced is produced from the investigator's own standpoint. The ethnographer purports to reconstruct a standpoint which is supposed to make the action of the people he observes subjectively meaningful, i.e., meaningful from their own point of view. But this cannot be established beyond peradventure, and it is always possible that the reconstruction corresponds to nothing in the feelings and experiences of the observed behavers and is only introduced by the observer because it makes the best sense of what he has observed. I am not saying that this must be the case and that the observer is never able to come to understand the standpoint of the community in which his investigation is being carried out. But I am saying that it is always possible to wonder if the reconstructed standpoint is the standpoint of the behavers, and that a strict account of its genesis and its function in the work of the social scientist makes it clear that its formulation in the way that the investigator formulates it has its origin in his need to understand what he observes. Hence, if we are required to choose between the phenomenological and naturalistic standpoints, it would seem that the latter must win out. But this notwithstanding, it also appears that the results of the two approaches point to each other and may even be thought to require one another. No one wants to assert that the social world in which we now find ourselves always was, and so we must recognize that any account of our social world or *Lebenswelt* is an account of something which is but the latest stage of a series which cannot be constituted in the same way that this latest stage itself can. And this is only another way of saying that what is constructed by the phenomenological approach to the study of the social cannot be said to stand by itself in the sense that it had no antecedents but simply came into the world fullblown the way it is. It clearly presupposes what can only be known through the naturalistic approach.

On the other hand, one may wonder how much sense the study of the social, from any standpoint you please, would make to us if we were not acquainted, even pre-reflectively, with the idea of a social world which comes to us from participating in one. Merely being social creatures ourselves does not enable us to understand the behavior of others who do not share our social life, but it is only because we are social beings that we can come to know that to understand that behavior we are required to understand the point of view that underlies it. That the data or evidence which is the starting point for naturalistic social or historical studies are recognized by us to be the starting point for such enterprises, and not merely objects in space and time, is precisely because we experience the world as social beings. And that way of experiencing the world which we take for granted is just what the phenomenological sociologist wants to make explicit, just as the ethnographer wants to do for contemporaries who do not share our *Lebenswelt*. We have seen that any such effort may be challenged and that we can never be absolutely certain that a reconstruction of this kind actually accords with the subjective standpoint of the people being studied.[23] But this only shows that the phenomenological standpoint cannot be made entirely independent of the naturalistic, not that the attempt to understand human behavior from the standpoint of subjectivity must be abandoned.

[23] The standpoint of the other may certainly be in question even if his otherness may not.

Common-Sense and Scientific Interpretation of Human Action[1]

ALFRED SCHUTZ

─────

I. Introduction: Content of Experience and Thought Objects

1. THE CONSTRUCTS OF COMMON-SENSE AND OF SCIENTIFIC THINKING

"NEITHER common sense nor science can proceed without departing from the strict consideration of what is actual in experience." This statement by A. N. Whitehead is at the foundation of his analysis of the Organization of Thought.[2] Even the thing perceived in everyday life is more than a simple sense presentation.[3] It is a thought object, a construct of a highly complicated nature, involving not only particular forms of time-successions in order to constitute it as an object of one single sense, say of

[1] This article appeared originally in *Philosophy and Phenomenological Research* (Vol. XIV, No. 1, September 1953, pp. 1–37), and is reprinted with corrections in Alfred Schutz, *Collected Papers I: The Problem of Social Reality*, ed. and with an intro. by Maurice Natanson with a preface by H. L. Van Breda, The Hague: Martinus Nijhoff, 1962, pp. 3–47. It is reprinted here with the permission of *Philosophy and Phenomenological Research* and Martinus Nijhoff. The 1962 text has been used.

[2] A. N. Whitehead, *The Organization of Thought*, now partially republished in *The Aims of Education*, also as a Mentor Book. The quotations refer to this edition. For the first quotation see p. 110.

[3] *Ibid.*, ch. 9, "The Anatomy of Some Scientific Ideas, I Fact, II Objects."

sight,[4] and of space relations in order to constitute it as a sense-object of several senses, say of sight and touch,[5] but also a contribution of imagination of hypothetical sense presentations in order to complete it.[6] According to Whitehead, it is precisely the last-named factor, the imagination of hypothetical sense presentation, "which is the rock upon which the whole structure of common-sense thought is erected"[7] and it is the effort of reflective criticism "to construe our sense presentation as actual realization of the hypothetical thought object of perceptions."[8] In other words, the so-called concrete facts of common-sense perception are not so concrete as it seems. They already involve abstractions of a highly complicated nature, and we have to take account of this situation lest we commit the fallacy of misplaced concreteness.[9]

Science always, according to Whitehead, has a twofold aim: First, the production of a theory which agrees with experience, and second, the explanation of common-sense concepts of nature at least in their outline; this explanation consists in the preservation of these concepts in a scientific theory of harmonized thought.[10] For this purpose physical science (which, in this context, is alone of concern to Whitehead) has to develop devices by which the thought objects of common-sense perception are superseded by the thought objects of science.[11] The latter, such as molecules, atoms, and electrons have shed all qualities capable of direct sense presentation in our consciousness and are known to us only by the series of events in which they are implicated, events, to be sure, which are represented in our consciousness by sense presentations. By this device a bridge is formed between the fluid vagueness of sense and the exact definition of thought.[12]

It is not our concern to follow here step by step the ingenious method by which Whitehead uses the principle briefly outlined

[4] *Ibid.*, pp. 128 f. and 131.
[5] *Ibid.*, p. 131 and 136.
[6] *Ibid.*, p. 133.
[7] *Ibid.*, p. 134.
[8] *Ibid.*, p. 135.
[9] A. N. Whitehead, *Science and the Modern World*, reprinted as a Mentor Book, p. 52 f.
[10] *The Aims of Education*, p. 126.
[11] *Ibid.*, p. 135.
[12] *Ibid.*, p. 136.

for his analysis of the organization of thought, starting from the "anatomy of scientific ideas" and ending with the mathematically formulated theories of modern physics and the procedural rules of symbolic logic.[13] We are, however, highly interested in the basic view which Whitehead shares with many other prominent thinkers of our time such as William James,[14] Dewey,[15] Bergson,[16] and Husserl.[17] This view can be, very roughly, formulated as follows:

All our knowledge of the world, in common-sense as well as in scientific thinking, involves constructs, i.e., a set of abstractions, generalizations, formalizations, idealizations specific to the respective level of thought organization. Strictly speaking, there are no such things as facts, pure and simple. All facts are from the outset facts selected from a universal context by the activities of our mind. They are, therefore, always interpreted facts, either facts looked at as detached from their context by an artificial abstraction or facts considered in their particular setting. In either case, they carry along their interpretational inner and outer horizon. This does not mean that, in daily life or in science, we are unable to grasp the reality of the world. It just means that we grasp merely certain aspects of it, namely those which are relevant to us either for carrying on our business of living or from the point of view of a body of accepted rules of procedure of thinking called the method of science.

2. PARTICULAR STRUCTURE OF THE CONSTRUCTS
OF THE SOCIAL SCIENCES

If, according to this view, all scientific constructs are designed to supersede the constructs of common-sense thought, then a

13 *Ibid.*, pp. 112–123, 136–155.

14 W. James, *Principles of Psychology*, I, ch. 9, "The Stream of Thought," p. 224 f.; esp. p. 289 f.

15 J. Dewey, *Logic: The Theory of Inquiry*, esp. chs. 3, 4, 7, 8, 12; see also the essay, "The Objectivism-Subjectivism of Modern Philosophy" (1941) now in the collection *Problems of Men*, p. 316 f.

16 H. Bergson, *Matière et mémoire*, ch. 1, "La Sélection des Images par la Représentation."

17 See for instance E. Husserl, *Logische Untersuchungen*, II, "Die ideale Einheit der Species und die neuen Abstraktions Theorien"; rendered excellently by M. Farber, *The Foundation of Phenomenology*, ch. 9, esp. p. 251 f.; Husserl, *Ideen zu einer reinen Phänomenologie*, English trans. B. Gibson, First Section; *Formale und transzedentale Logik*, Secs. 82–86, 94–96 (cf. Farber. l.c., p 501 f.); *Erfahrung und Urteil*, Secs. 6–10, 16–24, 41–43, and *passim*.

principal difference between the natural and the social sciences becomes apparent. It is up to the natural scientists to determine which sector of the universe of nature, which facts and events therein, and which aspects of such facts and events are topically and interpretationally relevant to their specific purpose. These facts and events are neither preselected nor preinterpreted; they do not reveal intrinsic relevance structures. Relevance is not inherent in nature as such, it is the result of the selective and interpretative activity of man within nature or observing nature. The facts, data, and events with which the natural scientist has to deal are just facts, data, and events within his observational field but this field does not "mean" anything to the molecules, atoms, and electrons therein.

But the facts, events, and data before the social scientist are of an entirely different structure. His observational field, the social world, is not essentially structureless. It has a particular meaning and relevance structure for the human beings living, thinking, and acting therein. They have preselected and preinterpreted this world by a series of common-sense constructs of the reality of daily life, and it is these thought objects which determine their behavior, define the goal of their action, the means available for attaining them—in brief, which help them to find their bearings within their natural and socio-cultural environment and to come to terms with it. The thought objects constructed by the social scientists refer to and are founded upon the thought objects constructed by the common-sense thought of man living his everyday life among his fellow-men. Thus, the constructs used by the social scientist are, so to speak, constructs of the second degree, namely constructs of the constructs made by the actors on the social scene, whose behavior the scientist observes and tries to explain in accordance with the procedural[18] rules of his science.

Modern social sciences find themselves faced with a serious dilemma. One school of thought feels that there is a basic difference in the structure of the social world and of the world of nature. This insight leads, however, to the erroneous conclusion that the social sciences are *toto coelo* different from the natural sciences, a view which disregards the fact that certain procedural

[18] On the concept of procedural rules, see F. Kaufmann, *Methodology of the Social Sciences*, esp. chs. 3, 4; on the divergent views of the relationship between the natural and the social sciences, *ibid.*, ch. 10.

rules relating to correct thought organization are common to all empirical sciences. The other school of thought tries to look at the behavior of man in the same way in which the natural scientist looks at the "behavior" of his thought objects, taking it for granted that the methods of the natural sciences (above all, mathematical physics), which have achieved such magnificent results, are the only scientific methods. On the other hand, it takes for granted that the very adoption of the methods of the natural sciences for establishing constructs will lead to reliable knowledge of social reality. Yet these two assumptions are incompatible with each other. An ideally refined and fully developed behavioristic system, for example, would lead far away from the constructs in terms of which men in the reality of daily life experience their own and their fellow-men's behavior.

To overcome this difficulty particular methodological devices are required, among them the constructs of patterns of rational action. For the purpose of further analysis of the specific nature of the thought objects of social sciences we have to characterize some of the common-sense constructs used by men in everyday life. It is upon the latter that the former are founded.

II. Constructs of Thought Objects in Common-Sense Thinking

1. THE INDIVIDUAL'S COMMON-SENSE KNOWLEDGE OF THE WORLD IS A SYSTEM OF CONSTRUCTS OF ITS TYPICALITY

Let us try to characterize the way in which the wide-awake[19] grown-up man looks at the intersubjective world of daily life within which and upon which he acts as a man amidst his fellowmen. This world existed before our birth, experienced and interpreted by others, our predecessors, as an organized world. Now it is given to our experience and interpretation. All interpretation of this world is based on a stock of previous experiences of it, our own or those handed down to us by parents or teachers; these experiences in the form of "knowledge at hand" function as a scheme of reference.

[19] As to the precise meaning of this term, see A. Schutz, "On Multiple Realities," *Philosophy and Phenomenological Research*, V, 1945, 533–576.

To this stock of knowledge at hand belongs our knowledge that the world we live in is a world of more or less well circumscribed objects with more or less definite qualities, objects among which we move, which resist us and upon which we may act. Yet none of these objects is perceived as insulated. From the outset it is an object within a horizon of familiarity and pre-acquaintanceship which is, as such, just taken for granted until further notice as the unquestioned, though at any time questionable stock of knowledge at hand. The unquestioned pre-experiences are, however, also from the outset, at hand as *typical*, that is, as carrying open horizons of anticipated similar experiences. For example, the outer world is not experienced as an arrangement of individual unique objects, dispersed in space and time, but as "mountains," "trees," "animals," "fellow-men." I may have never seen an Irish setter but if I see one, I know that it is an animal and in particular a dog, showing all the familiar features and the typical behavior of a dog and not, say, of a cat. I may reasonably ask: "What kind of dog is this?" The question presupposes that the dissimilarity of this particular dog from all other kinds of dogs which I know stands out and becomes questionable merely by reference to the similarity it has to my unquestioned experiences of typical dogs In the more technical language of Husserl, whose analysis of the typicality of the world of daily life we have tried to sum up,[20] what is experienced in the actual perception of an object is apperceptively transferred to any other similar object, perceived merely as to its type. Actual experience will or will not confirm my anticipation of the typical conformity with other objects. If confirmed, the content of the anticipated type will be enlarged; at the same time the type will be split up into sub-types; on the other hand the concrete real object will prove to have its individual characteristics, which, nevertheless, have a form of typicality.

Now, and this seems to be of special importance, I *may* take the typically apperceived object as an *exemplar* of the general type and allow myself to be led to this concept of the type, but I do not *need* by any means to think of the concrete dog as an

---

[20] E. Husserl, *Erfahrung und Urteil*, Secs. 18–21, 82–85; cf. also A. Schutz, "Language, Language Disturbances, and the Texture of Consciousness," *Social Research*, XVII, 1950, esp. 384–390.

exemplar of the general concept of "dog." "In general" my Irish setter Rover shows all the characteristics which the type "dog," according to my previous experience, implies. Yet exactly what he has in common with other dogs is of no concern to me. I look at him as my friend and companion Rover, as such distinguished from all the other Irish setters with which he shares certain typical characteristics of appearance and behavior. I am, without a special motive, not induced to look at Rover as a mammal, an animal, an object of the outer world, although I know that he is all this too.

Thus, in the natural attitude of daily life we are concerned merely with certain objects standing out over against the unquestioned field of pre-experienced other objects, and the result of the selecting activity of our mind is to determine which particular characteristics of such an object are individual and which typical ones. More generally, we are merely concerned with some aspects of this particular typified object. Asserting of this object S that it has the characteristic property p, in the form "S is p," is an elliptical statement. For S, taken without any question as it appears to me, is not merely p but also q and r and many other things. The full statement should read: "S is, among many other things, such as q and r, also p." If I assert with respect to an element of the world as taken for granted: "S is p," I do so because under the prevailing circumstances I am interested in the p-being of S, disregarding as not relevant its being also q and r.[21]

The terms "interest" and "relevant" just used are, however, merely headings for a series of complicated problems which cannot be elaborated upon within the frame of the present discussion. We have to restrict ourselves to a few remarks.

Man finds himself at any moment of his daily life in a biographically determined situation, that is, in a physical and sociocultural environment as defined by him,[22] within which he has his position, not merely his position in terms of physical space and outer time or of his status and role within the social system

[21] See literature referred to in Footnote 20.

[22] As to the concept of "Defining the Situation," see the various pertinent papers of W. I. Thomas, now collected in the volume, *Social Behavior and Personality, Contributions of W. I. Thomas to Theory and Social Research,* ed. E. H. Volkart. Consult index and the valuable introductory essay by the editor.

but also his moral and ideological position.[23] To say that this definition of the situation is biographically determined is to say that it has its history; it is the sedimentation of all man's previous experiences, organized in the habitual possessions of his stock of knowledge at hand, and as such his unique possession, given to him and to him alone. This biographically determined situation includes certain possibilities of future practical or theoretical activities which shall be briefly called the "purpose at hand." It is this purpose at hand which defines those elements among all the others contained in such a situation which are relevant for this purpose. This system of relevances in turn determines what elements have to be made a substratum of generalizing typification, what traits of these elements have to be selected as characteristically typical, and what others as unique and individual, that is, how far we have to penetrate into the open horizon of typicality. To return to our previous example: A change in my purpose at hand and the system of relevances attached thereto, the shifting of the "context" within which S is interesting to me, may induce me to become concerned with the q-being of S, its being also p having become irrelevant to me.

2. THE INTERSUBJECTIVE CHARACTER OF COMMON-SENSE KNOWLEDGE AND ITS IMPLICATION

In analyzing the first constructs of common-sense thinking in everyday life we proceeded, however, as if the world were my private world and as if we were entitled to disregard the fact that it is from the outset an intersubjective world of culture. It is intersubjective because we live in it as men among other men, bound to them through common influence and work, understanding others and being understood by them. It is a world of culture because, from the outset, the world of everyday life is a universe of significance to us, that is, a texture of meaning which we have to interpret in order to find our bearings within it and come to terms with it. This texture of meaning, however—and this distinguishes the realm of culture from that of nature—originates in and has been instituted by human actions, our own and our fellow-men's, contemporaries and predecessors. All cultural objects—tools, symbols, language systems, works of art, social in-

---

[23] Cf. M. Merleau-Ponty, *Phénoménologie de la perception*, p. 158.

stitutions, etc.–point back by their very origin and meaning to the activities of human subjects. For this reason we are always conscious of the historicity of culture which we encounter in traditions and customs. This historicity is capable of being examined in its reference to human activities of which it is the sediment. For the same reason I cannot understand a cultural object without referring it to the human activity from which it originates. For example, I do not understand a tool without knowing the purpose for which it was designed, a sign or symbol without knowing what it stands for in the mind of the person who uses it, an institution without understanding what it means for the individuals who orient their behavior with regard to its existence. Here is the origin of the so-called postulate of subjective interpretation of the social sciences which will call for our attention later on.

Our next task is, however, to examine the additional constructs which emerge in common-sense thinking if we take into account that this world is not my private world but an intersubjective one and that, therefore, my knowledge of it is not my private affair but from the outset intersubjective or socialized. For our purpose we have briefly to consider three aspects of the problem of the socialization of knowledge:

a) The reciprocity of perspectives or the structural socialization of knowledge;
b) The social origin of knowledge or the genetic socialization of knowledge;
c) The social distribution of knowledge.

a. The Reciprocity of Perspectives

In the natural attitude of common-sense thinking in daily life I take it for granted that intelligent fellow-men exist. This implies that the objects of the world are, as a matter of principle, accessible to their knowledge, i.e., either known to them or knowable by them. This I know and take for granted beyond question. But I know also and take for granted that, strictly speaking, the "same"object must mean something different to me and to any of my fellow-men. This is so because

i)   I, being "here," am at another distance from and experience other aspects as being typical of the objects than he, who is "there." For the same reason, certain objects are out of my reach (of my seeing, hearing, my manipulatory sphere, etc.) but within his, and vice versa.

ii) My and my fellow-man's biographically determined situations, and therewith our respective purposes at hand and our respective systems of relevances originating in such purposes, must differ, at least to a certain extent.

Common-sense thinking overcomes the differences in individual perspectives resulting from these factors by two basic idealizations:

i) The idealization of the interchangeability of the standpoints: I take it for granted—and assume my fellow-man does the same—that if I change places with him so that his "here" becomes mine, I shall be at the same distance from things and see them with the same typicality as he actually does; moreover, the same things would be in my reach which are actually in his. (The reverse is also true.)

ii) The idealization of the congruency of the system of relevances: Until counterevidence I take it for granted—and assume my fellow-man does the same—that the differences in perspectives originating in our unique biographical situations are irrelevant for the purpose at hand of either of us and that he and I, that "We" assume that both of us have selected and interpreted the actually or potentially common objects and their features in an identical manner or at least an "empirically identical" manner, i.e., one sufficient for all practical purposes.

It is obvious that both idealizations, that of the interchangeability of the standpoints and that of the congruency of relevances—together constituting the *general thesis of reciprocal perspectives*—are typifying constructs of objects of thought which supersede the thought objects of my and my fellow-man's private experience. By the operation of these constructs of common-sense thinking it is assumed that the sector of the world taken for granted by me is also taken for granted by you, my individual fellow-man, even more, that it is taken for granted by "Us." But this "We" does not merely include you and me but "everyone who is one of us," i.e., everyone whose system of relevances is substantially (sufficiently) in conformity with yours and mine. Thus, the general thesis of reciprocal perspectives leads to the apprehension of objects and their aspects actually known by me and potentially known by you as everyone's knowledge. Such knowledge is conceived to be objective and anonymous, i.e., detached from and independent of my and my fellow-man's definition of the situation, our unique biographical circumstances and the actual and potential purposes at hand involved therein.

We must interpret the terms "objects" and "aspect of objects" in the broadest possible sense as signifying objects of knowledge taken for granted. If we do so, we shall discover the importance of the constructs of intersubjective thought objects, originating in the structural socialization of knowledge just described, for many problems investigated, but not thoroughly analyzed, by eminent social scientists. What is supposed to be known in common by everyone who shares our system of relevances is the way of life considered to be the natural, the good, the right one by the members of the "in-group";[24] as such, it is at the origin of the many recipes for handling things and men in order to come to terms with typified situations, of the folkways and mores, of "traditional behavior," in Max Weber's sense,[25] of the "of-course statements" believed to be valid by the in-group in spite of their inconsistencies,[26] briefly, of the "relative natural aspect of the world."[27] All these terms refer to constructs of a typified knowledge of a highly socialized structure which supersede the thought objects of my and my fellow-man's private knowledge of the world as taken for granted. Yet this knowledge has its history, it is a part of our "social heritage," and this brings us to the second aspect of the problem of socialization of knowledge, its genetic structure.

[24] W. G. Sumner, *Folkways*.

[25] M. Weber, *The Theory of Social and Economic Organization*, p. 115 f.; see also T. Parsons, *The Structure of Social Action*, ch. 16.

[26] R. S. Lynd, *Middletown in Transition*, ch. 12, and *Knowledge for What?* pp. 38–63.

[27] M. Scheler, *Die Wissensformen und die Gesellschaft, Probleme einer Soziologie des Wissens*, p. 58 f. Cf. H. Becker and H. Dahlke, "Max Scheler's Sociology of Knowledge," *Philosophy and Phenomenological Research*, II, 1942, 310–322, esp. 315.

b. The Social Origin of Knowledge

Only a very small part of my knowledge of the world originates within my personal experience. The greater part is socially derived, handed down to me by my friends, my parents, my teachers and the teachers of my teachers. I am taught not only how to define the environment (that is, the typical features of the relative natural aspect of the world prevailing in the in-group as the unquestioned but always questionable sum total of things taken for granted until further notice), but also how typical constructs have to be formed in accordance with the system of relevances accepted from the anonymous unified point of view of the in-group. This includes ways of life, methods of coming to terms with the environment, efficient recipes for the use of typical means for bringing about typical ends in typical situations. The typifying medium *par excellence* by which socially derived knowledge is transmitted is the vocabulary and the syntax of everyday language. The vernacular of everyday life is primarily a language of named things and events, and any name includes a typification and generalization referring to the relevance system prevailing in the linguistic in-group which found the named thing significant enough to provide a separate term for it. The pre-scientific vernacular can be interpreted as a treasure house of ready made pre-constituted types and characteristics, all socially derived and carrying along an open horizon of unexplored content.[28]

c. The Social Distribution of Knowledge

Knowledge is socially distributed. The general thesis of reciprocal perspectives, to be sure, overcomes the difficulty that my actual knowledge is merely the potential knowledge of my fellow-men and vice versa. But the stock of *actual* knowledge at hand differs from individual to individual, and common-sense thinking takes this fact into account. Not only *what* an individual knows differs from what his neighbor knows, but also *how* both know the "same" facts. Knowledge has manifold degrees of clarity, distinctness, precision, and familiarity. To take as an

[28] See A. Schutz, "Language, Language Disturbances, and the Texture of Consciousness," *op. cit.,* p. 392 f.

example William James' [29] well known distinction between "knowledge of acquaintance" and "knowledge-about," it is obvious that many things are known to me just in the dumb way of mere acquaintance, whereas *you* have knowledge "about" what makes them what they are and vise versa. I am an "expert" in a small field and "layman" in many others; and so are you.[30] Any individual's stock of knowledge at hand is at any moment of his life structured as having zones of various degrees of clarity, distinctness and precision. This structure originates in the system of prevailing relevances and is thus biographically determined. The knowledge of these individual differences is itself an element of common-sense experience: I know whom and under what typical circumstances I have to consult as a "competent" doctor or lawyer. In other words, in daily life I construct types of the Other's field of acquaintance and of the scope and texture of his knowledge. In doing so, I assume that he will be guided by certain relevance structures, expressing themselves in a set of constant motives leading to a particular pattern of action and even co-determining his personality. But this statement anticipates the analysis of the common-sense constructs related to the understanding of our fellow-men, which is our next task.[31]

3. THE STRUCTURE OF THE SOCIAL WORLD
AND ITS TYPIFICATION BY COMMON-SENSE STANDARDS

I, the human being, born into the social world, and living my daily life in it, experience it as built around my place in it, as open to my interpretation and action, but always referring to my actual biographically determined situation. Only in reference to

[29] W. James, *op. cit.*, I, p. 221 f.

[30] A. Schutz, "The Well-Informed Citizen: an Essay on the Social Distribution of Knowledge," *Social Research*, XIII, 1946, 463–472.

[31] With the exception of some economists (e.g., F. A. Hayek, "Economics and Knowledge," in *Individualism and Economic Order*) the problem of the social distribution of knowledge has not attracted the attention of the social scientists it merits. It opens a new field for theoretical and empirical research which would truly deserve the name of a sociology of knowledge, now reserved for an ill-defined discipline which just takes for granted the social distribution of knowledge, upon which it is founded. It may be hoped that the systematic investigation of this field will yield significant contributions to many problems of the social sciences such as those of social role, of social stratification, of institutional or organizational behavior, of the sociology of occupations and professions, of prestige and status, etc.

me does a certain kind of my relations with others obtain the specific meaning which I designate with the word "We"; only with reference to "Us," whose center I am, do others stand out as "You," and in reference to "You," who refer back to me, third parties stand out as "They." In the dimension of time there are with reference to me in my actual biographical moment "contemporaries," with whom a mutual interplay of action and reaction can be established; "predecessors," upon whom I cannot act, but whose past actions and their outcome are open to my interpretation and may influence my own actions; and "successors," of whom no experience is possible but toward whom I may orient my actions in a more or less empty anticipation. All these relations show the most manifold forms of intimacy and anonymity, of familiarity and strangeness, of intensity and extensity.[32]

In the present context we are restricting ourselves to the interrelationship prevailing among contemporaries. Still dealing with common-sense experience we may just take for granted that man can understand his fellow-man and his actions and that he can communicate with others because he assumes they understand his actions; also, that this mutual understanding has certain limits but is sufficient for many practical purposes.

Among my contemporaries are some with whom I share, as long as the relation lasts, not only a community of time but also of space. We shall, for the sake of terminological convenience, call such contemporaries "consociates" and the relationship prevailing among them a "face-to-face" relationship, this term being understood in a sense other than that used by Cooley[33] and his successors; we designate by it merely a purely formal aspect of social relationship equally applicable to an intimate talk between friends and the co-presence of strangers in a railroad car.

Sharing a community of space implies that a certain sector of the outer world is equally within the reach of each partner, and contains objects of common interest and relevance. For each partner the other's body, his gestures, his gait and facial ex-

---

[32] A. Schutz, *Der sinnhafte Aufbau der sozialen Welt*. See also A. Stonier and K. Bode, "A New Approach to the Methodology of the Social Sciences," *Economica*, V, 1937, 406–424, esp. 416 f.

[33] C. H. Cooley, *Social Organization*, chs. 3–5; and A. Schutz, "The Homecomer," *American Journal of Sociology*, L, 1945, 371.

pressions, are immediately observable, not merely as things or events of the outer world but in their physiognomical significance, that is, as symptoms of the other's thoughts. Sharing a community of time—and this means not only of outer (chronological) time, but of inner time—implies that each partner participates in the on-rolling life of the other, can grasp in a vivid present the other's thoughts as they are built up step by step. They may thus share one another's anticipations of the future as plans, or hopes or anxieties. In brief, consociates are mutually involved in one another's biography; they are growing older together; they live, as we may call it, in a pure We-relationship.

In such a relationship, fugitive and superficial as it may be, the Other is grasped as a unique individuality (although merely one aspect of his personality becomes apparent) in its unique biographical situation (although revealed merely fragmentarily). In all the other forms of social relationship (and even in the relationship among consociates as far as the unrevealed aspects of the Other's self are concerned) the fellow-man's self can merely be grasped by a "contribution of imagination of hypothetical meaning presentation" (to allude to Whitehead's statement quoted earlier), that is, by forming a construct of a typical way of behavior, a typical pattern of underlying motives, of typical attitudes of a personality type, of which the Other and his conduct under scrutiny, both outside of my observational reach, are just instances or exemplars. We cannot here[34] develop a full taxonomy of the structuredness of the social world and of the various forms of constructs of course-of-action types and personality types needed for grasping the Other and his behavior. Thinking of my absent friend A, I form an ideal type of his personality and behavior based on my past experience of A as my consociate. Putting a letter in the mailbox, I expect that unknown people, called postmen, will act in a typical way, not quite intelligible to me, with the result that my letter will reach the addressee within typically reasonable time. Without ever having met a Frenchman or a German, I understand "Why France fears the rearmament of Germany." Complying with a rule of English grammar, I follow a socially approved behavior pattern of con-

[34] See footnote 32.

temporary English-speaking fellow-men to which I have to adjust my own behavior in order to make myself understandable. And, finally, any artifact or utensil refers to the anonymous fellow-man who produced it to be used by other anonymous fellow-men for attaining typical goals by typical means.

These are just a few examples but they are arranged according to the degree of increasing anonymity of the relationship among contemporaries involved and therewith of the construct needed to grasp the Other and his behavior. It becomes apparent that an increase in anonymity involves a decrease of fullness of content. The more anonymous the typifying construct is, the more detached it is from the uniqueness of the individual fellow-man involved and the fewer aspects of his personality and behavior pattern enter the typification as being relevant for the purpose at hand, for the sake of which the type has been constructed. If we distinguish between (subjective) personal types and (objective) course-of-action types, we may say that increasing anonymization of the construct leads to the superseding of the former by the latter. In complete anonymization the individuals are supposed to be interchangeable and the course-of-action type refers to the behavior of "whomsoever" acting in the way defined as typical by the construct.

Summing up, we may say that, except in the pure We-relation of consociates, we can never grasp the individual uniqueness of our fellow-man in his unique biographical situation. In the constructs of common-sense thinking the Other appears at best as a partial self, and he enters even the pure We-relation merely with a part of his personality. This insight seems to be important in several respects. It helped Simmel[35] to overcome the dilemma between individual and collective consciousness, so clearly seen by Durkheim;[36] it is at the basis of Cooley's[37] theory of the origin

[35] G. Simmel, "How Is Society Possible?", in this book, pp. 73–92; see also, *The Sociology of Georg Simmel*, trans., ed., and with an intro. by K. H. Wolff, and consult Index under "Individual and Group."

[36] An excellent presentation of Durkheim's view in G. Gurvitch, *La Vocation Actuelle de la Sociologie*, ch. 6, pp. 351–409; see also T. Parsons, *The Structure of Social Action*, ch. 10; É. Benoît-Smullyan, "The Sociologism of Emile Durkheim and His School," in H. E. Barnes, *An Introduction to the History of Sociology*, pp. 499–537, and R. K. Merton, *Social Theory and Social Structure*.

[37] C. H. Cooley, *Human Nature and the Social Order*, rev. ed., p. 184.

of the Self by a "looking glass effect"; it lead George H. Mead[38] to his ingenious concept of the "generalized other"; it is, finally, decisive for the clarification of such concepts as "social functions," "social role," and, last but not least, "rational action."

But this is merely half the story. My constructing the Other as a partial self, as the performer of typical roles or functions, has a corollary in the process of self-typification which takes place if I enter into interaction with him. I am not involved in such a relationship with my total personality but merely with certain layers of it. In defining the role of the Other I am assuming a role myself. In typifying the Other's behavior I am typifying my own, which is interrelated with his, transforming myself into a passenger, consumer, taxpayer, reader, bystander, etc. It is this self-typification which is at the bottom of William James'[39] and of George H. Mead's[40] distinction between the "I" and the "Me" in relation to the social self.

We have, however, to keep in mind that the common-sense constructs used for the typification of the Other and of myself are to a considerable extent socially derived and socially approved. Within the in-group the bulk of personal types and course-of-action types is taken for granted (until counter-evidence appears) as a set of rules and recipes which have stood the test so far and are expected to stand it in the future. Even more, the pattern of typical constructs is frequently institutionalized as a standard of behavior, warranted by traditional and habitual mores and sometimes by specific means of so-called social control, such as the legal order.

4. COURSE-OF-ACTION TYPES AND PERSONAL TYPES

We have now briefly to investigate the pattern of action and social interaction which underlies the construction of course-of-action and personal types in common-sense thinking.

[38] G. H. Mead: *Mind, Self, and Society,* pp. 152–163.
[39] W. James, *op. cit.,* I, Ch. 10.
[40] G. H. Mead, *op. cit.,* pp. 173–175, 196–198, 203; "The Genesis of the Self," reprinted in *The Philosophy of the Present,* pp. 176–195; "What Social Objects Must Psychology Presuppose?" *Journal of Philosophy,* X, 1913, 374–380.

a. Action, Project, Motive

The term "action" as used in this paper shall designate human conduct devised by the actor in advance, that is, conduct based upon a preconceived project. The term "act" shall designate the outcome of this ongoing process, that is, the accomplished action. Action may be covert (for example, the attempt to solve a scientific problem mentally) or overt, gearing into the outer world; it may take place by commission or omission, purposive abstention from acting being considered an action in itself.

All projecting consists in anticipation of future conduct by way of phantasying, yet it is not the ongoing process of action but the phantasied act as having been accomplished which is the starting point of all projecting. I have to visualize the state of affairs to be brought about by my future action before I can draft the single steps of such future acting from which this state of affairs will result. Metaphorically speaking, I must have some idea of the structure to be erected before I can draft the blueprints. Thus I have to place myself in my phantasy at a future time, when this action *will* already *have been* accomplished. Only then may I reconstruct in phantasy the single steps which *will have* brought forth this future act. In the terminology suggested, it is not the future action but the future act that is anticipated in the project, and it is anticipated in the Future Perfect Tense, *modo futuri exacti*. This time perspective peculiar to the project has rather important consequences.

i) All projects of my forthcoming acts are based upon my knowledge at hand at the time of projecting. To this knowledge belongs my experience of previously performed acts which are typically similar to the projected one. Consequently all projecting involves a particular idealization, called by Husserl the idealization of "I-can-do-it-again,"[41] i.e., the assumption that I may under typically similar circumstances act in a way typically similar to that in which I acted before in order to bring about a typically similar state of affairs. It is clear that this idealization involves a construction of a specific

[41] E. Husserl, *Formale und transzendentale Logik*, Sec. 74, p. 167; *Erfahrung und Urteil*, Sec. 24, Sec. 51b.

kind. My knowledge at hand at the time of projecting must, strictly speaking, be different from my knowledge at hand after having performed the projected act, if for no other reason than because I "grew older" and at least the experiences I had while carrying out my project have modified my biographical circumstances and enlarged my stock of experience. Thus, the "repeated" action will be something else than a mere re-performance. The first action A' started within a set of circumstances C' and indeed brought about the state of affairs S'; the repeated action A'' starts in a set of circumstances C'' and is expected to bring about the state of affairs S''. By necessity C'' will differ from C' because the experience that A' succeeded in bringing about S' belongs to my stock of knowledge, which is an element of C'', whereas to my stock of knowledge, which was an element of C', belonged merely the empty anticipation that this would be the case. Similarly S'' will differ from S' as A'' will from A'. This is so because all the terms—C', C'', A', A'', S', S''—are as such unique and irretrievable events. Yet exactly those features which make them unique and irretrievable in the strict sense are—to my common-sense thinking—eliminated as being irrelevant for my purpose at hand. When making the idealization of "I-can-do-it-again" I am merely interested in the typicality of A, C, and S, all of them without primes. The construction consists, figuratively speaking, in the suppression of the primes as being irrelevant, and this, incidentally, is characteristic of typifications of all kinds.

This point will become especially important for the analysis of the concept of so-called rational action. It is obvious that in the habitual and routine actions of daily life we apply the construction just described in following recipes and rules of thumb which have stood the test so far and in frequently stringing together means and ends without clear knowledge "about" their real connections. Even in common-sense thinking we construct a world of supposedly interrelated facts containing exclusively elements deemed to be relevant for our purpose at hand.

ii) The particular time perspective of the project sheds some light on the relationship between project and motive. In ordinary speech the term "motive" covers two different sets of concepts which have to be distinguished.

a) We may say that the motive of a murderer was to obtain the money of the victim. Here "motive" means the state of affairs, the end, which is to be brought about by the action undertaken. We shall call this kind of motive the "in-order-to motive." From the point of view of the actor this class of motives refers to the future. The state of affairs to be brought about by the future action, pre-phantasied in its project, is the in-order-to motive for carrying out the action.

b) We may say that the murderer has been motivated to commit his deed because he grew up in this or that environment, had these or those childhood experiences, etc. This class of motives, which we shall call "(genuine)[42] because-motives" refers from the point of view of the actor to his past experiences which have determined him to act as he did. What is motivated in an action in the form of "because" is the project of the action itself (for instance, to satisfy his need for money by killing a man).

We cannot enter here[43] into a more detailed analysis of the theory of motives. But it should be pointed out that the actor who lives in his ongoing process of acting has merely the in-order-to motive of his ongoing action in view, that is, the projected state of affairs to be brought about. Only by turning back to his accomplished act or to the past initial phases of his still ongoing action or to the once established project which anticipates the act *modo futuri exacti* can the actor grasp retrospectively the because-motive that determined him to do what he did or what he projected to do. But then the actor is not acting any more; he is an observer of himself.

---

[42] Linguistically in-order-to motives may be expressed in modern languages also by "because"-*sentences*. Genuine because-motives, however, cannot be expressed by "in-order-to" *sentences*. This distinction between the two possibilities of linguistic expressions relating to the in-order-to motive, important as it is in another context, will be disregarded in the following and the term "because-motive" or "because-sentence" will be exclusively reserved for the genuine because-motive and its linguistic expression.

[43] See footnote 32.

The distinction between the two kinds of motives becomes of vital importance for the analysis of human interaction to which we now turn.

b. Social Interaction

Any form of social interaction is founded upon the constructs already described relating to the understanding of the Other and the action pattern in general. Take as an example the interaction of consociates involved in questioning and answering. In projecting my question, I anticipate that the Other will understand my action (for instance my uttering an interrogative sentence) as a question and that this understanding will induce him to act in such a way that I may understand his behavior as an adequate response. (I: "Where is the ink?" The Other points at a table.) The in-order-to motive of my action is to obtain adequate information which, in this particular situation, presupposes that the understanding of my in-order-to motive will become the Other's because-motive to perform an action in-order-to furnish me this information—provided he is able and willing to do so, which I assume he is. I anticipate that he understands English, that he knows where the ink is, that he will tell me if he knows, etc. In more general terms, I anticipate that he will be guided by the same types of motives by which in the past, according to my stock of knowledge at hand, I myself and many others were guided under typically similar circumstances. Our example shows that even the simplest interaction in common life presupposes a series of common-sense constructs—in this case constructs of the Other's anticipated behavior—all of them based on the idealization that the actor's in-order-to motives will become because-motives of his partner and vice versa. We shall call this *idealization* that *of the reciprocity of motives*. It is obvious that this idealization depends upon the general thesis of the reciprocity of perspectives, since it implies that the motives imputed to the Other are typically the same as my own or that of others in typically similar circumstances; all this in accordance with my genuine or socially derived knowledge at hand.

Suppose now that I want to find some ink in order to refill my fountain pen so that I can write this application to the fellowship committee which, if granted, will change my entire way of life. I, the actor (questioner), and I alone know of this plan of mine to obtain the fellowship which is the ultimate in-order-to motive of my actual action, the state of affairs to be brought about. Of course, this can be done merely by a series of steps (writing an application, bringing writing tools within my reach, etc.) each of them to be materialized by an "action" with its particular project and its particular in-order-to motive. Yet all these "sub-actions" are merely phases of the total action and all intermediary steps to be materialized by them are merely means for attaining my final goal as defined by my original project. It is the span of this original project which welds together the chain of sub-projects into a unit. This becomes clear if we consider that in this chain of interrelated partial actions, designed to materialize states of affairs which are merely "means" for attaining the projected end, certain links can be replaced by others or even drop out without any change in the original project. If I cannot find some ink I may turn to the typewriter in order to prepare my application.

In other words, only the actor knows "when his action starts and where it ends," that is, why it will have been performed. It is the span of his projects which determines the unit of his action. His partner has neither knowledge of the projecting preceding the actor's action nor of the context of a higher unit in which it stands. He knows merely that fragment of the actor's action which has become manifest to him, namely, the performed act observed by him or the past phases of the still ongoing action. If the addressee of my question were asked later on by a third person what I wanted from him he would answer that I wanted to know where to find some ink. That is all he knows of my projecting and its context, and he has to look at it as a self-contained unit action. In order to "understand" what I, the actor, meant by my action he would have to start from the observed act and to construct from there my underlying in-order-to motive for the sake of which I did what he observed.

It is now clear that the meaning of an action is necessarily a different one (a) for the actor; (b) for his partner involved with him in interaction and having, thus, with him a set of relevances and purposes in common; and (c) for the observer not involved in such relationship. This fact leads to two important consequences: First, that in common-sense thinking we have merely a *chance* to understand the Other's action sufficiently for our purpose at hand; secondly that to increase this chance we have to search for the meaning the action has for the actor. Thus, the postulate of the "subjective interpretation of meaning," as the unfortunate term goes, is not a particularity of Max Weber's[44] sociology or of the methodology of the social sciences in general but a principle of constructing course-of-action types in common-sense experience.[45]

But subjective interpretation of meaning is merely possible by revealing the motives which determine a given course of action. By referring a course-of-action type to the underlying typical motives of the actor we arrive at the construction of a personal type. The latter may be more or less anonymous and, therewith, more or less empty of content. In the We-relationship among consociates the Other's course of action, its motives (insofar as they become manifest) and his person (insofar as it is involved in the manifest action) can be shared in immediacy and the constructed types, just described, will show a very low degree of anonymity and a high degree of fullness. In constructing course-of-action types of contemporaries other than consociates, we impute to the more or less anonymous actors a set of supposedly invariant motives which govern their actions. This set is itself a construct of typical expectations of the Other's behavior and has been investigated frequently in terms of social role or function or institutional behavior. In common-sense thinking such a construct has a particular significance for projecting actions which are oriented upon my contemporaries' (not my consociates') behavior. Its functions can be described as follows:

1) I take it for granted that my action (say putting a stamped and duly addressed envelope in a mailbox) will induce anonymous

---

[44] M. Weber, *op. cit.*, pp. 9, 18, 22, 90, esp. p. 88: "In 'action' is included all human behavior when and insofar as the acting individual attaches a subjective meaning to it . . . Action is social insofar as, by virtue of the subjective meaning attached to it by the acting individual (or individuals), it takes account of the behavior of others and is thereby oriented in its course." See T. Parsons, *op. cit.*, esp. pp. 82 f., 345–347, and 484 f.; F. Kaufmann, *op. cit.* p. 166 f.

[45] Cf. A. Schutz, "Concept and Theory Formation in the Social Sciences," this book, p. 239 f.

fellow-men (postmen) to perform typical actions (handling the mail) in accordance with typical in-order-to motives (to live up to their occupational duties) with the result that the state of affairs projected by me (delivery of the letter to the addressee within reasonable time) will be achieved. 2) I also take it for granted that my construct of the Other's course-of-action type corresponds substantially to his own self-typification and that to the latter belongs a typified construct of my, his anonymous partner's, typical way of behavior based on typical and supposedly invariant motives. ("Whoever puts a duly addressed and stamped envelope in the mailbox is assumed to intend to have it delivered to the addressee in due time.") 3) Even more, in my own self-typification—that is by assuming the role of a customer of the mail service—I have to project my action in such a typical way as I suppose the typical post office employee expects a typical customer to behave. Such a construct of mutually interlocked behavior patterns reveals itself as a construct of mutually interlocked in-order-to and because motives which are supposedly invariant. The more institutionalized or standardized such a behavior pattern is, that is, the more typified it is in a socially approved way by laws, rules, regulations, customs, habits, etc., the greater is the chance that my own self-typifying behavior will bring about the state of affairs aimed at.

c. The Observer

We have still to characterize the special case of the observer who is not a partner in the interaction patterns. His motives are not interlocked with those of the observed person or persons; he is "tuned in" upon them but not they upon him. In other words, the observer does not participate in the complicated mirror-reflexes involved by which in the interaction pattern among contemporaries, the actor's in-order-to motives become understandable to the partner as his own because motives and vice versa. Precisely this fact constitutes the so-called "disinterestedness" or detachment of the observer. He is not involved in the actor's hopes and fears whether or not they will understand one another and achieve their end by the interlocking of motives. Thus, his system of relevances differs from that of the interested parties and permits him to see at the same time more and less than what is seen by them. But under all circumstances, it is merely the manifested fragments of the actions of *both* partners that are accessible to his observation. In order to understand them the observer has to avail himself of his knowledge of typically similar patterns of interaction in typically similar situational settings and has to construct the motives of the actors from that sector of the course of action which is patent to his observation. The constructs of the observer are, therefore, different ones than those used by the participants in the interaction, if for no other reason than the fact that the purpose of the observer is different from that of the interactors and therewith the systems of relevances attached to such purposes are also different. There is a mere chance, although a chance sufficient for many practical purposes, that the observer in daily life can grasp the subjective meaning of the actor's acts. This chance increases with the degree of anonymity and standardization of the observed behavior. The scientific observer of human interrelation patterns, the social scientist, has to develop specific methods for the building of his constructs in order to assure their applicability for the interpretation of the subjective meaning the observed acts have for the actors. Among these devices we are here especially concerned with the constructs of models of so-called rational actions. Let us consider first the possible meaning of the term "rational action" within the common-sense experience of everyday life.

III. Rational Action Within Common-Sense Experience

Ordinary language does not sharply distinguish among a sensible, a reasonable, and a rational way of conduct. We may say that a man acted sensibly if the motive and the course of his action is understandable to us, his partners or observers. This will be the case if his action is in accordance with a socially approved set of rules and recipes for coming to terms with typical problems by applying typical means for achieving typical ends. If I, if We, if "Anybody who is one of us" found himself in typically similar circumstances he would act in a similar way. Sensible behavior, however, does not presuppose that the actor is guided by insight into his motives and the means-ends context. A strong emotional reaction against an offender might be sensible and refraining from it foolish. If an action seems to be sensible to the observer and is, in addition, supposed to spring from a judicious choice among different courses of action, we may call it reasonable even if such action follows traditional or habitual patterns just taken for granted. Rational action, however, presupposes that the actor has clear and distinct insight[46] into the ends, the means, and the secondary results, which "involves rational consideration of alternative means to the end, of the relations of the end to other prospective results of employment of any given means and, finally, of the relative importance of different possible ends. Determination of action, either in affectual or in traditional terms, is thus incompatible with this type."[47]

[46] This postulate of Leibniz obviously underlies the concept of rationality used by many students of this topic. Pareto, distinguishing between logical and non-logical actions, requires that the former have logically to conjoin means to ends not only from the standpoint of the subject performing the action but also from the standpoint of other persons who have a more extensive knowledge, that is, of the scientist. (V. Pareto, *Trattato de Sociologia Generale*, English trans. under the title *The Mind and Society*, ed. A. Livingston; see esp. I, secs. 150 ff.) Objective and subjective purpose have to be identical. Professor Talcott Parsons (*The Structure of Social Action*, p. 58) develops a similar theory. Pareto admits, however (l.c., sect. 150), that from the subjective point of view nearly all human actions belong to the logical class. Professor Howard Becker (*Through Values to Social Interpretation*, pp. 23–27) is of the opinion that action may be found (expediently) rational where it is completely centered upon means viewed by the actor as adequate for the attainment of ends which he conceives as unambiguous.

[47] M. Weber, *op. cit.*, p. 117. The characterization of "rational action" follows Max Weber's definition of one of the two types of rational actions distinguished by him (*op. cit.*, p. 115), namely, the so-called "*zweckrationales Handeln*" (rendered in Parsons' translation by "rational orientation to a system of discrete ends"). We disregard here Weber's second type of rational action, the "*wertrationales Handeln*" (rendered by "rational orientation to an absolute value") since the distinction between both types can be reduced in the terms of the present discussion to a distinction between two types of "because-motives" leading to the project of an action as such. "Zweckrationales Handeln" implies that within the system of hierarchial projects, which we have called the "plans," several courses of action stand to choice and that this choice has to be a rational one; "Wertrationales Handeln" cannot choose among several projects of action equally open to the actor within the system of his plan. The project is taken for granted, but there are alternatives open for bringing about the projected state of affairs, and they have to be determined by rational selection. Parsons has rightly pointed out (l.c., p. 115, footnote 38) that it is nearly impossible to find English terms for "*Zweckrational*" and "*Wertrational*," but the circumscription chosen by him for their translation already implies an interpretation of Weber's theory and obfuscates an important issue: Neither

These very preliminary definitions for sensible, reasonable, and rational actions are stated in terms of common-sense interpretations of other people's actions in daily life but, characteristically, they refer not only to the stock of knowledge taken for granted in the in-group to which the observer of this course of action belongs but also to the subjective point of view of the actor, that is, to his stock of knowledge at hand at the time of carrying out the action. This involves several difficulties. First, it is, as we have seen, our biographical situation which determines the problem at hand and, therewith, the systems of relevances under which the various aspects of the world are constructed in the form of types. Of necessity, therefore, the actor's stock of knowledge will differ from that of the observer. Even the general thesis of the reciprocity of perspectives is not sufficient to eliminate this difficulty because it presupposes that both the observed and the observer are sharing a system of relevances sufficiently homogeneous in structure and content for the practical purpose involved. If this is not the case, then a course of action which is perfectly rational from the point of view of the actor may appear as non-rational to the partner or observer and vice versa. Both attempts, to induce rain by performing the rain-dance or by seeding clouds with silver iodide, are subjectively seen, rational actions from the point of view of the Hopi Indian or the modern meteorologist respectively, but both would have been judged as non-rational by a meteorologist twenty years ago.

Secondly, even if we restrict our investigation to the subjective point of view, we have to ascertain whether there is a difference in the meaning of the term "rational," in the sense of reasonable, if applied to my own past acts or to the determination

---

is, in the case of "*Zweckrationalität*," a system of *discrete* ends presupposed nor, in the case of "*Wertrationalität*," an absolute value. (For Parsons' own theory, see pp. 16 ff. of his introduction to the Weber volume.)

Far more important for our problem than the distinction of two types of rational action is the distinction between rational actions of both types, on the one hand, and traditional and affectual actions on the other. The same holds good for the modifications suggested by Howard Becker (*op. cit.*, p. 22 f.) between "four types of means" followed by the members of any society in attaining their ends: (1) expedient rationality; (2) sanctioned rationality; (3) traditional non-rationality; (4) affective non-rationality. Whereas Weber and Parsons include the ends in their concept of rationality, Becker speaks of types of means.

of a future course of my actions. At first glance, it seems that the difference is considerable. What I did has been done and cannot be undone, although the state of affairs brought about by my actions might be modified or eliminated by countermoves. I do not have, with respect to past actions, the possibility of choice. Anything anticipated in an empty way in the project which had preceded my past action has been fulfilled or not by the outcome of my action. On the other hand, all future action is projected under the idealization of "I can do it again," which may or may not stand the test.

Closer analysis shows, however, that even in judging the reasonableness of our own past action we refer always to our knowledge at hand at the time of projecting such action. If we find, retrospectively, that what we had formerly projected as a reasonable course of action under the then known circumstances proved to be a failure, we may accuse ourselves of various mistakes: of an error in judgment if the then prevailing circumstances were incorrectly or incompletely ascertained; or of a lack of foresight if we failed to anticipate future developments, etc. We will, however, not say that we acted unreasonably.

Thus, in both cases, that of the past and of the future action, our judgment of reasonableness refers to the project determining the course of action and, still more precisely, to the choice among several projects of action involved. As has been shown elsewhere,[48] any projecting of future action involves a choice between at least two courses of conduct, namely, to carry out the projected action or to refrain from doing so.

Each of the alternatives standing to choice has, as Dewey says,[49] to be rehearsed in phantasy in order to make choice and decision possible. If this deliberation is to be strictly a rational one then the actor must have a clear and distinct knowledge of the following elements of each projected course-of-action standing to choice:

a) of the particular state of affairs within which his projected action has to start. This involves a sufficiently precise defi-

---

[48] A. Schutz, "Choosing Among Projects of Action," *Philosophy and Phenomenological Research*, XII, 1951, 161–184.
[49] J. Dewey, *Human Nature and Conduct*, p. 190.

nition of his biographical situation in the physical and sociocultural environment;

b) of the state of affairs to be brought about by his projected action, that is, its end. Yet since there is no such thing as
an isolated project or end, (all my projects, present to my mind
at a given time, being integrated into systems of projects, called
my plans and all my plans being integrated into my plan of life),
there are also no isolated ends. They are interconnected in
a hierarchical order, and the attaining of one might have repercussions on the other. I have, therefore, to have clear and distinct knowledge of the place of my project within the hierarchical order of my plans (or the interrelationship of the end to be
achieved with other ends), the compatibility of one with the
other, and the possible repercussions of one upon another, briefly:
of the secondary results of my future action, as Max Weber
calls it.[50]

c) of the various means necessary for attaining the established end, of the possibility of bringing them within my reach,
of the degree of the expediency of their application, of the possible employment of these same means for the attainment of
other potential ends, and of the compatibility of the selected
means with other means needed for the materialization of other
projects.

The complication increases considerably if the actor's project of a rational action involves the rational action or reaction of
a fellow-man, say of a consociate. Projecting rationally such a
kind of action involves sufficiently clear and distinct knowledge
of the situation of departure not only as defined by me but also
as defined by the Other. Moreover, there has to be sufficient
likelihood that the Other will be tuned in upon me and consider
my action as relevant enough to be motivated in the way of
because by my in-order-to motive. If this is the case, then there
has to be a sufficient chance that the Other will understand me,
and this means in the case of a rational interrelationship that he
will interpret my action rationally as being a rational one and
that he will react in a rational way. To assume that the Other
will do so implies, however, on the one hand, that he will have

[50] See quotation from Max Weber on p. 327 f.

sufficiently clear and distinct knowledge of my project and of its place in the hierarchy of my plans (at least as far as my overt actions makes them manifest to him) and of my system of relevances attached thereto; and, on the other hand, that the structure and scope of his stock of knowledge at hand will be in its relevant portion substantially similar to mine and that his and my system of relevances will, if not overlap, be at least partially congruent. If, furthermore, I assume in my projecting that the Other's reaction to my projected action will be a rational one, I suppose that he, in projecting his response, knows all the aforementioned elements (a), (b), and (c) of his reaction in a clear and distinct way. Consequently, if I project a rational action which requires an interlocking of my and the Other's motives of action to be carried out (e.g., I want the Other to do something for me), I must, by a curious mirror-effect, have sufficient knowledge of what he, the Other, knows (and knows to be relevant with respect to my purpose at hand), and this knowledge of his is supposed to include sufficient acquaintance with what I know. This is a condition of *ideally* rational interaction because without such mutual knowledge I could not "rationally" project the attainment of my goal by means of the Other's co-operation or reaction. Moreover, such mutual knowledge has to be clear and distinct; merely a more or less empty expectation of the Other's behavior is not sufficient.

It seems that under these circumstances rational social interaction becomes impracticable even among consociates. And yet we receive reasonable answers to reasonable questions, our commands are carried out, we perform in factories and laboratories and offices highly "rationalized" activities, we play chess together, briefly, we come conveniently to terms with our fellowmen. How is this possible?

Two different answers seem to offer themselves. First, if interaction among consociates is involved we may assume that the mutual participation in the consociate's onrolling life, the sharing of his anticipations so characteristic of the pure We-relation establishes the prerequisites for rational interaction just analyzed. Yet it is precisely this pure We-relation which is the irrational element of any interrelationship among consociates. The second answer refers not only to the interrelationship among consociates but among contemporaries in general. We may explain the rationality of human interaction by the fact that both actors orient their actions on certain standards which are socially approved as rules of conduct by the in-group to which they belong: norms, mores of good behavior, manners, the organizational framework provided for this particular form of division of labor, the rules of the chess game, etc. But neither the origin nor the import of the socially approved standard is "rationally" understood. Such standards might be traditionally or habitually accepted as just being taken for granted, and, within the meaning of our previous definitions, behavior of this kind will be sensible or even reasonable but not necessarily rational. At any rate, it will not be "ideally" rational, that is, meeting all the requirements worked out in the analysis of this concept.

We come, therefore, to the conclusion that "rational action" on the common-sense level is always action within an unquestioned and undetermined frame of constructs of typicalities of the setting, the motives, the means and ends, the courses of action and personalities involved and taken for granted. They are, however, not merely taken for granted by the actor but also supposed as being taken for granted by the fellow-man. From this frame of constructs, forming their undetermined horizon, merely particular sets of elements stand out which are clearly and distinctly determinable. To these elements refers the common-sense concept of rationality. Thus we may say that on this level actions are at best partially rational and that rationality has many degrees. For instance, our assumption that our fellow-man who is involved with us in a pattern of interaction knows its rational elements will never reach "empirical certainty" (certainty "until further notice" or "good until counter-evidence")[51] but will always bear the character of plausibility, that is, of subjective likelihood (in contradistinction to mathematical probability). We always have to "take chances" and to "run risks," and this situation is expressed by our hopes and fears which are merely the subjective corollaries of our basic uncertainty as to the outcome of our projected interaction.

To be sure, the more standardized the prevailing action pattern is, the more anonymous it is, the greater is the subjective

[51] E. Husserl, *Erfahrung und Urteil*, Sec. 77, p. 370.

chance of conformity and, therewith, of the success of inter-subjective behavior. Yet—and this is the paradox of rationality on the common-sense level—the more standardized the pattern is, the less the underlying elements become analyzable for common-sense thought in terms of rational insight.

All this refers to the criterion of rationality as applicable to the thinking of everyday life and its constructs. Only on the level of models of interaction patterns constructed by the social scientist in accordance with certain particular requirements defined by the methods of his science does the concept of rationality obtain its full significance. In order to make this clear we have first to examine the basic character of such scientific constructs and their relationship to the "reality" of the social world, as such reality presents itself to the common-sense thought of everyday life.

IV. Constructs of Thought Objects by the Social Sciences

I. THE POSTULATE OF SUBJECTIVE INTERPRETATION

There will be hardly any issue among social scientists that the object of the social sciences is human behavior, its forms, its organization, and its products. There will be, however, different opinions about whether this behavior should be studied in the same manner in which the natural scientist studies his object or whether the goal of the social sciences is the explanation of the "social reality" as experienced by man living his everyday life within the social world. The introductory section of the present discussion attempted to show that both principles are incompatible with each other. In the following pages we take the position that the social sciences have to deal with human conduct and its common-sense interpretation in the social reality, involving the analysis of the whole system of projects and motives, of relevances and constructs dealt with in the preceding sections. Such an analysis refers by necessity to the subjective point of view, namely, to the interpretation of the action and its settings in terms of the actor. Since this postulate of the subjective interpretation is, as we have seen, a general principle of constructing course-of-action types in common-sense experience, any social science aspiring to grasp "social reality" has to adopt this principle also.

Yet, at first glance, it seems that this statement is in contradiction to the well-established method of even the most advanced social sciences. Take as an example modern economics. Is it not the "behavior of prices" rather than the behavior of men in the market situation which is studied by the economist, the "shape of demand curves" rather than the anticipations of economic subjects symbolized by such curves? Does not the economist investigate successfully subject matters such as "savings," "capital," "business cycle," "wages" and "unemployment," "multipliers" and "monopoly" as if these phenomena were entirely detached from any activity of the economic subjects, even less without entering into the subjective meaning structure such activities may have for them? The achievements of modern economic theories would make it preposterous to deny that an abstract conceptual scheme can be used very successfully for the solution of many problems. And similar examples could be given from the field of almost all the other social sciences. Closer investigation, however, reveals that this abstract conceptual scheme is nothing else than a kind of intellectual shorthand and that the underlying subjective elements of human actions involved are either taken for granted or deemed to be irrelevant with respect to the scientific purpose at hand—the problem under scrutiny—and are, therefore, disregarded. Correctly understood, the postulate of subjective interpretation as applied to economics as well as to all the other social sciences means merely that we always *can*—and for certain purposes *must*—refer to the activities of the subjects within the social world and their interpretation by the actors in terms of systems of projects, available means, motives, relevances, and so on.[52]

But if this is true, two other questions have to be answered. First, we have seen from the previous analyses that the subjective meaning an action has for an actor is unique and individual because it originates in the unique and individual biographical situation of the actor. How is it then possible to grasp subjective meaning scientifically? Secondly, the meaning context of any system of scientific knowledge is objective knowledge but ac-

---

[52] L. Von Mises rightly calls his "Treatise on Economics" *Human Action*. See also F. A. Hayek, *The Counter-Revolution of Science*, pp. 25–36.

cessible equally to all his fellow scientists and open to their control, which means capable of being verified, invalidated, or falsified by them. How is it, then, possible to grasp by a system of objective knowledge subjective meaning structures? Is this not a paradox?

Both questions can be satisfactorily met by a few simple considerations. As to the first question, we learned from White-head that all sciences have to construct thought objects of their own which supersede the thought objects of common-sense thinking.[53] The thought objects constructed by the social sciences do not refer to unique acts of unique individuals occurring within a unique situation. By particular methodological devices, to be described presently, the social scientist replaces the thought objects of common-sense thought relating to unique events and occurrences by constructing a model of a sector of the social world within which merely those typified events occur that are relevant to the scientist's particular problem under scrutiny. All the other happenings within the social world are considered as being irrelevant, as contingent "data," which have to be put beyond question by appropriate methodological techniques as, for instance, by the assumption "all other things being equal."[54] Nevertheless, it is possible to construct a model of a sector of the social world consisting of typical human interaction and to analyze this typical interaction pattern as to the meaning it might have for the personal types of actors who presumptively originated them.

The second question has to be faced. It is indeed the particular problem of the social sciences to develop methodological devices for attaining objective and verifiable knowledge of a subjective meaning structure. In order to make this clear we have to consider very briefly the particular attitude of the scientist to the social world.

2. THE SOCIAL SCIENTIST AS DISINTERESTED OBSERVER

This attitude of the social scientist is that of a mere disinterested observer of the social world. He is not involved in the observed

[53] See above, pp. 304–306.
[54] On this concept see Felix Kaufmann, *op. cit.*, pp. 84 ff. and 213 ff., on the concept "scientific situation" pp. 52, 251 n. 4.

situation, which is to him not of practical but merely of cognitive interest. It is not the theater of his activities but merely the object of his contemplation. He does not act within it, vitally interested in the outcome of his actions, hoping or fearing what their consequences might be but he looks at it with the same detached equanimity with which the natural scientist looks at the occurrences in his laboratory.

A word of caution is necessary here to prevent possible misunderstandings. Of course, in his daily life the social scientist remains a human being, a man living among his fellow-men, with whom he is interrelated in many ways. And, surely, scientific activity itself occurs within the tradition of socially derived knowledge, is based upon co-operation with other scientists, requires mutual corroboration and criticism and can only be communicated by social interaction. But insofar as scientific activity is socially founded, it is one among all the other activities occurring within the social world. Dealing with science and scientific matters within the social world is one thing, the specific scientific attitude which the scientist has to adopt toward his object is another, and it is the latter which we propose to study in the following.

Our analysis of the common-sense interpretation of the social world of everyday life has shown how the biographical situation of man within the natural attitude determines at any given moment his purpose at hand. The system of relevances involved selects particular objects and particular typical aspects of such objects as standing out over against an unquestioned background of things just taken for granted. Man in daily life considers himself as the center of the social world which he groups around himself in layers of various degrees of intimacy and anonymity. By resolving to adopt the disinterested attitude of a scientific observer—in our language, by establishing the life-plan for scientific work—the social scientist detaches himself from his biographical situation within the social world. What is taken for granted in the biographical situation of daily life may become questionable for the scientist, and vice versa; what seems to be of highest relevance on one level may become entirely irrelevant on the other. The center of orientation has been radically shifted and so has the hierarchy of plans and projects. By making up his mind to carry out a plan for scientific work governed by the disinterested quest for truth in accordance with preestablished rules, called the scientific method, the scientist has entered a field of pre-organized knowledge, called the corpus of his science.[55] He has either to accept what is considered by his fellow-scientists as established knowledge or to "show cause" why he cannot do so. Merely within this frame may he select his particular scientific problem and make his scientific decisions. This frame constitutes his "being in a scientific situation" which supersedes his biographical situation as a human being within the world. It is henceforth the scientific problem once established which determines alone what is and what is not relevant to its solution, and thus what has to be investigated and what can be taken for granted as a "datum," and, finally, the level of research in the broadest sense, that is, the abstractions, generalizations, formalizations, idealizations, briefly, the constructs required and admissible for considering the problem as being solved. In other words, the scientific problem is the "locus" of all possible constructs relevant to its solution, and each construct carries along—to borrow a mathematical term—a subscript referring to the problem for the sake of which it has been established. It follows that any shifting of the problem under scrutiny and the level of research involves a modification of the structures of relevance and of the constructs formed for the solution of another problem or on another level; a great many misunderstandings and controversies, especially in the social sciences, originate from disregarding this fact.

3. DIFFERENCES BETWEEN COMMON-SENSE AND SCIENTIFIC CONSTRUCTS OF ACTION PATTERNS

Let us consider very briefly (and very incompletely) some of the more important differences between common-sense constructs and scientific constructs of interaction patterns originating in the transition from the biographically determined to the scientific situation. Common-sense constructs are formed from a "Here" within the world which determines the presupposed reciprocity of perspectives. They take a stock of socially derived and socially approved knowledge for granted. The social distribution of

[55] *Ibid.*, pp. 42 and 232.

knowledge determines the particular structure of the typifying construct, for instance, the assumed degree of anonymity of personal roles, the standardization of course-of-action patterns, and the supposed constancy of motives. Yet this social distribution itself depends upon the heterogeneous composition of the stock of knowledge at hand which itself is an element of common-sense experience. The concepts of "We," "You," "They," of "in-group" and "out-group," of consociates, contemporaries, predecessors, and successors, all of them with their particular structurization of familiarity and anonymity are at least implied in the common-sense typifications or even co-constitutive for them. All this holds good not only for the participants in a social interaction pattern but also for the mere observer of such interaction who still makes his observations from his biographical situation within the social world. The difference between both is merely that the participant in the interaction pattern, guided by the idealization of reciprocity of motives, assumes his own motives as being interlocked with that of his partners, whereas to the observer merely the manifest fragments of the actors' actions are accessible. Yet both, participants and observer, form their common-sense constructs relatively to their biographical situation. In either case, these constructs have a particular place within the chain of motives originating in the biographically determined hierarchy of the constructor's plans.

The constructs of human interaction patterns formed by the social scientist, however, are of an entirely different kind. The social scientist has no "Here" within the social world or, more precisely, he considers his position within it and the system of relevances attached thereto as irrelevant for his scientific undertaking. His stock of knowledge at hand is the corpus of his science, and he has to take it for granted—which means, in this context, as scientifically ascertained—unless he makes explicit why he cannot do so. To this corpus of science belong also the rules of procedure which have stood the test, namely, the methods of his science, including the methods of forming constructs in a scientifically sound way. This stock of knowledge is of quite another structure than that which man in everyday life has at hand. To be sure, it will also show manifold degrees of clarity and distinctness. But this structurization will depend upon knowledge of problems solved, of their still hidden implications and open horizons of other still not formulated problems. The scientist takes for granted what he defines to be a datum, and this is independent of the beliefs accepted by any in-group in the world of everyday life.[56] The scientific problem, once established, determines alone the structure of relevances.

Having no "Here" within the social world the social scientist does not organize this world in layers around himself as the center. He can never enter as a consociate in an interaction pattern with one of the actors on the social scene without abandoning, at least temporarily, his scientific attitude. The participant observer or field worker establishes contact with the group studied as a man among fellow-men; only his system of relevances which serves as the scheme of his selection and interpretation is determined by the scientific attitude, temporarily dropped in order to be resumed again.

Thus, adopting the scientific attitude, the social scientist observes human interaction patterns or their results insofar as they are accessible to his observation and open to his interpretation. These interaction patterns, however, he has to interpret in terms of their subjective meaning structure lest he abandon any hope of grasping "social reality."

In order to comply with this postulate, the scientific observer proceeds in a way similar to that of the observer of a social interaction pattern in the world of everyday life, although guided by an entirely different system of relevances.

4. THE SCIENTIFIC MODEL OF THE SOCIAL WORLD[57]

He begins to construct typical course-of-action patterns corresponding to the observed events. Thereupon he co-ordinates to these typical course-of-action patterns a personal type, a model of an actor whom he imagines as being gifted with consciousness. Yet it is a consciousness restricted to containing nothing but all the elements relevant to the performance of the course-of-action patterns under observation and relevant, therewith, to the scien-

[56] We intentionally disregard the problems of the so-called sociology of knowledge here involved.

[57] To this section cf. in addition to the literature mentioned in footnotes 32 and 48, A. Schutz, "The Problem of Rationality in the Social World," *Economica*, X, 1943, 130–149.

tist's problem under scrutiny. He ascribes, thus, to this fictitious consciousness a set of typical in-order-to motives corresponding to the goals of the observed course-of-action patterns and typical because-motives upon which the in-order-to motives are founded. Both types of motives are assumed to be invariant in the mind of the imaginary actor-model.

Yet these models of actors are not human beings living within their biographical situation in the social world of everyday life. Strictly speaking, they do not have any biography or any history, and the situation into which they are placed is not a situation defined by them but defined by their creator, the social scientist. He has created these puppets or homunculi to manipulate them for his purpose. A merely specious consciousness is imputed to them by the scientist, which is constructed in such a way that its presupposed stock of knowledge at hand (including the ascribed set of invariant motives) would make actions originating from it subjectively understandable, provided that these actions were performed by real actors within the social world. But the puppet and his artificial consciousness is not subjected to the ontological conditions of human beings. The homunculus was not born, he does not grow up, and he will not die. He has no hopes and no fears; he does not know anxiety as the chief motive of all his deeds. He is not free in the sense that his acting could transgress the limits his creator, the social scientist, has predetermined. He cannot, therefore, have other conflicts of interests and motives than those the social scientist has imputed to him. He cannot err, if to err is not his typical destiny. He cannot choose, except among the alternatives the social scientist has put before him as standing to his choice. Whereas man, as Simmel has clearly seen,[58] enters any social relationship merely with a part of his self and is, at the same time, always within and outside of such a relationship, the homunculus, placed into a social relationship is involved therein in his totality. He is nothing else but the originator of his typical function because the artificial consciousness imputed to him contains merely those elements which are necessary to make such functions subjectively meaningful.

Let us very briefly examine some of the implications of this

[58] See footnote 35 above.

general characterization. The homunculus is invested with a system of relevances originating in the scientific problem of his constructor and not in the particular biographically determined situation of an actor within the world. It is the scientist who defines what is to his puppet a Here and a There, what is within his reach, what is to him a We and a You or a They. The scientist determines the stock of knowledge his model has supposedly at hand. This stock of knowledge is not socially derived and, unless especially designed to be so, without reference to social approval. The relevance system pertinent to the scientific problem under scrutiny alone determines its intrinsic structure, namely, the elements "about" which the homunculus is supposed to have knowledge, those of which he has a mere knowledge of acquaintance and those others which he just takes for granted. With this is determined what is supposed to be familiar and what anonymous to him and on what level the typification of the experiences of the world imputed to him takes place.

If such a model of an actor is conceived as interrelated and interacting with others—they, too, being homunculi—then the general thesis of reciprocal perspectives, their interlocking, and, therewith, the correspondence of motives is determined by the constructor. The course-of-action and personal types supposedly formed by the puppet of his partners, including the definition of their systems of relevances, roles, motives, have not the character of a mere chance which will or will not be fulfilled by the supervening events. The homunculus is free from empty anticipations of the Other's reactions to his own actions and also from self-typifications. He does not assume a role other than that attributed to him by the director of the puppet show, called the model of the social world. It is he, the social scientist, who sets the stage, who distributes the roles, who gives the cues, who defines when an "action" starts and when it ends and who determines, thus, the "span of projects" involved. All standards and institutions governing the behavioral pattern of the model are supplied from the outset by the constructs of the scientific observer.

In such a simplified model of the social world pure rational acts, rational choices from rational motives are possible because all the difficulties encumbering the real actor in the everyday lifeworld have been eliminated. Thus, the concept of rationality in the strict sense already defined does not refer to actions within the common-sense experience of everyday life in the social world; it is the expression for a *particular* type of constructs of *certain specific* models of the social world made by the social scientist for certain specific methodological purposes.

Before discussing the particular functions of "rational" models of the social world, however, we have to indicate some principles governing the construction of scientific models of human action in general.

5. POSTULATES FOR SCIENTIFIC MODEL CONSTRUCTS OF THE SOCIAL WORLD

We said before that it is the main problem of the social sciences to develop a method in order to deal in an objective way with the subjective meaning of human action and that the thought objects of the social sciences have to remain consistent with the thought objects of common sense, formed by men in everyday life in order to come to terms with social reality. The model constructs as described before fulfill these requirements if they are formed in accordance with the following postulates:

a. The Postulate of Logical Consistency

The system of typical constructs designed by the scientist has to be established with the highest degree of clarity and distinctness of the conceptual framework implied and must be fully compatible with the principles of formal logic. Fulfillment of this postulate warrants the objective validity of the thought objects constructed by the social scientist, and their strictly logical character is one of the most important features by which scientific thought objects are distinguished from the thought objects constructed by common-sense thinking in daily life which they have to supersede.

b. The Postulate of Subjective Interpretation

In order to explain human actions the scientist has to ask what model of an individual mind can be constructed and what typical contents must be attributed to it in order to explain the observed facts as the result of the activity of such a mind in an understandable relation. The compliance with this postulate warrants the possibility of referring all kinds of human action or their result to the subjective meaning such action or result of an action had for the actor.

c. The Postulate of Adequacy

Each term in a scientific model of human action must be constructed in such a way that a human act performed within the life-world by an individual actor in the way indicated by the typical construct would be understandable for the actor himself as well as for his fellow-men in terms of common-sense interpretation of everyday life. Compliance with this postulate warrants the consistency of the constructs of the social scientist with the constructs of common-sense experience of the social reality.

V. Scientific Model Constructs of Rational Action Patterns

All model constructs of the social world in order to be scientific have to fulfill the requirements of these three postulates. But is not any construct complying with the postulate of logical consistency, is not any scientific activity by definition a rational one?

This is certainly true but here we have to avoid a dangerous misunderstanding. We have to distinguish between rational constructs of models of human actions on the one hand, and constructs of models of rational human actions on the other. Science may construct rational models of irrational behavior, as a glance in any textbook of psychiatry shows. On the other hand, common-sense thinking frequently constructs irrational models of highly rational behavior, for example, in explaining economic, political, military and even scientific decisions by referring them to sentiments or ideologies presupposed to govern the behavior of the participants. The rationality of the construction of the model is one thing and in this sense all properly constructed models of the sciences—not merely of the social sciences—are rational; the construction of models of rational behavior is quite another thing. It would be a serious misunderstanding to believe that it is the purpose of model constructs in the social sciences or a criterion for their scientific character that irrational behavior patterns be interpreted as if they were rational.

In the following we are mainly interested in the usefulness of scientific—therefore rational—models of rational behavior patterns.

It can easily be understood that the scientific construct of a perfect rational course-of-action type, of its corresponding personal type and also of rational interaction patterns is, as a matter of principle, possible. This is so because in constructing a model of a fictitious consciousness the scientist may select as relevant for his problem merely those elements which make rational actions or reactions of his homunculi possible. The postulate of rationality which such a construct would have to meet can be formulated as follows:

The rational course-of-action and personal types have to be constructed in such a way that an actor in the life-world would perform the typified action if he had a perfectly clear and distinct knowledge of all the elements, and only of the elements, assumed by the social scientist as being relevant to this action and the constant tendency to use the most appropriate means assumed to be at his disposal for achieving the ends defined by the construct itself.

The advantage of the use of such models of rational behavior in the social sciences can be characterized as follows:

1) The possibility of constructing patterns of social interaction under the assumption that all participants in such interaction act rationally within a set of conditions, means, ends, motives defined by the social scientist and supposed to be either common to all participants or distributed among them in a specific manner. By this arrangement standardized behavior such as so-called social roles, institutional behavior, etc., can be studied in isolation.

2) Whereas the behavior of individuals in the social life-world is not predictable unless in empty anticipations, the rational behavior of a constructed personal type is by definition supposed to be predictable, within the limits of the elements typified in the construct. The model of a rational action can, therefore, be used as a device for ascertaining deviating behavior in the real social world and for referring it to "problem-transcending data," that is, to non-typified elements.

3) By appropriate variations of some of the elements several models or even sets of models of rational actions can be constructed for solving the same scientific problem and compared with one another.

The last point, however, seems to require some comment.

Did we not state earlier that all constructs carry along a "sub-script" referring to the problem under scrutiny and have to be revised if a shift in the problem occurs? Is there not a certain contradiction between this insight and the possibility of constructing several competing models for the solution of one and the same scientific problem?

The contradiction disappears if we consider that any problem is merely a locus of implications which can be made explicit or, to use a term of Husserl's,[59] that it carries along its inner horizon of unquestioned but questionable elements.

In order to make the inner horizon of the problem explicit we may vary the conditions within which the fictitious actors are supposed to act, the elements of the world of which they are supposed to have knowledge, their assumed interlocked motives, the degree of familiarity or anonymity in which they are assumed to be interrelated, etc. For example, as an economist concerned with the theory of oligopoly,[60] I may construct models of a single firm or of an industry or of the economic system as a whole. If restricting myself to the theory of the individual firm (say, if analyzing the effects of a cartel agreement on the output of the commodity concerned), I may construct a model of a producer acting under conditions of unregulated competition, another of a producer with the same cost-conditions acting under the cartel restrictions imposed upon him and with the knowledge of similar restrictions imposed on the other suppliers of the "same" commodity. We can then compare the output of "the" firm in the two models.

All these models are models of rational actions but not of actions performed by living human beings in situations defined by them. They are assumed to be performable by the personal types constructed by the economist within the artificial environment in which he has placed his homunculi.

[59] As to the concept of horizon, see H. Kuhn, "The Phenomenological Concept of Horizon," in *Philosophical Essays in Memory of Edmund Husserl*, ed. Marvin Farber; and L. Landgrebe, in E. Husserl, *Erfahrung und Urteil*, Secs. 8–10.

[60] I gratefully acknowledge the permission of my friend, Professor Fritz Machlup, to borrow the following examples from his book *The Economics of Seller's Competition: Model Analysis of Seller's Conduct*, p. 4 f.

VI. Concluding Remarks

The relationship between the social scientist and the puppet he has created reflects to a certain extent an age-old problem of theology and metaphysics, that of the relationship between God and his creatures. The puppet exists and acts merely by the grace of the scientist; it cannot act otherwise than according to the purpose which the scientist's wisdom has determined it to carry out. Nevertheless, it is supposed to act as if it were not determined but could determine itself. A total harmony has been pre-established between the determined consciousness bestowed upon the puppet and the pre-constituted environment within which it is supposed to act freely, to make rational choices and decisions. This harmony is possible only because both, the puppet and its reduced environment, are the creation of the scientist. And by keeping to the principles which guided him, the scientist succeeds, indeed, in discovering within the universe, thus created, the perfect harmony established by himself.

For
FURTHER READING

....

Nagel's views on the methodology of the social sciences are systematically presented in his *Structure of Science*. For a further statement of Hempel's position see his monograph on *Fundamentals of Concept Formation in the Empirical Sciences* (International Encyclopedia of Unified Science). The first volume of the Collected Papers of Alfred Schutz is published as *The Problem of Social Reality*. For introductions to Schutz's position see Aron Gurwitsch, "The Common-Sense World as Social Reality: A Discourse on Alfred Schutz," *Social Research*, Vol. XXIX, 1962; Richard M. Zaner, "Theory of Intersubjectivity: Alfred Schutz," *Ibid.*, Vol. XXVIII, 1961; Alfred Stonier and Karl Bode, "A New Approach to the Methodology of the Social Sciences," *Economica*, Vol. IV, 1937. Also see the Introduction to *The Problem of Social Reality*.

Other relevant titles: *Naturalism and the Human Spirit* (ed. Y. H. Krikorian); Marvin Farber, *Naturalism and Subjectivism;* Paul F. Lazarsfeld, "Problems in Methodology," in *Sociology Today* (ed. Merton, Broom, and Cottrell); John C. McKinney, "Methodology, Procedures, and Techniques in Sociology," in

Modern Sociological Theory (ed. Becker and Boskoff). The reader should not miss Theodore Abel, "The Operation Called Verstehen," *American Journal of Sociology*, Vol. LIV, 1948, reprinted in *Readings in the Philosophy of Science* (ed. Feigl and Brodbeck) and in *The Structure of Scientific Thought* (ed. Edward H. Madden). Also see Fritz Machlup, "Operational Concepts and Mental Constructs in Model and Theory Formation," *Giornale Degli Economisti e Annali Di Economia*, Vol. XIX, 1960; Herbert A. Simon and Allen Newell, "Models: Their Uses and Limitations," in *The State of the Social Sciences* (ed. Leonard D. White); Morris R. Cohen and Ernest Nagel, *An Introduction to Logic and Scientific Method; An Introduction to Social Research* (ed. J. T. Doby); Howard Becker, "Interpretive Sociology and Constructive Typology," in *Twentieth Century Sociology* (ed. Gurvitch and Moore).

PART IV
Objectivity
and
Value

....

Introduction to PART IV

WRITING at the beginning of the century, Max Weber referred to the term "value" as "that unfortunate child of misery of our science" and deplored the vast confusion that had been generated by its ambiguous usage by social scientists. Today almost sixty years later, the situation, if better, is still a tangled one: the term "value" is used by scientists and philosophers in a variety of different senses, and the debates over value problems are far from resolution. Our concern in the essays which follow in this Part is with a limited though decisive segment of value theory, that of the relation between value and social science. And even with this delimitation of the field, there will be a number of very important methodological issues (the nature of "ideal types" for example) which will be left in the background. The focus of attention will be placed on the argument between Weber and Strauss, or, more precisely, on Leo Strauss's criticism of Weber. This criticism leads in its final thrust to an axial problem of all knowledge, what was described in our Introduction as the intellectual tension between commitment and nihilism.

Formulated in a very simple way, the problems of "value" in social science are (1) whether social scientists can reach objectively true conclusions about what is good in the same way that they can arrive at certain judgments about what is fact; and (2) if they can attain objective truth about matters of value, whether it is their proper business to make this a part of their scientific pursuits. Obviously, there are a number of possibilities here. It can be argued that whether they wish to or not, social scientists are incapable of securing absolute results with regard to value questions; or that science and value are disjunctive realms; or that a science of values can only mean a kind of "if-then" analysis of propositions and what they entail, quite apart from the truth value of those propositions. On the other hand, it can be argued that the very notion of error presupposes that of truth, and that objectivity in the realm of value is as necessary to science as it is essential to all knowledge. Furthermore, the very location and selection of problems in the course of scientific activity is said to be value-charged, for what is taken up as worthy of investigation is thereby deemed valuable. Finally, the rejection of a cleavage between science and value implies an affirmation of knowledge itself, the claim that philosophy is truly possible.

In the essays of Weber and Strauss which follow, these issues are given a concrete placement. Weber argues that value judgments cannot be derived from empirical science, that "it can never be the task of an empirical science to provide binding norms and ideals from which directives for immediate practical activity can be derived." Nor is it the function of the scientist qua scientist to choose between conflicting value claims; he can merely show the nature of those claims, clarify their methodological grounds, and, perhaps most important of all, point out their potential possibilities and consequences. As a citizen, as a man among men in everyday life, the social scientist does and indeed must make value choices, but then he operates outside the circle of his professional activity. To the extent that he remains a scientist, the economist or sociologist must remain on methodological guard, i.e., he must be critically aware of his own values, his fundamental commitments, etc., so that these transscientific elements will not interfere with his scientific practice or color his results. The man of action and the man of science cannot share the same mistress. This is perhaps the moral of Weber's secular sermon.

But if values are matters for the man of action, is there any reason for preferring one value to another, one moral outlook to another, one way of life to another? If a rational decision is not possible with respect to these questions, then what justifies one nonrational choice over another? Or are we then left with moral pandemonium? Strauss contends that "Weber's thesis necessarily leads to nihilism or to the view that every preference, however evil, base, or insane, has to be judged before the tribunal of reason to be as legitimate as any other preference." The criticism goes even further.

Strauss insists that on the basis of Weber's own formulation of the crisis of contemporary man in society, a radical choice emerges between a "spiritual renewal . . . or else 'mechanized petrifaction.'" How then are we to choose? Weber, according to Strauss, stops short of a real answer because his methodological strictures against entering the province of normative value judgment prohibit him from confronting social phenomena. The price paid for a "value-free" science is that the scientist is professionally incapable of expressing those judgments of preference he has no hesitation in voicing as a common-sense man. This axiological split between restraint and insight, between what may be said and what is known, between science and life goes to the root of the human condition. For Weber, the individual must follow his "demon" in making a primordial choice of value which antecedes scientific activity and which is indeed the very condition for there being intellectual activity at all. The rationale of that decision lies outside of science; if anything, its locus is in what we may call the existential subjectivity of the person. For Strauss, the divorce of value from science leads ultimately to the devastation of both. We come here to a disagreement that transcends methodological perspectives precisely because its theme is the cardinal presupposition of those perspectives. We are speaking of modernity as disenchantment. Weber writes: "The fate of an epoch which has eaten of the tree of knowledge is that it must know that we cannot learn the *meaning* of the world from the results of its analysis, be it ever so perfect; it must rather be in a position to create this meaning itself. It must recognize that general views of life and the universe can never be the products of increasing empirical knowledge, and that the highest ideals, which move us most forcefully, are always formed only in the struggle with other ideals which are just as sacred to others as ours are to us." Methodology is involved in this terrifying incertitude, and the methodologist must come to terms with it if he is to come to terms with himself.

The opposition between Strauss and Weber reflects a struggle within the history of philosophy between those who are convinced that reason can penetrate reality and locate truth and those for whom reason is in its ultimate fundament inadequate to the task of disclosing The Truth. In terms of the disenchanted outlook, it is the existential imperative of nonrational commitment alone that provides and sustains a bulwark against nihilism. The full weight of this concern can be felt only by those opponents of the view who are sensitive to a pathos at the heart of reason, and it is that sensitivity which makes Strauss's rejoinder to Weber more than a rejection of his views and which permits him to characterize Weber as "the greatest social scientist of our century."

"Objectivity" in Social Science and Social Policy[1]

MAX WEBER[2]

WHEN A SOCIAL SCIENCE journal which also at times concerns itself with a social policy, appears for the first time or passes into the hands of a new editorial board, it is customary to ask about

[1] Reprinted from Max Weber, *Methodology of the Social Sciences*, trans. and ed. Edward A. Shils and Henry A. Finch with a foreword by Edward A. Shils (Glencoe, Ill.: The Free Press, 1949), pp. 49–112, with the permission of the publisher. The essay originally appeared in the *Archiv für Sozialwissenschaft und Sozialpolitik*, XIX, 1904, pp. 22–87, as "Die 'Objektivität' sozialwissenschaftlicher und sozialpolitischer Erkenntnis." For further details concerning the publication of this essay, the reader should see Edward A. Shils' Foreword in the *Methodology of the Social Sciences*. The arrangement of this article follows, for the most part, the version reprinted in Max Weber's *Gesammelte Aufsätze zur Wissenschaftslehre*, zweite durchgesehene und ergänzte Auflage, besorgt von Johannes Winckelmann, Tübingen, J. C. B. Mohr, 1951, pp. 146–214.

[2] (Weber's note.)
Wherever assertions are explicitly made in the name of the editor or when tasks are set for the *Archiv* in the course of Section I of the following essay, the personal views of the author are not involved. Each of the points in question has the express agreement of the co-editors. The author alone bears the responsibility for the form and content of Section II.

The fact that the points of view, not only of the contributors but of the editors as well, are not identical even on methodological issues, stands as a guarantee that the *Archiv* will not fall prey to any sectarian outlook. On the other hand, agreement as to certain fundamental issues is a presup-

its "line."[3] We, too, must seek to answer this question and following up the remarks in our "Introductory Note" we will enter into the question in a more fundamental theoretical way. Even though or perhaps because, we are concerned with "self-evident truths," this occasion provides the opportunity to cast some light on the nature of the "social sciences" as we understand them, in such a manner that it can be useful, if not to the specialist, then to the reader who is more remote from actual scientific work.

In addition to the extension of our knowledge of the "social conditions of all countries," i.e., the facts of social life, the express purpose of the *Archiv* ever since its establishment has been the education of judgment about practical social problems—and in the very modest way in which such a goal can be furthered by private scholars—the criticism of practical social policy, extending even as far as legislation. In spite of this, the *Archiv* has firmly adhered, from the very beginning, to its intention to be an exclusively scientific journal and to proceed only with the methods of scientific research. Hence arises the question of whether the

position of the joint assumption of editorial responsibility. This agreement refers particularly to the value of *theoretical* knowledge from "one-sided" points of view, the *construction* of *precisely defined concepts* and the insistence on the rigorous distinction between *empirical knowledge* and *value-judgments* as here understood. Naturally we do not claim to present anything new therewith.

The extensiveness of the discussion (Section II) and the frequent repetition of the same thought are intended only to maximize the *general understanding of our argument in wider circles*. For the sake of this intention, much—let us hope not too much—precision in expression has been sacrificed. For the same reason, we have omitted the presentation of a *systematic* analysis in favor of the present listing of a few methodological viewpoints. A systematic inquiry would have required the treatment of a large number of epistemological questions which are far deeper than those raised here. We are not interested here in the furtherance of logical analysis *per se*. We are attempting only to apply the well-known results of modern logic to our own problems. Nor are we solving problems here; we are trying only to make their significance apparent to non-specialists. Those who know the work of the modern logicians—I cite only Windelband, Simmel, and for our purposes particularly Heinrich Rickert—will immediately notice that everything of importance in this essay is bound up with their work.

[3] This essay was published when the editorship of the *Archiv für Sozialwissenschaft und Sozialpolitik* was transferred to Edgar Jaffé, Werner Sombart and Max Weber. Its form was influenced by the occasion for which it was written and the content should be considered in this light.—Marianne Weber.

purpose stated above is compatible in principle with self-confine-
ment to the latter method. What has been the meaning of the
value-judgments found in the pages of the *Archiv* regarding legislative and administrative measures, or practical recommendations
for such measures? What are the standards governing these
judgments? What is the validity of the value-judgments which
are uttered by the critic, for instance, or on which a writer
recommending a policy founds his arguments for that policy? In
what sense, if the criterion of scientific knowledge is to be found
in the "objective" validity of its results, has he remained within
the sphere of *scientific* discussion? We will first present our own
attitude on this question in order later to deal with the broader
one: in what sense are there in general "objectively valid truths"
in those disciplines concerned with social and cultural phenomena? This question, in view of the continuous changes and
bitter conflict about the apparently most elementary problems of
our discipline, its methods, the formulation and validity of its
concepts, cannot be avoided. We do not attempt to offer solutions but rather to disclose problems—problems of the type to
which our journal, if it is to meet its past and future responsibilities, must turn its attention.

I

We all know that our science, as is the case with every
science treating the institutions and events of human culture,
(with the possible exception of political history) first arose in
connection with *practical* considerations. Its most immediate and
often sole purpose was the attainment of value-judgments concerning measures of State economic policy. It was a "technique"
in the same sense as, for instance, the clinical disciplines in the
medical sciences are. It is now become known how this situation
was gradually modified. This modification was not, however, accompanied by a formulation of the logical (*prinzipielle*) distinction between "existential knowledge," i.e., knowledge of what
"is," and "normative knowledge," i.e., knowledge of what "should
be." The formulation of this distinction was hampered, first, by
the view that immutably invariant natural laws,—later, by the
view that an unambiguous evolutionary principle—governed eco-

nomic life and that accordingly, *what was normatively right* was identical—in the former case—with the immutably *existent*—and in the latter—with the inevitably *emergent*. With the awakening of the historical sense, a combination of ethical evolutionism and historical relativism became the predominant attitude in our science. This attitude sought to deprive ethical norms of their formal character and through the incorporation of the totality of cultural values into the "ethical" (*Sittlichen*) sphere tried to give a *substantive content* to ethical norms. It was hoped thereby to raise economics to the status of an "ethical science" with empirical foundations. To the extent that an "ethical" label was given to all possible cultural ideals, the particular autonomy of the ethical imperative was obliterated, without however increasing the "objective" validity of those ideals. Nonetheless we can and must forego a discussion of the principles at issue. We merely point out that even today the confused opinion that economics does and should derive value-judgments from a specifically "economic point of view" has not disappeared but is especially current, quite understandably, among men of practical affairs.

Our journal as the representative of an empirical specialized discipline must, as we wish to show shortly, reject this view in principle. It must do so because, in our opinion, it can never be the task of an empirical science to provide binding norms and ideals from which directives for immediate practical activity can be derived.

What is the implication of this proposition? It is certainly not that value-judgments are to be withdrawn from scientific discussion in general simply because in the last analysis they rest on certain ideals and are therefore "subjective" in origin. Practical action and the aims of our journal would always reject such a proposition. Criticism is not to be suspended in the presence of value-judgments. The problem is rather: what is the meaning and purpose of the scientific criticism of ideals and value-judgments? This requires a somewhat more detailed analysis.

All serious reflection about the ultimate elements of meaningful human conduct is oriented primarily in terms of the categories "end" and "means." We desire something concretely either "for its own sake" or as a means of achieving something else which is more highly desired. The question of the appropriateness of the means for achieving a given end is undoubtedly accessible to scientific analysis. Inasmuch as we are able to determine (within the present limits of our knowledge) which means for the achievement of a proposed end are appropriate or inappropriate, we can in this way estimate the chances of attaining a certain end by certain available means. In this way we can indirectly criticize the setting of the end itself as practically meaningful (on the basis of the existing historical situation) or as meaningless with reference to existing conditions. Furthermore, when the possibility of attaining a proposed end appears to exist, we can determine (naturally within the limits of our existing knowledge) the consequences which the application of the means to be used will produce in addition to the eventual attainment of the proposed end, as a result of the interdependence of all events. We can then provide the acting person with the ability to weigh and compare the undesirable as over against the desirable consequences of his action. Thus, we can answer the question: what will the attainment of a desired end "cost" in terms of the predictable loss of other values? Since, in the vast majority of cases, every goal that is striven for does "cost" or can "cost" something in this sense, the weighing of the goal in terms of the incidental consequences of the action which realizes it cannot be omitted from the deliberation of persons who act with a sense of responsibility. One of the most important functions of the *technical criticism* which we have been discussing thus far is to make this sort of analysis possible. To apply the results of this analysis in the making of a decision, however, is not a task which science can undertake; it is rather the task of the acting, willing person: he weighs and chooses from among the values involved according to his own conscience and his personal view of the world. Science can make him realize that all action and naturally, according to the circumstances, inaction imply in their consequences the espousal of certain values—and herewith—what is today so willingly overlooked—the rejection of certain others. The act of choice itself is his own responsibility.

We can also offer the person, who makes a choice, insight into the significance of the desired object. We can teach him to think in terms of the context and the meaning of the ends he desires, and among which he chooses. We do this through making explicit and developing in a logically consistent manner the "ideas" which actually do or which can underlie the concrete end. It is self-evident that one of the most important tasks of every science of cultural life is to arrive at a rational understanding of these "ideas" for which men either really or allegedly struggle. This does not overstep the boundaries of a science which strives for an "analytical ordering of empirical reality," although the methods which are used in this interpretation of cultural (*geistiger*) values are not "inductions" in the usual sense. At any rate, this task falls at least partly beyond the limits of economics as defined according to the conventional division of labor. It belongs among the tasks of social philosophy. However, the historical influence of ideas in the development of social life has been and still is so great that our journal cannot renounce this task. It shall rather regard the investigation of this phenomenon as one of its most important obligations.

But the scientific treatment of value-judgments may not only understand and empathically analyze (*nacherleben*) the desired ends and the ideals which underlie them; it can also "judge" them critically. This criticism can of course have only a dialectical character, i.e., it can be no more than a formal logical judgment of historically given value-judgments and ideas, a testing of the ideals according to the postulate of the internal *consistency* of the desired end. It can, insofar as it sets itself this goal, aid the acting, willing person in attaining self-clarification concerning the final axioms from which his desired ends are derived. It can assist him in becoming aware of the ultimate standards of value which he does not make explicit to himself or, which he must presuppose in order to be logical. The elevation of these ultimate standards, which are manifested in concrete value-judgments, to the level of explicitness is the utmost that the scientific treatment of value-judgments can do without entering into the realm of speculation. As to whether the person expressing these value-judgments *should* adhere to these ultimate standards is his personal affair; it involves will and conscience, not empirical knowledge.

An empirical science cannot tell anyone what he *should* do— but rather what he *can* do—and under certain circumstances—

what he wishes to do. It is true that in our sciences, personal value-judgments have tended to influence scientific arguments without being explicitly admitted. They have brought about continual confusion and have caused various interpretations to be placed on scientific arguments even in the sphere of the determination of simple causal interconnections among facts according to whether the results increased or decreased the chances of realizing one's personal ideals, i.e., the possibility of desiring a certain thing. Even the editors and the collaborators of our journal will regard "nothing human as alien" to them in this respect. But it is a long way from this acknowledgement of human frailty to the belief in an "ethical" science of economics, which would derive ideals from its subject matter and produce concrete norms by applying general ethical imperatives. It is true that we regard as *objectively* valuable those innermost elements of the "personality," those highest and most ultimate value-judgments which determine our conduct and give meaning and significance to our life. We can indeed espouse these values only when they appear to us as valid, as derived from our highest values and when they are developed in the struggle against the difficulties which life presents. Certainly, the dignity of the "personality" lies in the fact that for it there exist values about which it organizes its life;—even if these values are in certain cases concentrated exclusively within the sphere of the person's "individuality," then "self-realization" in *those* interests for which it claims *validity* as *values* is the idea with respect to which its whole existence is oriented. Only on the assumption of belief in the validity of values is the attempt to espouse value-judgments meaningful. However, to *judge* the *validity* of such values is a matter of *faith*. It may perhaps be a task for the speculative interpretation of life and the universe in quest of their meaning. But it certainly does not fall within the province of an empirical science in the sense in which it is to be practised here. The empirically demonstrable fact that these ultimate ends undergo historical changes and are debatable does not affect this distinction between empirical science and value-judgments, contrary to what is often thought. For even the knowledge of the most certain proposition of our theoretical sciences—e.g., the exact natural sciences or mathematics, is, like the cultivation and refinement of the conscience, a product of culture. However, when we call to mind the practical problems of economic and social policy (in the usual sense), we see that there are many, indeed countless, practical questions in the discussion of which there seems to be general agreement about the self-evident character of certain goals. Among these we may mention emergency credit, the concrete problems of social hygiene, poor relief, factory inspection, industrial courts, employment exchanges, large sections of protective labor legislation—in short, all those issues in which, at least in appearance, only the *means* for the attainment of the goal are at issue. But even if we were to mistake the illusion of self-evidence for truth—which science can never do without damaging itself—and wished to view the conflicts immediately arising from attempts at practical realization as purely technical questions of expediency—which would very often be incorrect—even in this case we would have to recognize that this illusion of the self-evidence of normative standards of value is dissipated as soon as we pass from the concrete problems of philanthropic and protective social and economic services to problems of economic and social policy. The distinctive characteristic of a problem of social *policy* is indeed the fact that it cannot be resolved merely on the basis of purely technical considerations which assume already settled ends. Normative standards of value can and must be the objects of *dispute* in a discussion of a problem of social policy because the problem lies in the domain of general *cultural* values. And the conflict occurs not merely, as we are too easily inclined to believe today, between "class interests" but between general views on life and the universe as well. This latter point, however, does not lessen the truth that the particular ultimate value-judgment which the individual espouses is decided among other factors and certainly to a quite significant degree by the degree of affinity between it and his class interests—accepting for the time being this only superficially unambiguous term. One thing is certain under all circumstances, namely, the more "general" the problem involved, i.e., in this case, the broader its cultural *significance*, the less subject it is to a single unambiguous answer on the basis of the data of empirical sciences and the greater the role played by value-ideas (*Wertideen*) and the ultimate and highest personal axioms of belief. It is simply naive to believe, although there are many specialists who even now occasionally do, that it is possible to establish and to demonstrate as scientifically valid "a principle" for practical social science from which the norms for the solution of practical problems can be unambiguously derived. However much the social sciences need the discussion of practical problems in terms of fundamental principles, i.e., the reduction of unreflective value-judgments to the premises from which they are logically derived and however much our journal intends to devote itself specially to them—certainly the creation of a lowest common denominator for our problems in the form of generally valid ultimate value-judgments cannot be its task or in general the task of any empirical science. Such a thing would not only be impracticable; it would be entirely meaningless as well. Whatever the interpretation of the basis and the nature of the validity of the ethical imperatives, it is certain that from them, as from the norms for the concretely conditioned conduct of the *individual, cultural values* cannot be unambiguously derived as being normatively desirable; it can do so the less, the more inclusive are the values concerned. Only positive religions—or more precisely expressed: dogmatically bound *sects*—are able to confer on the content of *cultural values* the status of unconditionally valid *ethical* imperatives. Outside these sects, cultural ideals which the individual wishes to realize and ethical obligations which he *should* fulfil do not, in principle, share the same status. The fate of an epoch which has eaten of the tree of knowledge is that it must know that we cannot learn the *meaning* of the world from the results of its analysis, be it ever so perfect; it must rather be in a position to create this meaning itself. It must recognize that general views of life and the universe can never be the products of increasing empirical knowledge, and that the highest ideals, which move us most forcefully, are always formed only in the struggle with other ideals which are just as sacred to others as ours are to us.

Only an optimistic syncretism, such as is, at times, the product of evolutionary-historical relativism, can theoretically delude itself about the profound seriousness of this situation or practically shirk its consequences. It can, to be sure, be just as obligatory subjectively for the practical politician, in the individual case, to mediate between antagonistic points of view as to take sides with one of them. But this has nothing whatsoever to do with scientific "objectivity." *Scientifically the "middle course" is not truer even by a hair's breadth,* than the most extreme party ideals of the right or left. Nowhere are the interests of science more poorly served in the long run than in those situations where one refuses to see uncomfortable facts and the realities of life in all their starkness. The *Archiv* will struggle relentlessly against the severe self-deception which asserts that through the synthesis of several party points of view, or by following a line between them, practical norms of *scientific validity* can be arrived at. It is necessary to do this because, since this piece of self-deception tries to mask its own standards of value in relativistic terms, it is more dangerous to the freedom of research than the former naive faith of parties in the scientific "demonstrability" of their dogmas. The capacity to distinguish between empirical knowledge and value-judgments, and the fulfillment of the scientific duty to see the factual truth as well as the practical duty to stand up for our own ideals constitute the program to which we wish to adhere with ever increasing firmness.

There is and always will be—and this is the reason that it concerns us—an unbridgeable distinction among (1) those arguments which appeal to our capacity to become enthusiastic about and our feeling for concrete practical aims or cultural forms and values, (2) those arguments in which, once it is a question of the validity of ethical norms, the appeal is directed to our conscience, and finally (3) those arguments which appeal to our capacity and need for *analytically ordering* empirical reality in a manner which lays claim to *validity* as empirical truth. This proposition remains correct, despite, as we shall see, the fact that those highest "values" underlying the practical interest are and always will be decisively significant in determining the focus of attention of analytical activity (*ordnende Tätigkeit des Denkens*) in the sphere of the cultural sciences. It has been and remains true that a systematically correct scientific proof in the social sciences, if it is to achieve its purpose, must be acknowledged as correct even by a Chinese—or—more precisely stated—it must constantly *strive* to attain this goal, which perhaps may not be completely attainable due to faulty data. Furthermore, the successful *logical* analysis of the content of an ideal and its ultimate axioms and the discovery of the consequences which arise from pursuing it, logically and practically, must also be valid for the Chinese. At the same time, our Chinese can lack a "sense" for our ethical imperative and he can and certainly often will deny the ideal itself and the concrete value-judgments derived from it. Neither of these two latter attitudes can affect the scientific value of the analysis in any way. Quite certainly our journal will not ignore the ever and inevitably recurrent attempts to give an unambiguous interpretation to culture. On the contrary, these attempts themselves rank with the most important products of this cultural life and, under certain circumstances, among its dynamic forces. We will therefore constantly strive to follow with care the course of these discussions of "social philosophy" (as here understood). We are furthermore completely free of the prejudice which asserts that reflections on culture which go beyond the analysis of empirical data in order to interpret the world metaphysically can, because of their metaphysical character fulfill no useful cognitive tasks. Just what these cognitive tasks are is primarily an epistemological question, the answer to which we must and can, in view of our purpose, disregard at this point. There is one tenet to which we adhere most firmly in our work, namely, that a social science journal, in our sense, to the extent that it is *scientific* should be a place where those truths are sought, which—to remain with our illustration—can claim, even for a Chinese, the validity appropriate to an analysis of empirical reality.

Of course, the editors cannot once and for all deny to themselves or their contributors the possibility of expressing in value-judgment the ideals which motivate them. However, two important duties arise in connection with this. First, to keep the readers and themselves sharply aware at every moment of the standards by which they judge reality and from which the value-judgment is derived, instead of, as happens too often, deceiving themselves in the conflict of ideals by a value mélange of values of the most different orders and types, and seeking to offer something to everybody. If this obligation is rigorously heeded, the practical evaluative attitude can be not only harmless to scientific interests but even directly useful, and indeed mandatory. In the scientific criticism of legislative and other practical recommendations, the motives of the legislator and the ideals of the critic in all their scope often can not be clarified and analyzed in a tangible and intelligible form in any other way than through the confrontation of the standards of value underlying the ideas criticized with others, preferably the critic's own. Every meaningful *value-judgment* about someone else's *aspirations* must be a criticism from the standpoint of one's own *Weltanschauung;* it must be a struggle against *another's* ideals from the standpoint of one's *own.* If in a particular concrete case, the ultimate value-axioms which underlie practical activity are not only to be designated and scientifically analyzed but are also to be shown in their relationship to *other* value-axioms, "positive" criticism by means of a systematic exposition of the latter is unavoidable.

In the pages of this journal, especially in the discussion of legislation, there will inevitably be found social *policy*, i.e., the statement of ideals, in addition to social *science*, i.e., the analysis of facts. But we do not by any means intend to present such discussions as "science" and we will guard as best we can against allowing these two to be confused with each other. In such discussions, *science* no longer has the floor. For that reason, the second fundamental imperative of scientific freedom is that in such cases it should be constantly made clear to the readers (and —again we say it—above all to one's self!) exactly at which point the scientific investigator becomes silent and the evaluating and acting person begins to speak. In other words, it should be made explicit just where the arguments are addressed to the analytical understanding and where to the sentiments. The constant confusion of the scientific discussion of facts and their evaluation is still one of the most widespread and also one of the most damaging traits of work in our field. The foregoing arguments are directed against this confusion, and not against the clear-cut introduction of one's own ideals into the discussion. An *attitude of moral indifference* has no connection with *scientific* "objectivity." The *Archiv*, at least in its intentions, has never been and should never be a place where polemics against certain currents in politics or social policy are carried on, nor should it be a place where struggles are waged for or against ideals in politics or social-policy. There are other journals for these purposes. The peculiar characteristic of the journal has rather been from the very beginning and, insofar as it is in the power of the editors, shall continue to be that political antagonists can meet in it to carry on scientific work. It has not been a "socialist" organ hitherto and in the future it shall not be "bourgeois." It excludes no one from its circle of contributors who is willing to place himself within the framework of scientific discussion. It cannot be an arena for "objections," replies and rebuttals, but in its pages no one will be protected, neither its contributors nor its editors, from being subjected to the sharpest factual, scientific criticism. Whoever cannot bear this or who takes the viewpoint that he does not wish to work, in the service of scientific knowledge, with persons whose other ideals are different from his own, is free not to participate.

However, we should not deceive ourselves about it—this last sentence means much more in practice than it seems to do at first glance. In the first place, there are psychological limits everywhere and especially in Germany to the possibility of coming together freely with one's political opponents in a neutral forum, be it social or intellectual. This obstacle which should be relentlessly combatted as a sign of narrow-minded party fanaticism and backward political culture, is reenforced for a journal like ours through the fact that in social sciences the stimulus to the posing of scientific problems is in actuality always given by *practical* "questions." Hence the very recognition of the existence of a scientific problem coincides, personally, with the possession of specifically oriented motives and values. A journal which has come into existence under the influence of a general interest in a concrete problem, will always include among its contributors persons who are personally interested in these problems because certain concrete situations seem to be incompatible with, or seem to threaten, the realization of certain ideal values in which they believe. A bond of similar ideals will hold this circle of contributors together and it will be the basis of a further recruitment. This in turn will tend to give the journal, at least in its treatment of questions of practical social *policy*, a certain "*character*" which of course inevitably accompanies every collaboration of vigorously sensitive persons whose evaluative standpoint regarding the problems cannot be entirely expressed even in purely theoretical analysis; in the criticism of *practical* recommendations and measures it quite legitimately finds expression—under the particular conditions above discussed. The *Archiv* first appeared at a time in which certain practical aspects of the "labor problem" (as traditionally understood) stood in the forefront of social science discussions. Those persons for whom the problems which the *Archiv* wished to treat were bound up with ultimate and decisive value-judgments and who on that account became its most regular contributors also espoused at the same time the view of culture which was strongly influenced by these value-judgments. We all know that though this journal, through its explicit self-restriction to "scientific" discussions and through the express invitation to the "adherents of all political standpoints," denied that it would pursue a certain "tendency," it nonetheless possessed a "character" in the above sense. This "character" was created by the group of its regular contributors. In general they were men who, whatever may have been other divergences in their points of view, set as their goal the protection of the physical well-being of the laboring masses and the increase of the latters' share of the material and intellectual values of our culture. As a means, they employed the combination of state intervention into the arena of material interests with the freer shaping of the existing political and legal order. Whatever may have been their opinion as to the form of the social order in the more remote future—for the present, they accepted the emergent trends of the capitalist system, not because they seemed better than the older forms of social organization but because they seemed to be practically inevitable and because the attempt to wage a fundamental struggle against it appeared to hinder and not aid the cultural rise of the working class. In the situation which exists in Germany today—we need not be more specific at this point—this was not and is not to be avoided. Indeed, it bore direct fruit in the successful many-sidedness of the participation in the scientific discussion and it constituted a source of strength for the journal; under the given circumstances it was perhaps even one of its claims to the justification for its existence.

There can be no doubt that the development of a "charac-

- *Max Weber* -

ter," in this sense, in a scientific journal can constitute a threat to the freedom of scientific analysis; it really does amount to that when the selection of contributors is purposely one-sided. In this case the cultivation of a "character" in a journal is practically equivalent to the existence of a "tendency." The editors are aware of the responsibility which this situation imposes upon them. They propose neither the deliberate transformation of the character of the *Archiv* nor its artificial preservation by means of a careful restriction of the contributors to scholars of certain definite party loyalties. They accept it as given and await its further "development." The form which it takes in the future and the modifications which it may undergo as a result of the inevitable broadening of its circle of contributors will depend primarily on the character of those persons who, seeking to serve the cause of science, enter the circle and become or remain frequent contributors. It will be further affected by the broadening of the *problems*, the advancement of which is a goal of the journal.

With these remarks we come to the question on which we have not yet touched, namely, the factual delimitation of our field of operations. No answer can, however, be given without raising the question as to the goal of social science knowledge in general. When we distinguished in principle between "value-judgments" and "empirical knowledge," we presupposed the existence of an unconditionally valid type of knowledge in the social sciences, i.e., the analytical ordering of empirical social reality. This presupposition now becomes our problem in the sense that we must discuss the meaning of objectively "valid" truth in the social sciences. The genuineness of the problem is apparent to anyone who is aware of the conflict about methods, "fundamental concepts" and presuppositions, the incessant shift of "viewpoints," and the continuous redefinition of "concepts" and who sees that the theoretical and historical modes of analysis are still separated by an apparently unbridgeable gap. It constitutes, as a despairing Viennese examinee once sorrowfully complained, "*two* sciences of economics." What is the meaning of "objectivity" in this context? The following discussion will be devoted to this question.

II

This journal has from the beginning treated social-economic data as its subject-matter.[4] Although there is little point in entering here into the definition of terms and the delineation of the proper boundaries of the various sciences, we must nonetheless state briefly what we mean by this.

Most roughly expressed, the basic element in all those phenomena which we call, in the widest sense, "social-economic" is constituted by the fact that our physical existence and the satisfaction of our most ideal needs are everywhere confronted with the quantitative limits and the qualitative inadequacy of the necessary external means, so that their satisfaction requires planful provision and work, struggle with nature and the association of human beings. The quality of an event as a "social-economic" event is not something which it possesses "objectively." It is rather conditioned by the orientation of our cognitive interest, as it arises from the specific cultural significance which we attribute to the particular event in a given case. Wherever those aspects of a cultural event which constitute its specific significance for us are connected with a social-economic event either directly or most indirectly, they involve, or at least to the extent that this connection exists, can involve a problem for the social sciences. By a social science problem, we mean a task for a discipline the object of which is to throw light on the ramifications of that fundamental social-economic phenomenon: the scarcity of means.

Within the total range of social-economic problems, we are now able to distinguish events and constellations of norms, institutions, etc., the economic aspect of which constitutes their primary cultural significance for us. Such are, for example, the phenomena of the stock exchange and the banking world, which, in the main, interest us only in *this* respect. This will be the case regularly (but not exclusively) when institutions are involved which were *deliberately* created or used for economic ends. Such objects of our knowledge we may call "economic" events (or institutions, as the case may be). There are other phenomena,

---

[4] *Das Archiv für Sozialwissenschaft und Sozialpolitik.*

for instance, religious ones, which do not interest us, or at least do not primarily interest us with respect to their economic significance but which, however, under certain circumstances do acquire significance in this regard because they have consequences which are of interest from the economic point of view. These we shall call "economically relevant" phenomena. Finally there are phenomena which are *not* "economic" in our sense and the economic effects of which are of no, or at best slight, interest to us (e.g., the developments of the artistic taste of a period) but which in individual instances are in their turn more or less strongly influenced in certain important aspects by economic factors such as, for instance, the social stratification of the artistically interested public. We shall call these "economically *conditioned* phenomena." The constellation of human relationships, norms, and normatively determined conduct which we call the "state" is for example in its fiscal aspects, an "economic" phenomenon; insofar as it influences economic life through legislation or otherwise (and even where other than economic considerations deliberately guide its behavior), it is "economically relevant." To the extent that its behavior in non-"economic" affairs is partly influenced by economic motives, it is "economically conditioned." After what has been said, it is self-evident that: firstly), the boundary lines of "economic" phenomena are vague and not easily defined; secondly), the "economic" aspect of a phenomenon is by no means *only* "economically conditioned" or *only* "economically relevant"; thirdly), a phenomenon is "economic" only insofar as and *only* as long as our *interest* is exclusively focused on its constitutive significance in the material struggle for existence.

Like the science of social-economics since Marx and Roscher, our journal is concerned not only with economic phenomena but also with those which are "economically relevant" and "economically conditioned." The domain of such subjects extends naturally—and varyingly in accordance with the focus of our interest at the moment—through the totality of cultural life. Specifically economic motives—i.e., motives which, in their aspect most significant to us, are rooted in the above-mentioned fundamental fact—operate wherever the satisfaction of even the most immaterial need or desire is bound up with the application

of *scarce* material means. Their force has everywhere on that
account conditioned and transformed not only the mode in
which cultural wants or preferences are satisfied, but their content as well, even in their most subjective aspects. The indirect
influence of social relations, institutions and groups governed by
"material interests" extends (often unconsciously) into all
spheres of culture without exception, even into the finest nuances
of æsthetic and religious feeling. The events of everyday life no
less than the "historical" events of the higher reaches of political
life, collective and mass phenomena as well as the "individuated"
conduct of statesmen and individual literary and artistic achievements are influenced by it. They are "economically conditioned."
On the other hand, all the activities and situations constituting an
historically given culture affect the formation of the material
wants, the mode of their satisfaction, the integration of interest-
groups and the types of power which they exercise. They
thereby affect the course of "economic development" and are
accordingly "economically relevant." To the extent that our
science imputes particular causes—be they economic or non-
economic—to *economic* cultural phenomena, it seeks "historical"
knowledge. Insofar as it traces a specific element of cultural life
(the economic element in its cultural significance) through the
most diverse cultural contexts, it is making an historical interpretation from a specific point of view, and offering a partial picture, a *preliminary* contribution to a more complete historical
knowledge of culture.

Social economic *problems* do not exist everywhere that an
economic event plays a role as cause or effect—since problems
arise only where the significance of those factors is *problematical*
and can be precisely determined only through the application of
the methods of social-economics. But despite this, the range of
social-economics is almost overwhelming.

After due consideration our journal has generally excluded
hitherto the treatment of a whole series of highly important special fields in our discipline, such as descriptive economics, economic history in the narrower sense, and statistics. It has likewise
left to other journals, the discussion of technical fiscal questions
and the technical-economic problems of prices and markets in
the modern exchange economy. Its sphere of operations has been

the present significance and the historical development of certain conflicts and constellations of interests which have arisen through the dominant role of investment-seeking capital in modern societies. It has not thereby restricted itself to those practical and historical problems which are designated by the term "the social question" in its narrower sense, i.e., the place of the modern working class in the present social order. Of course, the scientific elaboration of the interest in this special question which became widespread in Germany in the '80's, has had to be one of its main tasks. The more the practical treatment of labor conditions became a permanent object of legislation and public discussion in Germany, the more the accent of scientific work had to be shifted to the analysis of the more universal dimensions of the problem. It had thereby to culminate in the analysis of all the cultural problems which have arisen from the peculiar nature of the economic bases of our culture and which are, in that sense, specifically modern. The journal soon began to deal historically, statistically and theoretically with the most diverse, partly "economically relevant," and partly "economically conditioned" conditions of the other great social classes of modern states and their interrelations. We are only drawing the conclusions of this policy when we state that the scientific investigation of the *general cultural significance of the social-economic structure of the human community* and its historical forms of organization is the central aim of our journal. This is what we mean when we call our journal the *Archiv für Sozialwissenschaft*. The title is intended to indicate the historical and theoretical treatment of the same problems, the practical solution of which constitutes "social *policy*" in the widest sense of this word. We thereby utilize the right to apply the word "social" in the meaning which concrete present-day problems give to it. If one wishes to call those disciplines which treat the events of human life with respect to their cultural significance "cultural sciences," then social science in our sense belongs in that category. We shall soon see what are the logical implications of this.

Undoubtedly the selection of the *social-economic* aspect of cultural life signifies a very definite delimitation of our theme. It will be said that the economic, or as it has been inaccurately called, the "materialistic" point of view, from which culture is here being considered, is "one-sided." This is true and the one-sidedness is intentional. The belief that it is the task of scientific work to cure the "one-sidedness" of the economic approach by broadening it into a *general* social science suffers primarily from the weakness that the "social" criterion (i.e., the relationships among persons) acquires the specificity necessary for the delimitation of scientific problems only when it is accompanied by some substantive predicate. Otherwise, as the subject matter of a science, it would naturally comprehend philology, for example, as well as church history and particularly all those disciplines which concern themselves with the state which is the most important form of the normative regulation of cultural life. The fact that social-economics concerns itself with "social" relations is no more justification for regarding it as the necessary precursor of a "general social science" than its concern with vital phenomena makes it a part of biology, or its preoccupation with events on one of the planets makes it a part of an extended and improved astronomy of the future. It is not the "actual" interconnections of "things" but the *conceptual* interconnections of *problems* which define the scope of the various sciences. A new "science" emerges where new problems are pursued by new methods and truths are thereby discovered which open up significant new points of view.

It is now no accident that the term: "social" which seems to have a quite general meaning, turns out to have, as soon as one carefully examines its application, a particular specifically colored though often indefinite meaning. Its "generality" rests on nothing but its ambiguity. It provides, when taken in its "general" meaning, no specific *point of view,* from which the *significance* of given elements of culture can be analyzed.

Liberated as we are from the antiquated notion that all cultural phenomena can be *deduced* as a product or function of the constellation of "material" interests, we believe nevertheless that the analysis of social and cultural phenomena with special reference to their economic conditioning and ramifications was a scientific principle of creative fruitfulness and with careful application and freedom from dogmatic restrictions, will remain such for a very long time to come. The so-called "materialistic conception of history" as a *Weltanschauung* or as a formula for the casual explanation of historical reality is to be rejected most emphatically. The advancement of the economic *interpretation* of history is one of the most important aims of our journal. This requires further explanation.

The so-called "materialistic conception of history" with the crude elements of genius of the early form which appeared, for instance, in the *Communist Manifesto* still prevails only in the minds of laymen and dilettantes. In these circles one still finds the peculiar condition that their need for a causal explanation of an historical event is never satisfied until somewhere or somehow economic causes are shown (or seem) to be operative. Where this however is the case, they content themselves with the most threadbare hypotheses and the most general phrases since they have then satisfied their dogmatic need to believe that the economic "factor" is the "real" one, the only "true" one, and the one which "in the last instance is everywhere decisive." This phenomenon is by no means unique. Almost all the sciences, from philology to biology have occasionally claimed to be the sources not only of specialized scientific knowledge but of *"Weltanschauungen"* as well. Under the impression of the profound cultural significance of *modern* economic transformations and especially of the far-reaching ramifications of the "labor question," the inevitable monistic tendency of every type of thought which is not self-critical naturally follows this path.

The same tendency is now appearing in anthropology where the political and commercial struggles of nations for world dominance are being fought with increasing acuteness. There is a widespread belief that "in the last analysis" all historical events are results of the interplay of innate "racial qualities." In place of uncritical descriptions of "national characters," there emerges the even more uncritical concoction of "social theories" based on the "natural sciences." We shall carefully follow the development of anthropological research in our journal insofar as it is significant from our point of view. It is to be hoped that the situation in which the causal explanation of cultural events by the invocation of "racial characteristics" testifies to our ignorance—just as the reference to the "milieu" or, earlier, to the "conditions of the age"—will be gradually overcome by research which is the fruit of systematic training. If there is anything that has hindered this type of research, it is the fact that eager dilettantes have thought that they could contribute something different and better to our knowledge of culture than the broadening of the possibility of the sure imputation of individual concrete cultural events occurring in historical reality to *concrete, historically* given causes through the study of precise empirical data which have been selected from specific points of view. Only to the extent that they are able to do this, are their results of interest to us and only then does "racial biology" become something more than a product of the modern passion for founding new sciences.

The problem of the significance of the economic interpretation of history is the same. If, following a period of boundless overestimation, the danger now exists that its scientific value will be underestimated, this is the result of the unexampled naiveté with which the economic interpretation of reality was applied as a "universal" canon which explained all cultural phenomena—i.e., all those which are meaningful to us—as, in the last analysis, economically conditioned. Its present logical form is not entirely unambiguous. Wherever the strictly economic explanation encounters difficulties, various devices are available for maintaining its general validity as the decisive causal factor. Sometimes every historical event which is *not* explicable by the invocation of economic motives is regarded *for that very reason* as a scientifically insignificant "accident." At others, the definition of "economic" is stretched beyond recognition so that all human interests which are related in any way whatsoever to the use of material means are included in the definition. If it is historically undeniable that different responses occur in two situations which are economically identical—due to political, religious, climatic and countless other non-economic determinants—then in order to maintain the primacy of the economic all these factors are reduced to historically accidental "conditions" upon which the economic factor operates as a "cause." It is obvious, however, that all those factors which are "accidental" according to the economic interpretation of history follow their own laws in the same sense as the economic factor. From a point of view which traces the specific meaning of these non-economic factors, the existing *economic* "conditions" are "historically accidental" in quite the same sense. A favorite attempt to preserve the supreme significance of the economic factor despite this consists in the interpretation of the constant interaction of the individual elements of cultural life as a causal or functional dependence of one on the other, or rather of all the others on one, namely, the economic element. When a certain *non*-economic institution has functioned for the benefit of certain economic class interests, as, for example, where certain religious institutions allowed themselves to be and actually were used as "black police," the whole institution is conceived either as having been created for this function or—quite metaphysically—as being impelled by a "developmental tendency" emanating from the economic factor.

It is unnecessary nowadays to go into detail to prove to the specialist that this interpretation of the purpose of the economic analysis of culture is in part the expression of a certain historical constellation which turned its scientific interest towards certain economically conditioned cultural problems, and in part the rabid chauvinism of a specialized department of science. It is clear that today it is antiquated at best. The explanation of everything by economic causes *alone* is never exhaustive in any sense whatsoever in *any* sphere of cultural phenomena, not even in the "economic" sphere itself. In principle, a banking history of a nation which adduces only economic motives for explanatory purposes is naturally just as unacceptable as an explanation of the Sistine Madonna as a consequence of the social-economic basis of the culture of the epoch in which it was created. It is no way more complete than, for instance, the explanation of capitalism by reference to certain shifts in the content of the religious ideas which played a role in the genesis of the capitalistic attitude; nor is it more exhaustive than the explanation of a political structure from its geographical background. In *all* of these cases, the degree of significance which we are to attribute to economic factors is decided by the class of causes to which we are to impute those specific elements of the phenomenon in question to which we attach significance in given cases and in which we are interested. The justification of the *one-sided* analysis of cultural reality from specific "points of view"—in our case with respect to its economic conditioning—emerges purely as a technical expedient from the fact that training in the observation of the effects of qualitatively similar categories of causes and the repeated utilization of the same scheme of concepts and hypotheses (*begrifflich-methodischen Apparates*) offers all the advantages of the division of labor. It is free from the charge of arbitrariness to the extent that it is successful in producing insights into interconnections which have been shown to be valuable for the causal explanation of concrete historical events. However—the "*one-sidedness*" and the unreality of the purely economic interpretation of history is in general only a special case of a principle which is generally valid for the scientific knowledge of cultural reality. The main task of the discussion to follow is to make explicit the logical foundations and the general methodological implications of this principle.

There is no absolutely "objective" scientific analysis of culture—or put perhaps more narrowly but certainly not essentially differently for our purposes—of "social phenomena" independent of special and "one-sided" viewpoints according to which—expressly or tacitly, consciously or unconsciously—they are selected, analyzed and organized for expository purposes. The reasons for this lie in the character of the cognitive goal of all research in social science which seeks to transcend the purely *formal* treatment of the legal or conventional norms regulating social life.

The type of social science in which we are interested is an *empirical science* of concrete *reality* (*Wirklichkeitswissenschaft*). Our aim is the understanding of the characteristic uniqueness of the reality in which we move. We wish to understand on the one hand the relationships and the cultural significance of individual events in their contemporary manifestations and on the other the causes of their being historically *so* and not *otherwise*. Now, as soon as we attempt to reflect about the way in which life confronts us in immediate concrete situations, it presents an infinite multiplicity of successively and coexistently emerging and disappearing events, both "within" and "outside" ourselves. The absolute infinitude of this multiplicity is seen to remain undiminished even when our attention is focused on a single "object," for instance, a concrete act of exchange, as soon as we seriously attempt an exhaustive description of *all* the individual components of this "individual phenomena," to say nothing of explaining it causally. All the analysis of infinite reality which the finite human mind can conduct rests on the tacit assumption that only a finite portion of this reality constitutes the object of scientific investigation, and that only it is "important" in the sense of being "worthy of being known." But what are the criteria by which this segment is selected? It has often been thought that the decisive criterion in the cultural sciences, too, was in the last analysis, the "regular" recurrence of certain causal relationships. The "laws" which we are able to perceive in the infinitely manifold stream of events must— according to this conception—contain the scientifically "essential" aspect of reality. As soon as we have shown some causal relationship to be a "law," i.e., if we have shown it to be universally valid by means of comprehensive historical induction or have made it immediately and tangibly plausible according to our subjective experience, a great number of similar cases order themselves under the formula thus attained. Those elements in each individual event which are left unaccounted for by the selection of their elements subsumable under the "law" are considered as scientifically unintegrated residues which will be taken care of in the further perfection of the system of "laws." Alternatively they will be viewed as "accidental" and therefore scientifically unimportant *because* they do not fit into the structure of the "law"; in other words, they are not typical of the event and hence can only be the objects of "idle curiosity." Accordingly, even among the followers of the Historical School we continually find the attitude which declares that the ideal which all the sciences, including the cultural sciences, serve and towards which they should strive even in the remote future is a system of propositions from which reality can be "deduced." As is well known, a leading natural scientist believed that he could designate the (factually unattainable) ideal goal of such a treatment of cultural reality as a sort of *"astronomical"* knowledge.

Let us not, for our part, spare ourselves the trouble of examining these matters more closely—however often they have already been discussed. The first thing that impresses one is that the "astronomical" knowledge which was referred to is not a system of laws at all. On the contrary, the laws which it presupposes have been taken from other disciplines like mechanics. But it too concerns itself with the question of the *individual* consequence which the working of these laws in an unique *configuration* produces, since it is these individual configurations which are *significant* for us. Every individual constellation which it "explains" or predicts is causally explicable only as the consequence of another equally individual constellation which has preceded it. As far back as we may go into the grey mist of the far-off past, the reality to which the laws apply always remains equally *individual*, equally *undeducible* from laws. A cosmic "primeval state" which had no individual character or less individual character than the cosmic reality of the present would naturally be a meaningless notion. But is there not some trace of similar ideas in our field in those propositions sometimes derived from natural law and sometimes verified by the observation of "primitives," concerning an economic-social "primeval state" free from historical "accidents," and characterized by phenomena such as "primitive agrarian communism," sexual "promiscuity," etc., from which individual historical development emerges by a sort of fall from grace into concreteness?

The social-scientific interest has its point of departure, of course, in the *real*, i.e., concrete, individually-structured configuration of our cultural life in its universal relationships which are themselves no less individually-structured, and in its development out of other social cultural conditions, which themselves are obviously likewise individually structured. It is clear here that the situation which we illustrated by reference to astronomy as a limiting case (which is regularly drawn on by logicians for the same purpose) appears in a more accentuated form. Whereas in astronomy, the heavenly bodies are of interest to us only in their *quantitative* and exact aspects, the *qualitative* aspect of phenomena concerns us in the social sciences. To this should be added that in the social sciences we are concerned with psychological and intellectual (*geistiger*) phenomena the empathic understanding of which is naturally a problem of a specifically different type from those which the schemes of the exact natural sciences in general can or seek to solve. Despite that, this distinction in itself is not a distinction in principle, as it seems at first glance. Aside from pure mechanics, even the exact natural sciences do not proceed without qualitative categories. Furthermore, in our own field we encounter the idea (which is obviously distorted) that at least the phenomena characteristic of a money-economy—which are basic to our culture— are quantifiable and on that account subject to formulation as "laws." Finally it depends on the breadth or narrowness of one's definition of "law" as to whether one will also include regularities which because they are not quantifiable are not subject to numerical analysis. Especially insofar as the influence of psychological and intellectual (*geistiger*) factors is concerned, it does not in any case exclude the establishment of *rules* governing rational conduct. Above all, the point of view still persists which claims that the task of psychology is to play a role comparable to mathematics for the *Geisteswissenschaften* in the sense that it analyzes the complicated phenomena of social life into their psychic conditions and effects, reduces them to their most elementary possible psychic factors and then analyzes their functional interdependences. Thereby, a sort of "chemistry" if not "mechanics" of the psychic foundations of social life would be created. Whether such investigations can produce valuable and—what is something else—useful results for the cultural sciences, we cannot decide here. But this would be irrelevant to the question as to whether the aim of social-economic knowledge in our sense, i.e., knowledge of *reality* with respect to its cultural *significance* and its causal relationships can be attained through the quest for recurrent sequences. Let us assume that we have succeeded by means of psychology or otherwise in analyzing all the observed and imaginable relationships of social phenomena into some ultimate elementary "factors," that we have made an exhaustive analysis and classification of them and then formulated rigorously exact laws covering their behavior,— What would be the significance of these results for our knowledge of the *historically* given culture or any individual phase thereof, such as capitalism, in its development and cultural significance? As an analytical tool, it would be as useful as a textbook of organic chemical combinations would be for our knowledge of the biogenetic aspect of the animal and plant world. In each case, certainly an important and useful preliminary step would have been taken. In neither case can concrete reality be deduced from "laws" and "factors." This is not because some higher mysterious powers reside in living phenomena (such as "dominants," "entelechies," or whatever they might be called). This, however, is a problem in its own right. The real reason is that the analysis of reality is concerned with the *configuration* into which those (hypothetical!) "factors" are arranged to form a cultural phenomenon which is historically significant to us. Furthermore, if we wish to "explain" this individual configuration "causally" we must invoke other equally individual configurations on the basis of which we will explain it with the aid of those (hypothetical!) "laws."

The determination of those (hypothetical) "laws" and "factors" would in any case only be the first of the many operations which would lead us to the desired type of knowledge. The analysis of the historically given individual configuration of those "factors" and their *significant* concrete interaction, conditioned by their historical context and especially the *rendering intelligible* of the basis and type of this significance would be the next task to be achieved. This task must be achieved, it is true, by the utilization of the preliminary analysis but it is nonetheless an entirely new and *distinct* task. The tracing as far into the past as possible of the individual features of these historically evolved configurations which are *contemporaneously* significant, and their historical explanation by antecedent and equally individual configurations would be the third task. Finally the prediction of possible future constellations would be a conceivable fourth task.

For all these purposes, clear concepts and the knowledge of those (hypothetical) "laws" are obviously of great value as heuristic means—but only as such. Indeed they are quite indispensable for this purpose. But even in this function their limitations become evident at a decisive point. In stating this, we arrive at the decisive feature of the method of the cultural sciences. We have designated as "cultural sciences" those disciplines which analyze the phenomena of life in terms of their cultural significance. The *significance* of a configuration of cultural phenomena and the basis of this significance cannot however be derived and rendered intelligible by a system of analytical laws (*Gesetzesbegriffen*), however perfect it may be, since the significance of cultural events presupposes a *value-orientation* towards these events. The concept of culture is a *value-concept*. Empirical reality becomes "culture" to us because and insofar as we relate it to value ideas. It includes those segments and only those segments of reality which have become significant to us because of this value-relevance. Only a small portion of existing concrete reality is colored by our value-conditioned interest and it alone is significant to us. It is significant because it reveals relationships which are important to us due to their connection with our values. Only because and to the extent that this is the case is it worthwhile for us to know it in its individual features. We cannot discover, however, what is meaningful to us by means of a "presuppositionless" investigation of empirical data. Rather perception of its meaningfulness to us is the presupposition of its becoming an *object* of investigation. Meaningfulness naturally does not coincide with laws as such, and the more general the law the less the coincidence. For the specific meaning which a phenomenon has for us is naturally *not* to be found in those relationships which it shares with many other phenomena.

The focus of attention on reality under the guidance of values which lend it significance and the selection and ordering of the phenomena which are thus affected in the light of their cultural significance is entirely different from the analysis of reality in terms of laws and general concepts. Neither of these two types of the analysis of reality has any necessary logical relationship with the other. They can coincide in individual instances but it would be most disastrous if their occasional coincidence caused us to think that they were not distinct *in principle*. The *cultural significance* of a phenomenon, e.g., the significance of exchange in a money economy, can be the fact that it exists on a mass scale as a fundamental component of modern culture. But the historical fact that it plays this role must be causally explained in order to render its cultural significance understandable. The analysis of the *general* aspects of exchange and the technique of the market is a—highly important and indispensable—*preliminary task*. For not only does this type of analysis leave unanswered the question as to how exchange historically acquired its fundamental significance in the modern world; but above all else, the fact with which we are primarily concerned, namely, the *cultural significance* of the money-economy, for the sake of which we are interested in the description of exchange technique and for the sake of which alone a science exists which deals with that technique—is not derivable from any "law." The *generic features* of exchange, purchase, etc., interest the jurist—but we are concerned with the analysis of the *cultural significance* of the concrete *historical* fact that today exchange exists on a mass scale. When we require an explanation, when we wish to understand what distinguishes the social-economic aspects of our culture for in-

stance from that of antiquity in which exchange showed precisely
the same generic traits as it does today and when we raise the
question as to where the significance of "money economy" lies,
logical principles of quite heterogeneous derivation enter into the
investigation. We will apply those concepts with which we are
provided by the investigation of the general features of economic
mass phenomena—indeed, insofar as they are relevant to the meaningful aspects of our culture, we shall use them as *means* of exposition. The *goal* of our investigation is not reached through the
exposition of those laws and concepts, precise as it may be. The
question as to what should be the object of universal conceptualization cannot be decided "presuppositionlessly" but only with
reference to the *significance* which certain segments of that infinite multiplicity which we call "commerce" have for culture.
We seek knowledge of an historical phenomenon, meaning by
historical: significant in its individuality (*Eigenart*). And the decisive element in this is that only through the presupposition that
a finite part alone of the infinite variety of phenomena is significant, does the knowledge of an individual phenomenon become
logically meaningful. Even with the widest imaginable knowledge
of "laws," we are helpless in the face of the question: how is the
causal explanation of an *individual* fact possible—since a *description* of even the smallest slice of reality can never be exhaustive?
The number and type of causes which have influenced any given
event are always infinite and there is nothing in the things themselves to set some of them apart as alone meriting attention. A
chaos of "existential judgments" about countless individual events
would be the only result of a serious attempt to analyze reality
"without presuppositions." And even this result is only seemingly
possible, since every single perception discloses on closer examination an infinite number of constituent perceptions which can
never be exhaustively expressed in a judgment. Order is brought
into this chaos only on the condition that in every case only a
part of concrete reality is interesting and *significant* to us, because only it is related to the *cultural values* with which we
approach reality. Only certain sides of the infinitely complex
concrete phenomenon, namely those to which we attribute a
general *cultural significance*—are therefore worthwhile knowing.
They alone are objects of causal explanation. And even this causal

explanation evinces the same character; an *exhaustive* causal investigation of any concrete phenomena in its full reality is not only practically impossible—it is simply nonsense. We select only those causes to which are to be imputed in the individual case, the "essential" feature of an event. Where the *individuality* of a phenomenon is concerned, the question of causality is not a question of *laws* but of concrete causal *relationships;* it is not a question of the subsumption of the event under some general rubric as a representative case but of its imputation as a consequence of some constellation. It is in brief a *question of imputation.* Wherever the causal explanation of a "cultural phenomenon"—an "historical individual"[5] is under consideration, the knowledge of causal *laws* is not the *end* of the investigation but only a *means.* It facilitates and renders possible the causal imputation to their concrete causes of those components of a phenomenon the individuality of which is culturally significant. So far and only so far as it achieves this, is it valuable for our knowledge of concrete relationships. And the more "general," i.e., the more abstract the laws, the less they can contribute to the causal imputation of *individual* phenomena and, more indirectly, to the understanding of the significance of cultural events.

What is the consequence of all this?

Naturally, it does not imply that the knowledge of *universal* propositions, the construction of abstract concepts, the knowledge of regularities and the attempt to formulate "*laws*" have no scientific justification in the cultural sciences. Quite the contrary, if the causal knowledge of the historians consists of the imputation of concrete effects to concrete causes, a *valid* imputation of any individual effect without the application of "*nomological*" knowledge—i.e., the knowledge of recurrent causal sequences—would in general be impossible. Whether a single individual component of a relationship is, in a concrete case, to be assigned causal responsibility for an effect, the causal explanation of which is at issue, can in doubtful cases be determined only by estimating the effects which we *generally* expect from it and from the other components of the same complex which are relevant to the explanation.

[5] We will use the term which is already occasionally used in the methodology of our discipline and which is now becoming widespread in a more precise formulation in logic.

In other words, the "*adequate*" effects of the causal elements involved must be considered in arriving at any such conclusion. The extent to which the historian (in the widest sense of the word) can perform this imputation in a reasonably certain manner with his imagination sharpened by personal experience and trained in analytic methods and the extent to which he must have recourse to the aid of special disciplines which make it possible, varies with the individual case. Everywhere, however, and hence also in the sphere of complicated economic processes, the more certain and the more comprehensive our general knowledge the greater is the *certainty* of imputation. This proposition is not in the least affected by the fact that even in the case of all so-called "economic laws" without exception, we are concerned here not with "laws" in the narrower exact natural science sense, but with *adequate* causal relationships expressed in rules and with the application of the category of "objective possibility." The establishment of such regularities is not the *end* but rather the *means* of knowledge. It is entirely a question of expediency, to be settled separately for each individual case, whether a regularly recurrent causal relationship of everyday experience should be formulated into a "law." Laws are important and valuable in the exact natural sciences, in the measure that those sciences are *universally valid*. For the knowledge of historical phenomena in their concreteness, the most general laws, because they are most devoid of content are also the least valuable. The more comprehensive the validity, —or scope—of a term, the more it leads us away from the richness of reality since in order to include the common elements of the largest possible number of phenomena, it must necessarily be as abstract as possible and hence *devoid* of content. In the cultural sciences, the knowledge of the universal or general is never valuable in itself.

The conclusion which follows from the above is that an "objective" analysis of cultural events, which proceeds according to the thesis that the ideal of science is the reduction of empirical reality of "laws," is meaningless. It is not meaningless, as is often maintained, because cultural or psychic events for instance are "objectively" less governed by laws. It is meaningless for a number of other reasons. Firstly, because the knowledge of social laws is not knowledge of social reality but is rather one of the various aids used by our minds for attaining this end; secondly, because knowledge of *cultural* events is inconceivable except on a basis of the *significance* which the concrete constellations of reality have for us in certain *individual* concrete situations. In *which* sense and in *which* situations this is the case is not revealed to us by any law; it is decided according to the *value-ideas* in the light of which we view "culture" in each individual case. "Culture" is a finite segment of the meaningless infinity of the world process, a segment on which *human beings* confer meaning and significance. This is true even for the human being who views a *particular* culture as a mortal enemy and who seeks to "return to nature." He can attain this point of view only after viewing the culture in which he lives from the standpoint of his values, and finding it "too soft." This is the purely logical-formal fact which is involved when we speak of the logically necessary rootedness of all historical entities (*historische Individuen*) in "evaluative ideas." The transcendental presupposition of every *cultural science* lies not in our finding a certain culture or any "culture" in general to be *valuable* but rather in the fact that we are *cultural beings*, endowed with the capacity and the will to take a deliberate attitude towards the world and to lend it *significance*. Whatever this significance may be, it will lead us to judge certain phenomena of human existence in its light and to respond to them as being (positively or negatively) meaningful. Whatever may be the content of this attitude—these phenomena have cultural significance for us and on this significance alone rests its scientific interest. Thus when we speak here of the conditioning of cultural knowledge through *evaluative* ideas (*Wertideen*) (following the terminology of modern logic), it is done in the hope that we will not be subject to crude misunderstandings such as the opinion that cultural significance should be attributed only to *valuable* phenomena. Prostitution is a *cultural* phenomenon just as much as religion or money. All three are cultural phenomena *only* because and *only* insofar as their existence and the form which they historically assume touch directly or indirectly on our cultural *interests* and arouse our striving for knowledge concerning problems brought into focus by the evaluative ideas which give *significance* to the fragments of reality analyzed by those concepts.

All knowledge of cultural reality, as may be seen, is always

knowledge from *particular points of view*. When we require
from the historian and social research worker as an elementary
presupposition that they distinguish the important from the trivial and that he should have the necessary "point of view" for this
distinction, we mean that they must understand how to relate the
events of the real world consciously or unconsciously to universal
"cultural values" and to select out those relationships which are
significant for us. If the notion that those standpoints can be derived from the "facts themselves" continually recurs, it is due to
the naive self-deception of the specialist who is unaware that it is
due to the evaluative ideas with which he unconsciously approaches his subject matter, that he has selected from an absolute
infinity a tiny portion with the study of which he *concerns* himself. In connection with this selection of individual special "aspects"
of the event which always and everywhere occurs, consciously or
unconsciously, there also occurs that element of cultural-scientific
work which is referred to by the often-heard assertion that the
"personal" element of a scientific work is what is really valuable
in it, and that personality must be expressed in every work if its
existence is to be justified. To be sure, without the investigator's
evaluative ideas, there would be no principle of selection of subject-
matter and no meaningful knowledge of the concrete reality. Just
as without the investigator's conviction regarding the significance
of particular cultural facts, every attempt to analyze concrete
reality is absolutely meaningless, so the direction of his personal
belief, the refraction of values in the prism of his mind, gives
direction to his work. And the values to which the scientific
genius relates the object of his inquiry may determine, i.e., decide
the "conception" of a whole epoch, not only concerning what is
regarded as "valuable" but also concerning what is significant or
insignificant, "important" or "unimportant" in the phenomena.

Accordingly, cultural science in our sense involves "subjective" presuppositions insofar as it concerns itself only with those
components of reality which have some relationship, however
indirect, to events to which we attach cultural *significance*. Nonetheless, it is entirely *causal* knowledge exactly in the same sense
as the knowledge of significant concrete (*individueller*) natural
events which have a qualitative character. Among the many confusions which the over-reaching tendency of a formal-juristic

outlook has brought about in the cultural sciences, there has recently appeared the attempt to "refute" the "materialistic conception of history" by a series of clever but fallacious arguments which state that since all economic life must take place in legally or conventionally *regulated forms*, all economic "development" must take the form of striving for the creation of new *legal* forms. Hence, it is said to be intelligible only through ethical maxims and is on this account essentially different from every type of "natural" development. Accordingly the knowledge of economic development is said to be "teleological" in character. Without wishing to discuss the meaning of the ambiguous term "development," or the logically no less ambiguous term "teleology" in the social sciences, it should be stated that such knowledge need not be "teleological" in the sense assumed by this point of view. The cultural significance of normatively regulated legal *relations* and even norms themselves can undergo fundamental revolutionary changes even under conditions of the formal identity of the prevailing legal norms. Indeed, if one wishes to lose one's self for a moment in phantasies about the future, one might theoretically imagine, let us say, the "socialization of the means of production" unaccompanied by any conscious "striving" towards this result, and without even the disappearance or addition of a single paragraph of our legal code; the statistical frequency of certain legally regulated relationships might be changed fundamentally, and in many cases, even disappear entirely; a great number of legal norms might become *practically* meaningless and their whole cultural significance changed beyond identification. *De lege ferenda* discussions may be justifiably disregarded by the "materialistic conception of history" since its central proposition is the indeed inevitable change in the *significance* of legal institutions. Those who view the painstaking labor of causally understanding historical reality as of secondary importance can disregard it, but it is impossible to supplant it by any type of "teleology." From our viewpoint, "purpose" is the conception of an *effect* which becomes a *cause* of an action. Since we take into account every cause which produces or can produce a significant effect, we also consider this one. Its specific significance consists only in the fact that we not only *observe* human conduct but can and desire to understand it.

Undoubtedly, all evaluative ideas are "subjective." Between the "historical" interest in a family chronicle and that in the development of the greatest conceivable cultural phenomena which were and are common to a nation or to mankind over long epochs, there exists an infinite gradation of "significance" arranged into an order which differs for each of us. And they are, naturally, historically variable in accordance with the character of the culture and the ideas which rule men's minds. But it obviously does not follow from this that research in the cultural sciences can only have results which are "subjective" in the sense that they are *valid* for one person and not for others. Only the degree to which they interest different persons varies. In other words, the choice of the object of investigation and the extent or depth to which this investigation attempts to penetrate into the infinite causal web, are determined by the evaluative ideas which dominate the investigator and his age. In the *method* of investigation, the guiding "point of view" is of great importance for the *construction* of the conceptual scheme which will be used in the investigation. In the mode of their *use*, however, the investigator is obviously bound by the norms of our thought just as much here as elsewhere. For scientific truth is precisely what is *valid* for all who *seek* the truth.

However, there emerges from this the meaninglessness of the idea which prevails occasionally even among historians, namely, that the goal of the cultural sciences, however far it may be from realization, is to construct a closed system of concepts, in which reality is synthesized in some sort of *permanently* and *universally* valid classification and from which it can again be deduced. The stream of immeasurable events flows unendingly towards eternity. The cultural problems which move men form themselves ever anew and in different colors, and the boundaries of that area in the infinite stream of concrete events which acquires meaning and significance for us, i.e., which becomes an "historical individual," are constantly subject to change. The intellectual contexts from which it is viewed and scientifically analyzed shift. The points of departure of the cultural sciences remain changeable throughout the limitless future as long as a Chinese ossification of intellectual life does not render mankind incapable of setting new questions to the eternally inexhaustible flow of life. A systematic science of culture, even only in the sense of a definitive, objectively valid, systematic fixation of the problems which it should treat, would be senseless in itself. Such an attempt could only produce a collection of numerous, specifically particularized, heterogeneous and disparate viewpoints in the light of which reality becomes "culture" through being significant in its unique character.

Having now completed this lengthy discussion, we can finally turn to the question which is *methodologically* relevant in the consideration of the "objectivity" of cultural knowledge. The question is: what is the logical function and structure of the *concepts* which our science, like all others, uses? Restated with special reference to the decisive problem, the question is: what is the significance of *theory* and theoretical conceptualization (*theoretische Begriffsbildung*) for our knowledge of cultural reality?

Economics was originally—as we have already seen—a "technique," at least in the central focus of its attention. By this we mean that it viewed reality from an at least ostensibly unambiguous and stable practical evaluative standpoint: namely, the increase of the "wealth" of the population. It was on the other hand, from the very beginning, more than a "technique" since it was integrated into the great scheme of the natural law and rationalistic *Weltanschauung* of the eighteenth century. The nature of that *Weltanschauung* with its optimistic faith in the theoretical and practical rationalizability of reality had an important consequence insofar as it *obstructed* the discovery of the *problematic* character of that standpoint which had been assumed as self-evident. As the rational analysis of society arose in close connection with the modern development of natural science, so it remained related to it in its whole method of approach. In the natural sciences, the practical evaluative attitude toward what was immediately and technically useful was closely associated from the very first with the hope, taken over as a heritage of antiquity and further elaborated, of attaining a purely "objective" (i.e., independent of all individual contingencies) monistic knowledge of the totality of reality in a *conceptual* system of metaphysical *validity* and mathematical *form*. It was thought that this hope could be realized by the method of generalizing abstraction and the formulation of laws based on empirical analysis. The natural sciences which were bound to evaluative standpoints, such as clinical medicine and even more what is conventionally called "technology" became purely practical "arts." The values for which they strove, e.g., the health of the patient, the technical perfection of a concrete productive process, etc., were fixed for the time being for all of them. The methods which they used could only consist in the application of the laws formulated by the theoretical disciplines. Every theoretical advance in the construction of these laws was or could also be an advance for the practical disciplines. With the end given, the progressive reduction of concrete practical questions (e.g., a case of illness, a technical problem, etc.) to special cases of generally valid laws, meant that extension of theoretical knowledge was closely associated and identical with the extension of technical-practical possibilities.

When modern biology subsumed those aspects of reality which interest us *historically*, i.e., in all their concreteness, under a universally valid evolutionary principle, which at least had the appearance—but not the actuality—of embracing everything essential about the subject in a scheme of universally valid laws, this seemed to be the final twilight of all evaluative standpoints in all the sciences. For since the so-called historical event was a segment of the totality of reality, since the principle of causality which was the presupposition of all scientific work, seemed to require the analysis of all events into generally valid "laws," and in view of the overwhelming success of the natural sciences which took this idea seriously, it appeared as if there was in general no conceivable meaning of scientific work other than the discovery of the *laws* of events. Only those aspects of phenomena which were involved in the "laws" could be essential from the scientific point of view, and concrete "individual" events could be considered only as "types," i.e., as representative illustrations of laws. An interest in such events in themselves did not seem to be a "scientific" interest.

It is impossible to trace here the important repercussions of this will-to-believe of naturalistic monism in economics. When socialist criticism and the work of the historians were beginning to transform the original evaluative standpoints, the vigorous development of zoological research on one hand and the influence of Hegelian panlogism on the other prevented economics from attaining a clear and full understanding of the relationship between concept and reality. The result, to the extent that we are interested in it, is that despite the powerful resistance to the infiltration of naturalistic dogma due to German idealism since Fichte and the achievement of the German Historical School in law and economics and partly because of the very work of the Historical School, the naturalistic viewpoint in certain decisive problems has not yet been overcome. Among these problems we find the relationship between "theory" and "history," which is still problematic in our discipline.

The "abstract"-theoretical method even today shows unmediated and ostensibly irreconcilable cleavage from empirical-historical research. The proponents of this method recognize in a thoroughly correct way the methodological impossibility of supplanting the historical knowledge of reality by the formulation of laws or, vice versa, of constructing "laws" in the rigorous sense through the mere juxtaposition of historical observations. Now in order to arrive at these laws—for they are certain that science should be directed towards these as its highest goal—they take it to be a fact that we always have a direct awareness of the structure of human actions in all their reality. Hence—so they think—science can make human behavior directly intelligible with axiomatic evidentness and accordingly reveal its laws. The only exact form of knowledge—the formulation of immediately and intuitively *evident* laws—is, however, at the same time the only one which offers access to events which have not been directly observed. Hence, at least as regards the fundamental phenomena of economic life, the construction of a system of abstract and therefore purely formal propositions analogous to those of the exact natural sciences, is the only means of analyzing and intellectually mastering the complexity of social life. In spite of the fundamental methodological distinction between historical knowledge and the knowledge of "laws" which the creator of the theory drew as the *first* and *only* one, he now claims empirical *validity*, in the sense of the *deducibility* of reality from "laws," for the propositions of abstract theory. It is true that this is not meant in the sense of empirical validity of the abstract economic laws as such, but in the sense that when equally "exact" theories have been constructed for all the other relevant factors, all these abstract theories together must contain the true reality of the object—i.e., whatever is worthwhile knowing about it. Exact economic theory deals with the operation of *one* psychic motive, the other theories have as their task the formulation of the behavior of all the other motives into similar sorts of propositions enjoying hypothetical validity. Accordingly, the fantastic claim has occasionally been made for economic theories—e.g., the abstract theories of price, interest, rent, etc.,—that they can, by ostensibly following the analogy of physical science propositions, be validly applied to the derivation of quantitatively stated conclusions from given real premises, since given the ends, economic behavior with respect to means is unambiguously "determined." This claim fails to observe that in order to be able to reach this result even in the simplest case, the totality of the existing historical reality including every one of its causal relationships must be assumed as "given" and presupposed as known. But if *this* type of knowledge were accessible to the finite mind of man, abstract theory would have no cognitive value whatsoever. The naturalistic prejudice that every concept in the cultural sciences should be similar to those in the exact natural sciences has led in consequence to the misunderstanding of the meaning of this theoretical construction (*theoretische Gedankengebilde*). It has been believed that it is a matter of the psychological isolation of a specific "impulse," the acquisitive impulse, or of the isolated study of a specific maxim of human conduct, the so-called economic principle. Abstract theory purported to be based on psychological *axioms* and as a result historians have called for an *empirical* psychology in order to show the invalidity of those axioms and to derive the course of economic events from psychological principles. We do not wish at this point to enter into a detailed criticism of the belief in the significance of a—still to be created—systematic science of "social psychology" as the future foundation of the cultural sciences, and particularly of social economics. Indeed, the partly brilliant attempts which have been made hitherto to interpret economic phenomena psychologically, show in any case that the procedure does not begin with the analysis of psychological qualities, moving then to the analysis of social institutions, but that, on the contrary, insight into the psychological preconditions and consequences of institutions presupposes a precise knowledge of the latter and the scientific analysis of their structure. In concrete cases, psychological analysis can contribute then an extremely valuable deepening of the knowledge of the historical cultural *conditioning* and cultural *significance* of institutions. The interesting aspect of the psychic attitude of a person in a social situation is specifically particularized in each case, according to the special cultural significance of the situation in question. It is a question of an extremely heterogeneous and highly concrete structure of psychic motives and influences. Social-psychological research involves the study of various very disparate *individual* types of cultural elements with reference to their interpretability by our empathic understanding. Through social-psychological research, with the knowledge of individual institutions as a point of departure, we will learn increasingly how to understand institutions in a psychological way. We will not however deduce the institutions from psychological laws or explain them by elementary psychological phenomena.

Thus, the far-flung polemic, which centered on the question of the psychological justification of abstract theoretical propositions, on the scope of the "acquisitive impulse" and the "economic principle," etc., turns out to have been fruitless.

In the establishment of the propositions of abstract theory, it is only apparently a matter of "deductions" from fundamental psychological motives. Actually, the former are a special case of a kind of concept-construction which is peculiar and to a certain extent, indispensable, to the cultural sciences. It is worthwhile at this point to describe it in further detail since we can thereby approach more closely the fundamental question of the significance of theory in the social sciences. Therewith we leave undiscussed, once and for all, whether *the* particular analytical concepts which we cite or to which we allude as illustrations, correspond to the purposes they are to serve, i.e., whether in fact they are well-adapted. The question as to how far, for example, contemporary "abstract theory" should be further elaborated, is ultimately also a question of the strategy of science, which must, however, concern itself with other problems as well. Even the "theory of marginal utility" is subsumable under a "law of marginal utility."

We have in abstract economic theory an illustration of those synthetic constructs which have been designated as *"ideas"* of historical phenomena. It offers us an ideal picture of events on the commodity-market under conditions of a society organized on the principles of an exchange economy, free competition and rigorously rational conduct. This conceptual pattern brings together certain relationships and events of historical life into a complex, which is conceived as an internally consistent system. Substantively, this construct in itself is like a *utopia* which has been arrived at by the analytical accentuation of certain elements of reality. Its relationship to the empirical data consists solely in the fact that where market-conditioned relationships of the type referred to by the abstract construct are discovered or suspected to exist in reality to some extent, we can make the *characteristic* features of this relationship pragmatically *clear* and *understandable* by reference to an *ideal-type*. This procedure can be indispensable for heuristic as well as expository purposes. The ideal typical concept will help to develop our skill in imputation in *research:* it *is* no "hypothesis" but it offers guidance to the construction of hypotheses. It is not a *description* of reality but it aims to give unambiguous means of expression to such a description. It is thus the "idea" of the *historically* given modern society, based on an exchange economy, which is developed for us by quite the same logical principles as are used in constructing the idea of the medieval "city economy" as a "genetic" concept. When we do this, we construct the concept "city economy" not as an average of the economic structures actually existing in all the cities observed but as an *ideal-type*. An ideal type is formed by the one-sided *accentuation* of one or more points of view and by the synthesis of a great many diffuse, discrete, more or less present and occasionally absent *concrete individual* phenomena, which are arranged according to those one-sidedly emphasized viewpoints into a unified *analytical* construct (*Gedankenbild*). In its conceptual purity, this mental construct (*Gedankenbild*) cannot be found empirically anywhere in reality. It is a *utopia*. Historical research faces the task of determining in each individual case, the extent to which this ideal-construct approximates to or diverges from reality, to what extent for example, the economic structure of a certain city is to be classified as a "city-economy." When carefully applied, those concepts are particularly useful in research and exposition. In very much the same way one can work the "idea" of "handicraft" into a utopia by arranging certain traits, actually found in an unclear, confused state in the industrial enterprises of the most diverse epochs and countries, into a consistent ideal-construct by an accentuation of their essential tendencies. This ideal-type is then related to the idea (*Gedankenausdruck*) which one finds expressed there. One can further delineate a society in which all branches of economic and even intellectual activity are governed by maxims which appear to be applications of the same principle which characterizes the ideal-typical "handicraft" system. Furthermore, one can juxtapose alongside the ideal typical "handicraft" system the antithesis of a correspondingly ideal-typical capitalistic productive system, which has been abstracted out of certain features of modern large scale industry. On the basis of this, one can delineate the utopia of a "capitalistic" culture, i.e., one in which the governing principle is the investment of private capital. This procedure would accentuate certain individual concretely diverse traits of modern material and intellectual culture in its unique aspects into an ideal construct which from our point of view would be completely self-consistent. This would then be the delineation of an *"idea"* of *capitalistic culture*. We must disregard for the moment whether and how this procedure could be carried out. It is possible, or rather, it must be accepted as certain that numerous, indeed a very great many, utopias of this sort can be worked out, of which *none* is like another, and *none* of which can be observed in empirical reality as an actually existing economic system, but *each* of which however claims that it is a representation of the "idea" of capitalistic culture. *Each* of these can claim to be a representation of the "idea" of capitalistic culture to the extent that it has really taken certain traits, meaningful in their essential features, from the empirical reality of our culture and brought them together into a unified ideal-construct. For those phenomena which interest us as cultural phenomena are interesting to us with respect to very different kinds of evaluative ideas to which we relate them. Inasmuch as the "points of view" from which they can become significant for us are very diverse, the most varied criteria can be applied to the selection of the traits which are to enter into the construction of an ideal-typical view of a particular culture.

What is the significance of such ideal-typical constructs for an *empirical* science, as we wish to constitute it? Before going any further, we should emphasize that the idea of an ethical *imperative*, of a "model" of what "ought" to exist is to be carefully distinguished from the analytical construct, which is "ideal" in the strictly logical sense of the term. It is a matter here of constructing relationships which our imagination accepts as plausibly motivated and hence as "objectively possible" and which appear as *adequate* from the nomological standpoint.

Whoever accepts the proposition that the knowledge of historical reality can or should be a "presuppositionless" copy of "objective" facts, will deny the value of the ideal-type. Even those who recognize that there is no "presuppositionlessness" in the logical sense and that even the simplest excerpt from a statute or from a documentary source can have scientific meaning only with reference to "significance" and ultimately to evaluative ideas, will more or less regard the construction of any such historical "utopias" as an expository device which endangers the autonomy of historical research and which is, in any case, a vain sport. And, in fact, *whether* we are dealing simply with a conceptual game or with a scientifically fruitful method of conceptualization and *theory*-construction can never be decided *a priori*. Here, too, there is only one criterion, namely, that of success in revealing concrete cultural phenomena in their interdependence, their causal conditions and their *significance*. The construction of abstract ideal-types recommends itself not as an end but as a *means*. Every conscientious examination of the conceptual elements of historical exposition shows, however, that the historian as soon as he attempts to go beyond the bare establishment of concrete relationships and to determine the *cultural* significance of even the simplest individual event in order to "characterize" it, *must* use concepts which are precisely and unambiguously definable only in the form of ideal types. Or are concepts such as "individualism," "imperialism," "feudalism," "mercantilism," "conventional," etc., and innumerable concepts of like character by means of which we seek analytically and empathically to understand reality constructed substantively by the "presuppositionless" *description* of some concrete phenomenon or through the abstract synthesis of those traits which are *common* to numerous concrete phenomena? Hundreds of words in the historian's vocabulary are ambiguous constructs created to meet the unconsciously felt need for adequate expression and the meaning of which is only concretely felt but not clearly thought out. In a great many cases, particularly in the field of descriptive political history, their ambiguity has not been prejudicial to the clarity of the presentation. It is sufficient that in each case the reader should *feel* what the historian had in mind; or, one can content one's self with the idea that the author used a *particular* meaning of the concept with special reference to the concrete case at hand. The greater the need however for a sharp appreciation of the significance of a cultural phenomenon, the more imperative is the need to operate with unambiguous concepts which are not only particularly but also systematically defined. A "definition" of such synthetic historical terms according to the scheme of *genus proximum* and *differentia specifica* is naturally nonsense. But let us consider it. Such a form of the establishment of the meanings of words is to be found only in axiomatic disciplines which use syllogisms. A simple "descriptive analysis" of these concepts into their components either does not exist or else exists only illusorily, for the question arises as to *which* of these components should be regarded as essential. When a genetic definition of the content of the concept is sought, there remains only the ideal-type in the sense explained above. It is a conceptual construct (*Gedankenbild*) which is neither historical reality nor even the "true" reality. It is even less fitted to serve as a schema under which a real situation or action is to be subsumed as one *instance*. It has the significance of a purely ideal *limiting* concept with which the real situation or action is *compared* and surveyed for the explication of certain of its significant components. Such concepts are constructs in terms of which we formulate relationships by the application of the category of objective possibility. By means of this category, the adequacy of our imagination, oriented and disciplined by reality, is *judged*.

In this function especially, the ideal-type is an attempt to analyze historically unique configurations or their individual components by means of genetic concepts. Let us take for instance the concepts "church" and "sect." They may be broken down purely classificatorily into complexes of characteristics whereby not only the distinction between them but also the content of the concept must constantly remain fluid. If, however, I wish to formulate the concept of "sect" genetically, e.g., with reference to certain important cultural significances which the "sectarian spirit" has had for modern culture, certain characteristics of both become *essential* because they stand in an adequate causal relationship to those influences. However, the concepts thereupon become ideal-typical in the sense that they appear in full conceptual *integrity* either not at all or only in individual instances. Here as elsewhere every concept which is not purely classificatory diverges from reality. But the discursive nature of our knowledge, i.e., the fact that we comprehend reality only through a chain of intellectual modifications, postulates such a conceptual shorthand. Our imagination can often dispense with explicit conceptual formulations as a means of *investigation*. But as regards exposition, to the extent that it wishes to be unambiguous, the use of precise formulations in the sphere of cultural analysis is in many cases absolutely necessary. Whoever disregards it entirely must confine himself to the formal aspect of cultural phenomena, e.g., to legal history. The universe of legal norms is naturally clearly definable and is valid (in the *legal* sense!) for historical reality. But social science in our sense is concerned with practical *significance*. This significance, however, can very often be brought unambiguously to mind only by relating the empirical data to an ideal limiting case. If the historian (in the widest sense of the word) rejects an attempt to construct such ideal types as a "theoretical construction," i.e., as useless or dispensable for his concrete heuristic purposes, the inevitable consequence is either that he consciously or unconsciously uses other similar concepts without formulating them verbally and elaborating them logically or that he remains stuck in the realm of the vaguely "felt."

Nothing, however, is more dangerous than the *confusion* of theory and history stemming from naturalistic prejudices. This confusion expresses itself firstly in the belief that the "true" content and the essence of historical reality is portrayed in such theoretical constructs or secondly, in the use of these constructs as a procrustean bed into which history is to be forced or thirdly, in the hypostatization of such "ideas" as real "forces" and as a "true" reality which operates behind the passage of events and which works itself out in history.

This latter danger is especially great since we are also, indeed primarily, accustomed to understand by the "ideas" of an epoch the thoughts or ideals which dominated the mass or at least an historically decisive number of the persons living in that epoch itself, and who were therefore significant as components of its culture. Now there are two aspects to this: in the first place, there are certain relationships between the "idea" in the sense of a tendency of practical or theoretical thought and the "idea" in the sense of the ideal-*typical* portrayal of an epoch constructed as a heuristic device. An ideal type of certain situations, which can be abstracted from certain characteristic social phenomena of an epoch, might—and this is indeed quite often the case—have also been present in the minds of the persons living in that epoch as an ideal to be striven for in practical life or as a maxim for the regulation of certain social relationships. This is true of the "idea" of "provision" (*Nahrungsschutz*) and many other Canonist doctrines, especially those of Thomas Aquinas, in relationship to the modern ideal type of medieval "city economy" which we discussed above. The same is also true of the much talked of "basic concept" of economics: economic "value." From Scholasticism to Marxism, the idea of an objectively "valid" value, i.e., of an *ethical imperative*, was amalgamated with an abstraction drawn from the empirical process of price formation. The notion that the "value" of commodities should be regulated by certain principles of natural law, has had and still has immeasurable significance for the development of culture—and not merely the culture of the Middle Ages. It has also influenced actual price formation very markedly. But what was meant and what can be meant by that *theoretical* concept can be made unambiguously clear *only* through precise, ideal-typical constructs. Those who are so contemptuous of the "Robinsonades" of classical theory should restrain themselves if they are unable to replace them with better concepts, which in this context means clearer concepts.

Thus the causal relationship between the historically determinable idea which governs the conduct of men and those components of historical reality from which their corresponding ideal-*type* may be abstracted, can naturally take on a considerable number of different forms. The main point to be observed is that *in principle* they are both fundamentally different things. There is still another aspect: those "ideas" which govern the behavior of the population of a certain epoch i.e., which are concretely influential in determining their conduct, can, if a somewhat complicated construct is involved, be formulated precisely only in the form of an ideal type, since empirically it exists in the minds of an indefinite and constantly changing mass of individuals and assumes in their minds the most multifarious nuances of form and content, clarity and meaning. Those elements of the spiritual life of the individuals living in a certain epoch of the Middle Ages, for example, which we may designate as the "Christianity" of those individuals, would, if they could be completely portrayed, naturally constitute a chaos of infinitely differentiated and highly contradictory complexes of ideas and feelings. This is true despite the fact that the medieval church was certainly able to bring about a unity of belief and conduct to a particularly high degree. If we raise the question as to what in this chaos was the "Christianity" of the Middle Ages (which we must nonetheless use as a stable concept) and wherein lay those "Christian" elements which we find in the institutions of the Middle Ages, we see that here too in every individual case, we are applying a purely analytical construct created by ourselves. It is a combination of articles of faith, norms from church law and custom, maxims of conduct, and countless concrete interrelationships which we have fused into an "idea." It is a synthesis which we could not succeed in attaining with consistency without the application of ideal-type concepts.

The relationship between the logical structure of the conceptual system in which we present such "ideas" and what is immediately given in empirical reality naturally varies considerably. It is relatively simple in cases in which one or a few easily formulated theoretical main principles as for instance Calvin's doctrine of predestination or clearly definable ethical postulates govern human conduct and produce historical effects, so that we can analyze the "idea" into a hierarchy of ideas which can be logically derived from those theses. It is of course easily overlooked that however important the significance even of the purely logically persuasive force of ideas—Marxism is an outstanding example of this type of force—nonetheless empirical-historical events occurring in men's minds must be understood as primarily *psychologically* and not logically conditioned. The ideal-typical character of such syntheses of historically effective ideas is revealed still more clearly when those fundamental main principles and postulates no longer survive in the minds of those individuals who are still dominated by ideas which were logically or associatively derived from them because the "idea" which was historically and originally fundamental has either died out or has in general achieved wide diffusion only for its broadest implications. The basic fact that the synthesis is an "idea" which *we* have created emerges even more markedly when those fundamental main principles have either only very imperfectly or not at all been raised to the level of explicit consciousness or at least have not taken the form of explicitly elaborated complexes of ideas. When we adopt this procedure, as it very often happens and must happen, we are concerned in these ideas, e.g., the "liberalism" of a certain period or "Methodism" or some intellectually unelaborated variety of "socialism," with a *pure* ideal type of much the same character as the synthetic "principles" of economic epochs in which we had our point of departure. The more inclusive the relationships to be presented, and the more many-sided their cultural *significance* has been, the *more* their comprehensive systematic exposition in a conceptual system approximates the character of an ideal type, and the less is it possible to operate with *one* such concept. In such situations the frequently repeated attempts to discover ever *new* aspects of significance by the construction of new ideal-typical concepts is all the more natural and unavoidable. All expositions, for example, of the "essence" of Christianity are ideal types enjoying only a necessarily very relative and problematic validity when they are intended to be regarded as the historical portrayal of empirically existing facts. On the other hand, such presentations are of great value for research and of high systematic value for expository purposes when they are used as conceptual instruments for *comparison* with and the *measurement* of reality. They are indispensable for this purpose.

There is still another, even more complicated significance implicit in such ideal-typical presentations. They regularly seek to be, or are unconsciously, ideal-types not only in the *logical* sense but also in the *practical* sense, i.e., they are *model types* which—in our illustration—contain what, from the point of view of the expositor, *should* be and what *to him* is "essential" in Christianity *because it is enduringly valuable*. If this is consciously or—as it is more frequently—unconsciously the case, they contain ideals *to* which the expositor *evaluatively* relates Christianity. These ideals are tasks and ends towards which he orients his "idea" of Christianity and which naturally can, and indeed doubtless always will, differ greatly from the values which other persons, for instance, the early Christians, connected with Christianity. In this sense, however, the "ideas" are naturally no longer purely *logical* auxiliary devices, no longer concepts with which reality is compared, but ideals by which it is evaluatively *judged*. Here it is no longer a matter of the purely theoretical procedure of treating empirical reality with respect to values but of *value-judgments* which are integrated into the concept of "*Christianity*." Because the ideal type claims empirical *validity* here, it penetrates into the realm of the evaluative *interpretation* of Christianity. The sphere of empirical science has been left behind and we are confronted with a profession of faith, not an ideal-typical construct. As fundamental as this distinction is in principle, the confusion of these two basically different meanings of the term "idea" appears with extraordinary frequency in historical writings. It is always close at hand whenever the descriptive historian begins to develop his "conception" of a personality or an epoch. In contrast with the fixed ethical standards which Schlosser applied in the spirit of rationalism, the modern relativistically educated historian who on the one hand seeks to "understand" the epoch of which he speaks "in its own terms," and on the other still seeks to "judge" it, feels the need to derive the standards for his judgment from the subject-matter itself, i.e., to allow the "idea" in the sense of the *ideal* to emerge from the "idea" in the sense of the "ideal-type." The esthetic satisfaction produced by such a procedure constantly tempts him to disregard the line where these two ideal types diverge—an error which on the one hand hampers the value-judgment and on the other, strives to free itself from the responsibility for its own judgment. In contrast with this, the *elementary duty of scientific self-control* and the only way to avoid serious and foolish blunders requires a sharp, precise distinction between the logically *comparative* analysis of reality by ideal-*types* in the logical sense and the *value-judgment* of reality *on the basis of ideals*. An "ideal type" in our sense, to repeat once more, has no connection at all with *value-judgments*, and it has nothing to do with any type of perfection other than a purely *logical* one. There are ideal types of brothels as well as of religions; there are also ideal types of those kinds of brothels which are technically "expedient" from the point of view of police ethics as well as those of which the exact opposite is the case.

It is necessary for us to forego here a detailed discussion of the case which is by far the most complicated and most interesting, namely, the problem of the logical structure of the *concept of the state*. The following however should be noted: when we inquire as to what corresponds to the idea of the "state" in empirical reality, we find an infinity of diffuse and discrete human actions, both active and passive, factually and legally regulated relationships, partly unique and partly recurrent in character, all bound together by an idea, namely, the belief in the actual or normative validity of rules and of the authority-relationships of some human beings towards others. This belief is in part consciously, in part dimly felt, and in part passively accepted by persons who, should they think about the "idea" in a really clearly defined manner, would not first need a "general theory of the state" which aims to articulate the idea. The scientific conception of the state, however it is formulated, is naturally always a synthesis which we construct for certain heuristic purposes. But on the other hand, it is also abstracted from the unclear syntheses which are found in the minds of human beings. The concrete content, however, which the historical "state" assumes in those syntheses in the minds of those who make up the state, can in its turn only be made explicit through the use of ideal-typical concepts. Nor, furthermore, can there be the least doubt that the manner in which those syntheses are made (always in a logically imperfect form) by the members of a state, or in other words, the "ideas" which *they* construct for themselves about the state—as for example, the German "organic" metaphysics of the state in contrast with the American "business" conception, is of great practical significance. In other words, here too the *practical idea* which should be *valid* or *is believed to be valid* and the heuristically intended, theoretically ideal type approach each

other very closely and constantly tend to merge with each other.
We have purposely considered the ideal type essentially—
if not exclusively—as a mental construct for the scrutiny and
systematic characterization of individual concrete patterns which
are significant in their uniqueness, such as Christianity, capitalism, etc. We did this in order to avoid the common notion that in
the sphere of cultural phenomena, the abstract *type* is identical
with the abstract *kind* (*Gattungsmässigen*). This is not the case.
Without being able to make here a full logical analysis of the
widely discussed concept of the "typical" which has been discredited through misuse, we can state on the basis of our previous
discussion that the construction of type-concepts in the sense
of the exclusion of the "accidental" also has a place in the analysis
of historically individual phenomena. Naturally, however, those
generic concepts which we constantly encountered as elements
of historical analysis and of concrete historical concepts, can
also be formed as ideal-types by abstracting and accentuating
certain conceptually essential elements. Practically, this is indeed
a particularly frequent and important instance of the application
of ideal-typical concepts. Every *individual* ideal type comprises
both *generic* and ideal-typically constructed conceptual *elements*.
In this case too, we see the specifically logical function of ideal-
typical concepts. The concept of "exchange" is for instance
a simple class concept (*Gattungsbegriff*) in the sense of a complex of traits which are common to many phenomena, as long
as we disregard the *meaning* of the component parts of the concept, and simply analyze the term in its everyday usage. If however we relate this concept to the concept of "marginal utility"
for instance, and construct the concept of "economic exchange"
as an economically rational event, this then contains as every
concept of "economic exchange" does which is fully elaborated
logically, a judgment concerning the "typical" *conditions* of exchange. It assumes a *genetic* character and becomes therewith
ideal-typical in the logical sense, i.e., it removes itself from empirical reality which can only be compared or related to it. The
same is true of all the so-called "fundamental concepts" of economics: they can be developed in genetic form only as ideal
types. The distinction between simple class or generic concepts
(*Gattungsbegriffe*) which merely summarize the common fea-

tures of certain empirical phenomena and the quasi-generic (*Gattungsmässigen*) *ideal type*—as for instance an ideal-typical concept of the "nature" of "handicraft"—varies naturally with each concrete case. But no class or generic concept as such has a "typical" character and there is no purely generic "average" type. Wherever we speak of typical magnitudes—as for example, in statistics—we speak of something more than a mere average. The more it is a matter of the simple classification of events which appear in reality as mass phenomena, the more it is a matter of class concepts. On the other hand, the greater the event to which we conceptualize complicated historical patterns with respect to those components in which their specific *cultural significance* is contained, the greater the extent to which the concept—or system of concepts—will be ideal-typical in character. The goal of ideal-typical concept-construction is always to make clearly explicit not the class or average character but rather the unique individual character of cultural phenomena.

The fact that ideal types, even classificatory ones, can be and are applied, first acquires methodological significance in connection with another fact.

Thus far we have been dealing with ideal-types only as abstract concepts of relationships which are conceived by us as stable in the flux of events, as historically individual complexes in which developments are realized. There emerges however a complication, which reintroduces with the aid of the concept of "type" the naturalistic prejudice that the goal of the social sciences must be the reduction of reality to "*laws.*" *Developmental* sequences too can be constructed into ideal types and these constructs can have quite considerable heuristic value. But this quite particularly gives rise to the danger that the ideal type and reality will be confused with one another. One can, for example, arrive at the theoretical conclusion that in a society which is organized on *strict* "handicraft" principles, the only source of capital accumulation can be ground rent. From this perhaps, one can—for the correctness of the construct is not in question here—construct a pure ideal picture of the shift, conditioned by certain specific factors—e.g., limited land, increasing population, influx of precious metals, rationalization of the conduct of life—from a handicraft to a capitalistic economic organization. Whether the empirical-historical course of development was actually identical with the constructed one, can be investigated only by using this construct as a heuristic device for the comparison of the ideal type and the "facts." If the ideal type were "correctly" constructed and the actual course of events did *not* correspond to that predicted by the ideal type, the hypothesis that medieval society was *not* in certain respects a *strictly* "handicraft" type of society would be proved. And if the ideal type were constructed in a heuristically *"ideal"* way—whether and in what way this could occur in our example will be entirely disregarded here—it will guide the investigation into a path leading to a more precise understanding of the non-handicraft components of medieval society in their peculiar characteristics and their historical significance. *If* it leads to this result, it fulfils its logical purpose, even though, in doing so, it demonstrates its divergence from reality. It was—in this case—the test of an hypothesis. This procedure gives rise to no methodological doubts so long as we clearly keep in mind that ideal-typical developmental *constructs* and *history* are to be sharply distinguished from each other, and that the construct here is no more than the means for explicitly and validly imputing an historical event to its real causes while eliminating those which on the basis of our present knowledge seem possible.

The maintenance of this distinction in all its rigor often becomes uncommonly difficult in practice due to a certain circumstance. In the interest of the concrete demonstration of an ideal type or of an ideal-typical developmental sequence, one seeks to *make it clear* by the use of concrete illustrative material drawn from empirical-historical reality. The danger of this procedure which in itself is entirely legitimate lies in the fact that historical knowledge here appears as a *servant* of theory instead of the opposite role. It is a great temptation for the theorist to regard this relationship either as the normal one or, far worse, to mix theory with history and indeed to confuse them with each other. This occurs in an extreme way when an ideal construct of a developmental sequence and a conceptual classification of the ideal-types of certain cultural structures (e.g., the forms of industrial production deriving from the "closed domestic economy" or the religious concepts beginning with the "gods of the moment") are integrated into a *genetic* classification. The series of types which results from the selected conceptual criteria appears then as an historical sequence unrolling with the necessity of a law. The logical classification of analytical concepts on the one hand and the empirical arrangements of the events thus conceptualized in space, time, and causal relationship, on the other, appear to be so bound up together that there is an almost irresistible temptation to do violence to reality in order to prove the real validity of the construct.

We have intentionally avoided a demonstration with respect to that ideal-typical construct which is the most important one from our point of view; namely, the Marxian theory. This was done in order not to complicate the exposition any further through the introduction of an interpretation of Marx and in order not to anticipate the discussions in our journal which will make a regular practice of presenting critical analyses of the literature concerning and following the great thinker. We will only point out here that naturally all specifically Marxian "laws" and developmental constructs—insofar as they are theoretically sound—are ideal types. The eminent, indeed unique, *heuristic* significance of these ideal types when they are used for the *assessment* of reality is known to everyone who has ever employed Marxian concepts and hypotheses. Similarly, their perniciousness, as soon as they are thought of as empirically valid or as real (*i.e.*, truly metaphysical) "effective forces," "tendencies," etc. is likewise known to those who have used them.

Class or generic concepts (*Gattungsbegriffe*)—ideal types—ideal-typical generic concepts—ideas in the sense of thought-patterns which actually exist in the minds of human beings—ideal types of such ideas—ideals which govern human beings—ideal types of such ideals—ideals with which the historian approaches historical facts—*theoretical* constructs using empirical data illustratively—*historical* investigations which utilize theoretical concepts as ideal limiting cases—the various possible combinations of these which could only be hinted at here; they are pure mental constructs, the relationships of which to the empirical reality of the immediately given is problematical in every individual case. This list of possibilities only reveals the infinite ramifications of the conceptual-methodological problems which face us in the sphere of the cultural sciences. We must renounce the serious discussion of the practical methodological issues the problems of which were only to be exhibited, as well as the detailed treatment of the relationships of ideal types to "laws," of ideal-typical concepts to collective concepts, etc. . . .

The historian will still insist, even after all these discussions, that the prevalence of ideal-typical concepts and constructs are characteristic symptoms of the adolescence of a discipline. And in a certain sense this must be conceded, but with other conclusions than he could draw from it. Let us take a few illustrations from other disciplines. It is certainly true that the harried fourth-form boy as well as the primitive philologist first conceives of a language "organically," i.e., as a meta-empirical totality regulated by norms, but the task of linguistic science is to establish which grammatical rules should be valid. The logical elaborations of the written language, i.e., the reduction of its content to rules, as was done for instance by the *Accademia della Crusca*, is normally the first task which "philology" sets itself. When, in contrast with this, a leading philologist today declares that the subject-matter of philosophy is the "speech of *every individual*," even the formulation of such a program is possible only after there is a relatively clear ideal type of the written language, which the otherwise entirely orientationless and unbounded investigation of the infinite variety of *speech* can utilize (at least tacitly). The constructs of the natural law and the organic theories of the state have exactly the same function and, to recall an ideal type in *our* sense, so does Benjamin Constant's theory of the ancient state. It serves as a harbor until one has learned to navigate safely in the vast sea of empirical facts. The coming of age of science in fact always implies the transcendence of the ideal-type, insofar as it was thought of as possessing empirical validity or as a class *concept* (*Gattungsbegriff*). However, it is still legitimate today to use the brilliant Constant hypothesis to demonstrate certain aspects and historically unique features of ancient political life, as long as one carefully bears in mind its ideal-typical character. Moreover, there are sciences to which eternal youth is granted, and the historical disciplines are among them—all those to which the eternally onward flowing stream of culture perpetually brings new problems. At the very heart of their task lies not only the transiency of *all* ideal types *but* also, at the same time, the inevitability of *new* ones.

The attempts to determine the "real" and the "true" meaning of historical concepts always reappear and never succeed in reaching their goal. Accordingly, the synthetic concepts used by historians are either imperfectly defined or, as soon as the elimination of ambiguity is sought for, the concept becomes an abstract ideal type and reveals itself therewith as a theoretical and hence "one-sided" viewpoint which illuminates the aspect of reality with which it can be related. But these concepts are shown to be obviously inappropriate as schema into which reality could be completely *integrated*. For none of those systems of ideas, which are absolutely indispensable in the understanding of those segments of reality which are meaningful at a particular moment, can exhaust its infinite richness. They are all attempts, on the basis of the present state of our knowledge and the available conceptual patterns, to bring order into the chaos of those facts which we have drawn into the field circumscribed by our *interest*. The intellectual apparatus which the past has developed through the analysis, or more truthfully, the analytical rearrangement of the immediately given reality, and through the latter's integration by concepts which correspond to the state of its knowledge and the focus of its interest, is in constant tension with the new knowledge which we can and *desire* to wrest from reality. The progress of cultural science occurs through this conflict. Its result is the perpetual reconstruction of those concepts through which we seek to comprehend reality. The history of the social sciences is and remains a continuous process passing from the attempt to order reality analytically through the construction of concepts—the dissolution of the analytical constructs so constructed through the expansion and shift of the scientific horizon—and the reformation anew of concepts on the foundations thus transformed. It is not the error of the attempt to construct conceptual systems *in general* which is shown by this process—every science, even simple descriptive history, operates with the conceptual stock-in-trade of its time. Rather, this process shows that in the cultural sciences concept-construction depends on the setting of the problem, and the latter varies with the content of culture itself. The relationship between concept and reality in the cultural sciences involves the transitoriness of all such syntheses. The great attempts at theory-construction in our science were always useful for revealing the limits of the significance of those points of view which provided their foundations. The greatest advances in the sphere of the social sciences are substantively tied up with the shift in practical cultural problems and take the guise of a critique of concept-construction. Adherence to the purpose of this critique, and therewith the investigation of the *principles of syntheses* in the social sciences, shall be among the primary tasks of our journal.

In the conclusions which are to be drawn from what has been said, we come to a point where perhaps our views diverge here and there from those of many, and even the most outstanding, representatives of the Historical School, among whose offspring we too are to be numbered. The latter still hold in many ways, expressly or tacitly, to the opinion that it is the end and the goal of every science to order its data into a system of concepts, the content of which is to be acquired and slowly perfected through the observation of empirical regularities, the construction of hypotheses, and their verification, until finally a "completed" and *hence* deductive science emerges. For this goal, the historical-inductive work of the present-day is a preliminary task necessitated by the imperfections of our discipline. Nothing can be more suspect, from this point of view, than the construction and application of clear-cut concepts since this seems to be an over-hasty anticipation of the remote future.

This conception was, in principle, impregnable within the framework of the classical-scholastic epistemology which was still fundamentally assumed by the majority of the research-workers identified with the Historical School. The function of concepts was assumed to be the *reproduction* of "objective" reality in the analyst's imagination. Hence the recurrent references to the *unreality* of all clear-cut concepts. If one perceives the implications of the fundamental ideas of modern epistemology which ultimately derives from Kant; namely, that concepts are primarily analytical instruments for the intellectual mastery of empirical data and can be only that, the fact that precise genetic concepts are necessarily ideal types will not cause him to desist from constructing them. The relationship between concept and historical research is reversed for those who appreciate this; the goal of the Historical School then appears as logically impossible, the concepts are not ends but are means to the end of understanding phenomena which are significant from concrete individual viewpoints. Indeed, it is just *because* the content of historical concepts is necessarily subject to change that they must be formulated precisely and clearly on all occasions. In their application, their character as ideal analytical constructs should be carefully kept in mind, and the ideal-type and historical reality should not be confused with each other. It should be understood that since really definitive historical concepts are not in general to be thought of as an ultimate end in view of the inevitable shift of the guiding value-ideas, the construction of sharp and unambiguous concepts relevant to the concrete *individual* viewpoint which directs our interest at any given time affords the possibility of clearly realizing the *limits* of their validity.

It will be pointed out, and we ourselves have already admitted, that in a particular instance the course of a concrete historical event can be made vividly clear without its being analyzed in terms of explicitly defined concepts. And it will accordingly be claimed for the historians in our field, that they may, as has been said of the political historians, speak the "language of life itself." Certainly! But it should be added that in this procedure, the attainment of a level of explicit awareness of the viewpoint from which the events in question get their significance remains highly accidental. We are in general not in the favorable position of the political historian for whom the cultural views to which he orients his presentation are usually unambiguous—or seem to be so. Every type of purely direct concrete description bears the mark of *artistic* portrayal. "Each sees what is in his own heart." Valid *judgments* always presuppose the *logical* analysis of what is concretely and immediately perceived, i.e., the use of *concepts*. It is indeed possible and often aesthetically satisfying to keep these *in petto* but it always endangers the security of the reader's orientation, and often that of the author himself concerning the content and scope of his judgments.

The neglect of clear-cut concept-construction in practical discussions of practical, economic and social policy can, however, become particularly dangerous. It is really unbelievable to an outsider what confusion has been fostered, for instance, by the use of the term "value"—that unfortunate child of misery of our science, which can be given an unambiguous meaning *only* as an ideal type—or terms like "productive," "from an economic viewpoint," et cetera, which in general will not stand up under a conceptually precise analysis. *Collective* concepts taken from the language of everyday life have particularly unwholesome effects. In order to have an illustration easy for the layman to understand, let us take the concept of "agriculture" especially as it appears in the term "the interests of agriculture." If we begin with "the interests of agriculture" as the empirically determinable, more or less clear *subjective* ideas of concrete economically active individuals about their own interests and disregard entirely the countless conflicts of interest taking place among the cattle breeders, the cattle growers, grain growers, corn consumers, corn-using, whiskey-distilling farmers, perhaps not all laymen, but certainly every specialist will know the great whirlpool of antagonistic and contradictory forms of value-relationship (*Wertbeziehung*) which are vaguely thought of under that heading. We will enumerate only a few of them here: the interests of farmers, who wish to sell their property and who are therefore interested in a rapid rise of the price of land; the diametrically opposed interest of those who wish to buy, rent or lease; the interest of those who wish to retain a certain property to the social advantage of their descendants and who are therefore interested in the stability of *landed* property; the antagonistic interests of those who, in their own or their children's interests, wish to see the land go to the most enterprising farmer—or what is not exactly the same—to the purchaser with the most capital; the purely economic interest in economic freedom of movement of the most "competent farmer" in the business sense; the antagonistic interests of certain dominating classes in the maintenance of the traditional social and political position of their own "class" and thereby of their descendants; the interest of the socially subordinated strata of farmers in the decline of the strata which are above them and which oppress them; in occasional contradiction to this the interest of this stratum in having the leadership of those above them to protect their economic interests. This list could be tremendously increased without coming to an end, although we have been as summary and imprecise as possible.

We will pass over the fact that most diverse purely ideal values are mixed and associated with, hinder and divert the more "egoistic" interests in order to remind ourselves, above all, that when we speak of the "interests of agriculture" we think not *only* of those material and ideal values to which the farmers themselves at a given time relate their interests, but rather those partly quite heterogeneous value-ideas which *we* can relate with agriculture. As instances of these value-ideas related to agriculture we may cite the *interests in production* derived from the interests in cheap and qualitatively good food, which two interests are themselves not always congruous and in connection with which many clashes between the interests of city and country can be found, and in which the interests of the present generation need not by any means always be identical with the interests of coming generations; *interests in a numerous population*, particularly in a large rural population, derived either from the foreign or domestic interests of the "State," or from other ideal interests of the most diverse sort, e.g., the expected influence of a large rural population on the character of the nation's culture. These "population-interests" can clash with the most diverse economic interests of all sections of the rural population, and indeed with all the present interests of the mass of rural inhabitants. Another instance is the interest in a certain type of social stratification of the rural population, because of the type of political or cultural influence which will be produced therefrom; this interest can, depending on its orientation, conflict with every conceivable (even the most urgent present and future) interests of the individual farmers as well as those "of the State." To this is added a further complication: the "state," to the "interests" of which we tend to relate such and numerous other similar individual interests, is often only a blanket term for an extremely intricate tangle of evaluative-ideas, to which it in its turn is related in individual cases, e.g., purely military security from external dangers; security of the dominant position of a dynasty or a certain class at home; interest in the maintenance and expansion of the formal-juridical unity of the nation for its own sake or in the interest of maintaining certain objective cultural values which in their turn again are very differentiated and which we as a politically unified people believe we represent; the reconstruction of the social aspects of the state according to certain once more diverse cultural ideas. It would lead us too far even merely to mention what is contained under the general label "state-interests" to which we can relate "agriculture." The illustrations which we have chosen and our even briefer analyses are crude and simplified. The non-specialist may now analyze similarly (and more thoroughly) for instance "the class interests of the worker" in order to see what contradictory elements, composed partly of the workers' interests and ideals, and partly of the ideals with which *we* view the workers, enter into this concept. It is impossible to overcome the slogans of the conflict of interests through a purely empirical emphasis on their "relative" character. The clear-cut, sharply defined analysis of the various possible standpoints is the only path which will lead us out of verbal confusion. The "free trade argument" as a *Weltanschauung* or as a valid *norm* is ridiculous but—and this is equally true whichever ideals of commercial policy the individual accepts—our underestimation of the heuristic value of the wisdom of the world's greatest merchants as expressed in such ideal-typical formulae has caused serious damage to our discussions of commercial policy. Only through ideal-typical concept-construction do the viewpoints with which we are concerned in individual cases become explicit. Their peculiar character is brought out by the *confrontation* of empirical reality with the ideal-type. The use of the undifferentiated collective concepts of everyday speech is always a cloak for confusion of thought and action. It is, indeed, very often an instrument of specious and fraudulent procedures. It is, in brief, always a means of obstructing the proper formulation of the problem.

We are now at the end of this discussion, the only purpose of which was to trace the course of the hair-line which separates science from faith and to make explicit the *meaning* of the quest for social and economic knowledge. The *objective* validity of all empirical knowledge rests exclusively upon the ordering of the given reality according to categories which are *subjective* in a specific sense, namely, in that they present the *presuppositions* of our knowledge and are based on the presupposition of the *value* of those *truths* which empirical knowledge alone is able to give us. The means available to our science offer nothing to those persons to whom this truth is of no value. It should be remembered that the belief in the value of scientific truth is the product of certain cultures and is not a product of man's original nature. Those for whom scientific truth is of no value will seek in vain for some other truth to take the place of science in just those respects in which it is unique, namely, in the provision of concepts and judgments which are neither empirical reality nor reproductions of it but which facilitate its analytical ordering in a valid manner. In the empirical social sciences, as we have seen, the possibility of meaningful knowledge of what is essential for us in the infinite richness of events is bound up with the unremitting application of viewpoints of a specifically particularized character, which, in the last analysis, are oriented on the basis of evaluative ideas. These evaluative ideas are for their part empirically discoverable and analyzable as elements of meaningful human conduct, but their validity can *not* be deduced from empirical data as such. The "objectivity" of the social sciences depends rather on the fact that the empirical data are always related to those evaluative ideas which alone make them worth knowing and the significance of the empirical data is derived from these evaluative ideas. But these data can never become the foundation for the empirically impossible proof of the validity of the evaluative ideas. The belief which we all have in some form or other, in the meta-empirical validity of ultimate and final values, in which the meaning of our existence is rooted, is not incompatible with the incessant changefulness of the concrete viewpoints, from which empirical reality gets its significance. Both these views are, on the contrary, in harmony with each other. Life with its irrational reality and its store of possible meanings is inexhaustible. The *concrete* form in which value-relevance occurs remains perpetually in flux, ever subject to change in the dimly seen future of human culture. The light which emanates from those highest evaluative ideas always falls on an ever changing finite segment of the vast chaotic stream of events, which flows away through time.

Now all this should not be misunderstood to mean that the proper task of the social sciences should be the continual chase for new viewpoints and new analytical constructs. *On the con-*

trary: nothing should be more sharply emphasized than the proposition that the knowledge of the *cultural significance* of *concrete historical events and patterns* is exclusively and solely the final end which, among other means, concept-construction and the criticism of constructs also seek to serve.

There are, to use the words of F. Th. Vischer, "subject matter specialists" and "interpretative specialists." The fact-greedy gullet of the former can be filled only with legal documents, statistical worksheets and questionnaires, but he is insensitive to the refinement of a new idea. The gourmandise of the latter dulls his taste for facts by ever new intellectual subtleties. That genuine artistry which, among the historians, Ranke possessed in such a grand measure, manifests itself through its ability to produce new knowledge by interpreting already *known* facts according to known viewpoints.

All research in the cultural sciences in an age of specialization, once it is oriented towards a given subject matter through particular settings of problems and has established its methodological principles, will consider the analysis of the data as an end in itself. It will discontinue assessing the value of the individual facts in terms of their relationships to ultimate value-ideas. Indeed, it will lose its awareness of its ultimate rootedness in the value-ideas in general. And it is well that should be so. But there comes a moment when the atmosphere changes. The significance of the unreflectively utilized viewpoints becomes uncertain and the road is lost in the twilight. The light of the great cultural problems moves on. Then science too prepares to change its standpoint and its analytical apparatus and to view the streams of events from the heights of thought. It follows those stars which alone are able to give meaning and direction to its labors:

>   . . . der neue Trieb erwacht,
>   Ich eile fort, ihr ewiges Licht zu trinken,
>   Vor mir den Tag und unter mir die Nacht,
>   Den Himmel über mir und unter mir die Wellen.[6]

---

[6] *Faust:* Act I, Scene II. (Trans. Bayard Taylor.)
  "The newborn impulse fires my mind,
  I hasten on, his beams eternal drinking,
  The Day before me and the Night behind,
  Above me Heaven unfurled, the floor of waves beneath me."

Natural Right and the Distinction Between Facts and Values[1]

LEO STRAUSS

‖‖

THE HISTORICIST CONTENTION can be reduced to the assertion that natural right is impossible because philosophy in the full sense of the term is impossible. Philosophy is possible only if there is an absolute horizon or a natural horizon in contradistinction to the historically changing horizons or the caves. In other words, philosophy is possible only if man, while incapable of acquiring wisdom or full understanding of the whole, is capable of knowing what he does not know, that is to say, of grasping the fundamental problems and therewith the fundamental alternatives, which are, in principle, coeval with human thought. But the possibility of philosophy is only the necessary and not the sufficient condition of natural right. The possibility of philosophy does not require more than that the fundamental problems always be the same; but there cannot be natural right if the fundamental problem of political philosophy cannot be solved in a final manner.

If philosophy in general is possible, political philosophy in particular is possible. Political philosophy is possible if man is capable of understanding the fundamental political alternative

[1] Reprinted from *Natural Right and History* (pp. 35–80), Charles R. Walgreen Foundation Lectures, by Leo Strauss by permission of The University of Chicago Press and with the approval of the author. Copyright 1953 by The University of Chicago.

which is at the bottom of the ephemeral or accidental alternatives. Yet if political philosophy is limited to understanding the fundamental political alternative, it is of no practical value. It would be unable to answer the question of what the ultimate goal of wise action is. It would have to delegate the crucial decision to blind choice. The whole galaxy of political philosophers from Plato to Hegel, and certainly all adherents of natural right, assumed that the fundamental political problem is susceptible of a final solution. This assumption ultimately rested on the Socratic answer to the question of how man ought to live. By realizing that we are ignorant of the most important things, we realize at the same time that the most important thing for us, or the one thing needful, is quest for knowledge of the most important things or quest for wisdom. That this conclusion is not barren of political consequences is known to every reader of Plato's *Republic* or of Aristotle's *Politics*. It is true that the successful quest for wisdom might lead to the result that wisdom is not the one thing needful. But this result would owe its relevance to the fact that it is the result of the quest for wisdom: the very disavowal of reason must be reasonable disavowal. Regardless of whether this possibility affects the validity of the Socratic answer, the perennial conflict between the Socratic and the anti-Socratic answer creates the impression that the Socratic answer is as arbitrary as its opposite, or that the perennial conflict is insoluble. Accordingly, many present-day social scientists who are not historicists or who do admit the existence of fundamental and unchanging alternatives deny that human reason is capable of solving the conflict between these alternatives. Natural right is then rejected today not only because all human thought is held to be historical but likewise because it is thought that there is a variety of unchangeable principles of right or of goodness which conflict with one another, and none of which can be proved to be superior to the others.

Substantially, this is the position taken by Max Weber. Our discussion will be limited to a critical analysis of Weber's view. No one since Weber has devoted a comparable amount of intelligence, assiduity, and almost fanatical devotion to the basic problem of the social sciences. Whatever may have been his errors, he is the greatest social scientist of our century.

Weber, who regarded himself as a disciple of the historical

school,[2] came very close to historicism, and a strong case can be made for the view that his reservations against historicism were halfhearted and inconsistent with the broad tendency of his thinking. He parted company with the historical school, not because it had rejected natural norms, i.e., norms that are both universal and objective, but because it had tried to establish standards that were particular and historical indeed, but still objective. He objected to the historical school not because it had blurred the idea of natural right but because it had preserved natural right in a historical guise, instead of rejecting it altogether. The historical school had given natural right a historical character by insisting on the ethnic character of all genuine right or by tracing all genuine right to unique folk minds, as well as by assuming that the history of mankind is a meaningful process or a process ruled by intelligible necessity. Weber rejected both assumptions as metaphysical, i.e., as based on the dogmatic premise that reality is rational. Since Weber assumed that the real is always individual, he could state the premise of the historical school also in these terms: the individual is an emanation from the general or from the whole. According to Weber, however, individual or partial phenomena can be understood only as effects of other individual or partial phenomena, and never as effects of wholes such as folk minds. To try to explain historical or unique phenomena by tracing them to general laws or to unique wholes means to assume gratuitously that there are mysterious or unanalyzable forces which move the historical actors.[3] There is no "meaning" of history apart from the "subjective" meaning or the intentions which animate the historical actors. But these intentions are of such limited power that the actual outcome is in most cases wholly unintended. Yet the actual outcome—historical fate—which is not planned by God or man, molds not only our way of life but our very thoughts, and especially does it determine our ideals.[4] Weber was, however, still too much impressed by the idea of science to accept

[2] M. Weber, *Gesammelte politische Schriften*, p. 22; *Gesammelte Aufsätze zur Wissenschaftslehre*, p. 208.

[3] M. Weber, *Wissenschaftslehre*, pp. 13, 15, 18, 19, 28, 35–37, 134, 137, 174, 195, 230; *Gesammelte Aufsätze zur Sozial- und Wirtschaftsgeschichte*, p. 517.

[4] M. Weber, *Wissenschaftslehre*, pp. 152, 183, 224 n.; *Politische Schriften*, pp. 19, 437; *Gesammelte Aufsätze zur Religionssoziologie*, I, pp. 82, 524.

historicism without qualification. In fact, one is tempted to suggest that the primary motive of his opposition to the historical school and to historicism in general was devotion to the idea of empirical science as it prevailed in his generation. The idea of science forced him to insist on the fact that all science as such is independent of Weltanschauung: both natural and social science claim to be equally valid for Westerners and for Chinese, i.e., for people whose "world views" are radically different. The historical genesis of modern science—the fact that it is of Western origin—is wholly irrelevant as regards its validity. Nor did Weber have any doubt that modern science is absolutely superior to any earlier form of thinking orientation in the world of nature and society. That superiority can be established objectively, by reference to the rules of logic.[5] There arose, however, in Weber's mind this difficulty in regard to the social sciences in particular. He insisted on the objective and universal validity of social science in so far as it is a body of true propositions. Yet these propositions are only a part of social science. They are the results of scientific investigation or the answers to questions. The questions which we address to social phenomena depend on the direction of our interest or on our point of view, and these on our value ideas. But the value ideas are historically relative. Hence the substance of social science is radically historical; for it is the value ideas and the direction of interest which determine the whole conceptual framework of the social sciences. Accordingly, it does not make sense to speak of a "natural frame of reference" or to expect a final system of the basic concepts: all frames of reference are ephemeral. Every conceptual scheme used by social science articulates the basic problems, and these problems change with the change of the social and cultural situation. Social science is necessarily the understanding of society from the point of view of the present. What is trans-historical are merely the findings regarding the facts and their causes. More precisely, what is trans-historical is the validity of these findings; but the importance or significance of any findings depends on value ideas and hence on historically changeable principles. Ultimately, this applies to every science. All science presupposes that science is valuable, but this presupposition is the product of certain cul-

[5] M. Weber, *Wissenschaftslehre*, pp. 58–60, 97, 105, 111, 155, 160, 184.

tures, and hence historically relative.[6] However, the concrete
and historical value ideas, of which there is an indefinitely large
variety, contain elements of a trans-historical character: the ultimate values are as timeless as the principles of logic. It is the
recognition of timeless values that distinguishes Weber's position
most significantly from historicism. Not so much historicism as
a peculiar notion of timeless values is the basis of his rejection
of natural right.[7]

Weber never explained what he understood by "values." He
was primarily concerned with the relations of values to facts.
Facts and values are absolutely heterogeneous, as is shown directly by the absolute heterogeneity of questions of fact and
questions of value. No conclusion can be drawn from any fact
as to its valuable character, nor can we infer the factual character of something from its being valuable or desirable. Neither
time-serving nor wishful thinking is supported by reason. By
proving that a given social order is the goal of the historical
process, one does not say anything as to the value or desirable
character of that order. By showing that certain religious or
ethical ideas had a very great effect or no effect, one does not
say anything about the value of those ideas. To understand a
factual or possible evaluation is something entirely different from
approving or forgiving that evaluation. Weber contended that
the absolute heterogeneity of facts and values necessitates the
ethically neutral character of social science: social science can
answer questions of facts and their causes; it is not competent to
answer questions of value. He insisted very strongly on the role
played by values in social science: the objects of social science
are constituted by "reference to values." Without such "reference," there would be no focus of interest, no reasonable selection of themes, no principles of distinction between relevant and
irrelevant facts. Through "reference to values" the objects of the
social sciences emerge out of the ocean or morass of facts. But
Weber insisted no less strongly on the fundamental difference
between "reference to values" and "value judgments": by saying
that something is relevant with regard to political freedom, for

[6] *Ibid.*, pp. 60, 152, 170, 184, 206–209, 213–214, 259, 261–262.
[7] *Ibid.*, pp. 60, 62, 152, 213, 247, 463, 467, 469, 472; *Politische Schriften*,
pp. 22, 60.

example, one does not take a stand for or against political freedom. The social scientist does not evaluate the objects constituted
by "reference to values"; he merely explains them by tracing
them to their causes. The values to which social science refers
and among which acting man chooses are in need of clarification.
This clarification is the function of social philosophy. But even
social philosophy cannot solve the crucial value problems. It cannot criticize value judgments that are not self-contradictory.[8]

Weber contended that his notion of a "value-free" or ethically neutral social science is fully justified by what he regarded
as the most fundamental of all oppositions, namely, the opposition of the Is and the Ought, or the opposition of reality and
norm or value.[9] But the conclusion from the radical heterogeneity
of the Is and the Ought to the impossibility of an evaluating
social science is obviously not valid. Let us assume that we had
genuine knowledge of right and wrong, or of the Ought, or of
the true value system. That knowledge, while not derived from
empirical science, would legitimately direct all empirical social
science; it would be the foundation of all empirical social science.
For social science is meant to be of practical value. It tries to
find means for given ends. For this purpose it has to understand
the ends. Regardless of whether the ends are "given" in a different manner from the means, the end and the means belong
together; therefore, "the end belongs to the same science as the
means."[10] If there were genuine knowledge of the ends, that
knowledge would naturally guide all search for means. There
would be no reason to delegate knowledge of the ends to social
philosophy and the search for the means to an independent social
science. Based on genuine knowledge of the true ends, social
science would search for the proper means to those ends; it
would lead up to objective and specific value judgments regard-

8 M. Weber, *Wissenschaftslehre*, pp. 90, 91, 124, 125, 150, 151, 154, 155,
461–465, 469–473, 475, 545, 550; *Gesammelte Aufsätze zur Soziologie und
Sozialpolitik*, pp. 417–418, 476–477, 482. As regards the connection between
the limitation of social science to the study of facts and the belief in the
authoritative character of natural science, see M. Weber, *Soziologie und
Sozialpolitik*, p. 478.
9 M. Weber, *Wissenschaftslehre*, pp. 32, 40 n., 127 n., 148, 401, 470–471,
501, 577.
10 Aristotle, *Physics* 194^{a}26–27.

ing policies. Social science would be a truly policy-making, not to say architectonic, science rather than a mere supplier of data for the real policy-makers. The true reason why Weber insisted on the ethically neutral character of social science as well as of social philosophy was, then, not his belief in the fundamental opposition of the Is and the Ought but his belief that there cannot be any genuine knowledge of the Ought. He denied to man any science, empirical or rational, any knowledge, scientific or philosophic, of the true value system: the true value system does not exist; there is a variety of values which are of the same rank, whose demands conflict with one another, and whose conflict cannot be solved by human reason. Social science or social philosophy can do no more than clarify that conflict and all its implications; the solution has to be left to the free, non-rational decision of each individual.

I contend that Weber's thesis necessarily leads to nihilism or to the view that every preference, however evil, base, or insane, has to be judged before the tribunal of reason to be as legitimate as any other preference. An unmistakable sign of this necessity is supplied by a statement of Weber about the prospects of Western civilization. He saw this alternative: either a spiritual renewal ("wholly new prophets or a powerful renaissance of old thoughts and ideals") or else "mechanized petrifaction, varnished by a kind of convulsive sense of self-importance," i.e., the extinction of every human possibility but that of "specialists without spirit or vision and voluptuaries without heart." Confronted with this alternative, Weber felt that the decision in favor of either possibility would be a judgment of value or of faith, and hence beyond the competence of reason.[11] This amounts to an admission that the way of life of "specialists without spirit or vision and voluptuaries without heart" is as defensible as the ways of life recommended by Amos or by Socrates.

To see this more clearly and to see at the same time why Weber could conceal from himself the nihilistic consequence of his doctrine of values, we have to follow his thought step by step. In following this movement toward its end we shall inevitably reach a point beyond which the scene is darkened by the

---

[11] Cf. M. Weber, *Religionssoziologie*, I, p. 204, with *Wissenschaftslehre*, pp. 469–470 and 150–151.

shadow of Hitler. Unfortunately, it does not go without saying that in our examination we must avoid the fallacy that in the last decades has frequently been used as a substitute for the *reductio ad absurdum:* the *reductio ad Hitlerum*. A view is not refuted by the fact that it happens to have been shared by Hitler.

Weber started out from a combination of the views of Kant as they were understood by certain neo-Kantians and of the views of the historical school. From neo-Kantianism he took over his general notion of the character of science, as well as of "individual" ethics. Accordingly, he rejected utilitarianism and every form of eudemonism. From the historical school he took over the view that there is no possible social or cultural order which can be said to be *the* right or rational order. He combined the two positions by means of the distinction between moral commands (or ethical imperatives) and cultural values. Moral commands appeal to our conscience, whereas cultural values appeal to our feelings: the individual ought to fulfil his moral duties, whereas it depends entirely on his arbitrary will whether he wishes to realize cultural ideals or not. Cultural ideals or values lack the specific obligatory character of the moral imperatives. These imperatives have a dignity of their own, with whose recognition Weber seemed to be greatly concerned. But, precisely because of the fundamental difference between moral commands and cultural values, ethics proper is silent in regard to cultural and social questions. Whereas gentlemen, or honest men, necessarily agree as to things moral, they legitimately disagree in regard to such things as Gothic architecture, private property, monogamy, democracy, and so on.[12]

One is thus led to think that Weber admitted the existence of absolutely binding rational norms, namely, the moral imperatives. Yet one sees immediately afterward that what he said about the moral commands is not much more than the residue of a tradition in which he was brought up and which, indeed, never ceased to determine him as a human being. What he really thought was that ethical imperatives are as subjective as cultural values. According to him, it is as legitimate to reject ethics in

---

[12] M. Weber, *Politische Schriften*, p. 22; *Religionssoziologie*, I, pp. 33–35; *Wissenschaftslehre*, pp. 30, 148, 154, 155, 252, 463, 466, 471; *Soziologie und Sozialpolitik*, p. 418.

the name of cultural values as it is to reject cultural values in the name of ethics, or to adopt any combination of both types of norm which is not self-contradictory.[13] This decision was the inevitable consequence of his notion of ethics. He could not reconcile his view that ethics is silent about the right social order with the undeniable ethical relevance of social questions, except by "relativizing" ethics. It was on this basis that he developed his concept of "personality" or of the dignity of man. The true meaning of "personality" depends on the true meaning of "freedom." Provisionally, one may say that human action is free to the extent to which it is not affected by external compulsion or irresistible emotions but is guided by rational consideration of means and ends. Yet true freedom requires ends of a certain kind, and these ends have to be adopted in a certain manner. The ends must be anchored in ultimate values. Man's dignity, his being exalted far above everything merely natural or above all brutes, consists in his setting up autonomously his ultimate values, in making these values his constant ends, and in rationally choosing the means to these ends. The dignity of man consists in his autonomy, i.e., in the individual's freely choosing his own values or his own ideals or in obeying the injunction: "Become what thou art."[14]

At this stage, we still have something resembling an objective norm, a categoric imperative: "Thou shalt have ideals." That imperative is "formal"; it does not determine in any way the content of the ideals, but it might still seem to establish an intelligible or nonarbitrary standard that would allow us to distinguish in a responsible manner between human excellence and depravity. Therewith it might seem to create a universal brotherhood of all noble souls; of all men who are not enslaved by their appetites, their passions, and their selfish interests; of all "idealists"—of all men who can justly esteem or respect one another. Yet this is only a delusion. What seems at first to be an invisible church proves to be a war of everybody against everybody or, rather, pandemonium. Weber's own formulation of his categoric im-

[13] M. Weber, *Wissenschaftslehre*, pp. 38, n. 2, 40–41, 155, 463, 466–469; *Soziologie und Sozialpolitik*, p. 423.

[14] M. Weber, *Wissenschaftslehre*, pp. 38, 40, 132–133, 469–470, 533–534, 555.

perative was "Follow thy demon" or "Follow thy god or demon." It would be unfair to complain that Weber forgot the possibility of evil demons, although he may have been guilty of underestimating them. If he had thought only of good demons, he would have been forced to admit an objective criterion that would allow him to distinguish in principle between good and evil demons. His categoric imperative actually means "Follow thy demon, regardless of whether he is a good or evil demon." For there is an insoluble, deadly conflict between the various values among which man has to choose. What one man considers following God another will consider, with equal right, following the Devil. The categoric imperative has then to be formulated as follows: "Follow God or the Devil as you will, but, whichever choice you make, make it with all your heart, with all your soul, and with all your power."[15] What is absolutely base is to follow one's appetites, passions, or self-interest and to be indifferent or lukewarm toward ideals or values, toward gods or devils.

Weber's "idealism," i.e., his recognition of all "ideal" goals or of all "causes," seems to permit of a nonarbitrary distinction between excellence and baseness or depravity. At the same time, it culminates in the imperative "Follow God or the Devil," which means, in nontheological language, "Strive resolutely for excellence or baseness." For if Weber meant to say that choosing value system A in preference to value system B is compatible with genuine respect for value system B or does not mean rejecting value system B as base, he could not have known what he was talking about in speaking of a choice between God and Devil; he must have meant a mere difference of tastes while talking of a deadly conflict. It thus appears that for Weber, in his capacity as a social philosopher, excellence and baseness completely lost their primary meaning. Excellence now means devotion to a cause, be it good or evil, and baseness means indifference to all causes. Excellence and baseness thus understood are excellence and baseness of a higher order. They belong to a dimension that is exalted far above the dimension of action. They can be seen only after one has completely broken away from the world in which we have to make decisions, although they present themselves as preceding any decision. They are the correlates of

[15] *Ibid.*, pp. 455, 466–469, 546; *Politische Schriften*, pp. 435–436.

a purely theoretical attitude toward the world of action. That theoretical attitude implies equal respect for all causes; but such respect is possible only for him who is not devoted to any cause. Now if excellence is devotion to a cause and baseness indifference to all causes, the theoretical attitude toward all causes would have to be qualified as base. No wonder, then, that Weber was driven to question the value of theory, of science, of reason, of the realm of the mind, and therewith of both the moral imperatives and the cultural values. He was forced to dignify what he called "purely 'vitalistic' values" to the same height as the moral commands and the cultural values. The "purely 'vitalistic' values" may be said to belong entirely to "the sphere of one's own individuality," being, that is, purely personal and in no way principles of a cause. Hence they are not, strictly speaking, values. Weber contended explicitly that it is perfectly legitimate to take a hostile attitude toward all impersonal and supra-personal values and ideals, and therewith toward every concern with "personality" or the dignity of man as previously defined; for, according to him, there is only one way to become a "personality," namely, through absolute devotion to a cause. At the moment when the "vitalistic" values are recognized as of equal rank with cultural values, the categoric imperative "Thou shalt have ideals" is being transformed into the command "Thou shalt live passionately." Baseness no longer means indifference to any of the incompatible great objects of humanity, but being engrossed with one's comfort and prestige. But with what right except that of arbitrary whim can one reject the way of life of the philistine in the name of "vitalistic" values, if one can reject the moral commands in the name of "vitalistic" values? It was in tacit recognition of the impossibility of stopping on the downward path that Weber frankly admitted that it is merely a subjective judgment of faith or value if one despises "specialists without spirit or vision and voluptuaries without heart" as degraded human beings. The final formulation of Weber's ethical principle would thus be "Thou shalt have preferences"—an Ought whose fulfilment is fully guaranteed by the Is.[16]

One last obstacle to complete chaos seems to remain. What-

<hr />

[16] M. Weber, *Wissenschaftslehre*, pp. 61, 152, 456, 468–469, 531; *Politische Schriften*, pp. 443–444.

ever preferences I may have or choose, I must act rationally: I must be honest with myself, I must be consistent in my adherence to my fundamental objectives, and I must rationally choose the means required by my ends. But why? What difference can this still make after we have been reduced to a condition in which the maxims of the heartless voluptuary as well as those of the sentimental philistine have to be regarded as no less defensible than those of the idealist, of the gentleman, or of the saint? We cannot take seriously this belated insistence on responsibility and sanity, this inconsistent concern with consistency, this irrational praise of rationality. Can one not very easily make out a stronger case for inconsistency than Weber has made out for preferring cultural values to the moral imperatives? Does one not necessarily imply the depreciation of rationality in every form at the moment in which one declares it legitimate to make "vitalistic" values one's supreme values? Weber would probably have insisted that, whatever preference one adopts, one has to be honest, at least with one's self, and especially that one must not make the dishonest attempt to give one's preferences an objective foundation which would necessarily be a sham foundation. But, should he have done so, he would merely have been inconsistent. For, according to him, it is equally legitimate to will or not to will truth, or to reject truth in favor of the beautiful and the sacred.[17] Why, then, should one not prefer pleasing delusions or edifying myths to the truth? Weber's regard for "rational self-determination" and "intellectual honesty" is a trait of his character which has no basis but his nonrational preference for "rational self-determination" and "intellectual honesty."

One may call the nihilism to which Weber's thesis leads "noble nihilism." For that nihilism stems not from a primary indifference to everything noble but from the alleged or real insight into the baseless character of everything thought to be noble. Yet one cannot make a distinction between noble and base nihilism except if one has some knowledge of what is noble and what is base. But such knowledge transcends nihilism. In order to be entitled to describe Weber's nihilism as noble, one must have broken with his position.

One could make the following objection to the foregoing

[17] M. Weber, *Wissenschaftslehre*, pp. 60–61, 184, 546, 554.

criticism. What Weber really meant cannot be expressed in terms of "values" or "ideals" at all; it is much more adequately expressed by his quotation "Become what thou art," i.e., "Choose thy fate." According to this interpretation, Weber rejected objective norms because objective norms are incompatible with human freedom or with the possibility of acting. We must leave it open whether this reason for rejecting objective norms is a good reason and whether the nihilistic consequence would be avoided by this interpretation of Weber's view. It is sufficient to remark that its acceptance would require a break with the notions of "value" and "ideal" on which Weber's actual doctrine is built and that it is that actual doctrine, and not the possible interpretation mentioned, which dominates present-day social science.

Many social scientists of our time seem to regard nihilism as a minor inconvenience which wise men would bear with equanimity, since it is the price one has to pay for obtaining that highest good, a truly scientific social science. They seem to be satisfied with any scientific findings, although they cannot be more than "barren truths which generate no conclusion," the conclusions being generated by purely subjective value judgments or arbitrary preferences. We have to consider, therefore, whether social science as a purely theoretical pursuit, but still as a pursuit leading to the understanding of social phenomena, is possible on the basis of the distinction between facts and values.

We remind ourselves again of Weber's statement about the prospects of Western civilization. As we observed, Weber saw the following alternative: either a spiritual renewal or else "mechanized petrifaction," i.e., the extinction of every human possibility except that of "specialists without spirit or vision and voluptuaries without heart." He concluded: "But by making this statement we enter the province of judgments of value and faith with which this purely historical presentation shall not be burdened." It is not proper, then, for the historian or social scientist, it is not permissible, that he truthfully describe a certain type of life as spiritually empty or describe specialists without vision and voluptuaries without heart as what they are. But is this not absurd? Is it not the plain duty of the social scientist truthfully and faithfully to present social phenomena? How can we give a causal explanation of a social phenomenon if we do not first see it as what it is? Do we not know petrifaction or spiritual emptiness when we see it? And if someone is incapable of seeing phenomena of this kind, is he not disqualified by this very fact from being a social scientist, just as much as a blind man is disqualified from being an analyst of painting?

Weber was particularly concerned with the sociology of ethics and of religion. That sociology presupposes a fundamental distinction between "ethos" and "techniques of living" (or "prudential" rules). The sociologist must then be able to recognize an "ethos" in its distinctive character; he must have a feel for it, an appreciation of it, as Weber admitted. But does such appreciation not necessarily imply a value judgment? Does it not imply the realization that a given phenomenon is a *genuine* "ethos" and not a *mere* "technique of living"? Would one not laugh out of court a man who claimed to have written a sociology of art but who actually had written a sociology of trash? The sociologist of religion must distinguish between phenomena which have a religious character and phenomena which are a-religious. To be able to do this, he must know what religion is, he must have understanding of religion. Now, contrary to what Weber suggested, such understanding enables and forces him to distinguish between genuine and spurious religion, between higher and lower religions: those religions are higher in which the specifically religious motivations are effective to a higher degree. Or shall we say that the sociologist is permitted to note the presence or absence of religion or of "ethos"—for this would be merely factual observation—but must not dare to pronounce on the degree to which it is present, i.e., on the rank of the particular religion or "ethos" he is studying? The sociologist of religion cannot help noting the difference between those who try to gain the favor of their gods by flattering and bribing them and those who try to gain it by a change of heart. Can he see this difference without seeing at the same time the difference of rank which it implies, the difference between a mercenary and a non-mercenary attitude? Is he not forced to realize that the attempt to bribe the gods is tantamount to trying to be the lord or employer of the gods and that there is a fundamental incongruity between such attempts and what men divine when speaking of gods? In fact, Weber's whole sociology of religion stands or falls by such distinctions as those between "ethics of intention" and "priestly formalism" (or "petrified maxims"); "sublime" religious thought and "pure sorcery"; "the fresh source of a really, and not merely apparently, profound insight" and "a maze of wholly unintuitive, symbolistic images"; "plastic imagination" and "bookish thinking." His work would be not merely dull but absolutely meaningless if he did not speak almost constantly of practically all intellectual and moral virtues and vices in the appropriate language, i.e., in the language of praise and blame. I have in mind expressions like these: "grand figures," "incomparable grandeur," "perfection that is nowhere surpassed," "pseudo-systematics," "this laxity was undoubtedly a product of decline," "absolutely unartistic," "ingenious explanations," "highly educated," "unrivaled majestic account," "power, plasticity, and precision of formulation," "sublime character of the ethical demands," "perfect inner consistency," "crude and abstruse notions," "manly beauty," "pure and deep conviction," "impressive achievement," "works of art of the first rank." Weber paid some attention to the influence of Puritanism on poetry, music, and so on. He noted a certain negative effect of Puritanism on these arts. This fact (if it is a fact) owes its relevance exclusively to the circumstance that a genuinely religious impulse of a very high order was the cause of the decline of art, i.e., of the "drying-up" of previously existing genuine and high art. For, clearly, no one in his senses would voluntarily pay the slightest attention to a case in which a languishing superstition caused the production of trash. In the case studied by Weber, the cause was a genuine and high religion, and the effect was the decline of art: both the cause and the effect become visible only on the basis of value judgments as distinguished from mere reference to values. Weber had to choose between blindness to the phenomena and value judgments. In his capacity as a practicing social scientist, he chose wisely.[18]

The prohibition against value judgments in social science

---

[18] *Ibid.*, pp. 380, 462, 481–483, 486, 493, 554; *Religionssoziologie*, I, pp. 33, 82, 112 n., 185 ff., 429, 513; II, pp. 165, 167, 173, 242 n., 285, 316, 370; III, pp. 2 n., 118, 139, 207, 209–210, 221, 241, 257, 268, 274, 323, 382, 385 n.; *Soziologie und Sozialpolitik*, p. 469; *Wirtschaft und Gesellschaft*, pp. 240, 246, 249, 266.

would lead to the consequence that we are permitted to give a strictly factual description of the overt acts that can be observed in concentration camps and perhaps an equally factual analysis of the motivation of the actors concerned: we would not be permitted to speak of cruelty. Every reader of such a description who is not completely stupid would, of course, see that the actions described are cruel. The factual description would, in truth, be a bitter satire. What claimed to be a straightforward report would be an unusually circumlocutory report. The writer would deliberately suppress his better knowledge, or, to use Weber's favorite term, he would commit an act of intellectual dishonesty. Or, not to waste any moral ammunition on things that are not worthy of it, the whole procedure reminds one of a childish game in which you lose if you pronounce certain words, to the use of which you are constantly incited by your playmates. Weber, like every other man who ever discussed social matters in a relevant manner, could not avoid speaking of avarice, greed, unscrupulousness, vanity, devotion, sense of proportion, and similar things, i.e., making value judgments. He expressed indignation against people who did not see the difference between Gretchen and a prostitute, i.e., who failed to see the nobility of sentiment present in the one but absent from the other. What Weber implied can be formulated as follows: prostitution is a recognized subject of sociology; this subject cannot be seen if the degrading character of prostitution is not seen at the same time; if one sees the fact "prostitution," as distinguished from an arbitrary abstraction, one has already made a value judgment. What would become of political science if it were not permitted to deal with phenomena like narrow party spirit, boss rule, pressure groups, statesmanship, corruption, even moral corruption, i.e., with phenomena which are, as it were, constituted by value judgments? To put the terms designating such things in quotation marks is a childish trick which enables one to talk of important subjects while denying the principles without which there cannot be important subjects—a trick which is meant to allow one to combine the advantages of common sense with the denial of common sense. Or can one say anything relevant on public opinion polls, for example, without realizing the fact that many answers to the questionnaires are given by unintelligent, uninformed, deceitful, and irrational people, and that not a few questions are formulated by people of the same caliber —can one say anything relevant about public opinion polls without committing one value judgment after another?[19]

Or let us look at an example that Weber himself discussed at some length. The political scientist or historian has, for example, to explain actions of statesmen and generals, i.e., he has to trace their actions to their causes. He cannot do this without answering the question of whether the action concerned was caused by rational consideration of means and ends or by emotional factors, for example. For this purpose he has to construct the model of a perfectly rational action in the given circumstances. Only thus will he be able to see which nonrational factors, if any, deflected the action from the strictly rational course. Weber admitted that this procedure implies evaluation: we are forced to say that the actor in question made this or that mistake. But, Weber argued, the construction of the model and the ensuing value judgment on the deviation from the model are merely a transitional stage in the process of causal explanation.[20] As good children, we are then to forget as soon as possible what, in passing by, we could not help noticing but were not supposed to notice. But, in the first place, if the historian shows, by objectively measuring the action of a statesman against the model of "rational action in the circumstances," that the statesman made one blunder after another, he makes an objective value judgment to the effect that the statesman was singularly inept. In another case the historian arrives by the same procedure at the equally objective value judgment that a general showed unusual resourcefulness, resolution, and prudence. It is impossible to understand phenomena of this kind without being aware of the standard of judgment that is inherent in the situation and accepted as a matter of course by the actors themselves; and it is impossible not to make use of that standard by actually evaluating. In the second place, one may wonder whether what Weber regarded as merely incidental or transitional—namely, the insight into the ways of folly and wis-

---

[19] M. Weber, *Wissenschaftslehre*, p. 158; *Religionssoziologie*, I, pp. 41, 170 n.; *Politische Schriften*, pp. 331, 435–436.

[20] M. Weber, *Wissenschaftslehre*, pp. 125, 129–130, 337–338; *Soziologie und Sozialpolitik*, p. 483.

dom, of cowardice and bravery, of barbarism and humanity, and so on—is not more worthy of the interest of the historian than any causal explanation along Weberian lines. As for the question whether the inevitable and unobjectionable value judgments should be expressed or suppressed, it is really the question of how they should be expressed, "where, when, by whom, and toward whom"; it belongs, therefore, before another tribunal than that of the methodology of the social sciences.

Social science could avoid value judgments only by keeping strictly within the limits of a purely historical or "interpretive" approach. The social scientist would have to bow without a murmur to the self-interpretation of his subjects. He would be forbidden to speak of "morality," "religion," "art," "civilization," and so on, when interpreting the thought of peoples or tribes who are unaware of such notions. On the other hand, he would have to accept as morality, religion, art, knowledge, state, etc., whatever claimed to be morality, religion, art, etc. As a matter of fact, there exists a sociology of knowledge according to which everything that pretends to be knowledge—even if it is notorious nonsense—has to be accepted as knowledge by the sociologist. Weber himself identified the types of legitimate rule with what are thought to be types of legitimate rule. But this limitation exposes one to the danger of falling victim to every deception and every self-deception of the people one is studying; it penalizes every critical attitude; taken by itself, it deprives social science of every possible value. The self-interpretation of a blundering general cannot be accepted by the political historian, and the self-interpretation of a silly rhymer cannot be accepted by the historian of literature. Nor can the social scientist afford to rest content with the interpretation of a given phenomenon that is accepted by the group within which it occurs. Are groups less liable to deceive themselves than individuals? It was easy for Weber to make the following demand: "What is alone important [for describing a given quality as charismatic] is how the individual is actually regarded by those subject to charismatic authority, by his 'followers' or 'disciples.'" Eight lines later, we read: "Another type [of charismatic leader] is that of Joseph Smith, the founder of Mormonism, who, however, cannot be classified in this way with absolute certainty since there is a possibility that he was a very sophisticated type of swindler," i.e., that he merely pretended to have a charisma. It would be unfair to insist on the fact that the German original is, to say the least, much less explicit and emphatic than the English translation; for the problem implicitly raised by the translator— namely, the problem concerning the difference between genuine and pretended charisma, between genuine prophets and pseudo-prophets, between genuine leaders and successful charlatans— cannot be disposed of by silence.[21] The sociologist cannot be obliged to abide by the legal fictions which a given group never dared to regard as legal fictions; he is forced to make a distinction between how a given group actually conceives of the authority by which it is ruled and the true character of the authority in question. On the other hand, the strictly historical approach, which limits itself to understanding people in the way in which they understand themselves, may be very fruitful if kept in its place. By realizing this, we grasp a legitimate motive underlying the demand for a nonevaluating social science.

Today it is trivial to say that the social scientist ought not to judge societies other than his own by the standards of his society. It is his boast that he does not praise or blame, but understands. But he cannot understand without a conceptual framework or a frame of reference. Now his frame of reference is more likely than not to be a mere reflection of the way in which his own society understands itself in his time. Accordingly, he will interpret societies other than his own in terms that are wholly alien to those societies. He will force these societies into the Procrustean bed of his conceptual scheme. He will not understand these societies as they understand themselves. Since the self-interpretation of a society is an essential element of its being, he will not understand these societies as they really are. And since one cannot understand one's own society adequately if one does not understand other societies, he will not even be able really to understand his own society. He has then to understand various societies of the past and present, or significant "parts" of those societies, exactly as they understand or understood themselves. Within the limits of this purely historical and

21 M. Weber, *The Theory of Social and Economic Organization,* pp. 359, 361; compare *Wirtschaft und Gesellschaft,* pp. 140–141, 753.

hence merely preparatory or ancillary work, that kind of objectivity which implies the foregoing of evaluations is legitimate and even indispensable from every point of view. Particularly in regard to such a phenomenon as a doctrine, it is obvious that one cannot judge of its soundness or explain it in sociological or other terms before one has understood it, i.e., before one has understood it exactly as its originator understood it.

It is curious that Weber, who was so fond of that kind of objectivity which requires the foregoing of value judgments, was almost blind in regard to the sphere which may be said to be the home, and the only home, of nonevaluating objectivity. He realized clearly that the conceptual framework which he used was rooted in the social situation of his time. It is easy to see, for instance, that his distinction of three ideal types of legitimacy (traditional, rational, and charismatic) reflects the situation as it existed in Continental Europe after the French Revolution when the struggle between the residues of the pre-Revolutionary regimes and the Revolutionary regimes was understood as a contest between tradition and reason. The manifest inadequacy of this scheme, which perhaps fitted the situation in the nineteenth century but hardly any other situation, forced Weber to add the charismatic type of legitimacy to the two types imposed on him by his environment. But this addition did not remove, it merely concealed, the basic limitation inherent in his scheme. The addition created the impression that the scheme was now comprehensive, but, in fact, it could not be made comprehensive by any additions because of its parochial origin: not a comprehensive reflection on the nature of political society but merely the experience of two or three generations had supplied the basic orientation. Since Weber believed that no conceptual scheme used by social science can be of more than ephemeral validity, he was not seriously disturbed by this state of affairs. In particular, he was not seriously disturbed by the danger that the imposition of his definitely "dated" scheme might prevent the unbiased understanding of earlier political situations. He did not wonder whether his scheme fitted the manner in which, say, the protagonists of the great political conflicts recorded in history had conceived of their causes, that is to say, the manner in which they had conceived of the principles of legitimacy. For funda-

mentally the same reason, he did not hesitate to describe Plato
as an "intellectual," without for one moment considering the
fact that the whole work of Plato may be described as a critique
of the notion of "the intellectual." He did not hesitate to consider the dialogue between the Athenians and Melians in
Thucydides' *History* as a sufficient basis for asserting that "in
the Hellenic polis of the classical time, a most naked 'Machiavellianism' was regarded as a matter of course in every respect
and as wholly unobjectionable from an ethical point of view."
To say nothing of other considerations, he did not pause to
wonder how Thucydides himself had conceived of that dialogue.
He did not hesitate to write: "The fact that Egyptian sages
praised obedience, silence, and absence of presumptuousness as
godly virtues, had its source in bureaucratic subordination. In
Israel, the source was the plebeian character of the clientele."
Similarly, his sociological explanation of Hindu thought is based
on the premise that natural right "of any kind" presupposes the
natural equality of all men, if not even a blessed state at the
beginning and at the end. Or, to take what is perhaps the most
telling example, when discussing the question of what has to be
regarded as the essence of a historical phenomenon like Calvinism, Weber said: By calling something the essence of a historical
phenomenon, one either means that aspect of the phenomenon
which one considers to be of permanent value, or else that aspect
through which it exercised the greatest historical influence. He
did not even allude to a third possibility, which is, in fact, the
first and most obvious one, namely, that the essence of Calvinism,
e.g., would have to be identified with what Calvin himself regarded as the essence, or as the chief characteristic, of his work.[22]

Weber's methodological principles were bound to affect his
work in an adverse manner. We shall illustrate this by glancing
at his most famous historical essay, his study on Protestant ethics
and the spirit of capitalism. He contended that Calvinist theology was a major cause of the capitalist spirit. He stressed the
fact that the effect was in no way intended by Calvin, that
Calvin would have been shocked by it, and—what is more im-

---

[22] M. Weber, *Religionssoziologie*, I, p. 89; II, pp. 136 n., 143–145; III, pp. 232–233; *Wissenschaftslehre*, pp. 93–95, 170–173, 184, 199, 206–209, 214, 249–250.

portant—that the crucial link in the chain of causation (a peculiar interpretation of the dogma of predestination) was rejected by Calvin but emerged "quite naturally" among the epigones and, above all, among the broad stratum of the general run of Calvinists. Now, if one speaks about a teaching of the rank of Calvin's, the mere reference to "epigones" and the "general run" of men implies a value judgment on that interpretation of the dogma of predestination which these people adopted: epigones and the general run of men are very likely to miss the decisive point. Weber's implied value judgment is fully justified in the eyes of everyone who has understood the theological doctrine of Calvin; the peculiar interpretation of the dogma of predestination that allegedly led to the emergence of the capitalistic spirit is based on a radical misunderstanding of Calvin's doctrine. It is a corruption of that doctrine or, to use Calvin's own language, it is a carnal interpretation of a spiritual teaching. The maximum that Weber could reasonably have claimed to have proved is, then, that a corruption or degeneration of Calvin's theology led to the emergence of the capitalist spirit. Only by means of this decisive qualification can his thesis be brought into even approximate harmony with the facts to which he refers. But he was prevented from making this crucial qualification because he had imposed on himself the taboo regarding value judgments. By avoiding an indispensable value judgment, he was forced into giving a factually incorrect picture of what had happened. For his fear of value judgments prompted him to identify the essence of Calvinism with its historically most influential aspect. He instinctively avoided identifying the essence of Calvinism with what Calvin himself considered essential, because Calvin's self-interpretation would naturally act as a standard by which to judge objectively the Calvinists who claimed to follow Calvin.[23]

[23] M. Weber, *Religionssoziologie*, I, pp. 81–82, 103–104, 112. One can hardly say that the problem stated by Weber in his study on the spirit of capitalism has been solved. To prepare a solution, one would have to free Weber's formulation of the problem from the particular limitation which was due to his "Kantianism." He may be said to have rightly identified the spirit of capitalism with the view that limitless accumulation of capital and profitable investment of capital is a moral duty, and perhaps the highest moral duty, and to have rightly contended that this spirit is characteristic of the modern Western world. But he also said that the spirit of capitalism consists in regarding the limitless accumulation of capital as an end in itself. He

The rejection of value judgments endangers historical objectivity. In the first place, it prevents one from calling a spade a spade. In the second place, it endangers that kind of objectivity which legitimately requires the forgoing of evaluations, namely, the objectivity of interpretation. The historian who takes it for

---

could not prove the latter contention except by referring to dubious or ambiguous impressions. He was forced to make that contention because he assumed that "moral duty" and "end in itself" are identical. His "Kantianism" also forced him to sever every connection between "moral duty" and "the common good." He was forced to introduce into his analysis of earlier moral thought a distinction, not warranted by the texts, between the "ethical" justification of the unlimited accumulation of capital and its "utilitarian" justification. As a consequence of his peculiar notion of "ethics," every reference to the common good in earlier literature tended to appear to him as a lapse into low utilitarianism. One may venture to say that no writer outside mental institutions ever justified the duty, or the moral right, to unlimited acquisition on any other ground than that of service to the common good. The problem of the genesis of the capitalist spirit is then identical with the problem of the emergence of the minor premise, "but the unlimited accumulation of capital is most conducive to the common good." For the major premise, "it is our duty to devote ourselves to the common good or to the love of our neighbors," was not affected by the emergence of the capitalist spirit. That major premise was accepted by both the philosophic and the theological tradition. The question, then, is which transformation of the philosophic or of the theological tradition or of both caused the emergence of the minor premise mentioned. Weber took it for granted that the cause must be sought in the transformation of the theological tradition, i.e., in the Reformation. But he did not succeed in tracing the capitalist spirit to the Reformation or, in particular, to Calvinism except by the use of "historical dialectics" or by means of questionable psychological constructions. The utmost one could say is that he traced the capitalist spirit to the corruption of Calvinism. Tawney rightly pointed out that the capitalist Puritanism studied by Weber was late Puritanism or that it was the Puritanism that had already made its peace with "the world." This means that the Puritanism in question had made its peace with the capitalist world already in existence: the Puritanism in question was then not the cause of the capitalist world or of the capitalist spirit. If it is impossible to trace the capitalist spirit to the Reformation, one is forced to wonder whether the minor premise under consideration did not emerge through the transformation of the philosophic tradition, as distinguished from the transformation of the theological tradition. Weber considered the possibility that the origin of the capitalist spirit might have to be sought in the Renaissance, but, as he rightly observed, the Renaissance as such was an attempt to restore the spirit of classical antiquity, i.e., a spirit wholly different from the capitalist spirit. What he failed to consider was that in the course of the sixteenth century there was a conscious break with the whole philosophic tradition, a break that took place on the plane of purely philosophic or rational or secular thought. This break was origi-

granted that objective value judgments are impossible cannot take very seriously that thought of the past which was based on the assumption that objective value judgments are possible, i.e., practically all thought of earlier generations. Knowing beforehand that that thought was based on a fundamental delusion, he lacks the necessary incentive for trying to understand the past as it understood itself.

Almost all that we have said up to this point was necessary in order to clear away the most important obstacles to an understanding of Weber's central thesis. Only now are we able to grasp its precise meaning. Let us reconsider our last example. What Weber should have said was that the corruption of Calvinist theology led to the emergence of the capitalist spirit. This would have implied an objective value judgment on vulgar Calvinism: the epigones unwittingly destroyed what they intended to preserve. Yet this implied value judgment is of very limited significance. It does not prejudge the real issue in any way. For, assuming that Calvinist theology were a bad thing, its corruption was a good thing. What Calvin would have considered a "carnal" understanding could, from another point of view, be approved as a "this-worldly" understanding, leading to such good things as secularist individualism and secularist democracy. Even from the latter point of view, vulgar Calvinism would appear as an impossible position, a halfway house, but preferable to Calvinism

---

nated by Machiavelli, and it led to the moral teachings of Bacon and Hobbes: thinkers whose writings preceded by decades those writings of their Puritan countrymen on which Weber's thesis is based. One can hardly say more than that Puritanism, having broken more radically with the "pagan" philosophic tradition (i.e., chiefly with Aristotelianism) than Roman Catholicism and Lutheranism had done, was more open to the new philosophy than were the latter. Puritanism thus could become a very important, and perhaps the most important, "carrier" of the new philosophy both natural and moral—of a philosophy which had been created by men of an entirely non-Puritan stamp. In brief, Weber overestimated the importance of the revolution that had taken place on the plane of theology, and he underestimated the importance of the revolution that had taken place on the plane of rational thought. By paying more careful attention than he did to the purely secular development, one would also be able to restore the connection, arbitrarily severed by him, between the emergence of the capitalist spirit and the emergence of the science of economics (cf. also E. Troeltsch, *The Social Teaching of the Christian Churches*, pp. 624, 894).

proper for the same reason that Sancho Panza may be said to be preferable to Don Quixote. The rejection of vulgar Calvinism is then inevitable from every point of view. But this merely means that only after having rejected vulgar Calvinism is one faced with the real issue: the issue of religion versus irreligion, i.e., of genuine religion versus noble irreligion, as distinguished from the issue of mere sorcery, or mechanical ritualism versus the irreligion of specialists without vision and voluptuaries without heart. It is this real issue which, according to Weber, cannot be settled by human reason, just as the conflict between different genuine religions of the highest rank (e.g., the conflict between Deutero-Isaiah, Jesus, and Buddha) cannot be settled by human reason. Thus, in spite of the fact that social science stands or falls by value judgments, social science or social philosophy cannot settle the decisive value conflicts. It is indeed true that one has already passed a value judgment when speaking of Gretchen and a prostitute. But this value judgment proves to be merely provisional the moment one comes face to face with a radically ascetic position which condemns all sexuality. From this point of view, the open degradation of sexuality through prostitution may appear to be a cleaner thing than the disguise of the true nature of sexuality through sentiment and poetry. It is indeed true that one cannot speak of human affairs without praising the intellectual and moral virtues and blaming the intellectual and moral vices. But this does not dispose of the possibility that all human virtues would ultimately have to be judged to be no more than splendid vices. It would be absurd to deny that there is an objective difference between a blundering general and a strategic genius. But if war is absolutely evil, the difference between the blundering general and the strategic genius will be on the same level as the difference between a blundering thief and a genius in thievery.

It seems, then, that what Weber really meant by his rejection of value judgments would have to be expressed as follows: The objects of the social sciences are constituted by reference to values. Reference to values presupposes appreciation of values. Such appreciation enables and forces the social scientist to evaluate the social phenomena, i.e., to distinguish between the genuine and the spurious and between the higher and the lower: between genuine religion and spurious religion, between genuine leaders and charlatans, between knowledge and mere lore or sophistry, between virtue and vice, between moral sensitivity and moral obtuseness, between art and trash, between vitality and degeneracy, etc. Reference to values is incompatible with neutrality; it can never be "purely theoretical." But nonneutrality does not necessarily mean approval; it may also mean rejection. In fact, since the various values are incompatible with one another, the approval of any one value necessarily implies the rejection of some other value or values. Only on the basis of such acceptance or rejection of values, of "ultimate values," do the objects of the social sciences come to sight. For all further work, for the causal analysis of these objects, it must be a matter of indifference whether the student has accepted or rejected the value in question.[24]

At any rate, Weber's whole notion of the scope and function of the social sciences rests on the allegedly demonstrable premise that the conflict between ultimate values cannot be resolved by human reason. The question is whether that premise has really been demonstrated, or whether it has merely been postulated under the impulse of a specific moral preference.

At the threshold of Weber's attempt to demonstrate his basic premise, we encounter two striking facts. The first is that Weber, who wrote thousands of pages, devoted hardly more than thirty of them to a thematic discussion of the basis of his whole position. Why was that basis so little in need of proof? Why was it self-evident to him? A provisional answer is supplied by the second observation we can make prior to any analysis of his arguments. As he indicated at the beginning of his discussion of the subject, his thesis was only the generalized version of an older and more common view, namely, that the conflict between ethics and politics is insoluble: political action is sometimes impossible without incurring moral guilt. It seems, then, that it was the spirit of "power politics" that begot Weber's position. Nothing is more revealing than the fact that, in a related context when speaking of conflict and peace, Weber put "peace" in quotation marks, whereas he did not take this precautionary measure when speaking of conflict. Conflict was for Weber an

[24] M. Weber, *Wissenschaftslehre*, pp. 90, 124–125, 175, 180–182, 199.

unambiguous thing, but peace was not: peace is phony, but war is real.[25]

Weber's thesis that there is no solution to the conflict between values was then a part, or a consequence, of the comprehensive view according to which human life is essentially an inescapable conflict. For this reason, "peace and universal happiness" appeared to him to be an illegitimate or fantastic goal. Even if that goal could be reached, he thought, it would not be desirable; it would be the condition of "the last men who have invented happiness," against whom Nietzsche had directed his "devastating criticism." If peace is incompatible with human life or with a truly human life, the moral problem would seem to allow of a clear solution: the nature of things requires a warrior ethics as the basis of a "power politics" that is guided exclusively by considerations of the national interest; or "the most naked Machiavellianism [would have to be] regarded as a matter of course in every respect, and as wholly unobjectionable from an ethical point of view." But we would then be confronted with the paradoxical situation that the individual is at peace with himself while the world is ruled by war. The strife-torn world demands a strife-torn individual. The strife would not go to the root of the individual, if he were not forced to negate the very principle of war: he must negate the war from which he cannot escape and to which he must dedicate himself, as evil or sinful. Lest there be peace anywhere, peace must not be simply rejected. It is not sufficient to recognize peace as the necessary breathing time between wars. There must be an absolute duty directing us toward universal peace or universal brotherhood, a duty conflicting with the equally high duty that directs us to participate in "the eternal struggle" for "elbow room" for our nation. Conflict would not be supreme if guilt could be escaped. The question of whether one can speak of guilt, if man is forced to become guilty, was no longer discussed by Weber: he needed the necessity of guilt. He had to combine the anguish bred by atheism (the absence of any redemption, of any solace) with the anguish bred by revealed religion (the oppressive sense of guilt).

[25] *Ibid.*, pp. 466, 479; *Politische Schriften*, pp. 17–18, 310.

Without that combination, life would cease to be tragic and thus lose its depth.[26]

Weber assumed as a matter of course that there is no hierarchy of values: all values are of the same rank. Now, precisely if this is the case, a social scheme that satisfies the requirements of two values is preferable to one whose scope is more limited. The comprehensive scheme might demand that some of the requirements of each of the two values would have to be sacrificed. In this case the question would arise as to whether the extreme or one-sided schemes are not so good as, or are better than, the apparently more comprehensive schemes. To answer that question, one would have to know whether it is at all possible to adopt one of the two values, while unqualifiedly rejecting the other. If it is impossible, some sacrifice of the apparent requirements of the two component values would be a dictate of reason. The optimal scheme might not be realizable except under certain very favorable conditions, and the actual conditions here and now may be very unfavorable. This would not deprive the optimal scheme of its importance, because it would remain indispensable as the basis for rational judgment about the various imperfect schemes. In particular, its importance would be in no way affected by the fact that in given situations one can choose only between two equally imperfect schemes. Last but not least, in all reflections on such matters one must not be oblivious for one moment of the general significance for social life of extremism, on the one hand, and moderation, on the other. Weber pushed all considerations of this character aside by declaring that "the middle line is no whit more scientifically correct than the most extreme party ideals of the right and the left" and that the middle line is even inferior to the extreme solutions, since it is less unambiguous.[27] The question, of course, is whether social science does not have to be concerned with sensible solutions to social problems and whether moderation is not more sensible than extremism. However sensible Weber may have been as a practical politician, however much he may have abhorred the spirit of narrow party fanaticism, as a social scientist he approached social problems in a spirit that had

[26] M. Weber, *Politische Schriften*, pp. 18, 20; *Wissenschaftslehre*, pp. 540, 550; *Religionssoziologie*, I, pp. 568–569.
[27] M. Weber, *Wissenschaftslehre*, pp. 154, 461.

nothing in common with the spirit of statesmanship and that could serve no other practical end than to encourage narrow obstinacy. His unshakable faith in the supremacy of conflict forced him to have at least as high a regard for extremism as for moderate courses.

But we can no longer delay turning to Weber's attempts to prove his contention that the ultimate values are simply in conflict with one another. We shall have to limit ourselves to a discussion of two or three specimens of his proofs.[28] The first one is the example that he used in order to illustrate the character of most issues of social policy. Social policy is concerned with justice; but what justice in society requires cannot be decided, according to Weber, by any ethics. Two opposed views are equally legitimate or defensible. According to the first view, one owes much to him who achieves or contributes much; according to the second view, one should demand much from him who can achieve or contribute much. If one adopts the first view, one would have to grant great opportunities to great talent. If one adopts the second view, one would have to prevent the talented

[28] While Weber referred rather frequently in general terms to a considerable number of insoluble value conflicts, his attempt to prove his basic contention is limited, as far as I can see, to the discussion of three or four examples. The example which will not be discussed in the text concerns the conflict between eroticism and all impersonal or supra-personal values: a genuine erotic relation between a man and a woman can be regarded, "from a certain standpoint," "as the sole or at any rate as the most royal road" to a genuine life; if someone opposes all saintliness or all goodness, all ethical or aesthetic norms, everything that is valuable from the point of view of culture or of personality, in the name of genuine erotic passion, reason has to be absolutely silent. The particular standpoint which permits or fosters this attitude is not, as one might expect, that of Carmen but that of intellectuals who suffer from the specialization or "professionalization" of life. To such people "marriage-free sexual life could appear as the only link that still connects man (who by then had completely left the cycle of the old, simple, and organic peasant existence) with the natural source of all life." It is probably sufficient to say that appearances may be deceptive. But we feel compelled to add that, according to Weber, this late return to the most natural in man is bound up with what he chose to call "die systematische Herauspräparierung der Sexualsphäre" (*Wissenschaftslehre*, pp. 468–469; *Religionssoziologie*, I, pp. 560–562). He thus proved indeed that eroticism as he understood it conflicts with "all esthetic norms"; but he proved at the same time that the intellectuals' attempt to escape specialization through eroticism merely leads to specialization in eroticism (cf. *Wissenschaftslehre*, p. 540). He proved, in other words, that his erotic Weltanschauung is not defensible before the tribunal of human reason.

individual from exploiting his superior opportunities. We shall not complain about the loose way in which Weber stated what he considered, rather strangely, an insuperable difficulty. We merely note that he did not think it necessary to indicate any reason by which the first view can be supported. The second view, however, seemed to require an explicit argument. According to Weber, one may argue, as Babeuf did, in the following way: the injustice of the unequal distribution of mental gifts and the gratifying feeling of prestige which attends the mere possession of superior gifts have to be compensated by social measures destined to prevent the talented individual from exploiting his great opportunities. Before one could say that this view is tenable, one would have to know whether it makes sense to say that nature committed an injustice by distributing her gifts unequally, whether it is a duty of society to remedy that injustice, and whether envy has a right to be heard. But even if one would grant that Babeuf's view, as stated by Weber, is as defensible as the first view, what would follow? That we have to make a blind choice? That we have to incite the adherents of the two opposed views to insist on their opinions with all the obstinacy that they can muster? If, as Weber contends, no solution is morally superior to the other, the reasonable consequence would be that the decision has to be transferred from the tribunal of ethics to that of convenience or expediency. Weber emphatically excluded considerations of expediency from the discussion of this issue. If demands are made in the name of justice, he declared, consideration of which solution would supply the best "incentives" is out of place. But is there no connection between justice and the good of society, and between the good of society and incentives to socially valuable activity? Precisely if Weber were right in asserting that the two opposite views are equally defensible, would social science as an objective science have to stigmatize as a crackpot any man who insisted that only one of the views is in accordance with justice?[29]

Our second example is Weber's alleged proof that there is an insoluble conflict between what he calls the "ethics of responsibility" and the "ethics of intention." According to the former, man's responsibility extends to the foreseeable conse-

[29] M. Weber, *Wissenschaftslehre*, p. 467.

quences of his actions, whereas, according to the latter, man's responsibility is limited to the intrinsic rightness of his actions. Weber illustrated the ethics of intention by the example of syndicalism: the syndicalist is concerned not with the consequences or the success of his revolutionary activity but with his own integrity, with preserving in himself and awakening in others a certain moral attitude and nothing else. Even a conclusive proof that in a given situation his revolutionary activity would be destructive, for all the foreseeable future, of the very existence of revolutionary workers would not be a valid argument against a convinced syndicalist. Weber's convinced syndicalist is an *ad hoc* construction, as is shown by his remark that if the syndicalist is consistent, his kingdom is not of this world. In other words, if he were consistent, he would cease to be a syndicalist, i.e., a man who is concerned with the liberation of the working class in this world, and by means belonging to this world. The ethics of intention, which Weber imputed to syndicalism, is, in reality, an ethics alien to all this-worldly social or political movements. As he stated on another occasion, within the dimension of social action proper "the ethics of intention and the ethics of responsibility are not absolute opposites, but supplement each other: both united constitute the genuine human being." That ethics of intention that is incompatible with what Weber once called the ethics of a genuine human being is a certain interpretation of Christian ethics or, more generally expressed, a strictly otherworldly ethics. What Weber really meant when speaking of the insoluble conflict between the ethics of intention and the ethics of responsibility was, then, that the conflict between this-worldly ethics and otherworldly ethics is insoluble by human reason.[30]

Weber was convinced that, on the basis of a strictly this-worldly orientation, no objective norms are possible: there cannot be "absolutely valid" and, at the same time, specific norms

---

[30] For a more adequate discussion of the problem of "responsibility" and "intention" compare Thomas Aquinas, *Summa theologica* i. 2. qu. 20, a. 5; Burke, *Present Discontents in The Works of Edmund Burke*, I, pp. 375–377); Lord Charnwood, *Abraham Lincoln*, pp. 136–137, 164–165; Churchill, *Marlborough*, VI, pp. 599–600. *Wissenschaftslehre*, pp. 467, 475, 476, 546; *Politische Schriften*, pp. 441–444, 448–449, 62–63; *Soziologie und Sozialpolitik*, pp. 512–514; *Religionssoziologie*, II, pp. 193–194.

except on the basis of revelation. Yet he never proved that the unassisted human mind is incapable of arriving at objective norms or that the conflict between different this-worldly ethical doctrines is insoluble by human reason. He merely proved that otherworldly ethics, or rather a certain type of otherworldly ethics, is incompatible with those standards of human excellence or of human dignity which the unassisted human mind discerns. One could say, without in the least becoming guilty of irreverence, that the conflict between this-worldly and otherworldly ethics need not be of serious concern to social science. As Weber himself pointed out, social science attempts to understand social life from a this-worldly point of view. Social science is human knowledge of human life. Its light is the natural light. It tries to find rational or reasonable solutions to social problems. The insights and solutions at which it arrives might be questioned on the basis of superhuman knowledge or of divine revelation. But, as Weber indicated, social science as such cannot take notice of such questionings, because they are based on presuppositions which can never be evident to unassisted human reason. By accepting presuppositions of this character, social science would transform itself into either Jewish or Christian or Islamic or Buddhistic or some other "denominational" social science. In addition, if genuine insights of social science can be questioned on the basis of revelation, revelation is not merely above reason but against reason. Weber had no compunction in saying that every belief in revelation is ultimately belief in the absurd. Whether this view of Weber, who, after all, was not a theological authority, is compatible with an intelligent belief in revelation need not concern us here.[31]

Once it is granted that social science, or this-worldly understanding of human life, is evidently legitimate, the difficulty raised by Weber appears to be irrelevant. But he refused to grant that premise. He contended that science or philosophy rests, in the last analysis, not on evident premises that are at the disposal of man as man but on faith. Granting that only science or philosophy can lead to the truth which man can know, he raised the

[31] M. Weber, *Wissenschaftslehre*, pp. 33, n. 2, 39, 154, 379, 466, 469, 471, 540, 542, 545–547, 550–554; *Politische Schriften*, pp. 62–63; *Religionssoziologie*, I, p. 566.

question of whether the search for knowable truth is good, and he decided that this question can no longer be answered by science or philosophy. Science or philosophy is unable to give a clear or certain account of its own basis. The goodness of science or philosophy was no problem as long as one could think that it is "the way to true being" or to "true nature" or to "true happiness." But these expectations have proved to be illusory. Henceforth, science or philosophy can have no other goal than to ascertain that very limited truth which is accessible to man. Yet, in spite of this amazing change in the character of science or philosophy, the quest for truth continues to be regarded as valuable in itself, and not merely with a view to its practical results—which, in their turn, are of questionable value: to increase man's power means to increase his power for evil as well as for good. By regarding the quest for truth as valuable in itself, one admits that one is making a preference which no longer has a good or sufficient reason. One recognizes therewith the principle that preferences do not need good or sufficient reasons. Accordingly, those who regard the quest for truth as valuable in itself may regard such activities as the understanding of the genesis of a doctrine, or the editing of a text—nay, the conjectural correction of any corrupt reading in any manuscript—as ends in themselves: the quest for truth has the same dignity as stamp collecting. Every pursuit, every whim, becomes as defensible or as legitimate as any other. But Weber did not always go so far. He also said that the goal of science is clarity, i.e., clarity about the great issues, and this means ultimately clarity not indeed about the whole but about the situation of man as man. Science or philosophy is then the way toward freedom from delusion; it is the foundation of a free life, of a life that refuses to bring the sacrifice of the intellect and dares to look reality in its stern face. It is concerned with the knowable truth, which is valid regardless of whether we like it or not. Weber went up to this point. But he refused to say that science or philosophy is concerned with the truth which is valid for all men regardless of whether they desire to know it or not. What stopped him? Why did he deny to the knowable truth its inescapable power?[32]

[32] M. Weber, *Wissenschaftslehre*, pp. 60–61, 184, 213, 251, 469, 531, 540, 547, 549; *Politische Schriften*, pp. 128, 213; *Religionssoziologie*, I, pp. 569–570.

He was inclined to believe that twentieth-century man has eaten of the fruit of the tree of knowledge, or can be free from the delusions which blinded all earlier men: we see the situation of man without delusions; we are disenchanted. But under the influence of historicism, he became doubtful whether one can speak of the situation of man as man or, if one can, whether this situation is not seen differently in different ages in such a manner that, in principle, the view of any age is as legitimate or as illegitimate as that of any other. He wondered, therefore, whether what appeared to be the situation of man as man was more than the situation of present-day man, or "the inescapable datum of our historical situation." Hence what originally appeared as freedom from delusions presented itself eventually as hardly more than the questionable premise of our age or as an attitude that will be superseded, in due time, by an attitude that will be in conformity with the next epoch. The thought of the present age is characterized by disenchantment or unqualified "this-worldliness," or irreligion. What claims to be freedom from delusions is as much and as little delusion as the faiths which prevailed in the past and which may prevail in the future. We are irreligious because fate forces us to be irreligious and for no other reason. Weber refused to bring the sacrifice of the intellect; he did not wait for a religious revival or for prophets or saviors; and he was not at all certain whether a religious revival would follow the present age. But he was certain that all devotion to causes or ideals has its roots in religious faith and, therefore, that the decline of religious faith will ultimately lead to the extinction of all causes or ideals. He tended to see before him the alternative of either complete spiritual emptiness or religious revival. He despaired of the modern this-worldly irreligious experiment, and yet he remained attached to it because he was fated to believe in science as he understood it. The result of this conflict, which he could not resolve, was his belief that the conflict between values cannot be resolved by human reason.[33]

Yet the crisis of modern life and of modern science does not necessarily make doubtful the idea of science. We must therefore try to state in more precise terms what Weber had in mind when

[33] M. Weber, *Wissenschaftslehre*, pp. 546–547, 551–555; *Religions-soziologie*, I, pp. 204, 523.

he said that science seemed to be unable to give a clear or certain account of itself.

Man cannot live without light, guidance, knowledge; only through knowledge of the good can he find the good that he needs. The fundamental question, therefore, is whether men can acquire that knowledge of the good without which they cannot guide their lives individually or collectively by the unaided efforts of their natural powers, or whether they are dependent for that knowledge on Divine Revelation. No alternative is more fundamental than this: human guidance or divine guidance. The first possibility is characteristic of philosophy or science in the original sense of the term, the second is presented in the Bible. The dilemma cannot be evaded by any harmonization or synthesis. For both philosophy and the Bible proclaim something as the one thing needful, as the only thing that ultimately counts, and the one thing needful proclaimed by the Bible is the opposite of that proclaimed by philosophy: a life of obedient love versus a life of free insight. In every attempt at harmonization, in every synthesis however impressive, one of the two opposed elements is sacrificed, more or less subtly but in any event surely, to the other: philosophy, which means to be the queen, must be made the handmaid of revelation or vice versa.

If we take a bird's-eye view of the secular struggle between philosophy and theology, we can hardly avoid the impression that neither of the two antagonists has ever succeeded in really refuting the other. All arguments in favor of revelation seem to be valid only if belief in revelation is presupposed; and all arguments against revelation seem to be valid only if unbelief is presupposed. This state of things would appear to be but natural. Revelation is always so uncertain to unassisted reason that it can never compel the assent of unassisted reason, and man is so built that he can find his satisfaction, his bliss, in free investigation, in articulating the riddle of being. But, on the other hand, he yearns so much for a solution of that riddle and human knowledge is always so limited that the need for divine illumination cannot be denied and the possibility of revelation cannot be refuted. Now it is this state of things that seems to decide irrevocably against philosophy and in favor of revelation. Philosophy has to grant that revelation is possible. But to grant that revelation is possible means to grant that philosophy is perhaps not the one thing needful, that philosophy is perhaps something infinitely unimportant. To grant that revelation is possible means to grant that the philosophic life is not necessarily, not evidently, *the* right life. Philosophy, the life devoted to the quest for evident knowledge available to man as man, would itself rest on an unevident, arbitrary, or blind decision. This would merely confirm the thesis of faith, that there is no possibility of consistency, of a consistent and thoroughly sincere life, without belief in revelation. The mere fact that philosophy and revelation cannot refute each other would constitute the refutation of philosophy by revelation.

It was the conflict between revelation and philosophy or science in the full sense of the term and the implications of that conflict that led Weber to assert that the idea of science or philosophy suffers from a fatal weakness. He tried to remain faithful to the cause of autonomous insight, but he despaired when he felt that the sacrifice of the intellect, which is abhorred by science or philosophy, is at the bottom of science or philosophy.

But let us hasten back from these awful depths to a superficiality which, while not exactly gay, promises at least a quiet sleep. Having come up to the surface again, we are welcomed by about six hundred large pages covered with the smallest possible number of sentences, as well as with the largest possible number of footnotes, and devoted to the methodology of the social sciences. Yet we notice very soon that we have not escaped trouble. For Weber's methodology is something different from what methodology usually is. All intelligent students of Weber's methodology have felt that it is philosophic. It is possible to articulate that feeling. Methodology, as reflection on the correct procedure of science, is necessarily reflection on the limitations of science. If science is indeed the highest form of human knowledge, it is reflection on the limitations of human knowledge. And if it is knowledge that constitutes the specific character of man among all earthly beings, methodology is reflection on the limitations of humanity or on the situation of man as man. Weber's methodology comes very close to meeting this demand.

To remain somewhat nearer to what he himself thought of his methodology, we shall say that his notion of science, both natural and social, is based on a specific view of reality. For, according to him, scientific understanding consists in a peculiar transformation of reality. It is therefore impossible to clarify the meaning of science without a previous analysis of reality as it is in itself, i.e., prior to its transformation by science. Weber did not say much about this subject. He was less concerned with the character of reality than with the different ways in which reality is transformed by the different types of science. For his primary concern was with preserving the integrity of the historical or cultural sciences against two apparent dangers: against the attempt to shape these sciences on the pattern of the natural sciences and against the attempt to interpret the dualism of natural and historical-cultural sciences in terms of a metaphysical dualism ("body-mind" or "necessity-freedom"). But his methodological theses remain unintelligible, or at any rate irrelevant, if one does not translate them into theses regarding the character of reality. When he demanded, for example, that interpretive understanding be subservient to causal explanation, he was guided by the observation that the intelligible is frequently overpowered by what is no longer intelligible or that the lower is mostly stronger than the higher. In addition, his preoccupations left him time to indicate his view of what reality is prior to its transformation by science. According to him, reality is an infinite and meaningless sequence, or a chaos, of unique and infinitely divisible events, which in themselves are meaningless: all meaning, all articulation, originates in the activity of the knowing or evaluating subject. Very few people today will be satisfied with this view of reality, which Weber had taken over from neo-Kantianism and which he modified merely by adding one or two emotional touches. It is sufficient to remark that he himself was unable to adhere consistently to that view. He certainly could not deny that there is an articulation of reality that precedes all scientific articulation: that articulation, that wealth of meaning, which we have in mind when speaking of the world of common experience or of the natural understanding of the world.[34] But he did not even attempt a coherent analysis of the social world as it is known to "common sense," or of social reality as it is known in social life or in action. The place of such an analysis is occupied in his work

[34] M. Weber, *Wissenschaftslehre*, pp. 5, 35, 50–51, 61, 67, 71, 126, 127 n., 132–134, 161–162, 166, 171, 173, 175, 177–178, 180, 208, 389, 503.

by definitions of ideal types, of artificial constructs which are not even meant to correspond to the intrinsic articulation of social reality and which, in addition, are meant to be of a strictly ephemeral character. Only a comprehensive analysis of social reality as we know it in actual life, and as men always have known it since there have been civil societies, would permit an adequate discussion of the possibility of an evaluating social science. Such an analysis would make intelligible the fundamental alternatives which essentially belong to social life and would therewith supply a basis for responsible judgment on whether the conflict between these alternatives is, in principle, susceptible of a solution.

In the spirit of a tradition of three centuries, Weber would have rejected the suggestion that social science must be based on an analysis of social reality as it is experienced in social life or known to "common sense." According to that tradition, "common sense" is a hybrid, begotten by the absolutely subjective world of the individual's sensations and the truly objective world progressively discovered by science. This view stems from the seventeenth century, when modern thought emerged by virtue of a break with classical philosophy. But the originators of modern thought still agreed with the classics in so far as they conceived of philosophy or science as the perfection of man's natural understanding of the natural world. They differed from the classics in so far as they opposed the new philosophy or science, as the truly natural understanding of the world, to the perverted understanding of the world had by classical and medieval philosophy or science, or by "the school."[35] The victory of the new philosophy or science was decided by the victory of its decisive part, namely, the new physics. That victory led eventually to the result that the new physics and the new natural science in general became independent of the rump of philosophy which from then on came to be called "philosophy" in contradistinction to "science"; and, in fact, "science" became the authority for "philosophy." "Science," we may say, is the successful part of modern philosophy or science, whereas "philosophy" is its less successful part. Thus not modern philosophy but modern natural science

[35] Cf. J. Klein, "Die griechische Logistik und die Entstehung der modernen Algebra," *Quellen und Studien zur Geschichte der Mathematik, Astronomie und Physik*, III, 1936, 125.

came to be regarded as the perfection of man's natural understanding of the natural world. But in the nineteenth century it became more and more apparent that a drastic distinction must be made between what was then called the "scientific" understanding (or "the world of science") and the "natural" understanding (or "the world in which we live"). It became apparent that the scientific understanding of the world emerges by way of a radical modification, as distinguished from a perfection, of the natural understanding. Since the natural understanding is the presupposition of the scientific understanding, the analysis of science and of the world of science presupposes the analysis of the natural understanding, the natural world, or the world of common sense. The natural world, the world in which we live and act, is not the object or the product of a theoretical attitude; it is a world not of mere objects at which we detachedly look but of "things" or "affairs" which we handle. Yet as long as we identify the natural or prescientific world with the world in which we live, we are dealing with an abstraction. The world in which we live is already a product of science, or at any rate it is profoundly affected by the existence of science. To say nothing of technology, the world in which we live is free from ghosts, witches, and so on, with which, but for the existence of science, it would abound. To grasp the natural world as a world that is radically prescientific or prephilosophic, one has to go back behind the first emergence of science or philosophy. It is not necessary for this purpose to engage in extensive and necessarily hypothetical anthropological studies. The information that classical philosophy supplies about its origins suffices, especially if that information is supplemented by consideration of the most elementary premises of the Bible, for reconstructing the essential character of "the natural world." By using that information, so supplemented, one would be enabled to understand the origin of the idea of natural right.

For
FURTHER READING

A companion essay to the Weber selection is his "The Meaning of 'Ethical Neutrality' in Sociology and Economics," in Max Weber, *The Methodology of the Social Sciences* (see the Foreword by Edward A. Shils). Also, the reader not already acquainted with them should read Weber's essays "Politics as a Vocation" and "Science as a Vocation" in *From Max Weber* (also see the "Biographical View" of Weber by the editors, H. H. Gerth and C. Wright Mills). An "Intellectual Portrait" of the man and his work is presented by Reinhard Bendix in his book *Max Weber*. A good short account is given by Talcott Parsons in "Max Weber's Sociological Analysis of Capitalism and Modern Institutions," in *An Introduction to the History of Sociology* (ed. Harry Elmer Barnes). Parsons' *Structure of Social Action* gives a more detailed discussion. Albert Salomon's "Max Weber's Methodology," *Social Research*, Vol. I, 1934, and his other articles on Weber in that journal are valuable contributions. For a critical view see the chapter on Weber in Carlo Antoni's *From History to Sociology*. Raymond Aron's *German Sociology* is helpful, and H. Stuart Hughes's *Consciousness and Society* is well worth reading, especially for those interested in history of ideas.

In addition to a study of the whole of Leo Strauss's *Natural Right and History*, see the following essays by Strauss: the title essay of his *What Is Political Philosophy?* and "Social Science and Humanism," in *The State of the Social Sciences* (ed. Leonard D. White).

Other relevant titles: Paul H. Furfey, *The Scope and Method of Sociology*, ch. 4; J. A. Passmore, "Can the Social Sciences Be Value-Free?" *Proceedings of the Tenth International Congress of Philosophy*, 1949, reprinted in *Readings in the Philosophy of Science* (ed. Feigl and Brodbeck); Howard Becker, *Through Values to Social Interpretation;* Felix Kaufmann, *Methodology of the Social Sciences*, chs. 9, 15; W. H. Werkmeister, "Social Science and the Problem of Value," in *Scientism and Values* (ed. Schoeck and Wiggins); Everett Hall, *Modern Science and Human Values;* Wolfgang Köhler, *The Place of Value in a World of Facts;* Bertrand Russell, *The Scientific Outlook.*

PART V

Philosophical Perspectives

————————————

Introduction to
PART V

THE THEMES of the first four Parts of this book—the nature of the social, the status of theory and practice, the problems of concept and theory formation, and the relationship between science and value—have been treated as more or less implicit representations of the underlying philosophic antagonism between the *Weltanschauungen* of "subjectivism" and "objectivism." The concluding part that now follows is a more explicit exemplification of those "world views" as they may be found in the actual practice of the philosopher's craft. The selections from Ayer and Merleau-Ponty clash at every level, from the stylistic to the conceptual. If the former writes cleanly and tartly, the latter builds his argument in a convoluted, almost tortured manner (nor will the reader find the original text of Merleau-Ponty's French more elegant); where Ayer states his case in unequivocal terms, Merleau-Ponty formulates his arguments obliquely. The one strikes the line like a game fish; the other circles the bait like a crab. If points are to be awarded on the basis of efficiency and economy of language, there is hardly a contest. However, the problematic style in which Merleau-Ponty writes is partly a matter of literary exactitude (and here he scores quite low) and, more importantly, partly a matter of the philosophic suggestive-ness of a more nearly magical function of language. The phe-nomenological framework and presence of a certain amount of jargon should not keep the reader from persisting in his effort to follow the argument. This is not to say that dark language is automatically justified in philosophical discourse; instead, we are confronted in this instance with a complex challenge: to follow a major figure in the existentialist vein of phenomenology in a relatively rare encounter with a topic directly concerned with the social sciences. To provide as much preparatory clarification as possible for the reader, we shall devote ourselves chiefly to Merleau-Ponty's essay. Such editorial emphasis should not be interpreted as a slight to Ayer's side of the discussion; rather, we are convinced that Ayer speaks very well, and clearly, for himself.

The traditional separation of philosophy and sociology still so evident today is the result, Merleau-Ponty thinks, of a false conception of the nature of the social, of the confusion of fact with reality and reality with a pyramid of facts. It is as if the individual, whether a scientific observer or a layman, were placed in an already understood world which really did not need any analysis of the meaning of "being placed in an already under-stood world." Yet perhaps the most crucial aspect of man's ex-istence is that he is a social being. Most often this phrase is taken for granted, but the effect of Merleau-Ponty's thesis of the underlying unity of philosophy and social science is to call into question what has thus been taken for granted. Man is a *social* being and he is also a social *being*. The first stress is on the indi-vidual's insertion into an intersubjectively structured reality—that of man with fellow men; the second emphasis is essentially ontological, i.e., man is a creature who has being, who partici-pates in being, whose existence is a mode of being. When phi-losophers and social scientists assume that they can speak of themselves and their fellow men as though they were describing inanimate objects, they forfeit their right to see the world directly, in its immediate givenness. The result is the silence that divides those who otherwise might communicate to mutual advantage.

If a *rapprochement* is possible between philosophers and social scientists, it must be undertaken by philosophers, for the grounds for a meaningful reconstruction of a conceptual grasp of social reality lie primarily in philosophy itself. Here Merleau-Ponty turns to the phenomenology of Husserl in order to find the foundation for such a reconstruction. For Husserl, philosophy holds within itself the creative clue to Western civilization to the extent that the historical unfolding and fulfillment of reason is a bastion against nihilism. The struggle of the philosopher to comprehend social reality is, at bottom, a way of committing himself to the validity and value of science, in a generic sense of that term. For the philosopher is not only a man who asks basic questions about reality; he is also defining himself in the essential act of questioning. His mode of inquiry becomes his mode of life, and implicitly he projects a certain style of being in the world. Here we return to a central problem posed in the Introduction—the paradoxical relationship between universals and particulars when those terms are understood in the context of social reality, when the particular individual philosophizing is in his concrete act fulfilling a universal meaning. And here as well the reader can begin to see the existential character of Merleau-Ponty's position. In calling for a reunion of philosophy and sociology, he is actually searching for the point of connection between the social scientist and the philosopher as agents of a conceptual-historical process in which their fundamental commitments are defined. At the same time, that process is phenomenologically conceived. What is the bond between Husserl and the existentialists? For an answer to this very difficult question we must substitute a scrap of reply.

There are two dimensions in Husserlian phenomenology, it might be suggested. One of them involves the idea of a rigorous discipline in which the fundamental terms of all discourse are to be given an absolute clarification by tracing their meaning back to the grounds of their constitution in consciousness. The other concerns a radically fresh way of seeing reality, a turning directly toward phenomena in the first flush of their perceptual innocence, and a complex willingness to confront a world and oneself in a world delivered from the philosophical safeguards of common sense and the dicta of natural science. Such a turn is indeed toward that life-world we discussed earlier. The phenomenologist's recovery of the *Lebenswelt* as a root theme for inquiry is itself an existential achievement. It is this combination of discipline and liberation that is reflected in the writings of Merleau-Ponty. Perhaps more than any of the existentialists his writings bear the imprint of Husserl's double heritage. The implications of that heritage for the philosophy of the social sciences come into sharpest view in regard to the problem of value. As a phenomenologically oriented existentialist Merleau-Ponty argues for that form of reunion between philosophers and sociologists in which both aspects of Husserl's legacy will find fulfillment: philosophy is both a critical instrument which clarifies concepts and an existential commitment to there being value in the world. Or more precisely, the philosopher is the agent who realizes these possibilities in his historical existence.

It is interesting to compare Merleau-Ponty's insistence on reunion in terms of both analysis and commitment with Ayer's divorce between the two. Where Merleau-Ponty's man faces the philosophic implications of his existential involvement, Ayer's man has done his professional task "when he has made the issues clear." As *Homo philosophicus*, Merleau-Ponty begins where Ayer, as a philosopher, leaves off. The fragmentation so deeply felt by the one is taken with good cheer by the other. That "the question how men ought to live is one to which there is no authoritative answer" and has "to be decided by each man for himself" is a source of anguish for the existentialist, a matter of good breeding for the positivist. Here at last the advocates of the *Weltanschauungen* stand revealed. Whether the reunion of philosophy and science can ever have the same meaning to both is doubtful, but perhaps the antagonists might be willing to have a fresh voice from a different quarter have the last word for the moment. Paul Henle wrote:

> Philosophy has been called the mother of the sciences including of course the social sciences, but the identity of their father is never mentioned. Rather than let such aspersions on their character stand, it is perhaps well to point out that they were born, as with the simplest animals, by fission. Philosophy developed two—or more—nuclei and the connection between them grew more and more tenuous till finally

with a violent effort they pulled apart. The impetus of that effort carried them far from each other but now that it is spent one may hope that they may turn toward each other and—to vary the figure—like the lovers whom Plato makes Aristophanes describe in the *Symposium* rush into each other's arms.

The Claims of Philosophy[1]

A. J. AYER

I

CONTEMPORARY PHILOSOPHERS may be divided into two classes: the pontiffs and the journeymen. As the names that I have chosen indicate, the basis of this division is not so much a difference of opinion as a difference of attitude. It is not merely that the journeyman denies certain propositions which the pontiff asserts, or that he asserts certain propositions which the pontiff denies. It is rather that he has a radically different conception of the method of philosophy and of the ends that it is fitted to achieve. Thus, it is characteristic of those whom I describe as pontiffs that they think it within the province of philosophy to compete with natural science. They may, indeed, be willing to admit that the scientist achieves valuable results in his own domain, but they insist that he does not, and cannot, attain to the complete and final truth about reality; and they think that it is open to the philosopher to make this deficiency good. In support of this view, they

[1] This article appeared originally in *Polemic* (March 1947, No. 7, pp. 18–33), and is reprinted in *Reflections on Our Age: Lectures Delivered at the Opening Session of UNESCO at the Sorbonne University, Paris*, intro. by David Hardman, foreword by Stephen Spender, London: Allan Wingate, 1948, pp. 51–66. It is reprinted here with the permission of UNESCO and with the approval of the author.

may, for example, argue that every scientific theory is based upon presuppositions which cannot themselves be scientifically proved; ✓ and from this they may infer, in the interests of their own "philosophical" brand of irrationality, that science itself is fundamentally irrational; or else they may have recourse to metaphysics to supply the missing proof. Alternatively, they may hold that the scientist deals only with the appearances of things, whereas the philosopher by the use of his special methods penetrates to the reality beyond. In general, the ideal of the pontiff is to construct a metaphysical system. Such a system may actually include some scientific hypotheses, either as premises or, more fre- ✓ quently, as deductions from metaphysical first principles. It may, on the other hand, be uncompromisingly metaphysical. In either case, the aim is to give a complete and definitive account of "ultimate" reality.

Unfortunately, as the journeymen on their side have been at pains to show, this "ultimate" reality is a fiction, and the ideal of a metaphysical system that is anything other than a scientific encyclopaedia is devoid of any basis in reason. To some extent, indeed, this fact has been borne in upon the pontiffs, and the result is that they now tend to desert reason and even to decry it. This separates them sharply from their philosophical ancestors, who at least professed to reason, even if they did not always reason well. Few men, indeed, can ever have reasoned worse than Hegel, the arch-pontiff of the nineteenth century, but at least he claimed the support of reason for his fantasies. His ground for thinking that a mobile logic is needed to describe a mobile world may have been no better than the principle that "who drives fat oxen must himself be fat"; but at least, if he rejected the "static" Aristotelian logic, he did so in favour of what he, no doubt mistakenly, believed to be a superior logic of his own. Though he misused logic abominably, he did not affect to be above it. But now if we turn to Heidegger, the high priest of the modern school of existentialists, and the leading pontiff of our times, we find ourselves in a country from which the ordinary processes of logic, or indeed reasoning of any kind, appear to have been banished. For what we learn from him is that it is only in the clear light of Nothing that Being has being, and consequently that it is the supreme privilege of the philosopher to concern himself with Nothing.[2] For this he requires no special intellectual discipline. It is sufficient that he experiences anguish, provided always that it is an anguish without any special object. For it is thus, according to Heidegger, that the Nothing reveals itself. This strange thesis is indeed backed by a pretence of argument, but since the argument depends upon the elementary fallacy of treating "nothing" as a name, it is hardly to be taken seriously. Nor does Heidegger himself appear to attach very much weight to it. For it is not by logic that he seeks to convince: nor is his the Socratic method of following an argument wherever it may lead. Like the sermons of Dr. Dodd,[3] his work is addressed to the passions; and it is no doubt for this reason that it has succeeded in becoming fashionable.

Now just as William James thought that all prigs must sooner or later end by becoming Hegelians, so it seems to me that the fate of the contemporary pontiff must be to go the way of Heidegger. I do not mean by this that he will have to subscribe to Heidegger's doctrines. There are other types of "deeply significant nonsense" available. But inasmuch as his quest for ultimate reality cannot be made to prosper by any rational means, he is likely, if he adheres to it, to seek some non-rational source of enlightenment. At this point he devolves into a mystic or a poet. As such he may express an attitude to life which is interesting in itself and even a source of inspiration to others; and perhaps it would be churlish to refuse him the title of philosopher. But it is to be remarked that when philosophy has been brought to this stage then, whatever its emotional value, it has ceased to be, in any ordinary sense, a vehicle of knowledge.

II

The history of philosophy, as it is taught in the text-books, is largely a parade of pontiffs; and it might be thought that the only course open to the budding philosopher was either to enrol himself under one of their banners, or else to try to become a

2 See M. Heidegger, *Was ist Metaphysik?*

3 See Boswell's *Life of Johnson*: "A clergyman (whose name I do not recollect): 'Were not Dodd's sermons addressed to the passions?' Johnson: 'They were nothing, sir, be they addressed to what they may.'" III, 248.

pontiff in his own right. But in this, as in so many other cases, the text-books are behind the times. For, at least in England and America, the philosophical scene has been dominated for the last fifty years, not by the pontiffs, but by those whom I describe as journeymen. Unlike the pontiffs, the journeymen do not set out in quest of ultimate reality. Nor do they try to bring philosophy into competition with the natural sciences. Believing, as they do, that the only way to discover what the world is like is to form hypotheses and test them by observation, which is in fact the method of science, they are content to leave the scientist in full possession of the field of speculative knowledge. Consequently they do not try to build systems. The task of the philosopher, as they see it, is rather to deal piecemeal with a special set of problems. Some of these problems are historical, in the sense that they involve the criticism and interpretation of the work of previous philosophers; others are primarily mathematical, as belonging to the specialized field of formal logic; others again are set by the sciences: they involve the analysis of scientific method, the evaluation of scientific theories, the clarification of scientific terms. It is, for example, a philosophical problem to decide what is meant by "probability": and the journeymen have already contributed much towards its solution. Finally, there are a number of problems, such as the problem of perception, the problem of our knowledge of other minds, the question of the significance of moral judgments, that arise out of the common usages and assumptions of everyday life. In a broad sense, all these problems are semantic: that is to say, they can all be represented as concerned with the use of language. But since the term "semantics" is technically applied to a particular formal discipline which does not, even for the journeymen, comprehend the whole of philosophy, I think it better to resume their philosophical activities under the general heading of logical analysis.

Essentially, the journeymen are technicians; and from this point of view the comparison with the pontiffs is very much to their advantage. They suffer, however, from a certain thinness of material. Consider, for example, the so-called philosophers of common-sense, who follow the distinguished leadership of Professor G. E. Moore. In the opinion of this school, it is not sensible for a philosopher to question the truth of such common-sense statements as that this is a sheet of paper or that I am wearing shoes on my feet. And if anyone were to question it they would reply simply that, on the relevant occasions, they knew for certain that statements of this sort were true. Thus, Professor Moore himself has proved, to his own satisfaction, the existence of external objects, a question much canvassed by philosophers, by the simple method of holding up his hands and saying that he knows for certain that they exist,[4] and indeed there is no denying that in its way this is a valid proof. At the same time these philosophers confess to being very doubtful of the correct analysis of the common-sense propositions which they know to be true. The question whether or not this really is a sheet of paper does not puzzle them at all; but the question of what precisely is implied by saying that it is puzzles them a great deal. In technical language, it is a matter of discovering the relationship between the sense-data which are immediately experienced and the physical objects which it is their function to present; and this is a problem which, in the opinion of our common-sense philosophers, has not yet been satisfactorily solved. Now I do not wish to suggest that this is not a difficult problem, or to belittle the ingenuity with which the journeymen have tackled it. But I am afraid that a layman who was told that a question of this sort was of sufficient interest to a modern philosopher to occupy him for a lifetime would be inclined to think that modern philosophy was degenerating into scholasticism. If he were told, as he might be by a pontiff, that there was serious doubt of the existence of this piece of paper he would be very properly incredulous, but he might also be impressed: he might even be brought to think that he himself had been excessively naïve in taking such a thing for granted. But once he had been assured that the truth of his common-sense assumption that the paper existed was not after all in doubt, I think it would be difficult to interest him in a meticulous analysis of its implications. He would remark that he understood very well what he meant by saying that this was a piece of paper, and that he did not see what was to be gained by a laborious attempt at further clarification. To this it could, indeed, be objected that he might think very differently if he had been

[4] See his "Proof of an External World," *Proceedings of the British Academy*, XXV, 1939, 273-300.

properly educated in philosophy; and that in any case there is no reason why the layman's judgments of value should be binding upon the philosopher. But even so it is difficult not to feel some sympathy for our layman. It is difficult not to suspect that the philosopher of common-sense must sometimes be inclined to say to himself what the poet Clough said when he found himself exclusively engaged in doing up parcels for Florence Nightingale: "This that I see is not all, and this that I do is but little. It is good but there is better than it."

Another prominent set of journeymen are the followers of Ludwig Wittgenstein, who has succeeded G. E. Moore as professor of philosophy at the University of Cambridge. More than twenty years ago, Professor Wittgenstein came to the conclusion, at the end of his remarkable *Tractatus Logico-Philosophicus*, that "the right method of philosophy would be this." "To say nothing except what can be said, i.e. the propositions of natural science, i.e. something that has nothing to do with philosophy: and then always when someone wished to say something metaphysical, to demonstrate to him that he had given no meaning to certain signs in his proposition. This method would be unsatisfying to the other—he would not have the impression that he was learning philosophy—but it would be the only strictly correct method." In other words, the philosopher is reduced, or elevated, to the position of a park keeper whose business it is to see that no one commits an intellectual nuisance; the nuisance in question being that of lapsing into metaphysics. I do not know whether Wittgenstein is still of this opinion; and even if his point of view has remained substantially the same I doubt if he would now express it in such terms as I have quoted. But what I do know is that the effect of his teaching upon his more articulate disciples has been that they tend to treat philosophy as a department of psychoanalysis. In their eyes, the *raison d'être* of the philosopher is the fact that people continually get themselves into states of metaphysical doubt. They are inclined to say, for example, that they can never really be sure of the existence of the material world, or that they can never really know what goes on in another person's mind, or even, more seriously, that he has a mind. Now these, according to the Wittgensteinians, are intellectually neurotic doubts; and it is the business of the philosopher to effect their cure. Admittedly, the people who feel them are usually those who have studied some philosophy: but equally the psycho-analyst finds his most profitable patients among those who have delved a little into psycho-analysis. In both cases, the method of cure is to enter sympathetically into the patient's neurosis and try to talk it out. As Mr. Wisdom puts it,[5] "the treatment is like psycho-analytic treatment in that the treatment is the diagnosis and the diagnosis is the description, the very full description, of the symptoms." That the description is full will hardly be denied by anyone who has read Mr. Wisdom. Whether it is effective is perhaps more doubtful; but, in his hands at any rate, it is a work of fascinating subtlety. Nevertheless one is again tempted to ask: "Is this all that the philosopher is fitted to achieve?"

Not all the contemporary philosophers whom I should classify as journeymen hold the views that I have quoted; but I think it can fairly be said that in the case of nearly all of them there is an unfortunate disparity between the richness of their technique and the increasing poverty of the material on which they are able to exercise it. The principal exceptions are those who, like Bertrand Russell and Professor Whitehead, at least in the days before he became a pontiff, combine a mastery of logic with an understanding of mathematics and natural science. And this suggests that the salvation of the journeymen may be the re-union of philosophy with science, just as the final resource of the pontiff is the passage of philosophy into mysticism, or at least into imaginative literature. In the meantime, however, there re-main a number of logical puzzles which the journeyman, who is relatively ignorant of science, may reasonably feel called upon to solve. The importance of his work may not indeed be immedi-ately obvious to the layman; and there may be times when the philosopher himself is reduced to wishing that the field of his achievement were rather more spectacular; but he may perhaps console himself with the words of John Locke that "it is ambi-tion enough to be employed as an under-labourer in clearing the ground a little, and removing some of the rubbish that lies in the way to knowledge."[6]

[5] In the first of his series of articles on "Other Minds," *Mind*, XLIX, 1940, 370.
[6] See *An Essay Concerning Human Understanding*, Epistle to the Reader.

III

On the side of the pontiffs, imaginative literature. On the side of the journeymen, the re-integration of philosophy with science, or the piecemeal solution of logical or linguistic puzzles. Surely, it will be said, this is not what the public expects of its philosophers. Surely, the business of the philosopher is to make clear the meaning of life, to show people how they ought to live. Call him a pontiff or a journeyman, according to his method of approach; the distinction is not of any great importance. What is important is the message that he has to give. It is wisdom that is needed, not merely scientific knowledge. Of what use to us is the understanding of nature if we do not know the purpose of our existence or how we ought to live? And who is to answer these supremely important questions if not the philosopher?

The reply to this is that there is no true answer to these questions; and since this is so it is no use expecting even the philosopher to provide one. What can be done, however, is to make clear why, and in what sense, these questions are unanswerable; and once this is achieved it will be seen that there is also a sense in which they can be answered. It will be found that the form of answer is not a proposition, which must be either true or false, but the adoption of a rule, which cannot properly be characterized as either true or false, but can nevertheless be judged as more or less acceptable. And with this the problem is solved, so far as reasoning can solve it. The rest is a matter of personal decision, and ultimately of action.

Let us begin then by considering the purpose of our existence. How is it possible for our existence to have a purpose? We know very well what it is for a man to have a purpose. It is a matter of his intending, on the basis of a given situation, to bring about some further situation, which for some reason or other he conceives to be desirable. And in that case it may be said that events have a meaning for him according as they conduce, or fail to conduce, towards the end that he desires. But how can life in general be said to have any meaning? A simple answer is that all events are tending towards a certain specifiable end: so that to understand the meaning of life it is necessary only to discover this end. But, in the first place, there is no good reason whatever for supposing this assumption to be true, and secondly, even if it were true, it would not do the work that is required of it. For what is being sought by those who demand to know the meaning of life is not an explanation of the facts of their existence, but a justification. Consequently a theory which informs them merely that the course of events is so arranged as to lead inevitably to a certain end does nothing to meet their need. For the end in question will not be one that they themselves have chosen. As far as they are concerned it will be entirely arbitrary; and it will be a no less arbitrary fact that their existence is such as necessarily to lead to its fulfilment. In short, from the point of view of justifying one's existence, there is no essential difference between a teleological explanation of events and a mechanical explanation. In either case, it is a matter of brute fact that events succeed one another in the ways that they do and are explicable in the ways that they are. And indeed what is called an explanation is nothing other than a more general description. Thus, an attempt to answer the question why events are as they are must always resolve itself into saying only how they are. But what is required by those who seek the meaning of life is precisely an answer to their question "Why?" that is something other than an answer to any question "How?" And just because this is so they can never legitimately be satisfied.

But now, it may be objected, suppose that the world is designed by a superior being. In that case the purpose of our existence will be the purpose that it realizes for him; and the meaning of life will be found in our conscious adaptation to his purpose. But here again, the answer is, first, that there is no good reason whatsoever for believing that there is any such superior being; and, secondly, that even if there were, he could not accomplish what is here required of him. For let us assume, for the sake of argument, that everything happens as it does because a superior being has intended that it should. As far as we are concerned, the course of events still remains entirely arbitrary. True, it can now be said to fulfil a purpose; but the purpose is not ours. And just as, on the previous assumption, it merely happened to be the case that the course of events conduced to the end that it did, so, on this assumption, it merely happens to be the case that the deity has

the purpose that he has, and not some other purpose, or no purpose at all. Nor does this unwarrantable assumption provide us
even with a rule of life. For even those who believe most firmly
that the world was designed by a superior being are not in a
position to tell us what his purpose can have been. They may
indeed claim that it has been mysteriously revealed to them, but
how can it be proved that the revelation is genuine? And even if
we waive this objection, even if we assume not only the world
as we find it is working out the purpose of a superior being, but
also that we are capable of discovering what this purpose is, we
are still not provided with a rule of life. For either his purpose
is sovereign or it is not. If it is sovereign, that is, if everything
that happens is necessarily in accordance with it, then this is true
also of our behavior. Consequently, there is no point in our deciding to conform to it, for the simple reason that we cannot do
otherwise. However we behave, we shall fulfil the purpose of
this deity; and if we were to behave differently, we should still
be fulfilling it; for if it were possible for us not to fulfil it it
would not be sovereign in the requisite sense. But suppose that it
is not sovereign, or, in other words, that not all events must
necessarily bear it out. In that case, there is no reason why we
should try to conform to it, unless we independently judge it to
be good. But that means that the significance of our behavior
depends finally upon our own judgments of value; and the con-
currence of a deity then becomes superfluous.

The point is, in short, that even the invocation of a deity does
not enable us to answer the question why things are as they are.
At the best it complicates the answer to the question how they
are by pushing the level of explanation to a further stage. For
even if the ways of the deity were clear to those who believed
in him, which they apparently are not, it would still be, even
to them, a matter of brute fact that he behaved as he did, just as
to those who do not believe in him it is a matter of brute fact
that the world is what it is. In either case the question "Why?"
remains unanswered, for the very good reason that it is unanswerable. That is to say, it may be answerable at any given
level, but the answer is always a matter of describing at a higher
level not why things are as they are, but simply how they are.
And so, to whatever level our explanations may be carried, the

final statement is never an answer to the question "Why?" but necessarily only an answer to the question "How?"

It follows, if my argument is correct, that there is no sense in asking what is the ultimate purpose of our existence, or what is the real meaning of life. For to ask this is to assume that there can be a reason for our living as we do which is somehow more profound than any mere explanation of the facts; and we have seen that this assumption is untenable. Moreover it is untenable in logic and not merely in fact. The position is not that our existence unfortunately lacks a purpose which, if the fates had been kinder, it might conceivably have had. It is rather that those who inquire, in this way, after the meaning of life are raising a question to which it is not logically possible that there should be an answer. Consequently, the fact that they are disappointed is not, as some romanticists would make it, an occasion for cynicism or despair. It is not an occasion for any emotional attitude at all. And the reason why it is not is just that it could not conceivably have been otherwise. If it were logically possible for our existence to have a purpose, in the sense required, then it might be sensible to lament the fact that it had none. But it is not sensible to cry for what is logically impossible. If a question is so framed as to be unanswerable, then it is not a matter for regret that it remains unanswered. It is, therefore, misleading to say that life has no meaning; for that suggests that the statement that life has a meaning is factually significant, but false; whereas the truth is that, in the sense in which it is taken in this context, it is not factually significant.

There is, however, a sense in which it can be said that life does have a meaning. It has for each of us whatever meaning we severally choose to give it. The purpose of a man's existence is constituted by the ends to which he, consciously or unconsciously, devotes himself. Some men have a single overriding purpose to which all their activities are subordinated. If they are at all successful in achieving it, they are probably the happiest, but they are the exceptions. Most men pass from one object to another; and at any one time they may pursue a number of different ends, which may or may not be capable of being harmonized. Philosophers, with a preference for tidiness, have sometimes tried to show that all these apparently diverse objects

can really be reduced to one: but the fact is that there is no
end that is common to all men, not even happiness. For setting
aside the question whether men ought always to pursue happiness,
it is not true even that they always do pursue it, unless the word
"happiness" is used merely as a description of any end that is in
fact pursued. Thus the question what is the meaning of life
proves, when it is taken empirically, to be incomplete. For there
is no single thing of which it can truly be said that this is the
meaning of life. All that can be said is that life has at various
times a different meaning for different people, according as they
pursue their several ends.

That different people have different purposes is an empirical
matter of fact. But what is required by those who seek to know
the purpose of their existence is not a factual description of the
way that people actually do conduct themselves, but rather a
decision as to how they should conduct themselves. Having been
taught to believe that not all purposes are of equal value, they
require to be guided in their choice. And thus the inquiry into
the purpose of our existence dissolves into the question "How
ought men to live?"

IV

The question how ought men to live is one that would
seem to fall within the province of moral philosophy; but it
cannot be said of every moral philosopher that he makes a serious
attempt to answer it. Moreover, those who do make a serious
attempt to answer it are mostly pontiffs, who approach it
wrongly. For having decided, on metaphysical grounds, that
reality is of such and such a character they try to deduce from
this the superiority of a certain rule of life. But, quite apart from
the merits or demerits of their metaphysics, it is a mistake on
their part to suppose that a mere description of reality is sufficient
to establish any rule of life at all. A familiar instance of this
mistake is the claim that men ought to live in such and such a
way because such and such is their real nature. But if what is
meant by their having such and such a real nature is that they
really are of the nature in question, then all that can possibly be
established is that they really do behave in the manner indicated.

For if they behaved differently, they would thereby show that they had a different nature. Thus in telling men that they ought to live in accordance with their real nature you are telling them to do what they do; and your pretended rule of life dissolves into nothing, since it is equally consistent with any course of conduct whatsoever. If, on the other hand, what is meant by a man's real nature is not the nature that he actually displays but the nature that he ought to display, then the moral rule that the argument is supposed to justify is assumed at the outset, and assumed without proof. As a moral rule, it may be acceptable in itself; but the supposed deduction of it from a non-moral premiss turns out inevitably to be a fraud.

It is not only metaphysicians who commit this fallacy. There is, for example, a brand of "scientific ethics" according to which the right rule of life is that which harmonizes with the course of human evolution. But here again the same ambiguity arises. For if "the course of human evolution" is understood as an actually existent process, then there is no sense in telling people that they ought to adapt themselves to it, for the very good reason that they cannot possibly do otherwise. However they may behave they will be acting rightly, since it is just their behaving as they do that makes the course of evolution what it is. In short, if progress is defined in terms of merely historical development, all conduct is progressive; for every human action necessarily furthers the course of evolution, in the straightforward sense of adding to its history. If on the other hand, it is only some among the many possible developments of human history that are considered to be progressive, then there is some sense in saying that we ought to strive to bring them about; but here again the moral rule which we are invited to adopt is not deduced but simply posited. It is neither itself a scientific statement of fact, nor a logical consequence of any such statement. By scientific methods we can indeed discover that certain events are more or less likely to occur; but the transition from this to deciding that some of these possible developments are more valuable than others carries us outside the domain of science altogether. In saying this, I do not wish to repudiate the humanistic values of those who put forward the claims of scientific ethics, or even to suggest that any other system of values is more securely founded. My objection to these moralists is simply that they fall into the logical error of confusing normative judgments of value with scientific statements of fact. They may have the advantage of the metaphysicians, in that their factual premises are more deserving of belief, but the fundamental mistake of trying to extract normative rules from supposedly factual descriptions is common to them both.

In moral, as in natural, philosophy it is characteristic of the journeymen to have detected the flaw in the method of the pontiffs, but here also they have purchased their freedom from error at the price of a certain aridity. For not only do they not attempt to prove their judgments of value; for the most part they refrain from expressing them at all. What they do instead, apart from criticizing other moral philosophers, is to subject the terminology of ethics to logical analysis. Thus the questions that they discuss are whether the term "good" or the term "right" is to be taken as fundamental, and whether either is definable; whether it is a man's duty to do an action or merely to set himself to do it; whether his duty is to do what is objectively right or merely what he thinks to be right; whether the rightness of an action depends upon its actual consequences, or upon its probable consequences, or upon its consequences as foreseen by the agent, or not upon its consequences at all; whether it is possible to fulfil an obligation unintentionally; whether the moral goodness of an action depends upon its motive; and many other questions of a similar sort. Such questions can be interesting, though they are not always made so, and I do not wish to say that they are not important; but to the practical man they must appear somewhat academic. By taking a course in this kind of moral philosophy a man may learn how to make the expression of his moral judgments secure from formal criticism. What he will not learn is what, in any concrete situation, he actually ought to do.

I think, then, that it can fairly be made a reproach to the journeymen that they have overlooked the Aristotelian principle that the end of moral philosophy is "not knowledge but action."[7] But their excuse is that once the philosopher who wishes to be practical has said this, there is very little more that he can say.

[7] See *Nicomachean Ethics*, Book I, Section 3.

Like anyone else, he can make moral recommendations, but he cannot legitimately claim for them the sanction of philosophy. He cannot prove that his judgments of value are correct, for the sufficient reason that no judgment of value is capable of proof. Or rather, if it is capable of proof, it is only by reference to some other judgment of value, which must itself be left unproved. The moral philosopher can sometimes affect men's conduct by drawing their attention to certain matters of fact; he may show, for example, that certain sorts of action have unsuspected consequences, or that the motives for which they are done are different from what they appear to be; and he may then hope that when his audience is fully aware of the circumstances it will assess the situation in the same way as he does himself. Nevertheless there may be some who differ from him, not on any question of fact, but on a question of value, and in that case he has no way of demonstrating that his judgment is superior. He lays down one rule, and they lay down another; and the decision between them is a subject for persuasion and finally a matter of individual choice.

Since judgments of value are not reducible to statements of fact, they are strictly speaking neither true nor false; and it is tempting to infer from this that no course of conduct is better or worse than any other. But this would be a mistake. For the judgment that no course of conduct is better or worse than any other is itself a judgment of value and consequently neither true nor false. And while an attitude of moral indifference is legitimate in itself, it is not easily maintained. For since we are constantly faced with the practical necessity of action, it is natural for most of us to act in accordance with certain principles; and the choice of principles implies the adoption of a positive set of values. That these values should be consistent is a necessary condition of their being fully realized; for it is logically impossible to achieve the complete fulfilment of an inconsistent set of ends. But, once their consistency is established, they can be criticized only on practical grounds, and from the standpoint of the critic's own moral system, which his adversary may or may not accept. No doubt, in practice, many people are content to follow the model rules that are prescribed to them by others; but the decision to submit oneself to authority on such a point is itself a judgment of value. In the last resort, therefore, each individual has the responsibility of choice; and it is a responsibility that is not to be escaped.

V

The same considerations apply to the philosophy of politics. That moral and political philosophy are intimately connected is fairly widely recognized; but the nature of their connection is still a subject of dispute. Thus some philosophers believe that morals can be logically subordinated to politics. They think that if they can establish the proper forms of political association they will be able to deduce from this how men ought to live. But, as we shall see, it is the opposite that is true. A political system may take one form or another; and, in any actual case, there will usually be an historical explanation of its taking the form that it does. But even if its existence can be historically accounted for, there still remains the question whether it is worthy of allegiance. Political institutions are not sacrosanct. It may, in certain circumstances, be beyond the power of a given individual to change them, but it does not follow that he is bound to think them good. That they are what they are is an unmistakable fact, but it does not follow that they are what they ought to be. And the question what they ought to be is ultimately a moral question. It is for the individual to answer it in accordance with the values that he himself adopts.

The confusion of fact with value, which we have seen to be a feature of certain moral systems, is equally a pitfall to political philosophers. Thus Plato seems, in his *Republic*, to look upon his ideal city-state as the unique embodiment of the reality of "justice"; and he seems even to suggest that in depicting the structure of this political community he has answered the moral question how men ought to live. But what he does not appear to have seen is that to assert that true, or real, justice is to be found in such and such a set of institutions is not to make a statement of fact at all, but rather to lay down a standard. It is not a way of describing the institutions in question, but of making a certain claim for them; and the claim is that they ought to be adopted. It may be objected that what is claimed is not merely that they ought to be adopted, but that they ought to be adopted because they are truly just. But the point is that to say that they are truly just is, in this usage, no more than another way of saying that they ought to be adopted: the one statement is not, as it is made to seem, a justification of the other, but simply a repetition of it. Thus, if anyone thinks, as he well may, that Plato's institutions are not the best possible, he may devise a different Utopia; and he too may seek to recommend it by saying that it alone fulfils the true conditions of justice. In saying this he will be disagreeing with Plato, but he will not be formally contradicting him: for neither party is making a statement of fact. What makes this easy to overlook is the occurrence in such a context of words like "true" or "real": for it is assumed that they are being given their ordinary descriptive use. But, in fact, their use in these contexts is not descriptive but persuasive. They serve only to put a little halo round the principles that the speaker wishes to recommend. Accordingly, the question whether one or other of two divergent political systems has the better claim to be considered just, is a question, not of truth or falsehood, in the ordinary sense, but of deciding where to give one's allegiance: and the answer to it will depend upon the system of values of the person who is called upon to judge. Thus, so far from its being the case, as Plato seems to have thought, that the choice of political institutions can determine how men ought to live, it is a previous conception of the way men ought to live that determines the value of the institutions themselves.

For Hegel, the perfect embodiment of justice was not an ideal republic but the contemporary Prussian State: and he based this illiberal view upon the principle that the real was the rational. But this convenient principle turned out to be two-edged. For while it was used by conservatives to prove that whatever happened to exist was best, it occurred to some followers of Hegel to argue that since the contemporary Prussian State was palpably irrational it was not wholly real; and they then conceived it to be their duty to try to put something more real in its place. In so doing they performed a political service: but they also unconsciously rendered a service to logic. For their inversion of Hegel's principle helps us to see how wretchedly ambiguous it is.

Thus, if the word "real" is used to mean "existent" and the word "rational" is used, as Hegel seems to have intended, to mean what is in accordance with logic, it will be necessarily true that everything that is real is rational; for what is logically impossible cannot exist. On the other hand, it will not be true that everything that is rational is real; for many states of affairs that do not exist are logically possible. The word "rational," however, can also be used, and is indeed most commonly used, as a term of value. As applied to a political system, it serves to claim that the system is such as to bring about the ends of which the speaker approves; and it carries the implication that the ends in question are such as any reasonable man would share. But if the word "rational" is used in this sense, the statement that the real is the rational is by no means necessarily true. For, whatever may be the set of values that is ascribed to the reasonable man, it is an open question whether they are satisfied. Assuredly much that exists will not come up to them, and very likely nothing exists that does. But, thirdly, the word "real" may itself be used as a term of values; and in that case the principle that the real is the rational becomes entirely verbal. It merely expresses the speaker's intention to use the words "real" and "rational" as equivalent terms of approbation. Thus in the sense in which it is true the principle is trivial, and in the sense in which it is not trivial it is not necessarily true.

The merit of this example is that it again brings out the point that, in politics as in morals, the fact that something is what it is does not by any means entail that it is what it ought to be; nor does the fact that something is considered valuable by any means entail that it exists. Within the domain of fact, the study of politics can yield us fruitful hypotheses about the ways in which political institutions develop. It can enable us to assess the probability that from a given set of circumstances a given situation will result. But over and above this, there remains the question what it is that we desire to bring about. Thus, when Marx said "Philosophers have previously offered various interpretations of the world. Our business is to change it,"[8] he was making a judgment of value. He was implying that the existing state of affairs was not what it ought to be, and consequently

8 See his *Eleven Theses on Feuerbach*.

that it ought to be changed. He himself, indeed, might not have admitted this, because of his historical determinism. He might have replied that in saying it was "our business" to change the world, he was merely calling upon his contemporaries to fulfil their necessary historical role. But if their role was really determined for them, then they were bound to fulfil it, and there was no sense in urging them to do so. The call to arms was needed to bring about something that Marx wished to happen; it was designed to influence events, not merely to encumber fate with help. That the future will be what it will be is indeed an analytic truth: but it does not prevent its also being true that the future will be what we make it. What changes are possible at any given moment is a subject for scientific inquiry; but the decision, which we then have to make, that one or other of these changes is the most desirable is not itself a scientific hypothesis but a judgment of value. It represents a moral choice.

No more than the scientist is the philosopher specially privileged to lay down the rules of conduct, or to prescribe an ideal form of life. If he has strong opinions on these points, and wishes to convert others to them, his philosophical training may give him a certain advantage in putting them persuasively: but, whether or not the values that he recommends are found to be acceptable, it is not from his philosophy that they can derive their title to acceptance. His professional task is done when he has made the issues clear. For in morals and in politics, at the stage where politics become a matter of morals, there is no repository of truth to which only the learned few have access. The question how men ought to live is one to which there is no authoritative answer. It has to be decided by each man for himself.

The Philosopher and Sociology[1]

MAURICE MERLEAU-PONTY

:::

PHILOSOPHY AND SOCIOLOGY have long lived separate lives, a state of affairs which succeeded in hiding their rivalry only by denying them any common ground, by hampering their growth, by rendering one incomprehensible to the other, by thus placing culture in a situation of permanent crisis. As always, the spirit of research has eluded these restrictions, and it seems to us that, today, the progress of both permits a reexamination of their relationships.

We should also like to call attention to Husserl's reflections upon these problems. Husserl seems to us exemplary in having felt, perhaps more profoundly than any other, that all the forms of thought are in a certain sense interdependent, that one has not to raze the science of man in order to lay the foundations of philosophy nor to raze philosophy in order to lay the foundations of the sciences of man, that any science secretes an ontology and that any ontology anticipates a knowing, and, finally, that

[1] Translated from the French by Harvey G. Rabbin. The original article, "Le Philosophe et la sociologie," appeared in *Cahiers internationaux de sociologie* (Vol. X, 1951, pp. 55–69), and is reprinted in Maurice Merleau-Ponty, *Signes*, Paris: Gallimard, 1960, pp. 123–142. The 1960 text has been used for translation. Permission to publish this article has been granted by Northwestern University Press, which plans to bring out a translation of *Signes* to be done by Richard C. McCleary.

it is up to us to adjust ourselves to this and see to it that philosophy and science are both possible.

Nowhere, perhaps, has the separation of philosophy and sociology been worded in the terms in which we are going to state it. Fortunately the labors of philosophers and sociologists are often less exclusive than their principles. But this separation is none the less part of a certain common sense understanding of philosophers and sociologists, who, reducing philosophy and the sciences of man to what they believe to be their pure type, finally endanger knowledge just as much as reflection.

While all great philosophers can be recognized by their effort to reflect upon the mind *and its dependence*—ideas and their movement, the understanding and the senses—there is a myth about philosophy which presents it as the authoritarian affirmation of the mind's absolute independence. Philosophy is no longer a questioning. It is a certain body of doctrines made to assure an absolutely *unattached* mind of its autonomy and that of its ideas. On the other hand, there is a myth of scientific knowledge which expects that from the mere notation of facts there should arise not only a science of worldly things, but in addition the science of that science, a sociology of knowledge (itself understood in an empirical manner), a knowledge having to constitute a closed universe of facts, and inserting therein everything down to the ideas we invent to interpret them, and to get rid, so to speak, of ourselves. These two myths, though antagonistic, are complementary. Philosopher and sociologist, thus opposed, agree at least upon the delimitation of frontiers, which assures them of never encountering one another. But if this quarantine were to be lifted, philosophy and sociology would mutually destroy each other. Already they are fighting for the possession of men's minds. The separation is cold war.

Any investigation wishing to take both ideas and facts into account is, in this atmosphere, immediately split in two. The facts, instead of being understood as stimulants and warrants of an effort of construction that joins their internal dynamic, are rather considered as some favor of the On-High, unique source of our salvation, while the ideas are exempted in principle from all confrontation with our experience of the world, of fellow-men and of ourselves. The movement back and forth from facts

to ideas and from ideas to facts is discredited as a bastard procedure—neither science nor philosophy; it denies the scientists a
final interpretation of the facts which they themselves, after all,
have gathered, and compromises philosophy with the ever-
provisional results of scientific research.

One must clearly see the *obscurantist* consequences of this
rigorism. If "mixed" investigations have indeed the inconveniences
just mentioned, then that amounts to recognizing that philosophical and scientific perspectives are incompatible and that philosophy and sociology will only attain certainty in ignoring one
another. One must then hide from the scientist that "idealization"
of the brute fact which, however, is the essential part of his work.
He will have to ignore the decoding of significations which is
his *raison d'être*, the construction of intellectual models of the
real without which sociology would no more exist today than
Galilean physics would have existed formerly. The blinders of
Baconian or "Millian" induction will have to be put on him, even
if his own investigations bypass, as it would appear, these canonic
recipes. He will pretend to face the social world as if it were
alien to him, as if his study were not indebted to the experience
he has, as a social subject, of intersubjectivity; on the pretext
that sociology is not yet made of this subjective experience
(*expérience vécue*), that it is the analysis, exposition and objectification of it, that it overthrows our initial consciousness of social
relationships and makes those in which we live appear as a very
particular variant of a dynamic of which initially we had no
inkling, and of which we learn only in contact with other
cultural formation; on this pretext then, objectivism forgets that
other evident fact, namely, that we can expand our experience
of social relationships and form the idea of social relationships
that hold true only by analogy or by contrast to those we ourselves have experienced, in a word, by an *imaginative variation*
of the latter, with regard to which they will doubtlessly receive
a new significance—as the fall of a body on an inclined plane is
placed in a new light by the pure idea of free fall—but to which
they will furnish everything it can have of sociological meaning.
Anthropology teaches us that in a particular kind of culture
children treat certain of their cousins as "parents," and this type
of fact permits us finally to draw a diagram of the family system

in the civilization under consideration. But the correlations thus noted give only the silhouette or contour of family relationships in that civilization, a cross-section of behavior called "parental" by nominal definition at certain significant but still anonymous points X .., Y .., Z ..; in a word: the correlations do not yet have sociological meaning—and the formulae which summarize them could just as well represent this or that physical or chemical process of the same form—as long as we have not succeeded in placing ourselves within the institution thus circumscribed, understood the family style to which all these facts allude, understood *in what sense* certain subjects in that culture perceive other subjects of their generation as their "parents," and, finally, grasped the basic personal and interpersonal structure, the institutional relationships with nature and fellow-man which render the observed correlations possible. To repeat: the dynamic in depth of the social whole is certainly not *given* in our narrow experience of life in small groups, but it is only by displacing the latter from the center of focus and then centering it again that we succeed in imagining this dynamic, just as number in general is number for us only by the relation that joins it to the integral number of elementary arithmetic. We can, beginning with the Freudian conceptions of pregenital sexuality, catalogue all possible modes of emphasis on the child's bodily orifices, and in this inventory those which are realized in our cultural system and have been described by the Freudians are represented as particular variants among a great number of possibilities perhaps actualized in civilizations as yet unknown to us. But this inventory tells us *nothing* of the relationships with fellow-men and with nature that define those cultural types, as long as we do not refer to the psychological significance of the mouth, the anus, or the genital apparatus within our own experience, in order that we may see the different usage which different cultures make of them, different crystallizations of the initial polymorphism of the body as vehicle of being-in-the-world. The catalogue presented to us is merely an invitation to imagine other techniques of the body, starting from our own experience of it. The one which happens to be actualized in us is never reduced to the status of a simple possible among all others, since it is against the background of this privileged experience in which we become acquainted with the body as a "structurizing" principle that the other possibles, however different they may be from our experience of our body, come into relief. It is essential never to disassociate sociological research from our experience of social subjects (which comprises, of course, not only what we have felt by ourselves but also the behavior we perceive through the gestures, the tales and writings of other human beings), since the sociologist's equations only begin to represent something social when the correlations they summarize are joined one to another and enveloped in a certain unique *view* of the social and of nature proper to the society considered and when this view, though it may be quite different from the official conceptions currently held within the society, has become institutionalized as a clandestine principle of the entire manifest functioning. If objectivism or scientism ever succeeded in denying sociology recourse to significations, they would keep it free of "philosophy" only by closing its mind to its object. Then perhaps we would do mathematics in the social; we would not have the mathematics *of* the society under consideration. The sociologist does philosophy to the extent to which he is not merely charged with noting facts but with understanding them. At the time of interpretation he is himself already a philosopher. That is, the professional philosopher is not disqualified from the reinterpretation of facts he himself has not observed if these facts say something other than, or more than, what the scientist has seen in them. As Husserl says, it is not with phenomenology that the eidetic of the physical thing has begun, but with Galileo. And reciprocally, the philosopher has the right to read and interpret Galileo.

The separation we are combating is not less prejudicial to philosophy than to the development of knowledge. How should the philosopher, conscious of his calling, seriously propose to refuse philosophy the company of science? For, after all, the philosopher always thinks *about something:* about the square traced in the sand, about the donkey, the horse, the mule, about the cubic-feet of a volume, about cinnabar, the Roman state, the hand plunged in iron filings. The philosopher reflects upon his experience and his world. How, if not by edict, could one give him the right to forget what science says about that same experience and that same world? Under the collective name of science there is nothing but the systematic arrangement, a methodological exercise—narrower or wider, more or less insightful—of that same experience which begins with our first perception. It is a collection of means of perceiving, of imagining and finally of living, oriented toward the same truth the necessity of which is established by our first experiences. It may happen that science buys its exactitude at the price of schematization. But the remedy is then to confront it with an integral experience and not to oppose it to a philosophical knowledge arriving from no one knows where.

Husserl's concepts of "viewing of essences," "morphological essences" and "phenomenological experience," which mark the maturity of his philosophy and thereafter its continual theme, enabled him to circumscribe with ever greater precision a domain and an attitude of investigation in which philosophy and effective knowledge would be able to encounter one another; and herein lies his very great merit. It is known that he began by affirming—and always maintained—a rigorous difference between them. It seems to us nevertheless, that his idea of a psycho-phenomenological parallelism—let us say in generalizing: his thesis that there is a parallelism between positive knowledge and philosophy, so that to each statement of the one there corresponds a statement of the other—leads really to the thesis of a *reciprocal envelopment*. In the case of the social, it becomes then a question of understanding how it can be at the same time a "thing" to be known without presuppositions, and a "signification" for which societies, those with which we become acquainted, furnish only the occasion of its appearance: how it can be in-itself and in us. Having entered this labyrinth, let us follow the steps by which Husserl makes his way toward his final conceptions, at which point, besides, they will be preserved as well as bypassed.

At his point of departure he claims rights for philosophy in terms such as would appear to abolish those of effective knowledge. Speaking of the eminently social relationship which is language, he postulates as a principle[2] that we shall not be able to understand the functioning of our proper language nor detach ourselves from the pseudo-evidence which arises from the fact that it is our own, and enter into the true understanding of other

<hr />

[2] E. Husserl, *Logische Untersuchungen*, 4th Untersuchung, II, 339.

languages without having first constituted an image of the "ideal form" *of* language and the modes of expression that belong to it by all necessity if it is to be language: only in this way will we be able to understand how German, Latin, Chinese participate, each in its own manner, in that eidetic universal, and then define each of these languages as a mixture, in their own original proportions, of the universal "forms of signification," a "dim" and incomplete realization of the "general and rational grammar." The factual language was then to be reconstructed by a synthetic operation out of the essential structures of any possible language, which, in their limpid clarity, envelop it. Philosophical thought appeared as absolutely autonomous, capable, and alone capable, of true understanding by referring to the essences that furnished it with the magic keys.

In general then one might say that our entire historical experience of social relationships is made problematical in the ✓ interest of viewing their essence. The former does present us with "social processes," "cultural formations," forms of law, of art, or religion, but as long as we keep to these empirical realizations we do not even know the meaning of these headings under which they are arranged, and consequently still less if the historical development of a particular religion, of this particular form of law or art truly conforms to their essence and thus truly judges of their value; or if, on the contrary, this law, this art, this religion contain yet other possibilities. History, Husserl then said, cannot judge an idea, and when it does, this "evaluative" (*wertende*) history borrows surreptitiously from the "ideal sphere" those necessary connections it pretends to make emerge from the facts.[3] As for the "world-views" (which can be nothing more than the inventory of what can be thought at any given moment, taking into account the available knowledge), Husserl does admit that they pose a real problem, but the form in which they state it prevents a serious solution. The true problem stems from the fact that philosophy would lose its meaning if it refused to judge the present. Just as a morality, "endless and transfinite in principle," would no longer be morality, so too a philosophy refusing to take a stand on the present would cease to be philos-

[3] E. Husserl, "Philosophie als strenge Wissenschaft," *Logos*, I, 1910, 325.

494 — Philosophical Perspectives —

ophy.[4] Except that as a matter of fact *Weltanschauung* philosophers fail all along the line by wishing to face current problems, "to have their system and yet soon enough so as to be able to live afterwards":[5] they can supply no more rigor than anyone else to the solution of these problems since they themselves are also within a *Weltanschauung* and have no science of the world (*Weltwissenschaft*); and while exhausting themselves in reflecting upon the present, they rob true philosophy of the unconditional devotion it demands. For, once constituted it permits us to reflect upon the present as well as the past and the eternal. Going straight to the present is to give up the solid for the illusory.

When Husserl in the second part of his career returns to the problems of history and primarily to that of language, we no longer find the idea of a philosopher-subject, master of the possible, who first has to distance himself from *his* language in order to find the ideal forms of a universal language beyond all actuality. The primary task of philosophy as regards language now seems to be the rediscovery of our inherence within a certain speech-system which we use with full efficacy just because it is as immediately present to us as our body. The philosophy of language need not be opposed to empirical linguistics, since the former is no longer the attempt to objectivize language completely nor is the latter a knowledge always menaced by the presuppositions of the native tongue; on the contrary, philosophy is the rediscovery of the subject in the act of speaking as opposed to linguistic science which inevitably treats him as a thing. Mr. Pos[6] has shown very well the distinction between the phenomenological attitude and the scientific attitude of observation—which considers a language as having already been built and thus belonging to the past, and then proceeds to decompose it into a sum of linguistic facts in which its unity then disappears. Phenomenology, on the other hand, allows us direct access to the living language, present within a linguistic community which

[4] *Ibid.*, p. 332.

[5] *Ibid.*, p. 338. (Translator's note: the translator would understand the German text as ". . . and soon enough so as to be able to live accordingly . . ." The German reads "*danach*.")

[6] H. Pos, "Phénoménologie et Linguistique," *Revue internationale de philosophie*, I, 1939, 354-365.

utilizes it not merely to conserve the past, but moreover to found, to aim at, and to define a future. It is evident that language as seen by phenomenology is no longer decomposed into elements to be added together little by little; it is rather like an organ within which all the tissues participate in a single function, irrespective of the difference in their origin and of how they happened to find their way into the whole. If this manner of approach is what really constitutes the essence of phenomenology, then it is no longer the synthetic determination of all the possibles; reflection can no longer be understood as the return to a pre-empirical subject, guardian of the keys to the world; no longer does it possess the constitutive elements of the real object, no longer can it grasp all its aspects. Reflection will have to learn about its object by long and intimate contact which at first transcends its power of understanding. The philosopher is primarily one who is aware of his situation within a language, aware that he *speaks;* and therefore phenomenological reflection can no longer be limited to the enumeration in full clarity of the "conditions without which" there would be no language. It must reveal why there is the spoken word, the paradox of a subject, turned toward the future, who speaks and understands, in spite of all we know about the accidents of language and the shifts of meaning that have occurred in the course of its formation. The presence of the spoken word enlightens us as no simple "possible" expression can; our linguistic "presence-field" contains an operation which serves as a model for conceiving other possible systems of expression, although the former is in no way a particular case of the latter. Reflection no longer passes over into another order of being which absorbs the order of actual things; it is first of all a consciousness more acutely aware of our being rooted in this order. From now on the absolute condition of a valid philosophy is its passage through the real world.

Actually, one does not have to await Husserl's recognition of the life-world (*Lebenswelt*) as the primary phenomenological theme in order to note his repudiation of a formal reflection. The reader of *Ideen I* will already have noticed that eidetic intuition has always been the act of "ascertaining" a truth, phenomenology an "experience" (a phenomenology of vision,

Husserl said, can be constituted only after having experienced the actual *conditions of visibility*,[7] and in general he refused the possibility of a "mathematics of the phenomena," a "geometry of the experienced"). The movement from fact upwards to essence was simply not emphasized. Thought hardly supported itself at all on factual structures in order to release their possible structures: a completely imaginative variation drew out of the most minute experience a treasure of eidetic statements. When in his last writings, the recognition of the world as experienced by us, and thus also of the language in which we live became characteristic of phenomenology, this is but a more resolute way of saying that philosophy is not from the very beginning in possession of the truth of language and the world; it is rather the recovery and the initial formulation of a Logos strewn in our world and our life, bound to their concrete structures—this "Logos of the aesthetic[8] world" already spoken of in *Formal and Transcendental Logic*. Husserl will merely complete the movement of his entire former thought when in a posthumous fragment he will write that the linguistic incarnation makes the transitory interior phenomenon pass into its ideal existence.[9] The ideal existence which at first was to found the possibility of language is now *its* most intimate possibility. But then, if philosophy is no longer the transition to the infinity of possibles or a leap into absolute objectivity, if it is first of all a contact with the actually present, we may then understand that certain linguistic investigations anticipate those of philosophy and that certain linguists without knowing it have already trodden the ground of phenomenology. Husserl does not say this (nor does Mr. Pos), but when he asks us to return from language considered as an object to the spoken word, it is difficult not to think of Saussure.

Basically, the entire relationship of philosophy to history is

[7] Translator's note: "Sichtigkeit" in the original French text left untranslated. To be understood in the sense navigators use the word "visibility," i.e., in reference to the specific conditions of the surrounding atmosphere which thus permit both the objects to come into sight and the eye to see.

[8] Translator's note: I.e., "of the senses," from "aisthesis."

[9] E. Husserl, "Die Frage nach dem Ursprung der Geometrie als intentional-historisches Problem," *Revue internationale de philosophie*, I, 1939, 210.

transformed in the very movement of reflection, which itself had sought to liberate philosophy from history. In the course of his reflections on the relation of eternal truths to those of fact, Husserl was obliged to substitute a much less simple relation for his initial delimitations. His meditations on transcendental reflection and its possibility, pursued for at least twenty years, show quite well that in his eyes this term did not designate some sort of distinct faculty, capable of being circumscribed, of being pointed to, really able to be isolated beside other modalities of experience. In spite of all the decisive formulations always reaffirming the radical distinction between the natural attitude and the transcendental attitude, Husserl knows quite well, from the very beginning, that as a matter of fact they encroach on one another and that any *fact of consciousness* carries in itself the transcendental. In any case, as for that which concerns the relation of fact and essence, a text as old as "Philosophie als strenge Wissenschaft," after having distinguished the "ideal sphere" and historical facts, clearly foresaw the eventual overlapping of the two orders. Husserl said that if an historical critique truly shows that a particular order of institutions is devoid of substantial reality and is finally nothing but a common term designating a mass of facts without internal relation, this only means that empirical history contains confused intuitions of essence and that a critique is always the reverse side or the emergence of a positive statement already there. He already admits in the same article that history is precious to the philosopher *because it reveals the Gemeingeist*[10] *to him.* The transition from these first formulations to later ones is not too difficult. To say that history teaches the philosopher what the *Gemeingeist* is, means that it makes him reflect upon the problem of communication of subjects. It compels him to understand how it is that there are not merely minds appointed each to its own perspective of the world—which the philosopher may inspect one after the other without it being permitted, and even less demanded, that he see them *together*— but rather a community of minds coexisting, each one for the other, and, this being the case, each one invested with an outside through which it becomes visible. The result is that the philos-

[10] Translator's note: "collective consciousness," as that which a group simply takes for granted as true, right, etc.

opher can no longer speak of minds in general, treat of them all
under the same heading, nor flatter himself at having constituted
them; rather he must see himself within the dialogue of minds,
situated just as all of them are, and recognize their dignity as
constituents at the very moment he claims this honor for himself.
We are at this point quite close to the formulation-enigma to
which Husserl comes in the texts of the *Krisis der europäischen
Wissenschaften* when he writes that "transcendental subjectivity
is intersubjectivity." If the transcendental is intersubjectivity
how could one prevent the frontiers between the transcendental
and the empirical from becoming hazy? Since, together with my
fellow-man (*autrui*) it is everything he sees of me, it is my entire
facticity that becomes reintegrated into subjectivity, or at least
posited as an indispensable element of its definition. Thus the
transcendental descends into history, or the historical, one might
say, is no longer the external relation of two or more absolutely
autonomous subjects, but it has an interior and belongs to their
very definition; each one knows himself a subject within a community of subjects and not simply as existing for itself.

In the unedited manuscripts of the final period, the opposition of fact and essence will be explicitly mediated by the idea
that the purest reflection discovers a "genesis of meaning"
(*Sinngenesis*) immanent in its objects, the requirement of a
development, of a "before" and "after" in their manifestation, a
series of steps each of which is replaced while being developed by
a subsequent one, this one not able to be "at the same time" as
that and presupposing it as its past horizon. It goes without saying
that this intentional history is not the simple sum of manifestations taken singly: it takes them up and orders them, it reanimates
and rectifies in the actuality of a present, a genesis which without
it might miscarry. But it can only do so in contact with the given,
seeking its motives in this. It is no longer as the result of an unfortunate accident that the study of significations and that of fact
trespass on one another: a signification would be empty if it did
not condense a certain development of truth.

It is to be hoped that soon we shall be able to read, in the
complete works of Husserl[11] the letter he wrote to Lévy-Bruhl

[11] Being published by Martinus Nijhoff, The Hague, under the direction
of H. L. Van Breda. We have not been officially authorized by the editors

on March 11, 1935, after having read *La Mythologie primitive*. He seems to admit here that the philosopher cannot immediately attain the universal of simple reflection, and that he is not in a position to do without anthropological experience, nor to construct the meanings of other experiences and of other civilizations by mere imaginative variation of his own experience. "It is a possible task and of great importance," he writes, "to project ourselves (*einzufühlen*) into a community enclosed within its living and traditional sociality and to understand it insofar as that community, in its total social life and on the basis of it, possesses the world which is not what that community simply imagines to be the world, but the world that is real for it." Now the access to archaic worlds is barred from us by our own world: the primitives of Lévy-Bruhl have no history; as far as they are concerned their life is but a flowing present (*ein Leben, das nur strömende Gegenwart ist*). We, on the other hand, live in an historical world, i.e., one which "has a future in part realized (the national 'past') and a future in part to be realized." Any intentional analysis wishing to discover and reconstruct the structures of the archaic world cannot be restricted to the exposition of those found in our own world: for what gives meaning to those structures is the milieu, the *Umwelt*, of which they are the typical style, and thus one cannot understand them without having first understood how time flows and how being is constituted in those cultures. Husserl goes so far as to write that historical relativism has its incontestible justification, as anthropological fact, within that intentional analysis already largely developed.

What finally does he make of philosophy? Toward the end of his letter he indicates: philosophy must accept the totality of what science has acquired, and thus historical relativism along with it, since science has the right to speak first in that which concerns knowledge. But, as philosophy, it is not satisfied with simply taking note of the variety of anthropological facts: "but

to quote the few unedited lines included in our article. We therefore ask the reader to accept them simply as a foretaste of the only authorized edition of the texts, being prepared by the Husserl Archives of Louvain. (The translator adds that 9 volumes of this exceptional collection have already been published.)

anthropology like any positive science and like the totality of these sciences, if it has the first word in knowledge, has not the last." There would be an autonomy of philosophy after positive knowledge, not before it. It does not exempt the philosopher from collecting all that anthropology may offer, which means fundamentally that we must put our communication with other cultures to the test. It can remove nothing from the competence of the scientist that might be accessible to his research methods. It will simply establish itself in a dimension where no scientific knowledge can contest it. Let us attempt to say which dimension.

If the philosopher no longer attributes to himself the unconditional power to think his own thoughts from beginning to end, if he admits that his "idea," his "evidences" are always naive to a certain extent, and, that caught within the fabric of his own culture, he can have no true knowledge of them merely by inspecting and varying them in thought, if, finally he must confront them with other cultural formations and see them against the background of other presuppositions, has he not then abdicated from this point on, handing over his rights to positive and empirical disciplines? Precisely not. The same historical dependence that prohibits the philosopher from claiming an immediate access to the universal or the eternal prohibits the sociologist from substituting himself for the philosopher in this function and from giving the scientific objectification of the social the value of an ontology. The most profound sense of the concept of history does not consist in chaining the thinking subject to a point of time and space. Thought would have to have a vantage point beyond all space and time in order to see the subject this way, in its particular place and moment of time. But it is just this presupposition that is discredited by our historical sense, namely, that we can liberate thought from its spatio-temporal restrictions. Simply to transfer to science the grand-mastery refused to systematic philosophy, as historicism does, is out of the question. You believe you are thinking for all times and for all men, the sociologist says to the philosopher, and in so doing you are merely expressing the prejudices or pretentions of your culture. True, but no less true of the dogmatic sociologist than of the philosopher. After all, where is the *relativist himself located?* The idea of an historical time containing the philosopher as a box contains an object can only be formed by the sociologist in that he in turn places himself beyond history, claiming for himself the privilege of an absolute spectator. Actually, historical consciousness invites us to shift the very notion of the relationship of the mind to its object. Precisely the inherence of my thinking within a certain historical situation, which is its own, and beyond this one its inherence in other historical situations that interest it—since the former is originary with regard to the objective relationships science tells us about—makes the understanding of the social an understanding of myself, calls for and authorizes a *view of intersubjectivity as being my own*, which is forgotten by science while utilized by it, and which is the specific field of philosophy. If history envelops us all, it is up to us to understand that whatever we can have of the truth is not to be obtained in spite of our historical situation but because of it. Considered superficially, history destroys all truth, though considered radically it founds a new idea of truth. As long as I hold the ideal of an absolute spectator before me, of knowledge without a point of view, I can see my situation only as a principle of error. But having once recognized that through this situation I have become part of all action and all knowledge that can be meaningful for me, and that it contains, in gradually widening horizons, all that can *be* for me, then my contact with the social in the finitude of my situation reveals itself as the origin of all truth, including that of science; and since we have an idea of truth, since we are in the truth and cannot escape it, then the only thing left for us to do is to define a truth within the situation. Knowledge will be founded upon the irrefutable fact that we are not in the situation as is the object in objective space, and that it is for us the principle of our curiosity, our research and interest in other situations as variants of ours, and in our own lives, illuminated by fellow-men, as variants of the lives of others. Finally it is that which unites us to the totality of human experience no less than that which separates us from it. Science and sociology will be called the attempt to construct ideal variables which objectivize and schematize the functioning of this effective communication. Philosophy will be called the consciousness we must keep of the open and successive community of living, speaking, and thinking *alter egos*, one in the presence of the other and all in relation to nature which can be grasped vaguely as a last reality, encircling us at the limit of our historical field—a nature whose functioning can be traced by our theoretical constructions but for which these cannot be substituted. Thus philosophy may not be defined by a certain domain that is specific to it alone: it speaks, as does sociology, only of the world, of men, and of the mind. It is distinguished by a certain *mode* of consciousness we have of other men, of nature and of ourselves; it is nature and man in the present, such as they offer themselves in the actual dealings we have with them, in our knowledge and action and not "leveled down" (Hegel) into an objectivity that comes second; it is that nature in us, the other in us, and we in them. This being the case, we must not merely say that philosophy is compatible with sociology, but rather that it is necessary to it as a constant reminder of its tasks, and that the sociologist does philosophy spontaneously whenever he returns to the living source of his knowledge, to that which operates within him as a means of understanding the most widely different forms of culture. Philosophy is not a certain kind of knowledge; it is the vigilance which does not permit us to forget the source of all knowledge.

We do not mean to say that Husserl would ever have accepted definitions of this kind, since until the very end he always considered the return to the living word and living history, the return to the *Lebenswelt*, as a preparatory step to be succeeded by the specifically philosophical task of universal constitution. It is nevertheless a fact that in his last published work rationality is but one of the two possibles before which we find ourselves, the other being chaos. And it is precisely in a consciousness menaced by a sort of anonymous adversity that Husserl searches for what can stimulate knowledge and action. The criterion of philosophy becomes Reason as a task and a calling (*appel*), "latent Reason" realizing the plenitude of its possibilities in the understanding of itself.

"Only in this way is it to be decided whether the motivation (*Telos*) innate in European man[12] since the birth of Greek philosophy: of wanting his humanity to be grounded in

[12] Translator: *Menschentum*. The human essence as manifested in the consciousness of an ethos, a culture, inter-subjectively created and shared.

philosophical Reason and being unable to exist otherwise—in the unending movement from latent to manifest Reason, and in the unending endeavor to give itself valid norms on the basis of this his human truth and authenticity—whether this is a mere historical-factual delusion, acquired accidentally by only one of the many different types of societies[13] and styles of history; or whether it is not rather the case that in the appearance of Greek man that which is by essence inherent in humanity as such, as an entelechy, has for the first time become manifest. Humanity, in the broadest sense, is by essence man's existence within human communities united both socially and by generations; and if man is a rational being (*animale rationale*) then he is this only to the extent to which his entire community is a rational community—either latently disposed to Reason or overtly to an entelechy having come into its own, manifest for itself, and now consciously conducting human development by the necessity of its essence. Philosophy, science would then be the historical movement of the self-manifestation of universal Reason, 'innate' in humanity as such."[14]

Thus the essence of man is not given, nor is the necessity entailed by an essence an unconditional necessity. The essence of man will become effective only if rationality, the ideal of which Greece has placed within us, instead of remaining an accident proves itself as essential by the knowledge and by the action it renders possible and makes itself recognized by the irrational humanities. The Husserlian essence is now carried by an "entelechy" as its vehicle.

The role of philosophy as consciousness of rationality in contingency is not some insignificant relic. In the final analysis only the philosophical consciousness of intersubjectivity permits us to understand scientific knowledge. Without this consciousness it remains indefinitely on reprieve, always deferred until the

---

[13] Translator: *Menschheit(-en)*. Here understood as a distinct community bound by primarily generative ties.

[14] E. Husserl, "Die Krisis der europäischen Wissenschaften und die transzendentale Phänomenologie," *Philosophia*, I, 1939, 92.

Translator's note: Cf. also *Husserliana*, VI, pp. 13–14. (The translator is well aware of the inadequacy of his rendition from the German which can only give a hint of Husserl's thought.)

discussions on causality have come to an end, which, it being a question of man, are by nature endless. It is asked, for example, if social relationships are, as psychoanalytical sociology would have it, merely the enlargement and generalization of the sexual-aggressive drama, or if on the contrary this drama itself, in the form described by psychoanalysis, is only a particular case of institutionalized relationships within occidental society. These discussions have their interest in provoking sociologists to observe, to reveal the facts, to give birth to analyses and intuitions. But they involve no conclusion as long as one remains within the field of causal and "objective" thinking, since one can neither eliminate one of the causal chains, nor consider them together as causal chains. One cannot hold these views to be true both at the same time, which of course they are, except on the condition of going over to acausal thinking, which is philosophy. It must be understood at the same time that the individual drama takes place among *roles* already inscribed in the institutional whole, that therefore from the very beginning of his life the infant proceeds, by the simple perception of the care given him and of the utensils about him, to an uncoding of significations which, from the start, generalizes his proper drama into a drama of his culture —and that nonetheless it is the entire symbolic consciousness that elaborates after all what the infant experiences or does not experience, suffers or does not suffer, feels or does not feel; with the result that there is not a detail of his most individual history which does not contribute something to that signification which is his own, and which he will manifest when, having first thought and lived according to what he believed good, and perceived according to the imagery of his culture, he arrives at last at the point of reversing the relationship and of sliding into the significations of his spoken word and his behavior, of converting his experience down to its most secretive corner into culture. It is inconceivable from the causal point of view that this centripetal movement and this centrifugal movement be possible together. These reversals, these "metamorphoses," this proximity and distance of the past and the present, of the archaic and the "modern," this rolling up of cultural time and space in themselves, this perpetual superdetermination of human events which makes the social fact, whatever the singularity of local or temporal conditions might be, always appear to us as a variant of a single life in which ours also participates, so that every *other fellow-man* appears as an *other ourself*—all of this then only becomes conceivable or even visible in the philosophical attitude.

Philosophy is certainly, is always, a breach with objectivism, a returning from the *constructa* to living experience, from the world to ourselves. Except that this indispensable step that characterizes philosophy no longer transports it into the rarified atmosphere of introspection or into a domain numerically distinct from that of science. It does not pose philosophy as a rival to knowledge once we have recognized that the "interior" to which it brings us is not a "private life" but an intersubjectivity connecting us, to an ever greater extent, to all of history. When I become aware that the social is not merely an object but first of all my situation, and when I awaken in myself the consciousness of this social which is my own, it is then my entire synchrony[15] that becomes present for me, and through this it is the entire past that I become able to reflect upon truly as the synchrony this past had been in its time (*à son heure*); it is the entire convergent and discordant action of the historical community that is effectively given to me in my living present. The renunciation of a systematic explicative apparatus does not reduce philosophy to the rank of an auxiliary or propagandist of objective knowledge since it has a proper dimension at its disposal which is that of coexistence, not as a ready made fact and object for contemplation, but as a perpetual event and field of universal *praxis*. Philosophy is irreplaceable because it reveals to us the movement by which lives become truths, and the circularity of that singular being who, in a certain sense, *is* already everything he *happens to think.*

[15] Translator's note: Cf. C. G. Jung, "Synchronicity: An Acausal Connecting Principle," in C. G. Jung and W. Pauli, *The Interpretation of Nature and the Psyche*, pp. 5–146.

For
FURTHER READING

A. J. Ayer's *Language, Truth and Logic* (2d ed.) is the best introduction to his thought. Ayer has also edited a collection of writings on *Logical Positivism* (which has a good bibliography). For a brief account see Herbert Feigl, "Logical Empiricism," in *Twentieth Century Philosophy*—also published under the title *Living Schools of Philosophy*—reprinted in *Readings in Philosophical Analysis* (ed. Feigl and Sellars). Other relevant titles: Karl Popper, *The Logic of Scientific Discovery;* Thomas Storer, "An Analysis of Logical Positivism," *Methodos*, Vol. III, 1951; J. Jorgenson, *The Development of Logical Empiricism* (International Encyclopedia of Unified Science); Victor Kraft, *The Vienna Circle;* Julius Weinberg, *An Examination of Logical Positivism;* Hans Reichenbach, *The Rise of Scientific Philosophy* and *Experience and Prediction;* Bertrand Russell, *Human Knowledge.*

Two of Merleau-Ponty's books have been translated into English: *Phenomenology of Perception* and *In Praise of Philosophy.* His article on "Cézanne's Doubt" appeared in *Partisan Review* XIII, 1946. In addition, there are a number of works on phenomenology and existential philosophy which the reader may consult: Marvin Farber, "Phenomenology," in *Twentieth Century Philosophy;* Alfred Schutz, "Some Leading Concepts of Phenomenology," *Social Research,* Vol. XII, 1945; Dorion Cairns, "Phenomenology," in *A History of Philosophical Systems* (ed. Ferm); Aron Gurwitsch, "The Phenomenological and the Psychological Approach to Consciousness," *Philosophy and Phenomenological Research,* Vol. XV, 1955. For a full-length survey see Herbert Spiegelberg, *The Phenomenological Movement,* 2 vols., 1960. For a critical view see Hans P. Neisser, "The Phenomenological Approach in Social Science," *Philosophy and Phenomenological Research,* Vol. XX, 1959. For something *by* Husserl to start with: "Philosophy as a Strict Science," *Cross Currents,* Vol. VI, 1956.

On existentialism: Ralph Harper, *Existentialism: A Theory of Man;* James Collins, *The Existentialists;* Helmut Kuhn, *Encounter with Nothingness; Existentialism from Dostoievski to Sartre* (ed. Walter Kaufmann). For a critical view see Sidney Hook, "The Quest for 'Being,' " *Journal of Philosophy,* Vol. L, 1953.

A few related titles: *Existence: A New Dimension in Psychology and Psychiatry* (ed. May, Angel, and Ellenberger); Edward A. Tiryakian, *Sociologism and Existentialism;* F. Copleston, *Contemporary Philosophy;* I. M. Bochenski, *Contemporary European Philosophy;* Stuart Hampshire, *Thought and Action.*

NOTE: The quotation from Paul Henle in the Preface to Part V is from an unpublished paper on "Philosophy and Social Science."

BIBLIOGRAPHY

..

NOTE. This selected list contains all titles mentioned in the corresponding Parts of the volume as well as other relevant books and
articles.[1] It is offered as an entrance into the massive literature of
philosophy of the social sciences.

FOR GENERAL REFERENCE

COLLECTIONS OF READINGS:

Coser, Lewis A., and Bernard Rosenberg (eds.), *Sociological Theory:
A Book of Readings*, New York: Macmillan, 1957.

Danto, Arthur, and Sidney Morgenbesser (eds.), *Philosophy of Science*,
Cleveland and New York: Meridian Books, World, 1960.

Feigl, Herbert, and May Brodbeck (eds.), *Readings in the Philosophy
of Science*, New York: Appleton-Century-Crofts, 1953.

Madden, Edward H. (ed.), *The Structure of Scientific Thought: An
Introduction to Philosophy of Science*, Boston: Houghton Mifflin,
1960.

Parsons, Talcott, Edward Shils, Kaspar D. Naegele, and Jesse R. Pitts
(eds.), *Theories of Society*, New York: Free Press of Glencoe,
1961, 2 vols.

[1] Occasionally, a title listed in one part of the bibliography is not repeated in another, even though reference may be made to it in the corresponding Part of the book. All authors referred to are included in the
Index.

Ruitenbeek, Hendrick M. (ed.), *Varieties of Classic Social Theory* and *Varieties of Modern Social Theory*, New York: Dutton, 1963.

Wiener, Philip (ed.), *Readings in the Philosophy of Science*, New York: Scribner's, 1953.

Wilson, Logan, and William L. Kolb (eds.), *Sociological Analysis: An Introductory Text and Case Book*, New York: Harcourt, Brace, 1949.

Professor Paul Diesing of the Department of Philosophy of the University of Colorado is preparing a collection of readings in the methodology of the social sciences.

ENCYCLOPEDIC SURVEYS:

Becker, Howard, and Harry Elmer Barnes (eds.), with the assistance of Émil Benoît-Smullyan and others, *Social Thought from Lore to Science*, 3d ed., New York: Dover, 1961, 3 vols.

Lindzey, Gardner (ed.), *Handbook of Social Psychology*, Reading, Mass.: Addison-Wesley, 1954, 2 vols.

Seligman, Edwin R. A., and Alvin Johnson (eds.), *Encyclopedia of the Social Sciences*, New York: Macmillan, 1930–1935, 15 vols.

BIBLIOGRAPHIES:

Albert, Ethel M., and Clyde Kluckhohn, with the assistance of Robert LeVine, Warren Seulowitz, and Miriam Gallaher, *A Selected Bibliography on Values, Ethics, and Esthetics*, Glencoe, Ill.: Free Press, 1959.

De Brie, A. A. (ed.), *Bibliographia Philosophica 1934–1945*, Brussels: Editiones Spectrum, 1950, 2 vols.

Hoselitz, Bert F. (ed.), *A Reader's Guide to the Social Sciences*, Glencoe, Ill.: Free Press, 1959.

The UNESCO International Committee for Social Sciences Documentation publishes a number of bibliographies of the literature of the social sciences.

Varet, Gilbert, *Manuel de Bibliographie Philosophique*, Vol. II: *Les Sciences Philosophiques*, Paris: Presses Universitaires de France, 1956.

INTRODUCTION

Agee, James, and Walker Evans, *Let Us Now Praise Famous Men*, Boston: Houghton Mifflin, 1941.

Anderson, John M., *The Individual and the New World: A Philosophical Exploration*, State College, Pa.: Bald Eagle Press, 1955.

Barnes, Harry Elmer (ed.), *An Introduction to the History of Sociology*, Chicago: University of Chicago Press, 1948.

Bendix, Reinhard, *Max Weber: An Intellectual Portrait*, Garden City, N.Y.: Doubleday Anchor Books, 1962.

Berger, Peter L., *Invitation to Sociology: A Humanistic Perspective*, Garden City, N.Y.: Doubleday Anchor Books, 1963.

———, *The Precarious Vision: A Sociologist Looks at Social Fictions and Christian Faith*, Garden City, N.Y.: Doubleday, 1961.

Briggs, Asa, "Sociology and History," in *Society: Problems and Methods of Study*, ed. A. T. Welford, Michael Argyle, D. V. Glass, and J. N. Morris, London: Routledge & Kegan Paul, 1962, pp. 91–98.

Chinoy, Ely, *Society: An Introduction to Sociology*, with a foreword by Charles H. Page, New York: Random House, 1961.

Coleridge, Samuel Taylor, *Select Poetry and Prose*, ed. Stephen Potter, London: Nonesuch Press, 1962.

Collingwood, R. G., *An Autobiography*, Oxford: Oxford University Press, 1939.

Dixon, James, "The Economic Influence of the Developments in Shipbuilding Techniques, 1450–1485" (for further details see Kingsley Amis, *Lucky Jim*, New York: Viking Press, 1958).

Dollard, Charles, "Strategy for Advancing the Social Sciences," in *The Social Sciences at Mid-Century*, Minneapolis, Minn.: University of Minnesota, 1952, pp. 12–20.

Gillin, John (ed.), *For A Science of Social Man: Convergences in Anthropology, Psychology and Sociology*, New York: Macmillan, 1954.

Gross, Llewellyn (ed.), *Symposium on Sociological Theory*, Evanston, Ill.: Row, Peterson, 1959.

Gurvitch, Georges, and Wilbert E. Moore (eds.), *Twentieth Century Sociology*, New York: Philosophical Library, 1945.

Hall, Everett W., *Philosophical Systems*, Chicago: University of Chicago Press, 1960.

Handy, Rollo, "Philosophy's Neglect of the Social Sciences," *Philosophy of Science*, XXV, 1958, pp. 117–124.

Johnstone, Henry W., Jr., *Philosophy and Argument*, State College, Pa.: Pennsylvania State University Press, 1959.

Kallen, H. M., "The Meaning of Unity Among the Sciences," in *Structure, Method, and Meaning: Essays in Honor of Henry M. Sheffer*, ed. Paul Henle, H. M. Kallen, and Susanne K. Langer, New York: Liberal Arts Press, 1951, pp. 225–241.

Kirk, Russell, "Is Social Science Scientific?" *New York Times Magazine*, June 25, 1961.

Klibansky, Raymond, and H. J. Paton (eds.), *Philosophy and History: Essays Presented to Ernst Cassirer*, Oxford: Clarendon Press, 1936.

Kracauer, Siegfried, *Theory of Film: The Redemption of Physical Reality*, New York: Oxford University Press, 1960.

Kubie, Lawrence S. and Hyman A. Israel, " 'Say You're Sorry,' " in *The Psychoanalytic Study of the Child*, New York: International Universities Press, X, 1955, pp. 289–299.

Lazarsfeld, Paul F., "Problems in Methodology," in *Sociology Today: Problems and Prospects*, ed. Robert K. Merton, Leonard Broom, and Leonard S. Cottrell, Jr., New York: Basic Books, 1959, pp. 39–78.

Machlup, Fritz, "Operational Concepts and Mental Constructs in Model and Theory Formation," *Giornale Degli Economisti e Annali Di Economia*, XIX (Sept.–Oct. 1960), pp. 553–582.

Mannheim, Karl, *Ideology and Utopia: An Introduction to the Sociology of Knowledge*, with a preface by Louis Wirth, New York: Harcourt, Brace, 1949.

Mead, George H., *The Philosophy of the Act*, ed. with an intro. by Charles W. Morris in collaboration with John M. Brewster, Albert M. Dunham, and David L. Miller, Chicago: University of Chicago Press, 1938.

Merton, Robert K., "Now the Case *for* Sociology," *New York Times Magazine*, July 16, 1961.

———, *Social Theory and Social Structure*, rev. and enl. ed., Glencoe, Ill.: Free Press, 1957.

Mills, C. Wright, "On Intellectual Craftsmanship," in *Symposium on Sociological Theory*, ed. Llewellyn Gross, Evanston, Ill.: Row, Peterson, 1959, pp. 25–53.

———, *The Sociological Imagination*, New York: Oxford University Press, 1959.

Mises, Ludwig von, *Human Action: A Treatise on Economics*, rev. ed., New Haven, Conn.: Yale University Press, 1962.

Page, Charles H., "Sociology as a Teaching Enterprise," in *Sociology Today: Problems and Prospects*, ed. Robert K. Merton, Leonard Broom, and Leonard S. Cottrell, Jr., New York: Basic Books, 1959, pp. 579–599.

Ray, Donald P. (ed.), *Trends in Social Science*, New York: Philosophical Library, 1961.

Salvemini, Gaetano, *Historian and Scientist: An Essay on the Nature of History and the Social Sciences*, Cambridge, Mass.: Harvard University Press, 1939.

Shils, Edward A., "The Calling of Sociology," in *Theories of Society*, ed. Talcott Parsons, Edward Shils, Kaspar D. Naegele, and Jesse R. Pitts, New York: Free Press of Glencoe, 1961, Vol. 2, pp. 1405–1448.

——, "Social Inquiry and the Autonomy of the Individual," in *The Human Meaning of the Social Sciences*, ed. Daniel Lerner, New York: Meridian Books, 1959, pp. 114–157.

Simon, Herbert A., and Allen Newell, "Models: Their Uses and Limitations," in *The State of the Social Sciences*, ed. Leonard D. White, Chicago: University of Chicago Press, 1956, pp. 66–83.

Stephenson, William, *The Study of Behavior: Q-Technique and its Methodology*, Chicago: University of Chicago Press, 1953.

Timasheff, Nicholas S., *Sociological Theory: Its Nature and Growth*, Garden City, N.Y.: Doubleday, 1955.

Voegelin, Eric, *The New Science of Politics: An Introduction*, Chicago: University of Chicago Press, 1952.

Wootton, Barbara, *Testament for Social Science: An Essay in the Application of Scientific Method to Human Problems*, London: George Allen & Unwin, 1950.

PART I. SCIENCE AND SOCIETY

Aristotle, *Natural Science, Psychology, and the Nicomachean Ethics*, trans. Philip H. Wheelwright, New York: Doubleday, 1935.

Arnold, Thurman W., *The Folklore of Capitalism*, New Haven, Conn.: Yale University Press, 1937.

Beck, Lewis W., "The 'Natural Science Ideal' in the Social Sciences," *Scientific Monthly*, LXVIII, 1949, pp. 386–394.

Bell, E. T., *The Handmaiden of the Sciences*, Baltimore: Williams & Wilkins, 1937.

Bentley, A. F., *Behavior, Knowledge, Fact*, Bloomington, Ind.: Principia Press, 1935.

——, "Sociology and Mathematics I and II," *Sociological Review*, XXIII, 1931, pp. 85–107 and 149–172.

Bergmann, Gustav, *Philosophy of Science*, Madison, Wisc.: University of Wisconsin Press, 1957.

Bernard, L. L., "The Evolution of Social Consciousness and of the Social Sciences," *Psychological Review*, XXXIX, 1932, pp. 147–164.

Blumer, Herbert, *An Appraisal of Thomas and Znaniecki's The Polish Peasant in Europe and America*, Critiques of Research in the Social Sciences: I (with statements by William I. Thomas and Florian Znaniecki, a panel discussion, and summary and analysis by Read Bain), New York: Social Science Research Council, 1939.

Bridgman, P. W., *The Intelligent Individual and Society*, New York: Macmillan, 1938.

———, *The Logic of Modern Physics*, New York: Macmillan, 1932.

Brodbeck, May, "On the Philosophy of the Social Sciences," *Philosophy of Science*, XXI, 1954, pp. 140–156.

Brown, J. F., *Psychology and the Social Order*, New York: McGraw-Hill, 1936.

Canetti, Elias, *Crowds and Power*, trans. Carol Stewart, New York: Viking Press, 1962.

Chase, Stuart, *The Tyranny of Words*, New York: Harcourt, Brace, 1938.

Cohen, Morris R., and Ernest Nagel, *An Introduction to Logic and Scientific Method*, New York: Harcourt, Brace, 1934.

Cooley, Charles H., "The Roots of Social Knowledge," *American Journal of Sociology*, XXXII, 1926, pp. 59–79; reprinted in Cooley's *Sociological Theory and Social Research*, New York: Henry Holt, 1930.

Copeland, M. A., "Desire, Choice and Purpose from a Natural-Evolutionary Viewpoint," *Psychological Review*, XXXIII, 1926, pp. 245–267.

Dewey, John, *Experience and Nature*, New York: Norton, 1925.

———, *Logic: The Theory of Inquiry*, New York: Henry Holt, 1939.

Dodd, Stuart C., *Dimensions of Society*, New York: Macmillan, 1942.

Durkheim, Émile, *Sociology and Philosophy*, trans. D. F. Pocock, with an intro. by J. G. Peristiany, Glencoe, Ill.: Free Press, 1953.

Einstein, Albert, and Leopold Infeld, *The Evolution of Physics*, New York: Simon & Schuster, 1938.

Faris, Ellsworth, "The Primary Group: Essence and Accident," *American Journal of Sociology*, XXXVIII, 1932, pp. 41–50.

Furfey, Paul Hanly, *The Scope and Method of Sociology: A Metasociological Treatise*, New York: Harper, 1953.

Gewirth, Alan, "Subjectivism and Objectivism in the Social Sciences," *Philosophy of Science*, XXI, 1954, pp. 157–163.

Goffman, Erving, *The Presentation of Self in Everyday Life*, Garden City, N.Y.: Doubleday Anchor Books, 1959.

Greenwood, Ernest, *Experimental Sociology: A Study in Method*, New York: King's Crown Press, 1945.

Hare, A. P., Edgar F. Borgatta, and Robert F. Bales (eds.), *Small Groups: Studies in Social Interaction*, New York: Alfred A. Knopf, 1955.

Hayek, Friedrich A., *The Counter-Revolution of Science: Studies on the Abuse of Reason*, Glencoe, Ill.: Free Press, 1952.

Heberle, Rudolf, "The Sociology of Georg Simmel: The Forms of Social Interaction," in *An Introduction to the History of Sociology*, ed. Harry Elmer Barnes, Chicago: University of Chicago Press, 1948, pp. 249–273.

Homans, George C., *The Human Group*, New York: Harcourt, Brace, 1950.

Hull, C. L., "Goal Attraction and Directing Ideas Conceived as Habit Phenomena," *Psychological Review*, XXXVIII, 1931, pp. 487–506.

James, William, *Principles of Psychology*, New York: Henry Holt, 1896, 2 vols.

Kattsoff, Louis O., *The Design of Human Behavior*, St. Louis, Mo.: Educational Publishers, 1953.

Kemeny, John G., *A Philosopher Looks at Science*, Princeton, N.J.: D. Van Nostrand, 1959.

Koffka, Kurt, *Principles of Gestalt Psychology*, New York: Harcourt, Brace, 1935.

Köhler, Wolfgang, *Gestalt Psychology*, New York: Liveright, 1929.

Korzybski, Alfred, *Science and Sanity*, 2d ed., Lancaster, Pa.: International Non-Aristotelian Library Publishing Co., 1941.

Lerner, Max (ed.), *The Portable Veblen*, New York: Viking Press, 1948.

Levy, Marion J., Jr., *The Structure of Society*, Princeton, N.J.: Princeton University Press, 1952.

Lewin, Kurt, *A Dynamic Theory of Personality*, New York: McGraw-Hill, 1935.

———, *Principles of Topological Psychology*, New York: McGraw-Hill, 1936.

Lundberg, George A., *Can Science Save Us?* New York: Longmans, Green, 1947.

———, *Foundations of Sociology*, New York: Macmillan, 1939.

———, "Is Sociology Too Scientific?" *Sociologus*, IX, 1933, pp. 298–322.

———, "Science, Scientists, and Values," *Social Forces*, XXX, 1952, pp. 373–379.

———, *Social Research*, 2d ed., New York: Longmans, Green, 1942.

MacIver, Robert M., *Social Causation*, Boston: Ginn, 1942.

———, *Society: A Textbook of Sociology*, New York: Farrar & Rinehart, 1931.

Mandelbaum, Maurice, "Societal Facts," *British Journal of Sociology*, VI, 1955, pp. 305–317; reprinted in *The Structure of Scientific Thought*, ed. Edward H. Madden.

———, "Societal Laws," *British Journal for the Philosophy of Science*, VIII, 1957, pp. 211–224.

Margenau, Henry, *The Nature of Physical Reality*, New York: McGraw-Hill, 1950.

Markey, J. F., *The Symbolic Process and its Integration in Children*, New York: Harcourt, Brace, 1928.

Maus, Heinz, *A Short History of Sociology*, London: Routledge & Kegan Paul, 1962.

Mead, George H., "The Genesis of the Self and Social Control," *International Journal of Ethics*, XXXV, 1924–1925, pp. 251–277.

Mehlberg, Henryk, *The Reach of Science*, Toronto: University of Toronto Press, 1958.

Merton, Robert K., "Durkheim's Division of Labor in Society," *American Journal of Sociology*, XL, 1934, pp. 319–328.

Metcalf, W. V., "The Reality of the Atom," *Philosophy of Science*, VI, 1939, pp. 367–371.

Morris, Charles W., *Foundation of the Theory of Signs*, in *International Encyclopedia of Unified Science*, I, No. 2, Chicago: University of Chicago Press, 1938.

Naegele, Kaspar D., "Some Observations on the Scope of Sociological Analysis," in *Theories of Society*, ed. Talcott Parsons, Edward Shils, Kaspar D. Naegele, and Jesse R. Pitts, New York: Free Press of Glencoe, 1961, I, pp. 3–29.

Ogden, C. K., and I. A. Richards, *The Meaning of Meaning*, rev. ed., New York: Harcourt, Brace, 1936.

Ratner, Sidney, "Evolution and the Rise of the Scientific Spirit in America," *Philosophy of Science*, III, 1936, pp. 104–122.

Robinson, James Harvey, "The Procession of Civilization," in *The Story of Human Error*, ed. Joseph Jastrow, New York: Appleton-Century, 1936, pp. 271–281.

Rose, Arnold M. (ed.), *Human Behavior and Social Processes*, Boston: Houghton Mifflin, 1962.

Ross, Ralph with Ernest Van Den Haag, *Symbols and Civilization: Science, Morals, Religion, Art*, New York: Harcourt, Brace, 1962.

Rouček, Joseph S. (ed.), *Contemporary Sociology*, London: Peter Owen, 1959.

Rudner, Richard S., "Philosophy and Social Science," *Philosophy of Science*, XXI, 1954, pp. 164–168.

———, *Philosophy of Social Science*, Englewood Cliffs, N.J.: Prentice-Hall (announced).

Seifriz, William, "A Materialistic Interpretation of Life," *Philosophy of Science*, VI, 1939, pp. 266–284.

Simmel, Georg, *Conflict* and *The Web of Group-Affiliations*, with a foreword by Everett C. Hughes, trans. Kurt H. Wolff and Reinhard Bendix, Glencoe, Ill.: Free Press, 1955.

———, *The Sociology of Georg Simmel*, trans., ed., and with an intro. by Kurt H. Wolff, Glencoe, Ill.: Free Press, 1950.

Singer, E. C., *Mind as Behavior*, Columbus, Ohio: R. G. Adams, 1924.

Sorokin, Pitirim A., *Social and Cultural Dynamics*, New York: American Book Co., 1937–1941, 4 vols.

Sprott, W. J. H., *Sociology*, London: Hutchinson's University Library, n.d.

Spykman, Nicholas J., *The Social Theory of Georg Simmel*, Chicago: University of Chicago Press, 1925.

Stevens, S. S., "Psychology: The Propaedeutic Science," *Philosophy of Science*, IV, 1936, pp. 90–103.

Strauss, Anselm L., *Mirrors and Masks*, Glencoe, Ill.: Free Press, 1957.

Thomas, W. I., and Florian Znaniecki, *The Polish Peasant in Europe and America*, New York: Dover, 1958, 2 vols.

Thomson, J. A., and P. Geddes, *Life: Outlines of General Biology*, New York: Harper, 1932.

Toulmin, Stephen, *The Philosophy of Science*, New York: Harper & Row (Torchbooks), 1960.

Veblen, Thorstein, *The Place of Science in Modern Civilization*, New York: Viking Press, 1932.

Watson, John B., *Behaviorism*, New York: Norton, 1924.

Weiss, A. P., *A Theoretical Basis of Human Behavior*, Columbus, Ohio: R. G. Adams, 1929.

Wiese, Leopold von, and Howard Becker, *Systematic Sociology on the Basis of the* Beziehungslehre *and* Gebildelehre *of Leopold von Wiese*, New York: John Wiley, 1932; reissued with a new preface, Gary, Ind.: Norman Paul Press, 1950.

Wolff, Kurt H. (ed.), *Georg Simmel 1858–1918: A Collection of Essays with Translations and a Bibliography*, Columbus, Ohio: Ohio State University Press, 1959.

Znaniecki, Florian, *The Method of Sociology*, New York: Farrar & Rinehart, 1934.

PART II. THEORY AND PRACTICE

Adorno, T. W., and Else Frenkel-Brunswik, Daniel J. Levinson, R. Nevitt Sanford, *The Authoritarian Personality*, New York: Harper, 1950.

Aristotle, *Nicomachean Ethics*, trans. and ed. W. D. Ross, Oxford: Oxford University Press, 1925.

Asch, Solomon E., *Social Psychology*, Englewood Cliffs, N.J.: Prentice-Hall, 1952.

Bacon, Francis, *The Great Instauration*, in *The New Organon: and Related Writings*, ed. with an intro. by Fulton H. Anderson, New York: Liberal Arts Press, 1960.

———, *Works*, ed. James Spedding and Robert L. Ellis, London: Douglas D. Heath, 1857–1874, III; also available in *Selected Writings of Francis Bacon*, New York: Modern Library, 1955.

Becker, Howard, "Interpretive Sociology and Constructive Typology," in *Twentieth Century Sociology*, ed. Georges Gurvitch and Wilbert E. Moore, New York: Philosophical Library, 1945, pp. 70–95.

———, "Vitalizing Sociological Theory," *American Sociological Review*, XIX, 1954, pp. 377–388.

Becker, Howard, Frances Bennett Becker, and Harry Elmer Barnes (eds.), *Contemporary Social Theory*, New York: Appleton-Century, 1940.

Becker, Howard, and Alvin Boskoff (eds.), *Modern Sociological Theory: In Continuity and Change*, New York: Dryden Press, 1957.

Berlin, Isaiah, *The Hedgehog and the Fox: An Essay on Tolstoy's View of History*, New York: Mentor Books, 1957.

Black, Max (ed.), *The Social Theories of Talcott Parsons: A Critical Examination*, Englewood Cliffs, N.J.: Prentice-Hall, 1961.

Blumer, Herbert, "What Is Wrong with Social Theory," *American Sociological Review*, XIX, 1954, pp. 3–10.

Borgatta, Edgar F., and Henry J. Meyer (eds.), *Sociological Theory: Present-Day Sociology from the Past*, New York: Alfred A. Knopf, 1956.

Braithwaite, Richard B., *Scientific Explanation: A Study of the Function of Theory, Probability and Law in Science*, Cambridge: Cambridge University Press, 1953.

Braybrooke, David, "Authority as a Subject of Social Science and Philosophy," *Review of Metaphysics*, XIII, 1960, pp. 469–485.

Brecht, Arnold, *Political Theory: The Foundations of Twentieth-Century Political Thought*, Princeton, N.J.: Princeton University Press, 1959.

Brown, Robert, *Explanation in Social Science*, Chicago: Aldine Publishing Co., 1963.

Burnet, John, *Greek Philosophy: Thales to Plato*, London: Macmillan, 1960.

Butler, D. E., *The Study of Political Behaviour*, 2d ed., London: Hutchinson University Library, 1959.

Caspari, Fritz, "Erasmus on the Social Functions of Christian Humanism," *Journal of the History of Ideas*, VIII, 1947, pp. 78–106.

Church, Joseph, *Language and the Discovery of Reality: A Developmental Psychology of Cognition*, with a foreword by Robert B. MacLeod, New York: Random House, 1961.

Cohen, Morris R., *Reason and Nature: An Essay on the Meaning of Scientific Method*, New York: Harcourt, Brace, 1931.

Descartes, René, *Philosophical Works*, trans. Elizabeth S. Haldane and G. R. T. Ross, New York: Dover, 1955, I.

Doby, J. T. (ed.), *An Introduction to Social Research*, Harrisburg, Pa.: Stackpole, 1954.

Durkheim, Émile, review of Antonio Labriola's "*Essais sur la conception matérialiste de l'histoire*," *Revue philosophique*, XLIV, 1897, pp. 645–651.

———, *The Rules of Sociological Method*, trans. Sarah A. Solovay and John H. Mueller, Chicago: University of Chicago Press, 1938.

Flew, A. G. N. (ed.), *Logic and Language*, First Series, Oxford: Basil Blackwell, 1960.

Foster, K., and S. Humphries (trans.), *Aristotle's De Anima, in the Version of William of Moerbeke and the Commentary of St. Thomas Aquinas*, New Haven, Conn.: Yale University Press, 1951.

Friedman, Milton, *Essays in Positive Economics*, Chicago: University of Chicago Press, 1953.

Gardiner, Patrick (ed.), *Theories of History*, Glencoe, Ill.: Free Press, 1959.

Goode, William J., and Paul K. Hatt, *Methods in Social Research*, New York: McGraw-Hill, 1952.

Hertz, Heinrich, *Die Prinzipien der Mechanik: in neuem Zusammenhange dargestellt*, with a foreword by H. von Helmholtz, in *Gesammelte Werke von Heinrich Hertz*, ed. Ph. Lenard, Leipzig: Johann Ambrosius Barth, 1894 (trans. D. E. Jones and J. T. Walley, as *The Principles of Mechanics*, New York: Dover, 1956).

Hume, David, *Enquiry into Human Understanding*, ed. L. A. Selby-Bigge, Oxford: Clarendon Press, 1844.

Hutchison, T. W., *The Significance and Basic Postulates of Economic Theory*, London: Macmillan, 1938.

Ibsen, Henrik, *Ghosts*, trans. James Walter McFarlane, London: Oxford University Press, 1961.

——, *The Wild Duck*, trans. James Walter McFarlane, London: Oxford University Press, 1960.

Jonas, Hans, *The Gnostic Religion: The Message of the Alien God and the Beginnings of Christianity*, Boston: Beacon Press, 1958.

Kariel, Henry S., "Political Science in the United States: Reflections on One of Its Trends," *Political Studies*, IV, 1956, pp. 113–127.

Kaufmann, Felix, *Methodology of the Social Sciences*, New York: Oxford University Press, 1944.

——, "The Significance of Methodology for the Social Sciences," *Social Research*, V, 1938, pp. 442–463.

Kelsen, Hans, *Allgemeine Staatslehre*, Berlin: Springer, 1925.

Landheer, Bart, *Mind and Society: Epistemological Essays on Sociology*, The Hague: Martinus Nijhoff, 1952.

Laslett, Peter (ed.), *Philosophy, Politics and Society*, Oxford: Basil Blackwell, 1956.

Lerner, Daniel (ed.), *The Human Meaning of the Social Sciences*, New York: Meridian Books, 1959.

Locke, John, *Essay Concerning Human Understanding*, ed. Alexander Campbell Fraser, New York: Dover, 1959, 2 vols.

Logan, Frank A., *Behavior Theory and Social Science*, New Haven, Conn.: Yale University Press, 1955.

Loomis, Charles P., and Zona K. Loomis (eds.), *Modern Social Theories: Selected American Writers*, Princeton, N.J.: D. Van Nostrand, 1961.

McKinney, John C., "Methodology, Procedures, and Techniques in Sociology," in *Modern Sociological Theory: In Continuity and Change*, ed. Howard Becker and Alvin Boskoff, New York: Dryden Press, 1957, pp. 186–235.

Machlup, Fritz, "The Inferiority Complex of the Social Sciences," in *On Freedom and Free Enterprise: Essays in Honor of Ludwig von Mises*, ed. Mary Sennholz, Princeton, N.J.: D. Van Nostrand, 1956, pp. 161–172.

——, "The Problems of Verification in Economics," *Southern Economic Journal*, XXII, 1955, pp. 1–21.

——, "Why Bother with Methodology?" *Economica*, New Series, III, 1936, pp. 39–45.

Mandler, George, and William Kessen, *The Language of Psychology*, New York: John Wiley, 1959.

Martindale, Don, *The Nature and Types of Sociological Theory*, Boston: Houghton Mifflin, 1960.

Mayer, Joseph, *Social Science Principles in the Light of Scientific Method: With Particular Application to Modern Economic Thought*, Durham, N.C.: Duke University Press, 1941.

Menegazzi, Guido, *Method and Foundations of Social Science*, Italy: University of Bari, 1957.

Moore, G. E., "Proof of an External World," *Proceedings of the British Academy*, XXV, 1939, pp. 273–300; and in George Edward Moore, *Philosophical Papers*, London: George Allen & Unwin, 1959.

Morgenthau, Hans J., *Dilemma of Politics*, Chicago: University of Chicago Press, 1958.

Nagel, Ernest, *The Structure of Science*, New York: Harcourt, Brace & World, 1961.

Northrop, F. S. C., *The Logic of the Sciences and the Humanities*, New York: Meridian Books, 1959.

Parsons, Talcott, *Essays in Sociological Theory, Pure and Applied*, 2d ed., Glencoe, Ill.: Free Press, 1954.

———, "General Theory in Sociology," in *Sociology Today: Problems and Prospects*, ed. Robert K. Merton, Leonard Broom, and Leonard S. Cottrell, Jr., New York: Basic Books, 1959, pp. 3–38.

———, "The Present Position and Prospects of Systematic Theory in Sociology," in *Twentieth Century Sociology*, ed. Georges Gurvitch and Wilbert E. Moore, New York: Philosophical Library, 1945, pp. 42–69.

———, *The Social System*, Glencoe, Ill.: Free Press, 1951.

Parsons, Talcott, Robert F. Bales, and Edward A. Shils, *Working Papers in the Theory of Action*, Glencoe, Ill.: Free Press, 1953.

Parsons, Talcott, and Edward A. Shils (eds.), *Toward a General Theory of Action*, Cambridge, Mass.: Harvard University Press, 1951.

Pirotta, Angelo M. (ed.), *Sancti Thomas Aquinatis in Aristotelis Librum de Anima Commentarium*, Turin: M. E. Marietti, 1936.

Planck, Max, *Scientific Autobiography and Other Papers*, New York: Philosophical Library, 1949.

Progoff, Ira, *Jung's Psychology and Its Social Meaning: An Introductory Statement of C. G. Jung's Psychological Theories and a First Interpretation of Their Significance for the Social Sciences*, with an introduction by Goodwin Watson, New York: Grove Press, 1955.

Rex, John, *Key Problems of Sociological Theory*, New York: Humanities Press, 1962.

Rhees, Rush, "Philosophy and Art," unpublished talk.

Rickert, Heinrich, *Die Grenzen der naturwissenschaftlichen Begriffsbildung*, Tübingen: Mohr-Siebeck, 1902.

Robbins, Lionel, *An Essay on the Nature and Significance of Economic Science*, 2d ed., London: Macmillan, 1935.

Rogow, Arnold A., "Comment on Smith and Apter: or, Whatever Happened to the Great Issues?" *American Political Science Review*, LI, 1957, pp. 763–775.

Rotwein, Eugene, "On the Methodology of Positive Economics," *Quarterly Journal of Economics*, LXXIII, 1959, pp. 554–575.

Ryle, Gilbert, *Dilemmas*, The Tanner Lectures 1953, Cambridge: Cambridge University Press, 1956.

Schutz, Alfred, *Der sinnhafte Aufbau der sozialen Welt: eine Einleitung in die verstehende Soziologie*, Wien: Springer, 1932; 2d unrevised ed., 1960.

Small, Albion W., *The Meaning of Social Science*, Chicago: University of Chicago Press, 1910.

Snow, C. P., *The Affair*, New York: Scribner's, 1960.

———, *The Two Cultures and the Scientific Revolution*, The Rede Lecture 1959. Cambridge: Cambridge University Press, 1961.

Snyder, Richard C., and Glen D. Paige, "The United States Decision to Resist Aggression in Korea: The Application of an Analytical Scheme," *Administrative Science Quarterly*, III, 1958, pp. 341–378.

Sorokin, Pitirim, *Contemporary Sociological Theories*, New York: Harper, 1928.

Strauss, Leo, *The Political Philosophy of Hobbes: Its Basis and Genesis*, trans. Elsa M. Sinclair, Chicago: University of Chicago Press, 1962.

Theory and Practice in Historical Study: A Report of the Committee on Historiography of the Social Science Research Council, New York, 1946.

Weldon, Thomas D., *The Vocabulary of Politics*, London: Pelican Books, 1953.

Werkmeister, W. H., *A Philosophy of Science*, New York: Harper, 1940.

Weyl, Hermann, *Philosophy of Mathematics and Natural Science*, Princeton, N.J.: Princeton University Press, 1949.

Winch, Peter, *The Idea of a Social Science: and Its Relation to Philosophy*, London: Routledge & Kegan Paul, 2d impression, 1960.

Wittgenstein, Ludwig, *Philosophical Investigations*, trans. G. E. M. Anscombe, Oxford: Basil Blackwell, 1958.

——, *Tractatus Logico-Philosophicus*, trans. D. F. Pears and B. F. McGuiness, with an intro. by Bertrand Russell, London: Routledge & Kegan Paul, 1961.

Wolfe, Dael, *America's Resources of Specialized Talent: The Report of the Commission on Human Resources and Advanced Training*, New York: Harper, 1954.

Wolff, Kurt, H. (ed.), *Émile Durkheim 1858–1917: A Collection of Essays with Translations and a Bibliography*, Columbus, Ohio: Ohio State University Press, 1960.

Zetterberg, Hans L., *On Theory and Verification in Sociology*, rev. ed., New York: Bedminister Press, 1962.

——, *Social Theory and Social Practice*, New York: Bedminster Press, 1962.

PART III. CONCEPTS, CONSTRUCTS, AND THEORY FORMATION

Abel, Theodore, "The Operation Called *Verstehen*," *American Journal of Sociology*, LIV, 1948, pp. 211–218; reprinted in *Readings in the Philosophy of Science*, ed. Herbert Feigl and May Brodbeck, and also in *The Structure of Scientific Thought*, ed. Edward H. Madden.

Beard, Charles A., *The Nature of the Social Sciences*, New York: Scribner's, 1934.

Becker, Howard, and Hellmuth Dahlke, "Max Scheler's Sociology of Knowledge," *Philosophy and Phenomenological Research*, II, 1942, pp. 310–322.

Benoît-Smullyan, Émile, "The Sociologism of Émile Durkheim and His School," in *An Introduction to the History of Sociology*, ed. Harry Elmer Barnes, Chicago: University of Chicago Press, 1948, pp. 499–537.

Bergson, Henri, *Matière et mémoire: essai sur la relation du corps à l'esprit*, Paris: Félix Alcan, 1913; trans. Nancy Margaret Paul and W. Scott Palmer as *Matter and Memory*, London: George Allen & Unwin, 1950.

Bierstedt, Robert, "The Common Sense World of Alfred Schutz," *Social Research*, XXX, 1963, pp. 116–121.

Brodbeck, May, "Methodological Individualism: Definition and Re-
duction," *Philosophy of Science*, XXV, 1958, pp. 1–22.
Burtt, Edwin A., *Right Thinking*, New York: Harper, 1946.
Cohen, Morris R., *The Meaning of Human History*, La Salle, Ill.:
Open Court, 1947.
Cooley, Charles H., *Human Nature and the Social Order*, rev. ed.,
New York: Scribner's, 1922.
———, *Social Organization*, New York: Scribner's, 1909.
Dalton, George, "A Note of Clarification on Economic Surplus,"
American Anthropologist, LXII, 1960, pp. 483–490.
de Laguna, Grace A., "The *Lebenswelt* and the Cultural World,"
Journal of Philosophy, LVII, 1960, pp. 777–791.
Dennes, William R., "The Categories of Naturalism," in *Naturalism
and the Human Spirit*, ed. Yervant H. Krikorian, New York:
Columbia University Press, 1944, pp. 270–294.
Dewey, John, *Democracy and Education: An Introduction to the
Philosophy of Education*, New York: Macmillan, 1961.
———, *Experience and Nature*, 2d ed., Chicago: Open Court, 1925.
———, *Human Nature and Conduct*, New York: Modern Library,
1930.
———, *Philosophy and Civilization*, New York: G. P. Putnam, 1931.
———, *Problems of Men*, New York: Philosophical Library, 1946.
Feigl, Herbert and Michael Scriven, Grover Maxwell (eds.), *Concepts,
Theories, and the Mind-Body Problem*, Minnesota Studies in the
Philosophy of Science, II, Minneapolis, Minn.: University of Min-
nesota Press, 1958.
Feuer, Lewis S., and Ethel M. Albert, Symposium on "Causality in the
Social Sciences," *Journal of Philosophy*, LI, 1954, pp. 681–706.
Firth, Raymond, *Elements of Social Organization*, New York: Philo-
sophical Library, 1951.
Garfinkel, Harold, "Common-Sense Knowledge of Social Structures:
The Documentary Method of Interpretation," in *Theories of the
Mind*, ed. Jordan M. Scher, New York: Free Press, 1962, pp. 689–
712.
Goldstein, Leon J., "Evidence and Events in History," *Philosophy of
Science*, XXIX, 1962, pp. 175–194.
———, review of *The Idea of a Social Science: and Its Relation to
Philosophy* by Peter Winch, *Philosophical Review*, LXIX, 1960,
pp. 411–414.
———, "The Inadequacy of the Principle of Methodological Indi-
vidualism," *Journal of Philosophy*, LIII, 1956, pp. 801–813.

———, "Mr. Watkins on the Two Theses," *British Journal for the Philosophy of Science*, X, 1959, pp. 240–241.

———, "The Two Theses of Methodological Individualism," *British Journal for the Philosophy of Science*, IX, 1958, pp. 1–11.

Greenhut, Melvin L., "Science, Art, and Norms in Economics," *Philosophy and Phenomenological Research*, XXI, 1960, pp. 159–172.

Gurvitch, Georges, *La Vocation actuelle de la sociologie*, Paris: Presses Universitaires de France, 1950.

Gurwitsch, Aron, "The Common-Sense World as Social Reality: A Discourse on Alfred Schutz," *Social Research*, XXIX, 1962, pp. 50–72.

Hayek, Friedrich A., *Individualism and Economic Order*, Chicago: University of Chicago Press, 1948.

Hegel, G. W. F., *Lectures on the Philosophy of History*, trans. J. Sibree, New York: Dover, 1956.

Helmer, Olaf, and Nicholas Rescher, "On the Epistemology of the Inexact Sciences," *Management Science*, VI, 1959, pp. 25–52.

Hempel, Carl G., "The Function of General Laws in History," *Journal of Philosophy*, XXXIX, 1942, pp. 35–48.

———, *Fundamentals of Concept Formation in the Empirical Sciences*, in *International Encyclopedia of Unified Science*, II, No. 7, Chicago: University of Chicago Press, 1952.

Hempel, Carl G., and Paul Oppenheim, "Studies in the Logic of Explanation," *Philosophy of Science*, XV, 1948, pp. 135–175.

———, *Der Typusbegriff im Lichte der neuen Logik*, Leiden: Sijthoff, 1936.

Hinshaw, Virgil G., Jr., "Levels of Analysis," *Philosophy and Phenomenological Research*, XI, 1950, pp. 213–220.

Hodges, H. A., *Wilhelm Dilthey: Selected Readings from His Works*, London: Routledge & Kegan Paul, 1944.

Husserl, Edmund, *Erfahrung und Urteil: Untersuchungen zur Genealogie der Logik*, ed. Ludwig Landgrebe, Prague: Academia Verlag, 1939.

———, *Formale und transzendentale Logik: Versuch einer Kritik der logischen Vernunft*, Halle: Niemeyer, 1929.

———, *Ideen zu einer reinen Phänomenologie und phänomenologischen Philosophie*, ed. Walter Biemel, The Hague: Martinus Nijhoff, 1950.

———, *Logische Untersuchungen*, Halle: Niemeyer, 1921, 2 vols.

Kaufmann, Felix, *Methodenlehre der Sozialwissenschaften*, Wien: Springer, 1936.

Kretschmer, Ernst, *Physique and Character*, trans. W. J. H. Sprott, New York: Harcourt, Brace, 1936.

Krikorian, Yervant H., "A Naturalistic View of Mind," in *Naturalism and the Human Spirit*, ed. Yervant H. Krikorian, New York: Columbia University Press, 1944, pp. 242–269.

—— (ed.), *Naturalism and the Human Spirit*, New York: Columbia University Press, 1944.

Kuhn, Helmut, "The Phenomenological Concept of Horizon," in *Philosophical Essays in Memory of Edmund Husserl*, ed. Marvin Farber, Cambridge, Mass.: Harvard University Press, 1940, pp. 106–124.

Lavine, Thelma Z., "Knowledge as Interpretation: An Historical Survey," *Philosophy and Phenomenological Research*, X, 1950, pp. 526–540; XI, 1950, pp. 88–103.

——, "Naturalism and the Sociological Analysis of Knowledge," in *Naturalism and the Human Spirit*, ed. Yervant H. Krikorian, New York: Columbia University Press, 1944, pp. 183–209.

——, "Reflections on the Genetic Fallacy," *Social Research*, XXIX, 1962, pp. 321–336.

Lazarsfeld, Paul F., and Allen H. Barton, "Qualitative Measurement in the Social Sciences: Classification, Typologies, and Indices," in *The Policy Sciences: Recent Developments in Scope and Method*, ed. Daniel Lerner and Harold D. Lasswell with the editorial collaboration of Harold H. Fisher, Ernest R. Hilgard, Saul K. Padover, Ithiel De Sola Pool, C. Easton Rothwell, Stanford, Calif.: Stanford University Press, 1951, pp. 155–192.

Lewis, C. I., *Mind and the World Order: Outline of a Theory of Knowledge*, New York: Scribner's, 1929.

Lynd, Robert S., *Knowledge for What?* Princeton, N.J.: Princeton University Press, 1939.

——, *Middletown in Transition*, New York: Harcourt, Brace, 1937.

Machlup, Fritz, *The Economics of Seller's Competition: Model Analysis of Seller's Conduct*, Baltimore: Johns Hopkins University Press, 1952.

——, *The Political Economy of Monopoly*, Baltimore: Johns Hopkins University Press, 1952.

MacIver, Robert M., *Society: A Textbook of Sociology*, New York: Farrar & Rinehart, 1931; new ed. with Charles H. Page, *Society: An Introductory Analysis*, New York: Rinehart, 1949.

Malinowski, Bronislaw, "Anthropology," in *The Encyclopaedia Britannica*, Supplementary Vol. I, 1936.

Marx, Melvin (ed.), *Psychological Theory: Contemporary Readings,* New York: Macmillan, 1951.

May, Rollo, "Kierkegaard and Freud," *The New School Bulletin,* XVII, February 15, 1960.

Mead, George H., *Mind, Self, and Society: From the Standpoint of a Social Behaviorist,* ed. with an intro. by Charles W. Morris, Chicago: University of Chicago Press, 1934.

———, *The Philosophy of the Present,* ed. Arthur E. Murphy with prefatory remarks by John Dewey, Lectures of the Paul Carus Foundation, Third Series, Chicago: Open Court, 1932.

———, "What Social Objects Must Psychology Presuppose?" *Journal of Philosophy,* X, 1913, pp. 374–380.

Miller, James G., "Toward a General Theory for the Behavioral Sciences," in *The State of the Social Sciences,* ed. Leonard D. White, Chicago: University of Chicago Press, 1956, pp. 29–65.

Nagel, Ernest, *Logic Without Metaphysics,* Glencoe, Ill.: Free Press, 1958.

———, "Logic Without Ontology," in *Naturalism and the Human Spirit,* ed. Yervant H. Krikorian, New York: Columbia University Press, 1944, pp. 210–241.

Natanson, Maurice, *The Social Dynamics of George H. Mead,* with an intro. by Horace M. Kallen, Washington, D.C.: Public Affairs Press, 1956.

Ortega y Gasset, José, *Man and People,* trans. Willard R. Trask, New York: Norton, 1957.

Pareto, Vilfredo, *The Mind and Society,* trans. Andrew Bongiorno and Arthur Livingston, ed. Arthur Livingston, New York: Harcourt, Brace, 1935, 4 vols.

———, *Trattato di Sociologia Generale,* 2d ed., Florence: G. Barbéra, 1923.

Randall, John Herman, Jr., "Epilogue: The Nature of Naturalism," in *Naturalism and the Human Spirit,* ed. Yervant H. Krikorian, New York: Columbia University Press, 1944, pp. 354–382.

Riezler, Kurt, *Man: Mutable and Immutable,* Chicago: Henry Regnery, 1950.

Scheler, Max, *Die Wissenformen und die Gesellschaft: Probleme einer Soziologie des Wissens,* Leipzig: Die Neue Geist Verlag, 1926.

Schelting, Alexander von, *Max Weber's Wissenschaftslehre,* Tübingen: J. C. B. Mohr, 1934.

Schutz, Alfred, "Choosing Among Projects of Action," *Philosophy and Phenomenological Research,* XII, 1951, pp. 161–184; reprinted in Alfred Schutz, *The Problem of Social Reality.*

———, Collected Papers, Vol. I: *The Problem of Social Reality* (ed. and intro. by Maurice Natanson with a preface by H. L. Van Breda), Phaenomenologica 10, The Hague: Martinus Nijhoff, 1962.

———, "The Homecomer," *American Journal of Sociology*, L, 1945, pp. 369–376.

———, "Husserl's Importance for the Social Sciences," in *Edmund Husserl 1859–1959*, Phaenomenologica 4, The Hague: Martinus Nijhoff, 1959, pp. 86–98; reprinted with minor deletions in Alfred Schutz, *The Problem of Social Reality*.

———, "Language, Language Disturbances, and the Texture of Consciousness," *Social Research*, XVII, 1950, pp. 365–394; reprinted in Alfred Schutz, *The Problem of Social Reality*.

———, "Making Music Together: A Study in Social Relationship," *Social Research*, XVIII, 1951, pp. 76–97.

———, "On Multiple Realities," *Philosophy and Phenomenological Research*, V, 1945, pp. 533–576; reprinted in Alfred Schutz, *The Problem of Social Reality*.

———, "Phenomenology and the Social Sciences," in *Philosophical Essays in Memory of Edmund Husserl*, ed. Marvin Farber, Cambridge, Mass.: Harvard University Press, 1940, pp. 164–186; reprinted in Alfred Schutz, *The Problem of Social Reality*.

———, "The Problem of Rationality in the Social World," *Economica*, New Series, X, 1943, pp. 130–149.

———, "The Social World and the Theory of Social Action," *Social Research*, XXVII, 1960, pp. 203–221.

———, "The Stranger: An Essay in Social Psychology," *American Journal of Sociology*, XLIX, 1944, pp. 499–507; reprinted in *Identity and Anxiety: Survival of the Person in Mass Society*, ed. Maurice Stein, Arthur J. Vidich, and David Manning White, Glencoe, Ill.: Free Press, 1960.

———, "The Well-Informed Citizen: An Essay on the Social Distribution of Knowledge," *Social Research*, XIII, 1946, pp. 463–472.

Science, Language, and Human Rights, American Philosophical Association, Eastern Division, I, Philadelphia: University of Pennsylvania Press, 1952.

Sheldon, W. H., "Critique of Naturalism," *Journal of Philosophy*, XLII, 1945, pp. 253–270.

———, *The Varieties of Human Physique*, New York: Harper, 1940.

———, *The Varieties of Temperament*, New York: Harper, 1942.

Stonier, Alfred, and Karl Bode, "A New Approach to the Methodology of the Social Sciences," *Economica*, New Series, IV, 1937, pp. 406–424.

Sumner, William Graham, *Folkways: A Study of the Sociological Importance of Manners, Customs, Mores and Morals*, New York: Ginn, 1906.

Tiryakian, E. A., "Methodology and Research," in *Contemporary Sociology*, ed. Joseph S. Roucek, London: Peter Owen, 1959, pp. 151–166.

Volkart, Edmund H. (ed.), *Social Behavior and Personality: Contributions of W. I. Thomas to Theory and Social Research*, New York: Social Science Research Council, 1951.

Waters, Bruce, "The Past and the Historical Past," *Journal of Philosophy*, LII, 1955, pp. 253–269.

Watkins, J. W. N., "The Alleged Inadequacy of Methodological Individualism," *Journal of Philosophy*, LV, 1958, pp. 390–395.

———, "Historical Explanation in the Social Sciences," *British Journal for the Philosophy of Science*, VIII, 1957, pp. 104–117.

———, "Ideal Types and Historical Explanation," *British Journal for the Philosophy of Science*, III, 1952, pp. 22–43.

———, "Methodological Individualism: A Reply," *Philosophy of Science*, XXII, 1955, pp. 58–62.

———, "Third Reply to Mr. Goldstein," *British Journal for the Philosophy of Science*, X, 1959, pp. 242–244.

Whitehead, Alfred North, *The Aims of Education*, New York: Macmillan, 1929; Mentor Books, 1949.

———, *The Organization of Thought*, London: Williams & Norgate, 1917.

———, *Science and the Modern World*, New York: Macmillan, 1925.

Winch, R. F., "Heuristic and Empirical Typologies: A Job for Factor Analysis," *American Sociological Review*, XII, 1947, pp. 68–75.

Yolton, John W., "Explanation," *British Journal for the Philosophy of Science*, X, 1959, pp. 194–208.

Zaner, Richard M., "Theory of Intersubjectivity: Alfred Schutz," *Social Research*, XXVII, 1961, pp. 71–93.

Znaniecki, Florian, *Social Actions*, New York: Farrar & Rinehart, 1935.

PART IV. OBJECTIVITY AND VALUE

Abel, Theodore F., *Systematic Sociology in Germany*, New York: Columbia University Press, 1929.

Antoni, Carlo, *From History to Sociology: The Transition in German Historical Thinking*, trans. Hayden V. White, Detroit, Mich.: Wayne State University Press, 1959.

Aquinas, St. Thomas, *Summa Theologica*, trans. Fathers of the English Dominican Province, New York: Benziger Brothers, 1947, 3 vols.

Aristotle, *Physics*, trans. R. P. Hardie and R. K. Gaye, Oxford: Oxford University Press, 1930.

Aron, Raymond, *German Sociology*, trans. Mary and Thomas Bottomore, Glencoe, Ill.: Free Press, 1957.

Becker, Howard, *Through Values to Social Interpretation: Essays on Social Contexts, Actions, Types, and Prospects*, Durham, N.C.: Duke University Press, 1950.

Bidney, David, *Theoretical Anthropology*, New York: Columbia University Press, 1953.

Bisbee, Eleanor, "Objectivity in the Social Sciences," *Philosophy of Science*, IV, 1937, pp. 371–382.

Boulding, Kenneth E., *The Image: Knowledge in Life and Society*, Ann Arbor, Mich.: University of Michigan Press, 1956.

Burke, Edmund, *Present Discontents*, in *The Works of Edmund Burke*, London: Bohn's Standard Library, 1853, I.

Cairns, Huntington, "Law as a Social Science," *Philosophy of Science*, II, 1935, pp. 484–498.

Charnwood, Lord, *Abraham Lincoln*, New York: Pocket Books, 1951.

Churchill, Winston S., *Marlborough: His Life and Times*, VI; and see the complete edition in 2 vols., London: George G. Harrap, 1947.

Furfey, Paul H., "Metasociological Value Judgments," ch. 4 of Paul H. Furfey, *The Scope and Method of Sociology: A Metasociological Treatise*, New York: Harper, 1953.

Gibson, Quentin, *The Logic of Social Inquiry*, New York: Humanities Press, 1960.

Goethe, Johann Wolfgang von, *Faust*, trans. Bayard Taylor, London: Ward, Lock, 1886. Compare with Sir Theodore Martin's trans. as rev. by W. H. Bruford, Goethe, *Faust*, Parts I and II, London: J. M. Dent, 1954.

Hall, Everett W., *Modern Science and Human Values: A Study in the History of Ideas*, Princeton, N.J.: D. Van Nostrand, 1956.

Horowitz, Irving Louis, *Philosophy, Science and the Sociology of Knowledge*, with a foreword by Robert S. Cohen, Springfield, Ill.: Charles C. Thomas, 1961.

Hughes, H. Stuart, *Consciousness and Society: The Reorientation of*

European Social Thought 1890–1930, New York: Alfred A. Knopf, 1958.

Irving, John A., *Science and Value: Explorations in Philosophy*, Toronto: Ryerson Press, 1952.

Kahler, Erich, *The Tower and the Abyss: or The Transformation of Man*, New York: George Braziller, 1957.

Kallen, H. M., "Social Philosophy and the War of the Faiths," *Social Research*, XX, 1953, pp. 1–18.

Klein, Jacob, "Die griechische Logistik und die Enstehung der modernen Algebra," *Quellen und Studien zur Geschichte der Mathematik, Astronomie und Physik*, III, 1936, pp. 18–105.

Knight, Frank H., "Fact and Value in Social Science," in *Freedom and Reform: Essays in Economics and Social Philosophy*, New York: Harper, 1947, pp. 225–245.

Köhler, Wolfgang, *The Place of Value in a World of Facts*, New York: Liveright, 1938.

Manasse, Ernst Moritz, "Max Weber's Influence on Jaspers," in *The Philosophy of Karl Jaspers*, ed. Paul Arthur Schilpp, Library of Living Philosophers, New York: Tudor, 1957, pp. 369–391.

Mandelbaum, Maurice, *The Problem of Historical Knowledge: An Answer to Relativism*, New York: Liveright, 1938.

Mannheim, Karl, *Essays on Sociology and Social Psychology*, ed. Paul Kecskemeti, New York: Oxford University Press, 1953.

———, *Essays on the Sociology of Culture*, ed. Ernest Manheim in cooperation with Paul Kecskemeti, New York: Oxford University Press, 1956.

———, *Essays on the Sociology of Knowledge*, ed. Paul Kecskemeti, New York: Oxford University Press, 1952.

Maquet, Jacques J., *The Sociology of Knowledge: Its Structure and Its Relation to the Philosophy of Knowledge, a Critical Analysis of the Systems of Karl Mannheim and Pitirim A. Sorokin*, trans. John F. Locke with a preface by F. S. C. Northrop, Boston: Beacon Press, 1951.

Mayer, J. P., *Max Weber and German Politics: A Study in Political Sociology*, 2d rev. and enl. ed., London: Faber & Faber, 1956.

Melden, A. I., "Judgments in the Social Sciences," in *Civilization*, Berkeley and Los Angeles, Calif.: University of California Press, 1959, pp. 121–146.

Merton, Robert K., Leonard Broom, and Leonard S. Cottrell, Jr. (eds.), *Sociology Today: Problems and Prospects*, New York: Basic Books, 1959.

Mises, Ludwig von, *Epistemological Problems of Economics*, Princeton, N.J.: Van Nostrand, 1960.

———, *Theory and History*, New Haven, Conn.: Yale University Press, 1957.

Myrdal, Gunnar, *Value in Social Theory: A Selection of Essays on Methodology*, ed. Paul Streeten, New York: Harper & Row, 1958.

Parsons, Talcott, "Max Weber's Sociological Analysis of Capitalism and Modern Institutions," in *An Introduction to the History of Sociology*, ed. Harry Elmer Barnes, Chicago: University of Chicago Press, 1948, pp. 287–308.

———, *The Structure of Social Action*, New York: McGraw-Hill, 1937.

Passmore, J. A., "Can the Social Sciences Be Value-Free?" in *Proceedings of the Tenth International Congress of Philosophy*, Amsterdam: North-Holland, 1949; reprinted in *Readings in the Philosophy of Science*, ed. Herbert Feigl and May Brodbeck.

Perry, Ralph Barton, *Realms of Value: A Critique of Human Civilization*, Cambridge, Mass.: Harvard University Press, 1954.

Popper, Karl R., *The Open Society and Its Enemies*, Princeton, N.J.: Princeton University Press, 1950.

———, *The Poverty of Historicism*, London: Routledge & Kegan Paul, 1961.

Reid, John R., "The Nature and Status of Values," in *Philosophy for the Future: The Quest of Modern Materialism*, ed. Roy Wood Sellars, V. J. McGill, and Marvin Farber, New York: Macmillan, 1949, pp. 453–475.

Rose, Arnold M., *Theory and Method in the Social Sciences*, Minneapolis, Minn.: University of Minnesota Press, 1954.

Roshwald, M., "Value-Judgments in the Social Sciences," *British Journal for the Philosophy of Science*, VI, 1955, pp. 186–208.

Salomon, Albert, "German Sociology," in *Twentieth Century Sociology*, ed. Georges Gurvitch and Wilbert E. Moore, New York: Philosophical Library, 1945, pp. 586–614.

———, "Max Weber's Methodology," *Social Research*, I, 1934, pp. 147–168.

———, "Max Weber's Political Ideas," *Social Research*, II, 1935, pp. 368–384.

———, "Max Weber's Sociology," *Social Research*, II, 1935, pp. 60–73.

Stark, Werner, *The Sociology of Knowledge: An Essay in Aid of a Deeper Understanding of the History of Ideas*, Glencoe, Ill.: Free Press, 1958.

Strauss, Leo, *Natural Right and History*, Charles R. Walgreen Foundation Lectures, Chicago: University of Chicago Press, 1953.

——, "Social Science and Humanism," in *The State of the Social Sciences*, ed. Leonard D. White, Chicago: University of Chicago Press, 1956, pp. 415–425.

——, *What Is Political Philosophy?* Glencoe, Ill.: Free Press, 1959.

Troeltsch, Ernst, *The Social Teaching of the Christian Churches*, trans. Olive Wyon, New York: Macmillan, 1931, 2 vols.

Ward, Leo R. (ed.), *Ethics and the Social Sciences*, Notre Dame, Indiana: University of Notre Dame Press, 1959.

Weber, Marianne, *Max Weber: Ein Lebensbild*, Heidelberg: Lambert Schneider, 1950.

Weber, Max, *Ancient Judaism*, trans. Hans Gerth and Don Martindale, Glencoe, Ill.: Free Press, 1951.

——, *The City*, trans. Don Martindale and Gertrud Neuwirth, Glencoe, Ill.: Free Press, 1958.

——, *From Max Weber: Essays in Sociology*, trans., ed., and with an intro. by H. H. Gerth and C. Wright Mills, New York: Oxford University Press, 1946.

——, *General Economic History*, trans. Frank H. Knight, New York: Greenberg, 1927.

——, *Gesammelte Aufsätze zur Religionssoziologie*, Tübingen: J. C. B. Mohr, 1920–1921, 3 vols.

——, *Gesammelte Aufsätze zur Sozial und Wirtschaftsgeschichte*, Tübingen: J. C. B. Mohr, 1924.

——, *Gesammelte Aufsätze zur Soziologie und Sozialpolitik*, Tübingen: J. C. B. Mohr, 1924.

——, *Gesammelte Aufsätze zur Wissenschaftslehre*, Tübingen: J. C. B. Mohr, 1922.

——, *Gesammelte Aufsätze zur Wissenschaftslehre*, zweite durchgesehene und ergänzte Auflage, besorgt von Johannes Winckelmann, Tübingen: J. C. B. Mohr, 1951.

——, *Gesammelte Politische Schriften*, München: Drei Masken Verlag, 1921.

——, *Max Weber on Law in Economy and Society*, trans. Edward A. Shils and Max Rheinstein, Cambridge, Mass.: Harvard University Press, 1954.

——, *The Methodology of the Social Sciences*, trans. and ed. Edward A. Shils and Henry A. Finch with a foreword by Edward A. Shils, Glencoe, Ill.: Free Press, 1949.

——, *The Protestant Ethic and the Spirit of Capitalism*, trans. Talcott Parsons, New York: Scribner's, 1930.

———, *The Rational and Social Foundations of Music*, trans. Don Martindale, Johannes Riedel, and Gertrud Neuwirth, Carbondale, Ill.: Southern Illinois University Press, 1958.

———, *The Religion of China*, trans. Hans Gerth, Glencoe, Ill.: Free Press, 1951.

———, *The Religion of India*, trans. Hans Gerth and Don Martindale, Glencoe, Ill.: Free Press, 1958.

———, *The Theory of Social and Economic Organization*, trans. A. M. Henderson and Talcott Parsons, New York: Oxford University Press, 1947.

———, *Wirtschaft und Gesellschaft*, 2d ed., Tübingen: J. C. B. Mohr, 1925, 2 vols.

———, *Wirtschaftsgeschichte*, München: Duncker & Humblot, 1924.

Werkmeister, W. H., "Social Science and the Problem of Value," in *Scientism and Values*, ed. Helmut Schoeck and James W. Wiggins, Princeton, N.J.: D. Van Nostrand, 1960, pp. 1–21.

White, Leonard D. (ed.), *The State of the Social Sciences*, Chicago: University of Chicago Press, 1956.

PART V. PHILOSOPHICAL PERSPECTIVES

Ayer, A. J., *The Foundations of Knowledge*, London: Macmillan, 1940.

———, *Language, Truth and Logic*, 2d ed., New York: Dover, 1946.

———, *The Problem of Knowledge*, London: Macmillan, 1956.

——— (ed.), *Logical Positivism*, Glencoe, Ill.: Free Press, 1959.

Ballard, Edward G., "Husserl's Philosophy of Intersubjectivity in Relation to his Rational Ideal," in *Studies in Social Philosophy*, Tulane Studies in Philosophy, XI, 1962, pp. 3–38.

———, "The Philosophy of Merleau-Ponty," in *Studies in Hegel*, Tulane Studies in Philosophy, IX, 1960, pp. 165–187.

Bannan, John F., "Philosophical Reflection and the Phenomenology of Merleau-Ponty," *Review of Metaphysics*, VIII, 1955, pp. 418–442.

Barrett, William, and Henry D. Aiken (eds.), *Philosophy in the Twentieth Century*, New York: Random House, 1962, 2 vols.

Bayer, Raymond, "Merleau-Ponty's Existentialism," in University of Buffalo Studies, XIX, 1951, pp. 95–104.

Bentley, Arthur F., *Inquiry into Inquiries: Essays in Social Theory*, ed. with an intro. by Sidney Ratner, Boston: Beacon Press, 1954.

Bergmann, Gustav, "Logical Positivism," in *A History of Philosophical Systems*, ed. Vergelius Ferm, New York: Philosophical Library, 1950, pp. 471–482.

Blanshard, Brand, *Reason and Analysis*, LaSalle, Ill.: Open Court, 1962.

Bochenski, I. M., *Contemporary European Philosophy*, trans. Donald Nicholl and Karl Aschenbrenner, Berkeley and Los Angeles, Calif.: University of California Press, 1961.

Boswell's Life of Johnson, ed. George Birkbeck Hill, Oxford: Clarendon Press, 1887, III.

Cairns, Dorion, "Phenomenology," in *A History of Philosophical Systems*, ed. Vergelius Ferm, New York: Philosophical Library, 1950, pp. 353–364.

Casserley, J. V. Langmead, *Morals and Man in the Social Sciences*, New York: Longmans, Green, 1951.

Cassirer, Ernst, *An Essay on Man: An Introduction to a Philosophy of Human Culture*, New Haven, Conn.: Yale University Press, 1945.

Chapman, Harmon M., "Realism and Phenomenology," in *The Return to Reason*, ed. John Wild, Chicago: Henry Regnery, 1953, pp. 3–35.

Collingwood, R. G., *An Essay on Philosophical Method*, New York: Oxford University Press, 1933.

Collins, James, *The Existentialists: A Critical Study*, Chicago: Henry Regnery, 1952.

Colodny, Robert G. (ed.), *Frontiers of Science and Philosophy*, Pittsburgh, Pa.: University of Pittsburgh Press, 1963.

Copleston, Frederick, *Contemporary Philosophy: Studies of Logical Positivism and Existentialism*, Westminster, Md.: Newman Press, 1956.

Desan, Wilfrid, *The Planetary Man: A Poetic Prelude to a United World*, Washington, D.C.: Georgetown University Press, 1961, I.

Dufrenne, Mikel, "Existentialisme et sociologie," *Cahiers internationaux de sociologie*, I, 1946, pp. 161–171.

———, *La Notion d'a priori*, Paris: Presses Universitaires de France, 1959.

———, *La Personalité de base: un concept sociologique*, Paris: Presses Universitaires de France, 1953.

Farber, Marvin, *The Foundations of Phenomenology: Edmund Husserl and the Quest for a Rigorous Science of Philosophy*, Cambridge, Mass.: Harvard University Press, 1943.

———, *Naturalism and Subjectivism*, Springfield, Ill.: Charles C. Thomas, 1959.

———, "Phenomenology," in *Twentieth Century Philosophy*, ed. Dagobert D. Runes, New York: Philosophical Library, 1943, pp. 345–370.

———— (ed.), *Philosophical Essays in Memory of Edmund Husserl*, Cambridge, Mass.: Harvard University Press, 1940.

Feigl, Herbert, "Logical Empiricism," in *Twentieth Century Philosophy*, ed. Dagobert D. Runes, New York: Philosophical Library, 1943, pp. 373–416 (republished as *Living Schools of Philosophy*, Ames, Iowa: Littlefield, Adams, 1956).

————, "Some Major Issues and Developments in the Philosophy of Science of Logical Empiricism," in *The Foundations of Science and the Concepts of Psychology and Psychoanalysis*, ed. Herbert Feigl and Michael Scriven, Minnesota Studies in the Philosophy of Science, Minneapolis, Minn.: University of Minnesota Press, 1956, pp. 3–37.

Feigl, Herbert and Grover Maxwell (eds.), *Current Issues in the Philosophy of Science*, New York: Holt, Rinehart, and Winston, 1961.

Feigl, Herbert, and Wilfred Sellars (eds.), *Readings in Philosophical Analysis*, New York: Appleton-Century-Crofts, 1949.

Ferm, Vergelius (ed.), *A History of Philosophical Systems*, New York: Philosophical Library, 1950.

Ferrater Mora, José, *Philosophy Today*, New York: Columbia University Press, 1960.

Gellner, Ernest, *Words and Things*, with an intro. by Bertrand Russell, Boston: Beacon Press, 1960.

Gurwitsch, Aron, "The Last Work of Edmund Husserl," *Philosophy and Phenomenological Research*, XVI, 1956, pp. 380–399; XVII, 1957, pp. 370–398.

————, "The Phenomenological and the Psychological Approach to Consciousness," *Philosophy and Phenomenological Research*, XV, 1955, pp. 303–319.

————, *Théorie du champ de la conscience*, Paris: Desclée de Brouwer, 1957 (Duquesne University Press plans to bring out an English translation).

Hampshire, Stuart, "Can There Be a General Science of Man?" *Commentary*, XXIV, 1957, pp. 164–167.

————, *Thought and Action*, New York: Viking Press, 1960.

Harper, Ralph, *Existentialism: A Theory of Man*, Cambridge, Mass.: Harvard University Press, 1948.

Heidegger, Martin, *Being and Time*, trans. John Macquarrie and Edward Robinson, New York: Harper & Row, 1962.

———, *Existence and Being*, with an intro. by Werner Brock, Chicago: Henry Regnery, 1949.

———, *Was ist Metaphysik?* Bonn: Friedrich Cohen, 1929 (trans. in Martin Heidegger, *Existence and Being*).

Heider, Fritz, "Consciousness, the Perceptual World, and Communications with Others," in *Person Perception and Interpersonal Behavior*, ed. Renato Tagiuri and Luigi Petrullo, Stanford, Calif.: Stanford University Press, 1958, pp. 27–53.

Henle, Paul, "Philosophy and Social Science," unpublished paper read at the 1957 meeting of the Western Division of the American Philosophical Association.

Hook, Sidney, "The Quest for 'Being,'" *Journal of Philosophy*, L, 1953, pp. 709–731.

Husserl, Edmund, *Cartesian Meditations: An Introduction to Phenomenology*, trans. Dorion Cairns, The Hague: Martinus Nijhoff, 1960.

———, "The Crisis of European Humanity and Philosophy," in *The Search for Being: Essays from Kierkegaard to Sartre on the Problem of Existence*, trans. and ed. Jean T. Wilde and William Kimmel, New York: Twayne Publishers, 1962, pp. 378–413.

———, "Die Frage nach dem Ursprung der Geometrie als intentional-historisches Problem (with a foreword by Eugen Fink)," *Revue internationale de philosophie* I, 1939, pp. 203–225.

———, *Ideas: General Introduction to Pure Phenomenology*, trans. W. R. Boyce Gibson, New York: Macmillan, 1931.

———, "Die Krisis der europäischen Wissenschaften und die transzendentale Phänomenologie," *Philosophia*, I, 1936, pp. 77–176.

———, *Die Krisis der europäischen Wissenschaften und die transzendentale Phänomenologie*, ed. Walter Biemel, Husserliana 6, The Hague: Martinus Nijhoff, 1954.

———, "Phenomenology and Anthropology," trans. Richard G. Schmitt, in *Realism and the Background of Phenomenology*, ed. Roderick M. Chisholm, Glencoe, Ill.: Free Press, 1960, 129–142.

———, "Philosophie als strenge Wissenschaft," *Logos*, I, 1910, pp. 289–314; trans. Quentin Lauer as "Philosophy as a Strict Science," *Cross Currents*, VI, 1956, pp. 227–246, 325–344.

Jones, J. R., "Self-Knowledge," *Proceedings of the Aristotelian Society*, Supplementary XXX, 1956, pp. 120–142.

Jorgenson, Jorgen, *The Development of Logical Empiricism*, in *International Encyclopedia of Unified Science*, II, No. 9, Chicago: University of Chicago Press, 1951.

Jung, C. G., "Synchronicity: An Acausal Connecting Principle," trans. R. F. Hull, in C. G. Jung and W. Pauli, *The Interpretation of Nature and the Psyche*, Bollingen Series LI, New York: Pantheon Books, 1955, pp. 5-146.

Kaelin, Eugene F., *An Existentialist Aesthetic: The Theories of Sartre and Merleau-Ponty*, Madison, Wis.: University of Wisconsin Press, 1962.

Kaufmann, Fritz, "In Memoriam Edmund Husserl," *Social Research*, VII, 1940, pp. 61-91.

Kaufmann, Walter (ed.), *Existentialism from Dostoievski to Sartre*, New York: Meridian Books, 1957.

Komarovsky, Mira (ed.), *Common Frontiers of the Social Sciences*, Glencoe, Ill.: Free Press, 1957.

Kracauer, Siegfried, *Soziologie als Wissenschaft: Eine erkenntnistheoretische Untersuchung*, Dresden: Sibyllen-Verlag, 1922.

Kraft, Victor, *The Vienna Circle*, trans. Arthur Pap, New York: Philosophical Library, 1953.

Kuhn, Helmut, *Encounter with Nothingness*, Hinsdale, Ill.: Henry Regnery, 1949.

Kullman, Michael and Charles Taylor, "The Pre-Objective World," *Review of Metaphysics*, XII, 1958, pp. 108-132.

Landgrebe, Ludwig, "The World as a Phenomenological Problem," *Philosophy and Phenomenological Research*, I, 1940, pp. 38-58.

Lauer, Quentin, *The Triumph of Subjectivity: An Introduction to Transcendental Phenomenology*, with a preface by Aron Gurwitsch, New York: Fordham University Press, 1958.

Lévy-Bruhl, Lucien, *La Mythologie primitive*, Paris: Félix Alcan, 1935.

Lins, Mario, *Foundations of Social Determinism: An Inquiry into Its Epistemological Problematics*, Rio de Janeiro, 1959.

MacLeod, Robert B., "The Phenomenological Approach to Social Psychology," in *Person Perception and Interpersonal Behavior*, ed. Renato Tagiuri and Luigi Petrullo, Stanford, Calif.: Stanford University Press, 1958, pp. 33-53.

———, "The Place of Phenomenological Analysis in Social Psychological Theory," in *Social Psychology at the Crossroads*, ed. J. H. Rohrer and Muzafer Sherif, New York: Harper, 1951, pp. 215-241.

Margenau, Henry, *Open Vistas: Philosophical Perspectives of Modern Science*, New Haven, Conn.: Yale University Press, 1961.

Marx, Karl, *Eleven Theses on Feuerbach*, in *Basic Writings on Politics and Philosophy: Karl Marx and Friedrich Engels*, ed. Lewis S. Feuer, Garden City, N.Y.: Doubleday, 1959.

May, Rollo, Ernest Angel, and Henri F. Ellenberger (eds.), *Ex-*

istence: A New Dimension in Psychiatry and Psychology, New York: Basic Books, 1958.

Mehta, Ved, "A Battle Against the Bewitchment of Our Intelligence," *The New Yorker*, XXXVII, (December 9, 1961), p. 59 f.

Merlan, Philip, "Time Consciousness in Husserl and Heidegger," *Philosophy and Phenomenological Research*, VIII, 1947, pp. 23–53.

Merleau-Ponty, Maurice, "Cézanne's Doubt," *Partisan Review*, trans. Juliet Bigney, XIII (September–October, 1946), pp. 464–478.

——, *In Praise of Philosophy*, trans. John Wild and James M. Edie, Evanston, Ill.: Northwestern University Press, 1963.

——, *Phénoménologie de la perception*, Paris: Gallimard, 1945 and trans. Colin Smith as *Phenomenology of Perception*, New York: Humanities Press, 1962.

——, *Les Sciences de l'homme et la phénoménologie*, Paris: Centre de Documentation Universitaire, n.d.

——, "What Is Phenomenology?" trans. John F. Bannan, *Cross Currents*, VI, 1956, pp. 59–70.

Molina, Fernando, *Existentialism as Philosophy*, Englewood Cliffs, N.J.: Prentice-Hall, 1962.

Natanson, Maurice, *A Critique of Jean-Paul Sartre's Ontology*, University of Nebraska Studies, New Series No. 6, Lincoln, Nebr.: University of Nebraska Press, 1951.

——, *Literature, Philosophy, and the Social Sciences: Essays in Existentialism and Phenomenology*, The Hague: Martinus Nijhoff, 1962.

——, "Philosophische Grundfragen der Psychiatrie I: Philosophie und Psychiatrie," trans. Robert O. Weiss, in *Psychiatrie der Gegenwart*, ed. H. W. Gruhle, R. Jung, W. Mayer-Gross, and M. Müller, Berlin: Springer-Verlag, 1963, Band ½, pp. 903–925.

Neisser, Hans P., "The Phenomenological Approach in Social Science," *Philosophy and Phenomenological Research*, XX, 1959, pp. 198–212.

Pap, Arthur, *An Introduction to the Philosophy of Science*, with an epilogue by Brand Blanshard, New York: Free Press of Glencoe, 1962.

Peursen, C. A. van, "Edmund Husserl and Ludwig Wittgenstein," *Philosophy and Phenomenological Research*, XX, 1959, pp. 181–197.

Pfuetze, Paul E., *Self, Society, Existence: Human Nature and Dialogue in the Thought of George Herbert Mead and Martin Buber*, with a foreword by H. Richard Niebuhr, New York: Harper Torchbooks, 1961.

La Philosophie analytique, Cahiers de Royaumont, Philosophie No. IV, Paris: Les Editions de Minuit, 1962.

Popper, Karl, *The Logic of Scientific Discovery,* New York: Basic Books, 1959.

Pos, H.-J., "Phénoménologie et Linguistique," *Revue internationale de philosophie,* I, 1939, pp. 354–365.

Quinton, Anthony, Stuart Hampshire, Iris Murdoch, and Isaiah Berlin, "Philosophy and Beliefs," a discussion of Oxford Philosophy in *The Twentieth Century,* CLVII, 1955, pp. 495–521.

Reflections on Our Age: Lecture Delivered at the Opening Session of UNESCO at the Sorbonne University, Paris, introduction by David Hardman, foreword by Stephen Spender, London: Allan Wingate, 1948.

Reichenbach, Hans, *Experience and Prediction,* Chicago: University of Chicago Press, 1938.

———, *The Rise of Scientific Philosophy,* Berkeley, Calif.: University of California Press, 1951.

The Revolution in Philosophy, with an intro. by Gilbert Ryle, London: Macmillan, 1960.

Rosen, Stanley, "Wisdom: The End of Philosophy," *Review of Metaphysics,* XVI, 1962, pp. 181–211.

Russell, Bertrand, *Human Knowledge,* New York: Simon & Schuster, 1948.

———, *The Scientific Outlook,* New York: W. W. Norton, 1962.

Sartre, Jean-Paul, *Being and Nothingness: An Essay on Phenomenological Ontology,* trans. with an intro. by Hazel E. Barnes, New York: Philosophical Library, 1956.

Schaff, Adam, *Introduction to Semantics,* trans. Olgierd Wojtasiewicz, Oxford: Pergamon Press, 1962.

Scheler, Max, *Man's Place in Nature,* trans. Hans Meyerhoff, Boston: Beacon Press, 1961.

Schutz, Alfred, "Some Leading Concepts of Phenomenology," *Social Research,* XII, 1945, pp. 77–97; reprinted in Alfred Schutz, *The Problem of Social Reality.*

Spiegelberg, Herbert, *The Phenomenological Movement: A Historical Introduction,* Phaenomenologica 5 and 6, The Hague: Martinus Nijhoff, 1960, 2 vols.

Storer, Thomas, "An Analysis of Logical Positivism," *Methodos,* III, 1951, pp. 245–272 (a discussion of this article by Ferruccio Rossi-Landi follows on pp. 273–274).

Strasser, Stephan, *The Soul in Metaphysical and Empirical Psychology,* trans. Henry J. Koren, Duquesne Studies, Philosophical Series 7, Pittsburgh, Pa.: Duquesne University Press, 1957.

Straus, Erwin W., "Philosophische Grundfragen der Psychiatrie II: Psychiatrie und Philosophie," in *Psychiatrie der Gegenwart*, ed. H. W. Gruhle, R. Jung, W. Mayer-Gross, and M. Müller, Berlin: Springer-Verlag, 1963, Band ½, pp. 926–994.

———, *Vom Sinn der Sinne: Ein Beitrag zur Grundlegung der Psychologie*, 2d ed., Berlin: Springer, 1956 (English trans. forthcoming under the title *The Primary World: A Vindication of Sensory Experience*, New York: Free Press of Glencoe).

Taylor, Charles, and A. J. Ayer, "Phenomenology and Linguistic Analysis," *Proceedings of the Aristotelian Society*, Supplementary Vol. XXXIII, 1959, pp. 93–124.

Thévenaz, Pierre, *What Is Phenomenology?* trans. James M. Edie, Chicago: Quadrangle Books, 1962.

Tiryakian, Edward A., *Sociologism and Existentialism: Two Perspectives on the Individual and Society*, Englewood Cliffs, N.J.: Prentice-Hall, 1962.

Toulemont, René, *L'Essence de la société selon Husserl*, Paris: Presses Universitaires de France, 1962.

Tymieniecka, Anna-Teresa, *Phenomenology and Science in Contemporary European Thought*, New York: Farrar, Straus, and Cudahy, 1962.

Waismann, F., "How I See Philosophy," in *Contemporary British Philosophy: Personal Statements*, ed. H. D. Lewis, London: George Allen & Unwin, 1956, pp. 447–490.

Weinberg, Julius, *An Examination of Logical Positivism*, New York: Harcourt, Brace, 1936.

Werkmeister, W. H., *The Basis and Structure of Knowledge*, New York: Harper, 1948.

Wild, John, "The Exploration of the Life-World," *Proceedings and Addresses of The American Philosophical Association*, XXXIV, 1961, pp. 5–23.

———, "Is There a World of Ordinary Language?" *Philosophical Review*, LXVII, 1958, pp. 460–476.

———, "Man and His Life-World," in *For Roman Ingarden: Nine Essays in Phenomenology*, with an editorial note by Anna-Teresa Tymieniecka, The Hague: Martinus Nijhoff, 1959, pp. 90–109.

Wisdom, John, "Other Minds," *Mind*, XLIX, 1940, pp. 369–402.

Wolman, Benjamin B., *Contemporary Theories and Systems in Psychology*, New York: Harper, 1960.

INDEX

The Contributors

MAURICE NATANSON is the Editor of this book and also a contributor. He received his Ph.D. from the University of Nebraska and holds the Doctor of Social Science degree from the New School for Social Research. He has taught at the University of Nebraska, the Graduate Faculty of the New School for Social Research, the University of Houston, and the University of North Carolina. For the spring term of 1963 he was Distinguished Visiting Professor at Pennsylvania State University. He is the author of *A Critique of Jean-Paul Sartre's Ontology, The Social Dynamics of George H. Mead,* and *Literature, Philosophy, and the Social Sciences.* In addition to editing *The Problem of Social Reality* by Alfred Schutz, he has contributed chapters to several books. Mr. Natanson was American Council of Learned Societies Scholar from 1951 to 1953 and held a fellowship from the same Council for study in Europe during the year 1961–1962. He is a member of the editorial board of the journal *Philosophy and Phenomenological Research.* Dr. Natanson is Professor of Philosophy at the University of California, Santa Cruz.

SOLOMON E. ASCH is Professor of Psychology at Swarthmore College. He studied at Columbia University, has been a member of the Institute for Advanced Study at Princeton, and has been a visiting lecturer at Harvard. He is the author of *Social Psychology* and has contributed to psychological journals.

A. J. AYER is Wykenham Professor of Logic in the University of Oxford and Fellow of New College. He studied at Christ Church, Oxford, and has taught at the University of London. In addition to *Language, Truth, and Logic*, he is the author of *The Foundations of Empirical Knowledge* and *The Problem of Knowledge*.

LEON J. GOLDSTEIN received his Ph.D. from Yale and has taught philosophy at Brandeis University. His articles have appeared in the *British Journal for the Philosophy of Science, Inquiry*, and *Philosophy of Science*. He is now an Associate Professor at Harpur College.

CARL G. HEMPEL is Stuart Professor of Philosophy at Princeton University and has also taught at Yale. His Ph.D. is from the University of Berlin. Together with Paul Oppenheim he wrote *Der Typusbegriff im Lichte der neuen Logik*, and he has contributed a monograph to the *Encyclopedia of Unified Science* as well as numerous articles to philosophical and scientific journals.

ERICH HULA is Professor of Political Science, Constitutional, and International Law in the Graduate Faculty of the New School for Social Research. He received his doctorate at the University of Vienna and has been a visiting professor at Cornell. He is the author of articles on political theory as well as public and labor law.

HANS JONAS is Professor of Philosophy in the Graduate Faculty of the New School for Social Research. He received his Ph.D. at Marburg and has taught and lectured at Carleton College in Ottawa, McGill University, the Hebrew University, as well as at Princeton, Columbia, and Harvard. In addition to several books in German, he is the author of *The Gnostic Religion*.

THELMA Z. LAVINE is Professor of Philosophy at the University of Maryland and has also taught at Brooklyn College. She took her

Ph.D. at Radcliffe. *Naturalism and the Human Spirit* includes one of her essays, and she has also published in the *Journal of Philosophy, Philosophy and Phenomenological Research*, and *Social Research*.

ADOLPH LOWE is Professor of Economics in the Graduate Faculty of the New School for Social Research. He studied at the University of Tübingen and has taught at Kiel University and lectured at the University of Manchester and the Hebrew University. He is the author of a number of books concerned with economics and the social sciences.

GEORGE A. LUNDBERG is Professor of Sociology at the University of Washington and has also taught at Pittsburgh, Stanford, and Columbia. His Ph.D. is from the University of Minnesota and he holds the LL.D. from the University of North Dakota. His books include *Social Research, Can Science Save Us?* and *Foundations of Sociology*. He is a past President of the American Sociological Association.

FRITZ MACHLUP is Walker Professor of Economics and International Finance at Princeton University and has also taught at Johns Hopkins University. He holds the Dr. rer. pol. degree from the University of Vienna and the LL.D. from Lawrence College. Among his books are *The Economics of Seller's Competition* and *The Political Economy of Monopoly*.

MAURICE MERLEAU-PONTY (1907–1961) studied at the École Normale Supérieur and taught at the Collège de France. His name is often associated with that of Jean-Paul Sartre and the "Paris School" of existentialism. In addition to phenomenological studies in psychology and language, he also wrote on politics. His major work is *Phénoménologie de la perception*.

ERNEST NAGEL is Dewey Professor of Philosophy at Columbia University and also studied there. He has been a member of the Center for Advanced Study in the Behavioral Sciences at Stanford. In addition to some volumes of his essays, he is the coauthor of

An Introduction to Logic and Scientific Method and has written *The Structure of Science.*

ALFRED SCHUTZ (1899–1959) studied at the University of Vienna and was Professor of Philosophy and Sociology in the Graduate Faculty of the New School for Social Research. He is the author of *Der sinnhafte Aufbau der sozialen Welt,* and the first volume of his Collected Papers appeared in 1962 as *The Problem of Social Reality.*

GEORG SIMMEL (1858–1918) studied at the University of Berlin where he received his doctorate and where he also taught. He spent the last years of his academic career at the University of Strasbourg. Among the English translations of his writings are *The Sociology of Georg Simmel* and *Conflict* and *The Web of Group-Affiliations.*

LEO STRAUSS is Robert Maynard Hutchins Distinguished Service Professor of Political Science at the University of Chicago. He studied at the universities of Marburg, Berlin, Hamburg, and Freiburg and has taught in the Graduate Faculty of the New School for Social Research. In addition to books on Hobbes and Machiavelli, he has written on classical political philosophy.

MAX WEBER (1864–1920) studied at the universities of Heidelberg, Göttingen, and Berlin and taught at Berlin, Freiburg, and Heidelberg. The vast range of his interests is reflected in his writings, from his Ph.D. dissertation on the history of trading companies during the Middle Ages to his works on the religions of China and India.

PETER WINCH is Senior Lecturer in Philosophy at the University College of Swansea, University of Wales. In 1961–1962 he was a visiting professor at the University of Rochester. He studied at St. Edmund Hall, Oxford. In addition to *The Idea of a Social Science,* he has published articles in *Philosophical Quarterly, Analysis,* and the *British Journal of Sociology.*

A Note on the Type

The text of this book was set on the Linotype in Janson, a recutting made direct from type cast from matrices long thought to have been made by the Dutchman Anton Janson, who was a practicing type founder in Leipzig during the years 1668–87. However, it has been conclusively demonstrated that these types are actually the work of Nicholas Kis (1650–1702), a Hungarian, who most probably learned his trade from the master Dutch type founder Dirk Voskens. The type is an excellent example of the influential and sturdy Dutch types that prevailed in England up to the time William Caslon developed his own incomparable designs from these Dutch faces.